THE PAPERS OF DANIEL WEBSTER

CHARLES M. WILTSE, EDITOR-IN-CHIEF

SERIES FOUR:

SPEECHES AND FORMAL WRITINGS

THE UNIVERSITY PRESS

OF NEW ENGLAND

Sponsoring Institutions

BRANDEIS UNIVERSITY

BROWN UNIVERSITY

CLARK UNIVERSITY

UNIVERSITY OF CONNECTICUT

DARTMOUTH COLLEGE

UNIVERSITY OF NEW HAMPSHIRE

UNIVERSITY OF RHODE ISLAND

TUFTS UNIVERSITY

UNIVERSITY OF VERMONT

The Papers of
Daniel Webster

Speeches and Formal Writings, Volume 1

1800–1833

CHARLES M. WILTSE, EDITOR

ALAN R. BEROLZHEIMER, ASSISTANT EDITOR

PUBLISHED FOR

DARTMOUTH COLLEGE BY THE

UNIVERSITY PRESS OF NEW ENGLAND

HANOVER, NEW HAMPSHIRE AND

LONDON, ENGLAND 1986

*The edition of the Papers of Daniel Webster, of which this is volume one
in the Speeches and Formal Writings series, has been made possible
through grants from the Program for Editions and Publications of the
National Endowment for the Humanities, an independent federal
agency, and through the continuing support, both administrative and
financial, of the National Historical Publications and Records Commission. The edition is sponsored and published by Dartmouth College.*

Contents

Acknowledgments

For these volumes of *Speeches and Formal Writings* our obligations are no less extensive than for the Correspondence series, where they are perhaps more conspicuous. Our thanks are due to all those librarians, editors, and historians who contributed in countless quiet ways to make these books both significant and accurate. There were those who searched out for us newspaper and pamphlet texts, those who answered countless inquiries that matured into explanatory notes, and those who discussed with us the merits of individual items to be included or passed over.

The number of institutions on which we have drawn for support is relatively small but of enduring quality. At the National Historical Publications and Records Commission, and its parent organization, the National Archives, Mary Giunta, Sara Jackson, and Anne Henry seemed at times almost an extension of our own staff. Manuscript historian John McDonough at the Library of Congress cheerfully sought out facts and documents in our behalf; and we relied heavily on the Massachusetts and New Hampshire Historical Societies, whose generous help was never more than a phone call away. Above all, we are indebted to Baker Library of Dartmouth College, where our project itself is housed, and where the entire organization seemed always at our disposal. There are few indeed associated with Baker whose skills we have not tapped, directly or indirectly, but we can mention only a few: Margaret A. Otto, Librarian of the College; Virginia Close and her efficient staff of reference librarians; Stanley W. Brown, chief of Special Collections; Kenneth C. Cramer, Archivist, who has been a tower of strength since the very inception of the Webster Papers; Patricia A. Carter and Susan C. Hall, Interlibrary Loan Officers; L. Sue Marcoulier, Circulation Supervisor; and Erin Sweeney and Nancy Markee of the Jones Microtext Center. Finally, we thank the Trustees of the Boston Public Library for permitting us to publish the reported version of the Second Reply to Hayne.

The Dartmouth History Department has stood ready at all times to respond to our inquiries, and to route in our direction exceptional students. Two of these, William Cole and Jennifer Kern, contributed measurably to these volumes.

Our colleagues of the Webster Papers have given generously of their

own time, especially Michael J. Birkner, Associate Editor, and Wendy Tilghman, Assistant Editor, for Correspondence; Kenneth E. Shewmaker and Kenneth R. Stevens of the Diplomatic Papers; Alfred S. Konefsky and Andrew J. King of the Legal Papers; and by all odds the most diligent and productive of our associates, Mary Virginia Anstruther, Assistant to the Editor-in-Chief. Mrs. Anstruther's special skills in keeping track of myriad details, in ferreting out obscure identities, and in locating long lost publications are awesome.

And now we come to the most taxing, most physically debilitating, and yet the most necessary of tasks connected with *Speeches and Formal Writings*—the word by word comparison of variant texts, showing as it does how expressions were changed for different audiences; how speeches grew and were modified in those days of imperfect reporting, compensated by flawless political shrewdness. For this most exacting assignment we are indebted to the patience and dedication of Frank W. Barham and Robert H. Ross.

In addition to these intellectual obligations, we owe others of a more concrete nature. The financial support that has made it all possible has come from the National Endowment for the Humanities, where Kathy Fuller, Program Specialist, has given freely of her time and expertise; from the National Historical Publications and Records Commission, where Executive Director Frank G. Burke and Roger Bruns, Director of Publications, have added administrative support to monetary assistance; and from Dartmouth College, which has given generously, both in financial aid and in all those numerous supporting services the smooth provision of which has enabled the editors to get on with the job. At Dartmouth we must acknowledge in particular the contributions of Provost Agnar Pytte, Assistant to the Provost Barbara D. Klunder, Associate Dean of the Faculty Gregory S. Prince, and Assistant Comptroller Nancy J. Atkins.

Introduction

For half a century after his death in 1852 the very name of Daniel Webster conjured the image of the peerless orator: a man who could cast a spell over any audience, however large or small, who could sway the doubters, win the admiration of opponents, and move to tears even the venerable justices of the Supreme Court. All of this he was, as those who heard him universally attest: but he also appealed to the minds of his listeners as well as to their emotions. His arguments in debate, always clear, concise and effectively organized, carried conviction to those who merely read them in the press, quite removed from the hypnotic quality of their delivery. His arguments before the courts were close and learned, relying not on oratorical flourishes but on a skilled marshalling of the facts and a thorough knowledge of the law. Similarly, his formal writings, such as reports and memorials, were tightly reasoned and presented with simplicity, clarity, and force.

Although Webster had been too shy at Exeter to mount a platform, he was an accomplished and popular speaker before he graduated from Dartmouth in 1801. He chose a career—or rather, two careers: the law and politics—that kept him constantly on his feet. His total rhetorical output, if one might measure it, must have been enormous. Even the body of speeches, pleadings, reports, and abbreviated debates in Congress that has survived is staggering. To achieve anything like the representative selection aimed at in these volumes has therefore required drastic pruning. Many criteria have been applied in making the selection, but the final determination has rested with our own editorial judgment.

It is to be noted that while Webster never committed to paper any formal statement of his political philosophy, he acted for the most part consistently throughout his life as though he had such a creed. Only from his public utterances may one deduce the long-standing principles which guided his public conduct. Conservative that he was, he never doubted that power would follow property nor that the nation would grow and prosper with her merchants, her manufacturers, and her farmers. The documents selected appear in chronological sequence, showing some evolution of his thinking as well as development of his style. At the same time we have tried to avoid redundancy. Inevitably,

Webster spoke many times over a considerable span of years on certain recurring issues: the tariff, banking, constitutional interpretation to name only the most obvious. We have chosen among these on the basis of content rather than sequence. The only tariff speech we have included, for example, is that of 1824, opposing a policy whose defense later became a major part of his own faith. It is the most intellectual and best reasoned of his tariff speeches. He clearly explains his shift of ground in his 1827 letter to the editor of the *New York Evening Post* (*Correspondence*, 2: 160–163): that his Massachusetts constituency after the passage of the tariff of 1824 had shifted from shipping to manufacturing. His speeches on that subject thereafter are little more than special pleading for special interests.

We have tried to show Webster as the multidimensional character that he was by offering his opinions on a wide variety of topics, and we have followed him in many different roles: as leader of the opposition, as spokesman for the administration, as stump speaker, as maverick, as popular orator, as debater, legislator, diplomatist, advocate, and prosecutor. In each of these areas there have been choices, which have been influenced by the quality of the speech, by its importance in time and place, by comparison with others in the same genre, and finally by the personal judgment of the editors. As representative of his popular oratory, for example, we have chosen the eulogy of Adams and Jefferson in 1826, and the Addition to the Capitol of 1851, but we might with equal justification have selected the Plymouth Oration, either or both of the Bunker Hill Addresses, or the Character of Washington. Other choices, like that of the Second Reply to Hayne, have been inevitable. In this case our choice lay between versions: the transcription of Joseph Gales's shorthand notes, representing the speech as actually delivered, or Webster's revision of the transcript for publication. In this single instance we have printed both texts. Equally inevitable choices were Webster's defense of the Treaty of Washington, and the great compromise speech of March 7, 1850. Banking and currency, on the other hand, offered multiple choices over three decades in such widely differing contexts as to invite several examples.

Although Webster's legal arguments were often extraordinary productions, important in a number of ways, they are not represented here. Many of them have been published in volume three of the *Legal Papers*, in a context that is more appropriate for their particular subject matter. The single exception is Webster's jury speech in the Salem murder trials, where he appeared for the first and only time on behalf of the prosecution. We have included this because it is unique, showing an aspect of Webster's genius that would otherwise not be revealed in these papers.

We have held commentary to what appears to us to be the necessary

minimum. Each speech or paper is preceded by an historical note explaining the circumstances surrounding it and placing it in context. Footnotes have been used where necessary to identify some now obscure character or event, to cite other sources and documents, and to indicate significant textual variations. Each document is also accompanied by a provenance note tracing its publication history.

Most of Webster's speeches appeared first in one or more newspaper versions. As his fame as an orator grew, and as the art of shorthand reporting improved, interested newspapers sent their own reporters to cover important debates. Their reports, however, were by no means equally precise. Webster's own favorite was Joseph Gales, editor and publisher with William Winston Seaton of the Washington *National Intelligencer*. From 1812 to 1829 the two men were respectively the official reporters for the House and Senate. Indeed, it was at Webster's request that Gales personally reported the Reply to Hayne. In the 1840's Webster considered Henry Jarvis Raymond of the New York *Courier and Enquirer* as the most accurate. The Massachusetts senator once postponed a speech to allow Raymond time to reach the Capitol. (*Correspondence*, 6: 274). Although some papers were clearly favored over others, the *National Intelligencer* remained the preferred source until the 1840's. It is the Congressional reporting of the *Intelligencer* that is reprinted as the *Annals of Congress* and its successor, the *Register of Debates*. Gales and Seaton generally submitted transcriptions from their shorthand notes to the respective speakers for editing and sometimes full scale revision.

Of each of Webster's more important speeches there was generally one or more pamphlet versions, appearing in different cities. These might follow exactly a newspaper report and perhaps be issued simultaneously from the same press; or one version might bear the marks of Webster's editing prior to publication. Alterations were normally minor, but could amount to a virtual rewriting if he regarded the speech as of special importance. The two versions of the Reply to Hayne illustrate the process. Many of Webster's contemporaries wrote out their own speeches, before or more commonly after delivery. The printed text was thus very apt to be an improvement on the words actually spoken. So far as we know, Webster did this only rarely, generally with formal orations such as the Eulogy of Adams and Jefferson. In this case, we know that the manuscript was written out in advance, but not strictly followed. His speech of December 9, 1814, against conscription, on the other hand, was not reported and was written out by Webster after the fact. The delay gave him time to reflect, and the speech was withheld from publication. It did not appear in print until the twentieth century.

Although most of Webster's speeches appear spontaneous, they were

in fact carefully prepared. He often made notes, which he usually did not follow, but the matter and generally the manner of the speech had been worked out beforehand, stored in his memory for instant recall. Preparation was the key to his success, both in Congress and before the courts. His mind was quick, his memory exceptional, his command of language hardly equalled in his time. His study of history included great speeches, classical and modern, from which he derived or reinforced his skill in building an argument, his sense of timing, and his marvellous use of words to flesh out and to reinforce the structure of his creation.

The first bound collection of productions, entitled *Speeches and Forensic Arguments* came from the press of Perkins and Marvin in Boston late in 1830. It was no doubt Webster's own idea, inspired by the widespread popular approval of the Reply to Hayne. The evidence seems conclusive that the Massachusetts senator had already determined to run for president. The debate with Hayne convinced him that the time was near; a volume of his speeches for general distribution was a necessary first step. Within a month of the Reply, Webster's nephew, Charles Brickett Haddock, then Professor of Rhetoric and Oratory at Dartmouth, was at work on the volume. (*Correspondence*, 3: 22). Needless to say, Webster himself made final selection of the contents, which significantly did not include the Rockingham Memorial or the antiwar speeches of the 13th Congress.

Before the election of 1836, in which Webster carried only Massachusetts, a second volume of *Speeches and Forensic Arguments* appeared, this one edited anonymously by Edward Everett who also contributed a short, unsigned biographical sketch. The third and final volume of the series was published in 1843. This too was edited by Everett, with the biographical sketch somewhat enlarged. Everett made still another contribution in 1848 with the *Diplomatic and Official Papers of Daniel Webster while Secretary of State*, but by that date both Webster and his editor were thinking in terms of a more comprehensive edition.

The *Works of Daniel Webster* in six volumes, were again edited by Everett with the assistance of George Jacob Abbot, a clerk in the State Department. The books were actually distributed in early April 1852, although they carried an 1851 publication date. The biographical memoir was expanded into a full length monograph, but the basis of the work remained the volumes earlier published, with additions to bring them up to date. The antiwar speeches and documents of the period of the second war with England were still omitted—presumably because their author continued to regard them as unworthy of the great nationalist of the later years. They might also have been embarrassing to the prospects of a man who still hoped to be president. The *Works* went through numerous printings before being superseded in 1903 by the

National Edition of the Writings and Speeches of Daniel Webster, edited in 18 volumes by James W. McIntyre.

The first 12 volumes of the *Writings and Speeches* follow page by page the 6 volumes of the *Works*; the last two volumes are a reissue of Fletcher Webster's two volume edition of his father's *Private Correspondence*; but the other four volumes include speeches and other documents omitted from the earlier publications. We have taken the *Writings and Speeches* (short title *W & S*) as our basic text, collating with manuscripts where we have them, or with newspaper or pamphlet versions.

PLAN OF WORK

From the outset the Papers of Daniel Webster was planned as an integrated project, using both microfilm and letterpress publication. The persistent pressure of time and the steadily rising cost of book publication were important factors in the choice of the dual media, but the overriding consideration was the desire to bring all of Webster together, without abridgment or gloss, for those who were equipped to use it that way, while providing the less dedicated scholar and the general reader with the essential Webster in convenient annotated form. The microfilm edition, in four different groupings, is as complete as the surviving records permit. Webster's correspondence, including letters received as well as letters sent, together with miscellaneous notes, memoranda, briefs, drafts, formal writings, reports, petitions, and business papers have been issued with printed guide and index as *The Papers of Daniel Webster* by University Microfilms, Ann Arbor, Michigan. *The Legal Papers of Daniel Webster*, also to be issued with guide and alphabetical list of cases by University Microfilms, consists of records drawn primarily from the county courts of New Hampshire and Massachusetts and from the state and lower federal courts in New England. Records of the Department of State and of the Supreme Court are available on film from the National Archives and Records Service of the General Services Administration, but the user must select for himself the reels that may contain Webster material.

The value of these films, including as they do virtually all known Webster papers, cannot be overstated; but the very magnitude of the material makes it unmanageable. The films, moreover, are relatively expensive, require special equipment to use, are hard on the eyes, and effectively bury the grains of wheat by mixing them unevenly with an enormous amount of chaff. The user must decipher for himself often difficult or faded handwriting. He must search out the identity of persons and the nature of events alluded to. and finally he must rely upon his own judgment as to the significance of the given document. In the letterpress edition all this has been done for him, even to the selection of documents in terms of their significance, by editors totally immersed in the time and place and almost as familiar with the central characters as was Webster himself.

The letterpress edition in effect complements and renders more useful these various microfilm collections, whose very existence has made it possible to select more rigorously the documents important enough to be offered to the larger audience reached by the printed book. Each volume of correspondence, moreover, includes a calendar of letters written in the same time period but not selected for publication. For each of these the

microfilm frame number is cited, as is volume and page citation for any document now available only in a printed version. Footnote references are also made to the film wherever appropriate. Items found subsequent to publication of the appropriate volume will be calendared at the end of the Correspondence Series. For the general reader and for the student of the period rather than of the man, the editors believe the selection of items printed will be ample. The biographer, and the scholar pursuing an in-depth study of some segment of the times, will need the film, to which he will find the printed volumes an indispensable annotated guide.

The letterpress edition is being published in four different series, overlapping in time but not in content, in order to make maximum use of subject matter specialists as technical editors. The edition has been planned in a total of fourteen volumes, of which seven are correspondence, three are legal papers, two are diplomatic papers, and two are speeches and formal writings. The present volume covering the period of Webster's life from his first entry into politics through 1833, is the first of the Speeches and Formal Writings series.

EDITORIAL METHOD

The speeches and formal writings included in this volume have been selected by the editors for their significance. Some are important because they affected Webster's political or legal career; others demonstrate the evolution of his thoughts about the issues of the day. The documents are arranged in chronological order, with the date placed to the right of the title. Each speech or writing is preceded by introductory and provenance notes. The introduction is intended to enhance the reader's understanding of the importance of the work by placing it in a historical context. The provenance note traces the origins of the version of the work being published here, and notes the relevant details about revisions and alterations. Footnotes are used to point out variations between the major versions of a text, as well as to identify people, events, quotations, or other matters that help to clarify the context of a particular reference.

For most of the documents reproduced, the text has been taken exactly as it appears in *Writings and Speeches*, published by Scribner in 1903. This is the last collected edition of Webster, including without change the materials published in the 1851 *Works*, together with items originating after that date and others not chosen for the earlier edition.

Speeches and formal writings not selected for inclusion in this volume are listed and described in a calendar at the end of the book.

Symbols used in the provenance notes and the calendar entries are the standard descriptive symbols, and the location symbols developed by the Catalog Publication Division of the Library of Congress. Those appearing in the present volume are listed below under Abbreviations and Symbols.

Abbreviations and Symbols

DESCRIPTIVE SYMBOLS

AD   Autograph Document
AD draft   Autograph Document, draft
AD incomplete   Autograph Document, incomplete
ADS   Autograph Document Signed
Copy   Copy, not by writer

LOCATION SYMBOLS

DLC   Library of Congress
MassSJC,E   Massachusetts Supreme Judicial Court, Essex County
MassSJC,S   Massachusetts Supreme Judicial Court, Suffolk County
NN   New York Public Library
NhD   Dartmouth College, Hanover, N.H.
NhHi   New Hampshire Historical Society, Concord
USCC,DMass   United States Circuit Court, District of Massachusetts

SHORT TITLES

Adams, *Memoirs*   Charles Francis Adams, ed., *Memoirs of John Quincy Adams, Comprising Portions of His Diary from 1795 to 1848* (12 vols., Philadelphia, 1874–1877).

Annals   *Annals of the Congress of the United States, 1789–1824* (18 vols., Washington, D.C., 1834–1856).

Correspondence   Charles M. Wiltse and others, eds., *The Papers of Daniel Webster, Correspondence* (7 vols., Hanover, N.H. and London, 1974–1985).

Elliot, *Debates*   Jonathan Elliot, ed., *The Debates in the Several State Conventions, on the Adoption of the Federal Constitution* (5 vols., Philadelphia, 1845).

Legal Papers   Alfred S. Konefsky and Andrew J. King, eds., *The Papers of Daniel Webster, Legal Papers* (3 vols., Hanover, N.H. and London, 1982–).

mDW Microfilm Edition of the Papers of Daniel Webster (Ann Arbor, 1971). References are followed by frame numbers.

mDWs Microfilm Edition of the Papers of Daniel Webster, Supplementary Reel.

Messages and Papers James D. Richardson, ed., *A Compilation of the Messages and Papers of the Presidents . . . 1789–1897* (10 vols., Washington, D.C., 1896–1899).

Register of Debates *Register of Debates in Congress, 1824–1837* (14 vols., Washington, D.C., 1825–1837).

Speeches and Forensic Arguments Daniel Webster, *Speeches and Forensic Arguments* (3 vols., Boston, 1830, 1835, 1843).

U.S. Stat. *United States Statutes at Large.* References are preceded by volume numbers and followed by page numbers.

Van Tyne Claude H. Van Tyne, ed., *The Letters of Daniel Webster* (New York, 1902).

W & S James W. McIntyre, ed., *The Writings and Speeches of Daniel Webster* (18 vols., New York, 1903).

Works Edward Everett, ed., *The Works of Daniel Webster* (6 vols., Boston, 1851).

In citing legal cases we have used the nominative reporters. Citations to Wheaton and Peters refer to cases decided by the United States Supreme Court. Citations to Mason correspond to cases before the United States Circuit Court, reported alphabetically in *Federal Cases*. Citations to Tyng and Pickering refer to cases from the Massachusetts Supreme Judicial Court, found in *Massachusetts Reports*.

SERIES FOUR:
SPEECHES AND FORMAL WRITINGS

VOLUME ONE: 1800–1833

Rockingham Memorial, August 5, 1812

The *Rockingham Memorial* of 1812 was the springboard for launching Daniel Webster's political career. It was also the ultimate statement of New England Federalism, going back for its origins to Adams's defeat in the election of 1800, and to a succession of Jeffersonian policies thereafter. When France and Great Britain resumed their interrupted war in 1803, Napoleon realized that he could not hold Louisiana against the superior naval power of his enemy. He seized the moment and sold the territory to the United States. New England, foreseeing the dilution of her own influence in the Union, reacted angrily. A handful of Federalist leaders, soon known as the "Essex Junto," even contemplated withdrawal to a northern confederacy of their own, until Alexander Hamilton, titular head of the party, repudiated the movement.

At this point young Daniel Webster, newly established in the practice of law in Boscawen, produced "An Appeal to the Old Whigs of New Hampshire," a pamphlet in support of the Federalist candidate for governor. The work was entirely his own, but the argument was the classic conservative appeal to stability and order that he had imbibed from the distinguished Federalists with whom he read law: Thomas W. Thompson in New Hampshire and Christopher Gore in Boston.

The mighty conflict in Europe, meanwhile, was assuming the proportions of a life and death struggle, engaging economic as well as military weapons. In May of 1805 Great Britain closed American trade with the West Indies, lest some of the products of that trade find their way to the support of Napoleon's armies. A year later, after the destruction of the French fleet at Trafalgar, the coast of Europe from Brest to the Elbe was declared blockaded. It was the United States, as the only neutral maritime nation in a world at war, that was the principal sufferer from these restrictions, which were added to other long-standing grievances: the continued impressment of American seamen by British ships of war, and the reputed tampering with the Indians in the West by British agents. Yet New England, deeply committed to Britain by her commerce as well as by her heritage, reserved her wrath for Bonaparte, who still represented to them all the excesses of the Jacobins. No exception was the 24-year-old Webster, who delivered a Fourth of July address at

Concord in 1806. It was a partisan Federalist speech, pro-British and anti-French.

Napoleon's next move did nothing to appease New England. Flushed with military victories, he issued a decree from Berlin on November 21, 1806 proclaiming a blockade of the British Isles and closing the entire continent of Europe to British trade. The British responded in kind. An Order in Council of January 7, 1807 closed to neutrals the coasting trade between French ports; and another, of November 11, blockaded the European coast from Copenhagen to Trieste. Between these two dates a vessel of the British Navy, plying American coastal waters with contemptuous arrogance, fired upon the U.S. frigate *Chesapeake* off Hampton Roads when her demand for the surrender of deserters was refused. For a short while even New England was outraged; but Great Britain hastened to disavow the incident and to make amends, while Napoleon, in a new decree issued from Milan, reaffirmed and extended his blockade of England.

Spurred by the lure of measureless profits, sleek, swift-sailing Yankee merchantmen continued to thread their way between the British and the French, but American prestige was at its lowest ebb. Faced with the alternatives of entering the war on one side or the other, or halting the flow of foodstuffs and raw materials to both, the choice was clear. Jefferson asked for and obtained an embargo, holding all American vessels in port.

New England went immediately into opposition, and the Federalist party, all but destroyed by the Essex Junto, took a new lease on life. Webster, meanwhile, had moved to Portsmouth, then a thriving seaport, where his new clients included many of the merchants and shipowners who now faced ruin. In 1808 he published for their benefit *Considerations on the Embargo Laws*, in which he challenged the constitutionality of the restrictive system. In port cities from Maine to the Carolinas opposition slowly mounted until it could no longer be withstood. As Jefferson gave way to Madison in 1809, the embargo was repealed, to be replaced by a form of non-intercourse that permitted commerce with all nations excepting only France and Great Britain. The new approach proved no more satisfactory than the old, and after a year of turmoil it too was repealed. There was, however, a curious proviso, that if either belligerent should rescind its own restrictions, non-intercourse would be reimposed against the other.

The wily Bonaparte lost no time in letting it be known that the Berlin and Milan decrees were repealed as of November 1, 1810, although no change was observable in his treatment of American vessels; but a too-credulous Madison, desperately seeking to escape his own dilemma, took the French emperor at his word. Non-intercourse was reimposed

against Great Britain early in 1811, but events had already passed beyond the control of the president. The elections of 1810 had returned to Congress, primarily from the South and West, a younger, more aggressive breed, soon to be called the "War Hawks," who were ready to redress long-standing grievances in arms. President Madison's message to the new Congress, meeting early in November 1811, recommended preparation for war with Great Britain. The following April a 90-day embargo was imposed to give ships at sea time to make port; and on June 19, 1812 war was declared.

The news was in the Portsmouth papers on the 30th. Daniel Webster, now a successful lawyer and popular speaker, delivered the Fourth of July address before the Washington Benevolent Society at Brentwood. He repudiated the stated causes of the war, and denounced the war itself, which was exactly what his audience wanted to hear. The speech won him immediate acclaim, and a seat as delegate to a Rockingham County convention of citizens opposed to the war. There he was named chairman of a committee to prepare a memorial to the president. Having been warned that such might be the case, he had the document ready when the convention met. With relatively minor changes his draft was adopted and sent forth to the world as the *Rockingham Memorial*.

The same convention, in its political capacity, nominated Webster for Congress. He was elected easily and took his seat at the special session of the 13th Congress in May 1813.

The text of the Rockingham Memorial printed below follows the first published version in the Portsmouth *Oracle* of August 8, 1812, as reproduced in *Writings and Speeches*, 15: 599–610. This is the document as it came from Webster's committee. The manuscript, in an unidentified hand, is now at the New Hampshire Historical Society.

In addition to this committee product, there are two earlier manuscript versions in Webster's hand. The shorter of the two is in the New Hampshire Historical Society, where it is mistakenly endorsed "Minutes of Mr. Webster's Brentwood Speech in 1812." It is also available in the microfilm edition of the Webster Papers, mDW 1344–1353. The second, enlarged draft, now in the Dartmouth College Archives (mDW 1355–1381) is the manuscript with which we have collated the *Oracle* text.

Although variations are relatively numerous, they are for the most part changes in wording or in the order of presentation that do not alter the meaning. To indicate these variations by brackets, italics, footnotes, or in some other form would render the text virtually unreadable. To publish only Webster's draft, on the other hand, would be misleading, since it was the committee product as disseminated in the press and in pamphlet from that helped to channel New England's opposition to the

war and brought Webster to national attention. It is therefore this final version that appears below. Those interested in textual variants may compare the extant drafts for themselves. Significant changes have been footnoted, but there is of course now no way of knowing which are Webster's own modifications, based on committee discussion, and which may have been suggested by others.

More than fifteen hundred of the inhabitants and free electors of the county of Rockingham in the state of New Hampshire, being assembled in an orderly and peaceable manner, according to our undoubted constitutional rights, at Brentwood, in said county, on the fifth day of August, 1812, to consult on the common good and public welfare, do now address you, with the respect due to the Chief Magistrate of the nation.

In assembling to express our opinions on the present state of our national affairs, we are influenced, not only by a wish to contribute, as far as in us lies, towards removing the evils which we feel, and averting the greater evils which we fear, but also by a sense of the duty we owe to the Supreme Executive of the nation.

The Chief Magistrate of a Government, which rests on public opinion, and which can only look for the support of its measures to the approbation of the people, has a right to be informed, distinctly and unequivocally, of the sentiments entertained by the community, concerning measures of great national importance. As one portion of the community, deeply interested in the present state of things, and solicitously concerned about their future progress, we beg leave to present to you a brief view of our sentiments and opinions.

We have witnessed, with sincere and deep regret, a system of policy pursued by the General Government, from the Embargo of 1807, to the present time, tending most obviously, in our view, to the destruction of the commerce of these states. We have not been indifferent spectators of this course of measures. Being inhabitants of the Atlantic coast, we regard commerce, as a great and essential interest. It is not only in itself a leading pursuit, but it is most intimately blended with all our other interests and occupations. Habits, arising naturally from our local situation, and the nature of our soil and products, and now confirmed by the usage of two centuries, are not to be[1] changed. We hold the right of judging for ourselves, and have never yet delegated to any government the power of deciding for us, what pursuits and occupations, best comport with our interests, and our situation. When we assented to the National Constitution, it was among other, (but none more important) reasons, to the end that our commerce might be better protected, and the

1. Manuscript reads "not to be lightly changed."

farther extended. Taught to regard our right of traversing the seas, as sacred, (and it is to us as important) as our right of tilling the ground, we have supposed that we should never be deprived of the former, but for reasons, so weighty and important, as would equally justify the prohibition of the latter. We originally saw nothing, and can now see nothing, either in the letter, or the spirit, of the national compact,[2] which makes it our duty, to acquiesce in a system, tending to compel us to abandon our natural and accustomed pursuits. We regard the Constitution as "an instrument of preservation, not of change." We take its intention to have been, to protect, by the strong arm of the whole nation, the interests of each particular section. It could not therefore be without alarm and apprehension, that we perceived in the General Government a disposition to embarrass and enthrall commerce by repeated restrictions, and to make war, by shutting up our own ports. Still greater was our concern, when we heard ourselves admonished, finally to retire from the seas, and "to provide for ourselves, those comforts and conveniences of life, for which it would be unwise ever more to recur to distant countries."[3] We do not hesitate to say, that we deem this language equally unconstitutional and arrogant; and it would be with infinite regret, mingled with other strong emotions, that we should perceive a fixed and settled resolution in the General Government, to enforce this exhortation by the authority of law, and to accumulate upon us, in the intervals of war, a ponderous and crushing system of restriction, non-importation, non-intercourse, and embargo.

The alarm excited in our minds by the favorite and long continued "Restrictive System," is raised still higher, by the late declaration of war against Great Britain,[4] an event which we believe, in the present defenceless circumstances of the country, will be productive of evils of incalculable magnitude.

We are not, sir, among those who feel an unmanly reluctance to the privations, or a nervous sensibility to the dangers of war. Many of us had

2. Over the next few years, Webster's thinking changed significantly. By 1830 he denied categorically that the Constitution was a compact. See Reply to Hayne, pp.285–348, below.

3. Thomas Jefferson to the Legislature of New Hampshire, August 2, 1808, polygraph copy, DLC. We are indebted to the Jefferson Papers, Princeton University, for a copy of this letter, which was enclosed with a private communication of the same date to Governor John Langdon. The sentence from which Webster extracted his quotation reads:

It gave us time too, to make a last appeal to the reason & reputation of nations; in the meanwhile, I see that this measure of self-denial is approved and supported by the great body of our real citizens: that they meet with chearfulness the temporary privations it occasions, and are preparing with spirit to provide for themselves, those comforts and conveniences of life, for which it would be unwise ever more to recur to distant countries.

4. Manuscript reads "the greatest maritime power on earth."

the honor of aiding, by our humble efforts, in the establishment of our independence, and of exposing our lives, in more than one field of danger and blood, in our country's service. We are ready to meet those scenes again, whenever it can be shown that the vindication of our national honor, or the preservation of our essential rights, demands it. We shall not be more slow than others, to aspire after distinction, in any cause in which distinction would be honorable.[5]

If we could perceive that the present war was just; if we could perceive that our rights and liberties required it; if we could perceive that no Administration, however wise, honest, or impartial, could have carried us clear of it; if we could perceive its expediency, and a reasonable hope of obtaining its professed objects; if we could perceive those things, the war would, in some measure, cease to be horrible. It would grow tolerable, in idea, as its expediency should be made manifest. Its iron and bloody features would soften, as its justice grew apparent. Give us but to see, that this war hath clear justice, necessity, and expediency on its side, and we are ready to pour out our treasure, and our blood in its prosecution.

But we are constrained to say, that we cannot, in conscience, ascribe the foregoing characteristics, to the present war. We are not, sir, the apologists of other nations, nor will our voice ever be heard, to varnish wrongs, inflicted either on the interest or honor of our native land. But we deem it necessary, to every justifiable war, not only that its justice be as plain and visible as the light of Heaven, but that its objects be distinct and clear, in order that every man may see them; that they be great, in order that every man perceive their importance; that they be probably attainable, in order that every citizen may be encouraged to contend for them. We are wholly mistaken, if the causes assigned for the present war against England will bear the test of these principles.

The impressment of our seamen, which forms the most plausible and popular of the alleged causes of war, we believe to have been the subject of great misrepresentation. We have as much sympathy as others, for those who suffer under this abuse of power. We know there are instances of this abuse. We know that native American citizens[6] have been, in some cases, in too many cases, impressed from American merchant

5. Webster's original version of this last sentence is more florid: "We have sons, and brethren, as ambitious as other men to distinguish themselves by martial prowess. They are ready to draw their swords in any cause in which distinction would be honorable."

6. Webster is careful to confine the argument that follows to "native American citizens." Impressment of seamen was one of the long-standing complaints against Great Britain, but so far as records are available, the bulk of them were naturalized Americans, mostly Englishmen; since

ships, and compelled to serve on board British ships of war. But the number of these cases has been extravagantly exaggerated. Every inquiry on the subject strengthens our conviction, that the reputed number bears little relation to the true number. We are among those, to whom instances of impressment, if they did actually exist to any considerable extent, must be known. Yet we cannot find them out. Some of the members of this meeting have been constantly employed in commercial pursuits, and have had ships on the ocean from the Peace of 1783, until the ocean became unnavigable, as to us, by the Embargo of 1807, and yet during all that time have never suffered the loss of one native American seaman, by impressment. Other members of this meeting have, as masters of vessels, long inhabited, as it were, on the seas, and have been visited hundreds of times by British ships of war, and never had an American seaman taken from them by impressment.

The people of the neighboring Commonwealth, as we understand, have been as unable as ourselves, to discover instances of impressment, in any degree equal to the alleged numbers. It is impossible, under these circumstances, for us to believe, that the evil of impressment does exist, in the degree of enormity pretended. If so many of our seafaring fellow-citizens were actually in bondage, they must have been taken from among the inhabitants of the Atlantic coast. They would be from among our brethren, sons, relations and friends. We should be acquainted with them, and their misfortunes. We should hear the cries of their wives and children, their parents and relatives, quite as soon as our fellow-citizens of the South and the West.

It is well worthy of notice, that the greatest apparent feeling on this subject of impressments, and the greatest disposition to wage war on that account, are entertained by the representatives of those states, which have no seamen at all of their own; while those sections of the community, in which more than three-fourths of the mariners of the United States have their homes, are, by great majorities, against that war, among the professed objects of which, the release of impressed seamen forms so principal a figure.

It is well known that England pretends to no right of impressing our seamen. She insists, only, that she has a right to the service of her own subjects, in time of war, even though found serving on board the merchant ships of other nations. This claim we suppose to be neither unfounded, nor novel. It is recognized by the public law of Europe, and of the civilized world. Writers of the highest authority maintain, that the right belongs to all nations. For the same reason, say they, that the

---

Britain recognized no right of expatriation she held them to be Englishmen still.

father of a family may demand the aid of his children to defend himself and his house, a nation may call home her subjects to her defence and protection, in time of war.[7]

But if this were not so, is our nation to plunge into a ruinous war, in order to settle a question of relative right, between the government of a foreign nation and the subjects of that government? Are[8] we to fight the battles of British seamen? Nay more—are we to espouse their cause, in opposition to the cause of our own native mariners? Shall we contend for the free and privileged admission of foreigners into our merchant service, and thereby exclude the seamen of New England from that service? Do we profess to be at war, for the support of our seamen's rights, when we contend for a point, which, if gained, will shut them out from the most lucrative part of their employment, and "sacrifice their interest, that British and other foreign seamen may have equal privileges with themselves?"

Fatal,[9] indeed, would it be to important interests of the navigating states, if the consequence of this war should be that the American flag shall give the American character to all who sail under it, and thus invite thousands of foreign seamen to enter into our service, and thrust aside our own native citizens.

But this evil of impressment, however great it may be, is at least not greater now, than it was in the time of Washington. That great man did not, however, deem it an evil to be remedied by war. Neither did it occur to President Adams, nor even to President Jefferson, that it would be wise or politic, for the purpose of attempting to rescue a very small portion of our seamen from captivity, to commence a war, which must inevitably, as this war will, consign ten times as many to a captivity as bad.

England[10] has always professed a willingness to adjust this subject by amicable arrangement. She has repeatedly called on us to do our part,

7. Webster's law library contained several editions of Vattel's *Law of Nations* and Grotius's *Rights of War and Peace*.

8. This passage, to the end of the paragraph, does not appear in Webster's manuscript.

9. In the manuscript, this paragraph reads: "It would be fatal to the navigating interest of New England, it would deprive her seamen of their employment, if this War should terminate in the establishment of a doctrine, that the American flag shall make American seamen of all who serve under it. Such a doctrine would encourage foreigners & discourage and injure ourselves."

10. For this paragraph, except for the last sentence which is retained, the manuscript reads: "Yet England never pretended to any right to take native Americans, and always professed to be willing to form arrangements that should guard against such consequences, it has heretofore appeared to all men to be a fit subject of negotiation, not of war."

towards affecting such adjustment. She has reminded us of the facility—we may say the falsity, with which American protections are obtained; of the frequent instances, in which Irishmen and others, that cannot speak a word of our language, are found with American protections in their pockets. She has, expressly, and officially, offered to prohibit, by severe laws, all impressments from American vessels, if the American Government would enact laws prohibiting American officers from granting protections, of certificates of citizenship to British subjects. She has also, through her Ministers, offered to restore every native seaman, that our Government could name, as being under impressment. For years preceding the Declaration of War, our Government has been, in a manner, silent on this subject. Under an expectation (which has never been broken off) of an amicable arrangement, Government seems to have ceased to make it a topic of complaint. When the arrangement was made with Mr. [David M.] Erskine, the present Administration themselves did not consider any existing difficulties on the subject of impressment as insuperable obstacles to peace.

What is it, then, that hath since given to this subject a sudden and unusual importance? What is it, that hath so completely stifled the voice of the friends of the seamen, and at the same time called into action such powerful sympathies in the bosom of strangers? What is it, that hath raised the voice, beyond the western mountains, so loud and clamorous for their protection by war, while the fathers and brethren, the friends and relatives, the wives and children of these very seamen—nay even the seamen themselves, deprecate this war, as the greatest calamity that could fall upon them?

The blockade, and Orders in Council, the other causes of war, bear no better examination than the subject of impressment. The blockade, now so grievous to be endured, we know was regarded, at the time it was laid, as a measure favorable to our interests. We know this, upon the express declaration of Mr. Monroe, then our Minister in England. We have his own words, that it should be regarded "in a favorable light," and that it "promised to be highly satisfactory to our commercial interests."[11]

By what train of reasoning this favor is now turned into an injury, and an injury of such magnitude as to justify war, we are utterly at a loss to comprehend.

We are equally unsatisfied with the arguments used, to prove that

11. Monroe's remarks, taken out of context, are in his despatches nos. 48 and 49, May 17 and 20, 1806, commenting on Foreign Secretary Charles J. Fox's note to him of May 16. See *Annals*, 10th Cong., 1st sess., pp. 2466, 2469.

the Decrees of France were repealed in November, 1810, and that there-fore, without departing from impartial policy, we are justified in under-taking to compel England, by war, to abandon her Orders in Council. Against such supposed repeal of the French Decrees we have the express declaration of the French Government itself, as late as March, 1812, alleging that those decrees did then exist. We have also, had daily evi-dence of their operation, in the destruction of our property,[12] and some members of this meeting have convictions of the existence and opera-tion of those decrees, down to the very moment of our declaration of war; which convictions, being produced by great and repeated personal losses, in the seizures, detentions, confiscations, and burnings, under those very decrees, are not likely to be removed, by any ingenious comments on the terms of an ambiguous, deceptive, and fallacious instrument, like the Duke of Cadore's letter.

But this question is now at rest. The recent appearance of the French Decree, purporting to be dated April 28, 1811, leaves no foothold for persistence and partiality longer to stand upon. That decree declares, that in consequence of measures adopted by our Government against En-gland in March, 1811, the Decrees of Berlin and Milan shall now be considered as having ceased to operate, as against us, in November, 1810. This proves beyond contradiction, that those decrees were not re-pealed, at the time when our government adopted measures against England, founded on their supposed repeal.

A more singular incongruity, than is here manifest, never character-ized the intercourse of nations. In March, 1811, this Government took measures against England, because France had actually repealed her decrees. Afterwards, in May, 1811, France repealed her decrees, because our government had actually taken measures against England.

The conduct of France, in relation to the repeal of her edicts, exhibits, to our view a scene of the most contemptible fraud and juggling that ever disgraced the court of any nation.

The British[13] Orders in Council, we are informed, are now revoked. We cannot but lament, that the declaration of war was forced and hur-ried, as if to put us beyond the benefit of favorable events. Every attempt at postponement was ineffectual, and the question was taken, at a mo-ment, when, perhaps, a month's delay would have removed the principal ground of complaint, and averted the awful calamity.

12. In the manuscript the phrase reads: "in the detention and destruc-tion of our ships."

13. This paragraph does not ap-pear in Webster's manuscript. He had probably completed his draft of the document before it was known in Portsmouth that the Orders in Council had been repealed. They were repealed on June 23, 1812 but the news did not reach New Hamp-shire until the first of August.

As none of the complaints against England are of recent origin; as[14] they must all have been long in the contemplation of Government, it was reasonably expected, that if Government intended war, it would have made adequate provision and preparation for that event. In this expectation we have been disappointed. The nation is totally unprepared for war. We say totally unprepared; because the degree of preparation bears no definable relation to the magnitude of the occasion, or to the greatness of the interests which are at stake.

Without mentioning the situation of our inland frontier, it is sufficient to advert to the exposed state of our sea coast, and commerce. It is unheard of, and beyond imagination strange, in our opinion, that such great and important interests as the navigation and commerce of a whole country, should be put to hazard,—nay to certain loss—for want of that protection, which is in the power, and which we presume to say it was the duty, of Government, to have afforded.

On the subject of naval defence, we do not feel ourselves confined to the mere language of supplication. On that topic we do not address ourselves to the favor and clemency only, of any Administration. We hold it to be our right, to demand, at the hand of the General Government, adequate protection to our lawful commerce. When the Constitution empowered the Government to build and maintain a navy, it was not supposed, that that provision would remain inoperative parchment, and a dead letter. On the contrary, it was confidently expected that that power would be exercised, as cheerfully as the power to levy and collect taxes. We[15] consider protection on the sea to be as solemnly guaranteed to us by the Constitution, as protection on the land; and we shall as readily assent, to a practical construction of that instrument, which deprives us of the one, as to that which deprives us of the other.

When the commercial and navigating states surrendered to the General Government the riches of their custom-houses, and thereby parted with the fairest portion of their revenue, leaving to themselves nothing to defray the expenses of their own establishments, but an unpleasant resort to direct taxation, they had a right to expect, and they did expect, from the wisdom and justice of that Government, adequate and ample means of protection and defence. They[16] entered into the union under this full expectation. It was an expectation, raised and excited, not only by the express words of the Constitution itself, but also by the declarations and assurances of those, who recommended its adoption.

It is not disrespectful to remind you sir, that a distinguished advocate

14. "as they . . . of Government," absent from manuscript.

15. This sentence is absent from the manuscript.

16. The remainder of this paragraph is not included in the manuscript.

for the union of these states, urged the adoption of the Federal Constitution upon the inhabitants of the Atlantic frontier in the following manner:[17]

> The palpable necessity of the power to provide and maintain a navy, has protected that part of the Constitution, against a spirit of censure which has spared few other parts. It must be numbered among the greatest blessings of America, that as her union will be the only source of her maritime strength, so this will be the principal source of her security against danger from abroad.
>
> The inhabitants of the Atlantic frontier are all of them deeply interested, in this provision for naval protection, and if they have hitherto been suffered to sleep quietly in their beds, if their property has remained safe against the predatory spirit of licentious adventurers; if their maritime towns have not yet been compelled to ransom themselves from the terrors of conflagration, by yielding to the exactions of daring and sudden invaders, these instances of good fortune are not to be ascribed to the capacities of the existing Government (in 1788).

The same distinguished gentleman, at a later period, gave to the people of this nation a solemn and official pledge of his sentiments on this important subject, in his station as a leading member of Congress. in the following manner.

> I consider an acquisition of maritime strength essential, to this country; should we ever be so unfortunate as to be engaged in war, what but this can defend our towns and cities upon the sea coast? or what but this can enable us to repel an invading enemy.[18]

May we now, sir, be permitted to ask, whether these hopes have been realized, and these assurances performed? Has this solemn pledge been redeemed? Does the present actual administration of the Constitution

17. The "distinguished advocate" is of course Madison himself. The quotation that follows is from *The Federalist*, No. 41, but Webster makes the passage better serve his own purposes by omitting from the end of the first paragraph the following: "In this respect our situation bears another likeness to the insular advantage of Great Britain. The batteries most capable of repelling foreign enterprizes on our safety, are happily such as can never be turned by a perfidious government against our liberties."

The second paragraph, as Webster quotes it, ends in mid-sentence, which should continue: ". . . existing government for the protection of those from whom it claims allegiance, but to causes that are fugitive and fallacious." The paragraph continues at considerable length, but the remainder is not relevant.

18. With inconsiderable changes, the quotation is from Madison's speech in Congress, April 21, 1789, *Annals:* 197.

comport with these principles? Is a sufficient navy provided and maintained? Is this naval protection in which the inhabitants of the Atlantic frontier are so deeply interested, afforded to them? Can they, now, sleep quietly in their beds? Is[19] their property now safe against the licentious spirit of predatory adventurers? Are their maritime towns secure from the terrors of conflagration, or the exactions of daring and sudden invaders? We put these questions, not merely to the wisdom and policy, but to the duty and the conscience of our Government. Alas! it is notorious that we have not this navy; we are not protected; we cannot be quiet, or secure; our maritime towns are not safe against invasion and burning; our best interests are at the mercy of our enemies, and we can do nothing, but sit still, and see the fruits of thirty years of laborious industry swept away with the besom of destruction!

We are, sir, from principle and habit[20] attached to the union of the states. But our attachment is to the substance, and not to the form. It is to the good which this union is capable of producing, and not to the evil, which is suffered unnaturally to grow out of it. If the time should ever arrive, when this union shall be holden together by nothing but the authority of law; when its incorporating, vital principle shall become extinct; when its principal exercises shall consist in acts of power and authority, not of protection and beneficence; when[21] it shall lose the strong bond which it hath hitherto had in the public affection; and when, consequently, we shall be one, not in interest and mutual regard, but in name and form only; we, sir, shall look on that hour, as the closing scene of our country's prosperity.

We[22] shrink from the separation of the states, as an event fraught with incalculable evils, and it is among our strongest objections to the present course of measures, that they have, in our opinion, a very dan-

19. This passage, down through "of our Government," absent from the manuscript.

20. Manuscript adds "firmly."

21. "when it shall . . . public affection" absent from manuscript.

22. In Webster's manuscript the paragraph reads:

We shrink from a separation of the states, as an event fraught with incalculable evils, and it is among our strongest objections to the recent, & present measures, that they seem directly calculated, if not intended, <to raise an idea of that event> and presume to bring the contemplation of that event to the mind, and present to the minds of <our> the People as a thing possible to happen. We <solemnly> devoutly believe, that if ever the separation of these States takes place, it will be on some occasion, when a small and heated majority in the Government, contemptuously disregarding the interest, & perhaps stopping the mouths of a large and respectable minority, taking counsel not of their pride & their passion not of their reason & candor, shall by hasty rash & ruinous measures, threaten the system, in particular expose to certain loss the best interests of the people, their lives and their properties.

gerous and alarming bearing on such an event. If a separation of the states ever should take place, it will be, on some occasion, when one portion of the country undertakes to control, to regulate, and to sacrifice the interest of another; when a small and heated majority in the Government, taking counsel of their passions, and not of their reason, contemptuously disregarding the interests, and perhaps stopping the mouths, of a large and respectable minority, shall by hasty, rash, and ruinous measures, threaten to destroy essential rights; and lay waste the most important interests.

It[23] shall be our most fervent supplication to Heaven to avert both the event and the occasion, and the Government may be assured, that the tie that binds us to the Union, will never be broken, by us.

But although we lament the present war, on all accounts, yet do we deprecate it, most of all, as we view in it, as we fear, the harbinger of French Alliance. Our apprehensions, on this head, are not unnatural. The United States, and Napoleon, emperor and king, have a common enemy, and, in some sort, a common cause. They wage war against England, for objects, in some degree, the same. There has been, really or apparently, a series of remarkable coincidences in the measures of the two Governments. Add to this the known character of the French court for intrigue, circumvention, and perfidy, and the world will judge, whether our fears are either groundless, or unwarrantable.

On the subject, of any French connection, either close, or the more remote, we have made up our minds.[24] We will, in no event, assist in uniting the Republic of America with the military despotism of France. We will have no connection with her principles or her power. If[25] her armed troops, under whatever name or character, should come here, we shall regard them as enemies. No pressure, domestic or foreign, shall ever compel us to connect our interests with those of the house of Corsica; or to yoke ourselves, to the triumphal car of the conqueror and the tyrant of continental Europe. In forming this resolution, we have not been thoughtless of possible consequences. We[26] have weighed them. We have reflected on the measures, which an adherence to this resolution might hereafter occasion. We have considered the events which may grow out

23. This paragraph absent from manuscript.

24. Manuscript adds: "We do solemnly assure Your Excellency that no persuasion shall induce, and no power compel us to acquiesce in such a measure."

25. This sentence absent from manuscript.

26. This and the two following sentences, through ". . . out of it." read in DW's manuscript: "We have reflected on the events that may grow out of it, and on the measures that it may make necessary to be adopted. We have considered the enticements that it may call on us to withstand, & the power which it may oblige us to resist."

of it. In the full and undisguised view of these consequences, we have formed this our resolution, and we affirm to you, sir, and to the world, that it is deep, fixed, and unchangeable.

It only remains for us, to express our conscientious convictions, that the present course of measures will[27] prove most prejudicial and ruinous to the country, and to supplicate the government to adopt such a system as shall restore to us the blessings of peace and of commerce.

27. For "will prove . . . to the country." manuscript reads: "will be attended with the most disastrous & ruinous consequences."

The Conscription Bill, December 9, 1814

The United States has never been so near prostration as it was in December 1814, when Webster spoke out against a military draft. The Treasury was empty and the nation's bankers refused to lend more money to sustain a losing cause; the Army, always inadequate, was melting away as militia enlistments expired; the Navy was hopelessly outnumbered and outgunned in its own home waters by an enemy fleet based on Cape Cod; the Capitol, the "palace," and most of Washington City were in ashes; the last word received from the peace commissioners at Ghent conveyed an offer from the British so humiliating that it had been rejected out of hand; the New England states, disaffected even before the war began, were about to meet at Hartford in a convention whose purpose might well be disunion; and most alarming of all, with Napoleon defeated and in exile, battle-hardened British troops were on the way to America.

Although money to pay them appeared most unlikely, the secretary of war, when the special session of Congress met in September, asked for 80,000 more militia to be called into the federal service, and for an additional 40,000 troops to be conscripted. The Senate reluctantly passed the required legislation, but the House added amendments which the upper chamber refused to accept. The House version, following closely the War Department recommendations, provided "for the division of the whole free male population of the United States . . . into classes of twenty-five men each; each class to be compelled . . . to furnish . . . an able-bodied recruit for the service of the United States." (*Annals*, 13th Cong., 3d sess., p. 482.) It was this bill, involved and heavy with detail, that Webster took the floor to oppose on December 9.

The speech was not reported save for a two-line entry in the *Annals of Congress*: "Mr. Webster, of New Hampshire, spoke in favor of the motion," (*Annals*, 13th Cong., 3d sess., p. 800), the motion on the floor being one to strike out the first section of the bill. Webster himself wrote out the speech immediately after its delivery, but wisely decided not to publish it (DW to his brother Ezekiel, Dec. 22, 1814, *Correspondence*, 1: 178). The Hartford Convention, even though neither its purposes nor its outcome were yet known, was being roundly condemned, and it behooved a New England man who looked to a political future to tread

with great caution. Yet those who heard the speech long remembered its impact. More than a decade and a half later, after the first volume of Webster's *Speeches and Forensic Arguments* was published late in 1830, Chief Justice John Marshall recalled the speech and wondered why it had been omitted from the collection (Marshall to DW, Jan. 23, 1831, mDW 9150).

The text reproduced below is from Webster's *Writings and Speeches*, 14: 55–69, which follows exactly, save for occasional variations in spelling, capitalization, and punctuation, a manuscript in the New Hampshire Historical Society (mDW 1747). Both the editors of W & S and C. H. Van Tyne, who also reproduced it (Van Tyne, pp. 56–68), assume this to be the manuscript Webster wrote out in December 1814. It is not, however, in Webster's hand. The original manuscript had already been lost by the time Curtis wrote his *Life of Webster* in the 1860's (1: 139). Just when the manuscript was copied, and by whom, is pure conjecture. It may have been copied by Charles Brickett Haddock, or at his direction, when he was editing the first volume of *Speeches and Forensic Arguments* in 1830, with a view to including it. It was probably Webster himself who determined the omission. After the Reply to Hayne (see pp. 285–348, below) he began to see himself as a presidential candidate, and he wanted no reminder of the role New England, or Daniel Webster had played in the War of 1812.

Mr. Chairman: After the best reflection which I have been able to bestow on the subject of the bill before you, I am of opinion that its principles are not warranted by any provision of the Constitution. It appears to me to partake of the nature of those other propositions for military measures which this session, so fertile in inventions, has produced. It is of the same class with the plan of the Secretary of War [James Monroe], with the bill reported to this House by its own Committee for filling the ranks of the regular army, by classifying the free male population of the United States, and with the resolution recently introduced by an honorable gentleman from Pennsylvania [Charles Jared Ingersoll]; and which now lies on your table, carrying the principle of compulsory service in the regular army to its utmost extent.

This bill indeed is less undisguised in its object, and less direct in its means, than some of the measures proposed. It is an attempt to exercise the power of forcing the free men of this country into the ranks of an army, for the general purposes of war, under color of a military service. To this end it commences with a classification which is no way connected with the general organization of the militia, nor, to my apprehension, included within any of the powers which Congress possesses

over them. All the authority which this Government has over the militia, until actually called into its service, is to enact laws for their organization and discipline. This power it has exercised. It now possesses the further power of calling into its service any portion of the militia of the States, in the particular exigencies for which the Constitution provides, and of governing them during the continuance of such service. Here its authority ceases. The classification of the whole body of the militia, according to the provisions of this bill, is not a measure which respects either their general organization or their discipline. It is a distinct system, introduced for new purposes, and not connected with any power which the Constitution has conferred on Congress.

But, sir, there is another consideration. The services of the men to be raised under this act are not limited to those cases in which alone this Government is entitled to the aid of the militia of the States. These cases are particularly stated in the Constitution, "to repel invasion, suppress insurrection, or execute the laws." But this bill has no limitation in this respect. The usual mode of legislating on the subject is abandoned. The only section which would have confined the service of the militia, proposed to be raised, within the United States has been stricken out; and if the President should not march them into the Provinces of England at the north, or of Spain at the south, it will not be because he is prohibited by any provision in this act.

This, sir, is a bill for calling out the militia, not according to its existing organization, but by draft from new created classes;—not merely for the purpose of "repelling invasion, suppressing insurrection, or executing the laws," but for the general objects of war—for defending ourselves, or invading others, as may be thought expedient;—not for a sudden emergency, or for a short time, but for long stated periods; for two years, if the proposition of the Senate should finally prevail; for one year, if the amendment of the House should be adopted. What is this, sir, but raising a standing army out of the militia by draft, and to be recruited by draft, in like manner, as often as occasion may require?

This bill, then, is not different in principle from the other bills, plans, and resolutions which I have mentioned. The present discussion is properly and necessarily common to them all. It is a discussion, sir, of the last importance. That measures of this nature should be debated at all, in the councils of a free government, is cause of dismay. The question is nothing less than whether the most essential rights of personal liberty shall be surrendered, and despotism embraced in its worst form.

I have risen, on this occasion, with anxious and painful emotions, to add my admonition to what has been said by others. Admonition and remonstrance, I am aware, are not acceptable strains. They are duties of unpleasant performance. But they are, in my judgment, the duties

which the condition of a falling State imposes. They are duties which sink deep in his conscience, who believes it probable that they may be the last services which he may be able to render to the Government of his country. On the issue of this discussion, I believe the fate of this Government may rest. Its duration is incompatible, in my opinion, with the existence of the measures in contemplation. A crisis has at last arrived, to which the course of things has long tended, and which may be decisive upon the happiness of present and of future generations. If there be anything important in the concerns of men, the considerations which fill the present hour are important. I am anxious, above all things, to stand acquitted before God and my own conscience, and in the public judgment, of all participations in the counsels which have brought us to our present condition and which now threaten the dissolution of the Government. When the present generation of men shall be swept away, and that this Government ever existed shall be matter of history only, I desire that it may be known that you have not proceeded in your course unadmonished and unforewarned. Let it then be known, that there were those who would have stopped you, in the career of your measures, and held you back, as by the skirts of your garments, from the precipice over which you are plunging and drawing after you the Government of your country.

I had hoped, sir, at an early period of the session, to find gentlemen in another temper. I trusted that the existing state of things would have impressed on the minds of those who decide national measures, the necessity of some reform in the administration of affairs. If it was not to have been expected that gentlemen would be convinced by argument, it was still not unreasonable to hope that they would listen to the solemn preaching of events. If no previous reasoning could satisfy them, that the favorite plans of Government would fail, they might yet be expected to regard the fact, when it happened, and to yield to the lesson which it taught. Although they had, last year, given no credit to those who predicted the failure of the campaign against Canada, yet they had seen that failure. Although they then treated as idle all doubts of the success of the loan, they had seen the failure of that loan. Although they then held in derision all fears for the public credit, and the national faith, they had yet seen the public credit destroyed, and the national faith violated and disgraced. They had seen much more than was predicted; for no man had foretold that our means of defence would be so far exhausted in foreign invasion, as to leave the place of our own deliberations insecure, and that we should this day be legislating in view of the crumbling monuments of our national disgrace.[1] No one had anticipated that this

1. Congress was meeting in the Patent Office, the only public building spared when the British burned the capital late in August.

city would have fallen before a handful of troops, and that British generals and British admirals would have taken their airings along the Pennsylvania Avenue, while the Government was in full flight, just awaked perhaps from one of its profound meditations on the plan of a conscription for the conquest of Canada. These events, sir, with the present state of things, and the threatening aspect of what is future, should have brought us to a pause. They might have reasonably been expected to induce Congress to review its own measures, and to exercise its great duty of inquiry relative to the conduct of others. If this was too high a pitch of virtue for the multitude of party men, it was at least to have been expected from gentlemen of influence and character, who ought to be supposed to value something higher than mere party attachment, and to act from motives somewhat nobler than a mere regard to party consistency. All that we have yet suffered will be found light and trifling in comparison with what is before us, if the Government shall learn nothing from experience but to despise it, and shall grow more and more desperate in its measures, as it grows more and more desperate in its affairs.

It is time for Congress to examine and decide for itself. It has taken things on trust long enough. It has followed executive recommendation, till there remains no hope of finding safety in that path. What is there, sir, that makes it the duty of this people now to grant new confidence to the administration, and to surrender their most important rights to its discretion? On what merits of its own does it rest this extraordinary claim? When it calls thus loudly for the treasure and the lives of the people, what pledge does it offer that it will not waste all in the same preposterous pursuits which have hitherto engaged it? In the failure of all past promises, do we see any assurance of future performance? Are we to measure out our confidence in proportion to our disgrace and now at last to grant away everything, because all that we have heretofore granted has been wasted or misapplied? What is there in our condition that bespeaks a wise or an able government? What is the evidence that the protection of the country is the object principally regarded? In every quarter that protection has been more or less abandoned to the States. That every town on the coast is not now in possession of the enemy, or in ashes, is owing to the vigilance and exertions of the States themselves, and to no protection granted to them by those on whom the whole duty of their protection rested.

Or shall we look to the acquisition of the professed objects of the war, and there find grounds for approbation and confidence. The professed objects of the war are abandoned in all due form. The contest for sailors' rights is turned into a negotiation about boundaries and military roads, and the highest hope entertained by any man of the issue, is that we

may be able to get out of the war without a cession of territory.

Look, sir, to the finances of the country. What a picture do they exhibit of the wisdom and prudence and foresight of Government. "The revenue of a State," says a profound writer, "is the State."[2] If we are to judge of the condition of the country by the condition of its revenues, what is the result? A wise government sinks deep the fountain of its revenues—not only till it can touch the first springs, and slake the present thirst of the treasury, but till lasting sources are opened, too abundant to be exhausted by demand, too deep to be affected by heats and droughts. What sir, is our present supply, and what our provision for the future resource? I forbear to speak of the present condition of the treasury; and as to public credit, the last reliance of government, I use the language of government itself only, when I say it does not exist. This is a state of things calling for the soberest counsels, and yet it seems to meet only the wildest speculations. Nothing is talked of but banks, and a circulating paper medium, and exchequer notes, and the thousand other contrivances which ingenuity, vexed and goaded by the direst necessity, can devise, with the vain hope of giving value to mere paper. All these things are not revenue, nor do they produce it. They are the effect of a productive commerce, and a well ordered system of finance, and in their operation may be favorable to both, but are not the cause of either. In other times these facilities existed. Bank paper and government paper circulated because both rested on substantial capital or solid credit. Without these they will not circulate, nor is there a device more shallow or more mischievous, than to pour forth new floods of paper without credit as a remedy for the evils which paper without credit has already created. As was intimated the other day by my honorable friend from North Carolina [William Gaston] this is an attempt to act over again the farce of the Assignats of France. Indeed, sir, our politicians appear to have but one school. They learn everything of modern France; with this variety only, that for examples of revenue they go to the Revolution, when her revenue was in the worst state possible, while their model for military force is sought after in her imperial era, when her military was organized on principles the most arbitrary and abominable.

Let us examine the nature and extent of the power which is assumed by the various military measures before us. In the present want of men and money, the Secretary of War has proposed to Congress a military conscription. For the conquest of Canada, the people will not enlist; and if they would, the treasury is exhausted, and they could not be paid. Conscription is chosen as the most promising instrument, both of over-

2."Revenues, the sinews of the state." Cicero, *Pro Lege Manilia,* Ch. 7, sec. 17.

coming reluctance to the service, and of subduing the difficulties which arise from the deficiencies of the exchequer. The administration asserts the right to fill the ranks of the regular army by compulsion. It contends that it may now take one out of every twenty-five men, and any part, or the whole of the rest, whenever its occasions require. Persons thus taken by force, and put into an army, may be compelled to serve there during the war, or for life. They may be put on any service, at home or abroad, for defence or for invasion, according to the will and pleasure of the Government. This power does not grow out of any invasion of the country, or even out of a state of war. It belongs to government at all times, in peace as well as in war, and it is to be exercised under all circumstances, according to its mere discretion. This, sir, is the amount of the principle contended for by the Secretary of War.

Is this, sir, consistent with the character of a free government? Is this civil liberty? Is this the real character of our Constitution? No, sir, indeed it is not. The Constitution is libelled, foully libelled. The people of this country have not established for themselves such a fabric of despotism. They have not purchased at a vast expense of their own treasure and their own blood a Magna Charta to be slaves. Where is it written in the Constitution, in what article or section is it contained, that you may take children from their parents, and parents from their children, and compel them to fight the battles of any war in which the folly or the wickedness of government may engage it? Under what concealment has this power lain hidden which now for the first time comes forth, with a tremendous and baleful aspect, to trample down and destroy the dearest rights of personal liberty? Who will show me any constitutional injunction which makes it the duty of the American people to surrender everything valuable in life, and even life itself, not when the safety of their country and its liberties may demand the sacrifice, but whenever the purposes of an ambitious and mischievous government may require it? Sir, I almost disdain to go to quotations and references to prove that such an abominable doctrine has no foundation in the Constitution of the country. It is enough to know that that instrument was intended as the basis of a free government, and that the power contended for is incompatible with any notion of personal liberty. An attempt to maintain this doctrine upon the provisions of the Constitution is an exercise of perverse ingenuity to extract slavery from the substance of a free government. It is an attempt to show, by proof and argument, that we ourselves are subjects of despotism, and that we have a right to chains and bondage, firmly secured to us and our children by the provisions of our government. It has been the labor of other men, at other times, to mitigate and reform the powers of government by construction; to support the rights of personal security by every species of

favorable and benign interpretation, and thus to infuse a free spirit into governments not friendly in their general structure and formation to public liberty.

The supporters of the measures before us act on the opposite principle. It is their task to raise arbitrary powers, by construction, out of a plain written charter of National Liberty. It is their pleasing duty to free us of the delusion, which we have fondly cherished, that we are the subjects of a mild, free, and limited government, and to demonstrate, by a regular chain of premises and conclusions, that government possesses over us a power more tyrannical, more arbitrary, more dangerous, more allied to blood and murder, more full of every form of mischief, more productive of every sort and degree of misery than has been exercised by any civilized government, with a single exception, in modern times.

The Secretary of War has favored us with an argument on the constitutionality of this power. Those who lament that such doctrines should be supported by the opinion of a high officer of government, may a little abate their regret, when they remember that the same officer, in his last letter of instructions to our ministers abroad, maintained the contrary. In that letter he declares, that even the impressment of seamen, for which many more plausible reasons may be given than for the impressment of soldiers, is repugnant to our Constitution. It might therefore be a sufficient answer to his argument, in the present case, to quote against it the sentiments of its own author, and to place the two opinions before the House, in a state of irreconcilable conflict. Further comment on either might then be properly forborne, until he should be pleased to inform us which he retracted, and to which he adhered. But the importance of the subject may justify a further consideration of the arguments.

Congress, having, by the Constitution, a power to raise armies, the secretary contends that no restraint is to be imposed on the exercise of this power, except such as is expressly stated in the written letter of the instrument. In other words, that Congress may execute its powers, by any means it chooses, unless such means are particularly prohibited. But the general nature and object of the Constitution impose as rigid a restriction on the means of exercising power as could be done by the most explicit injunctions. It is the first principle applicable to such a case, that no construction shall be admitted which impairs the general nature and character of the instrument. A free constitution of government is to be construed upon free principles, and every branch of its provisions is to receive such an interpretation as is full of its general spirit. No means are to be taken by implication which would strike us absurdly if expressed. And what would have been more absurd than for this Constitution to have said that to secure the great blessings of liberty it gave

to government an uncontrolled power of military conscription? Yet such is the absurdity which it is made to exhibit, under the commentary of the Secretary of War.

But it is said that it might happen that an army could not be raised by voluntary enlistment, in which case the power to raise armies would be granted in vain, unless they might be raised by compulsion. If this reasoning could prove anything, it would equally show, that whenever the legitimate power of the Constitution should be so badly administered as to cease to answer the great ends intended by them, such new powers may be assumed or usurped, as any existing administration may deem expedient. This is the result of his own reasoning, to which the secretary does not profess to go. But it is a true result. For if it is to be assumed, that all powers were granted, which might by possibility become necessary, and that government itself is the judge of this possible necessity, then the powers of government are precisely what it chooses they should be. Apply the same reasoning to any other power granted to Congress, and test its accuracy by the result. Congress has power to borrow money. How is it to exercise this power? Is it confined to voluntary loans? There is no express limitation to that effect, and, in the language of the secretary, it might happen, indeed it has happened, that persons could not be found willing to lend. Money might be borrowed then in any other mode. In other words, Congress might resort to a *forced* loan. It might take the the money of any man by force, and give him in exchange exchequer notes or certificates of stock. Would this be quite constitutional, sir? It is entirely within the reasoning of the secretary, and it is a result of his argument, outraging the rights of individuals in a far less degree than the practical consequences which he himself draws from it. A compulsory loan is not to be compared, in point of enormity, with a compulsory military service.

If the Secretary of War has proved the right of Congress to enact a law enforcing a draft of men out of the militia into the regular army, he will at any time be able to prove, quite as clearly, that Congress has power to create a Dictator. The arguments which have helped him in one case, will equally aid him in the other, the same reason of a supposed or possible state necessity, which is urged now, may be repeated then, with equal pertinency and effect.

Sir, in granting Congress the power to raise armies, the people have granted all the means which are ordinary and usual, and which are consistent with the liberties and security of the people themselves, and they have granted no others. To talk about the unlimited power of the Government over the means to execute its authority, is to hold a language which is true only in regard to despotism. The tyranny of arbitrary governments consists as much in its means as in its ends; and it would be a ridiculous

and absurd constitution which should be less cautious to guard against abuses in the one case than in the other. All the means and instruments which a free government exercises, as well as the ends and objects which it pursues, are to partake of its own essential character, and to be conformed to its genuine spirit. A free government with arbitrary means to administer it is a contradiction; a free government without adequate provision for personal security is an absurdity; a free government, with an uncontrolled power of military conscription, is a solecism, at once the most ridiculous and adominable that ever entered into the head of man.

Sir, I invite the supporters of the measures before you to look to their actual operation. Let the men who have so often pledged their own fortunes and their own lives to the support of this war, look to the wanton sacrifice which they are about to make of their lives and fortunes. They may talk as they will about substitutes, and compensations, and exemptions. It must come to the draft at last. If the Government cannot hire men voluntarily to fight its battles, neither can individuals. If the war should continue, there will be no escape, and every man's fate and every man's life will come to depend on the issue of the military draft. Who shall describe to you the horror which your orders of conscription shall create in the once happy villages of this country? Who shall describe the distress and anguish which they will spread over those hills and valleys, where men have heretofore been accustomed to labor, and to rest in security and happiness. Anticipate the scene, sir, when the class shall assemble to stand its draft, and to throw the dice for blood. What a group of wives and mothers and sisters, of helpless age and helpless infancy, shall gather round the theatre of this horrible lottery, as if the stroke of death were to fall from heaven before their eyes on a father, a brother, a son, or a husband. And in a majority of cases, sir, it will be the stroke of death. Under present prospects of the continuance of the war, not one half of them on whom your conscription shall fall will ever return to tell the tale of their sufferings. They will perish of disease and pestilence, or they will leave their bones to whiten in fields beyond the frontier. Does the lot fall on the father of a family? His children, already orphans, shall see his face no more. When they behold him for the last time, they shall see him lashed and fettered, and dragged away from his own threshold, like a felon and an outlaw. Does it fall on a son, the hope and the staff of aged parents? That hope shall fail them. On that staff they shall lean no longer. They shall not enjoy the happiness of dying before their children. They shall totter to their grave, bereft of their offspring and unwept by any who inherit their blood. Does it fall on a husband? The eyes which watch his parting steps may swim in tears forever. She is a wife no longer. There is no relation so tender or so sacred that by these accursed measures you do not propose to violate it. There is no happiness so per-

fect that you do not propose to destroy it. Into the paradise of domestic life you enter, not indeed by temptations and sorceries, but by open force and violence.

But this father, or this son, or this husband goes to the camp. With whom do you associate him? With those only who are sober and virtuous and respectable like himself? No, sir. But you propose to find him companions in the worst men of the worst sort. Another bill lies on your table offering a bounty to deserters from your enemy.[3] Whatever is most infamous in his ranks you propose to make your own. You address yourselves to those who will hear you advise them to perjury and treason. All who are ready to set heaven and earth at defiance at the same time, to violate their oaths and run the hazard of capital punishment, and none others, will yield to your solicitations. And these are they whom you are allowing to join your ranks, by holding out to them inducements and bounties with one hand, while with the other you are driving thither the honest and worthy members of your own community, under the lash and scourge of conscription. In the line of your army, with the true levelling of despotism, you propose a promiscuous mixture of the worthy and the worthless, the virtuous and the profligate; the husbandman, the merchant, the mechanic of your own country, with the beings whom war selects from the excess of European population, who possess neither interest, feeling, nor character in common with your own people, and who have no other recommendation to your notice than their propensity to crimes.

Nor is it, sir, for the defence of his own house and home, that he who is the subjct of military draft is to perform the task allotted to him. You will put him upon a service equally foreign to his interests and abhorrent to his feelings. With his aid you are to push your purposes of conquest. The battles which he is to fight are the battles of invasion,—battles which he detests perhaps and abhors, less from the danger and the death that gather over them, and the blood with which they drench the plain, than from the principles in which they have their origin. Fresh from the peaceful pursuits of life, and yet a soldier but in name, he is to be opposed to veteran troops, hardened under every scene, inured to every privation, and disciplined in every service. If, sir, in this strife he fall— if, while ready to obey every rightful command of government, he is forced from his home against right, not to contend for the defence of

3. On September 28, 1814, Senator James Fisk of Vermont introduced a resolution before the House of Representatives, that the Committee on Military Affairs be instructed "to inquire into the expediency of giving to each deserter from the British Army during the present war, one hundred acres of public land. . . ." The House authorized this investigation; Webster did not vote. See *Journal of the House of Representatives*, 13th Cong., 3d sess., pp. 32, 190.

his country, but to prosecute a miserable and detestable project of invasion, and in that strife he fall, 'tis murder. It may stalk above the cognizance of human law, but in the sight of Heaven it is murder; and though millions of years may roll away, while his ashes and yours lie mingled together in the earth, the day will yet come when his spirit and the spirits of his children must be met at the bar of omnipotent justice. May God, in his compassion, shield me from any participation in the enormity of this guilt.

I would ask, sir, whether the supporters of these measures have well weighed the difficulties of their undertaking. Have they considered whether it will be found easy to execute laws which bear such marks of despotism on their front, and which will be so productive of every sort and degree of misery in their execution? For one, sir, I hesitate not to say that they cannot be executed. No law professedly passed for the purpose of compelling a service in the regular army, nor any law which, under color of military draft, shall compel men to serve in the army, not for the emergencies mentioned in the Constitution, but for long periods, and for the general objects of war, can be carried into effect. In my opinion it ought not to be carried into effect. The operation of measures thus unconstitutional and illegal ought to be prevented by a resort to other measures which are both both constitutional and legal. It will be the solemn duty of the State Governments to protect their own authority over their own militia, and to interpose between their citizens and arbitrary power. These are among the objects for which the State Governments exist; and their highest obligations bind them to the preservation of their own rights and the liberties of their people. I express these sentiments here, sir, because I shall express them to my constituents. Both they and myself live under a constitution which teaches us that "the doctrine of non-resistance against arbitrary power and oppression is absurd, slavish, and destructive of the good and happiness of mankind."[4] With the same earnestness with which I now exhort you to forbear from these measures, I shall exhort them to exercise their unquestionable right of providing for the security of their own liberties.

In my opinion, sir, the sentiments of the free population of this country are greatly mistaken here. The nation is not yet in a temper to submit to conscription. The people have too fresh and strong a feeling of the blessings of civil liberty to be willing thus to surrender it. You may talk to them as much as you please, of the victory and glory to be obtained in the enemy's provinces; they will hold these objects in light estimation if the means be a forced military service. You may sing to them the song of Canada Conquest in all its variety, but they will not be charmed out of the remembrance of their substantial interests and true happiness.

4. Article 10, The Right of Revolution, New Hampshire Bill of Rights.

Similar pretences, they know, are the grave in which the liberties of other nations have been buried, and they will take warning.

Laws, sir, of this nature can create nothing but opposition. If you scatter them abroad, like the fabled serpents' teeth, they will spring up into armed men. A military force cannot be raised in this manner, but by the means of a military force. If administration has found that it cannot form an army without conscription, it will find, if it venture on these experiments, that it cannot enforce conscription without an army. The Government was not constituted for such purposes. Framed in the spirit of liberty, and in the love of peace, it has no powers which render it able to enforce such laws. The attempt, if we rashly make it, will fail; and having already thrown away our peace, we may thereby throw away our government.

Allusions have been made, sir, to the state of things in New England, and, as usual, she has been charged with an intention to dissolve the Union.[5] The charge is unfounded. She is much too wise to entertain such purposes. She has had too much experience, and has too strong a recollection of the blessings which the Union is capable of producing under a just administration of government. It is her greatest fear, that the course at present pursued will destroy it, by destroying every principle, every interest, every sentiment, and every feeling which have hitherto contributed to uphold it. Those who cry out that the Union is in danger are themselves the authors of that danger. They put its existence to hazard by measures of violence, which it is not capable of enduring. They talk of dangerous designs against government, when they are overthrowing the fabric from its foundations. They alone, sir, are friends to the union of the States, who endeavor to maintain the principles of civil liberty in the country, and to preserve the spirit in which the Union was framed.

5. Such charges went back to the Essex Junto in 1803. The reference here is to popular speculation as to the purposes of the Hartford Convention.

The Legal Currency, April 26, 1816

The War of 1812 left the country in financial chaos. Failure to recharter the Bank of the United States in 1811 brought a proliferation of state-chartered banks, each issuing its own paper, extending loans, and discounting notes with no rules but the judgment and morality of individual bankers, within widely varying frameworks established by state laws. The financial needs of the government during the war had all but destroyed the national credit, and left it to the first peacetime Congress, the 14th, to restore prosperity. By December 1815, when the new Congress met, only New England banks still redeemed their own notes in gold or silver. There was no standard for a circulating medium, and the Treasury had no choice but to accept for taxes paper that differed from state to state in the degree of its depreciation, and left the government itself with insufficient funds to finance its operations or to pay the interest on the national debt.

While the war continued, all efforts to reestablish a national bank failed, but the state of the currency had so far deteriorated by the end of 1815 that even President Madison, who had vetoed one bank bill, now called for another in his annual message. After a bitter legislative battle, the Second Bank of the United States was finally chartered, the bill being signed by the president on April 10, 1816. The bank was to commence operations in January, 1817, but there was nothing in its charter that would restrain the flow of unequally depreciated paper from the state banks into the Treasury, which could ill-afford the loss of revenue.

The bank bill was still on the president's desk when John C. Calhoun on April 6 offered a bill "for the more effectual collection of revenue in the lawful currency of the United States." The purport of the bill was to require that after December 31, 1816 all moneys due to the United States for any reason must be paid in metallic currency, in treasury notes, or if authorized by the secretary of the treasury in the notes of banks that redeemed their own notes in specie on demand. The bill was debated, amended, and debated once more over the next two and one-half weeks; then brought to a vote on April 25 and defeated, 60 to 59. The following day Webster offered three resolutions, designed to accomplish the same purpose. The speech reproduced below is his accompanying argument. The first two of Websters' resolutions were merely declaratory of policy,

and were presently dropped. The third, containing the meat of his proposal, follows:

> *And resolved further,* That the Secretary of the Treasury be, and he is hereby, required and directed to adopt such measures as he may deem necessary, to cause, as soon as may be, all duties, taxes, debts, or sums of money accruing or becoming payable to the United States, to be collected and paid in the legal currency of the United States, or Treasury notes, or notes of the Bank of the United States, as aforesaid; and that from and after the 1st day of February next on such duties, taxes, debts, or sums of money accruing or becoming payable to the United States as aforesaid, ought to be collected or received otherwise than in the legal currency of the United States, or Treasury notes, or notes of the Bank of the United States as aforesaid (*Annals*, 14th Cong., 1st sess., p. 1440).

Webster's speech was followed by a debate "of much length and no little warmth," but all attempts at amendment were defeated and the resolution passed on the same day it was offered, 71 to 34. The Senate added minor amendments which the House accepted on April 30, a few hours before the session ended.

The text is reproduced from Webster's *Writings and Speeches*, 5: 48–59, identical with *Works*, 3: 48–59. There are a very few, mainly verbal, differences between this version and that contemporaneously published in the *National Intelligencer* and later in *Annals*, 14th Cong., 1st sess., pp. 1440–1449. Those deemed of any significance are footnoted.

I[1] have felt it to be my duty to call the attention of the House once more to the subject of the collection of the revenue, and to present the resolutions which are now submitted. I have been the more inclined to do this from an apprehension that the rejection, yesterday, of the bill which had been introduced, may be construed into an abandonment, on the part of the House, of all hope of remedying the existing evil. I have had, it is true, some objection against proceeding by way of bill; because the case is not one in which the law is deficient, but one in which the execution of the law is deficient. The great object, however, is to obtain a decision of this and the other house, that the present mode of receiving the revenue shall not be continued; and as this might be substantially effected by the bill, I had hoped that it might pass. This hope has been disap-

---

1. In its original publication in the *National Intelligencer*, May 18, 1816, reprinted in *Annals*, 14th Cong., 1st sess., pp. 1440–1449, the first two paragraphs of this speech are cast in the third person: "Mr. Webster said, that he had felt it to be his duty," etc. The conversion is made in *W & S*, which we have followed.

pointed. The bill has been rejected. The House has put its negative upon the only proposition which has been submitted to it, for correcting a state of things which every body knows to exist in plain violation of the Constitution, and in open defiance of the written letter of the law. For one, I can never consent to adjourn, leaving this implied sanction of the House upon all that has taken place, and all that may hereafter take place. I hope not to hear again that there is not now time to act on this question. If other gentlemen consider the question as important as I do, they will not forbear to act on it from any desire, however strong, to bring the session to an early close.

The situation of the country, in regard to its finances and [2] the collection of its revenues, is most deplorable. With a perfectly sound legal currency, the national revenues are not collected in this currency, but in paper of various sorts and various degrees of value. The origin and progress of this evil are distinctly known, but it is not easy to see its duration or its future extent, if an adequate remedy be not soon found. Before the war, the business of the country was conducted principally by means of the paper of the different State banks. As these were in good credit, and paid their notes in gold and silver on demand, no great evil was experienced from the circulation of their paper. Not being, however, a part of the legal money of the country, it could not, by law, be received in the payment of duties, taxes, or other debts to government. But being payable, and hitherto regularly paid, on demand, the collectors and agents of government had generally received it as cash; it had been deposited as cash in the banks which received the deposits of government, and from them it had been drawn as cash, and paid off to creditors of the public.

During the war this state of things changed. Many of the banks had been induced to make loans to a very great amount to the government. These loans were made by an issue of their own bills. This proceeding threw into circulation an immense quantity of bank paper, in no degree corresponding with the mercantile business of the country, and resting, for its payment and redemption, on nothing but the government stocks, which were held by the banks. The consequence immediately followed, which it would be imputing a great degree of blindness both to the government and to the banks to suggest that they had not foreseen. The excess of paper which was found everywhere created alarm. Demands began to be made on the banks, and they all stopped payment. No contrivance to get money without inconvenience to the people ever had a shorter course of experiment, or a more unequivocal termination. The depreciation of bank-notes was the necessary consequence of a neglect or refusal to pay them, on the part of those who issued them. It took

2. "its finances and" omitted in *Annals*.

place immediately, and has continued, with occasional fluctuations in the depression,[3] to the present moment. What still further increases the evil is, that this bank paper, being the issue of very many institutions, situated in different parts of the country, and possessing different degrees of credit, the depreciation has not been, and is not now, uniform throughout the United States. It is not the same at Baltimore as at Philadelphia, nor the same at Philadelphia as at New York. In New England, the banks have not stopped payment in specie, and of course their paper has not been depressed at all. But the notes of banks which have ceased to pay specie have, nevertheless, been, and still are, received for duties and taxes, in the places where such banks exist. The consequence of all this is, that the people of the United States pay their duties and taxes in currencies of different values in different places. In other words, taxes and duties are higher in some places than they are in others, by as much as the value of gold and silver is greater than the value of the several descriptions of bank paper which are received by government. This difference in relation to the paper of the District where we now are, is twenty-five per cent. Taxes and duties, therefore, collected in Massachusetts, are one quarter higher than the taxes and duties which are collected, by virtue of the same laws, in the District of Columbia.

By the Constitution of the United States, it is certain that all duties, taxes, and excises ought to be uniform throughout the country; and that no preference should be given, by any regulation of commerce or revenue, to the ports of one State over those of another. This constitutional provision, it is obvious, is flagrantly violated. Duties and taxes are not uniform. They are higher in some places than in others. A citizen of New England pays his taxes in gold and silver, or their equivalent. From his hand the collector will not receive, and is instructed by government not to receive, the paper of the banks which do not pay their notes on demand, and which notes he could obtain twenty or twenty-five per cent. cheaper than that which is demanded of him. Yet a citizen of the Middle States pays his taxes in these notes at par. Can a greater injustice than this be conceived? Can constitutional provisions be disregarded in a more essential point? Commercial preferences also are given, which, if they should be continued, would be sufficient to annihilate the commerce of some cities and some States, while they would greatly promote that of others. The importing merchant of Boston pays the duties upon his goods, either in specie or cash notes, which are at least twenty per cent., or in treasury-notes, which are ten per cent. more valuable than the notes which are paid for duties, at par, by the importing merchant at Baltimore. Surely this is not to be endured. Such monstrous inequality

3. *Annals* reads "in the degree of depression."

and injustice cannot continue.[4] Since the commencement of this course of things, it can be shown that the people of the Northern States have paid a million of dollars more than their just proportion of the public burdens. A similar inequality, though somewhat less in degree, has fallen upon the States south of the Potomac, in which the paper in circulation, although not equivalent to specie, is yet of higher value than the bank-notes of this District, Maryland, and the Middle States.

But it is not merely the inequality and injustice of this system, if that may be called system which is rather the want of all system, that need reform. It throws the whole revenue into derangement and endless confusion. It prevents the possibility of order, method, or certainty in the public receipts or disbursements. This mass of depressed paper, thrown out at first in loans to accommodate government, has done little else than embarrass and distress government. It can hardly be said to circulate, but it lies in the channel of circulation, and chokes it up by its bulk and its sluggishness. In a great portion of the country the dues are not paid, or are badly paid; and in an equal portion of the country the public creditors are not paid, or are paid badly.

It is quite clear, that by the statute all duties and taxes are required to be paid in the legal money of the United States, or in treasury-notes, agreeably to recent provisions. It is just as clear, that the law has been disregarded, and that the notes of banks of a hundred different descriptions, and almost as many different values, have been received, and still are received, where the statute requires legal money or treasury-notes to be paid.

In these circumstances, I cannot persuade myself that Congress will adjourn, without attempting something by way of remedy. In my opinion, no greater evil has threatened us. Nothing can more endanger, either the existence and preservation of the public revenue, or the security of private property, than the consequences which are to be apprehended from the present course of things, if they be not arrested by a timely and effectual interference. Let gentlemen consider what will probably happen, if Congress should rise without the adoption of any measure on the subject.

Virginia, having passed a law for compelling the banks in that State to limit the circulation of their paper, and resume specie payments by the autumn, will, doubtless, repeal it. The States farther to the south will probably fall into a similar relaxation, for it is hardly to be expected that they will have firmness and perseverance enough to persist in their present most prudent and commendable course, without the countenance of the general government. If, in addition to these events, an abandon-

4. For "cannot continue," *Annals* reads "are not to be tolerated."

ment of the wholesome system which has thus far prevailed in the Northern States, or any relaxation of that system, should take place, the government is in danger of falling into a condition, from which it will hardly be able to extricate itself for twenty years, if indeed it shall ever be able to extricate itself; and if that state of things, instead of being changed by the government, shall not change the government.

It is our business to foresee this danger, and to avoid it. There are some political evils which are seen as soon as they are dangerous, and which alarm at once as well the people as the government. Wars and invasions, therefore, are not always the most certain destroyers of national prosperity. They come in no questionable shape. They announce their own approach, and the general security is preserved by the general alarm. Not so with the evils of a debased coin, a depreciated paper currency, or a depressed and falling public credit. Not so with the plausible and insidious mischiefs of a paper-money system. These insinuate themselves in the shape of facilities, accommodation, and relief. They hold out the most fallacious hope of an easy payment of debts, and a lighter burden of taxation. It is easy for a portion of the people to imagine that government may properly continue to receive depreciated paper, because they have received it, and because it is more convenient to obtain it than to obtain other paper or specie. But on these subjects it is that government ought to exercise its own peculiar wisdom and caution. It is supposed to possess, on subjects of this nature, somewhat more of foresight than has fallen to the lot of individuals. It is bound to foresee the evil before every man feels it, and to take all necessary measures to guard against it, although they may be measures attended with some difficulty and not without temporary inconvenience. In my humble judgment, the evil demands the immediate attention of Congress. It is not certain, and in my opinion not probable, that it will ever cure itself. It is more likely to grow by indulgence, while the remedy which must in the end be applied will become less efficacious by delay.

The only power which the general government possesses of restraining the issues of the State banks, is to refuse their notes in the receipts of the treasury. This power it can exercise now, or at least it can provide now for exercising in reasonable time, because the currency of some part of the country is yet sound, and the evil is not universal. If it should become universal, who that hesitates now will then propose any adequate means of relief? If a measure like the bill of yesterday, or the resolutions of to-day, can hardly pass here now, what hope is there that any efficient measure will be adopted hereafter?

The conduct of the treasury department in receiving the notes of the banks, after they had suspended payment, might, or might not, have

been excused by the necessity of the case. That is not now the subject of inquiry. I wish such inquiry had been instituted. It ought to have been. It is of dangerous consequence to permit plain omissions to execute the law to pass off, under any circumstances, without inquiry. It would probably be easier to prove that the treasury must have continued to receive such notes, or that all payments to government would have been suspended, than it would be to justify the previous negotiations of great loans at the banks, which was a voluntary transaction, induced by no particular necessity, and which is, nevertheless, beyond doubt, the principal cause of their present condition. But I have expressed my belief on more than one occasion, and I repeat the opinion, that it was the duty, and in the power, of the Secretary of the Treasury [Alexander J. Dallas], on the return of peace, to return to the legal and proper mode of collecting the revenue. The paper of the banks rose on that occasion almost to an equality with specie; that was the favorable moment. The banks in which the public money was deposited ought to have been induced to lead the way, by the sale of their government stocks, and other measures calculated to bring about, moderately and gradually, but regularly and certainly, the restoration of the former and only safe state of things. It can hardly be doubted, that the influence of the treasury could have affected all this. If not, it could have withdrawn the deposits and countenance of government from institutions which, against all rule and propriety, were holding great sums in government stocks, and making enormous profits from the circulation of their own dishonored paper. That which was most wanted was the designation of a time for the corresponding operation of banks in different places. This could have been made by the head of the treasury, better than by any body or every body else. But the occasion was suffered to pass by unimproved, and the credit of the banks soon fell again, when it was found they used none of the means which the opportunity afforded them for enabling them to fulfil their engagements.

As to any power of compulsion to be exercised over the State banks, they are not subject to the direct control of the general government. It is for the State authorities which created them to decide whether they have acted according to their charters, and if not, what shall be the remedy for their irregularities. But from such of them as continued to receive deposits of public money, government had a right to expect that they would conduct their concerns according to the safe and well-known principles which should properly govern such institutions.[5] It is bound

5. *Annals* adds: "And this government has in all cases a right to protect its own revenues, and to guard them against defalcation by bad or depreciated paper."

also to collect its taxes of the people on a uniform system. These rights and these duties are too important to be surrendered to the accommodation of any particular interest or any temporary purpose.

The resolutions before the House take no notice of the State banks. They express neither praise nor censure of them. They neither commend them for their patriotism in the loans made to government, nor propose to tax them for their neglect or refusal to pay their debts. They assume no power of interfering with these institutions. They say not one word about compelling them to resume their payments; they leave that to the consideration of the banks themselves, or to those who have a right to call them to account for any misconduct in that respect. But the resolutions declare that taxes ought to be equal; that preferences ought not to be given; that the revenues of the country ought not to be diminished in amount, nor hazarded altogether, by the receipt of varying and uncertain paper; and that the present state of things, in which all these unconstitutional, illegal, and dangerous ingredients are mixed, ought not to exist.

It has been said, that these resolutions may be construed into a justification of the past conduct of the treasury department. Such an objection has been anticipated. It was made, in my opinion, with much more justice to the bill rejected yesterday, and a provision was therefore subsequently introduced into that bill to exclude such an inference. This is certainly not the time to express any justification or approbation of the conduct of that department on this subject, and I trust these resolutions do not imply it. Nor do the resolutions propose to express any censure. A sufficient reason for declining to do either is, that the facts are not sufficiently known. What loss has actually happened, what amount—it is said to be large—may be now in the treasury, in notes which will not pass, or under what circumstances these were received, is not now sufficiently ascertained.

But before these resolutions are rejected, on the ground that they may shield the treasury department from responsibility, it ought to be clearly shown that they are capable of such a construction. The mere passing of any resolution cannot have that effect. A declaration of what ought to be done does not necessarily imply any sanction of what has been done. It may sometimes imply the contrary. These resolutions cannot be made to imply any more than this,—that the financial affairs of the country are in such a condition that the revenue cannot be instantly collected in legal currency. This they do imply, and this I suppose almost all admit to be true. An instantaneous execution of the law, without warning or notice, could in my opinion produce nothing, in a portion of the country, but an entire suspension of payments.

But to whose fault it is owing that the affairs of the country are re-

duced to this condition, they do not declare. They do not prevent, or in any degree embarrass, future inquiry on that subject. They speak to the fact that the finances are deranged. They say, also, that reformation, though it must be gradual, ought to be immediately begun, and to be carried to perfection in the shortest time practicable. They cannot by any fair construction be made to express the approbation of Congress on the past conduct of any high officer of government; and if the time shall ever come when this House shall deem investigation necessary, it must be a case of very unpromising aspect, and of most fearful issue, which shall afford no other hope of escape than by setting up these resolutions by way of bar to an inquiry.

Nor is it any objection to this measure that inquiry has not first been had. Two duties may be supposed to have rested on the House: the one, to inquire into the origin of the evil, if it needed inquiry; and the other, to find and apply the remedy. Because one of these duties has not hitherto been discharged, is no reason why the other should be longer neglected. While we are deciding which to do first, the time of the session is going by us, and neither may be done. In the mean time, public mischiefs of unknown magnitude and incalculable duration threaten the country. I see no equivalent, no consolation, no mitigation, for these evils in the future responsibility of departments. Let gentlemen show me any responsibility which will not be a name and a mockery. If, when we meet here again, it shall be found that all the barriers which have hitherto, in any degree, restrained the emissions of a paper money of the very worst sort, have given way, and that the floods have broken in upon us and come over us,—if it shall be found that revenues have failed, that the public credit, now a little propped and supported by a state of peace and commerce, has again tottered and fallen to the ground, and that all the operations of government are at a stand,—what then will be the value of the responsibility of departments? How great, then, the value of inquiry, when the evil is past prevention, when officers may have gone out of place, and when, indeed, the whole administration will necessarily be dissolving by the expiration of the term for which the chief executive magistrate was chosen? I cannot consent to stake[6] the chance of the greatest public mischiefs upon a reliance on any such responsibility. The stakes are too unequal.

As to the opinion advanced by some, that the object of the resolutions cannot in any way be answered, that the revenues cannot be collected otherwise than as they are now, in the paper of any and every banking association which chooses to issue paper, it cannot for a moment be admitted. This would be at once giving up the government; for what is government without revenue, and what is a revenue that is gathered to-

6. *Annals* reads "take."

gether in the varying, fluctuating, discredited, depreciated, and still falling promissory notes of two or three hundred distinct, and, as to this government, irresponsible banking companies? If it cannot collect its revenues in a better manner than this, it must cease to be a government. This thing, therefore, is to be done; at any rate it is to be attempted. That it will be accomplished by the treasury department, without the interference of Congress, I have no belief. If from that source no reformation came when reformation was easy, it is not now to be expected. Especially after the vote of yesterday, those whose interest it is to continue the present state of things will arm themselves with the authority of Congress. They will justify themselves by the decision of this House. They will say, and say truly, that this House, having taken up the subject and discussed it, has not thought fit so much as to declare that it is expedient ever to relieve the country or its revenues from a paper-money system. Whoever believes that the treasury department will oppose this tide, aided as it will be by strong feeling and great interest, has more faith in that department than has fallen to my lot. It is the duty of this House to interfere with its own authority. Having taxed the people with no light hand, it is now its duty to take care that the people do not sustain these burdens in vain. The taxes are not borne without feeling. They will not be borne without complaint, if, by mismanagement in collection, their utility to government should be lost, and they should get into the treasury at last only in discredited and useless paper.

A bank of thirty-five millions has been created for the professed purpose of correcting the evils of our circulation, and facilitating the receipts and expenditures of government. I am not so sanguine in the hope of great benefit from this measure as others are. But the treasury is also authorized to issue twenty-five millions of treasury-notes, eighteen or twenty millions of which remain yet to be issued, and which are also allowed by law to be received for duties and taxes. In addition to these is the coin which is in the country, and which is sure to come forth into circulation whenever there is a demand for it. These means, if wisely and skilfully administered, are sufficient to prevent any particular pressure, or great inconvenience, in returning to the legal mode of collecting the revenue. It is true, it may be easier for the people in the States in which the depreciated paper exists to pay their taxes in such paper than in the legal currency of[7] treasury notes, because they can get it cheaper. But this is only saying that it is easier to pay a small tax than to pay a large one, or that money costs more than that which is less valuable than money, a proposition not to be disputed. But a medium of payment convenient for the people and safe for the government will be furnished, and may everywhere be obtained for a reasonable price. This

7. *Annals* reads "or."

is all that can justly be expected of Congress. Having provided this, they ought to require all parts of the country to conform to the same measure of justice. If taxes be not necessary, they should not be laid. If laid, they ought to be collected without preference or partiality.

But while some gentlemen oppose the resolutions because they fix a day too near, others think they fix a day too distant. In my own judgment, it is not so material what the time is, as it is to fix a time. The great object is to settle the question, that our legal currency is to be preserved, and that we are not about to embark on the ocean of paper money. The State banks, if they consult their own interest, or the interest of the community, will dispose of their government stocks, and prepare themselves to redeem their paper and fulfil their contracts. If they should not adopt this course, there will be time for the people to be informed that the paper of such institutions will not answer the demands of government, and that duties and taxes must be paid in the manner provided by law.

I cannot say, indeed, that this measure will certainly produce the desired effect. It may fail. Its success, as is obvious, must essentially depend on the course pursued by the treasury department. But its tendency, I think, will be to produce good. It will, I hope, be a proof that Congress is not regardless of its duty. It will be evidence that this great subject has not passed without notice. It will record our determination to resist the introduction of a most destructive and miserable policy into our system; and if there be any sanction or authority in the Constitution and the law, if there be any regard for justice and equality, if there be any care for the national revenue, or any concern for the public interest, let gentlemen consider whether they will relinquish their seat here before this or some other measure be adopted.

Memorial to Congress on Restraining the Increase of Slavery, December 15, 1819

The Missouri Compromise was a watershed in American history—a turning point from which there was no retreat. When the Missouri debate began in mid-February 1819 the country was deeply mired in its first major depression, for which many blamed the second Bank of the United States; Congress was preoccupied with the bank question and with General Jackson's unauthorized foray into Spanish Florida; and the moot question of state versus national sovereignty, never far beneath the surface, was about to be tested in the Supreme Court. The atmosphere was already charged when a bill granting statehood to Missouri reached the floor of the House of Representatives. By a narrow sectional majority the bill was amended to exclude slavery. The rather brief debate revolved around two questions: whether Congress had power to attach such a condition to statehood, and whether it was expedient to exercise the power, if it existed. The amended bill was then adopted by a margin of almost two to one.

Debate in the Senate, where slave and free states were equally represented, is not reported, but from the tenor of Rufus King's remarks, written out later for pamphlet publication, we may assume a pattern similar to that in the House. As the session drew to a close the Senate rejected the restrictive amendments. The House refused to recede and for the time being Missouri statehood was lost.

After the adjournment the debate began in earnest. Southern leaders saw all too clearly that the power to restrict slavery in future states would one day become the power to abolish slavery wherever it existed. The Supreme Court's decision in *McCulloch* v. *Maryland*, holding the nation sovereign over the states, only served to further exacerbate southern sensitivities. Faced with the prospect of ultimate abolition, the slaveholders reconsidered their position. Before the Missouri question was compromised by the next Congress the South had begun a reluctant transition from apology to active defense of her peculiar institution, and the stage was set for the sectional conflict of the 60's.

While the South was sharpening her weapons for the defense of slavery in Missouri, the free states were reacting quite as positively in their own way, with mass meetings, resolutions and memorials favoring

restriction. Such is the memorial from Webster's hand, printed below. A large meeting in the Massachusetts statehouse on December 3, 1819— just three days before the 16th Congress was to meet—voted in favor of such a memorial and named a committee to prepare it. Webster, although he had lived in Boston only three years, was an almost inevitable choice for chairman. His powers of reasoning and his undeviating nationalism had been reaffirmed earlier in the year in *McCulloch* v. *Maryland*. He held no political office and he had been in Washington while the Missouri debates were going on. Associated with him were George Blake, former United States attorney for Boston; Josiah Quincy, former member of Congress and future president of Harvard; James Trecothick Austin, county attorney for Suffolk County; and John Gallison, a court reporter.

The memorial, dated December 15, 1819, takes essentially the same position as to the power of Congress to impose restrictions on statehood that Rufus King had taken in the Senate (DW to King, Dec. 27, 1819, *Correspondence*, 1: 268; and compare *Papers Relative to the Restriction of Slavery: Speeches of Mr. King in the Senate and of Messrs. Taylor & Talmadge in the House of Representatives* (Philadelphia, 1819), and *The Substance of Two Speeches on the Missouri Bill Delivered by Mr. King in the Senate* (New York, 1819), reprinted in Charles R. King, ed., *Life and Correspondence of Rufus King* (6 vols., New York, 1894–1900), 6: 690–703. Webster, however, converts the arguments into an all but impregnable bastion. His succeeding argument in favor of the restriction of slavery is put gently, almost apologetically that it must be made at all, for surely the advantages of freedom must be clear to everyone. Tactfully, he states the case in language least likely to offend.

The text here reproduced is that of the pamphlet issued contemporaneously by Boston printer Sewall Phelps, *A Memorial to the Congress of the United States on the subject of Restraining the Increase of Slavery in New States to be Admitted into the Union*. The pamphlet version in all probability preceded publication in the newspapers which used it as their own text. It appeared without change in *W & S*, 15: 55–72.

The undersigned, inhabitants of Boston and its vicinity, beg leave most respectfully and humbly to represent; That the question of the introduction of slavery into the new States, to be formed on the west side of the Mississippi River, appears to them to be a question of the last importance to the future welfare of the United States. If the progress of this great evil is ever to be arrested, it seems to the undersigned that this is the time to arrest it. A false step taken now cannot be retracted; and it appears to us that the happiness of unborn millions rests on the measures, which Con-

gress may on this occasion, adopt. Considering this is no local question, nor a question to be decided by a temporary expediency, but as involving great interests of the whole of the United States, and affecting deeply and essentially those objects of common defense, general welfare, and the perpetuation of the blessings of liberty, for which the Constitution itself was formed, we have presumed, in this way, to offer our sentiments and express our wishes to the National Legislature. And as various reasons have been suggested, against prohibiting slavery in the new States, it may perhaps be permitted to us to state our reasons, both for believing that Congress possesses the constitutional power to make such prohibition a condition, on the admission of a new State into the Union, and that it is just and proper that they should exercise that power.

And, in the first place, as to the constitutional authority of Congress. The Constitution of the United States has declared, that "the Congress shall have power to dispose of and make all needful rules and regulations respecting the territory, or other property belonging to the United States; and nothing in this Constitution shall be so construed as to prejudice the claims of the United States, or of any particular State." It is very well known that the savings in this clause of the claims of any particular State was designed to apply to claims by the then existing States of territory, which was also claimed by the United States as their own property. It has, therefore, no bearing on the present question. The power, then, of Congress over its own territories is, by the very terms of the Constitution, unlimited. It may make all "needed rules and regulations;" which of course include all such regulations as its own views of policy or expediency shall from time to time dictate. If, therefore, in its judgment, it be needful for the benefit of a Territory to enact a prohibition of slavery, it would seem to be as much within its power of legislation, as any other ordinary act of local policy. Its sovereignty being complete and universal, as to the Territory, it may exercise over it the most ample jurisdiction in every respect. It possesses in this view all the authority which any State Legislature possesses over its own territory; and if a State Legislature may, in its discretion, abolish or prohibit slavery within its own limits, in virtue of its general legislative authority, for the same reason Congress also may exercise the like authority over its own Territories. And that a State Legislature, unless restrained by some constitutional provision, may so do, is unquestionable, and has been established by general practice.

If, then, Congress possesses unlimited powers of government over its Territories, it may certainly from time to time vary, control, and modify its legislation as it pleases. The Territories, as such, can have no rights but such as are conferred by Congress; and it is morally bound to adopt such measures as are best calculated to promote the permanent interest

and security of these Territories, as well as to secure the future well-being of the Union. Without an enabling act of Congress, no Territory or portion of Territory belonging to the United States can be created into a State, or form a constitution of government, or become discharged of its territorial obedience; and if Congress may grant to any of its Territories this privilege, it may also most clearly, as it seems to us, in its discretion, refuse it. It is not obliged to admit it to become a State, if it be not satisfied that such admission will conduce as well to its own good as to the good of the Union. In this respect Congress stands, in relation to its Territories, like a State in relation to any portion of its own territory which requests to be separated and formed into a new State. No person has ever doubted that the question as to such separation was a question of expediency, resting in the sound discretion of the State; and that it could not be claimed as matter of right, unless in virtue of ˙some compact, establishing such right. No person has ever doubted that any State, in acceding to a division of its territory, and the formation of a new State, has always possessed the right to impose its own terms and conditions as a part of the grant. The ground of this right is the exclusive possession of sovereignty, with which the State is not compellable to part, and if it does part with it, it may annex all such conditions and rules as it deems fit for its own security and for the permanent good of the citizens of the divided territory. Such was the case of Virginia, when she acceded to the separation of the District of Kentucky, and allowed it to become an independent State. Such is the case of the recent separation of the District of Maine from Massachusetts. In each of these cases, a considerable number of fundamental conditions were offered to the districts as the sole grounds upon which the separation could be allowed; and not a doubt was ever entertained, that these conditions were within the legitimate exercise and authority of these States. These conditions were accepted by Kentucky, and have been accepted by Maine; and it was never imagined, that they in any respect prevented either from possessing all the proper attributes of State sovereignty. They have never been viewed in any other light than as just restrictions, not upon essential state rights, but upon an unlimited exercise of sovereignty, which might be injurious to rights already vested in the parent State, or its citizens. And if Virginia and Massachusetts may, by virtue of their sovereign rights, impose conditions upon their grants of their own territorial jurisdiction; for the same reason, it would seem, the United States may impose any like conditions, according to their own sound discretion. And a construction of this clause of the Constitution of the United States, which should inhibit Congress from annexing conditions to the act enabling any Territory to form a State government, because it would impair the sovereignty of the State so formed, would equally affect the like conditions annexed by a State to a like act in

favor of a portion of its own territory. A construction, which would lead to such consequences, cannot be a sound one. It would lead to the most injurious results, and absolve all the new States, which have been admitted into the Union since the year 1791, from conditions which have hitherto been held to be inviolably binding upon them. It would also be repugnant to the comprehensive language of this clause of the Constitution, and to the uniform practice which has prevailed under it from the earliest period of the formation of new States to the present time. No State has ever admitted a new State to be formed in its own bosom without annexing conditions, and no act has passed Congress enabling any of its Territories to become States, which has not, in like manner, annexed important fundamental conditions to the act. And if conditions may be annexed, it depends solely upon the wisdom of Congress what such conditions shall be. They may embrace everything not incompatible with the possession of those federal rights which an admission into the Union confers upon the new State. As to such rights, there must, by the very nature of the case, be an implied exception. The remarks, that have hitherto been made, have proceeded upon the supposition that Congress are not morally bound, either by the Treaty of Cession, or by any compact with the inhabitants, to pass an act for the erection of the new State, without imposing conditions.

These observations, so far, have been confined to the constitutional authority of Congress flowing directly from the clause which has been mentioned. Here, then, is the case of an express power given in plain terms; and by another clause of the Constitution, Congress have express authority "to make all laws necessary and proper for carrying that power into execution." But other clauses may well be called in aid of this construction, applicable to all cases whatsoever in which a new State seeks to be admitted into the Union. The Constitution provides that "new States may be admitted into the Union." The only parties to the Constitution, contemplated by it originally, were the thirteen confederated States. It was perceived that the territory, already included within these States, might be beneficially divided and organized under separate governments, and that the Territories already belonging to the United States might, and in good faith ought, to participate in the privileges of the federal Union. It was therefore wisely provided that Congress, in which all the old States were represented, should have authority to admit new States into the Union, whenever in its judgment such an act would be beneficial to the public interests. But it was at the same time provided that no new State should be formed or erected within the jurisdiction of any other State, etc., without the consent of the Legislatures of the States concerned, as well as of the Congress. It is observable, that the language of the Constitution is, that new States may (not shall) be admitted into

the Union. It is, therefore, a privilege which Congress may withhold or grant, according to its discretion. If it may give its consent, it may also refuse it, and no new State can have a right to compel Congress to do that which, in its judgment, is not fit to be done. If Congress have authority to withhold its consent, it has also authority to give that consent, either absolutely, or upon condition; for there is nothing in the Constitution which restricts the manner or the terms of that consent. It is observable, too, that where a new State is to be erected within the limits of an old State, the consent of the State Legislature is as necessary as that of Congress. Now it will not, we suppose, be contended, that the State Legislature may not grant its consent upon condition; and, if so, Congress must have the same right also, for the consent of the State Legislatures and of Congress is required by the same clause, and the construction which fixes the meaning of "consent" as to the one, must, in order to maintain consistency, fix it as to the other. And here it might be again asked, if the conditions of Virginia, annexed to her consent that Kentucky should become a State, were not binding upon the latter, and upon Congress? It appears to the memorialists perfectly clear, that since Congress has a discretionary authority as to the admission of new States into the Union, it may impose whatever conditions it pleases as terms of that consent; and that this clause, alone, which applies as well to new States formed from old States, as to those formed from the Territories of the Union, completely establishes the right, for which the memorialists contend.

The creation of a new State is, in effect, a compact between Congress and the inhabitants of the proposed State. Congress would not probably claim the power of compelling the inhabitants of Missouri to form a Constitution of their own, and come into the Union as a State. It is as plain, that the inhabitants of that Territory have no right to admission into the Union, as a State, without the consent of Congress. Neither party is bound to form this connection. It can be formed only by the consent of both. What, then, prevents Congress, as one of the stipulating parties, to propose its terms? And if the other party assents to these terms, why do they not effectually bind both parties? Or if the inhabitants of the Territory do not choose to accept the proposed terms, but prefer to remain under a territorial government, has Congress deprived them of any right, or subjected them to any restraint, which, in its discretion, it had not authority to do? If the admission of new States be not discretionary exercise of a constitutional power, but, in all cases, an imperative duty, how is it to be performed? If the Constitution means that Congress shall admit new States, does it mean that Congress shall do this on every application, and under all circumstances? Or, if this

construction cannot be admitted, and if it must be conceded that Congress must, in some respects, exercise its discretion, on the admission of new States, how is it to be shown that the discretion may not be exercised, in regard to this subject, as well as in regard to others?

The Constitution declares, "that the migration or importation of such persons as any of the States, now existing, shall think proper to admit, shall not be prohibited by the Congress, prior to the year 1808." It is most manifest that the Constitution does contemplate, in the very terms of this clause, that Congress possess the authority to prohibit the migration or importation of slaves; for it limits the exercise of this authority for a specific period of time, leaving it to its full operation ever afterwards. And this power seems necessarily included in the authority, which belongs to Congress, "to regulate commerce with foreign nations and among the several States." No person has ever doubted that the prohibition of the foreign slave trade was completely within the authority of Congress since the year 1808. And why? Certainly only because it is embraced in the regulation of foreign commerce: and if so, it may for the like reason be prohibited since that period, between the States. Commerce in slaves since the year 1808, being as much subject to the regulation of Congress as any other commerce, if it should see fit to enact that no slave should ever be sold from one State to another, it is not perceived how its constitutional right to make such provision could be questioned. It would seem to be too plain to be questioned, that Congress did possess the power, before the year 1808, to prohibit the migration or importation of slaves into its Territories (and in point of fact it exercised that power), as well as into any new States; and that its authority, after that year, might be as fully exercised to prevent the migration or importation of slaves into any of the old States. And if it may prohibit new States from importing slaves, it may surely, as we humbly submit, make it a condition of the admission of such States into the Union, that they shall never import them. In relation, too, to its own territories, Congress possesses a more extensive authority, and may, in various other ways, effect the same object. It might, for example, make it an express condition of its grants of the soil, that the owners shall never hold slaves; and thus prevent the possession of slaves from ever being connected with the ownership of the soil.

As corroborative of the views, which have been already suggested, the memorialists would respectfully call the attention of Congress to the history of the national legislation, under the confederation as well as under the present Constitution, on this interesting subject. Unless the memorialists greatly mistake, it will demonstrate the sense of the nation at every period of its legislation to have been, that the prohibition of

slavery was no infringement of any just rights belonging to free States, and was not incompatible with the enjoyment of all the rights and immunities which an admission into the Union was supposed to confer.

It will be recollected that Congress, by a resolve of the 10th of October, 1780, declared that the unappropriated lands that might be ceded to the United States, pursuant to a previous recommendation of Congress, should be disposed of for the common benefit of the United States, and be settled and formed into distinct republican States, which should become members of the federal Union and have the same rights of sovereignty, freedom, and independence as the other States. This language is exceedingly strong, and guarantees to the new States the same rights of sovereignty as the old States possessed. It was undoubtedly with this resolve in view, that the territory northwest of the Ohio was ultimately ceded to the United States by the several States claiming title to it; viz., by Massachusetts, Connecticut, New York, and Virginia. New York made a cession on the 1st of March, 1781, without annexing any condition; Virginia, on the 1st of March, 1784, upon certain conditions, and, among others, a condition embracing the substance of the resolve of the 10th of October, 1780. Massachusetts made a cession on the 19th of April, 1785, stating no conditions, but expressly to the uses stated in the resolve of 1780. And lastly, Connecticut made a cession on the 13th of September, 1786, without any condition, but expressly for the common use and benefit of the United States. On the 13th of July, 1787, Congress passed an ordinance for the government of the territory so added, which has ever since continued in force, and has formed the basis of the territorial governments of the United States. This ordinance was passed by the unanimous voice of all the States present at its passage; viz., Massachusetts, New York, Pennsylvania, Delaware, Virginia, North Carolina, South Carolina, and Georgia. It contains six fundamental articles as a compact between the United States and the inhabitants who might occupy that Territory, which are introduced by a preamble, declaring them to be "for extending the fundamental principles of civil and religious liberty, which form the basis whereon these republics, their laws and constitutions, are created; to fix and establish those principles as the basis of all laws, constitutions, and governments, which forever hereafter shall be formed in said Territory; to provide also for the establishment of States and a government therein, and for their admission into a share *in the federal councils, on an equal footing with the original States*, at as early a period as might be consistent with the general interest." The 6th article declares, that "there shall neither be slavery nor involuntary servitude in the said territory, otherwise than for the punishment of crimes, whereof the party shall become convicted." It is observable, that no objection occurred to this article, on the ground that it was incom-

patible with the equal sovereignty, freedom, and independence with the original States, to which the new States, to be formed in the ceded Territory, were entitled, by the resolve of the 10th of October, 1780, and by the express reference to that resolve, in the conditions of some of the cessions. It is observable, also, that by the preamble already recited, to which all the States present acceded, and among these were three of the ceding States, and a majority of the slave-holding States, it was expressly admitted that the restrictions of the 6th article would not deprive the new States, upon their admission into the federal councils, of their equal footing with the original States. This is a high legislative construction, by independent States, acting in their sovereign capacity, and entitled to the greater weight because it was a subject of common interest; and to all it could not but be deemed a precedent which would justly influence the subsequent measures of the general Government. Since the adoption of the Constitution, three new States, forming a part of this territory, viz., Ohio, Indiana, and Illinois, have been admitted into the Union. In the acts enabling them to form State governments and a State constitution, Congress has, among other very important conditions, made it a fundamental condition that their constitutions should contain nothing repugnant to the ordinance of 1787. These conditions were acceded to by these States, and have ever been deemed obligatory upon them and inviolable; and these States, notwithstanding these conditions, are universally considered as admitted into the Union upon the same footing as the original States, and as possessing, in respect to the Union, the same rights of sovereignty, freedom, and independence as the other States, in the sense in which those terms are used in the resolve of 1780. During a period of thirty years, not a doubt has been suggested that the provisions of this ordinance were perfectly compatible with the implied and express conditions of the cessions of this territory; and that Congress might justly impose the conditions which it contains upon all the States formed within its limits.

In the year 1791, Vermont was admitted into the Union, without any condition being annexed respecting slavery. The reason was obvious. It had already formed a constitution which excluded slavery; and it may be also asserted, that, looking to the habits and feelings of its population, and the habits and feelings and constitutional provisions of neighboring States, it was morally impossible that slavery could be adopted in that State.

Kentucky was admitted into the Union in June, 1792. The State was formed from the State of Virginia, and the latter, in granting its consent, imposed certain conditions, which have since been supposed to form a fundamental compact, which neither is at liberty to violate. Congress did not impose any restrictions as to slavery on its admission, and for

reasons which cannot escape the most careless observer. It would have been manifestly unjust, as well as impolitic.

Tennessee was admitted into the Union in June, 1796. It was ceded by North Carolina, more than six years before, as a Territory, upon certain conditions, and among them that Congress should assume the government of the Territory, and govern it according to the ordinance of 1787; with a proviso, however, "that no regulation made or to be made by Congress shall tend to emancipate slaves." In good faith, therefore, Congress could not justly insist upon a prohibition of slavery upon its admission into the Union.

Mississippi was admitted into the Union in December, 1817, upon condition that its constitution should contain nothing repugnant to the ordinance of 1787; so far as the same had been extended to the Territory by the agreement of cession made between the United States and Georgia; and Alabama was authorized to become a State by the act of 2d of March, 1819, upon a similar condition. Both of these States were ceded as one Territory to the United States by Georgia in April, 1802, upon condition, among other things, that it should be admitted into the Union in the same manner as the Territory northwest of the Ohio might be under the ordinance of 1787; "which ordinance (it is declared) shall extend to the territory contained in the present act of cession, *that article only excepted which forbids slavery.*" The prohibition of slavery could not, therefore, without the grossest breach of faith, be applied to this Territory. And the very circumstances of this exception in this cession of Georgia, as well as in that of North Carolina, shows strongly the sense of those States that, without such an exception, Congress would possess the authority in question.

The memorialists, after this general survey, would respectfully ask the attention of Congress to the state of the question of the right of Congress to prohibit slavery in that part of the former territory of Louisiana, which now forms the Missouri Territory. Louisiana was purchased of France by the Treaty of the 30th of April, 1803. The third article of that Treaty is as follows: "The inhabitants of the ceded Territory shall be incorporated into the Union of the United States, and admitted as soon as possible, *according to the principles of the federal Constitution,* to the enjoyment of all the *rights, advantages,* and *immunities* of *citizens of the United States;* and in the mean time they shall be maintained and protected in the free enjoyment of their liberty, property, and the religion which they profess."

Although the language of this article is not very precise or accurate, the memorialists conceive that its real import and intent cannot be mistaken. The first clause provides for the admission of the ceded Territory into the Union, and the succeeding clause shows this must be according

to the principles of the federal Constitution; and this very qualification necessarily excludes the idea that Congress were not to be at liberty to impose any conditions upon such admission which were consistent with the principles of that Constitution, and which had been or might justly be applied to other new States. The language is not by any means so pointed as that of the resolve of 1780: and yet it has been seen that that resolve was never supposed to inhibit the authority of Congress, as to the introduction of slavery. And it is clear, upon the plainest rules of construction, that in the absence of all restrictive language, a clause, merely providing for the admission of a Territory into the Union, must be construed to authorize an admission in the manner, and upon the terms, which the Constitution itself would justify. This construction derives additional support from the next clause. The inhabitants "shall be admitted as soon as possible, according to the principles of the federal Constitution, to the enjoyment of all the *rights, advantages,* and *immunities of citizens of the United States.*" The rights, advantages, and immunities here spoken of must, from the very force of the terms of the clause, be such as are recognized or communicated by the Constitution of the United States; such as are common to all citizens, and are uniform throughout the United States. The clause cannot be referred to rights, advantages, and immunities derived exclusively from the State governments, for these do not depend upon the federal Constitution. Besides, it would be impossible that all the rights, advantages, and immunities of citizens of the different States could be at the same time enjoyed by the same persons. These rights are different in different States; a right exists in one State which is denied in others, or is repugnant to other rights enjoyed in others. In some of the States, a freeholder alone is entitled to vote in elections; in some, a qualification of personal property is sufficient; and in others, age and freedom are the sole qualifications of electors. In some States, no citizen is permitted to hold slaves; in others, he possesses that power absolutely; in others, it is limited. The obvious meaning, therefore, of the clause is, that the rights derived under the federal Constitution shall be enjoyed by the inhabitants of Louisiana in the same manner as by the citizens of other states. The United States, by the Constitution, are bound to guarantee to every state in the Union a republican form of government; and the inhabitants of Louisiana are entitled, when a State, to this guarantee. Each State has a right to two senators, and to representatives according to a certain enumeration of population pointed out in the Constitution. The inhabitants of Louisiana, upon their admission into the Union, are also entitled to these privileges. The Constitution further declares "that the citizens of each State shall be entitled to all the privileges and immunities of citizens *in* the several States." It would seem as if the meaning of this clause could not well be misinterpreted.

It obviously applies to the case of the removal of a citizen of one State to another State; and in such a case it secures to the migrating citizen all the privileges and immunities of citizens *in* the State to which he removes. It cannot surely be contended, upon any rational interpretation, that it gives to the citizens of each State all the privileges and immunities of the citizens of every other State, at the same time and under all circumstances. Such a construction would lead to the most extraordinary consequences. It would at once destroy all the fundamental limitations of the State constitutions upon the rights of their own citizens; and leave all those rights at the mercy of the citizens of any other State which should adopt different limitations. According to this construction, if all the State constitutions save one prohibited slavery, it would be in the power of that single State, by the admission of the right of its citizens to hold slaves, to communicate the same right to the citizens of all the other States within their own exclusive limits, in defiance of their own constitutional prohibitions; and to render the absurdity still more apparent, the same construction would communicate the most opposite and irreconcilable rights to the citizens of different States at the same time. It seems, therefore, to be undeniable, upon any rational interpretation, that this clause of the Constitution communicated no rights in any State which its own citizens do not enjoy; and that the citizens of Louisiana, upon their admission into the Union, in receiving the benefit of this clause, would not enjoy higher or more extensive rights than the citizens of Ohio. It would communicate to the former no right of holding slaves, except in States where the citizens already possessed the same right under their own State constitutions and laws.

The Treaty, then, by providing for the inhabitants of Louisiana the enjoyment of all the rights, advantages, and immunities of citizens of the United States, seems distinctly to have pointed to those derived from the federal Constitution, and not to those which, being derived from other sources, were enjoyed by some and denied to others of the citizens of the United States.

The remaining clause of the Treaty, "that in the mean time" the inhabitants "shall be maintained and protected in the free enjoyment of their liberty, property, and the religion which they profess," requires no examination. It manifestly applies to the period of its territorial government, and has no reference to the terms of its admission into the Union, or to the condition of the Territory after it becomes a State. But it may be confidently asked whether, if the whole ordinance of 1787, which contains the prohibition of slavery, had been extended to Louisiana, there would have been anything inconsistent with the enjoyment of liberty, property, or religion? So far as slaves are deemed property, it might be just that the then real owners within the Territory should be

secured in the enjoyment of that property; but the permission to acquire such property in future, like every other right of property, ought to depend upon sound legislation, and be granted or denied by Congress, as its own judgment should direct. And the memorialists cannot perceive, in this clause of the Treaty, any restriction upon the right of Congress to exercise the utmost freedom of legislation as to the future introduction of slaves into the ceded Territory.

Congress, after this cession, divided the Territory into two territorial governments; and by an act passed on the 2d of March, 1805, in the exercise of its legislative discretion, directed that the Orleans Territory (which has since become the State of Louisiana) should be governed by the ordinance of 1787, excepting as to the descent and distribution of estates, and the article respecting slavery. By a subsequent act of the 11th of April, 1811, authorizing the inhabitants of this Territory to become a State, Congress annexed several highly important conditions to the exercise of this high act of sovereignty. Among other conditions, it required that the River Mississippi, and the water thereof, should be highways, and remain forever free to all the inhabitants of the United States and its Territories, without any tax, toll, or impost laid by the State therefor; that the constitution should contain the fundamental principles of civil and religious liberty, and should allow the trial by jury in criminal cases, and the privilege of the writ of habeas corpus; that all the laws, records, and judicial proceedings of the State, judicial and legislative, should be in the language in which the laws of the United States are written; that the people should disclaim all right to the unappropriated territory within the limits of the State, and that the same should be at the disposal of the United States; that lands sold by the United States should be exempt from taxation for five years from the sale; and that lands of non-residents should not be taxed higher than those of residents. These conditions are certainly very striking limitations of sovereignty, and embrace most of the fundamental regulations of the ordinance of 1787, excepting the article touching slavery. It is not known to the memorialists that any doubt of their constitutionality, or of their perfect harmony with the Treaty of 1803, was ever entertained, either in Congress or in Louisiana; and yet they contained some principles as repugnant to the original jurisprudence of the Territory, at the time of its cession, as could well be devised; and if Congress could then impose such conditions, what reason is there to say that it may not now impose the same conditions on the Missouri Territory? and if such conditions, why not any others which its wisdom, its justice, or its policy may dictate?

Upon the whole, the memorialists would most respectfully submit that the terms of the Constitution, as well as the practice of the governments

under it, must, as they humbly conceive, entirely justify the conclusion, that Congress may prohibit the further introduction of slavery into its own Territories, and also make such prohibition a condition of the admission of any new State into the Union.

If the constitutional power of Congress to make the proposed prohibition be satisfactorily shown, the justice and policy of such prohibition seem to the undersigned to be supported by plain and strong reasons. The permission of slavery in a new State necessarily draws after it an extension of that inequality of representation which already exists in regard to the original States. It cannot be expected that those of the original States which do not hold slaves can look on such an extension as being politically just. As between the original States, the representation rests on compact and plighted faith; and your memorialists have no wish that that compact should be disturbed, or that plighted faith in the slightest degree violated. But the subject assumes an entirely different character when a new State proposes to be admitted. With her there is no compact, and no faith plighted; and where is the reason that she should come into the Union with more than an equal share of political importance and political power? Already the ratio of representation, established by the Constitution, has given to the States holding slaves twenty members in the House of Representatives more than they would have been entitled to, except under the particular provision of the Constitution. In all probability, this number will be doubled in thirty years. Under these circumstances, we deem it not an unreasonable expectation that the inhabitants of Missouri should propose to come into the Union, renouncing the right in question, and establishing a constitution prohibiting it forever. Without dwelling on this topic, we have still thought it our duty to present it to the consideration of Congress. We present it with a deep and earnest feeling of its importance, and we respectfully solicit for it the full consideration of the National Legislature.

Your memorialists were not without the hope that the time had at length arrived when the inconvenience and the danger of this description of population had become apparent in all parts of this country, and in all parts of the civilized world. It might have been hoped that the new States themselves would have had such a view of their own permanent interests and prosperity, as would have led them to prohibit its extension and increase. The wonderful increase and prosperity of the States north of the Ohio is unquestionably to be ascribed in a great measure to the consequences of the ordinance of 1787; and few, indeed, are the occasions, in the history of nations, in which so much can be done by a single act, for the benefit of future generations, as was done by that ordinance, and as may now be done by the Congress of the United States. We appeal to the justice and the wisdom of the national councils to pre-

vent the further progress of a great and serious evil. We appeal to those who look forward to the remote consequences of their measures, and who cannot balance a temporary or trifling convenience, if there were such, against a permanent, growing, and desolating evil.

We cannot forbear to remind the two Houses of Congress that the early and decisive measures adopted by the American Government for the abolition of the slave trade are among the proudest memorials of our nation's glory. That slavery was ever tolerated in the republic is, as yet, to be attributed to the policy of another government. No imputation, thus far, rests on any portion of the American Confederacy. The Missouri Territory is a new country. If its extensive and fertile fields shall be opened as a market for slaves, the Government will seem to become a party to a traffic which, in so many acts, through so many years, it has denounced as impolitic, unchristian, inhuman. To enact laws to punish the traffic, and at the same time to tempt cupidity and avarice by the allurements of an insatiable market, is inconsistent and irreconcilable. Government, by such a course, would only defeat its own purposes, and render nugatory its own measures. Nor can the laws derive support from the manners of the people, if the power of moral sentiment be weakened by enjoying, under the permission of Government, great facilities to commit offences. The laws of the United States have denounced heavy penalties against the traffic in slaves, because such traffic is deemed unjust and inhuman. We appeal to the spirit of these laws; we appeal to this justice and humanity. We ask whether they ought not to operate, on the present occasion, with all their force? We have a strong feeling of the injustice of any toleration of slavery. Circumstances have entailed it on a portion of our community which cannot be immediately relieved from it without consequences more injurious than the suffering of the evil. But to permit it in a new country, where yet no habits are formed which render it indispensable, what is it, but to encourage that rapacity, fraud, and violence against which we have so long pointed the denunciations of our penal code? What is it, but to tarnish the proud fame of the country? What is it, but to throw suspicion on its good faith, and to render questionable all its professions of regard for the rights of humanity and the liberties of mankind?

As inhabitants of a free country, as citizens of a great and rising republic, as members of a Christian community, as living in a liberal and enlightened age, and as feeling ourselves called upon by the dictates of religion and humanity,—we have presumed to offer our sentiments to Congress on this question, with a solicitude for the event far beyond what a common occasion could inspire.

Basis of the Senate, December 15, 1820

The Revolution was over in New England although heavy fighting was still ahead in the south when Massachusetts adopted her first state constitution in 1780. It was drawn up by a convention whose members were elected for that purpose, and was duly ratified by town meetings throughout the state. Largely the work of John Adams, the document was an ingenious blending of the conservative and the democratic, balancing property and people. The system worked; the state prospered and her merchants, and later her manufacturers, grew wealthy. As time passed, however, many began to feel that the conservative elements had come to outweigh the democratic. A move to revise the constitution gradually gained momentum, and a convention for that purpose was called to meet in Boston on November 15, 1820.

Webster, fresh from drafting Boston's protest against the Missouri Compromise, was a delegate, along with former President John Adams, Supreme Court Justice Joseph Story, and a large sampling of the great and soon to be great of Massachusetts. The convention quickly resolved itself into two factions—those who sought decisive changes to liberalize the fundamental law, and those who preferred, with only minimal alterations, to keep it as it was. The dominant figure of the larger, radical group was Levi Lincoln, a future long-term governor, whose father had helped to draft the constitution of 1780 and had later served as attorney general in Jefferson's cabinet. Among the conservatives, none played a more important role than Daniel Webster. He participated freely and persuasively in debate; he worked effectively in committee; and spoke eloquently when the occasion seemed to require it.

Webster made only three convention speeches of lasting significance. In one of these he argued, unsuccessfully, for an amendment that would have abolished the last lingering connection between church and state— a provision in the constitution of 1780 requiring the governor, lieutenant governor, members of the council, and members of the legislature to declare under oath that they believed in the Christian religion. In another speech he favored, again without success, an amendment that would have made judges removable by the governor and council only upon the address of two-thirds, instead of a simple majority, of each

house of the legislature. His third major effort, in which he carried the day, was the speech reproduced below.

Under the constitution of 1780 the state senate was so chosen as to represent property rather than numbers or geographical areas. A proposed amendment would have replaced this basis with a choice of senators by district. Webster argues here, as he had some two years earlier in *McCulloch* v. *Maryland,* that property is an essential ingredient of political power. This conviction was basic to his thinking, recurring again and again in his speeches and legal arguments, but nowhere better stated than in this speech on the basis of the senate.

The right to report and publish the proceedings of the Massachusetts Constitutional Convention of 1820–1821, went to the *Boston Daily Advertiser*, with the understanding that each day's record would appear the following day. The confident publishers of the paper were Nathan Hale, brother-in-law of Edward Everett who would later edit Webster's *Works*, and Octavius Pickering, state supreme court reporter. The schedule, however, quickly proved unrealistic, as reports fell farther and farther behind. Webster's "Basis of the Senate" speech was delivered on December 15, 1820 but did not appear in the *Advertiser* until January 17, 1821, more than a month later. It was reprinted on January 25 in the weekly edition of the same paper, the *Boston Weekly Messenger.* The official *Journal of Debates and Proceedings in the Convention of Delegates, Chosen to Revise the Constitution of Massachusetts* followed two months later, compiled by Hale and Pickering from the daily reports in the *Advertiser.* The edition was limited and was soon exhausted but was reprinted without change in 1853.

The "Basis of the Senate" was among the selections chosen by Charles Brickett Haddock for inclusion in the first volume of Webster's *Speeches and Forensic Arguments*, with text unaltered from that of the *Journal*. The version that appears in *Works*, 3: 8–25, and in the fifth volume of *Writings and Speeches*, pp. 8–25, was considerably shortened by Everett, who deleted several pages with no indication that he had done so.

The text below is taken from the *Journal of Debates and Proceedings*, with Everett's omissions bracketed.

Mr. Webster spoke in substance as follows:

I know not, sir, whether it be probable that any opinions or votes of mine are ever likely to be of more permanent importance, than those which I may give in the discharge of my duties in this body. And of the questions which may arise here, I anticipate no one of greater consequence than the present. I ask leave therefore to submit a few remarks to the consideration of the committee.

The subject before us, is the manner of constituting the legislative department of government. We have already decided that the legislative power shall exist, as it has heretofore existed, in two separate and distinct branches, a senate and a house of representatives. We propose also, at least I have heard no intimation of a contrary opinion, that these branches shall, in form, possess a negative on each other. And I presume I may take it for granted, that the members of both these houses are to be chosen annually. The immediate question, now under discussion is, *in what manner* shall the senators be elected? They are to be chosen in districts; but shall they be chosen, in proportion to the *number of inhabitants* in each district, or, in other words, *in proportion to the part which each district bears in the public burdens of the State.* The latter is the existing provision of the constitution; and to this I give my support. The proposition[1] of the honorable member from Roxbury [Henry A. S. Dearborn], proposes to divide the State into certain *legislative districts,* and to choose a given number of senators, and a given number of representatives, in each district, *in proportion to population.* This I understand. It is a simple and plain system. The honorable member from Pittsfield, [Henry H. Childs] and the honorable member from Worcester [Levi Lincoln] support the first part of this proposition—that is to say, that part which provides for the choice of *senators,* according to population—without explaining entirely their views, as to the latter part, relative to the choice of *representatives.* They insist that the questions are distinct, and capable of a separate consideration and decision. I confess myself, sir, unable to view the subject in that light. It seems to me there is an essential propriety in considering the questions together; and in forming our opinions on the constitution of one, with reference to that of the other.[2] The Legislature is one great machine of government, not two machines; the two houses are its parts, and its utility will as it seems to me, depend, not merely on the materials of these parts, or their separate construction, but on their accommodation also, and adaptation to each other. Their balanced and regulated movement, when united, is that which is expected to insure safety to the State; and who can give any opinion on this, without first seeing the construction of both, and considering how they are formed and arranged, with respect to their mutual relation. I cannot imagine, therefore, how the member from Worcester should think it uncandid to inquire of him, since he supports this mode of choosing senators, *what mode* he proposes for the choice of representatives.

It has been said, that the constitution, as it now stands, gives more than an equal and proper number of senators to the county of Suffolk.

1. *Works,* 3: 8 reads "resolution."
2. *Works,* 3: 9 reads ". . . our opinions of them, as parts respectively of one legislative system."

I hope I may be thought to contend for the general principle, without being influenced by any regard to its local application. I do not inquire, whether the senators whom this principle brings into the government, will come from the county of Suffolk, or from the Housatonic River, or the extremity of Cape Cod. I wish to look only to the principle, and as I believe that to be sound and salutary, I give my vote in favor of maintaining it.

In my opinion, sir, there are two questions before the committee; the first is, shall the legislative department be constructed with any other *check,* than such as arises simply from dividing the members of this department into two houses? The second is, if such other and further check ought to exist, *in what manner* shall it be created?

If the two houses are to be chosen in the manner proposed by the resolution of the member from Roxbury, there is obviously no other check or control than a division into separate chambers. The members of both houses are to be chosen at the same time, by the same electors, in the same districts, and for the same term of office. They will of course all be actuated by the same feelings and interests. Whatever motives may at the moment exist, to elect particular members of one house, will operate equally on the choice of members of the other. There is so little of real utility in this mode that, if nothing more be done, it would be more expedient to choose all the members of the Legislature, without distinction, simply as members of the Legislature, and to make the division into two houses, either by lot, or otherwise, after these members, thus chosen, should have come up to the Capital.

I understand the reason of *checks* and *balances,* in the legislative power, to arise from the truth that, in representative governments, that department is the leading and predominating power; and if its will may be, at any time, suddenly and hastily expressed, there is great danger that it may overthrow all other powers. Legislative bodies naturally feel strong, because they are numerous, and because they consider themselves as the immediate representatives of the people. They depend on public opinion to sustain their measures, and they undoubtedly possess great means of influencing public opinion. With all the guards which can be raised by constitutional provisions, we are not likely to be too well secured against cases of improper, or hasty, or intemperate legislation. It may be observed, also, that the executive power, so uniformly the object of jealousy to republics, has become, in the states of this Union, deprived of the greatest part, both of its importance and its splendor, by the establishment of the general government. While the states possessed the power of making war and peace, and maintained military forces by their own authority, the power of the state executives was very considerable, and respectable. It might then even be an object, in some cases, of

a just and warrantable jealousy. But a great change has been wrought. The care of foreign relations, the maintenance of armies and navies, and their command and control, have devolved on another government. Even the power of appointment, so exclusively, one would think, an executive power, is, in very many of the states, held or controlled by the legislature; that department either making the principal appointments, itself, or else surrounding the chief executive magistrate with a council of its own election, possessing a negative upon his nominations.

Nor has it been found easy, nor in all cases possible, to preserve the judicial department from the progress of legislative encroachment. Instead, in some of the states all judges are appointed by the legislature; in others, although appointed by the executive, they are removable at the pleasure of the legislature. In all, the provision for their maintenance is necessarily to be made by the legislature. As if Montesquieu had never demonstrated the necessity of separating the departments of government; as if Mr. Adams had not done the same thing, with equal ability, and more clearness, in his defence of the American Constitutions; as if the sentiments of Mr. Hamilton and Mr. Madison were already forgotten; we see, all around us, a tendency to extend the legislative power over the proper sphere of the other departments. And as the legislature, from the very nature of things, is the most powerful department, it becomes necessary to provide, in the mode of forming it, some check which shall ensure deliberation and caution in its measures. If all legislative power rested in one house, it is very problematical, whether any proper independence could be given, either to the executive or the judiciary. Experience does not speak encouragingly on that point. If we look through the several constitutions of the states, we shall perceive that generally the departments are most distinct and independent, where the legislature is composed of two houses, with equal authority, and mutual checks. If all legislative power be in one popular body, all other power, sooner or later, will be there also.

I wish now, sir, to correct a most important mistake, in the manner in which this question has been stated. It has been said, that we propose to give to property, merely as such, a control over the people numerically considered. But this I take not to be at all the true nature of the proposition. The senate is not to be a check on the *people*, but on the *house of representatives*. It is the case of an authority, given to *one* agent, to check or control the acts of *another*. The people, having conferred on the house of representatives, powers which are great, and, from their nature, liable to abuse, require for their own security another house, which shall possess an effectual negative on the first. This does not limit the power of the people; but only the authority of their agents. It is not a restraint on their rights, but a restraint on that power which they have

delegated. It limits the authority of agents, in making laws to bind their principles. And if it be wise to give one agent the power of checking or controlling another, it is equally wise, most manifestly, that there should be some difference of character, sentiment, feeling, or origin, in that agent, who is to possess this control. Otherwise, it is not at all probable that the control will ever be exercised. To require the consent of two agents to the validity of an act, and yet to appoint agents so similar, in all respects, as to create a moral certainty that what one does the other will do also, would be inconsistent and nugatory. There can be no effectual control without some difference of origin, or character, or interest, or feeling, or sentiment. And the great question, in this country, has been, where to find, or how to create this difference, in governments entirely elective and popular? Various modes have been attempted, in various states. In some, a difference of qualification has been required, in the persons to be elected. This obviously produces little or no effect. All property qualification, even the highest, is so low as to produce no exclusion, to any extent, in any of the states. A difference of age, in the persons elected, is sometimes required; but this is found to be equally unimportant. It has not happened, either, that any consideration of the relative rank of the members of the two houses has had much effect on the character of their constituent members. Both in the state governments, and in the United States government, we daily see persons elected into the house of representatives who have been members of the senate. Public opinion does not attach so much weight and importance to the distinction, as to lead individuals greatly to regard it. In some of the states, a different sort of qualification in the electors is required, for the two houses; and this is probably the most proper and efficient check. But such has not been the provision in this Commonwealth, and there are strong objections to introducing it. In other cases, again, there is a double election for senators; electors being first chosen, who elect senators. Such is the constitution of Maryland; in which the senators are elected, for five years, by electors, appointed in equal numbers by the counties; a mode of election not unlike that of choosing representatives in Parliament for the boroughs of Scotland. In this State the qualification of the voters is the same,[3] and there is no essential difference in that of the persons chosen. But, in apportioning the senate to the different districts of the State, the present constitution assigns to each district, a number proportioned to its public taxes. Whether this be the best mode of producing a difference in the construction of the two houses, is not now the question; but the question is, whether this be better than no mode.

The gentleman from Roxbury called for authority on this subject. He

3. *Works*, 3: 13 inserts "for the two houses."

asked what writer of reputation had approved the principle for which we contend. I should hope, sir, that even if this call could not be answered, it would not necessarily follow that the principle should be expunged. Governments are instituted for practical benefit, not for subjects of speculative reasoning merely. The best authority for the support of a particular principle or provision in government, is experience; and, of all experience, our own, if it have been long enough to give the principle a fair trial, should be most decisive. This provision has existed for forty years; and while so many gentlemen contend that it is wrong in theory, no one has shown that it has been either injurious or inconvenient in practice. No one pretends that it has caused a bad law to be enacted or a good one to be rejected. To call on us, then, to strike out this provision, because we should be able to find no authority for it in any book on government, would seem to be like requiring a mechanic to abandon the use of an implement, which had always answered all the purposes designed by it, because he could find no model of it in the patent office.

But, sir, I take the *principle* to be well established by writers of the greatest authority. In the first place, those who have treated of natural law have maintained, as a principle of that law, that, as far as the object of society is the protection of something in which the members possess unequal shares, it is just that the weight of each person in the common councils, should bear a relation and proportion to his interest. Such is the sentiment of Grotius, and he refers, in support of it, to several institutions among the ancient states.

Those authors, who have written more particularly on the subject of political institutions, have, many of them, maintained similar sentiments. Not indeed, that every man's power should be in exact proportion to his property, but that, in a general sense, and in a general form, property, as such, should have its weight and influence in political arrangement. Montesquieu speaks, with approbation, of the early Roman regulation, made by Servius Tullius, by which the people were distributed into classes according to their property, and the public burdens apportioned to each individual, according to the degree of power which he possessed in the government. By which regulation, he observes, some bore with the greatness of their tax, because of their proportionable participation in power and credit; others consoled themselves for the smallness of their power and credit, by the smallness of their tax. One of the most ingenious of political writers is Mr. [James] Harrington, an author not now read as much as he deserves. It is his leading object, in his "Oceana," to prove, that power *naturally* and *necessarily* follows property. He maintains that a government, founded on property is legitimately founded; and that a government founded on the disregard of property is founded in injustice, and can only be maintained by military

force. "If one man," says he, "be sole landlord, like the grand seignior, his empire is absolute. If a few possess the land, this makes the gothic or feudal constitution. If the *whole* people be landlords, then it is a Commonwealth." "It is strange," says[4] Mr. [Alexander] Pope, in one of his recorded conversations, "that Harrington should be the first man to find out so evident and demonstrable a truth, as that of property being the true basis and *measure* of power."[5] In truth he was not the first: the idea is as old as political science itself. It may be found in Aristotle, Lord Bacon, Sir Walter Raleigh, and other writers. Harrington seems, however, to be the first writer who has illustrated and expanded the principle, and given to it the effect and prominence which justly belong to it. To this sentiment, sir, I entirely agree. It seems to me to be plain, that, in the absence of military force, political power naturally and necessarily goes into the hands which hold the property. In my judgment, therefore, a republican form of government rests not more on political constitutions than on those laws which regulate the descent and transmission of property. [Governments[6] like ours could not have been maintained, where property was holden according to the principles of the feudal system; nor, on the other hand, could the feudal constitution possibly exist with us. Our New England ancestors brought hither no great capitals from Europe; and if they had, there was nothing productive in which they could have been invested. They left behind them the whole feudal system of the other continent. They broke away at once from that system of military service, established in the dark ages, and which continues, down even to the present time, more or less to affect the condition of property all over Europe. They came to a new country. There were, as yet, no lands yielding rent, and no tenants rendering service. The whole soil was unreclaimed from barbarism. They were, themselves, either from their original condition, or for the necessity of their common interest, nearly on a general level in respect to property. Their situation demanded a parcelling out and division of the lands; and it may be fairly said, that this necessary act *fixed the future frame and form of their government.* The character of their political institutions was determined by the fundamental laws respecting property. The laws rendered estates divisible among sons and daughters. The right of primogeniture, at first limited and curtailed, was afterwards abolished. The property was all freehold.

4. *Works*, 3: 14 reads "says an ingenious person in the last century, 'that Harrington. . . .' "

5. *Works*, 3: 14 cites "Spence's Anecdotes of Books and Men, p. 75." Joseph Spence, *Anecdotes, Observations, and Characters of Books and Men* (London, 1820). In the source a parenthetical phrase "(so short a time ago)" follows "Harrington."

6. The next six paragraphs, bracketed here, are omitted in *Works*, 3: 15.

The entailment of estates, long trusts, and the other processes for fetter-
ing and tying up inheritances, were not applicable to the condition of
society, and seldom made use of. On the contrary, alienation of the land
was every way facilitated, even to the subjecting of it to every species of
debt. The establishment of public registries, and the simplicity of our
forms of conveyance, have greatly facilitated the change of real estate
from one proprietor to another. The consequence of all these causes has
been, a great subdivision of the soil, and a great equality of condition;
the true basis, most certainly, of a popular government. "If the people,"
says Harrington, "hold three parts in four of the territory, it is plain there
can neither be any single person nor nobility able to dispute the government with them; in this case, therefore, *except force be interposed*, they
govern themselves."

[The history of other nations may teach us how favorable to public
liberty is the division of the soil into small freeholds, and a system of
laws, of which the tendency is, without violence or injustice, to produce
and to preserve a degree of equality of property. It has been estimated,
if I mistake not, that about the time of Henry the Seventh, four fifths of
the land in England was holden by the great barons and ecclesiastics.
The effects of a growing commerce soon afterwards began to break in
on this state of things, and before the Revolution in 1688, a vast change
had been wrought. It is probable, perhaps, that for the last half century,
the process of subdivision in England has been retarded, if not reversed;
that the great weight of taxation has compelled many of the lesser freeholders to dispose of their estates, and to seek employment in the army
and navy, in the professions of civil life, in commerce, or in the colonies.
The effect of this on the British constitution cannot but be most unfavorable. A few large estates grow larger; but the number of those who
have no estates also increases; and there may be danger lest the inequality of property become so great, that those who possess it may be
dispossessed by force. In other words, that the government may be over-
turned.

[A most interesting experiment of the effect of a subdivision of property, on government, is now making in France. It is understood that the
law regulating the transmission of property, in that country, now divides
it, real and personal, among all the children equally, both sons and
daughters; and that there is, also, a very great restraint on the power
of making dispositions of property by will. It has been supposed that the
effect of this might probably be, in time, to break up the soil into such
small subdivisions, that the proprietors would be too *poor* to resist the
encroachments of executive power. I think far otherwise. What is lost in
individual wealth will be more than gained in numbers, in intelligence,
and in a sympathy of sentiment. If indeed only one or a few landholders

were to resist the crown, like the barons of England, they must, of course, be great and powerful landholders, with multitudes of retainers, to promise success. But if the proprietors of a given extent of territory are summoned to resistance, there is no reason to believe that such resistance would be less forcible or less successful, because the number of such proprietors should be great. Each would perceive his own importance, and his own interest, and would feel that natural elevation of character which the consciousness of property inspires. A common sentiment would unite all, and numbers would not only add strength, but excite enthusiasm. It is true that France possesses a vast military force, under the direction of an hereditary executive government; and military power, it is possible, may overthrow any government. It is in vain, however, in this period of the world, to look for security against military power to the arm of the great landholders. That notion is derived from a state of things long since past; a state in which a feudal baron, with his retainers, might stand against the sovereign, who was himself but the greatest baron, and his retainers. But at present, what could the richest landholder do against one regiment of disciplined troops? Other securities, therefore, against the prevalence of military power must be provided. Happily for us, we are not so situated as that any purpose of national defence requires, ordinarily and constantly, such a military force as might seriously endanger our liberties.

[In respect, however, sir, to the recent law of succession in France, to which I have alluded, I would, presumptuously perhaps, hazard a conjecture, that if the government do not change the law, the law, in half a century, will change the government; and that this change will be not in favor of the power of the crown, as some European writers have supposed, but against it. Those writers only reason upon what they think correct general principles in relation to this subject. They acknowledge a want of experience. Here we have had that experience; and we know that a multitude of small proprietors, acting with intelligence, and that enthusiasm which a common cause inspires, constitute not only a formidable, but an invincible power.

[The true principle of a free and popular government would seem to be, so to construct it as to give to all, or at least to a very great majority, an interest in its preservation; to found it, as other things are founded, on men's interest. The stability of government requires that those who desire its continuance should be more powerful than those who desire its dissolution. This power, of course, is not always to be measured by mere numbers. Education, wealth, talents, are all parts and elements of the general aggregate of power. But numbers, nevertheless, constitute ordinarily, the most important consideration, unless indeed there be a *military force* in the hands of the few, by which they can control the

many. In this country, we have actual existing systems of government, in the protection of which it would seem a great majority, both in numbers and in other means of power and influence, must see their interest. But this state of things is not brought about merely by written political constitutions, or the mere manner of organizing the government; but also by the laws which regulate the descent and transmission of property. The freest government, if it could exist, would not be long acceptable, if the tendency of the laws were to create a rapid accumulation of property in few hands, and to render the great mass of the population dependent and penniless. In such a case the popular power must break in upon the rights of property, or else the influence of property must limit and control the exercise of popular power. Universal suffrage, for example, could not long exist in a community where there was great inequality of property. The holders of estates would be obliged in such case, either in some way to restrain the right of suffrage, or else such right of suffrage would ere long divide the property. In the nature of things, those who have not property, and see their neighbors possess much more than they think them to need, cannot be favorable to laws made for the protection of property. When this class becomes numerous, it grows clamorous. It looks on property as its prey and plunder, and is naturally ready, at all times, for violence and revolution.

[It would seem, then, to be the part of political wisdom to found government on property; and to establish such distribution of property, by the laws which regulate its transmission and alienation, as to interest the great majority of society in the protection of the government. This is, I imagine, the true theory and the actual practice of our republican institutions. With property divided, as we have it, no other government than that of a republic could be maintained, even were we foolish enough to desire it. There is reason, therefore, to expect a long continuance of our systems. Party and passion, doubtless, may prevail at times, and much temporary mischief be done. Even modes and forms may be changed, and perhaps for the worse. But a great revolution in regard to property must take place, before our governments can be moved from their republican basis, unless they be violently struck off by military power. The people possess the property, more emphatically than it could ever be said of the people of any other country, and they can have no interest to overturn a government which protects that property by equal laws.]

If the nature of our institutions be to found government on property, and that it should look to those who hold property for its protection, it is entirely just that property should have its due weight and consideration in political arrangements. Life and personal liberty are, no doubt, to be protected by law; but property is also to be protected by law, and is the

fund out of which the means for protecting life and liberty are usually furnished. We have no experience that teaches us, that any other rights are safe, where property is not safe. Confiscation and plunder are generally, in revolutionary commotions, not far behind banishment, imprisonment and death. It would be monstrous to give even the name of government, to any association, in which the rights of property should not be competently secured. The disastrous revolutions which the world has witnessed; those political thunder-storms and earthquakes which have overthrown the pillars of society from their very deepest foundations, have been revolutions *against property*. Since the honorable member from Quincy [President John Adams] has alluded, on this occasion, to the history of the ancient states, it would be presumption, in me, to dwell upon it. It may be truly said, however, I think, that Rome herself is an example of the mischievous influence of the popular power, when disconnected with property, and in a corrupt age. It is true, the arm of Caesar prostrated her liberty; but Caesar found his support within her very walls. Those who were profligate, and necessitous, and factious, and desperate, and capable, therefore, of being influenced by bribes and largesses, which were distributed with the utmost prodigality, outnumbered and outvoted, in the tribes and centuries, the substantial, sober, prudent and faithful citizens. Property was in the hands of one description of men, and power in those of another; and the balance of the constitution was destroyed. Let it never be forgotten that it was the popular magistrates, elevated to office where the bad outnumbered the good, where those who had no stake in the Commonwealth, by clamor, and noise, and numbers, drowned the voice of those who had, that laid the neck of Rome at the foot of her conqueror. When Caesar, manifesting a disposition to march his army into Italy, approached that little stream, which has become so memorable from its association with his character and conduct, a decree was proposed in the senate, declaring him a public enemy, if he did not disband his troops. To this decree, the popular tribunes, the sworn protectors of the people, interposed their negative; and thus opened the high road of Italy, and the gates of Rome herself, to the approach of her conqueror.

The English revolution of 1688 was a revolution *in favor of property*, as well as of other rights. It was brought about by the men of property, for their security; and our own immortal revolution was undertaken, not to shake or plunder property, but to protect it. The acts of which the country complained, were such as violated rights of property. An immense majority of all those who had an interest in the soil were in favor of the revolution; and they carried it through, looking to its results for the security of their possessions. It was the property of the frugal yeomanry of New-England, hard earned, but freely given, that enabled her

to act her proper part, and perform her full duty, in achieving the independence of the country.

I would not be thought, Mr. Chairman, to be among those who underrate the value of military service. My heart beats, I trust, as responsive as any one's, to a soldier's claim for honor and renown. It has ever been my opinion, however, that while celebrating the military achievements of our countrymen, in the revolutionary contest, we have not always done equal justice to the merits, and the sufferings of those who sustained, on their property, and on their means of subsistence, the great burden of the war. Any one, who has had occasion to be acquainted with the records of the New-England towns, knows well how to estimate those merits, and those sufferings. Nobler records of patriotism exist nowhere. Nowhere can there be found higher proofs of a spirit, that was ready to hazard all, to pledge all, to sacrifice all, in the cause of the country. Instances were not unfrequent, in which small freeholders parted with their last hoof, and the last measure of corn from their granaries, to supply provisions for the troops, and hire service for the ranks. The voice of [James] Otis and of [Samuel] Adams in Faneuil Hall, found its full and true echo. In the little councils of the interior towns; and if, within the continental congress, patriotism shone more conspicuously, it did not there exist more truly, nor burn more fervently; it did not render the day more anxious, or the night more sleepless; it sent up no more ardent prayer to God for succor; and it put forth, in no greater degree, the fullness of its effort, and the energy of its whole soul and spirit, in the common cause, than it did in the small assemblies of the towns. I cannot, therefore, sir, agree that it is in favor of society, or in favor of the people, to constitute government, with an entire disregard to those who bear the public burdens, in times of great exigency. This question has been argued, as if it were proposed only to give an advantage to a few rich men. I do not so understand it. I consider it as giving property, generally, a representation in the senate, both because it is just that it should have such representation, and because it is a convenient mode of providing that *check*, which the constitution of the Legislature requires. I do not say that such check might not be found in some other provision; but this is the provision already established, and it is, in my opinion, a and justice?

I will beg leave to ask, sir, whether property may not be said to *deserve* this portion of respect and power in the government? It pays, at this moment, I think, *five sixths* of all the public taxes; *one sixth* only being raised on persons. Not only, sir, do these taxes support those burdens, which all governments require, but we have, in New-England, from early times holden property to be subject to *another* great public use;—I mean the support of SCHOOLS.

[In [7] this particular we may be allowed to claim a merit of a very high and peculiar character. This Commonwealth, with other of the New England States, early adopted, and has constantly maintained the principle, that it is the undoubted right, and the bounden duty of government, to provide for the instruction of all youth. That which is elsewhere left to chance, or to charity, we secure by law. For the purpose of public instruction, we hold every man subject to taxation, in proportion to his property, and we look not to the question, whether he, himself, have, or have not, children to be benefited by the education for which he pays. We regard it as a wise and liberal system of police, by which property, and life, and the peace of society are secured. We seek to prevent, in some measure, the extension of the penal code, by inspiring a salutary and conservative principle of virtue and of knowledge, in an early age. We hope to excite a feeling of respectability and a sense of character, by enlarging the capacity, and increasing the sphere of intellectual enjoyment. By general instruction, we seek, as far as possible, to purify the whole moral atmosphere; to keep good sentiments uppermost, and to turn the strong current of feeling and opinion, as well as the censures of the law, and the denunciations of religion, against immorality and crime. We hope for a security, beyond the law, and above the law, in the prevalence of enlightened and well-principled moral sentiment. We hope to continue, and to prolong the time, when, in the villages and farm houses of New-England, there may be undisturbed sleep, within unbarred doors. And knowing that our government rests directly on the public will, that we may preserve it, we endeavor to give a safe and proper direction to that public will. We do not, indeed, expect all men to be philosophers, or statesmen; but we confidently trust, and our expectation of the duration of our system of government rests on that trust, that by the diffusion of general knowledge, and good and virtuous sentiments, the political fabric may be secure, as well against open violence and overthrow, as against the slow but sure undermining of licentiousness.

[We know, sir, that at the present time an attempt is making in the English parliament to provide by law for the education of the poor, and that a gentleman of distinguished character, (Henry Peter Brougham) has taken the lead, in presenting a plan to government for carrying that purpose into effect. And yet, although the representatives of the three kingdoms listened to him with astonishment, as well as delight, we hear no principles with which we ourselves have not been familiar from youth; we see nothing in the plan, but an approach towards that system which has been established in this State, for more than a century and a half. It is said, that in England, not more than *one child in fifteen*, pos-

7. The bracketed passage is omitted in *Works*, 3:17

sesses the means of being taught to read and write; in Wales, *one in twenty;* in France, until lately, when some improvement was made, not more than *one in thirty-five.* Now, sir, it is hardly too strong to say that in this State, *every child possesses* such means. It would be difficult to find an instance to the contrary unless where it was owing to the negligence of the parent—and in truth the means are actually used and enjoyed by nearly every one. A youth of fifteen, of either sex, who cannot both read and write, is very unfrequently to be found. How many such can any member of this Convention remember to have met with in ten years? Sir, who can make this comparison, or contemplate this spectacle, without delight, and a feeling of just pride? And yet, sir, what is it, but the *property* of the rich, devoted, by law, to the education of the poor, which has produced this state of things? Does any history show property more beneficently applied? Did any government ever subject the property of those who have estates, to a burden, for a purpose more favorable to the poor, or more useful to the whole community?] Sir, *property* and the power which the law exercises over it, for the purpose of instruction, is the basis of the system. It is entitled to the respect and protection of government, because, in a very vital respect, it aids and sustains government. The honorable member from Worcester, in contending for the admission of the mere popular principle in all branches of the government, told us, that our system rested on the intelligence of the community. He told us truly. But allow me, sir, to ask the honorable gentleman, what, but property, supplies the means of that intelligence? What living fountain feeds this ever-flowing, ever-refreshing, ever-fertilizing stream, of public instruction and general intelligence? If we take away from the towns the power of assessing taxes on property, will the school houses remain open? If we deny to the poor, the benefit which they now derive from the property of the rich, will their children remain on their forms, or will they not, rather, be in the streets, in idleness and in vice?

I might ask, again, sir, how is it with religious instruction? Do not the towns and parishes raise money, by vote of the majority, assessed on property, for the maintenance of religious worship? Are not the poor, as well as the rich, benefited by the means of attending on public worship, and do they not, equally with the rich, possess a voice and vote, in the choice of the minister, and in all other parish concerns? Does any man, sir, wish to try the experiment of striking out of the constitution the regard which it has hitherto maintained for property, and of foregoing also the extraordinary benefit which society among us, for near two centuries, has derived, from laying the burden of religious and literary instruction of all classes upon property? Does any man wish to see those only worshipping God, who are able to build churches and maintain

ministers for themselves; and those children only educated, whose parents possess the means of educating them? Sir, it is as unwise as it is unjust, to make property an object of jealousy. Instead of being, in any just sense, a popular course, such a course would be most injurious and destructive to the best interest of the people. The nature of our laws sufficiently secures us against any dangerous accumulations; and, used and diffused, as we have it, the whole operation of property is in the highest degree useful, both to the rich and to the poor. I rejoice, sir, that every man in this community may call all property his own, as far as he has occasion for it, to furnish for himself and his children the blessings of religious instruction and the elements of knowledge. This celestial,[8] and this earthly light, he is entitled to by the fundamental laws. It is every poor man's undoubted birthright, it is the great blessing which this constitution has secured to him, it is his solace in life, and it may well be his consolation in death, that his country stands pledged by the faith which it has plighted to all its citizens, to protect his children from ignorance, barbarism and vice.

I will now proceed to ask sir, whether we have not seen, and whether we do not at this moment see, the advantage and benefit of giving security to property by this and all other reasonable and just provisions? The constitution has stood, on its present basis, forty years. Let me ask, what state has been more distinguished for wise and wholesome legislation? I speak sir, without the partiality of a native, and also without intending the compliment of a stranger; and I ask, what example have we had of better legislation? No violent measures, affecting property, have been attempted. Stop-laws, suspension laws, tender laws, all the tribe of those arbitrary and tyrannical interferences between creditor and debtor which, wheresoever practised, generally end in the ruin of both, are strangers to our statute book. An upright and intelligent judiciary has come in aid of wholesome legislation; and general security for public and private rights has been the result. I do not say that this is peculiar, I do not say that others have not done as well. It is enough, that in these respects we shall be satisfied that we are not behind our neighbors. No doubt, sir, there are benefits of every kind, and of great value, in possessing a character of government, both in legislative and judicial administration, which secures well the rights of property; and we should find it so, by unfortunate experience, should that character be lost. There are millions of personal property now in this Commonwealth, which are easily transferable, and would be instantly transferred elsewhere, if any doubt existed of its entire security. I do not know how much of this stability of government and of the general respect for it,

8. *Works*, 3: 18 reads "heavenly."

may be fairly imputed to this particular mode of organizing the senate. It has, no doubt, had some effect. It has shown a respect for the rights of property, and may have operated on opinion, as well as upon measures. Now to strike out and obliterate it, as it seems to me, would be in a high degree unwise and improper.

As to the *right* of apportioning senators upon this principle, I do not understand how there can be a question about it. All government is a modification of general principles and general truths, with a view to practical utility. Personal liberty, for instance, is a clear right, and is to be provided for; but it is not a clearer right than the right of property, though it may be more important. It is therefore entitled to protection. But property is also to be protected; and when it is remembered how great a portion of the people of this State possess property, I cannot understand how its protection or its influence is hostile to their rights and privileges.

For these reasons, sir, I am in favor of maintaining that *check* in the constitution of the Legislature, which has so long existed there.

I understand the gentlemen from Worcester [Levi Lincoln], to be in favor of a check, but it seems to me he would place it in the wrong house. Besides, the sort of *check* he proposes appears to me to be of a novel nature, as a balance, in government. He proposes to choose the senators according to the number of inhabitants; and to choose representatives, not according to that number, but in proportions greatly unequal in the town corporations. It has been stated to result from computation, and I do not understand it is denied, that on his system a majority of the representatives will be chosen by towns not containing *one third part* of the whole population of the State. I would beg to ask, sir, on what principle this can stand; especially in the judgment of those who regard *population* as the only just basis of representation? But, sir, I have a preliminary objection to this system; which is, that it reverses all our common notions, and constitutes the *popular* house upon *anti-popular* principles. We are to have a popular senate of thirty-six members, and we are to place the *check* of the system in a house of representatives of two hundred and fifty members! All money bills are to originate in the house, yet the house is not to be the popular branch. It is to exceed the senate seven or eight to one, in point of numbers—yet the senate is to be chosen on the popular principle, and the house on some other principle.

It is necessary here, sir, to consider the manner of electing representatives in this Commonwealth as heretofore practised, the necessity which exists of reducing the present number of representatives, and the propositions which have been submitted for that purpose. Representation by towns or townships, (as they might have been originally more properly called) is peculiar to New England. It has existed, however, since

the first settlement of the country. These local districts are so small, and of such unequal population, that if every town is to have one representative, and larger towns as many more as their population, compared with the smallest town, would numerically entitle them to, a very numerous body must be the consequence, in any large state. Five hundred members, I understand, may now be constitutionally elected to the house of representatives; the very statement of which number shows the necessity of reduction. I agree, sir, that this is a very difficult subject. Here are three hundred towns, all possessing the right of representation; and representation by towns, is an ancient habit of the people. For one, I am disposed to preserve this mode, so far as may be practicable. There is always an advantage in making the revisions which circumstances may render necessary, in a manner which does no violence to ancient habits and established rules. I prefer, therefore, a representation by towns, even though it should necessarily be somewhat numerous, to a division of the State into new districts, the parts of which might have little natural connection or little actual intercourse with one another. But I ground my opinion in this respect on fitness and expediency, and the sentiments of the people; not on absolute right. The town corporations, simply as such, cannot be said to have any *right* to representation; except so far as the constitution creates such right. And this I apprehend to be the fallacy of the argument of the hon. member from Worcester. He contends, that the smallest town has a *right* to its representative. This is true; but the largest town (Boston) has a *right* also to fifty. These rights are precisely equal. They stand on the same ground, that is, on the provisions of the existing constitution. The hon. member thinks it quite just to reduce the right of the large town from fifty to ten, and yet that there is no power to affect the right of the small town; either by uniting it with another small town, for the choice of a representative, or otherwise. But I do not assent to that opinion. If it be right to take away half, or three fourths of the representation of the large towns, it cannot be right to leave that of the small towns undiminished. The report of the committee proposes that these small towns shall elect a member every other year, half of them sending one year, and half the next; or else that two small towns shall unite and send one member every year. There is something apparently irregular and anomalous in sending a member every other year; yet, perhaps, it is no great departure from former habits; because these small towns being, by the present constitution, compelled to pay their own members, have not, ordinarily, sent them oftener, on the average, than once in two years.

The honorable member from Worcester founds his argument on the *right* of town corporations, as such, to be represented in the Legislature. If he only means that right which the constitution at present secures,

his observation is true, while the constitution remains unaltered. But if he intend to say that such right exists, *prior* to the constitution, and independent of it, I ask whence it is derived? Representation of the PEOPLE has heretofore been by towns, because such a mode has been thought convenient. Still it has been the representation of the people. It is no *corporate right,* to partake in the sovereign power and form a part of the Legislature. To establish this right, as a corporate right, the gentleman has enumerated the *duties* of the town corporation; such as the maintenance of public worship, public schools, and public highways; and insists that the performance of these duties gives the town a right to a representative in the Legislature. But I would ask, sir, what possible ground there is for this argument? The burden of these duties falls not on any corporate funds belonging to the towns, but on the people, under assessments made on them individually, in their town meetings. As distinct from their individual *inhabitants,* the towns have no interest in these affairs. These duties are imposed by general laws; they are to be performed by the people, and if the people are represented in the making of these laws, the object is answered, whether they should be represented in one mode or another. But, further, sir; are these municipal duties rendered to the State, or are they not rather performed by the people of the towns for their own benefit? The general treasury derives no supplies from all these contributions. If the towns maintain religious instruction, it is for the benefit of their own inhabitants. If they support schools, it is for the education of the children of their inhabitants; and if they maintain roads and bridges, it is also for their own convenience. And therefore, sir, although I repeat that for reasons of expediency, I am in favor of maintaining town representation, as far as it can be done with a proper regard to equality of representation, I entirely disagree to the notion, that every town has a *right,* which an alteration of the constitution cannot divest, if the general good require such alteration, to have a representative in the Legislature. The honorable member has declared that we are about to *disfranchise* corporations, and destroy chartered rights. He pronounces this system of representation an outrage, and declares that we are forging *chains and fetters* for the people of Massachusetts. "Chains and fetters!" This Convention of delegates, chosen by the people, within this month, and going back to the people, divested of all power within another month, yet occupying their span of time here, in forging chains and fetters for themselves and their constituents! "Chains and fetters!" A popular assembly of four hundred men, by combining to fabricate these manacles for the people, and nobody, but the honorable member from Worcester, with sagacity enough to detect the horrible conspiracy, or honesty enough to disclose it! "Chains and fetters!" An assembly most variously composed; men of all

professions, and all parties; of different ages, habits and associations—
all freely and recently chosen by their towns and districts; yet this assembly, in one short month, contriving to fetter and enslave itself and
its constituents! Sir, there are some things too extravagant for the ornament and decoration of oratory; some things too excessive, even for the
fictions of poetry; and I am persuaded that a little reflection would satisfy the honorable member, that when he speaks of this assembly as
committing outrages on the rights of the people, and as forging chains
and fetters for their subjugation, he does as great injustice to his own
character as a correct and manly debater, as he does to the motives and
the intelligence of this body.

I do not doubt, sir, that some inequality exists in the mode of representatives proposed by the committee. A precise and exact equality is not
attainable, in any mode. Look to the gentleman's own proposition. By
that, Essex, with twenty thousand inhabitants more than Worcester,
would have twenty representatives less. Suffolk, which according to
numbers would be entitled to twenty, would have, if I mistake not, eight
or nine only. Whatever else, sir, this proposition may be a specimen of,
it is hardly a specimen of equality. As to the house of representatives,
my view of the subject is this. Under the present constitution the towns
have all a right to send representatives to the Legislature, in a certain
fixed proportion to their numbers. It has been found, that the full exercise of this right fills the house of representatives with too numerous a
body. What then is to be done? Why, sir, the delegates of the towns are
here assembled, to agree, mutually, on some reasonable mode of reduction. Now, sir, it is not for one party to stand sternly on its right, and
demand all the concession from another. As to right, all are equal. The
right which *Hull* possesses to send one, is the same as the right of *Boston*
to send fifty. Mutual concession and accommodation, therefore, can
alone accomplish the purpose of our meeting. If Boston consents, instead
of fifty, to send but twelve or fifteen, the small towns must consent, either to be united in the choice of their representatives with other small
towns, or to send a representative less frequently than every year; or to
have an option to do one or the other of these, hereafter, as shall be
found most convenient. This is what the report of the committee proposes, and, as far as we have yet learned, a great majority of the delegates from small towns approve the plan. I am willing, therefore, to vote
for this part of the report of the committee; thinking it as just and fair
a representation, and as much reduced in point of numbers, as can be
reasonably hoped for, without giving up entirely the system of representation by towns. It is to be considered also, that according to the report of the committee, the pay of the members is to be out of the public
treasury. Every body must see how this will operate on the large towns.

Boston, for example, with its twelve or fourteen members, will pay for fifty. Be it so; it is incident to its property, and not at all an injustice, if proper weight be given to that property, and proper provision be made for its security.

To recur again to the subject of the senate—there is one remark, made by gentlemen on the other side, of which I wish to take notice. It is said, that if the principle of representation in the senate by property be correct, it ought to be carried through; whereas it is limited and restrained by a provision that no district shall be entitled to more than six senators. But this is a prohibition on the making of great districts, generally; not merely a limitation of the effect of the property principle. It prevents great districts from being made where the valuation is small, as well as where it is large. Were it not for this, or some similar prohibition, Worcester and Hampshire might have been joined, under the present constitution, and have sent perhaps ten or twelve senators. The limitation is a general one, introduced for general purposes; and if, in a particular instance, it bears hard on any county, this should be regarded as an evil incident to a good and salutary rule, and ought to be, as I doubt not it will be, quietly borne.

I forbear, Mr. Chairman, to take notice of many minor objections to the report of the committee. The defence of that report, especially in its details, properly belongs to other and abler hands. My purpose in addressing you was simply to consider the propriety of providing, in one branch of the Legislature, a real check upon the other. And as I look upon that principle to be of the highest practical importance, and as it has seemed to me that the doctrines contended for would go to subvert it, I hope I may be pardoned for detaining the committee so long.

The Revolution in Greece, January 19, 1824

As Webster journeyed to Washington in November 1823 to attend the first session of the 18th Congress, he was keenly aware that he had been six years out of public life. He was no stranger to Washington, where he had spent the better part of the past three years arguing for clients before the Spanish Claims Commission (*Legal Papers*, 2: 175–275), but in parliamentary matters he was rusty. His election to the House of Representatives from Massachusetts, so short a time after moving his residence to that state was ample evidence of his standing at home, but he wanted to advertise his presence to the country at large. To that end, he devoted much attention to the choice of subject for his maiden speech. He selected the ongoing revolution in Greece, unaware that President Monroe, in his forthcoming annual message to Congress, would pledge non-intervention in future European controversies.

Greece had been a subjugated part of the Ottoman Empire for almost 400 years when sporadic local revolts became national revolution in 1821. The American people, incurably romantic and forever ready to side with the underdog, were quick to see in the movement the heritage of ancient Greece, which was also their own heritage, and they made no secret of their feelings. It was both to channel this widespread public sentiment to his own support and to afford a vehicle for the statement of a political creed that Webster chose his topic. If he could lead the United States to a recognition of Greek independence it would be at once a moral and a political triumph; if he could help to exert pressure upon the "Great Powers" (as the Holy Alliance now called itself) to intervene on behalf of Greece he would be an international as well as a national force. On the other hand, if he failed he would still have won, to the extent that he marshalled public feeling in his own behalf. In January 1824 the adventure seemed safe enough, for up to that time the Revolution had been a success.

Aside from numerous articles in the press, many of dubious accuracy, Webster's material came from Edward Everett, editor of the *North American Review*, professor of Greek literature at Harvard, and only two years returned from a four-year sojourn in Europe. Not only did Webster study Everett's publications on Greece, he read also the manuscript of "Ali Pacha," destined to appear in the January 1824 issue of

the *North American Review* (DW to Everett, Nov. 16, 28; Dec. 5, 6, 1823; Jan. 2, 1824, *Correspondence*, 1: 332–333; 335–336; 338–340; 344–345). He was well on the way to a mastery of the history of the Greek revolution when he made his first move on December 8, 1823. In the resolution he then introduced he was careful to avoid any seeming conflict with the Monroe Doctrine, laid down only six days earlier:

> *Resolved*, that provisions ought to be made, by law, for defraying the expense incident to the appointment of an Agent or Commissioner to Greece, whenever the President shall deem it expedient to make such appointment.

The resolution was not cleared in advance with Secretary of State John Quincy Adams, who let it be known after the fact that he was opposed to the whole proceeding (Adams, *Memoirs*, 6: 240).

The resolution was not adopted, but Webster himself had "nothing to regret." In the words of his friend Jeremiah Mason he had "acquired all the credit the subject & occasion were capable of giving, without any responsibility for the success of the proposed measure" (Mason to DW, Feb. 1, 1824, *Correspondence*, 1: 351). Within months the tide turned in Greece; Egypt joined Turkey to wipe out the revolution, and the cause seemed lost. The Greeks were at last saved by the timely intervention of Russia and Great Britain. Webster's friends would later find in the speech below a spark that may indeed have fired the sympathies of the Christian world. (See Everett's headnote to the speech in *Works*, 3: 60–61.)

The text reproduced below is the final version, taken for convenience from *Writings and Speeches*, 5: 60–93. It is identical with *Works*, 3:60–93, and with *Speeches and Forensic Arguments*, 1:241–264, where it is only very slightly edited from the contemporary pamphlet. The pamphlet, however, represents a substantial departure from the speech as it appeared in the *National Intelligencer* of January 20, 1824 and in the *Annals*, 18th Cong., 1st sess., pp. 1084–1099.

The *Intelligencer* published the speech, as transcribed by its own reporter, the day after its delivery. Such speed, in that day of hand-set type, was to say the least unusual, but the editors of the paper—Joseph Gales and William Winston Seaton, both friends of Webster's—justified the procedure. "The debate," explained the editors, "on Mr. Webster's motion respecting the cause of the Greeks commenced yesterday. Knowing the desire of our readers to understand the views of the mover of this proposition, we have, to make room for an immediate sketch of them, deferred other matter of much interest. . . ."

In return for this quick publication, Webster sacrificed the privilege

of revision before the speech appeared. He had worked on it long and carefully and was presumably satisfied to give it to the world as delivered. Rereading it, however, and perhaps mindful of reactions to it, he undertook almost at once a general overhauling, published separately before the end of January, not by Gales and Seaton, who usually did such things, but by John S. Meehan, publisher of the Washington *Columbian Star* (DW to Ezekiel Webster, Jan. 27, 1824, *Correspondence*, 1:350). This was the version Webster supplied to his nephew, Charles B. Haddock, for inclusion in the first published volume of his works, *Speeches and Forensic Arguments*; and it is the version we have selected for inclusion here.

Any comparison of the respective texts will have to be made by the reader. It has proved quite impractical to footnote variations, even those of substantive significance, because the entire text has been rewritten. The meaning and purport of the speech have not been altered, but the language and structure have been changed, sometimes beyond recognition. Wherever ambiguity might lurk, wherever meaning might be obscure, wherever the message did not leap instantly from the page, Webster amplified, clarified, or emended. The pamphlet version was the same but not the same, calculated in its final form to carry conviction to eye and heart; to let the people the country over know that Daniel Webster was back in Congress, ready to be their champion.

I am afraid, Mr. Chairman, that, so far as my part in this discussion is concerned, those expectations which the public excitement existing on the subject, and certain associations easily suggested by it, have conspired to raise, may be disappointed. An occasion which calls the attention to a spot so distinguished, so connected with interesting recollections, as Greece, may naturally create something of warmth and enthusiasm. In a grave, political discussion, however, it is necessary that those feelings should be chastised. I shall endeavor properly to repress them, although it is impossible that they should be altogether extinguished. We must, indeed, fly beyond the civilized world; we must pass the dominion of law and the boundaries of knowledge; we must, more especially, withdraw ourselves from this place, and the scenes and objects which here surround us,—if we would separate ourselves entirely from the influence of all those memorials of herself which ancient Greece has transmitted for the admiration and the benefit of mankind. This free form of government, this popular assembly, the common council held for the common good,—where have we contemplated its earliest models? This practice of free debate and public discussion, the contest of mind with mind, and that popular eloquence, which, if it were now

here, on a subject like this, would move the stones of the Capitol,—whose was the language in which all these were first exhibited? Even the edifice in which we assemble, these proportioned columns, this ornamented architecture, all remind us that Greece has existed, and that we, like the rest of mankind, are greatly her debtors.

But I have not introduced this motion in the vain hope of discharging any thing of this accumulated debt of centuries. I have not acted upon the expectation, that we, who have inherited this obligation from our ancestors, should now attempt to pay it to those who may seem to have inherited from *their* ancestors a right to receive payment. My object is nearer and more immediate. I wish to take occasion of the struggle of an interesting and gallant people, in the cause of liberty and Christianity, to draw the attention of the House to the circumstances which have accompanied that struggle, and to the principles which appear to have governed the conduct of the great states of Europe in regard to it; and to the effects and consequences of these principles upon the independence of nations, and especially upon the institutions of free governments. What I have to say of Greece, therefore, concerns the modern, not the ancient; the living, and not the dead. It regards her, not as she exists in history, triumphant over time, and tyranny, and ignorance; but as she now is, contending, against fearful odds, for being, and for the common privileges of human nature.

As it is never difficult to recite commonplace remarks and trite aphorisms, so it may be easy, I am aware, on this occasion, to remind me of the wisdom which dictates to men a care of their own affairs, and admonishes them, instead of searching for adventures abroad, to leave other men's concerns in their own hands. It may be easy to call this resolution *Quixotic*, the emanation of a crusading or propagandist spirit. All this, and more, may be readily said; but all this, and more, will not be allowed to fix a character upon this proceeding, until that is proved which it takes for granted. Let it first be shown, that in this question there is nothing which can affect the interest, the character, or the duty of this country. Let it be proved, that we are not called upon, by either of these considerations, to express an opinion on the subject to which the resolution relates. Let this be proved, and then it will indeed be made out, that neither ought this resolution to pass, nor ought the subject of it to have been mentioned in the communication of the President to us. But, in my opinion, this cannot be shown. In my judgment, the subject is interesting to the people and the government of this country, and we are called upon, by considerations of great weight and moment, to express our opinions upon it. These considerations, I think, spring from a sense of our own duty, our character, and our own interest. I wish to treat the subject on such grounds, exclusively, as are truly *American;*

but then, in considering it as an American question, I cannot forget the age in which we live, the prevailing spirit of the age, the interesting questions which agitate it, and our own peculiar relation in regard to these interesting questions. Let this be, then, and as far as I am concerned I hope it will be, purely an American discussion; but let it embrace, nevertheless, every thing that fairly concerns America. Let it comprehend, not merely her present advantage, but her permanent interest, her elevated character as one of the free states of the world, and her duty towards those great principles which have hitherto maintained the relative independence of nations, and which have, more especially, made her what she is.

At the commencement of the session, the President, in the discharge of the high duties of his office, called our attention to the subject to which this resolution refers. "A strong hope," says that communication, "has been long entertained, founded on the heroic struggle of the Greeks, that they would succeed in their contest, and resume their equal station among the nations of the earth. It is believed that the whole civilized world takes a deep interest in their welfare. Although no power has declared in their favor, yet none, according to our information, has taken part against them. Their cause and their name have protected them from dangers which might ere this have overwhelmed any other people. The ordinary calculations of interest, and of acquisition with a view to aggrandizement, which mingle so much in the transactions of nations, seem to have had no effect in regard to them. From the facts which have come to our knowledge, there is good cause to believe that their enemy has lost for ever all dominion over them; that Greece will become again an independent nation."

It has appeared to me that the House should adopt some resolution reciprocating these sentiments, so far as it shall approve them. More than twenty years have elapsed since Congress first ceased to receive such a communication from the President as could properly be made the subject of a general answer. I do not mean to find fault with this relinquishment of a former and an ancient practice. It may have been attended with inconveniences which justified its abolition. But, certainly, there was one advantage belonging to it; and that is, that it furnished a fit opportunity for the expression of the opinion of the houses of Congress upon those topics in the executive communication which were not expected to be made the immediate subjects of direct legislation. Since, therefore, the President's message does not now receive a general answer, it has seemed to me to be proper that, in some mode, agreeable to our own usual form of proceeding, we should express our sentiments upon the important and interesting topics on which it treats.

If the sentiments of the message in respect to Greece be proper, it is

equally proper that this House should reciprocate those sentiments. The present resolution is designed to have that extent, and no more. If it pass, it will leave any future proceedings where it now is, in the discretion of the executive government. It is but an expression, under those forms in which the House is accustomed to act, of the satisfaction of the House with the general sentiments expressed in regard to this subject in the message, and of its readiness to defray the expense incident to any inquiry for the purpose of further information, or any other agency which the President, in his discretion, shall see fit, in whatever manner and at whatever time, to institute. The whole matter is still left in his judgment, and this resolution can in no way restrain its unlimited exercise.

I might well, Mr. Chairman, avoid the responsibility of this measure, if it had, in my judgment, any tendency to change the policy of the country. With the general course of that policy I am quite satisfied. The nation is prosperous, peaceful, and happy; and I should very reluctantly put its peace, prosperity, or happiness at risk. It appears to me, however, that this resolution is strictly conformable to our general policy, and not only consistent with our interests, but even demanded by a large and liberal view of those interests.

It is certainly true that the just policy of this country is in the first place, a peaceful policy. No nation ever had less to expect from forcible aggrandizement. The mighty agents which are working out our greatness are time, industry, and the arts. Our augmentation is by growth, not by acquisition; by internal development, not by external accession. No schemes can be suggested to us so magnificent as the prospects which a sober contemplation of our own condition, unaided by projects, uninfluenced by ambition, fairly spreads before us. A country of such vast extent, with such varieties of soil and climate, with so much public spirit and private enterprise, with a population increasing so much beyond former example, with capacities of improvement not only unapplied or unexhausted, but even, in a great measure, as yet unexplored,—so free in its institutions, so mild in its laws, so secure in the title it confers on every man to his own acquisitions,—needs nothing but time and peace to carry it forward to almost any point of advancement.

In the next place, I take it for granted that the policy of this country, springing from the nature of our government and the spirit of all our institutions, is, so far as it respects the interesting questions which agitate the present age, on the side of liberal and enlightened sentiments. The age is extraordinary; the spirit that actuates it is peculiar and marked; and our own relation to the times we live in, and to the questions which interest them, is equally marked and peculiar. We are placed, by our good fortune and the wisdom and valor of our ancestors, in a

condition in which we *can* act no obscure part. Be it for honor, or be it for dishonor, whatever we do is sure to attract the observation of the world. As one of the free states among the nations, as a great and rapidly rising republic, it would be impossible for us, if we were so disposed, to prevent our principles, our sentiments, and our example from producing some effect upon the opinions and hopes of society throughout the civilized world. It rests probably with ourselves to determine whether the influence of these shall be salutary or pernicious.

It cannot be denied that the great political question of this age is that between absolute and regulated governments. The substance of the controversy is whether society shall have any part in its own government. Whether the form of government shall be that of limited monarchy, with more or less mixture of hereditary power, or wholly elective or representative, may perhaps be considered as subordinate. The main controversy is between that absolute rule, which, while it promises to govern well, means, nevertheless, to govern without control, and that constitutional system which restrains sovereign discretion, and asserts that society may claim as matter of right some effective power in the establishment of the laws which are to regulate it. The spirit of the times sets with a most powerful current in favor of these last-mentioned opinions. It is opposed, however whenever and wherever it shows itself, by certain of the great potentates of Europe; and it is opposed on grounds as applicable in one civilized nation as in another, and which would justify such opposition in relation to the United States, as well as in relation to any other state or nation, if time and circumstances should render such opposition expedient.

What part it becomes this country to take on a question of this sort, so far as it is called upon to take any part, cannot be doubtful. Our side of this question is settled for us, even without our own volition. Our history, our situation, our character, necessarily decide our position and our course, before we have even time to ask whether we have an option. Our place is on the side of free institutions. From the earliest settlement of these States, their inhabitants were accustomed, in a greater or less degree, to the enjoyment of the powers of self-government; and for the last half-century they have sustained systems of government entirely representative, yielding to themselves the greatest possible prosperity, and not leaving them without distinction and respect among the nations of the earth. This system we are not likely to abandon; and while we shall no farther recommend its adoption to other nations, in whole or in part, than it may recommend itself by its visible influence on our own growth and prosperity, we are, nevertheless, interested to resist the establishment of doctrines which deny the legality of its foundations. We stand as an equal among nations, claiming the full benefit of the estab-

lished international law; and it is our duty to oppose, from the earliest to the latest moment, any innovations upon that code which shall bring into doubt or question our own equal and independent rights.

I will now, Mr. Chairman, advert to those pretensions put forth by the allied sovereigns of Continental Europe, which seem to me calculated, if unresisted, to bring into disrepute the principles of our government, and, indeed, to be wholly incompatible with any degree of national independence. I do not introduce these considerations for the sake of topics. I am not about to declaim against crowned heads, nor to quarrel with any country for preferring a form of government different from our own. The right of choice that we exercise for ourselves, I am quite willing to leave also to others. But it appears to me that the pretensions to which I have alluded are wholly inconsistent with the independence of nations generally, without regard to the question whether their governments be absolute, monarchical and limited, or purely popular and representative. I have a most deep and thorough conviction, that a new era has arisen in the world, that new and dangerous combinations are taking place, promulgating doctrines and fraught with consequences wholly subversive in their tendency of the public law of nations and of the general liberties of mankind. Whether this be so, or not, is the question which I now propose to examine, upon such grounds of information as are afforded by the common and public means of knowledge.

Every body knows that, since the final restoration of the Bourbons to the throne of France, the Continental powers have entered into sundry alliances, which have been made public, and have held several meetings or congresses, at which the principles of their political conduct have been declared. These things must necessarily have an effect upon the international law of the states of the world. If that effect be good, and according to the principles of that law, they deserve to be applauded. If, on the contrary, their effect and tendency be most dangerous, their principles wholly inadmissible, their pretensions such as would abolish every degree of national independence, then they are to be resisted.

I begin, Mr. Chairman, by drawing your attention to the treaty concluded at Paris in September, 1815, between Russia, Prussia, and Austria, commonly called the Holy Alliance. This singular alliance appears to have originated with the Emperor of Russia; for we are informed that a draft of it was exhibited by him, personally, to a plenipotentiary of one of the great powers of Europe, before it was presented to the other sovereigns who ultimately signed it. This instrument professes nothing, certainly, which is not extremely commendable and praiseworthy. It promises only that the contracting parties, both in relation to other states, and in regard to their own subjects, will observe the rules of justice and Christianity. In confirmation of these promises, it makes the

most solemn and devout religious invocations. Now, although such an alliance is a novelty in European history, the world seems to have received this treaty, upon its first promulgation, with general charity. It was commonly understood as little or nothing more than an expression of thanks for the successful termination of the momentous contest in which those sovereigns had been engaged. It still seems somewhat unaccountable, however, that these good resolutions should require to be confirmed by treaty. Who doubted that these august sovereigns would treat each other with justice, and rule their own subjects in mercy? And what necessity was there for a solemn stipulation by treaty, to insure the performance of that which is no more than the ordinary duty of every government? It would hardly be admitted by these sovereigns, that by this compact they consider themselves bound to introduce an entire change, or any change, in the course of their own conduct. Nothing substantially new, certainly, can be supposed to have been intended. What principle, or what practice, therefore, called for this solemn declaration of the intention of the parties to observe the rules of religion and justice?

It is not a little remarkable, that a writer of reputation upon the Public Law, described, many years ago, not inaccurately, the character of this alliance. I allude to Puffendorf. "It seems useless," says he, "to frame any pacts or leagues, barely for the defence and support of universal peace; for by such a league nothing is superadded to the obligation of natural law, and no agreement is made for the performance of any thing which the parties were not previously bound to perform; nor is the original obligation rendered firmer or stronger by such an addition. Men of any tolerable culture and civilization might well be ashamed of entering into any such compact, the conditions of which imply only that the parties concerned shall not offend in any clear point of duty. Besides, we should be guilty of great irreverence towards God, should we suppose that his injunctions had not already laid a sufficient obligation upon us to act justly, unless we ourselves voluntarily consented to the same engagement; as if our obligation to obey his will depended upon our own pleasure.

"If one engage to serve another, he does not set it down expressly and particularly among the terms and conditions of the bargain, that he will not betray nor murder him, nor pillage nor burn his house. For the same reason, that would be a dishonorable engagement, in which men should bind themselves to act properly and decently, and not break the peace."

Such were the sentiments of that eminent writer. How nearly he had anticipated the case of the Holy Alliance will appear from the preamble to that alliance. After stating that the allied sovereigns had become persuaded, by the events of the last three years, that "their relations with

each other ought to be regulated exclusively by the sublime truths taught by the eternal religion of God the Saviour," they solemnly declare their fixed resolution "to adopt as the sole rule of their conduct, both in the administration of their respective states, and in their political relations with every other government, the precepts of that holy religion, namely, the precepts of justice, charity, and peace, which, far from being applicable to private life alone, ought, on the contrary, to have a direct influence upon the counsels of princes, and guide all their steps, as being the only means of consolidating human institutions, and remedying their imperfections."

This measure, however, appears principally important, as it was the first of a series, and was followed afterwards by others of a more marked and practical nature. These measures, taken together, profess to establish two principles, which the Allied Powers would introduce as a part of the law of the civilized world; and the establishment of which is to be enforced by a million and a half of bayonets.

The first of these principles is, that all popular or constitutional rights are held no otherwise than as grants from the crown. Society, upon this principle, has no rights of its own; it takes good government, when it gets it, as a boon and a concession, but can demand nothing. It is to live by that favor which emanates from royal authority, and if it have the misfortune to lose that favor, there is nothing to protect it against any degree of injustice and oppression. It can rightfuly make no endeavor for a change, by itself; its whole privilege is to receive the favors that may be dispensed by the sovereign power, and all its duty is described in the single word *submission*. This is the plain result of the principal Continental state papers; indeed, it is nearly the identical text of some of them.

The circular despatch addressed by the sovereigns assembled at Laybach, in the spring of 1821, to their ministers at foreign courts, alleges, "that useful and necessary changes in legislation and in the administration of states ought only to emanate from the free will and intelligent and well-weighed conviction of those whom God has rendered responsible for power. All that deviates from this line necessarily leads to disorder, commotions, and evils far more insufferable than those which they pretend to remedy." Now, Sir, this principle would carry Europe back again, at once, into the middle of the Dark Ages. It is the old doctrine of the Divine right of kings, advanced now by new advocates, and sustained by a formidable array of power. That the people hold their fundamental privileges as matter of concession or indulgence from the sovereign power, is a sentiment not easy to be diffused in this age, any farther than it is enforced by the direct operation of military means. It is true, certainly, that some six centuries ago the early founders of

English liberty called the instrument which secured their rights a *charter*. It was, indeed, a concession; they had obtained it sword in hand from the king; and in many other cases, whatever was obtained, favorable to human rights, from the tyranny and despotism of the feudal sovereigns, was called by the names of *privileges and liberties*, as being matter of special favor. Though we retain this language at the present time, the principle itself belongs to ages that have long passed by us. The civilized world has done with "the enormous faith, of many made for one." Society asserts its own rights, and alleges them to be original, sacred, and unalienable. It is not satisfied with having kind masters; it demands a participation in its own government; and in states much advanced in civilization, it urges this demand with a constancy and an energy that cannot well nor long be resisted. There are, happily, enough of regulated governments in the world, and those among the most distinguished, to operate as constant examples, and to keep alive an unceasing panting in the bosoms of men for the enjoyment of similar free institutions.

When the English Revolution of 1688 took place, the English people did not content themselves with the example of Runnymede; they did not build their hopes upon royal charters; they did not, like the authors of the Laybach circular, suppose that all useful changes in constitutions and laws must proceed from those only whom God has rendered responsible for power. They were somewhat better instructed in the principles of civil liberty, or at least they were better lovers of those principles than the sovereigns of Laybach. Instead of petitioning for charters, they declared their rights, and while they offered to the Prince of Orange the crown with one hand, they held in the other an enumeration of those privileges which they did not profess to hold as favors, but which they demanded and insisted upon as their undoubted rights.

I need not stop to observe, Mr. Chairman, how totally hostile are these doctrines of Laybach to the fundamental principles of our government. They are in direct contradiction; the principles of good and evil are hardly more opposite. If these principles of the sovereigns be true, we are but in a state of rebellion or of anarchy, and are only tolerated among civilized states because it has not yet been convenient to reduce us to the true standard.

But the second, and, if possible, the still more objectionable principle, avowed in these papers, is the right of forcible interference in the affairs of other states. A right to control nations in their desire to change their own government, wherever it may be conjectured, or pretended, that such change might furnish an example to the subjects of other states, is plainly and distinctly asserted. The same Congress that made the declaration at Laybach had declared, before its removal from Troppau, "that the powers have an undoubted right to take a hostile attitude in

regard to those states in which the overthrow of the government may operate as an example."

There cannot, as I think, be conceived a more flagrant violation of public law, or national independence, than is contained in this short declaration.

No matter what be the character of the government resisted; no matter with what weight the foot of the oppressor bears on the neck of the oppressed; if he struggle, or if he complain, he sets a dangerous example of resistance,—and from that moment he becomes an object of hostility to the most powerful potentates of the earth. I want words to express my abhorrence of this abominable principle. I trust every enlightened man throughout the world will oppose it, and that, especially, those who, like ourselves, are fortunately out of the reach of the bayonets that enforce it, will proclaim their detestation of it, in a tone both loud and decisive. The avowed object of such declarations is to preserve the peace of the world. But by what means is it proposed to preserve this peace? Simply, by bringing the power of all governments to bear against all subjects. Here is to be established a sort of double, or treble, or quadruple, or, for aught I know, quintuple allegiance. An offence against one king is to be an offence against all kings, and the power of all is to be put forth for the punishment of the offender. A right to interfere in extreme cases, is the case of contiguous states, and where imminent danger is threatened to one by what is occurring in another, is not without precedent in modern times, upon what has been called the law of vicinage; and when confined to extreme cases, and limited to a certain extent, it may perhaps be defended upon principles of necessity and self-defence. But to maintain that sovereigns may go to war upon the subjects of another state to repress an example, is monstrous indeed. What is to be the limit to such a principle, or to the practice growing out of it? What, in any case, but sovereign pleasure, is to decide whether the example be good or bad? And what, under the operation of such a rule, may be thought of our example? Why are we not as fair objects for the operation of the new principle, as any of those who may attempt a reform of government on the other side of the Atlantic?

The ultimate effect of this alliance of sovereigns, for objects personal to themselves, or respecting only the permanence of their own power, must be the destruction of all just feeling, and all natural sympathy, between those who exercise the power of government and those who are subject to it. The old channels of mutual regard and confidence are to be dried up, or cut off. Obedience can now be expected no longer than it is enforced. Instead of relying on the affections of the governed, sovereigns are to rely on the affections and friendship of other sovereigns. There are, in short, no longer to be nations. Princes and people are no longer

to unite for interests common to them both. There is to be an end of all patriotism, as a distinct national feeling. Society is to be divided horizontally; all sovereigns above, and all subjects below; the former coalescing for their own security, and for the more certain subjection of the undistinguished multitude beneath. This, Sir, is no picture drawn by imagination. I have hardly used language stronger than that in which the authors of this new system have commented on their own work. M. de Chateaubriand, in his speech in the French Chamber of Deputies, in February last, declared, that he had a conference with the Emperor of Russia at Vernon, in which that august sovereign uttered sentiments which appeared to him so precious, that he immediately hastened home, and wrote them down while yet fresh in his recollection. "The Emperor declared," said he, "that there can no longer be such a thing as an English, French, Russian, Prussian, or Austrian policy; there is henceforth but one policy, which, for the safety of all, should be adopted both by people and kings. It was for me first to show myself convinced of the principles upon which I founded the alliance; an occasion offered itself,—the rising in Greece. Nothing certainly could occur more for my interests, for the interests of my people; nothing more acceptable to my country, than a religious war in Turkey. But I have thought I perceived in the troubles of the Morea the sign of revolution, and I have held back. Providence has not put under my command eight hundred thousand soldiers to satisfy my ambition, but to protect religion, morality, and justice, and to secure the prevalence of those principles of order on which human society rests. It may well be permitted, that kings may have public alliances to defend themselves against secret enemies."

These, Sir, are the words which the French minister thought so important that they deserved to be recorded; and I, too, Sir, am of the same opinion. But if it be true that there is hereafter to be neither a Russian policy, nor a Prussian policy, nor an Austrian policy, nor a French policy, nor even, which yet I will not believe, an English policy, there will be, I trust in God, an American policy. If the authority of all these governments be hereafter to be mixed and blended, and to flow, in one augmented current of prerogative, over the face of Europe, sweeping away all resistance in its course, it will yet remain for us to secure our own happiness by the preservation of our own principles; which I hope we shall have the manliness to express on all proper occasions, and the spirit to defend in every extremity. The end and scope of this amalgamated policy are neither more nor less than this, to interfere, by force, for any government, against any people who may resist it. Be the state of the people what it may, they shall not rise; be the government what it will, it shall not be opposed.

The practical commentary has corresponded with the plain language

of the text. Look at Spain, and at Greece. If men may not resist the Spanish Inquisition, and the Turkish cimeter, what is there to which humanity must not submit? Stronger cases can never arise. Is it not proper for us, at all times, is it not our duty, at this time, to come forth, and deny, and condemn, these monstrous principles? Where, but here, and in one other place, are they likely to be resisted? They are advanced with equal coolness and boldness; and they are supported by immense power. The timid will shrink and give way, and many of the brave may be compelled to yield to force. Human liberty may yet, perhaps, be obliged to repose its principal hopes on the intelligence and the vigor of the Saxon race. As far as depends on us, at least, I trust those hopes will not be disappointed; and that, to the extent which may consist with our own settled, pacific policy, our opinions and sentiments may be brought to act on the right side, and to the right end, on an occasion which is, in truth, nothing less than a momentous question between an intelligent age, full of knowledge, thirsting for improvement, and quickened by a thousand impulses, on one side, and the most arbitrary pretensions, sustained by unprecedented power, on the other.

This asserted right of forcible intervention in the affairs of other nations is in open violation of the public law of the world. Who has authorized these learned doctors of Troppau to establish new articles in this code? Whence are their diplomas? Is the whole world expected to acquiesce in principles which entirely subvert the independence of nations? On the basis of this independence has been reared the beautiful fabric of international law. On the principle of this independence, Europe has seen a family of nations flourishing within its limits, the small among the large, protected not always by power, but by a principle above power, by a sense of propriety and justice. On this principle, the great commonwealth of civilized states has been hitherto upheld. There have been occasional departures or violations, and always disastrous, as in the case of Poland; but, in general, the harmony of the system has been wonderfully preserved. In the production and preservation of this sense of justice, this predominating principle, the Christian religion has acted a main part. Christianity and civilization have labored together; it seems, indeed, to be a law of our human condition, that they can live and flourish only together. From their blended influence has arisen that delightful spectacle of the prevalence of reason and principle over power and interest, so well described by one who was an honor to the age;—

> "And sovereign Law, the state's collected will,
>   O'er thrones and globes elate,
>   Sits empress,—crowning good, repressing ill:
>   Smit by her sacred frown,

The fiend, Discretion, like a vapor, sinks,
　　And e'en the all-dazzling crown
Hides his faint rays, and at her bidding shrinks."

But this vision is past. While the teachers at Laybach give the rule, there will be no law but the law of the strongest.

It may now be required of me to show what interest *we* have in resisting this new system. What is it to *us*, it may be asked, upon what principles, or what pretences, the European governments, assert a right of interfering in the affairs of their neighbors? The thunder, it may be said, rolls at a distance. The wide Atlantic is between us and danger; and, however others may suffer, *we* shall remain safe.

I think it is a sufficient answer to this to say, that we are one of the nations of the earth; that we have an interest, therefore, in the preservation of that system of national law and national intercourse which has heretofore subsisted, so beneficially for all. Our system of government, it should also be remembered, is, throughout, founded on principles utterly hostile to the new code; and if we remain undisturbed by its operation, we shall owe our security either to our situation or our spirit. The enterprising character of the age, our own active, commercial spirit, the great increase which has taken place in the intercourse among civilized and commercial states, have necessarily connected us with other nations, and given us a high concern in the preservation of those salutary principles upon which that intercourse is founded. We have as clear an interest in international law, as individuals have in the laws of society.

But apart from the soundness of the policy, on the ground of direct interest, we have, Sir, a duty connected with this subject, which I trust we are willing to perform. What do *we* not owe to the cause of civil and religious liberty? to the principle of lawful resistance? to the principle that society has a right to partake in its own government? As the leading republic of the world, living and breathing in these principles, and advanced, by their operation, with unequalled rapidity in our career, shall we give *our* consent to bring them into disrepute and disgrace? It is neither ostentation nor boasting to say, that there lies before this country, in immediate prospect, a great extent and height of power. We are borne along towards this, without effort, and not always even with a full knowledge of the rapidity of our own motion. Circumstances which never combined before have coöperated in our favor, and a mighty current is setting us forward which we could not resist even if we would, and which, while we would stop to make an observation, and take the sun, has set us, at the end of the operation, far in advance of the place where we commenced it. Does it not become us, then, is it not a duty imposed on us, to give our weight to the side of liberty and justice, to let

mankind know that we are not tired of our own institutions, and to protest against the asserted power of altering at pleasure the law of the civilized world?

But whatever we do in this respect, it becomes us to do upon clear and consistent principles. There is an important topic in the message to which I have yet hardly alluded. I mean the rumored combination of the European Continental sovereigns against the newly established free states of South America. Whatever position this government may take on that subject, I trust it will be one which can be defended on known and acknowledged grounds of right. The near approach or the remote distance of danger may affect policy, but cannot change principle. The same reason that would authorize us to protest against unwarrantable combinations to interfere between Spain and her former colonies, would authorize us equally to protest, if the same combinations were directed against the smallest state in Europe, although our duty to ourselves, our policy, and wisdom, might indicate very different courses as fit to be pursued by us in the two cases. We shall not, I trust, act upon the notion of dividing the world with the Holy Alliance, and complain of nothing done by them in their hemisphere if they will not interfere with ours. At least this would not be such a course of policy as I could recommend or support. We have not offended, and I hope we do not intend to offend, in regard to South America, against any principle of national independence or of public law. We have done nothing, we shall do nothing, that we need to hush up or compromise by forbearing to express our sympathy for the cause of the Greeks, or our opinion of the course which other governments have adopted in regard to them.

It may, in the next place, be asked, perhaps, Supposing all this to be true, what can *we* do? Are we to go to war? Are we to interfere in the Greek cause, or any other European cause? Are we to endanger our pacific relations? No, certainly not. What, then, the question recurs, remains for us? If we will not endanger our own peace, if we will neither furnish armies nor navies to the cause which we think the just one, what is there within our power?

Sir, this reasoning mistakes the age. The time has been, indeed, when fleets, and armies, and subsidies, were the principal reliances even in the best cause. But, happily for mankind, a great change has taken place in this respect. Moral causes come into consideration, in proportion as the progress of knowledge is advanced; and the public opinion of the civilized world is rapidly gaining an ascendency over mere brutal force. It is already able to oppose the most formidable obstruction to the progress of injustice and oppression; and as it grows more intelligent and more intense, it will be more and more formidable. It may be silenced by military power, but it cannot be conquered. It is elastic, irrepressible, and

invulnerable to the weapons of ordinary warfare. It is that impassible, unextinguishable enemy of mere violence and arbitrary rule, which, like Milton's angels,

> "Vital in every part, ...
> Cannot, but by annihilating, die."

Until this be propitiated or satisfied, it is vain for power to talk either of triumphs or of repose. No matter what fields are desolated, what fortresses surrendered, what armies subdued, or what provinces overrun. In the history of the year that has passed by us, and in the instance of unhappy Spain, we have seen the vanity of all triumphs in a cause which violates the general sense of justice of the civilized world. It is nothing, that the troops of France have passed from the Pyrenees to Cadiz; it is nothing that an unhappy and prostrate nation has fallen before them; it is nothing that arrests, and confiscation, and execution, sweep away the little remnant of national resistance. There is an enemy that still exists to check the glory of these triumphs. It follows the conquerer back to the very scene of his ovations; it calls upon him to take notice that Europe, though silent, is yet indignant; it shows him that the sceptre of his victory is a barren sceptre; that it shall confer neither joy nor honor, but shall moulder to dry ashes in his grasp. In the midst of his exultation, it pierces his ear with the cry of injured justice; it denounces against him the indignation of an enlightened and civilized age; it turns to bitterness the cup of his rejoicing, and wounds him with the sting which belongs to the consciousness of having outraged the opinion of mankind.

In my opinion, Sir, the Spanish nation is now nearer, not only in point of time, but in point of circumstance, to the acquisition of a regulated government, than at the moment of the French invasion. Nations must, no doubt, undergo these trials in their progress to the establishment of free institutions. The very trials benefit them, and render them more capable both of obtaining and of enjoying the object which they seek.

I shall not detain the committee, Sir, by laying before it any statistical, geographical, or commercial, account of Greece. I have no knowledge on these subjects which is not common to all. It is universally admitted, that, within the last thirty or forty years, the condition of Greece has been greatly improved. Her marine is at present respectable, containing the best sailors in the Mediterranean, better even, in that sea, than our own, as more accustomed to the long quarantines and other regulations which prevail in its ports. The number of her seamen has been estimated as high as 50,000, but I suppose that estimate must be much too large. She has, probably, 150,000 tons of shipping. It is not easy to ascertain the amount of the Greek population. The Turkish government

does not trouble itself with any of the calculations of political economy, and there has never been such a thing as an accurate census, probably, in any part of the Turkish empire. In the absence of all official information, private opinions widely differ. By the tables which have been communicated, it would seem that there are 2,400,000 Greeks in Greece proper and the islands; an amount, as I am inclined to think, somewhat overrated. There are, probably, in the whole of European Turkey, 5,000,000 Greeks, and 2,000,000 more in the Asiatic dominions of that power.

The moral and intellectual progress of this numerous population, under the horrible oppression which crushes it, has been such as may well excite regard. Slaves, under barbarous masters, the Greeks have still aspired after the blessings of knowledge and civilization. Before the breaking out of the present revolution, they had established schools, and colleges, and libraries, and the press. Wherever, as in Scio, owing to particular circumstances, the weight of oppression was mitigated, the natural vivacity of the Greeks, and their aptitude for arts, were evinced. Though certainly not on an equality with the civilized and Christian states of Europe,—and how is it possible, under such oppression as they endured, that they should be?—they yet furnished a striking contrast with their Tartar masters. It has been well said, that it is not easy to form a just conception of the nature of the despotism exercised over them. Conquest and subjugation, as known among European states, are inadequate modes of expression by which to denote the dominion of the Turks. A conquest in the civilized world is generally no more than an acquisition of a new dominion to the conquering country. It does not imply a never-ending bondage imposed upon the conquered, a perpetual mark,—an opprobrious distinction between them and their masters; a bitter and unending persecution of their religion; and habitual violation of their rights of person and property, and the unrestrained indulgence towards them of every passion which belongs to the character of a barbarous soldiery. Yet such is the state of Greece. The Ottoman power over them, obtained originally by the sword, is constantly preserved by the same means. Wherever it exists, it is a mere military power. The religious and civil code of the state being both fixed in the Koran, and equally the object of an ignorant and furious faith, have been found equally incapable of change. "The Turk," it has been said, "has been *encamped* in Europe for four centuries." He has hardly any more participation in European manners, knowledge, and arts, than when he crossed Bosphorus. But this is not the worst. The power of the empire is fallen into anarchy, and as the principle which belongs to the head belongs also to the parts, there are as many despots as there are pachas, beys, and viziers. Wars are almost perpetual between the Sultan and some

rebellious governor of a province; and in the conflict of these despotisms, the people are necessarily ground between the upper and the nether millstone. In short, the Christian subjects of the Sublime Porte feel daily all the miseries which flow from despotism, from anarchy, from slavery, and from religious persecution. If any thing yet remains to heighten such a picture, let it be added, that every office in the government is not only actually, but professedly, venal; the pachalics, the vizierates, the cadi-ships, and whatsoever other denomination may denote the depositary of power. In the whole world, Sir, there is no such oppression felt as by the Christian Greeks. In various parts of India, to be sure, the government is bad enough; but then it is the government of barbarians over barbarians, and the feeling of oppression is, of course, not so keen. There the oppressed are perhaps not better than their oppressors; but in the case of Greece, there are millions of Christian men, not without knowledge, not without refinement, not without a strong thirst for all the pleasures of civilized life, trampled into the very earth, century after century, by a pillaging, savage, relentless soldiery. Sir, the case is unique. There exists, and has existed, nothing like it. The world has no such misery to show; there is no case in which Christian communities can be called upon with such emphasis of appeal.

But I have said enough, Mr. Chairman, indeed I need have said nothing, to satisfy the House, that it must be some new combination of circumstances, or new views of policy in the cabinets of Europe, which have caused this interesting struggle not merely to be regarded with indifference, but to be marked with opprobrium. The very statement of the case, as a contest between the Turks and Greeks, sufficiently indicates what must be the feeling of every individual, and every government, that is not biased by a particular interest, or a particular feeling, to disregard the dictates of justice and humanity.

And now, Sir, what has been the conduct pursued by the Allied Powers in regard to this contest? When the revolution broke out, the sovereigns were assembled in congress in Laybach; and the papers of that assembly sufficiently manifest their sentiments. They proclaimed their abhorrence of those "criminal combinations which had been formed in the eastern parts of Europe"; and, although it is possible that this denunciation was aimed, more particularly, at the disturbances in the provinces of Wallachia and Moldavia, yet no exception is made, from its general terms, in favor of those events in Greece which were properly the commencement of her revolution, and which could not but be well known at Laybach, before the date of these declarations. Now it must be remembered, that Russia was a leading party in this denunciation of the efforts of the Greeks to achieve their liberation; and it cannot but be expected by Russia, that the world should also remember what part

she herself has heretofore acted in the same concern. It is notorious, that within the last half-century she has again and again excited the Greeks to rebellion against the Porte, and that she has constantly kept alive in them the hope that she would, one day, by her own great power, break the yoke of their oppressor. Indeed, the earnest attention with which Russia has regarded Greece goes much farther back than to the time I have mentioned. Ivan the Third, in 1482, having espoused a Grecian princess, heiress of the last Greek Emperor, discarded St. George from the Russian arms, and adopted the Greek two-headed black eagle, which has continued in the Russian arms to the present day. In virtue of the same marriage, the Russian princes claim the Greek throne as their inheritance.

Under Peter the Great, the policy of Russia developed itself more fully. In 1696, he rendered himself master of Azof, and in 1698, obtained the right to pass the Dardanelles, and to maintain, by that route, commercial intercourse with the Mediterranean. He had emissaries throughout Greece, and particularly applied himself to gain the clergy. He adopted the *Labarum* of Constantine, "In hoc signo vinces"; and medals were struck, with the inscription, "Petrus I. Russo-Græcorum Imperator." In whatever new direction the principles of the Holy Alliance may now lead the politics of Russia, or whatever course she may suppose Christianity now prescribes to her, in regard to the Greek cause, the time has been when she professed to be contending for that cause, as identified with Christianity. The white banner under which the soldiers of Peter the First usually fought, bore, as its inscription, "In the name of the Prince, and for our country." Relying on the aid of the Greeks, in his war with the Porte, he changed the white flag to red, and displayed on it the words, "In the name of God, and for Christianity." The unfortunate issue of this war is well known. Though Anne and Elizabeth, the successor of Peter, did not possess his active character, they kept up a constant communication with Greece, and held out hopes of restoring the Greek empire. Catharine the Second, as is well known, excited a general revolt in 1769. A Russian fleet appeared in the Mediterranean, and a Russian army was landed in the Morea. The Greeks in the end were disgusted at being expected to take an oath of allegiance to Russia, and the Empress was disgusted because they refused to take it. In 1774, peace was signed between Russia and the Porte, and the Greeks of the Morea were left to their fate. By this treaty the Porte acknowledged the independence of the khan of the Crimea; a preliminary step to the acquisition of that country by Russia. It is not unworthy of remark, as a circumstance which distinguished this from most other diplomatic transactions, that it conceded to the cabinet of St. Petersburg the right of intervention in the interior affairs of Turkey, in regard to whatever concerned the

religion of the Greeks. The cruelties and massacres that happened to the Greeks after the peace between Russia and the Porte, notwithstanding the general pardon which had been stipulated for them, need not now be recited. Instead of retracing the deplorable picture, it is enough to say, that in this respect the past is justly reflected in the present. The Empress soon after invaded and conquered the Crimea, and on one of the gates of Kerson, its capital, caused to be inscribed, "The road to Byzantium." The present Emperor, on his accession to the throne, manifested an intention to adopt the policy of Catharine the Second as his own, and the world has not been right in all its suspicions, if a project for the partition of Turkey did not form a part of the negotiations of Napoleon and Alexander at Tilsit.

All this course of policy seems suddenly to be changed. Turkey is no longer regarded, it would appear, as an object of partition or acquisition, and Greek revolts have all at once become, according to the declaration of Laybach, "criminal combinations." The recent congress at Verona exceeded its predecessor at Laybach in its denunciations of the Greek struggle. In the circular of the 14th of December, 1822, it declared the Grecian resistance to the Turkish power to be rash and culpable, and lamented that "the firebrand of rebellion had been thrown into the Ottoman empire." This rebuke and crimination we know to have proceeded on those settled principles of conduct which the Continental powers had prescribed for themselves. The sovereigns saw, as well as others, the real condition of the Greeks; they knew as well as others that it was most natural and most justifiable, that they should endeavor, at whatever hazard, to change that condition. They knew that they themselves, or at least one of them, had more than once urged the Greeks to similar efforts; that they themselves had thrown the same firebrand into the midst of the Ottoman empire. And yet, so much does it seem to be their fixed object to discountenance whatsoever threatens to disturb the actual government of any country, that, Christians as they were, and allied, as they professed to be, for purposes most important to human happiness and religion, they have not hesitated to declare to the world that they have wholly forborne to exercise any compassion to the Greeks, simply because they thought that they saw, in the struggles of the Morea, the sign of revolution. This, then, is coming to a plain, practical result. The Grecian revolution has been discouraged, discountenanced, and denounced, solely because it *is* a revolution. Independent of all inquiry into the reasonableness of its causes or the enormity of the oppression which produced it; regardless of the peculiar claims which Greece possesses upon the civilized world; and regardless of what has been their own conduct towards her for a century; regardless of the interest of the Christian religion,—the sovereigns at Verona seized upon the case of the

Greek revolution as one above all others calculated to illustrate the fixed principles of their policy. The abominable rule of the Porte on one side, the value and the sufferings of the Christian Greeks on the other, furnished a case likely to convince even an incredulous world of the sincerity of the professions of the Allied Powers. They embraced the occasion with apparent ardor; and the world, I trust, is satisfied.

We see here, Mr. Chairman, the direct and actual application of that system which I have attempted to describe. We see it in the very case of Greece. We learn, authentically and indisputably, that the Allied Powers, holding that all changes in legislation and administration ought to proceed from kings alone, were wholly inexorable to the sufferings of the Greeks, and entirely hostile to their success. Now it is upon this practical result of the principle of the Continental powers that I wish this House to intimate its opinion. The great question is a question of principle. Greece is only the signal instance of the application of that principle. If the principle be right, if we esteem it conformable to the law of nations, if we have nothing to say against it, or if we deem ourselves unfit to express an opinion on the subject, then, of course, no resolution ought to pass. If, on the other hand, we see in the declarations of the Allied Powers principles not only utterly hostile to our own free institutions, but hostile also to the independence of all nations, and altogether opposed to the improvement of the condition of human nature; if, in the instance before us, we see a most striking exposition and application of those principles, and if we deem our opinions to be entitled to any weight in the estimation of mankind,—then I think it is our duty to adopt some such measure as the proposed resolution.

It is worthy of observation, Sir, that as early as July, 1821, Baron Strogonoff [Grigorii Aleksandrovich Stroganov, 1770–1857], the Russian minister at Constantinople, represented to the Porte, that if the undistinguished massacres of the Greeks, both of such as were in open resistance and of those who remained patient in their submission were continued, and should become a settled habit, they would give just cause of war against the Porte to all Christian states. This was in 1821. It was followed, early in the next year, by that indescribable enormity, that appalling monument of barbarian cruelty, the destruction of Scio; a scene I shall not attempt to describe; a scene from which human nature shrinks shuddering away; a scene having hardly a parallel in the history of fallen man. This scene, too, was quickly followed by the massacres in Cyprus; and all these things were perfectly known to the Christian powers assembled at Verona. Yet these powers, instead of acting upon the case supposed by Baron Strogonoff and which one would think had been then fully made out,—instead of being moved by any compassion for the sufferings of the Greeks,—these powers, these Christian powers, rebuke

their gallantry and insult their sufferings by accusing them of "throwing a firebrand into the Ottoman empire." Such, Sir, appear to me to be the principles on which the Continental powers of Europe have agreed hereafter to act; and this, an eminent instance of the application of those principles.

I shall not detain the committee, Mr. Chairman, by any attempt to recite the events of the Greek struggle up to the present time. Its origin may be found, doubtless, in that improved state of knowledge which, for some years, has been gradually taking place in that country. The emancipation of the Greeks has been a subject frequently discussed in modern times. They themselves are represented as having a vivid remembrance of the distinction of their ancestors, not unmixed with an indignant feeling that civilized and Christian Europe should not ere now have aided them in breaking their intolerable fetters.

In 1816 a society was founded in Vienna for the encouragement of Grecian literature. It was connected with a similar institution at Athens, and another in Thessaly, called the "Gymnasium of Mount Pelion." The treasury and general office of the institution were established at Munich. No political object was avowed by these institutions, probably none contemplated. Still, however, they had their effect, no doubt, in hastening that condition of things in which the Greeks felt competent to the establishment of their independence. Many young men have been for years annually sent to the universities in the western states of Europe for their education; and, after the general pacification of Europe, many military men, discharged from other employment, were ready to enter even into so unpromising a service as that of the revolutionary Greeks.

In 1820, war commenced between the Porte and Ali, the well-known Pacha of Albania. Differences existed also with Persia and with Russia. In this state of things, at the beginning of 1821, an insurrection broke out in Moldavia, under the direction of Alexander Ypsilanti, a well-educated soldier, who had been major-general in the Russian service. From his character, and the number of those who seemed inclined to join him, he was supposed to be countenanced by the court of St. Petersburg. This, however, was a great mistake, which the Emperor, then at Laybach, took an early opportunity to rectify. The Turkish government was alarmed at these occurrences in the northern provinces of European Turkey, and caused search to be made of all vessels entering the Black Sea, lest arms or other military means should be sent in that manner to the insurgents. This proved inconvenient to the commerce of Russia, and caused some unsatisfactory correspondence between the two powers. It may be worthy of remark, as an exhibition of national character, that, agitated by these appearances of intestine commotion, the Sultan issued a proclamation, calling on all true Mussulmans to renounce the

pleasures of social life, to prepare arms and horses, and to return to the manner of their ancestors, the life of the plains. The Turk seems to have thought that he had, at last, caught something of the dangerous contagion of European civilization, and that it was necessary to reform his habits, by recurring to the original manners of military roving barbarians.

It was about this time, that is to say, at the commencement of 1821, that the revolution burst out in various parts of Greece and the isles. Circumstances, certainly, were not unfavorable to the movement, as one portion of the Turkish army was employed in the war against Ali Pacha in Albania, and another part in the provinces north of the Danube. The Greeks soon possessed themselves of the open country of the Morea and drove their enemy into the fortresses. Of these, that of Tripolitza, with the city, fell into their hands, in the course of the summer. Having after these first movements obtained time to breathe, it became, of course, an early object to establish a government. For this purpose delegates of the people assembled, under that name which describes the assembly in which we ourselves sit, that name which "freed the Atlantic," a *Congress*. A writer, who undertakes to render to the civilized world that service which was once performed by Edmund Burke, I mean the compiler of the English Annual Register, asks, by what authority this assembly could call itself a Congress. Simply, Sir, by the same authority by which the people of the United States has given the same name to their own legislature. We, at least, should be naturally inclined to think, not only as far as names, but things also, are concerned, that the Greeks could hardly have begun their revolution under better auspices; since they have endeavored to render applicable to themselves the general principles of our form of government, as well as its name. This constitution went into operation at the commencement of the next year. In the mean time, the war with Ali Pacha was ended, he having surrendered, and being afterwards assassinated, by an instance of treachery and perfidy, which, if it had happened elsewhere than under the government of the Turks, would have deserved notice. The negotiation with Russia, too, took a turn unfavorable to the Greeks. The great point upon which Russia insisted, beside the abandonment of the measure of searching vessels bound to the Black Sea, was, that the Porte should withdraw its armies from the neighborhood of the Russian frontiers; and the immediate consequence of this, when effected, was to add so much more to the disposable force ready to be employed against the Greeks. These events seemed to have left the whole force of the Ottoman empire, at the commencement of 1822, in a condition to be employed against the Greek rebellion; and, accordingly, very many anticipated the immediate destruction of the cause. The event, however, was ordered otherwise. Where the great-

est effort was made, it was met and defeated. Entering the Morea with an army which seemed capable of bearing down all resistance, the Turks were nevertheless defeated and driven back, and pursued beyond the isthmus, within which, as far as it appears, from that time to the present, they have not been able to set their foot.

It was in April of this year that the destruction of Scio took place. That island, a sort of appanage of the Sultana mother, enjoyed many privileges peculiar to itself. In a population of 130,000 or 140,000, it had no more than 2,000 or 3,000 Turks; indeed, by some accounts, not near as many. The absence of these ruffian masters had in some degree allowed opportunity for the promotion of knowledge, the accumulation of wealth, and the general cultivation of society. Here was the seat of modern Greek literature; here were libraries, printing-presses, and other establishments, which indicate some advancement in refinement and knowledge. Certain of the inhabitants of Samos, it would seem, envious of this comparative happiness of Scio, landed upon the island in an irregular multitude, for the purpose of compelling its inhabitants to make common cause with their countrymen against their oppressors. These, being joined by the peasantry, marched to the city and drove the Turks into the castle. The Turkish fleet, lately reinforced from Egypt, happened to be in the neighboring seas, and, learning these events, landed a force on the island of fifteen thousand men. There was nothing to resist such an army. These troops immediately entered the city and began an indiscriminate massacre. The city was fired; and in four days the fire and sword of the Turk rendered the beautiful Scio a clotted mass of blood and ashes. The details are too shocking to be recited. Forty thousand women and children, unhappily saved from the general destruction, were afterwards sold in the market of Smyrna, and sent off into distant and hopeless servitude. Even on the wharves of our own cities, it has been said, have been sold the utensils of those hearths which now exist no longer. Of the whole population which I have mentioned, not above nine hundred persons were left living upon the island. I will only repeat, Sir, that these tragical scenes were as fully known at the Congress of Verona, as they are now known to us; and it is not too much to call on the powers that constituted that congress, in the name of conscience and in the name of humanity, to tell us if there be nothing even in these unparalleled excesses of Turkish barbarity to excite a sentiment of compassion; nothing which they regard as so objectionable as even the very idea of popular resistance to power.

The events of the year which has just passed by, as far as they have become known to us, have been even more favorable to the Greeks than those of the year preceding. I omit all details, as being as well known to others as to myself. Suffice it to say, that with no other enemy to con-

tend with, and no diversion of his force to other objects, the Porte has not been able to carry the war into the Morea; and that, by the last accounts, its armies were acting defensively in Thessaly. I pass over, also, the naval engagements of the Greeks, although that is a mode of warfare in which they are calculated to excel, and in which they have already performed actions of such distinguished skill and bravery, as would draw applause upon the best mariners in the world. The present state of the war would seem to be, that the Greeks possess the whole of the Morea, with the exception of the three fortresses of Patras, Coron, and Modon; all Candia, but one fortress; and most of the other islands. They possess the citadel of Athens, Missolonghi, and several other places in Livadia. They have been able to act on the offensive, and to carry the war beyond the isthmus. There is no reason to believe their marine is weakened; more probably, it is strengthened. But, what is most important of all, they have obtained time and experience. They have awakened a sympathy throughout Europe and throughout America; and they have formed a government which seems suited to the emergency of their condition.

Sir, they have done much. It would be great injustice to compare their achievements with our own. We began our Revolution, already possessed of government, and, comparatively, of civil liberty. Our ancestors had from the first been accustomed in a great measure to govern themselves. They were familiar with popular elections and legislative assemblies, and well acquainted with the general principles and practice of free governments. They had little else to do than to throw off the paramount authority of the parent state. Enough was still left, both of law and of organization, to conduct society in its accustomed course, and to unite men together for a common object. The Greeks, of course, could act with little concert at the beginning; they were unaccustomed to the exercise of power, without experience, with limited knowledge, without aid, and surrounded by nations which, whatever claims the Greeks might seem to have upon them, have afforded them nothing but discouragement and reproach. They have held out, however, for three campaigns; and that, at least, is something. Constantinople and the northern provinces have sent forth thousands of troops;—they have been defeated. Tripoli, and Algiers, and Egypt, have contributed their marine contingents;—they have not kept the ocean. Hordes of Tartars have crossed the Bosphorus; —they have died where the Persians died. The powerful monarchies in the neighborhood have denounced their cause and admonished them to abandon it and submit to their fate. They have answered them, that, although two hundred thousand of their countrymen have offered up their lives, there yet remain lives to offer; and that it is the determination of *all*, "yes, of ALL," to persevere until they shall have established their

liberty, or until the power of their oppressors shall have relieved them from the burden of existence.

It may now be asked, perhaps, whether the expression of our own sympathy, and that of the country, may do them good? I hope it may. It may give them courage and spirit, it may assure them of public regard, teach them that they are not wholly forgotten by the civilized world, and inspire them with constancy in the pursuit of their great end. At any rate, Sir, it appears to me that the measure which I have proposed is due to our own character, and called for by our own duty. When we shall have discharged that duty, we may leave the rest to the disposition of Providence.

I do not see how it can be doubted that this measure is entirely *pacific*. I profess my inability to perceive that it has any possible tendency to involve our neutral relations. If the resolution pass, it is not of necessity to be immediately acted on. It will not be acted on at all, unless, in the opinion of the President, a proper and safe occasion for acting upon it shall arise. If we adopt the resolution to-day, our relations with every foreign state will be to-morrow precisely what they now are. The resolution will be sufficient to express our sentiments on the subjects to which I have adverted. Useful for that purpose, it can be mischievous for no purpose. If the topic were properly introduced into the message, it cannot be improperly introduced into discussion in this House. If it were proper, which no one doubts, for the President to express his opinions upon it, it cannot, I think, be improper for us to express ours. The only certain effect of this resolution is to signify, in a form usual in bodies constituted like this, our approbation of the general sentiment of the message. Do we wish to withhold that approbation? The resolution confers on the President no new power, nor does it enjoin on him the exercise of any new duty; nor does it hasten him in the discharge of any existing duty.

I cannot imagine that this resolution can add any thing to those excitements which it has been supposed, I think very causelessly, might possibly provoke the Turkish government to acts of hostility. There is already the message, expressing the hope of success to the Greeks and disaster to the Turks, in a much stronger manner than is to be implied from the terms of this resolution. There is the correspondence between the Secretary of State and the Greek Agent in London, already made public, in which similar wishes are expressed, and a continuance of the correspondence apparently invited. I might add to this, the unexampled burst of feeling which this cause has called forth from all classes of society, and the notorious fact of pecuniary contributions made throughout the country for its aid and advancement. After all this, whoever can see cause of danger to our pacific relations from the adoption of this resolution has a keener vision than I can pretend to. Sir, there is no aug-

mented danger; there is no danger. The question comes at last to this, whether, on a subject of this sort, this House holds an opinion which is worthy to be expressed.

Even suppose, Sir, an agent or commissioner were to be immediately sent,—a measure which I myself believe to be the proper one,—there is no breach of neutrality, nor any just cause of offence. Such an agent, of course, would not be accredited; he would not be a public minister. The object would be inquiry and information; inquiry which we have a right to make, information which we are interested to possess. If a dismemberment of the Turkish empire be taking place, or has already taken place; if a new state be rising, or be already risen, in the Mediterranean, —who can doubt, that, without any breach of neutrality, we may inform ourselves of these events for the government of our own concerns? The Greeks have declared the Turkish coasts in a state of blockade; may we not inform ourselves whether this blockade be *nominal* or *real*? and, of course, whether it shall be regarded or disregarded? The greater our trade may happen to be with Smyrna, a consideration which seems to have alarmed some gentlemen, the greater is the reason, in my opinion, why we should seek to be accurately informed of those events which may affect its safety. It seems to me impossible, therefore, for any reasonable man to imagine that this resolution can expose us to the resentment of the Sublime Porte.

As little reason is there for fearing its consequences upon the conduct of the Allied Powers. They may, very naturally, dislike our sentiments upon the subject of the Greek revolution; but what those sentiments are they will much more explicitly learn in the President's message than in this resolution. They might, indeed, prefer that we should express no dissent from the doctrines which they have avowed, and the application which they have made of those doctrines to the case of Greece. But I trust we are not disposed to leave them in any doubt as to our sentiments upon these important subjects. They have expressed their opinions, and do not call that expression of opinion an interference; in which respect they are right, as the expression of opinion in such cases is not such an interference as would justify the Greeks in considering the powers at war with them. For the same reason, any expression which we may make of different principles and different sympathies is no interference. No one would call the President's message an interference; and yet it is much stronger in that respect than this resolution. If either of them could be construed to be an interference, no doubt it would be improper, at least it would be so according to my view of the subject; for the very thing which I have attempted to resist in the course of these observations is the right of foreign interference. But neither the message nor the resolution has that character. There is not a power in Europe which can

suppose, that, in expressing our opinions on this occasion, we are governed by any desire of aggrandizing ourselves or of injuring others. We do no more than to maintain those established principles in which we have an interest in common with other nations, and to resist the introduction of new principles and new rules, calculated to destroy the relative independence of states, and particularly hostile to the whole fabric of our government.

I close, then, Sir, with repeating, that the object of this resolution is to avail ourselves of the interesting occasion of the Greek revolution to make our protest against the doctrines of the Allied Powers, both as they are laid down in principle and as they are applied in practice. I think it right, too, Sir, not to be unseasonable in the expression of our regard, and, as far as that goes, in a manifestation of our sympathy with a long oppressed and now struggling people. I am not of those who would, in the hour of utmost peril, withhold such encouragement as might be properly and lawfully given, and, when the crisis should be past, overwhelm the rescued sufferer with kindness and caresses. The Greeks address the civilized world with a pathos not easy to be resisted. They invoke our favor by more moving considerations than can well belong to the condition of any other people. They stretch out their arms to the Christian communities of the earth, beseeching them, by a generous recollection of their ancestors, by the consideration of their desolated and ruined cities and villages, by their wives and children sold into an accursed slavery, by their blood, which they seem willing to pour out like water, by the common faith, and in the name, which unites all Christians, that they would extend to them at least some token of compassionate regard.

The Tariff, April 1–2, 1824

Ever since Alexander Hamilton's *Report on Manufactures* of 1791 there had been in the United States a modest but growing demand for the encouragement of industry. The simplest way of accomplishing this was by imposing duties on imports, not for revenue alone but to equalize the cost of foreign and domestic production. The War of 1812 greatly accelerated the shift of capital from commerce to manufacturing, and convinced most of the doubters that industrial self-sufficiency was prerequisite to political independence. In 1816, with the wartime double duties about to expire, the first frankly protective tariff was imposed.

Webster objected. Except for certain specific items such as hemp, iron, and sailcloth needed by his merchant constituency, he saw only loss to the shipping interest from possible curtailment of imports. He opposed also the tariff increase of 1820, justified by its proponents as a means of overcoming the current depression. His constituents, now of Boston rather than Portsmouth, remained dominantly merchants rather than manufacturers.

The situation was unchanged in 1824, but the debate in the House was more wide-ranging, dealing with broad principles rather than specific items alone. This time Webster made a major speech, reprinted below. He was answering Henry Clay who had turned the debate from the merits of individual duties to a sweeping endorsement of the principle of protection, cornerstone of his "American System." (See James F. Hopkins and others, eds., *Papers of Henry Clay* (8 vols. to date, Lexington, 1954–1985), 3: 683–730). Webster's reply was a penetrating defense of free trade. Clay drew heavily on Mathew Carey, whose *Essays on Political Economy* had recently been published in Philadelphia; Webster relied largely on British sources, particularly William Huskisson, then president of the Board of Trade. The speech is by far the best reasoned and most persuasive of many tariff utterances Webster would make over the next two decades on the other side of the question.

Webster's change of position, from free trade to the protection of domestic industry, came three years later. Under attack by the New York *Evening Post* for his vote in support of a tariff increase on imported woolens early in 1827, Webster justified his switch in a letter to the *Post's* editor, William Coleman. The tariff of 1824, he argued, had so far

increased New England's stake in manufacturing that the interest of his constituents now required continuation and even extension of the protective system. His Boston supporters, who had made fortunes trading in the world's goods, had invested a substantial share of their profits in manufacturing enterprises. (DW to Coleman, Feb. 23, 1827, *Correspondence*, 2: 160–163.)

By 1828, when the "tariff of abominations" was enacted with Webster's active help, he had been elected to the Senate, where he represented not commercial Boston alone but all of Massachusetts with her growing industrial empire, typified by Lowell, Waltham, and Lawrence. Thereafter Webster rather than Clay was the very high priest of protection. He supported the tariff of 1832, opposed South Carolina's nullification of that and the preceding measure, opposed Clay's tariff compromise of 1833. As Tyler's secretary of state he was instrumental in getting the president to sign the Fillmore tariff of 1842, and he led the opposition to the McKay-Walker tariff reduction of 1846—the last tariff bill to be presented in his lifetime. His method was to circularize leading men of his home state for their views in general and in particular detail, on whatever bill might be pending. His arguments then closely followed the consensus thus obtained.

Only in his tariff speech of 1824 did he allow himself the luxury of argument uncoerced by pressure from his constituents and unmolded by local interests. Perhaps for that reason the many arguments of later years never rang quite as true as those of 1824.

The text is from *Writings and Speeches*, 5: 94–149, but except for trivial variations in punctuation, capitalization, or spelling, an occasional synonym, or italicized passage, there are no other versions. The speech was first published in the National Intelligencer on May 1, 1824, a month after its delivery, which allowed ample time for any revising that Webster felt to be necessary. The *Intelligencer* furnished the text later published in *Annals of Congress*. The same text was issued by Gales and Seaton in pamphlet form, and similarly by Wells and Lilly, and Cummings, Hilliard, & Co. in Boston. One of these pamphlets was the text for the speech as reproduced in *Speeches and Forensic Arguments*, 1: 265–304, and from that volume found its way without change into *Works*, 3:94–149, and *Writings and Speeches*.

Mr. Chairman,—I will avail myself of the present occasion to make some remarks on certain principles and opinions which have been recently advanced, and on those considerations which, in my judgment, ought to govern us in deciding upon the several and respective parts of this very

important and complex measure. I can truly say that this is a painful duty. I deeply regret the necessity which is likely to be imposed upon me of giving a general affirmative or negative vote on the whole of the bill. I cannot but think this mode of proceeding liable to great objections. It exposes both those who support and those who oppose the measure to very unjust and injurious misapprehensions. There may be good reasons for favoring some of the provisions of the bill, and equally strong reasons for opposing others; and these provisions do not stand to each other in the relation of principal and incident. If that were the case, those who are in favor of the principal might forego their opinions upon incidental and subordinate provisions. But the bill proposes enactments entirely distinct and different from one another in character and tendency. Some of its clauses are intended merely for revenue; and of those which regard the protection of home manufactures, one part stands upon very different grounds from those of other parts. So that probably every gentleman who may ultimately support the bill will vote for much which his judgment does not approve; and those who oppose it will oppose something which they would very gladly support.

Being intrusted with the interests of a district highly commercial, and deeply interested in manufactures also, I wish to state my opinions on the present measure, not as on a whole, for it has no entire and homogeneous character, but as on a collection of different enactments, some of which meet my approbation and some of which do not.

And allow me, Sir, in the first place, to state my regret, if indeed I ought not to express a warmer sentiment at the names or designations which Mr. Speaker [Henry Clay] has seen fit to adopt for the purpose of describing the advocates and the opposers of the present bill. It is a question, he says, between the friends of an "American policy" and those of a "foreign policy." This, Sir, is an assumption which I take the liberty most directly to deny. Mr. Speaker certainly intended nothing invidious or derogatory to any part of the House by this mode of denominating friends and enemies. But there is power in names, and this manner of distinguishing those who favor and those who oppose particular measures may lead to inferences to which no member of the House can submit. It may imply that there is a more exclusive and peculiar regard to American interests in one class of opinions than in another. Such an implication is to be resisted and repelled. Every member has a right to the presumption, that he pursues what he believes to be the interest of his country with as sincere a zeal as any other member. I claim this in my own case; and while I shall not, for any purpose of description or convenient arrangement, use terms which may imply any disrespect to other men's opinions, much less any imputation upon other men's mo-

tives, it is my duty to take care that the use of such terms by others be not, against the will of those who adopt them, made to produce a false impression.

Indeed, Sir, it is a little astonishing, if it seemed convenient to Mr. Speaker, for the purposes of distinction, to make use of the terms "American policy" and "foreign policy," that he should not have applied them in a manner precisely the reverse of that in which he has in fact used them. If names are thought necessary, it would be well enough. one would think, that the name should be in some measure descriptive of the thing; and since Mr. Speaker denominates the policy which he recommends "a new policy in this country"; since he speaks of the present measure as a new era in our legislation; since he professes to invite us to depart from our accustomed course, to instruct ourselves by the wisdom of others, and to adopt the policy of the most distinguished foreign states,—one is a little curious to know with what propriety of speech this imitation of other nations is denominated an "American policy," while, on the contrary, a preference for our own established system, as it now actually exists and always has existed, is called a "foreign policy." This favorite American policy is what America has never tried; and this odious foreign policy is what, as we are told, foreign states have never pursued. Sir, that is the truest American policy which shall most usefully employ American capital and American labor, and best sustain the whole population. With me it is a fundamental axiom, it is interwoven with all my opinions, that the great interests of the country are united and inseparable; that agriculture, commerce, and manufactures will prosper together or languish together; and that all legislation is dangerous which proposes to benefit one of these without looking to consequences which may fall on the others.

Passing from this, Sir, I am bound to say that Mr. Speaker began his able and impressive speech at the proper point of inquiry; I mean the present state and condition of the country, although I am so unfortunate, or rather although I am so happy, as to differ from him very widely in regard to that condition. I dissent entirely from the justice of that picture of distress which he has drawn. I have not seen the reality, and know not where it exists. Within my observation, there is no cause for so gloomy and terrifying a representation. In respect to the New England States, with the condition of which I am of course best acquainted. the present appears to me a period of very general prosperity. Not, indeed, a time for sudden acquisition and great profits, not a day of extraordinary activity and successful speculation. There is no doubt a considerable depression of prices, and, in some degree, a stagnation of business. But the case presented by Mr. Speaker was not one of *depression*, but of

distress; of universal, pervading, intense distress, limited to no class and to no place. We are represented as on the very verge and brink of national ruin. So far from acquiescing in these opinions, I believe there has been no period in which the general prosperity was better secured, or rested on a more solid foundation. As applicable to the Eastern States, I put this remark to their representatives, and ask them if it is not true. When has there been a time in which the means of living have been more accessible and more abundant? When has labor been rewarded, I do not say with a larger, but with a more certain success? Profits, indeed, are low; in some pursuits of life, which it is not proposed to benefit, but to *burden,* by this bill, very low. But still I am unacquainted with any proofs of extraordinary distress. What, indeed, are the general indications of the state of the country? There is no famine nor pestilence in the land, nor war, nor desolation. There is no writhing under the burden of taxation. The means of subsistence are abundant; and at the very moment when the miserable condition of the country is asserted, it is admitted that the wages of labor are high in comparison with those of any other country. A country, then, enjoying a profound peace, perfect civil liberty, with the means of subsistence cheap and abundant, with the reward of labor sure, and its wages higher than anywhere else, cannot be represented as in gloom, melancholy, and distress, but by the effort of extraordinary powers of tragedy.

Even if, in judging of this question, we were to regard only those proofs to which we have been referred, we shall probably come to a conclusion somewhat different from that which has been drawn. Our exports, for example, although certainly less than in some years, were not, last year, so much below an average formed upon the exports of a series of years, and putting those exports at a fixed value, as might be supposed. The value of the exports of agricultural products, of animals, of the products of the forest and of the sea, together with gunpowder, spirits, and sundry unenumerated articles, amounted in the several years to the following sums, viz.: —

In 1790,	$27,716,152
1804,	33,842,316
1807,	38,465,854

Coming up now to our own times, and taking the exports of the years 1821, 1822, and 1823, of the same articles and products, at the same prices, they stand thus: —

In 1821,	$45,643,175
1822,	48,782,295
1823,	55,863,491

Mr. Speaker has taken the very extraordinary year of 1803, and, adding to the exportation of that year what he thinks ought to have been a just augmentation, in proportion to the increase of our population, he swells the result to a magnitude, which, when compared with our actual exports, would exhibit a great deficiency. But is there any justice in this mode of calculation? In the first place, as before observed, the year 1803 was a year of extraordinary exportation. By reference to the accounts, that of the article of flour, for example, there was an export that year of thirteen hundred thousand barrels; but the very next year it fell to eight hundred thousand, and the next year to seven hundred thousand. In the next place, there never was any reason to expect that the increase of our exports of agricultural products would keep pace with the increase of our population. That would be against all experience. It is, indeed, most desirable, that there should be an augmented demand for the products of agriculture; but, nevertheless, the official returns of our exports do not show that absolute want of all foreign market which has been so strongly stated.

But there are other means by which to judge of the general condition of the people. The quantity of the means of subsistence consumed, or, to make use of a phraseology better suited to the condition of our own people, the quantity of the comforts of life enjoyed, is one of those means. It so happens, indeed, that it is not so easy in this country as elsewhere to ascertain facts of this sort with accuracy. Where most of the articles of subsistence and most of the comforts of life are taxed, there is, of course, great facility in ascertaining, from official statements, the amount of consumption. But in this country, most fortunately, the government neither knows, nor is concerned to know, the annual consumption; and estimates can only be formed in another mode, and in reference only to a few articles. Of these articles, tea is one. It is not quite a luxury, and yet is something above the absolute necessaries of life. Its consumption, therefore, will be diminished in times of adversity, and augmented in times of prosperity. By deducting the annual export from the annual import, and taking a number of years together, we may arrive at a probable estimate of consumption. The average of eleven years, from 1790 to 1800, inclusive, will be found to be two millions and a half of pounds. From 1801 to 1812, inclusive, the average was three millions seven hundred thousand; and the average of the last three years, to wit, 1821, 1822, and 1823, was five millions and a half. Having made a just allowance for the increase of our numbers, we shall still find, I think, from these statements, that there is no distress which has limited our means of subsistence and enjoyment.

In forming an opinion of the degree of general prosperity, we may regard, likewise, the progress of internal improvements, the investment

of capital in roads, bridges, and canals. All these prove a balance of income over expenditure; they afford evidence that there is a surplus of profits, which the present generation is usefully vesting for the benefiit of the next. It cannot be denied, that, in this particular, the progress of the country is steady and rapid.

We may look, too, to the sums expended for education. Are our colleges deserted? Do fathers find themselves less able than usual to educate their children? It will be found, I imagine, that the amount paid for the purpose of education is constantly increasing, and that the schools and colleges were never more full than at the present moment. I may add, that the endowment of public charities, the contributions to objects of general benevolence, whether foreign or domestic, the munificence of individuals towards whatever promises to benefit the community, are all so many proofs of national prosperity. And, finally, there is no defalcation of revenue, no pressure of taxation.

The general result, therefore, of a fair examination of the present condition of things, seems to me to be, that there is a considerable depression of prices, and curtailment of profit; and in some parts of the country, it must be admitted, there is a great degree of pecuniary embarrassment, arising from the difficulty of paying debts which were contracted when prices were high. With these qualifications, the general state of the country may be said to be prosperous; and these are not sufficient to give to the whole face of affairs any appearance of general distress.

Supposing the evil, then, to be a depression of prices, and a partial pecuniary pressure, the next inquiry is into the causes of that evil; and it appears to me that there are several; and in this respect, I think, too much has been imputed by Mr. Speaker to the single cause of the diminution of exports. Connected, as we are, with all the commercial nations of the world, and having observed great changes to take place elsewhere, we should consider whether the causes of those changes have not reached us, and whether we are not suffering by the operation of them, in common with others. Undoubtedly, there has been a great fall in the price of all commodities throughout the commercial world, in consequence of the restoration of a state of peace. When the Allies entered France in 1814, prices rose astonishingly fast, and very high. Colonial produce, for instance, in the ports of this country, as well as elsewhere, sprung up suddenly from the lowest to the highest extreme. A new and vast demand was created for the commodities of trade. These were the natural consequences of the great political changes which then took place in Europe.

We are to consider, too, that our own war created new demand, and that a government expenditure of twenty-five or thirty million dollars a

year had the usual effect of enhancing prices. We are obliged to add, that the paper issues of our banks carried the same effect still further. A depreciated currency existed in a great part of the country; depreciated to such an extent, that, at one time, exchange between the centre and the North was as high as twenty per cent. The Bank of the United States was instituted to correct this evil; but, for causes which it is not necessary now to enumerate, it did not for some years bring back the currency of the country to a sound state. This depreciation of the circulating currency was so much, of course, added to the nominal prices of commodities, and these prices, thus unnaturally high, seemed, to those who looked only at the appearance, to indicate great prosperity. But such prosperity is more specious than real. It would have been better, probably, as the shock would have been less, if prices had fallen sooner. At length, however, they fell; and as there is little doubt that certain events in Europe had an influence in determining the time at which this fall took place, I will advert shortly to some of the principal of those events.

In May, 1819, the British House of Commons decided, by a unanimous vote, that the resumption of cash payments by the Bank of England should not be deferred beyond the ensuing February. The restriction had been continued from time to time, and from year to year, Parliament always professing to look to the restoration of a specie currency whenever it should be found practicable. Having been, in July, 1818, continued to July, 1819, it was understood that, in the interim, the important question of the time at which cash payments should be resumed should be finally settled. In the latter part of the year 1818, the circulation of the bank had been greatly reduced, and a severe scarcity of money was felt in the London market. Such was the state of things in England. On the Continent, other important events took place. The French Indemnity Loan had been negotiated in the summer of 1818, and the proportion of it belonging to Austria, Russia, and Prussia had been sold. This created an unusual demand for gold and silver in those countries. It has been stated, that the amount of the precious metals transmitted to Austria and Russia in that year was at least twenty millions sterling. Other large sums were sent to Prussia and to Denmark. The effect of this sudden drain of specie, felt first at Paris, was communicated to Amsterdam and Hamburg, and all other commercial places in the North of Europe.

The paper system of England had certainly communicated an artificial value to property. It had encouraged speculation, and excited overtrading. When the shock therefore came, and this violent pressure for money acted at the same moment on the Continent and in England, inflated and unnatural prices could be kept up no longer. A reduction took place, which has been estimated to have been at least equal to a fall of thirty, if not forty per cent. The depression was universal; and the change

was felt in the United States severely, though not equally so in every part. There are those, I am aware, who maintain that the events to which I have alluded did not cause the great fall of prices, but that that fall was natural and inevitable, from the previously existing state of things, the abundance of commodities, and the want of demand. But that would only prove that the effect was produced in another way, rather than by another cause. If these great and sudden calls for money did not reduce prices, but prices fell, as of themselves, to their natural state, still the result is the same; for we perceive that, after these new calls for money, prices could not be kept longer at their unnatural height.

About the time of these foreign events, our own bank system under-went a change; and all these causes, in my view of the subject, con-curred to produce the great shock which took place in our commercial cities, and in many parts of the country. The year 1819 was a year of numerous failures, and very considerable distress, and would have fur-nished far better grounds than exist at present for that gloomy repre-sentation of our condition which has been presented. Mr. Speaker has alluded to the strong inclination which exists, or has existed, in various parts of the country, to issue paper money, as a proof of great existing difficulties. I regard it rather as a very productive cause of those difficulties; and the committee will not fail to observe, that there is, at this moment, much the loudest complaint of distress precisely where there has been the greatest attempt to relieve it by systems of paper credit. And, on the other hand, content, prosperity, and happiness are most observable in those parts of the country where there has been the least endeavor to administer relief by law. In truth, nothing is so baneful, so utterly ruinous to all true industry, as interfering with the legal value of money, or attempting to raise artificial standards to supply its place. Such remedies suit well the spirit of extravagant speculation, but they sap the very foundation of all honest acquisition. By weakening the se-curity of property, they take away all motive for exertion. Their effect is to transfer property. Whenever a debt is allowed to be paid by any thing less valuable than the legal currency in respect to which it was con-tracted, the difference between the value of the paper given in payment and the legal currency is precisely so much property taken from one man and given to another, by legislative enactment.

When we talk, therefore, of protecting industry, let us remember that the first measure for that end is to secure it in its earnings; to assure it that it shall receive its own. Before we invent new modes of raising prices, let us take care that existing prices are not rendered wholly un-available, by making them capable of being paid in depreciated paper. I regard, Sir, this issue of irredeemable paper as the most prominent and deplorable cause of whatever pressure still exists in the country; and,

further, I would put the question to the members of this committee, whether it is not from that part of the people who have tried this paper system, and tried it to their cost, that this bill receives the most earnest support? And I cannot forbear to ask, further, whether this support does not proceed rather from a general feeling of uneasiness under the present condition of things, than from the clear perception of any benefit which the measure itself can confer? Is not all expectation of advantage centred in a sort of vague hope, that change may produce relief? Debt certainly presses hardest where prices have been longest kept up by artificial means. They find the shock lightest who take it soonest; and I fully believe that, if those parts of the country which now suffer most, had not augmented the force of the blow by deferring it, they would have now been in a much better condition than they are. We may assure ourselves, once for all, Sir, that there can be no such thing as payment of debts by legislation. We may abolish debts indeed; we may transfer property by visionary and violent laws. But we deceive both ourselves and our constituents, if we flatter either ourselves or them with the hope that there is any relief against whatever pressure exists, but in economy and industry. The depression of prices and the stagnation of business have been in truth the necessary result of circumstances. No government could prevent them, and no government can altogether relieve the people from their effect. We have enjoyed a day of extraordinary prosperity; we had been neutral while the world was at war, and had found a great demand for our products, our navigation, and our labor. We had no right to expect that that state of things would continue always. With the return of peace, foreign nations would struggle for themselves, and enter into competition with us in the great objects of pursuit.

Now, Sir, what is the remedy for existing evils? What is the course of policy suited to our actual condition? Certainly it is not our wisdom to adopt any system that may be offered to us, without examination, and in the blind hope that whatever changes our condition may improve it. It is better that we should

> "bear those ills we have,
> Than fly to others that we know not of."

We are bound to see that there is a fitness and an aptitude in whatever measures may be recommended to relieve the evils that afflict us; and before we adopt a system that professes to make great alterations, it is our duty to look carefully to each leading interest of the community, and see how it may probably be affected by our proposed legislation.

And, in the first place, what is the condition of our commerce? Here we must clearly perceive, that it is not enjoying that rich harvest which fell to its fortune during the continuance of the European wars. It has

been greatly depressed, and limited to small profits. Still, it is elastic and active, and seems capable of recovering itself in some measure from its depression. The shipping interest, also, has suffered severely, still more severely, probably, than commerce. If any thing should strike us with astonishment, it is that the navigation of the United States should be able to sustain itself. Without any government protection whatever, it goes abroad to challenge competition with the whole world; and, in spite of all obstacles, it has yet been able to maintain eight hundred thousand tons in the employment of foreign trade. How, Sir, do the ship-owners and navigators accomplish this? How is it that they are able to meet, and in some measure overcome, universal competition? It is not, Sir, by protection and bounties; but by unwearied exertion, by extreme economy, by unshaken perseverance, by that manly and resolute spirit which relies on itself to protect itself. These causes alone enable American ships still to keep their element, and show the flag of their country in distant seas. The rates of insurance may teach us how thoroughly our ships are built, and how skilfully and safely they are navigated. Risks are taken, as I learn, from the United States to Liverpool, at one per cent; and from the United States to Canton and back, as low as three per cent. But when we look to the low rate of freight, and when we consider, also, that the articles entering into the composition of a ship, with the exception of wood, are dearer here than in other countries, we cannot but be utterly surprised that the shipping interest has been able to sustain itself at all. I need not say that the navigation of the country is essential to its honor and its defence. Yet, instead of proposing benefits for it in this hour of its depression, we threaten by this measure to lay upon it new and heavy burdens. In the discussion, the other day, of that provision of the bill which proposes to tax tallow for the benefit of the oil-merchants and whalemen, we had the pleasure of hearing eloquent eulogiums upon that portion of our shipping employed in the whale-fishery, and strong statements of its importance to the public interest. But the same bill proposes a severe tax upon that interest, for the benefit of the iron-manufacturer and the hemp-grower. So that the tallow-chandlers and soapboilers are sacrificed to the oil-merchants, in order that these again may contribute to the manufacturers of iron and the growers of hemp.

If such be the state of our commerce and navigation, what is the condition of our home manufactures? How are they amidst the general depression? Do they need further protection? and if any, how much? On all these points, we have had much general statement, but little precise information. In the very elaborate speech of Mr. Speaker, we are not supplied with satisfactory grounds of judging with respect to these various particulars. Who can tell, from any thing yet before the committee, whether the proposed duty be too high or too low on any one article?

Gentlemen tell us, that they are in favor of domestic industry; so am I. They would give it protection; so would I. But then all domestic industry is not confined to manufactures. The employments of agriculture, commerce, and navigation are all branches of the same domestic industry; they all furnish employment for American capital and American labor. And when the question is, whether new duties shall be laid, for the purpose of giving further encouragement to particular manufactures, every reasonable man must ask himself, both whether the proposed new encouragement be necessary, and whether it can be given without injustice to other branches of industry.

It is desirable to know, also, somewhat more distinctly, how the proposed means will produce the intended effect. One great object proposed, for example, is the increase of the home market for the consumption of agricultural products. This certainly is much to be desired; but what provisions of the bill are expected wholly or principally to produce this, is not stated. I would not deny that some increase of the home market may follow, from the adoption of this bill, but all its provisions have not an equal tendency to produce this effect. Those manufactures which employ most labor, create, of course, most demand for articles of consumption; and those create least in the production of which capital and skill enter as the chief ingredients of cost. I cannot, Sir, take this bill merely because a committee has recommended it. I cannot espouse a side, and fight under a flag. I wholly repel the idea that we must take this law, or pass no law on the subject. What should hinder us from exercising our own judgments upon these provisions, singly and severally? Who has the power to place us, or why should we place ourselves, in a condition where we cannot give to every measure, that is distinct and separate in itself, a separate and distinct consideration? Sir, I presume no member of the committee will withhold his assent from what he thinks right, until others will yield their assent to what they think wrong. There are many things in this bill acceptable, probably, to the general sense of the House. Why should not these provisions be passed into a law, and others left to be decided upon their own merits, as a majority of the House shall see fit? To some of these provisions, I am myself decidedly favorable; to others I have great objections; and I should have been very glad of an opportunity of giving my own vote distinctly on propositions which are, in their own nature, essentially and substantially distinct from one another.

But, Sir, before expressing my own opinion upon the several provisions of this bill, I will advert for a moment to some other general topics. We have heard much of the policy of England, and her example has been repeatedly urged upon us, as proving, not only the expediency of encouragement and protection, but of exclusion and direct prohibition

also. I took occasion the other day to remark, that more liberal notions were becoming prevalent on this subject; that the policy of restraints and prohibitions was getting out of repute, as the true nature of commerce became better understood; and that, among public men, those most distinguished were most decided in their reprobation of the broad principle of exclusion and prohibition. Upon the truth of this representation, as matter of fact, I supposed there could not be two opinions among those who had observed the progress of political sentiment in other countries, and were acquainted with its present state. In this respect, however, it would seem that I was greatly mistaken. We have heard it again and again declared, that the English government still adheres, with immovable firmness, to its old doctrines of prohibition; that although journalists, theorists, and scientific writers advance other doctrines, yet the practical men, the legislators, the government of the country, are too wise to follow them. It has even been most sagaciously hinted, that the promulgation of liberal opinions on these subjects is intended only to delude other governments, to cajole them into the folly of liberal ideas, while England retains to herself all the benefits of the admirable old system of prohibition. We have heard from Mr. Speaker a warm commendation of the complex mechanism of this system. The British empire, it is said, is, in the first place, to be protected against the rest of the world; then the British Isles against the colonies; next, the isles respectively against each other, England herself, as the heart of the empire, being protected most of all, and against all.

Truly, Sir, it appeals to me that Mr. Speaker's imagination has seen system, and order, and beauty, in that which is much more justly considered as the result of ignorance, partiality, or violence. This part of English legislation has resulted, partly from considering Ireland as a conquered country, partly from the want of a complete union, even with Scotland, and partly from the narrow views of colonial regulation, which in early and uninformed periods influenced the European states.

Nothing, I imagine, would strike the public men of England more singularly, than to find gentlemen of real information and much weight in the councils of this country expressing sentiments like these, in regard to the existing state of these English laws. I have never said, indeed, that prohibitory laws do not exist in England; we all know they do; but the question is, Does she owe her prosperity and greatness to these laws? I venture to say, that such is not the opinion of public men now in England, and the continuance of the laws, even without any alteration, would not be evidence that their opinion is different from what I have represented it; because the laws having existed long, and great interests having been built up on the faith of them, they cannot now be repealed without great and overwhelming inconvenience. Because a thing has

been wrongly done, it does not therefore follow that it can now be undone; and this is the reason, as I understand it, for which exclusion, prohibition, and monopoly are suffered to remain in any degree in the
English system; and for the same reason, it will be wise in us to take our
measures, on all subjects of this kind, with great caution. We may not
be able, but at the hazard of much injury to individuals, hereafter to re-
trace our steps. And yet, whatever is extravagant or unreasonable is not
likely to endure. There may come a moment of strong reaction; and if
no moderation be shown in laying on duties, there may be as little
scruple in taking them off.

It may be here observed, that there is a broad and marked distinction
between entire prohibition and reasonable encouragement. It is one
thing, by duties or taxes on foreign articles, to awaken a home competition in the production of the same articles; it is another thing to remove
all competition by a total exclusion of the foreign article; and it is quite
another thing still, by total prohibition, to raise up at home manufactures
not suited to the climate, the nature of the country, or the state of the
population. These are substantial distinctions, and although it may not
be easy in every case to determine which of them applies to a given
article, yet the distinctions themselves exist, and in most cases will be
sufficiently clear to indicate the true course of policy; and, unless I have
greatly mistaken the prevailing sentiment in the councils of England, it
grows every day more and more favorable to the diminution of restrictions, and to the wisdom of leaving much (I do not say every thing, for
that would not be true) to the enterprise and the discretion of individuals.
I should certainly not have taken up the time of the committee to state
at any length the opinions of other governments, or of the public men of
other countries, upon a subject like this; but an occasional remark made
by me the other day, having been so directly controverted, especially by
Mr. Speaker, in his observations yesterday, I must take occasion to refer
to some proofs of what I have stated.

What, then, is the state of English opinion? Every body knows that,
after the termination of the late European war, there came a time of
great pressure in England. Since her example has been quoted, let it be
asked in what mode her government sought relief. Did it aim to maintain
artificial and unnatural prices? Did it maintain a swollen and extravagant paper circulation? Did it carry further the laws of prohibition and
exclusion? Did it draw closer the cords of colonial restraint? No, Sir,
but precisely the reverse. Instead of relying on legislative contrivances
and artificial devices, it trusted to the enterprise and industry of the
people, which it sedulously sought to excite, not by imposing restraint,
but by removing it, wherever its removal was practicable. In May, 1820,
the attention of the government having been much turned to the state of

foreign trade, a distinguished member [Lord Lansdowne] of the House of Peers brought forward a Parliamentary motion[1] upon that subject, followed by an ample discussion and a full statement of his own opinions. In the course of his remarks, he observed, "that there ought to be no prohibitory duties, as such; for that it was evident, that, where a manufacture could not be carried on, or a production raised, but under the protection of a prohibitory duty, that manufacture, or that produce, could not be brought to market but at a loss. In his opinion, the name of strict prohibition might, therefore, in commerce, be got rid of altogether; but he did not see the same objection to protecting duties, which, while they admitted of the introduction of commodities from abroad similar to those which we ourselves manufactured, placed them so much on a level as to allow a competition between them." "No axiom," he added, "was more true than this: that it was by growing what the territory of a country could grow most cheaply, and by receiving from other countries what it could not produce except at too great an expense, that the greatest degree of happiness was to be communicated to the greatest extent of population."

In assenting to the motion, the first minister [Lord Liverpool] of the crown expressed his own opinion of the great advantage resulting from unrestricted freedom of trade. "Of the soundness of that general principle," he observed, "I can entertain no doubt. I can entertain no doubt of what would have been the great advantages to the civilized world, if the system of unrestricted trade had been acted upon by every nation from the earliest period of its commercial intercourse with its neighbors. If to those advantages there could have been any exceptions, I am persuaded that they would have been but few; and I am also persuaded that the cases to which they would have referred would not have been, in themselves, connected with the trade and commerce of England. But we are now in a situation in which, I will not say that a reference to the principle of unrestricted trade can be of no use, because such a reference may correct erroneous reasoning, but in which it is impossible for us, or for any country in the world but in the United States of America, to act unreservedly on that principle. The commercial regulations of the European world have been long established, and cannot suddenly be departed from." Having supposed a proposition to be made to England by a foreign state for free commerce and intercourse, and an unrestricted exchange of agricultural products and of manufactures, he proceeds to observe: "It would be impossible to accede to such a proposition. We have risen to our present greatness under a different system. Some suppose that we have risen in consequence of that system; *others, of whom*

1. *The Parliamentary Debates*, n.s. (25 vols., London, 1820–1830), 1: 546 ff.

I am one, believe that we have risen in spite of that system. But, whichever of these hypotheses be true, certain it is that we have risen under
a very different system than that of free and unrestricted trade. It is
utterly impossible, with our debt and taxation, even if they were but
half their existing amount, that we can suddenly adopt the system of
free trade."

Lord Ellenborough, in the same debate, said, "that he attributed the
general distress then existing in Europe to the regulations that had taken
place since the destruction of the French power. Most of the states on
the Continent had surrounded themselves as with walls of brass, to
inhibit intercourse with other states. Intercourse was prohibited, even in
districts of the same state, as was the case in Austria and Sardinia. Thus,
though the taxes on the people had been lightened, the severity of their
condition had been increased. He believed that the discontent which pervaded most parts of Europe, and especially Germany, was more owing
to commercial restrictions than to any theoretical doctrines on government; and that a free communication among them would do more to
restore tranquillity, than any other step that could be adopted. He objected to all attempts to frustrate the benevolent intentions of Providence, which had given to various countries various wants, in order to
bring them together. He objected to it as anti-social; he objected to it,
as making commerce the means of barbarizing, instead of enlightening
nations. The state of the trade with France was most disgraceful to both
countries; the two greatest civilized nations of the world, placed at a
distance of scarcely twenty miles from each other, had contrived, by
their artificial regulations, to reduce their commerce with each other to
a mere nullity." Every member speaking on this occasion agreed in the
general sentiments favorable to unrestricted intercourse, which had thus
been advanced; one of them remarking, at the conclusion of the debate,
that "the principles of free trade, which he was happy to see so fully recognized, were of the utmost consequence; for, though, in the present circumstances of the country, a free trade was unattainable, yet their task
hereafter was to approximate to it. Considering the prejudices and interests which were opposed to the recognition of that principle, it was no
small indication of the firmness and liberality of government to have so
fully conceded it."

Sir, we have seen, in the course of this discussion, that several gentlemen have expressed their high admiration of the *silk manufacture* of
England. Its commendation was begun, I think, by the honorable member from Vermont, who sits near me, who thinks that alone gives conclusive evidence of the benefits produced by attention to manufactures,
inasmuch as it is a great source of wealth to the nation, and has amply
repaid all the cost of its protection. Mr. Speaker's approbation of this

part of the English example was still warmer. Now, Sir, it does so happen, that both these gentlemen differ very widely on this point from the opinions entertained in England, by persons of the first rank, both as to knowledge and power. In the debate to which I have already referred, the proposer of the motion urged the expediency of providing for the admission of the silks of France into England. "He was aware," he said, "that there was a poor and industrious body of manufacturers, whose interests must suffer by such an arrangement; and therefore he felt that it would be the duty of Parliament to provide for the present generation by a large Parliamentary grant. It was conformable to every principle of sound justice to do so, when the interests of a particular class were sacrificed to the good of the whole." In answer to these observations, Lord Liverpool said that, with reference to several branches of manufactures, time, and the change of circumstances, had rendered the system of protecting duties merely nominal; and that, in his opinion, if all the protecting laws which regarded both the woollen and cotton manufactures were to be repealed, no injurious effects would thereby be occasioned. "But," he observes, "with respect to silk, that manufacture in this kingdom is so completely artificial, that any attempt to introduce the principles of free trade with reference to it might put an end to it altogether. I allow that the silk manufacture is not natural to this country. *I wish we had never had a silk manufactory.* I allow that it is natural to France; I allow that it might have been better, had each country adhered exclusively to that manufacture in which each is superior; and had the silks of France been exchanged for British cottons. But I must look at things as they are; and when I consider the extent of capital, and the immense population, consisting, I believe, of about fifty thousand persons, engaged in our silk manufacture, I can only say, that one of the few points in which I totally disagree with the proposer of the motion is the expediency, under existing circumstances, of holding out any idea, that it would be possible to relinquish the silk manufacture, and to provide for those who live by it, by Parliamentary enactment. Whatever objections there may be to the continuance of the protecting system, I repeat, that it is impossible altogether to relinquish it. I may regret that the system was ever commenced; but as I cannot recall that act, I must submit to the inconvenience by which it is attended, rather than expose the country to evils of greater magnitude." Let it be remembered, Sir, that these are not the sentiments of a theorist, nor the fancies of speculation; but the operative opinions of the first minister of England, acknowledged to be one of the ablest and most practical statesmen of his country.

Gentlemen could have hardly been more unfortunate than in the selection of the silk manufacture in England as an example of the beneficial effects of that system which they would recommend. It is, in the

language which I have quoted, completely artificial. It has been sustained by I know not how many laws, breaking in upon the plainest principles of general expediency. At the last session of Parliament, the manufacturers petitioned for the repeal of three or four of these statutes, complaining of the vexatious restrictions which they impose on the wages of labor; setting forth, that a great variety of orders has from time to time been issued by magistrates under the authority of these laws, interfering in an oppressive manner with the minutest details of the manufacture: such as limiting the number of threads to an inch, restricting the widths of many sorts of work, and determining the quantity of labor not to be exceeded without extra wages; that by the operation of these laws, the rate of wages, instead of being left to the recognized principles of regulation, has been arbitrarily fixed by persons whose ignorance renders them incompetent to a just decision; that masters are compelled by law to pay an equal price for all work, whether well or ill performed; and that they are wholly prevented from using improved machinery, it being ordered, that work, in the weaving of which machinery is employed, shall be paid precisely at the same rate as if done by hand; that these acts have frequently given rise to the most vexatious regulations, the unintentional breach of which has subjected manufacturers to ruinous penalties; and that the introduction of all machinery being prevented, by which labor might be cheapened, and the manufacturers being compelled to pay at a fixed price, under all circumstances, they are unable to afford employment to their workmen, in times of stagnation of trade, and are compelled to stop their looms. And finally, they complain, that, notwithstanding these grievances under which they labor, while carrying on their manufacture in London, the law still prohibits them, while they continue to reside there, from employing any portion of their capital in the same business in any other part of the kingdom, where it might be more beneficially conducted. Now, Sir, absurd as these laws must appear to be to every man, the attempt to repeal them did not, as far as I recollect, altogether succeed. The weavers were too numerous, their interests too great, or their prejudices too strong; and this notable instance of protection and monopoly still exists, to be lamented in England with as much sincerity as it seems to be admired here.

In order further to show the prevailing sentiment of the English government, I would refer to a report of a select committee of the House of Commons, at the head of which was the Vice-President of the Board of Trade (Mr. Wallace), in July, 1820.[2] "The time," say that committee,

2. "Report from the Select Committee Appointed to Consider of the Means of Maintaining and Improving the Foreign Trade of the Country," July 18, 1820, in *British Sessional Papers*, House of Commons, 1820, Vol. 2, pp. 365 ff.

"when monopolies could be successfully supported, or would be patiently endured, either in respect to subjects against subjects, or particular countries against the rest of the world, seems to have passed away. Commerce, to continue undisturbed and secure, must be, as it was intended to be, a source of reciprocal amity between nations, and an interchange of productions to promote the industry, the wealth, and the happiness of mankind." In moving for the reappointment of the committee in February, 1823, the same gentleman said: "We must also get rid of that feeling of appropriation which exhibited itself in a disposition to produce every thing necessary for our own consumption, and to render ourselves independent of the world. No notion could be more absurd or mischievous; it led, even in peace, to an animosity and rancor greater than existed in time of war. Undoubtedly there would be great prejudices to combat; both in this country and elsewhere, in the attempt to remove the difficulties which are most obnoxious. It would be impossible to forget the attention which was in some respects due to the present system of protections, although that attention ought certainly not to be carried beyond the absolute necessity of the case." And in a second report of the committee, drawn by the same gentleman, in that part of it which proposes a diminution of duties on timber from the North of Europe, and the policy of giving a legislative preference to the importation of such timber in the log, and a discouragement of the importation of deals, it is stated that the committee reject this policy, because, among other reasons, "it is founded on a principle of exclusion, which they are most averse to see brought into operation, in any *new instance*, without the warrant of some evident and great political expediency." And on many subsequent occasions the same gentleman has taken occasion to observe, that he differed from those who thought that manufactures could not flourish without restrictions on trade; that old prejudices of that sort were dying away, and that more liberal and just sentiments were taking their place.

These sentiments appear to have been followed by important legal provisions, calculated to remove restrictions and prohibitions where they were most severely felt; that is to say, in several branches of navigation and trade. They have relaxed their colonial system, they have opened the ports of their islands, and have done away the restriction which limited the trade of the colony to the mother country. Colonial products can now be carried directly from the islands to any part of Europe; and it may not be improbable, considering our own high duties on spirits, that that article may be exchanged hereafter by the English West India colonies directly for the timber and deals of the Baltic. It may be added that Mr. Lowe, whom the gentleman has cited, says, that nobody supposes that the three great staples of English manufactures, cotton, woollen, and hardware, are benefited by any existing protecting duties; and that

one object of all these protecting laws is usually overlooked, and that is, that they have been intended to reconcile the various interests to taxation; the corn law, for example, being designed as some equivalent to the agricultural interest for the burden of tithes and of poor-rates.

In fine, Sir, I think it is clear, that, if we now embrace the system of prohibitions and restrictions, we shall show an affection for what others have discarded, and be attempting to ornament ourselves with cast-off apparel.

Sir, I should not have gone into this prolix detail of opinions from any consideration of their special importance on the present occasion; but having happened to state that such was the actual opinion of the government of England at the present time, and the accuracy of this representation having been so confidently denied, I have chosen to put the matter beyond doubt or cavil, although at the expense of these tedious citations. I shall have occasion hereafter to refer more particularly to sundry recent British enactments, by way of showing the diligence and spirit with which that government strives to sustain its navigating interest, by opening the widest possible range to the enterprise of individual adventurers. I repeat, that I have not alluded to these examples of a foreign state as being fit to control our own policy. In the general principle, I acquiesce. Protection, when carried to the point which is now recommended, that is, to entire prohibition, seems to me destructive of all commercial intercourse between nations. We are urged to adopt the system upon general principles; and what would be the consequence of the universal application of such a general principle, but that nations would abstain entirely from all intercourse with one another? I do not admit the general principle; on the contrary, I think freedom of trade to be the general principle, and restriction the exception. And it is for every state, taking into view its own condition, to judge of the propriety, in any case, of making an exception, constantly preferring, as I think all wise governments will, not to depart without urgent reason from the general rule.

There is another point in the existing policy of England to which I would most earnestly invite the attention of the committee; I mean the warehouse system, or what we usually call the system of drawback. Very great prejudices appear to me to exist with us on that subject. We seem averse to the extension of the principle. The English government, on the contrary, appear to have carried it to the extreme of liberality. They have arrived, however, at their present opinions and present practice by slow degrees. The transit system was commenced about the year 1803, but the first law was partial and limited. It admitted the importation of raw materials for exportation, but it excluded almost every sort of manufactured goods. This was done for the same reason that we propose to prevent the transit of Canadian wheat through the United States, the

fear of aiding the competition of the foreign article with our own in foreign markets. Better reflection or more experience has induced them to
abandon that mode of reasoning, and to consider all such means of influencing foreign markets as nugatory; since, in the present active and
enlightened state of the world, nations will supply themselves from the
best sources, and the true policy of all producers, whether of raw materials or of manufactured articles, is, not vainly to endeavor to keep
other vendors out of the market, but to conquer them in it by the quality
and the cheapness of their articles. The present policy of England, therefore, is to allure the importation of commodities into England, there to
be deposited in English warehouses, thence to be exported in assorted
cargoes, and thus enabling her to carry on a general export trade to all
quarters of the globe. Articles of all kinds, with the single exception of
tea, may be brought into England, from any part of the world, in foreign
as well as British ships, there warehoused, and again exported, at the
pleasure of the owner, without the payment of any duty or government
charge whatever.

While I am upon this subject, I would take notice also of the recent
proposition in the English Parliament to abolish the tax on imported
wool; and it is observable that those who support this proposition give
the same reasons that have been offered here, within the last week,
against the duty which we propose on the same article. They say that
their manufacturers require a cheap and coarse wool, for the supply of
the Mediterranean and Levant trade, and that, without a more free admission of the wool of the Continent, that trade will fall into the hands
of the Germans and Italians, who will carry it on through Leghorn and
Trieste. While there is this duty on foreign wool to protect the wool-
growers of England, there is, on the other hand, a prohibition on the
exportation of the native article in aid of the manufacturers. The opinion
seems to be gaining strength, that the true policy is to abolish both.

Laws have long existed in England preventing the emigration of
artisans and the exportation of machinery; but the policy of these, also,
has become doubted, and an inquiry has been instituted in Parliament
into the expediency of repealing them. As to the emigration of artisans,
say those who disapprove the laws, if that were desirable, no law could
effect it; and as to the exportation of machinery, let us make it and
export it as we would any other commodity. If France is determined to
spin and weave her own cotton, let us, if we may, still have the benefit
of furnishing the machinery.

I have stated these things, Sir, to show what seems to be the general
tone of thinking and reasoning on these subjects in that country, the
example of which has been so much pressed upon us. Whether the
present policy of England be right or wrong, wise or unwise, it cannot, as

it seems clearly to me, be quoted as an authority for carrying further the restrictive and exclusive system, either in regard to manufactures or trade. To rëestablish a sound currency, to meet at once the shock, tremendous as it was, of the fall of prices, to enlarge her capacity for foreign trade, to open wide the field of individual enterprise and competition, and to say plainly and distinctly that the country must relieve itself from the embarrassments which it felt, by economy, frugality, and renewed efforts of enterprise,—these appear to be the general outline of the policy which England has pursued.

Mr. Chairman, I will now proceed to say a few words upon a topic, but for the introduction of which into this debate I should not have given the committee on this occasion the trouble of hearing me. Some days ago, I believe it was when we were settling the controversy between the oil-merchants and the tallow-chandlers, the *balance of trade* made its appearance in debate, and I must confess, Sir, that I spoke of it, or rather spoke to it, somewhat freely and irreverently. I believe I used the hard names which have been imputed to be, and I did it simply for the purpose of laying the spectre, and driving it back to its tomb. Certainly, Sir, when I called the old notion on this subject nonsense, I did not suppose that I should offend any one, unless the dead should happen to hear me. All the living generation, I took it for granted, would think the term very properly applied. In this, however, I was mistaken. The dead and the living rise up together to call me to account, and I must defend myself as well as I am able.

Let us inquire, then, Sir, what is meant by an unfavorable balance of trade, and what the argument is, drawn from that source. By an unfavorable balance of trade, I understand, is meant that state of things in which importation exceeds exportation. To apply it to our own case, if the value of goods imported exceed the value of those exported, then the balance of trade is said to be against us, inasmuch as we have run in debt to the amount of this difference. Therefore it is said, that, if a nation continue long in a commerce like this, it must be rendered absolutely bankrupt. It is in the condition of a man that buys more than he sells; and how can such a traffic be maintained without ruin? Now, Sir, the whole fallacy of this argument consists in supposing, that, whenever the value of imports exceeds that of exports, a debt is necessarily created to the extent of the difference, whereas, ordinarily, the import is no more than the result of the export, augmented in value by the labor of transportation. The excess of imports over exports, in truth, usually shows the gains, not the losses, of trade; or, in a country that not only buys and sells goods, but employs ships in carrying goods also, it shows the profits of commerce, and the earnings of navigation. Nothing is more certain than that, in the usual course of things, and taking a series of years

together, the value of our imports is the aggregate of our exports and our freights. If the value of commodities imported in a given instance did not exceed the value of the outward cargo, with which they were purchased, then it would be clear to every man's common sense, that the voyage had not been profitable. If such commodities fell far short in value of the cost of the outward cargo, then the voyage would be a very losing one; and yet it would present exactly that state of things, which, according to the notion of a balance of trade, can alone indicate a prosperous commerce. On the other hand, if the return cargo were found to be worth much more than the outward cargo, while the merchant, having paid for the goods exported, and all the expenses of the voyage, finds a handsome sum yet in his hands, which he calls profits, the balance of trade is still against him, and, whatever he may think of it, he is in a very bad way. Although one individual or all individuals gain, the nation loses; while all its citizens grow rich, the country grows poor. This is the doctrine of the balance of trade.

Allow me, Sir, to give an instance tending to show how unaccountably individuals deceive themselves, and imagine themselves to be somewhat rapidly mending their condition. while they ought to be persuaded that, by that infallible standard, the balance of trade, they are on the high road to ruin. Some years ago, in better times than the present, a ship left one of the towns of New England with 70,000 specie dollars. She proceeded to Mocha, on the Red Sea, and there laid out these dollars in coffee, drugs, spices, and other articles procured in that market. With this new cargo she proceeded to Europe; two thirds of it were sold in Holland for $130,000, which the ship brought back, and placed in the same bank from the vaults of which she had taken her original outfit. The other third was sent to the ports of the Mediterranean, and produced a return of $25,000 in specie, and $15,000 in Italian merchandise. These sums together make $170,000 imported, which is $100,000 more than was exported, and is therefore proof of an unfavorable balance of trade, to that amount, in this adventure. We should find no great difficulty, Sir, in paying off our balances, if this were the nature of them all.

The truth is, Mr. Chairman, that all these obsolete and exploded notions had their origin in very mistaken ideas of the true nature of commerce. Commerce is not a gambling among nations for a stake, to be won by some and lost by others. It has not the tendency necessarily to impoverish one of the parties to it, while it enriches the other; all parties gain, all parties make profits, all parties grow rich, by the operations of just and liberal commerce. If the world had but one clime and but one soil; if all men had the same wants and the same means, on the spot of their existence, to gratify those wants,—then, indeed, what one obtained from the other by exchange would injure one party in the same degree

that it benefited the other; then, indeed, there would be some foundation for the balance of trade. But Providence has disposed our lot much more kindly. We inhabit a various earth. We have reciprocal wants, and reciprocal means for gratifying one another's wants. This is the true origin of commerce, which is nothing more than an exchange of equivalents, and, from the rude barter of its primitive state, to the refined and complex condition in which we see it, its principle is uniformly the same, its only object being, in every stage, to produce that exchange of commodities between individuals and between nations which shall conduce to the advantage and to the happiness of both. Commerce between nations has the same essential character as commerce between individuals, or between parts of the same nation. Cannot two individuals make an interchange of commodities which shall prove beneficial to both, or in which the balance of trade shall be in favor of both? If not, the tailor and the shoemaker, the farmer and the smith, have hitherto very much misunderstood their own interests. And with regard to the internal trade of a country, in which the same rule would apply as between nations, do we ever speak of such an intercourse as prejudicial to one side because it is useful to the other? Do we ever hear that, because the intercourse between New York and Albany is advantageous to one of those places, it must therefore be ruinous to the other?

May I be allowed, Sir, to read a passage on this subject from the observations of a gentleman, in my opinion one of the most clear and sensible writers and speakers of the age upon subjects of this sort?[3] "There is no political question on which the prevalence of false principles is so general, as in what relates to the nature of commerce and to the pretended balance of trade; and there are few which have led to a greater number of practical mistakes, attended with consequences extensively prejudicial to the happiness of mankind. In this country, our Parliamentary proceedings, our public documents, and the works of several able and popular writers, have combined to propagate the impression, that we are indebted for much of our riches to what is called the balance of trade." "Our true policy would surely be to profess, as the object and

3. William Huskisson, member of parliament and president of the Board of Trade. Both of the quotations that follow, with minor changes, come from Huskisson's *The Question Concerning the Depreciation of Our Currency Stated and Examined* (London, 1810), the first on pages 67–68 and the second on pages 68–69. These two quotations by no means represent Webster's indebtedness to this small volume. More than two years later Webster's British friend, John Evelyn Denison wrote, after a meeting with Huskisson: ". . . he desired me, when I wrote to you, . . . to say, how greatly struck he was with your speech on the Tariff, wh[ich] he had read with the greatest pleasure." (Denison to DW, July 11, 1826, *Correspondence*, 2: 124).

guide of our commercial system, that which every man who has studied
the subject must know to be the true principle of commerce, the interchange of reciprocal and equivalent benefit. We may rest assured that it
is not in the nature of commerce to enrich one party at the expense of the
other. This is a purpose at which, if it were practicable, we ought not to
aim; and which, if we aimed at, we could not accomplish." These remarks, I believe, Sir, were written some ten or twelve years ago. They
are in perfect accordance with the opinions advanced in more elaborate
treatises, and now that the world has returned to a state of peace, and
commerce has resumed its natural channels, and different nations are
enjoying, or seeking to enjoy, their respective portions of it, all see the
justness of these ideas; all see, that, in this day of knowledge and of
peace, there can be no commerce between nations but that which shall
benefit all who are parties to it.

If it were necessary, Mr. Chairman, I might ask the attention of the
committee to refer to a document before us, on this subject of the balance
of trade. It will be seen by reference to the accounts, that, in the course
of the last year, our total export to Holland exceeded two millions and a
half; our total import from the same country was but seven hundred
thousand dollars. Now, can any man be wild enough to make any inference from this as to the gain or loss of our trade with Holland for that
year? Our trade with Russia for the same year produced a balance the
other way; our import being two millions, and our export but half a
million. But this has no more tendency to show the Russian trade a losing trade, than the other statement has to show that the Dutch trade
has been a gainful one. Neither of them, by itself, proves any thing.

Springing out of this notion of a balance of trade, there is another
idea, which has been much dwelt upon in the course of this debate; that
is, that we ought not to buy of nations who do not buy of us; for example,
that the Russian trade is a trade disadvantageous to the country, and
ought to be discouraged, because, in the ports of Russia, we buy more
than we sell. Now allow me to observe, in the first place, Sir, that we
have no account showing how much we do sell in the ports of Russia.
Our official returns show us only what is the amount of our direct trade
with her ports. But then we all know that the proceeds of another portion of our exports go to the same market, though indirectly. We send
our own products, for example, to Cuba, or to Brazil; we there exchange
them for the sugar and the coffee of those countries, and these articles
we carry to St. Petersburg, and there sell them. Again; our exports to
Holland and Hamburg are connected directly or indirectly with our imports from Russia. What difference does it make, in sense or reason,
whether a cargo of iron be bought at St. Petersburg, by the exchange of
a cargo of tobacco, or whether the tobacco has been sold on the way, in a

better market, in a port of Holland, the money remitted to England, and the iron paid for by a bill on London? There might indeed have been an augmented freight, there might have been some saving of commissions, if tobacco had been in brisk demand in the Russian market. But still there is nothing to show that the whole voyage may not have been highly profitable. That depends upon the original cost of the article here, the amount of freight and insurance to Holland, the price obtained there, the rate of exchange between Holland and England, the expense, then, of proceeding to St. Petersburg, the price of iron there, the rate of exchange between that place and England, the amount of freight and insurance at home, and, finally, the value of the iron when brought to our own market. These are the calculations which determine the fortune of the adventure; and nothing can be judged of it, one way or the other, by the relative state of our imports or exports with Holland, England, or Russia.

I would not be understood to deny, that it may often be our interest to cultivate a trade with countries that require most of such commodities as we can furnish, and which are capable also of directly supplying our own wants. This is the original and the simplest form of all commerce, and is no doubt highly beneficial. Some countries are so situated, that commerce, in this original form, or something near it, may be all that they can, without considerable inconvenience, carry on. Our trade, for example, with Madeira and the Western Islands[4] has been useful to the country, as furnishing a demand for some portion of our agricultural products, which probably could not have been bought had we not received their products in return. Countries situated still farther from the great marts and highways of the commercial world may afford still stronger instances of the necessity and utility of conducting commerce on the original principle of barter, without much assistance from the operations of credit and exchange. All I would be understood to say is, that it by no means follows that we can carry on nothing but a losing trade with a country from which we receive more of her products than she receives of ours. Since I was supposed, the other day, in speaking upon this subject, to advance opinions which not only this country ought to reject, but which also other countries, and those the most distinguished for skill and success in commercial intercourse, do reject, I will ask leave to refer again to the discussion which I first mentioned in the English Parliament, relative to the foreign trade of that country. "With regard," says the mover [Lord Lansdowne] of the proposition, "to the argument employed against renewing our intercourse with the North of Europe, namely, that those who supplied us with timber from that quarter would not receive British manufactures in return, it appeared to him

4. Probably Madeira, Canary, and Cape Verde Islands.

futile and ungrounded. If they did not send direct for our manufactures at home, they would send for them to Leipsic and other fairs of Germany. Were not the Russian and Polish merchants purchasers there to a great amount? But he would never admit the principle, that a trade was not profitable because we were obliged to carry it on with the precious metals, or that we ought to renounce it, because our manufactures were not received by the foreign nation in return for its produce. Whatever we received must be paid for in the produce of our land and labor, directly or circuitously, and he was glad to have the noble Earl's [Lord Liverpool] marked concurrence in this principle."

Referring ourselves again, Sir, to the analogies of common life, no one would say that a farmer or a mechanic should buy *only* where he can do so by the exchange of his own produce, or of his own manufacture. Such exchange may be often convenient; and, on the other hand, the cash purchase may be often more convenient. It is the same in the intercourse of nations. Indeed, Mr. Speaker has placed this argument on very clear grounds. It was said, in the early part of the debate, that, if we cease to import English cotton fabrics, England will no longer continue to purchase our cotton. To this Mr. Speaker replied, with great force and justice, that, as she must have cotton in large quantities, she will buy the article where she can find it best and cheapest; and that it would be quite ridiculous in her, manufacturing as she still would be, for her own vast consumption and the consumption of millions in other countries, to reject our uplands because we had learned to manufacture a part of them for ourselves. Would it not be equally ridiculous in us, if the commodities of Russia were both cheaper and better suited to our wants than could be found elsewhere, to abstain from commerce with her, because she will not receive in return other commodities which we have to sell, but which she has no occasion to buy?

Intimately connected, Sir, with this topic, is another which has been brought into the debate; I mean the evil so much complained of, the exportation of specie. We hear gentlemen imputing the loss of market at home to a want of money, and this want of money to the exportation of the precious metals. We hear the India and China trade denounced, as a commerce conducted on our side, in a great measure, with gold and silver. These opinions, Sir, are clearly void of all just foundation, and we cannot too soon get rid of them. There are no shallower reasoners than those political and commercial writers who would represent it to be the only true and gainful end of commerce, to accumulate the precious metals. These are articles of use, and articles of merchandise, with this additional circumstance belonging to them, that they are made, by the general consent of nations, the standard by which the value of all other merchandise is to be estimated. In regard to weights and measures,

something drawn from external nature is made a common standard, for the purposes of general convenience; and this is precisely the office performed by the precious metals, in addition to those uses to which, as metals, they are capable of being applied. There may be of these too much or too little in a country at a particular time, as there may be of any other articles. When the market is overstocked with them, as it often is, their exportation becomes as proper and as useful as that of other commodities, under similar circumstances. We need no more repine, when the dollars which have been brought here from South America are despatched to other countries, than when coffee and sugar take the same direction. We often deceive ourselves, by attributing to a scarcity of money that which is the result of other causes. In the course of this debate, the honorable member from Pennsylvania [John Tod] has represented the country as full of every thing but money. But this I take to be a mistake. The agricultural products, so abundant in Pennsylvania, will not, he says, sell for money; but they will sell for money as quick as for any other article which happens to be in demand. They will sell for money, for example, as easily as for coffee or for tea, at the prices which properly belong to those articles. The mistake lies in imputing that to want of money which arises from want of demand. Men do not buy wheat because they have money, but because they want wheat. To decide whether money be plenty or not, that is, whether there be a large portion of capital unemployed or not, when the currency of a country is metallic, we must look, not only to the prices of commodities, but also to the rate of interest. A low rate of interest, a facility of obtaining money on loans, a disposition to invest in permanent stocks, all of which are proofs that money is plenty, may nevertheless often denote a state not of the highest prosperity. They may, and often do, show a want of employment for capital; and the accumulation of specie shows the same thing. We have no occasion for the precious metals as money, except for the purposes of circulation, or rather of sustaining a safe paper circulation. And whenever there is a prospect of a profitable investment abroad, all the gold and silver, except what these purposes require, will be exported. For the same reason, if a demand exist abroad for sugar and coffee, whatever amount of those articles might exist in the country, beyond the wants of its own consumption, would be sent abroad to meet that demand.

Besides, Sir, how should it ever occur to any body, that we should continue to export gold and silver, if we did not continue to import them also? If a vessel take our own products to the Havana, or elsewhere, exchange them for dollars, proceed to China, exchange them for silks and teas, bring these last to the ports of the Mediterranean, sell them

there for dollars, and return to the United States; this would be a voyage resulting in the importation of the precious metals. But if she had returned from Cuba, and the dollars obtained there had been shipped direct from the United States to China, the China goods sold in Holland, and the proceeds brought home in the hemp and iron of Russia, this would be a voyage in which they were exported. Yet every body sees that both might be equally beneficial to the individual and to the public. I believe, Sir, that, in point of fact, we have enjoyed great benefit in our trade with India and China, from the liberty of going from place to place all over the world, without being obliged in the mean time to return home, a liberty not heretofore enjoyed by the private traders of England, in regard to India and China. Suppose the American ship to be at Brazil, for example; she could proceed with her dollars direct to India, and, in return, could distribute her cargo in all the various ports of Europe or America; while an English ship, if a private trader, being at Brazil, must first return to England, and then could only proceed in the direct line from England to India. This advantage our countrymen have not been backward to improve; and in the debate to which I have already so often referred, it was stated, not without some complaint of the inconvenience of exclusion, and the natural sluggishness of monopoly, that American ships were at that moment fitting out in the Thames, to supply France, Holland, and other countries on the Continent, with tea; while the East India Company would not do this of themselves; nor allow any of their fellow-countrymen to do it for them.

There is yet another subject, Mr. Chairman, upon which I would wish to say something, if I might presume upon the continued patience of the committee. We hear sometimes in the House, and continually out of it, of the rate of exchange, as being one proof that we are on the downward road to ruin. Mr. Speaker himself has adverted to that topic, and I am afraid that his authority may give credit to opinions clearly unfounded, and which lead to very false and erroneous conclusions. Sir, let us see what the facts are. Exchange on England has recently risen one or one and a half per cent., partly owing, perhaps, to the introduction of this bill into Congress. Before this recent rise, and for the last six months, I understand its average may have been about seven and a half per cent. advance. Now, supposing this to be the *real*, and not merely, as it is, the nominal, par of exchange between us and England, what would it prove? Nothing, except that funds were wanted by American citizens in England for commercial operations, to be carried on either in England or elsewhere. It would not necessarily show that we were indebted to England; for, if we had occasion to pay debts in Russia or Holland, funds in England would naturally enough be required for such a purpose. Even if

it did prove that a balance was due England at the moment, it would have no tendency to explain to us whether our commerce with England had been profitable or unprofitable.

But it is not true, in point of fact, that the *real* price of exchange is seven and a half per cent. advance, nor, indeed, that there is at the present moment any advance at all. That is to say, it is not true that merchants will give such an advance, or any advance, for *money* in England, beyond what they would give for the same amount, in the same currency, here. It will strike every one who reflects upon it, that, if there were a real difference of seven and a half per cent., money would be immediately shipped to England; because the expense of transportation would be far less than that difference. Or commodities of trade would be shipped to Europe, and the proceeds remitted to England. If it could so happen, that American merchants should be willing to pay ten per cent. premium for money in England, or, in other words, that a real difference to that amount in the exchange should exist, its effects would be immediately seen in new shipments of our own commodities to Europe, because this state of things would create new motives. A cargo of tobacco, for example, might sell at Amsterdam for the same price as before; but if its proceeds, when remitted to London, were advanced, as they would be in such a case, ten per cent. by the state of exchange, this would be so much added to the price, and would operate therefore as a motive for the exportation; and in this way national balances are, and always will be, adjusted.

To form any accurate idea of the true state of exchange between two countries, we must look at their currencies, and compare the quantities of gold and silver which they may respectively represent. This usually explains the state of the exchanges; and this will satisfactorily account for the apparent advance now existing on bills drawn on England. The English standard of value is gold; with us that office is performed by gold, and by silver also, at a fixed relation to each other. But our estimate of silver is rather higher, in proportion to gold, than most nations give it; it is higher, especially, than in England, at the present moment. The consequence is, that silver, which remains a legal currency with us, stays here, while the gold has gone abroad; verifying the universal truth, that, if *two* currencies be allowed to exist, of different values, that which is cheapest will fill up the whole circulation. For as much gold as will suffice to pay here a debt of a given amount, we can buy in England more silver than would be necessary to pay the same debt here; and from this difference in the value of silver arises wholly or in a great measure the present apparent difference in exchange. Spanish dollars sell now in England for four shillings and nine pence sterling per ounce, equal to one dollar and six cents. By our standard the same ounce is

worth one dollar and sixteen cents, being a difference of about nine per cent. The true par of exchange, therefore, is nine per cent. If a merchant here pay one hundred Spanish dollars for a bill on England, at nominal par, in sterling money, that is for a bill of £ 22 10s., the proceeds of this bill, when paid in England in the legal currency, will there purchase, at the present price of silver, one hundred and nine Spanish dollars. Therefore, if the nominal advance on English bills do not exceed nine per cent., the real exchange is not against this country; in other words, it does not show that there is any pressing or particular occasion for the remittance of funds to England.

As little can be inferred from the occasional transfer of United States stock to England. Considering the interest paid on our stocks, the entire stability of our credit, and the accumulation of capital in England, it is not at all wonderful that investments should occasionally be made in our funds. As a sort of countervailing fact, it may be stated that English stocks are now actually held in this country, though probably not to any considerable amount.

I will now proceed, Sir, to state some objections of a more general nature, to the course of Mr. Speaker's observations.

He seems to me to argue the question as if all domestic industry were confined to the production of manufactured articles; as if the employment of our own capital and our own labor, in the occupations of commerce and navigation, were not as emphatically domestic industry as any other occupation. Some other gentlemen, in the course of the debate, have spoken of the price paid for every foreign manufactured article as so much given for the encouragement of foreign labor, to the prejudice of our own. But is not every such article the product of our own labor as truly as if we had manufactured it ourselves? Our labor has earned it, and paid the price for it. It is so much added to the stock of national wealth. If the commodity were dollars, nobody would doubt the truth of this remark; and it is precisely as correct in its application to any other commodity as to silver. One man makes a yard of cloth at home; another raises agricultural products and buys a yard of imported cloth. Both these are equally the earnings of domestic industry, and the only questions that arise in the case are two: the first is, which is the best mode, under all the circumstances, of obtaining the article; the second is, how far this first question is proper to be decided by government, and how far it is proper to be left to individual discretion. There is no foundation for the distinction which attributes to certain employments the peculiar appellation of American industry; and it is, in my judgment, extremely unwise to attempt such discriminations.

We are asked, What nations have ever attained eminent prosperity without encouraging manufactures? I may ask, What nation ever reached

the like prosperity without promoting foreign trade? I regard these interests as closely connected, and am of opinion that it should be our aim to cause them to flourish together. I know it would be very easy to promote manufactures, at least for a time, but probably for a short time only, if we might act in disregard of other interests. We could cause a sudden transfer of capital, and a violent change in the pursuits of men. We could exceedingly benefit some classes by these means. But what, then, becomes of the interests of others? The power of collecting revenue by duties on imports, and the habit of the government of collecting almost its whole revenue in that mode, will enable us, without exceeding the bounds of moderation, to give great advantages to those classes of manufactures which we may think most useful to promote at home. What I object to is the immoderate use of the power,—exclusions and prohibitions; all of which, as I think, not only interrupt the pursuits of individuals, with great injury to themselves and little or no benefit to the country, but also often divert our own labor, or, as it may very properly be called, our own domestic industry, from those occupations in which it is well employed and well paid, to others in which it will be worse employed and worse paid. For my part, I see very little relief to those who are likely to be deprived of their employments, or who find the prices of the commodities which they need, raised, in any of the alternatives which Mr. Speaker has presented. It is nothing to say that they may, if they choose, continue to buy the foreign article; the answer is, the price is augmented: nor that they may use the domestic article; the price of that also is increased. Nor can they supply themselves by the substitution of their own fabric. How can the agriculturist make his own iron? How can the ship-owner grow his own hemp?

But I have a yet stronger objection to the course of Mr. Speaker's reasoning; which is, that he leaves out of the case all that has been already done for the protection of manufactures, and argues the question as if those interests were now for the first time to receive aid from duties on imports. I can hardly express the surprise I feel that Mr. Speaker should fall into the common mode of expression used elsewhere, and ask if we will give our manufacturers no protection. Sir, look to the history of our laws; look to the present state of our laws. Consider that our whole revenue, with a trifling exception, is collected at the custom-house, and always has been; and then say what propriety there is in calling on the government for protection, as if no protection had heretofore been afforded. The real question before us, in regard to all the important clauses of the bill, is not whether we will *lay* duties, but whether we will *augment* duties. The demand is for something more than exists, and yet it is pressed as if nothing existed. It is wholly forgotten that iron and hemp, for example, already pay a very heavy and burdensome duty; and,

in short, from the general tenor of Mr. Speaker's observations, one would infer that, hitherto, we had rather taxed our own manufactures than fostered them by taxes on those of other countries. We hear of the fatal policy of the tariff of 1816; and yet the law of 1816 was passed avowedly for the benefit of manufactures, and, with very few exceptions, imposed on imported articles very great additions of tax; in some important instances, indeed, amounting to a prohibition.

Sir, on this subject, it becomes us at least to understand the real posture of the question. Let us not suppose that we are *beginning* the protection of manufactures, by duties on imports. What we are asked to do is, render those duties much higher and therefore, instead of dealing in general commendations of the benefits of protection, the friends of the bill, I think, are bound to make out a fair case for each of the manufactures which they propose to benefit. The government has already done much for their protection, and it ought to be presumed to have done enough, unless it be shown, by the facts and considerations applicable to each, that there is a necessity for doing more.

On the general question, Sir, allow me to ask if the doctrine of prohibition, as a general doctrine, be not preposterous. Suppose all nations to act upon it; they would be prosperous, then, according to the argument, precisely in the proportion in which they abolished intercourse with one another. The less of mutual commerce the better, upon this hypothesis. Protection and encouragement may be, and doubtless are, sometimes, wise and beneficial, if kept within proper limits; but when carried to an extravagant height, or the point of prohibition, the absurd character of the system manifests itself. Mr. Speaker has referred to the late Emperor Napoleon, as having attempted to naturalize the manufacture of cotton in France. He did not cite a more extravagant part of the projects of that ruler, that is, his attempt to naturalize the growth of that plant itself, in France; whereas, we have understood that considerable districts in the South of France, and in Italy, of rich and productive lands, were at one time withdrawn from profitable uses, and devoted to raising, at great expense, a little bad cotton. Nor have we been referred to the attempts, under the same system, to make sugar and coffee from common culinary vegetables; attempts which served to fill the print-shops of Europe, and to show us how easy is the transition from what some think sublime to that which all admit to be ridiculous. The folly of some of these projects has not been surpassed, nor hardly equalled, unless it be by the philosopher in one of the satires of Swift, who so long labored to extract sunbeams from cucumbers.[5]

The poverty and unhappiness of Spain have been attributed to the

5. Jonathan Swift, *Gulliver's Travels*, ed. Herbert Davis (Oxford, 1965), Part 3, Ch. 5, p. 179.

want of protection to her own industry. If by this it be meant that the poverty of Spain is owing to bad government and bad laws, the remark is, in a great measure, just. But these very laws are bad because they are restrictive, partial, and prohibitory. If prohibition were protection, Spain would seem to have had enough of it. Nothing can exceed the barbarous rigidity of her colonial system, or the folly of her early commercial regulations. Unenlightened and bigoted legislation, the multitude of holidays, miserable roads, monopolies on the part of government, restrictive laws, that ought long since to have been abrogated, are generally, and I believe truly, reckoned the principal causes of the bad state of the productive industry of Spain. Any partial improvement in her condition, or increase of her prosperity, has been, in all cases, the result of relaxation, and the abolition of what was intended for favor and protection.

In short, Sir, the general sense of this age sets, with a strong current, in favor of freedom of commercial intercourse, and unrestrained individual action. Men yield up their notions of monopoly and restriction, as they yield up other prejudices, slowly and reluctantly; but they cannot withstand the general tide of opinion.

Let me now ask, Sir, what relief this bill proposes to some of those great and essential interests of the country, the condition of which has been referred to as proof of national distress; and which condition, although I do not think it makes out a case of *distress*, yet does indicate depression.

And first, Sir, as to our foreign trade. Mr. Speaker has stated that there has been a considerable falling off in the tonnage employed in that trade. This is true, lamentably true. In my opinion, it is one of those occurrences which ought to arrest our immediate, our deep, our most earnest attention. What does this bill propose for its relief? It proposes nothing but new burdens. It proposes to diminish its employment, and it proposes, at the same time, to augment its expense, by subjecting it to heavier taxation. Sir, there is no interest, in regard to which a stronger case for protection can be made out, than the navigating interest. Whether we look at its present condition, which is admitted to be depressed, the number of persons connected with it, and dependent upon it for their daily bread, or its importance to the country in a political point of view, it has claims upon our attention which cannot be surpassed. But what do we propose to do for it? I repeat, Sir, simply to burden and to tax it. By a statement which I have already submitted to the committee, it appears that the shipping interest pays, annually, more than half a million of dollars in duties on articles used in the construction of ships. We propose to add nearly, or quite, fifty per cent. to this amount, at the very moment that we appeal to the languishing state of this interest as a

proof of national distress. Let it be remembered that our shipping employed in foreign commerce has, at this moment, not the shadow of government protection. It goes abroad upon the wide sea to make its own way, and earn its own bread, in a professed competition with the whole world. Its resources are its own frugality; its own skill, its own enterprise. It hopes to succeed, if it shall succeed at all, not by extraordinary aid of government, but by patience, vigilance, and toil. This right arm of the nation's safety strengthens its own muscle by its own efforts, and by unwearied exertion in its own defence becomes strong for the defence of the country.

No one acquainted with this interest can deny that its situation, at this moment, is extremely critical. We have left it hitherto to maintain itself or perish; to swim if it can, and to sink if it must. But at this moment of its apparent struggle, can we as men, can we as patriots, add another stone to the weight that threatens to carry it down? Sir, there is a limit to human power, and to human effort. I know the commercial marine of this country can do almost every thing, and bear almost every thing. Yet some things are impossible to be done, and some burdens may be impossible to be borne; and as it was the last ounce that broke the back of the camel, so the last tax, although it were even a small one, may be decisive as to the power of our marine to sustain the conflict in which it is now engaged with all the commercial nations on the globe.

Again, Mr. Chairman, the failures and the bankruptcies which have taken place in our large cities have been mentioned as proving the little success attending *commerce*, and its general decline. But this bill has no balm for those wounds. It is very remarkable, that when the losses and disasters of certain manufacturers, those of iron, for instance, are mentioned, it is done for the purpose of invoking aid for the distressed. Not so with the losses and disasters of commerce; these last are narrated, and not unfrequently much exaggerated, to prove the ruinous nature of the employment, and to show that it ought to be abandoned, and the capital engaged in it turned to other objects.

It has been often said, Sir, that our manufacturers have to contend, not only against the natural advantages of those who produce similar articles in foreign countries, but also against the action of foreign governments, who have great political interest in aiding their own manufactures to suppress ours. But have not these governments as great an interest to cripple our marine, by preventing the growth of our commerce and navigation? What is it that makes us the object of the highest respect, or the most suspicious jealousy, to foreign states? What is it that most enables us to take high relative rank among the nations? I need not say that this results, more than from any thing else, from that

quantity of military power which we can cause to be water-borne, and from that extent of commerce which we are able to maintain throughout the world.

Mr. Chairman, I am conscious of having detained the committee much too long with these observations. My apology for now proceeding to some remarks upon the particular clauses of the bill is, that, representing a district at once commercial and highly manufacturing, and being called upon to vote upon a bill containing provisions so numerous and so various, I am naturally desirous to state as well what I approve, as what I would reject.

The first section proposes an augmented duty upon woollen manufactures. This, if it were unqualified, would no doubt be desirable to those who are engaged in that business. I have myself presented a petition from the woollen manufacturers of Massachusetts, praying an augmented *ad valorem* duty upon imported woollen cloths; and I am prepared to accede to that proposition, to a reasonable extent. But then this bill proposes, also, a very high duty upon imported wool; and, as far as I can learn, a majority of the manufacturers are at least extremely doubtful whether, taking these two provisions together, the state of the law is not better for them now than it would be if this bill should pass. It is said, this tax on raw wool will benefit the agriculturist; but I know it to be the opinion of some of the best informed of that class, that it will do them more hurt than good. They fear it will check the manufacturer, and consequently check his demand for their article. The argument is, that a certain quantity of coarse wool, cheaper than we can possibly furnish, is necessary to enable the manufacturer to carry on the general business, and that if this cannot be had, the consequence will be, not a greater, but a less, manufacture of our own wool. I am aware that very intelligent persons differ upon this point; but if we may safely infer from that difference of opinion, that the proposed benefit is at least doubtful, it would be prudent perhaps to abstain from the experiment. Certain it is, that the same reasoning has been employed, as I have before stated, on the same subject, when a renewed application was made to the English Parliament to repeal the duty on imported wool, I believe scarcely two months ago; those who supported the application pressing urgently the necessity of an unrestricted use of the cheap, imported raw material, with a view to supply with coarse cloths the markets of warm climates, such as those of Egypt and Turkey, and especially a vast newly created demand in the South American states.

As to the manufactures of cotton, it is agreed, I believe, that they are generally successful. It is understood that the present existing duty operates pretty much as a prohibition over those descriptions of fabrics to which it applies. The proposed alteration would probably enable the

American manufacturer to commence competition with higher-priced fabrics; and so, perhaps, would an augmentation less than is here proposed. I consider the cotton manufactures not only to have reached, but to have passed, the point of competition. I regard their success as certain, and their growth as rapid as the most impatient could well expect. If, however, a provision of the nature of that recommended here were thought necessary, to commence new operations in the same line of manufacture, I should cheerfully agree to it, if it were not at the cost of sacrificing other great interests of the country. I need hardly say, that whatever promotes the cotton and woollen manufactures promotes most important interests of my constituents. They have a great stake in the success of those establishments, and, as far as those manufactures are concerned, would be as much benefited by the provisions of this bill as any part of the community. It is obvious, too, I should think, that, for some considerable time, manufactures of this sort, to whatever magnitude they may rise, will be principally established in those parts of the country where population is most dense, capital most abundant, and where the most successful beginnings have already been made.

But if these be thought to be advantages, they are greatly counterbalanced by other advantages enjoyed by other portions of the country. I cannot but regard the situation of the West as highly favorable to human happiness. It offers, in the abundance of its new and fertile lands, such assurances of permanent property and respectability to the industrious, it enables them to lay such sure foundations for a competent provision for their families, it makes such a nation of freeholders, that it need not envy the happiest and most prosperous of the manufacturing communities. We may talk as we will of well-fed and well-clothed day-laborers or journeymen; they are not, after all, to be compared, either for happiness or respectability, with him who sleeps under his own roof and cultivates his own fee-simple inheritance.

With respect to the proposed duty on glass, I would observe, that, upon the best means of judging which I possess, I am of opinion that the chairman of the committee is right in stating that there is in effect a bounty upon the exportation of the British article. I think it entirely proper, therefore, to raise our own duty by such an amount as shall be equivalent to that bounty.

And here, Mr. Chairman, before proceeding to those parts of the bill to which I most strenuously object, I will be so presumptuous as to take up a challenge which Mr. Speaker has thrown down. He has asked us, in a tone of interrogatory indicative of the feeling of anticipated triumph, to mention any country in which manufactures have flourished without the aid of prohibitory laws. He has demanded if it be not policy, protection, ay, and prohibition, that have carried other states to the height

of their prosperity, and whether any one has succeeded with such tame and inert legislation as ours. Sir, I am ready to answer this inquiry.

There is a country, not undistinguished among the nations, in which the progress of manufactures has been far more rapid than in any other, and yet unaided by prohibitions or unnatural restrictions. That country, the happiest which the sun shines on, is our own.

The woollen manufactures of England have existed from the early ages of the monarchy. Provisions designed to aid and foster them are in the black-letter statutes of the Edwards and the Henrys. Ours, on the contrary, are but of yesterday; and yet, with no more than the protection of existing laws, they are already at the point of close and promising competition. Sir, nothing is more unphilosophical than to refer us, on these subjects, to the policy adopted by other nations in a very different state of society, or to infer that what was judged expedient by them, in their early history, must also be expedient for us, in this early part of our own. This would be reckoning our age chronologically, and estimating our advance by our number of years; when, in truth, we should regard only the state of society, the knowledge, the skill, the capital, and the enterprise which belong to our times. We have been transferred from the stock of Europe, in a comparatively enlightened age, and our civilization and improvement date as far back as her own. Her original history is also our original history; and if, since the moment of separation, she has gone ahead of us in some respects, it may be said, without violating truth, that we have kept up in others, and, in others again, are ahead ourselves. We are to legislate, then, with regard to the present actual state of society; and our own experience shows us, that, commencing manufactures at the present highly enlightened and emulous moment, we need not resort to the clumsy helps with which, in less auspicious times, governments have sought to enable the ingenuity and industry of their people to hobble along.

The English cotton manufactures began about the commencement of the last reign. Ours can hardly be said to have commenced, with any earnestness, until the application of the power-loom, in 1814, not more than ten years ago. Now, Sir, I hardly need again speak of its progress, its present extent, or its assurance of future enlargement. In some sorts of fabrics we are already exporters, and the products of our factories are, at this moment, in the South American markets. We see, then, what *can* be done without prohibition, or extraordinary protection, because we see what *has* been done; and I venture to predict, that, in a few years, it will be thought wonderful that these branches of manufactures, at least, should have been thought to require additional aid from government.

Mr. Chairman, the best apology for laws of prohibition and laws of monopoly will be found in that state of society, not only unenlightened but sluggish, in which they are most generally established. Private industry, in those days, required strong provocatives, which governments were seeking to administer by these means. Something was wanted to actuate and stimulate men, and the prospects of such profits as would, in our times, excite unbounded competition, would hardly move the sloth of former ages. In some instances, no doubt, these laws produced an effect, which, in that period, would not have taken place without them. But our age is of a wholly different character, and its legislation takes another turn. Society is full of excitement; competition comes in place of monopoly; and intelligence and industry ask only for fair play and an open field. Profits, indeed, in such a state of things, will be small, but they will be extensively diffused; prices will be low, and the great body of the people prosperous and happy. It is worthy of remark, that, from the operation of these causes, commercial wealth, while it is increased beyond calculation in its general aggregate, is, at the same time, broken and diminished in its subdivisions. Commercial prosperity should be judged of, therefore, rather from the extent of trade, than from the magnitude of its apparent profits. It has been remarked, that Spain, certainly one of the poorest nations, made very great profits on the amount of her trade; but with little other benefit than the enriching of a few individuals and companies. Profits to the English merchants engaged in the Levant and Turkey trade were formerly very great, and there were richer merchants in England some centuries ago, considering the comparative value of money, than at the present highly commercial period. When the diminution of profits arises from the extent of competition, it indicates rather a salutary than an injurious change.[6]

The true course then, Sir, for us to pursue, is, in my opinion, to consider what our situation is; what our means are; and how they can be best applied. What amount of population have we in comparison with our extent of soil, what amount of capital, and labor at what price? As to skill, knowledge, and enterprise, we may safely take it for granted that

6. Quote by DW reads, "'The present equable diffusion of moderate wealth cannot be better illustrated, than by remarking that in this age many palaces and superb mansions have been pulled down, or converted to other purposes, while none have been erected on a like scale. The numberless baronial castles and mansions, in all parts of England, now in ruins, may all be adduced as examples of the decrease of inordinate wealth. On the other hand, the multiplication of commodious dwellings for the upper and middle classes of society, and the increased comforts of all ranks, exhibit a picture of individual happiness, unknown in any other age.' Sir G. Blane's Letter to Lord Spencer, in 1800."

in these particulars we are on an equality with others. Keeping these considerations in view, allow me to examine two or three of those provisions of the bill to which I feel the strongest objections.

To begin with the article of iron. Our whole annual consumption of this article is supposed by the chairman of the committee to be forty-eight or fifty thousand tons. Let us suppose the latter. The amount of our own manufacture he estimates, I think, at seventeen thousand tons. The present duty on the imported article is $15 per ton, and as this duty causes, of course, an equivalent augmentation of the price of the home manufacture, the whole increase of price is equal to $750,000 annually. This sum we pay on a raw material, and on an absolute necessary of life. The bill proposes to raise the duty from $15 to $22.50 per ton, which would be equal to $1,125,000 on the whole annual consumption. So that, suppose the point of prohibition which is aimed at by some gentlemen to be attained, the consumers of the article would pay this last-mentioned sum every year to the producers of it, over and above the price at which they could supply themselves with the same article from other sources. There would be no mitigation of this burden, except from the prospect, whatever that might be, that iron would fall in value, by domestic competition, after the importation should be prohibited. It will be easy, I think, to show that it cannot fall; and supposing for the present that it shall not, the result will be, that we shall pay annually the sum of $1,125,000, constantly augmented, too, by increased consumption of the article, *to support a business that cannot support itself.*

It is of no consequence to the argument, that this sum is expended at home; so it would be if we taxed the people to support any other useless and expensive establishment, to build another Capitol, for example, or incur an unnecessary expense of any sort. The question still is, Are the money, time, and labor well laid out in these cases? The present price of iron at Stockholm, I am assured by importers, is $53 per ton on board, $48 in the yard before loading, and probably not far from $40 at the mines. Freight, insurance, &c., may be fairly estimated at $15, to which add our present duty of $15 more, and these two last sums, together with the cost on board at Stockholm, give $83 as the cost of Swedes iron in our market. In fact, it is said to have been sold last year at $81.50 to $82 per ton. We perceive, by this statement, that the cost of the iron is doubled in reaching us from the mine in which it is produced. In other words, our present duty, with the expense of transportation, gives an advantage to the American over the foreign manufacturer of one hundred per cent. Why, then, cannot the iron be manufactured at home? Our ore is said to be as good, and some of it better. It is under our feet, and the chairman of the committee tells us that it might be wrought by persons who otherwise will not be employed. Why, then, is it

not wrought? Nothing could be more sure of constant sale. It is not an article of changeable fashion, but of absolute, permanent necessity, and such, therefore, as would always meet a steady demand. Sir, I think it would be well for the chairman of the committee to revise his premises, for I am persuaded that there is an ingredient properly belonging to the calculation which he has misstated or omitted. Swedes iron in England pays a duty, I think, of about $27 per ton; yet it is imported in considerable quantities, notwithstanding the vast capital, the excellent coal, and, more important than all perhaps, the highly improved state of inland navigation in England; although I am aware that the English use of Swedes iron may be thought to be owing in some degree to its superior quality.

Sir, the true explanation of this appears to me to lie in the different prices *of labor;* and here I apprehend is the grand mistake in the argument of the chairman of the committee. He says it would cost the nation, as a nation, nothing, to make our ore into iron. Now, I think it would cost us precisely that which we can worst afford; that is, great *labor.* Although bar-iron is very properly considered a raw material in respect to its various future uses, yet, as bar-iron, the principal ingredient in its cost is labor. Of manual labor, no nation has more than a certain quantity, nor can it be increased at will. As to some operations, indeed, its place may be supplied by machinery; but there are other services which machinery cannot perform for it, and which it must perform for itself. A most important question for every nation, as well as for every individual, to propose to itself, is, how it can best apply that quantity of labor which it is able to perform. Labor is the great producer of wealth; it moves all other causes. If it call machinery to its aid, it is still employed, not only in using the machinery, but in making it. Now, with respect to the quantity of labor, as we all know, different nations are differently circumstanced. Some need, more than any thing, work for hands, others require hands for work; and if we ourselves are not absolutely in the latter class, we are still most fortunately very near it. I cannot find that we have those idle hands, of which the chairman of the committee speaks. The price of labor is a conclusive and unanswerable refutation of that idea; it is known to be higher with us than in any other civilized state, and this is the greatest of all proofs of general happiness. Labor in this country is independent and proud. It has not to ask the patronage of capital but capital solicits the aid of labor. This is the general truth in regard to the condition of our whole population, although in the large cities there are doubtless many exceptions. The mere capacity to labor in common agricultural employments, gives to our young men the assurance of independence. We have been asked, Sir, by the chairman of the committee, in a tone of some pathos, whether we will

allow to the serfs of Russia and Sweden the benefit of making iron for us. Let me inform the gentleman, Sir, that those same serfs do not earn more than seven cents a day, and that they work in these mines for that compensation because they are serfs. And let me ask the gentleman further, whether we have any labor in this country that cannot be better employed than in a business which does not yield the laborer more than seven cents a day? This, it appears to me, is the true question for our consideration. There is no reason for saying that we will work iron because we have mountains that contain the ore. We might for the same reason dig among our rocks for the scattered grains of gold and silver which might be found there. The true inquiry is, Can we produce the article in a useful state at the same cost, or nearly at the same cost, or at any reasonable approximation towards the same cost, at which we can import it?

Some general estimates of the price and profits of labor, in those countries from which we import our iron, might be formed by comparing the reputed products of different mines, and their prices, with the number of hands employed. The mines of Danemora are said to yield about 4,000 tons, and to employ in the mines twelve hundred workmen. Suppose this to be worth $50 per ton; any one will find by computation, that the whole product would not pay, in this country, for one quarter part of the necessary labor. The whole export of Sweden was estimated, a few years ago, at 400,000 ship pounds, or about 54,000 tons. Comparing this product with the number of workmen usually supposed to be employed in the mines which produce iron for exportation, the result will not greatly differ from the foregoing. These estimates are general, and might not conduct us to a precise result; but we know, from intelligent travellers, and eyewitnesses, that the price of labor in the Swedish mines does not exceed seven cents a day.[7]

7. DW's note here reads, "The price of labor in Russia may be pretty well collected from Tooke's *View of the Russian Empire*. 'The workmen in the mines and the foundries are, indeed, all called master-people; but they distinguish themselves into masters, under-masters, apprentices, delvers, servants, carriers, washers, and separators. In proportion to their ability their wages are regulated, which proceed from fifteen to upwards of thirty roubles per annum. The provisions which they receive from the magazines are deducted from this pay.' The value of the rouble at that time (1799) was about twenty-four pence sterling, or forty-five cents of our money.

" 'By the edict of 1799,' it is added, 'a laborer with a horse shall receive, daily, in summer, twenty, and in winter, twelve copecks; a laborer without a horse, in summer, ten, in winter, eight copecks.'

"A copeck is the hundredth part of a rouble, or about half a cent of our money. The price of labor may have risen, in some degree, since that period, but probably not much."

The date 1799, twice repeated in the note, should be 1779. The first

The true reason, Sir, why it is not our policy to compel our citizens to manufacture our own iron, is, that they are far better employed. It is an unproductive business, and they are not poor enough to be obliged to follow it. If we had more of poverty, more of misery, and something of servitude, if we had an ignorant, idle, starving population, we might set up for iron makers against the world.

The committee will take notice, Mr. Chairman, that, under our present duty, together with the expense of transportation, our manufacturers are able to supply their own immediate neighborhood; and this proves the magnitude of that substantial encouragement which these two causes concur to give. There is litte or no foreign iron, I presume, used in the county of Lancaster. This is owing to the heavy expense of land carriage; and, as we recede farther from the coast, the manufacturers are still more completely secured, as to their own immediate market, against the competition of the imported article. But what they ask is to be allowed to supply the sea-coast, at such a price as shall be formed by adding to the cost at the mines the expense of land carriage to the sea; and this appears to me most unreasonable. The effect of it would be to compel the consumer to pay the cost of two land transportations; for, in the first place, the price of iron at the inland furnaces will always be found to be at, or not much below, the price of the imported article in the seaport, and the cost of transportation to the neighborhood of the furnace; and to enable the home product to hold a competition with the imported in the seaport, the cost of another transportation downward, from the furnace to the coast, must be added. Until our means of inland commerce be improved, and the charges of transportation by that means lessened, it appears to me wholly impracticable, with such duties as any one would think of proposing, to meet the wishes of the manufacturers of this article. Suppose we were to add the duty proposed by this bill, although it would benefit the capital invested in works near the sea and the navigable rivers, yet the benefit would not extend far in the interior. Where, then, are we to stop, or what limit is proposed to us?

The freight of iron has been afforded from Sweden to the United States as low as eight dollars per ton. This is not more than the price of fifty miles of land carriage. Stockholm, therefore, for the purpose of this argument, may be considered as within fifty miles of Philadelphia. Now, it is at once a just and a strong view of this case, to consider, that there

---

few words of the second paragraph should not be in quotation marks, and the remainder of the quote begins with a capital letter. Figures in Tooke are in Arabic numerals. See William Tooke, *View of the Rus-* *sian Empire During the Reign of Catherine the Second, and to the Close of the Eighteenth Century*, 2d. ed. (3 vols., London, 1800; reprinted New York, 1970), pp. 310, 338.

are, within fifty miles of our market, vast multitudes of persons who are willing to labor in the production of this article for us, at the rate of seven cents per day, while we have no labor which will not command, upon the average, at least five or six times that amount. The question is, then, shall we buy this article of these manufacturers, and suffer our own labor to earn its greater reward, or shall we employ our own labor in a similar manufacture, and make up to it, by a tax on consumers, the loss which it must necessarily sustain.

I proceed, Sir, to the article of hemp. Of this we imported last year, in round numbers, 6,000 tons, paying a duty of $30 a ton, or $180,000 on the whole amount; and this article, it is to remembered, is consumed almost entirely in the uses of navigation. The whole burden may be said to fall on one interest. It is said we can produce this article if we will raise the duties. But why is it not produced now? or why, at least, have we not seen some specimens? for the present is a very high duty, when expenses of importation are added. Hemp was purchased at St. Petersburg, last year, at $101.67 per ton. Charges attending shipment, &c., $14.25. Freight may be stated at $30 per ton, and our existing duty $30 more. These three last sums, being the charges of transportation, amount to a protection of near seventy-five per cent. in favor of the home manufacturer, if there be any such. And we ought to consider, also, that the price of hemp at St. Petersburg is increased by all the expense of transportation from the place of growth to that port; so that probably the whole cost of transportation, from the place of growth to our market, including our duty, is equal to the first cost of the article; or, in other words, is a protection in favor of our own product of one hundred per cent.

And since it is stated that we have great quantities of fine land for the production of hemp, of which I have no doubt, the question recurs, Why is it not produced? I speak of the water-rotted hemp, for it is admitted that that which is dew-rotted is not sufficiently good for the requisite purposes. I cannot say whether the cause be in climate, in the process of rotting, or what else, but the fact is certain, that there is no American water-rotted hemp in the market. We are acting, therefore, upon an hypothesis. Is it not reasonable that those who say that they *can* produce the article shall at least prove the truth of that allegation, before new taxes are laid on those who use the foreign commodity? Suppose this bill passes; the price of hemp is immediately raised $14.80 per ton, and this burden falls immediately on the ship-builder; and no part of it, for the present, will go for the benefit of the American grower, because he has none of the article that can be used, nor is it expected that much of it will be produced for a considerable time. Still the tax takes

effect upon the imported article; and the ship-owners, to enable the Kentucky farmer to receive an additional $14 on his ton of hemp, whenever he may be able to raise and manufacture it, pay, in the meantime, an equal sum per ton into the treasury on all the imported hemp which they are still obliged to use; and this is called "protection!" Is this just or fair? A particular interest is here burdened, not only for the benefit of another particular interest, but burdened also beyond that, for the benefit of the treasury. It is said to be important for the country that this article should be raised in it; then let the country bear the expense, and pay the bounty. If it be for the good of the whole, let the sacrifice be made by the whole, and not by a part. If it be thought useful and necessary, from political considerations, to encourage the growth and manufacture of hemp, government has abundant means of doing it. It might give a direct bounty, and such a measure would, at least, distribute the burden equally; or, as government itself is a great consumer of this article, it might stipulate to confine its own purchases to the home product, so soon as it should be shown to be of the proper quality. I see no objection to this proceeding, if it be thought to be an object to encourage the production. It might easily, and perhaps properly, be provided by law, that the navy should be supplied with American hemp, the quality being good, at any price not exceeding, by more than a given amount, the current price of foreign hemp in our market. Every thing conspires to render some such course preferable to the one now proposed. The encouragement in that way would be ample, and, if the experiment should succeed, the whole object would be gained; and if it should fail, no considerable loss or evil would be felt by any one.

I stated, some days ago, and I wish to renew the statement, what was the amount of the proposed augmentation of the duties on iron and hemp, in the cost of a vessel. Take the case of a common ship of three hundred tons, not coppered, nor copper-fastened. It would stand thus, by the present duties: —

14½ tons of iron, for hull, rigging, and anchors, at $15 per ton,	$217.50
10 tons of hemp, at $30,	300.00
40 bolts Russia duck, at $2,	80.00
20 bolts Ravens duck, at $1.25,	25.00
On articles of ship-chandlery, cabin furniture, hardware, &c.,	40.00
	$662.50

The bill proposes to add,—

$7.40 per ton on iron, which will be	$107.30

$14.80 per ton on hemp, equal to 148.00
And on duck, by the late amendment of the bill,
  say 25 per cent., 25.00
  $280.30

But to the duties on iron and hemp should be added those paid on copper, whenever that article is used. By the statement I furnished the other day, it appeared that the duties received by government on articles used in the construction of a vessel of three hundred and fifty-nine tons, with copper fastenings, amounted to $1,056. With the augmentations of this bill, they would be equal to $1,400.

Now I cannot but flatter myself, Mr. Chairman, that, before the committee will consent to this new burden upon the shipping interest, it will very deliberately weigh the probable consequences. I would again urgently solicit its attention to the condition of that interest. We are told that government has protected it, by discriminating duties, and by an exclusive right to the coasting trade. But it would retain the coasting trade, by its own natural efforts, in like manner, and with more certainty, than it now retains any portion of foreign trade. The discriminating duties are now abolished, and while they existed, they were nothing more than countervailing measures; not so much designed to give our navigation an advantage over that of other nations, as to put it upon an equality; and we have, accordingly, abolished ours, when they have been willing to abolish theirs. Look to the rate of freights. Were they ever lower, or even so low? I ask gentlemen who know, whether the harbor of Charleston, and the river of Savannah, be not crowded with ships seeking employment, and finding none? I would ask the gentlemen from New Orleans, if their magnificent Mississippi does not exhibit, for furlongs, a forest of masts? The condition, Sir, of the shipping interest is not that of those who are insisting on high profits, or struggling for monopoly; but it is the condition of men content with the smallest earnings, and anxious for their bread. The freight of cotton has formerly been three pence sterling, from Charleston to Liverpool, in time of peace. It is now I know not what, or how many fractions of a penny; I think, however, it is stated at five eighths. The producers, then, of this great staple, are able, by means of this navigation, to send it, for a cent a pound, from their own doors to the best market in the world.

Mr. Chairman, I will now only remind the committee that, while we are proposing to add new burdens to the shipping interest, a very different line of policy is followed by our great commercial and maritime rival. It seems to be announced as the sentiment of the government of England, and undoubtedly it is its real sentiment, that the first of all manufactures is the manufacture of ships. A constant and wakeful at-

tention is paid to this interest, and very important regulations, favorable to it, have been adopted within the last year, some of which I will beg leave to refer to, with the hope of exciting the notice, not only of the committee, but of all others who may feel, as I do, a deep interest in this subject. In the first place, a general amendment has taken place in the register acts, introducing many new provisions, and, among others, the following: —

A direct mortgage of the interest of a ship is allowed, without subjecting the mortgagee to the responsibility of an owner.

The proportion of interest held by each owner is exhibited in the register, thereby facilitating both sales and mortgages, and giving a new value to shipping among the moneyed classes.

Shares, in the ships of copartnerships, may be registered as joint property, and subject to the same rules as other partnership effects.

Ships may be registered in the name of trustees, for the benefit of joint-stock companies.

And many other regulations are adopted, with the same general view of rendering the mode of holding the property as convenient and as favorable as possible.

By another act, British registered vessels, of every description, are allowed to enter into the general and the coasting trade in the India seas, and may now trade to and from India, with any part of the world, except China.

By a third, all limitations and restrictions, as to latitude and longitude, are removed from ships engaged in the Southern whale-fishery. These regulations, I presume, have not been made without first obtaining the consent of the East India Company; so true is it found, that real encouragement of enterprise oftener consists, in our days, in restraining or buying off monopolies and prohibitions, than in imposing or extending them.

The trade with Ireland is turned into a free coasting trade; light duties have been reduced, and various other beneficial arrangements made, and still others proposed. I might add, that, in favor of general commerce, and as showing their confidence in the principles of liberal intercourse, the British government has perfected the warehouse system, and authorized a reciprocity of duties with foreign states, at the discretion of the Privy Council.

This, Sir, is the attention which our great rival is paying to these important subjects, and we may assure ourselves that, if we do not cherish a proper sense of our own interests, she will not only beat us, but will deserve to beat us.

Sir, I will detain you no longer. There are some parts of this bill which I highly approve; there are others in which I should acquiesce;

but those to which I have now stated my objections appear to me so destitute of all justice, so burdensome and so dangerous to that interest which has steadily enriched, gallantly defended, and proudly distinguished us, that nothing can prevail upon me to give it my support.[8]

8. The pamphlet adds a three-page excerpt from a speech made by Chancellor of the Exchequer Frederick John Robinson subsequent to Webster's delivery of this speech but prior to its publication as a pamphlet. See *The Parliamentary Debates*, n.s., 10: 327 ff.

The Cumberland Road Bill, January 18, 1825

In March of 1806 Congress appropriated $30,000 "to defray the expenses of laying out and making" a road from Cumberland, Maryland to the Ohio River. Its purpose was to provide a link between the new state of Ohio and the Atlantic seaboard. The Cumberland Road, or National Pike as it came to be called, was included in Albert Gallatin's farseeing program of public transportation in 1808; but the walls of strict construction were closing in. The road had been justified, tacitly if not overtly, by the same logic that had justified the Louisiana purchase: it was necessary to insure the continuance of the Union.

After the war of 1812, the argument no longer held. Each request for funds, to continue or to resurface portions of the road met new opposition from those who held highway construction to be outside the constitutional power of the Federal Government. President Madison vetoed a sweeping internal improvement program on his last day of office, and Monroe tended to follow the lead of his predecessor. It was this matter of power as well as the aspect of expediency to which Webster addressed himself in the brief speech printed below. The road then terminated just below Wheeling on the Ohio River, fulfilling its original authorization. The new appropriation was to carry it to Zanesville, a third of the way across the state of Ohio.

Creeping west by small increments and mighty arguments but still not too far behind the advancing settlements, the National Road got as far as Vandalia, Illinois, by 1838. It got no farther, halted by economic depression and the growing competition of the railroads.

The text below is from *Writings & Speeches*, 14: 92–100, which follows the *National Intelligencer*, January 20, 1825, and *Register of Debates*, 18th Cong., 2d sess., pp. 249–252, 254–255.

Mr. Webster of Massachusetts then rose and said, that, as he was in favor of the bill, he should say a few words in explanation of the reasons which led him to vote for it. As to the question of power in this House to make appropriations for objects of internal improvement, he should at this time say nothing. When that question was so much agitated in 1816,

he had made his opinions respecting it openly known,[1] he was, of course, ready to change them whenever he could be brought to doubt the constitutional foundation on which that power rests.

At present the question was a different one, inasmuch as the present bill might be passed without the assumption of any power different from what has been exercised by this House for these twenty years. The bill, it is true, carries the principle of former acts somewhat further, but it does not alter the principle.[2]

On this subject, as on all others, Mr. Webster said, he wished to bring to the discussion a right feeling—that is, a feeling truly national. It mattered nothing to him who was to be immediately benefited. *Tros Tyriusque*, whether an inhabitant of the banks of the Merrimac of New Hampshire, or the Merrimac of the Missouri, he cared not; provided he be a subject of our legislation, he has claims, said Mr. Webster, on my impartial consideration. If he had been led, since the discussion of 1816, to alter his opinion on any part of the general subject then debated, it was that which respects an equal distribution of the public expenditures through the different parts of the Union, according to their population. He doubted, extremely, the propriety, and even the power of Congress to carry on legislation on the principle of balancing the local interests of different sections of the country. If the business of legislation has been committed to us at all, the whole subject is in our power and under our discretion. He doubted whether Congress had power to adopt a system which should go on the professed principle of distributing the public moneys *pro rata*; having respect to the different portions of the Union merely in a numerical view of them. When Congress legislates at all, it must legislate for a whole, and not for twenty-four parts. The idea had been brought forward, as being calculated to prevent a merely local legislation; but it was, in truth, itself a local idea. Such a system would rest on a foundation essentially vicious. When going into a system of improvement, the House has simply to inquire, where is improvement most wanted? He cared not whether it was beyond the Alleghanies, or beyond the Missouri; wherever it was most needed, there it must first be made. He supposed the House had power to decide which of the various objects was most pressing; but he denied that it had the power to enter into the consideration of a principle of mere numerical calculation, in under-

1. The record indicates that Webster did not participate in the public discussion of internal improvements at this time. He did, however, vote in favor of Calhoun's "Bonus Bill" and again to sustain that bill over Madison's veto.

2. In the legislation authorizing the Cumberland Road, Congress resolved the constitutional issue by entering into "compacts" with the states. These compacts set aside 2% of the proceeds from the sale of public lands for internal improvements, and exempted federal lands from state taxation for five years.

takings for the public good. On the present subject, it was his opinion that the States which had been admitted under the stipulations[3] which had been stated, had, in fairness, a right to expect the Government to proceed with this road.

Taking the different statutes together, it seemed to be holden out that Government would make a road leading to those States. Congress had acted again and again on this idea; and he asked, where was the difference between the present appropriation and those which had been formerly granted for this same road? All that can be said is, that the Government has made advances on a fund which is incompetent to repay them, and so the present amounts to a direct grant. Well; had not this been done before? The appropriations for the Cumberland road had, many of them, been made when it was known that that fund was inadequate. The case is no worse now. The degree only is different. The principle is the same; and he thought that the Western States might fairly expect this object to be effected on the ground of their several contracts. The next question was, is this a fit object for which to appropriate? Gentlemen say it is not a national object. But he knew of no work equally beneficial to all the twenty-four States. What, asked Mr. Webster, is a national object? Is nothing to be so denominated except what benefits every part of the United States? Congress last year voted a sum to improve certain harbors on Lake Erie; was this of any benefit to Alabama or New Orleans? They had appropriated money for the repairs of Plymouth beach; could this be any benefit to the citizens of Indiana? Works surely may be denominated national which are of extensive importance, although the benefit may not be strictly universal. The fortifications, for instance, which had been erected on the Chesapeake are national only because many have an interest in them. The degree of interest in these works between those who lived on the shores of the Chesapeake and the shores of Lake Michigan was so widely different that the latter may, in comparison, be said to have no interest in them. Yet certainly those fortifications were a fit subject of appropriation, and it was the duty of Congress to erect them.

With respect to the present road, he asked, how did the concern of the General Government in it begin? He presumed the origin of that concern was to be found in the connection of Government with its great territory of public lands. This was the idea out of which grew the reser-

3. In March, 1803 Congress passed an addendum to the act granting Ohio statehood, establishing a compact to set aside 2% of the revenues from the sale of public lands for the construction of a road to the Ohio border. The federal government entered into similar compacts with Indiana, Illinois, and Missouri. See 2 *U.S. Stat.* 226; 3 *U.S. Stat.* 290, 430, 547.

vation of the two per cent fund. It was intended, doubtless, as an inducement to the settlement of the public lands; and none, surely, can doubt that Government may rightfully hold out considerations calculated to bring the public lands to a better market. The reason for making the road is still the same. Those lands are still in market, and every rod which is added to this road increases the value and is calculated to raise the price of those lands.

Another consideration was, the great accommodation which such a line of road would furnish to all the Western States. With respect to those States, the object was strictly a general one. Let me ask, said Mr. Webster, if Government were about to erect a fort or an arsenal, or to build ships of war, and it was possible that any of these objects would require so small a sum as that now asked for, whether anybody would then hesitate? If, then, the object was legitimate, if it was useful to all our citizens, and especially so to those who now ask it, might not Congress lawfully make it? As to the incidental advantages accruing from the expenditure of so much of the public money as was now proposed to be appropriated, he was confident they had been overrated. The expenditure of one hundred and fifty thousand dollars could be no great boon to any of the States. For his own part, he felt glad that this money was to be laid out beyond the mountains. He did not hesitate to avow that he should be yet more glad, could more of the public money be expended there. Such were his feelings, whether right or wrong; and such his views, whether correct or erroneous.

And here he would state what he conceived to be the true situation of that part of the Union. The people he considered as being substantially rich; yet, having no markets, they were without the means of converting their riches to many desirable purposes of common life. And, in such a situation, the expenditure of comparatively a small sum of money might do much in promoting the comfort of the people. There could be no doubt, if gentlemen looked at the money received into the Treasury from the sale of the public lands to the West, and then looked to the whole amount expended by Government, even including the whole of what was laid out for the army, the latter must be allowed to be very inconsiderable, and there must be a constant drain of money from the West, to pay for the public lands. It might, indeed, be said that this was no more than the refluence of capital which had previously gone over the mountains. Be it so. Still, its practical effect was to produce inconvenience, if not distress, by absorbing the money of the people. It was as true of the West as of other parts of the country, that the consumer pays the tax. The public revenue was not raised in Boston, or New York, or Charleston. The West paid as much of that revenue as the East, in proportion to its consumption; nay, on a strict calculation, something more. They pay

the tax, and a profit on transportation. True, indeed, the money was collected in the custom-house, yet it was first paid where the imported articles were consumed. It could not be paid in the seaports, if it had not first been received in the interior. Some gentlemen said we must wait till a system is formed—that is, some system of internal improvement so equal in its bearings and so satisfactory in its details that all shall agree in adopting it. He feared, if gentlemen waited till then, they would have to wait till they grew very old. He suspected that few of those who heard him would travel over the roads or sail upon the canals constructed after the adoption of the system. How long would it take merely to make the surveys for such a system? Was any man to be found bold enough to undertake to sketch out a system of internal improvements extending for twenty years to come? He would venture to say that no one man could form a plan in which he could get five others to agree. The thing was impracticable—and impracticable for this reason: that our entire condition was merely in a process of development. The country was changing every day and every hour; new views were continually presenting themselves; new wants were continually discovered; new resources were constantly unfolding themselves; new connections were every day taking place; individuals were doing much; States were doing much; and he was satisfied that, if Congress was never to act on individual cases, but only on a universal system, it would never act at all.

This road was wanted; it was wanted now; it was wanted more now than it would be to-morrow; and the expense of making it to-day would be no more than of making it to-morrow. In the settlement of a new country, roads were all-important. The sooner they were opened, the greater was their value and importance to the settlers. Ought not the road, then, if it is to be made at all, to be made now?

As to the burden of this appropriation, he agreed, indeed, with the gentleman from South Carolina, that it was proper to limit the public expenditure within reasonable bounds, and to keep down the public debt. Yet he must be permitted to ask, what was likely to be the prodigious effect of this one hundred and fifty thousand dollars upon the public debt? If this was a question which might not be asked now, how could it be asked when the system had been adopted, and an expenditure, not of one hundred and fifty thousand dollars, but fifty millions of dollars, would be called for to carry it into effect? That, indeed, would be a formidable subject of consideration (and one which he suspected would always operate to prevent the adoption of such a system); but now the amount was certainly too small to be in the least degree onerous to the public resources. In illustration of the principle that a general system was slow in being adopted, and that it would be necessary to commence with some particular object, Mr. Webster referred to the act

of last session, for removing obstructions in the Mississippi and Ohio rivers. It was then thought extraordinary, by many gentlemen, that an object in which nine different States were each greatly interested should have remained so long unaccomplished. But that circumstance was, perhaps, the most operative reason why it had not been done. Among so many States, it was difficult to obtain mutual counsel and united effort; and they thus continued to neglect an improvement, the want of which had occasioned, at different times, the loss of half a million of dollars, although it was found that responsible individuals were now ready to undertake it for sixty-five thousand dollars; a sum which, at least in the Eastern States, would not be viewed as a heavy burden for one single county, or even for a single town. He regarded the country as under a general expectation of aid from the General Government in respect to the subject of roads. Congress had virtually said to the people of the West, that the road should be carried on till it reached them all; and though it might not have said this in any formal act, yet it had virtually been given out in the speeches made on this floor. The people consider it as under pledge; and the present bill, in carrying on the road for eighty miles, does but carry Congress eighty miles further towards the redeeming of its pledge.

Government, he believed, had received eighteen or twenty millions of dollars from the public lands, and it was with the greatest satisfaction he adverted to the change which had been introduced in the mode of paying for them,[4] yet he could never think that the national domain was to be regarded as any great source of revenue. The great object of the Government, in respect to those lands, was not so much the money derived from their sale as it was the getting of them settled. What he meant to say was, that he did not think they ought to hug that domain as a great treasure, which was to enrich the exchequer; yet the consideration that Government has already received large sums from it had great weight with them, when the persons who proposed it came to this House, and asked a small appropriation to aid them in doing so.

Mr. [George] McDuffie of South Carolina having made some remarks in opposition to the bill, Mr. Webster observed in reply, that the gentleman from South Carolina had mistaken him if he supposed that it was his wish so to hasten the sales of the public lands as to throw them into the hands of purchasers who would sell again. His idea only went as far as this: that the price should be fixed as low as not to prevent the settlement of the lands, yet not so low as to tempt speculators to pur-

---

4. Congress passed a law on April 24, 1820 that abolished the credit system for purchasing public land; reduced the price of land from $2 to $1.25 per acre; and reduced the minimum purchase from 160 to 80 acres. 3 *U.S. Stat.* 566.

chase. Mr. Webster observed that he could not at all concur with the gentleman from South Carolina, in wishing to restrain the laboring classes of population in the Eastern States from going to any part of our territory where they could better their condition;[5] nor did he suppose that such an idea was anywhere entertained. The observations of the gentleman had opened to him new views of policy on this subject, and he thought he now could perceive why some of our States continued to have such bad roads; it must be for the purpose of preventing people from going out of them. The gentleman from South Carolina supposes that if our population had been confined to the old thirteen States, the aggregate wealth of the country would have been greater than it now is. But, sir, it is an error, that the increase of the aggregate of the national wealth is the object chiefly to be pursued by Government. The distribution of the national wealth is an object quite as important as its increase. He was not surprised that the old States not increasing in population so fast as was expected (for he believed nothing like a decrease was pretended) should be an idea by no means agreeable to gentlemen from those States; we are all reluctant in submitting to the loss of relative importance; but this was nothing more than the natural condition of a country densely populated in one part, and possessing in another a vast tract of unsettled lands. The plan of the gentleman went to reverse the order of nature, vainly expecting to retain men within a small and comparatively unproductive territory, "who have all the world before them, where to choose."[6] For his own part, he was in favor of letting population take its own course; he should experience no feeling of mortification if any of his constituents liked better to settle on the Kansas, or the Arkansas, or the Lord knows where, within our territory; let them go and be happier if they could. The gentleman says our aggregate of wealth would have been greater if our population had been restrained within the limits of the old States; but does he not consider population to be wealth? And has not this been increased by the settlement of a new and fertile country? Such a country presents the most alluring of all prospects to a young and laboring man; it gives him a freehold; it offers to him weight and respectability in society; and, above all, it presents to him a prospect of a permanent provision for his children. Sir, these are inducements which never were resisted, and never will be; and, were the whole extent of country filled with population up to the Rocky Mountains, these inducements would carry that population forward to the shores of the Pacific Ocean. Sir, it is in vain to talk; individuals will seek their own good, and not any artificial aggregate of the national wealth; a young, enter-

5. McDuffie's comments are found in *Register of Debates*, 18th Cong., 2d sess., pp. 245–255.

6. Milton, *Paradise Lost*, Book 12, line 646.

prising, and hardy agriculturist can conceive of nothing better to him than plenty of good, cheap land.

I may have misunderstood what the gentleman from South Carolina first said, in relation to the collection and disbursement of the revenue. I now understand his remarks as only applying to the disturbance in the currency of any portion of the country where large amounts of the revenue are collected, without being again expended. It is true that those who make an immediate advance of the revenue to Government must suffer if it does not return into their hands by means of sale and consumption; but I believe that the credit usually allowed by Government to importing merchants is about equal to that allowed by them to the purchasers of goods.

Speech at Faneuil Hall on the Election of 1825, April 3, 1825

"I made a small speech here, a week ago, in Faneuil Hall," Webster wrote to a friend, "of which I shall send you a copy, as reported. There is little in it, of good or evil." (DW to Julius von Wallenstein, April 10, 1825, *Correspondence*, Supplementary Calendar, 7: 606.) Indeed, at the time, it must have seemed innocuous enough. The scars left by the election of 1824 were not yet as discernible as they would soon become. Although John Quincy Adams had been fairly elected as the Constitution provided, his majority in the House of Representatives, where the ultimate choice was made, included the support of three states carried at the polls by Henry Clay. Andrew Jackson had won a larger electoral vote, and his partisans were resentful. When Adams offered the State Department to Clay, and Clay accepted, the Jacksonians were outraged. Charges that a "corrupt bargain" had been struck between the two men were current even before the inauguration and were to persist through the four years of Adams's term.

It was a term characterized by the emergence of a new party alignment, with chronic infighting as the two coalitions tested their strength. Clay's following joined Adams's partisans to form the "National Republican" party. Conservative in its philosophy and nationalist in its aims, it drew elements from both Jeffersonians and Federalists of an earlier day. Jackson became the rallying point of the opposition, calling his party "The Democracy," but the Jacksonians too absorbed both doctrine and partisans from the predecessor parties. The Democrats were soon joined by the followers of William H. Crawford, the other casualty of 1824; by the adherents of Martin Van Buren's "Albany Regency"; and eventually by Vice President John C. Calhoun.

Webster had turned his considerable power of persuasion to securing Adams's election, but he well understood how brittle the initial situation was. In the speech printed below he is appealing to all factions in Massachusetts for political harmony. The state elections were about to be held, he hoped without rancor, and without in any way jeopardizing the Adams administration's chances of success.

The text here is from *Writings and Speeches*, 2: 5–10, which merely reprints *Works*, 1: 155–160. The same text, which was in turn the source

for *Works*, appears in *Speeches and Forensic Arguments*, 1: 97–101. The original source, duplicated with no change more serious than variations in punctuation and capitalization, is the report in the Boston *Courier*, April 5, 1825.

Mr. Webster said, he was quite unaccustomed to appear in that place; having on no occasion addressed his fellow-citizens there, either to recommend or to oppose the support of any candidates for public office. He had long been of opinion, that to preserve the distinction and the hostility of political parties was not consistent with the highest degree of public good. At the same time, he did not find fault with the conduct, nor question the motives, of those who thought otherwise. But, entertaining this opinion, he had habitually abstained from attending on those occasions on which the merits of public men, and of candidates for office, were discussed, necessarily with more or less reference to party attachment and party organization.

The present was an occasion of a different kind. The sentiment which had called this meeting together was one of union and conciliation; a sentiment so congenial to his own feelings, and to his opinion of the public interest, that he could not resist the inclination to be present, and to express his entire and hearty concurrence.

He should forbear, he said, from all remarks upon the particular names which had been recommended by the committee. They had been selected, he must presume, fairly, and with due consideration, by those who were appointed for that purpose. In cases of this sort, every one cannot expect to find every thing precisely as he might wish it; but those who concurred in the general sentiment which dictated the selection would naturally allow that sentiment to prevail as far as possible over particular objections.

On the general question he would make a few remarks, begging the indulgence of the meeting if he should say any thing which might with more propriety proceed from others.

He hardly conceived how well disposed and intelligent minds could differ as to the question, whether party contest and party strife, organized, systematic, and continued, were of themselves desirable ingredients in the composition of society. Difference of opinion on political subjects, honorable competition, and emulous rivalry, may indeed be useful. But these are very different things from organized and systematic party combinations. He admitted, it was true, that party associations were sometimes unavoidable, and perhaps necessary to the accomplishment of other ends and purposes. But this did not prove that, of themselves, they were good; or that they should be continued and preserved

for their own sake, when there had ceased to be any object to be effected by them.

But there were those who supposed, that, whether political party distinctions were or were not useful, it was impossible to abolish them. Now he thought, on the contrary, that, under present circumstances, it was quite impossible to continue them. New parties, indeed, might arise, growing out of new events or new questions; but as to those old parties which had sprung from controversies now no longer pending, or from feelings which time and other causes had now changed, or greatly allayed, he did not believe that they could long remain. Efforts, indeed, made to that end, with zeal and perseverance, might delay their extinction, but, he thought, could not prevent it. There was nothing to keep alive these distinctions in the interests and objects which now engaged society. New questions and new objects arise, having no connection with the subjects of past controversies, and present interest overcomes or absorbs the recollection of former controversies. Those who are united on these existing questions and present interests will not be disposed to weaken their efforts to promote them, by angry reflections on past differences. If there were nothing *in things* to divide about, he thought the people not likely to maintain systematic controversies about *men*. They have no interest in so doing. Associations formed to support *principles* may be called *parties*; but if they have no bond of union but adherence to particular *men*, they become *factions*.

The people, in his opinion, were at present grateful to all parties for whatever of good they had accomplished, and indulgent to all for whatever of error they had committed; and, with these feelings, were now mainly intent on the great objects which affected their present interests. There might be exceptions to this remark; he was afraid there were; but, nevertheless, such appeared to him to be the general feeling in the country. It was natural that some prejudices should remain longer than their causes, as the waves lash the shore for a time after the storm has subsided; but the tendency of the elements was to repose. Monopolies of all sorts were getting out of fashion; they were yielding to liberal ideas, and to the obvious justice and expediency of fair competition.

An administration of the general government, which had been in general highly satisfactory to the country, had now closed. He was not aware that it could with propriety be said, that that administration had been either supported or opposed, by any party associations or on any party principles. Certain it was, that, as far as there had been any organized opposition to the administration, it had nothing to do with former parties. A new administration had now commenced, and he need hardly say that the most liberal and conciliatory principles had been

avowed in the Inaugural Address of the newly elected President.[1] It could not be doubted that his administration would conform to those principles. Thus far, he believed, its course had given general satisfaction. After what they all had seen in relation to the gentleman holding the highest appointment in the executive department under the President,[2] he would take this opportunity to say, that, having been a member of the House of Representatives for six years, during the greater part of which time Mr. Clay had presided in that House, he was most happy in being able, in a manner less formal and more explicit than by concurring in the usual vote of thanks, to express his own opinion of his liberality, independence, and honorable feeling. And he would take this occasion also to add, if his opinion could be of any value in such a case, that he thought nothing more unfounded than that that gentleman owed his present situation to any unworthy compromise or arrangement whatever. He owed it to his talent, to his prominent standing in the community, to his course of public service, not now a short one, and to the high estimation in which he stands with that part of the country to which he belongs.

Remarks, Mr. Webster proceeded to say, had been made from the chair, very kind and partial, as to the manner in which he had discharged the duties which he owed to his constituents in the House of Representatives. He wished to say, that if he had been able to render any, the humblest services, either to the public or his constituents, in that place, it was owing wholly to the liberal manner in which his efforts there had been received.

Having alluded to the Inaugural Address, he did not mean in the slightest degree to detract from its merits, when he now said, that, in his opinion, if either of the other candidates[3] had succeeded in the election, he also would have adopted a liberal course of policy. He had no reason to believe that the sentiments of either of those gentlemen were, in this respect, narrow or contracted. He fully believed the contrary, in regard to both of them; but if they had been otherwise, he thought still that expediency or necessity would have controlled their inclinations.

I forbear, said Mr. Webster, from pursuing these remarks farther. I repeat, that I do not complain of those who have hitherto thought, or who still think, that party organization is necessary to the public good. I do not question their motives; and I wish to be tolerant even to those who think that toleration ought not to be indulged.

It is said, Sir, that prosperity sometimes hardens the heart. Perhaps,

1. See *Messages and Papers*, 2: 294.

2. Henry Clay, appointed secretary of state. See headnote for a brief description of the "corrupt bargain" charge.

3. Andrew Jackson, (1767–1845), and William Harris Crawford (1772–1834).

also, it may sometimes have a contrary effect, and elevate and liberalize the feelings. If this can ever be the result of such a cause, there is certainly in the present condition of the country enough to inspire the most grateful and the kindest feelings. We have a common stock both of happiness and of distinction, of which we are all entitled, as citizens of the country, to partake. We may all rejoice in the general prosperity, in the peace and security which we enjoy, and in the brilliant success which has thus far attended our republican institutions. These are circumstances which may well excite in us all a noble pride. Our civil and political institutions, while they answer for us all the great ends designed by them, furnish at the same time an example to others, and diffuse blessings beyond our own limits. In whatever part of the globe men are found contending for political liberty, they look to the United States with a feeling of brotherhood, and put forth a claim of kindred. The South American states, especially, exhibit a most interesting spectacle. Let the great men who formed our constitutions of government, who still survive, and let the children of those who have gone to their graves, console themselves with the reflection, that, whether they have risen or fallen in the little contests of party, they have not only established the liberty and happiness of their own native land, but have conferred blessings beyond their own country, and beyond their own thoughts, on millions of men and on successions of generations. Under the influence of these institutions, received and adopted in principle from our example, the whole southern continent has shaken off its colonial subjection. A new world, filled with fresh and interesting nations, has risen to our sight. America seems again discovered; not to geography, but to commerce, to social intercourse, to intelligence, to civilization, and to liberty. Fifty years ago, some of those who now hear me, and the fathers of many others, listened in this place to those mighty leaders, [James] Otis and [Samuel] Adams. When they then uttered the spirit-stirring sounds of Independence and Liberty, there was not a foot of land on the continent, inhabited by civilized man, that did not acknowledge the dominion of European power. Thank God, at this moment, from this place to the south pole, and from sea to sea, there is hardly a foot of land that does.

And, Sir, when these states, thus newly disenthralled and emancipated, assume the tone and bear the port of independence, what language and what ideas do we find associated with their newly acquired liberty? They speak, Sir, of constitutions, of declarations of rights, of the liberty of the press, of a congress, and of representative government. Where, Sir, did they learn these? And when they have applied to their great leader, and the founder of their states,[4] the language of praise and

4. Simon Bolivar (1783–1830), Venezuelan general known as the Liberator.

commendation till they have exhausted it, when unsatisfied gratitude can express itself no otherwise, do they not call him their WASHINGTON? Sir, the Spirit of Continental Independence, the Genius of American Liberty, which in earlier times tried her infant voice in the halls and on the hills of New England, utters it now, with power that seems to wake the dead, on the plains of Mexico, and along the sides of the Andes.

> "Her path, where'er the goddess roves,
> Glory pursues, and generous shame,
> The unconquerable mind, and Freedom's holy flame." [5]

There is one other point of view, Sir, in regard to which I will say a few words, though perhaps at some hazard of misinterpretation.

In the wonderful spirit of improvement and enterprise which animates the country, we may be assured that each quarter will naturally exert its power in favor of objects in which it is interested. This is natural and unavoidable. Each portion, therefore, will use its best means. If the West feels a strong interest in clearing the navigation of its mighty streams, and opening roads through its vast forests, if the South is equally zealous to push the production and augment the prices of its great staples, it is reasonable to expect that these objects will be pursued by the best means which offer themselves. And it may therefore well deserve consideration, whether the commercial and navigating and manufacturing interests of the North do not call on us to aid and support them, by united counsels and united efforts. But I abstain from enlarging on this topic. Let me rather say, that in regard to the whole country a new era has arisen. In a time of peace, the proper pursuits of peace engage society with a degree of enterprise and an intenseness of application heretofore unknown. New objects are opening, and new resources developed, on every side. We tread on a broader theatre; and if, instead of acting our parts according to the novelty and importance of the scene, we waste our strength in mutual crimination and recrimination concerning the past, we shall resemble those navigators, who, having escaped from some crooked and narrow river to the sea, now that the whole ocean is before them, should, nevertheless, occupy themselves with the differences which happened as they passed along among the rocks and the shallows, instead of opening their eyes to the wide horizon around them, spreading their sail to the propitious gale that woos it, raising their quadrant to the sun, and grasping the helm with the conscious hand of a master.

5. Thomas Gray, "The Progress of Poesy," line 64.

The Judiciary, January 4 and 25, 1826

By 1825 the 13 original states had expanded to 24 and the population of the Union had grown from the four million enumerated in the first census to eleven million or more. Yet the system of Federal courts, with only minimal extensions, remained as it had been organized under the Judiciary Act of 1789. There were now some 30 district courts instead of 13, and seven Supreme Court justices instead of six; but the work load had increased enormously, both in volume and in complexity. Especially was this true of the seven United States circuit courts, each presided over by a justice of the Supreme Court. Six of the seven circuits lay in the east where the nation's wealth was concentrated. Only one, comprising the states of Ohio, Kentucky and Tennessee, lay beyond the Appalachians, although the west, aggressive and turbulent, generated its full share and more of legal business. Some of the newer states belonged to no circuit at all, and were forced to rely on the district courts. Dockets were crowded, with little hope of catching up; judges were overworked while litigants grew tired of waiting.

Since the early years of the century there had been agitation for judicial reform, in and out of Congress. A bill making needed changes in the system actually passed the Senate in 1819, but died quietly in the House. Potentially the most effective, the most carefully prepared and most skillfully managed was Webster's attempt of 1825–1826, which among other changes increased the number of Supreme Court justices to ten. A corresponding increase in the number of circuits added two in the west. As chairman of the House Judiciary Committee, Webster introduced his bill in December 1825, called it up after the holidays, and opened the debate on January 4, 1826. Over the next three weeks he remained in control, but limited his own direct participation to occasional explanatory comments. Then on January 25 he summed up the case for his bill, called for a vote, and secured passage by a substantial majority.

The fate of judicial reform for that Congress and for several more to come was decided by politics as usual in the Senate. The House bill was kept on ice until the Panama Mission was disposed of. It then came from the Judiciary Committee, chaired by Martin Van Buren, with amendments. Most significant was a provision joining Ohio with Kentucky,

rather than with Indiana, to form one of the new Western circuits, and requiring that judges should be residents of their circuits. The amendment was designed, as all Washington understood, to preclude the appointment of Postmaster General John McLean of Ohio to the Supreme Court, which already had a Kentucky member. The Senate passed the bill as amended, the House refused to concur, and judiciary reform was again lost between the houses.

The speech printed below joins Webster's opening exposition and his concluding remarks in a single document. This follows Edward Everett's arrangement in *Works*, 3: 150–177, which had Webster's own approval. The text here used is from *Writings and Speeches*, 5: 150–177, which is identical with *Works*. The original source is the *National Intelligencer* of January 5 and of February 4, 1826, from which the version in *Register of Debates*, 19th Cong., 1st sess., pp. 872–880, 1139–1148 is reprinted verbatim. A manuscript of the second portion of this speech, the remarks of January 25 in Webster's hand, belongs to the Chicago Historical Society. The manuscript, with all its numerous interlinings, does not differ from the version noted above. We may assume that the delay in publication from January 25 to February 4 occurred while he was preparing the text for the press. With the first segment of the speech no such delay was needed, since he knew well ahead of time that he would speak, and what he would say.

The bill which is under the consideration of the committee is so simple in its provisions, and so unembarrassed with detail, that little or nothing in the way of explanation merely is probably expected from the committee. But the general importance of the subject, and the material change which the proposed measure embraces, demands some exposition of the reasons which have led the Committee on the Judiciary to submit it to the consideration of the House.[1]

The occasion naturally presents two inquiries: first, whether any evils exist in the administration of justice in the courts of the United States; and secondly, whether, if there be such evils, the proposed bill is a proper and suitable remedy. On both these points it is my duty to express the sentiments which the Committee on the Judiciary entertain. Perhaps, however, Mr. Chairman, before entering into a discussion of these two questions, I may be allowed to state something of the history of this department of the government, and to advert to the several laws which have been, from time to time, enacted respecting its organization.

1. The *National Intelligencer*, Jan. 5, 1826, and *Register of Debates*, 19th Cong., 1st sess., p. 872, reprinted from it, cast the first paragraph in third person indirect discourse and past tense.

The judicial power, which, by the Constitution, was to be exercised by the present government, necessarily engaged the attention of the first Congress. The subject fell into the hands of very able men, and it may well excite astonishment that the system which they prepared and recommended, and which was adopted in the hurried session of the summer of 1789, has thus far been found to fulfil, so well and for so long a time, the great purposes which it was designed to accomplish. The general success of the general system, so far, may well inspire some degree of caution in the minds of those who are called on to alter or amend it.

By the original act of September, 1789,[2] there was to be a Supreme Court, according to the Constitution, which was to consist of six judges, and to hold two sessions a year at the seat of government. The United States, or such of them as had then adopted the Constitution, were to be divided into circuits and districts, and there was to be a District Court in each district, holden by a district judge. The districts were divided into three circuits, the Eastern, the Middle, and the Southern; and there was to be a Circuit Court in each district, to be composed of two of the justices of the Supreme Court, and the district judge for the district. This Circuit Court was to hold two sessions a year in each district, and I need not inform the committee, that the great mass of business, excepting only that of admiralty and maritime jurisdiction, belonged to the Circuit Court as a court of original jurisdiction. It entertained appeals, or writs of error, also, from the decisions of the District Courts, in all cases.

By this arrangement, then, the justices of the Supreme Court were required to hold two sessions of that court annually, at the seat of government, to hear appeals and causes removed by writs of error; and it was required of them also, that two of them should attend in each district twice a year, to hold, with the district judge, a Circuit Court.

It was found that these duties were so burdensome, that they could not be performed. In November, 1792, the judges addressed the President on the subject, (who laid their communication before Congress,) setting forth their inability to perform the services imposed on them by law, without exertions and sacrifices too great to be expected from any men. It was, doubtless, this communication which produced the law of March, 1793,[3] by which it was provided that one judge of the Supreme Court, with the district judge, should constitute the Circuit Court. And, inasmuch as the courts would now consist of two judges, provision was made, perhaps sufficiently awkward and inconvenient, for the case of difference of opinion. It will be observed, Mr. Chairman, that by these laws, thus far, particular justices are not assigned to particular circuits. Any two judges of the Supreme Court, under the first law, and any one, under

2. Sept. 24, 1789. 1 *U.S. Stat.* 73.   3. March 2, 1793. 1 *U.S. Stat.* 333.

that of 1793, with the district judge, constituted a Circuit Court. A change, or alternation, of the judges was contemplated by the law. It was accordingly provided by the act of 1793, that, in case of division of opinion, as the court consisted of but two judges, the question should be continued to the next session, and, if a different judge then appeared, and his opinion coincided with that of his predecessor, judgment should go accordingly.

And here, Mr. Chairman, I wish to observe, that, in my opinion, the original plan of holding the Circuit Courts by different judges, from time to time, was ill-judged and founded on a false analogy. It seems to have been borrowed from the English Courts of Assize and *Nisi Prius;* but the difference in the powers and jurisdiction of the judges in the two cases rendered what was proper for one not a fit model for the other. The English judges at *Nisi Prius,* so far as civil causes are concerned, have nothing to do but try questions of fact by the aid of a jury, on issues or pleadings already settled in the court from which the record proceeds. They give no final judgments; nor do they make interlocutory orders respecting the proceeding and progress of the cause. They take a verdict of the jury on the issues already joined between the parties, and give no other directions in matters of law, than such as become necessary in the course of this trial by jury. Every case begun, therefore, is ordinarily finished. Nothing of that case remains for the judge's successor. If it be tried, the record is taken back with the verdict to Westminster Hall; if it be not tried, the whole case remains for a subsequent occasion. It is, perhaps, surprising, that the very able men who framed the first judicial act did not see the great difference between this manner of proceeding at the English Assizes, and the necessary course of proceeding in our Circuit Courts, with the powers and jurisdictions conferred on those courts. These are courts of final jurisdiction; they not only take verdicts, but give judgments. Here suits are brought, proceeded with through all their stages, tried, and finally determined. And as, in the progress of suits, especially those of equity jurisdiction, it necessarily happens that there are different stages, and successive orders become necessary from term to term, it happened, of course, that the judge was often changed before the cause was decided; he who heard the end had not heard the beginning. When to this is added, that these judges were bred in different schools, and, as to matters of practice, especially, accustomed to different usages, it will be easy to perceive that no small difficulties were to be encountered in the ordinary despatch of business. So, in cases reserved for advisement and further consideration, the judges reserving the question was not the judge to decide it. He who heard the argument was not to make the decision. Without pursuing this part of the case farther, it is quite obvious that such a system could not answer the ends of justice.

The courts, indeed, were called Circuit Courts, which seemed to imply an itinerant character; but, in truth, they resembled much more, in their power and jurisdiction, the English courts sitting in bench, than the Assizes, to which they appear to have been likened.

The act of 1793, by requiring the attendance of only one, instead of two, of the judges of the Supreme Court on the circuits, of course diminished by one half the circuit labors of those judges.

We then come to the law of February, 1801.[4] By this act, the judges of the Supreme Court were relieved from all circuit duties. Provision was made that their number should be reduced, on the first vacancy, from six to five. They were still to hold two sessions annually of the Supreme Court, and circuit judges were appointed to hold the Circuit Court in each district. The provisions of this law are generally known, and it is not necessary to recite them particularly. It is enough to say, that, in five of the six circuits, the Circuit Court was to consist of three judges, specially appointed to constitute such court; and in the sixth, of one judge, specially appointed, and the district judge of the district.

We all know, Sir, that this law lasted but a twelvemonth. It was repealed in toto by the act of the 8th of March, 1802;[5] and a new organization of the Circuit Courts was provided for by the act of the 29th of April of that year.[6] It must be admitted, I think, Sir, that this act made considerable improvements upon the system, as it existed before the act of February, 1801. It took away the itinerary character of the Circuit Courts, by assigning particular justices to particular circuits. This, in my opinion, was a great improvement. It conformed the constitution of the court to the nature of the powers which it exercised. The same judges now heard the cause through all the stages of its progress, and the court became, what its duties properly made it, a court of record, with permanent judges, exercising a various jurisdiction, trying causes at its bar by jury, in cases proper for the intervention of a jury, and rendering final judgments. This act also provided another mode of proceeding with cases in which the two judges composing the Circuit Court should differ in opinion. It prescribed, that such difference should be stated, certified to the Supreme Court, and that that court should decide the question, and certify its decision to the Circuit Court.

In this state of things, the judicial system remained, without material change, until the year 1807, when a law was passed for the appointment of an additional judge of the Supreme Court, and a circuit allotted to him in the Western States.

It may be here observed, that, from the commencement, the system has not been uniform. From the first, there was an anomaly in it. By the origi-

4. Feb. 13, 1801. 2 *U.S. Stat.* 89.   6. 2 *U.S. Stat.* 156.
5. 2 *U.S. Stat.* 132.

nal act of September, 1789, a District Court was established for Kentucky (then part of Virginia) and for Maine (then part of Massachusetts), and, in addition to the powers of District Courts, there was conferred on these all the jurisdiction which elsewhere belongs to Circuit Courts, and, in other cases, as new States were added to the Union, District Courts were established with the powers of Circuit Courts. The same thing has happened, too, when States have been divided into two districts. There are, at present, several States which have no Circuit Court except the District Court, and there are other States which are divided into more than one district, and in some of which Districts there is but a District Court with Circuit Court jurisdiction; so that it cannot be said that the system has been at any time entirely uniform.

So much, Mr. Chairman, for the history of our legislation on the judicial department.

I am not aware, Mr. Chairman, that there is any public complaint of the operation of the present system, so far as it applies to the Atlantic States. So far as I know, justice has been administered efficiently, promptly, and satisfactorily, in all those circuits. The judges, perhaps, have a good deal of employment: but they have been able to go through their arduous duties in such manner as to leave no cause of complaint, as far as I am informed. For my own part, I am not sanguine enough to expect, as far as those circuits are concerned, that any improvement can be made. In my opinion, none is needed. But it is not so in the Western States. Here exists a great deficiency. The country has outgrown the system. This is no man's fault, nor does it impute want of usual foresight to any one. It would have seemed chimerical in the framers of the law of 1789, if they had professed to strike out a plan which should have been adequate to the exigencies of the country, as it actually exists in 1826. From a period as far back as the close of the late war, the people of the West have applied to Congress on the subject of the courts. No session of Congress has passed without an attempt, in one or the other house, to produce some change; and although various projects have been presented, the inherent difficulties of the subject have prevented any efficient action of the legislature. I will state shortly, Sir, and as nearly as I remember, what has been at different times proposed.

In the first place, it has been proposed to recur to the system of Circuit Courts, upon the principle, although not exactly after the model, of the act of February, 1801. A bill of this character passed the Senate in 1819,[7] dividing the country into nine circuits, and providing for the appointment of one circuit judge to each circuit, who with the district judge of the district should constitute the Circuit Court. It also provided, that the

7. This bill was introduced on Dec. 1, 1818, and passed on Jan. 26, 1819. See *Annals*, 15th Cong., 2d sess., pp. 31, 186.

Supreme Court, as vacancies should occur, should be reduced to five members. This bill, I believe, was not acted upon in this House. Again, it has been proposed to constitute Circuit Courts by the union of the district judges in the circuit. It has been proposed, also, to extend the existing system somewhat in conformity to the object of the present bill, by adding to the number of the judges in the Supreme Court. And a different arrangement still has been suggested, which contemplates the appointment of circuit judges for some districts, and the continued performance of circuit duties by the supreme judges in others, with such legal provision as shall not attach the judges of the Supreme Court, in the performance of their circuit duties, unequally to any part of the country, but allow them to be distributed equally and fairly over the whole. This system, though somewhat complex, and perhaps liable to be misunderstood, is, I confess, what appears to me best of all suited to our condition. It would not make the Supreme Court too numerous; and it would still require from its members the performance of circuit duties; it would allow a proper distribution of these members to every part of the country; and, finally, it would furnish an adequate provision for the despatch of business in the Circuit Courts. Upon this plan, a bill was presented to the House of Representatives at the first session of the last Congress, but it did not meet with general favor; and the fate of a similar proposition elsewhere, at a subsequent period, discourages any revival of it.

I now come, Sir, to consider whether any, and what, evils exist; and then, whether the present bill be a suitable remedy. And in the first place, it is said, perhaps with some justice, that the business of the Supreme Court itself is not gone through with sufficient promptitude; that it is accumulating; that great delays are experienced, and greater delays feared. As to this, I would observe, that the annual session of the court cannot last above six or seven weeks, because it commences in February, and the circuit duties of the judges require them to leave this place the latter part of March. But I know no reason why the judges should not assemble earlier. I believe it would not materially interfere with their circuit duties, to commence the session here in the early part of January; and if that were the case, I have little doubt that, in two years, they would clear the docket. A bill to make this change passed this House two years ago[8]; I regret to say, it was not acted upon in the Senate.

As to returning to the original practice of having two sessions of the Supreme Court within the year, I incline to think it wholly inexpedient. The inconvenience arising from the distance of suitors and counsel from the seat of government forms a decisive objection to that proposition.

The great evil, however, Sir, at present experienced, and that which

8. May 18, 1824. *Annals*, 18th Cong., 1st sess., pp. 2635, 2648.

calls most loudly and imperatively for a remedy, is the state of business in the Circuit Courts in the Western States. The seventh circuit consists of Kentucky, Ohio, and Tennessee. All the other Western States have District Courts, with the powers of Circuit Courts. I am clearly of opinion, that some further provision is required of us for the administration of justice in these States. The existing means are not equal to the end. The judicial organization is not competent to exercise the jurisdiction which the laws confer upon it. There is a want of men, and a want of time. In this respect, it appears to me that our constitutional duty is very plain. The Constitution confers certain judicial powers on the government of the United States; we undertake to provide for the exercise of these powers; but the provision is inadequate, and the powers are not exercised. By the Constitution, the judicial power of this government extends, as well as to other things, to causes between citizens of different States. We open courts professedly to exercise that jurisdiction; but they are not competent to it; it is not exercised with reasonable promptitude; the suitor is delayed, and the end of the constitutional provision, in some measure, defeated. Now, it appears to me very plain, that we should either refuse to confer this jurisdiction on the courts, or that we should so constitute them that it may be efficiently exercised.

I hold, Sir, the certificate of the clerk for the District and Circuit Court of the District of Kentucky, that there are now pending in those courts nine hundred and fifty causes. As this is not a maritime district, most of these causes, doubtless, are in the Circuit Court. This accumulation has not arisen from any want of diligence in the judges themselves, for the same paper states, that two thousand causes have been disposed of within the last three years. The Memorial of the Bar of Nashville informs us that one hundred and sixty cases are pending in the Circuit Court for the Western District of Tennessee; a number, perhaps, not much less, is on the docket of the court for the Eastern District of Tennessee; and I am authorized to state that two hundred or two hundred and fifty may be taken as the number of suits pending in the Circuit Court of Ohio. These three States, Sir, constitute one circuit; they extend over a wide region; the places for holding the courts are at vast distances from one another; and it is not within the power of man, that the judge assigned to this circuit should get through the duties of his station. With the state of the courts in the other Western and Southwestern States, I am not so particularly acquainted. Gentlemen from those States will make it known to the committee. I know enough, however, to be satisfied that the whole case calls for attention. It grows no better by delay, and, whatever difficulties embarrass it, we may as well meet them at once, and agree upon such remedy as shall, upon the whole, seem most expedient.

And this, Sir, brings me to the most difficult part of our inquiry; that

is to say, whether such a measure as this bill proposes be the proper remedy. I beg to say, Sir, that I feel this difficulty as deeply as it can be felt by any member of the committee; and while I express my own opinions, such as they are, I shall be most happy to derive light from the greater experience, or the better intelligence, of any gentleman. To me it appears, that we are brought to the alternative of deciding between something like what this bill proposes, and the Circuit Court system, as provided in the bill of the Senate in 1819. As a practical question, I think it has come to this point: Shall we extend the present system, by increasing the number of the judges, or shall we recur to the system of Circuit Courts? I invoke the attention of the committee to this question, because, thinking the one or the other inevitable, I wish for the mature judgment of the House on both.

In favor of the Circuit Court system, it may be said, that it is uniform, and may be made to apply to all the States equally; so that if new States come into the Union, Circuit Courts may be provided for them without derangement to the general organization. This, doubtless, is a consideration entitled to much weight. It is said, also, that by separating the judges of the Supreme Court from the circuits, we shall leave them ample time for the discharge of the high duties of their appellate jurisdiction. This, no doubt, is true; but then, whether it be desirable, upon the whole, to withdraw the judges of the Supreme Court from the circuits, and to confine their labors entirely to the sessions at Washington, is a question which has most deeply occupied my reflections, and in regard to which I am free to confess some change has been wrought in my opinions. With entire respect for the better judgment of others, and doubting, therefore, when I find myself differing from those who are wiser and more experienced, I am still constrained to say, that my judgment is against withdrawing the judges of the Supreme Court from the circuits, if it can be avoided. The reasons which influence this sentiment are general, and perhaps may be thought too indefinite and uncertain to serve as a guide in measures of public importance; they nevertheless appear to me to have weight, and I will state them with frankness, in the hope that, if they are without reasonable foundation, they will be shown to be so, when certainly I shall cheerfully relinquish them.

In the first place, it appears to me that such an intercourse as the judges of the Supreme Court are enabled to have with the profession, and with the people, in their respective circuits, is itself an object of no inconsiderable importance. It naturally inspires respect and confidence, and it produces a reciprocal communication of information through all the branches of the judicial department. This leads to a harmony of opinion and of action. The Supreme Court, by itself, is in some measure insulated; it has not frequent occasions of contact with the community.

The bar that attends it is neither numerous nor regular in its attendance. The gentlemen who appear before it, in the character of counsel, come for the occasion, and depart with the occasion. The profession is occupied mainly in the objects which engage it in its own domestic forums; it belongs to the States, and their tribunals furnish its constant and principal theatre. If the judges of the Supreme Court, therefore, are wholly withdrawn from the circuits, it appears to me there is danger of leaving them without the means of useful intercourse with other judicial characters, with the profession of which they are members, and with the public. But, without pursuing these general reflections, I would say, in the second place, that I think it useful that judges should see in practice the operation and effect of their own decisions. This will prevent theory from running too far, or refining too much. We find, in legislation, that general provisions of law, however cautiously expressed, often require limitation and modification. Something of the same sort takes place in judicature. However beautiful may be the theory of general principles, such is the infinite variety of human affairs, that those most practised in them and conversant with them see at every turn a necessity of imposing restraints and qualifications on such principles. The daily application of their own doctrines will necessarily inspire courts with caution; and, by a knowledge of what takes place upon the circuits and occurs in constant practice, they will be able to decide finally, without the imputation of having overlooked, or not understood, any of the important elements and ingredients of a just decision.

But further, Sir, I must take the liberty of saying, that, in regard to the judicial office, constancy of employment is of itself, in my judgment, a good, and a great good. I appeal to the conviction of the whole profession, if, as a general rule, they do not find that those judges who decide most causes decide them best. Exercise strengthens and sharpens the faculties in this more than in almost any other employment. I would have the judicial office filled by him who is wholly a judge, always a judge, and nothing but a judge. With proper seasons, of course, for recreation and repose, his serious thoughts should all be turned to his official duties; he should be *omnis in hoc*. I think, Sir, there is hardly a greater mistake than has prevailed occasionally in some of the States, of creating many judges, assigning them duties which occupy but a small part of their time, and then making this the ground for allowing them a small compensation. The judicial power is incompatible with any other pursuit in life; and all the faculties of every man who takes it ought to be constantly exercised, and exercised to one end. Now, Sir, it is natural, that, in reasoning on this subject, I should take my facts from what passes within my own means of observation. If I am mistaken in my premises, the conclusion, of course, ought to be rejected. But I suppose

it will be safe to say, that a session of eight weeks in the year will probably be sufficient for the decision of causes in the Supreme Court; and, reasoning from what exists in one of the most considerable circuits in the Atlantic States, I suppose that eight, ten, or at most twelve weeks, may be the average of the time requisite to be spent by a circuit judge in his court in those circuits. If this be so, then, if the courts be separated, we have supreme judges occupied two months out of twelve, and circuit judges occupied three months out of twelve. In my opinion, this is not a system either to make or to keep good judges. The Supreme Court exercises a great variety of jurisdiction. It reverses decisions at common law, in equity, and in admiralty; and with the theory and the practice of all these systems it is indispensable that the judges should be accurately and intimately acquainted. It is for the committee to judge how far the withdrawing them from the circuits, and confining them to the exercise of an appellate jurisdiction, may increase or diminish this information. But, again, Sir, we have a great variety of local laws existing in this country, which are the standard of decision where they prevail. The laws of New England, Maryland, Louisiana, and Kentucky are almost so many different codes. These laws are to be construed and administered, in many cases, in the courts of the United States. Is there any doubt that a judge coming on the bench of the Supreme Court with a familiar acquaintance with these laws, derived from daily practice and decisions, must be more able both to form his own judgment correctly, and to assist that of his brethren, than a stranger who only looks at the theory? This is a point too plain to be argued. Of the weight of the suggestion the committee will judge. It appears to me, I confess, that a court remotely situated, a stranger to these local laws in their application and practice, with whatever diligence or with whatever ability, must be liable to fall into great mistakes.

May I ask your indulgence, Mr. Chairman, to suggest one other idea. With no disposition whatever to entertain doubts as to the manner in which the executive duty of appointments shall at any time hereafter be performed, the Supreme Court is so important, that, in whatever relates to it, I am willing to make assurance doubly sure, and to adopt, therefore, whatever fairly comes in my way likely to increase the probability that able and efficient men will be placed upon that bench. Now I confess that I know nothing which I think more conducive to that end than the assigning to the members of that court important, responsible, individual duties. Whatsoever makes the individual prominent, conspicuous, and responsible increases the probability that he will be some one possessing the proper requisites for a judge. It is one thing to give a vote upon a bench (especially if it be a numerous bench) for plaintiff or defendant, and quite another thing to act as the head of a court of various

jurisdiction, civil and criminal, to conduct trials by jury, and render judgments in law, equity, and admiralty. While these duties belong to the condition of a judge on the bench, that place will not be a sinecure, nor likely to be conferred without proofs of proper qualifications. For these reasons, I am inclined to wish that the judges of the Supreme Court may not be separated from the circuits, if any other suitable provision can be made.

As to the present bill, Mr. Chairman, it will doubtless be objected, that it makes the Supreme Court too numerous. In regard to that, I am bound to say that my own opinion was, that the present exigency of the country could have been answered by the addition of two members of the court. I believe the three Northwestern States might well enough go on for some time longer, and form a circuit of themselves, perhaps, hereafter, as the population shall increase, and the state of their affairs require it. The addition of the third judge is what I assent to, rather than what I recommend. It is what I would gladly avoid, if I could with propriety. I admit that, for some causes, the court as constituted by the bill will be inconveniently large; for such, especially, as require investigation into matters of fact, such as those of equity and admiralty, and perhaps for all private causes generally. But the great and leading character of the Supreme Court, its most important duties, and its highest functions, have not yet been alluded to. It is its peculiar relation to this government and the State governments, it is the power which it rightfully holds and exercises, of revising the opinions of other tribunals on constitutional questions, as the great practical expounder of the powers of the government, which attaches to this tribunal the greatest attention, and makes it worthy of the most deliberate consideration. Duties at once so important and so delicate impose no common responsibility, and require no common talent and weight of character. A very small court seems unfit for these high functions. These duties, though essentially judicial, partake something of a political character. The judges are called on to sit in judgment on the acts of independent States; they control the will of sovereigns; they are liable to be exposed, therefore, to the resentment of wounded sovereign pride; and from the very nature of our system, they are sometimes called on, also, to decide whether Congress has not exceeded its constitutional limits. Sir, there exists not upon the earth, and there never did exist, a judicial tribunal clothed with powers so various, and so important. I doubt the safety of rendering it small in number. My own opinion is, that, if we were to establish Circuit Courts, and to confine their judges to their duties on the bench, their number should not be at all reduced; and if, by some moderate addition to it, other important objects may well be answered, I am prepared to vote for such addition. In a government like ours, entirely popular, care should

be taken in every part of the system, not only to do right, but to satisfy the community that right is done. The opinions of mankind naturally attach more respect and confidence to the decisions of a court somewhat numerous, than to those of one composed of a less number. And, for myself, I acknowledge my fear, that, if the number of the court were reduced, and its members wholly withdrawn from the circuits, it might become an object of unpleasant jealousy and great distrust.

Mr. Chairman, I suppose I need not assure the committee that, if I saw any thing in this bill which would lessen the respectability or shake the independence of the Supreme Court, I should be the last man to favor it. I look upon the judicial department of this government as its main support. I am persuaded that the Union could not exist without it. I shall oppose whatever I think calculated to disturb the fabric of government, to unsettle what is settled, or to shake the faith of honest men in the stability of the laws, or the purity of their administration. If any gentleman shall show me that any of these consequences is like to follow the adoption of this measure, I shall hasten to withdraw from it my support. But I think we are bound to do something; and shall be most happy if the wisdom of the House shall suggest a course more free from difficulties than that which is now proposed to it.

Further remarks made on the same subject, on the 25th of January, 1826, in reply to the arguments used against the bill, and in favor of its postponement.

I had not intended, Sir, to avail myself of the indulgence which is generally allowed, under circumstances like the present, of making a reply. But the House has been invited with such earnestness to postpone this measure to another year, it has been pressed, with so much apparent alarm, to give no further countenance or support now to the bill, that I reluctantly depart from my purpose, and ask leave to offer a few brief remarks upon the leading topics of the discussion.

This, Sir, must be allowed, and is, on all hands allowed, to be a measure of great and general interest. It respects that important branch of government, the judiciary; and something of a judicial tone of discussion is not unsuitable to the occasion. We cannot treat the question too calmly, or too dispassionately. For myself, I feel that I have no pride of opinion to gratify, no eagerness of debate to be indulged, no competition to be pursued. I hope I may say, without impropriety, that I am not insensible to the responsibility of my own situation as a member of the House, and a member of the committee. I am aware of no prejudice which should draw my mind from the single and solicitous contemplation of what may be best; and I have listened attentively, through the

whole course of this debate, not with the feelings of one who is meditating the means of replying to objections, or escaping from their force, but with an unaffected anxiety to give every argument its just weight, and with a perfect readiness to abandon this measure, at any moment, in favor of any other which should appear to have solid grounds of preference. But I cannot say that my opinion is altered. The measure appears to my mind in the same light as when it was first presented to the House. I then saw some inconveniences attending it, and admitted them. I see them now; but while the effect of this discussion on my own mind has not been to do away entirely the sense of these inconveniences, it has not been, on the other hand, to remove the greater objections which exist to any other plan. I remain fully convinced, that this course is, on the whole, that which is freest from difficulties. However plausible other systems may seem in their general outline, objections arise, and thicken as we go into their details. It is not now at all certain that those who are opposed to this bill are agreed as to what other measure should be preferred. On the contrary, it is certain that no plan unites them all; and they act together only on the ground of their common dissatisfaction with the proposed bill. That system which seems most favored is the circuit system, as provided for in the Senate's bill of 1819. But as to that there is not an entire agreement. One provision in that bill was, to reduce the number of the judges of the Supreme Court to five. This was a part, too, of the original resolution of amendment moved by the gentleman from Virginia [Alfred H. Powell][9]; but it was afterwards varied; probably to meet the approbation of the gentleman from Pennsylvania [James Buchanan] and others who preferred to keep the court at its present number. But other gentlemen who are in opposition to this bill have still recommended a reduction of that number. Now, Sir, notwithstanding such reduction was one object, or was to be one effect, of the law of 1801, [it][10] was contemplated, also, in the Senate's bill of 1819, and has been again recommended by the gentleman from Virginia, and other gentlemen, yet I cannot persuade myself that any ten members of the House, upon mature reflection, would now be in favor of such reduction. It could only be made to take place when vacancies should occur on the bench, by death or resignation. Of the seven judges of which the court consists, six are now assigned to circuits in the Atlantic States; one

9. Everett identifies the gentleman from Virginia as Alfred H. Powell, but the discussion reported in the *Register of Debates* seems to indicate that the speaker was Charles Fenton Mercer. See *Register of Debates*, 19th Cong., 1st sess., pp. 888–912.

10. "It" appears in the *National Intelligencer*, Feb. 2, 1826, and in *Register of Debates*, 19th Cong., 1st sess., p. 1140, but seems to have been inadvertently omitted in *Works*, 3: 165. The omission was repeated in *W&S*, 5: 165.

only is attached to the Western Districts. Now, Sir, if we were to provide for a reduction, it might happen that the first vacancy would be in the situation of the single Western judge. In that event, no appointment could be made until two other vacancies should occur, which might be several years. I suppose that no man would think it just, or wise, or prudent, to make a legal provision, in consequence of which it might happen that there should be no Western judge at all on the supreme bench for several years to come. This part of the plan, therefore, was wisely abandoned by the gentleman. The court cannot be reduced; and the question is only between seven justices of the Supreme Court, with ten circuit judges, and ten justices of the Supreme Court, with no circuit judges.

I will take notice here of another suggestion made by the gentleman from Pennsylvania, who is generally so sober-minded and considerate in his observations, that they deserve attention, from respect to the quarter whence they proceed. That gentleman recommends that the justices of the Supreme Court should be relieved from circuit duties, as individuals, but proposes, nevertheless, that the whole court should become migratory, or ambulatory, and that its sessions should be holden, now in New York or Boston, now in Washington or Richmond, and now in Kentucky or Ohio. And it is singular enough, that this arrangement is recommended in the same speech in which the authority of a late President is cited,[11] to prove that considerations arising from the usually advanced age of some of the judges, and their reasonable desire for repose, ought to lead us to relieve them from all circuit duties whatever. Truly, Sir, this is a strange plan of relief. Instead of holding courts in his own State, and perhaps in his own town, and visiting a neighboring State, every judge on this plan is to join every other judge, and the whole bench to make, together, a sort of judicial progress. They are to visit the North, and the South, and to ascend and descend the Alleghanies. Sir, it is impossible to talk seriously against such a proposition. To state it, is to refute it. Let me merely ask, whether, in this peregrination of the court, it is proposed that they take all their records of pending suits, and the whole calendar of causes, with them. If so, then the Kentucky client, with his counsel, is to follow the court to Boston; and the Boston client to pursue it back to Kentucky. Or is it, on the contrary, proposed that there shall be grand judicial divisions in the country, and that while at the North, for example, none but Northern appeals shall be heard? If this be intended, then I ask, How often could the court sit in each one of

11. Buchanan's remarks are found in *Register of Debates*, 19th Cong., 1st sess., pp. 916–925, 927–932. Although he does comment on the problem of advanced age in judges, the *Register* does not report that Buchanan invoked the authority of an ex-president (pp. 924–925).

these divisions? Certainly, not oftener than once in two years; probably, not oftener than once in three. An appeal, therefore, might be brought before the appellate court in two or three years from the time of rendering the first judgment; and supposing judgment to be pronounced in the appellate court at the second term, it would be decided in two or three years more. But it is not necessary to examine this suggestion further. Sir, every thing conspires to prove, that, with respect to the great duties of the Supreme Court, they must be discharged at one annual session, and that session must be holden at the seat of government. If such provision be made as that the business of the year in that court may be despatched within the year, reasonable promptitude in the administration of justice will be attained; and such provision, I believe, is practicable.

Another objection advanced by the member from Pennsylvania applies as well to the system as it now exists, as to that which will be substituted if this bill shall pass. The honorable member thinks that the appellate court and the court from which the appeal comes should, in all cases, be kept entirely distinct and separate. True principle requires, in his judgment, that the circuit judge should be excluded from any participation in the revision of his own judgments. I believe, Sir, that, in the early history of the court, the practice was for the judge whose opinion was under revision not to partake in the deliberations of the court. This practice, however, was afterwards altered, and the court resolved that it could not discharge the judge from the duty of assisting in the decision of the appeal. Whether the two courts ought to be kept so absolutely distinct and separate as the member from Pennsylvania recommends, is not so clear a question that persons competent to form an opinion may not differ upon it. On the other hand, it may very well be said, that, if the judgment appealed from has been rendered by one of the judges of the appellate court, courtesy, kindness, or sympathy may inspire some disposition in the members of the same bench to affirm that judgment; and that the general habit of the court may thus become unfriendly to a free and unbiased revision. On the other hand, it may be contended, that, if there be no medium of communication between the court of the first instance, and the court of appellate jurisdiction, there may be danger that the reasons of the first may not be always well understood, and its judgments consequently liable, sometimes, to be erroneously reversed. It certainly is not true, that the chance of justice, in an appellate court, is always precisely equal to the chance of reversing the judgment below; although it is necessary for the peace of society and the termination of litigation to take it for granted, as a general rule, that what is decided by the ultimate tribunal is decided rightly.

To guard against too great a tendency to reversals in appellate courts,

it has often been thought expedient to furnish a good opportunity at least of setting forth the grounds and reasons of the original judgment. Thus, in the British House of Lords a judgment of the King's Bench is not ordinarily reversed until the judges have been called in, and the reason of their several opinions stated by themselves. Thus, too, in the Court of Errors of New York, the Chancellor and the judges are members of the court; and, although they do not vote upon the revision of their own judgments or decrees, they are expected to assign and explain the reasons of the original judgment. In the modern practice of the courts of common law, causes are constantly and daily revised on motions for new trials founded on the supposed misdirection of the judge in matter of law. In these cases the judge himself is a component member of the court, and constantly takes part in its proceedings. It certainly may happen in such cases that some bias of preconceived opinion may influence the individual judge, or some undue portion of respect for the judgment already pronounced may unconsciously mingle itself with the judgments of others. But the universality of the practice sufficiently shows that no great practical evil is experienced from this cause.

It has been said in England, that the practice of revising the opinions of judges by motions for new trial, instead of filing bills of exception and suing out writs of error, has greatly diminished the practical extent of the appellate jurisdiction of the House of Lords. This shows that suitors are not advised that they have no hope to prevail against the first opinions of individual judges, or the sympathy of their brethren. Indeed, Sir, judges of the highest rank of intellect have always been distinguished for the candor with which they reconsider their own judgments. A man who should commend himself for never having altered his opinion might be praised for firmness of purpose; but men would think of him, either that he was a good deal above all other mortals, or somewhat below the most enlightened of them. He who is not wise enough to be always right, should be wise enough to change his opinion when he finds it wrong. The consistency of a truly great man is proved by his uniform attachment to truth and principle, and his devotion to the better reason; not by obstinate attachment to first-formed notions. Whoever has not candor enough, for good cause, to change his own opinions, is not safe authority to change the opinions of other men. But at least, Sir, the member from Pennsylvania will admit, that, if an evil in this respect exist under the present law, this bill will afford some mitigation of that evil. By augmenting the number of the judges, it diminishes the influence of the individual whose judgment may be under revision; and so far, I hope, the honorable member may himself think the measure productive of good.

But, Sir, before we postpone to another year the consideration of this

bill, I beg again to remind the House that the measure is not new. It is not new in its general character; it is not entirely new in its particular provisions. The necessity of some reform in the judicial establishment of the country has been presented to every Congress, and every session of Congress, since the peace of 1815. What has been recommended, at different times, has been already frequently stated. It is enough, now, to say, that the measure of extending the system by increasing the number of the judges of the Supreme Court was presented to the House, among other measures, in 1823, by the Judiciary Committee; and that so late as the last session it received a distinct expression of approbation in the other branch of the legislature. Gentlemen have referred to the bill introduced into this House two years ago. That bill had my approbation; I so declared at the commencement of this debate. It proposed to effect the object of retaining the judges upon their circuits without increasing their number. But it was complex. It was thought to be unequal, and it was unsatisfactory. There appeared no disposition in the House to adopt it; and when the same measure in substance was afterwards proposed in the other branch of the legislature, it received the approbation of no more than a half dozen voices. This led me to make a remark, at the opening of the debate, which I have already repeated, that, in my opinion, we are brought to the narrow ground of deciding between the system of the Circuit Courts and the provisions of this bill. Shall we keep the judges upon the circuits and augment their number, or shall we relieve them from circuit duties and appoint special circuit judges in their places? This, as it seems to me, is the only practical question remaining for our decision.

I do not intend, Sir, to go again into the general question of continuing the justices of the Supreme Court in the discharge of circuit duties. My opinion has been already expressed, and I have heard nothing to alter it. The honorable gentleman from Virginia does me more than justice in explaining any expression of his own which might refer this opinion to a recent origin, or to any new circumstances. I confess, Sir, that four-and-twenty years ago, when this matter was discussed in Congress, my opinion, as far as I can be supposed to have had any opinion then on such subjects, inclined to the argument that recommended the separation of the judges from the circuits. But, if I may be pardoned for referring to any thing so little worthy the regard of the House as my own experience, I will say that that experience early led me to doubt the correctness of the first impression, and that I became satisfied that it was desirable in itself that the judges of the Supreme Court should remain in the active discharge of the duties of the circuits. I have acted in conformity to this sentiment so often as this subject has been before

Congress in the short periods that I have been a member. I still feel the same conviction; and though I shall certainly yield the point, rather than that no provision for the existing exigency should be made, yet I should feel no inconsiderable pain in submitting to such necessity. I do not doubt, indeed, Sir, that, if the judges were separated from circuit duties, we should go on very well for some years to come. But looking to it as a permanent system, I view it with distrust and anxiety.

My reasons are already before the House. I am not about to repeat them. I beg to take this occasion, however, to correct one or two mis-apprehensions of my meaning into which gentlemen have fallen. I did not say, Sir, that I wished the judges of the Supreme Court to go upon the circuits, to the end that they might see in the country the impression which their opinions made upon the public sentiment. Nothing like it. What I did say was, that it was useful that the judge of the Supreme Court should be able to perceive the application and bearing of the opinions of that court upon the variety of causes coming before him at the circuit. And is not this useful? Is it not probable that the judge will lay down a general rule with the greatest wisdom and precision, who comprehends in his view the greatest number of instances to which that rule is to be applied? As far as I can now recall the train of my own ideas, the expression was suggested by a reflection upon the laws of the Western States, respecting title to land. We hear often in this House of "judicial legislation." If any such thing exist in this country, an instance of it doubtless is to be found in the land laws of some of the Western States. In Kentucky, for example, titles to the soil appear to depend, to a very great extent, upon a series of judicial decisions, growing out of an act of the Legislature of Virginia passed in 1779, for the sale and disposi-tion of her public domain. The legislative provision was very short and general; and as rights were immediately acquired under it, the want of legislative detail could only be supplied by judicial construction and de-termination. Hence a system has grown up, which is complex, artificial, and argumentative. I do not impute blame to the courts; they had no option but to decide cases as they arose, upon the best reasons. And al-though I am a very incompetent judge in the case, yet as far as I am informed, it appears to me that the courts, both of the State and of the United States, have applied just principles to the state of things which they found existing. But, Sir, as a rule laid down at Washington in one of these cases may be expected to affect five hundred others, is it not obvious that a judge, bred to this peculiar system of law, and having also many of these cases in judgment before him in his own circuit, is better enabled to state, to limit, and to modify the general rule, than another judge, though of equal talents, who should be a stranger to the decisions

of the State tribunals, a stranger to the opinions and practice of the profession, and a stranger to all cases except the single one before him for judgment?

The honorable member from Pennsylvania asks, Sir, whether a statute of Vermont cannot be as well understood at Washington, as at Windsor or Rutland. Why, Sir, put in that shape, the question has very little meaning. But if the gentleman intends to ask, whether a judge who has been for years in the constant discharge of the duties incumbent upon him as the head of the Circuit Court in Vermont, and who, therefore, has had the statutes of that State frequently before him, has learned their interpretation by the State judicatures, and their connection with other laws, local or general,—if the question be, whether such a judge is not probably more competent to understand that statute than another, who, with no knowledge of its local interpretation or local application, shall look at its letter for the first time in the hall of the Supreme Court,—if this be the question, Sir, which the honorable gentleman means to propound, I cheerfully refer him to the judgment of this House, and to his own good understanding, for an answer. Sir, we have heard a tone of observation upon this subject which quite surprises me. It seems to imply that one intelligent man is as fit to be a judge of the Supreme Court as another. The perception of the true rule, and its rightful application, whether of local or general law, are supposed to be entirely easy, because there are many volumes of statutes and of decisions. There can be no doubt, it seems, that a Supreme Court, however constituted, would readily understand, in the instance mentioned, the law of Vermont, because the statutes of Vermont are accessible. Nor need Louisiana fear that her peculiar code will not be thoroughly and practically known, inasmuch as a printed copy will be found in the public libraries.

Sir, I allude to such arguments, certainly not for the purpose of undertaking a refutation of them, but only to express my regret that they should have found place in this discussion. I have not contended, Sir, for any thing like judicial representation. I care not in what terms of reproach such an idea be spoken of. It is none of mine. What I said was, and I still say it, with so many States, having various and different systems, with such a variety of local laws and usages and practices, it is highly important that the Supreme Court should be so constituted as to allow a fair prospect, in every case, that these laws and usages should be known; and that I know nothing so naturally conducive to this end, as the knowledge and experience obtained by the judges on the circuits. Let me ask, Sir, the members from New England, if they have ever found any man this side of the North River[12] who thoroughly understood our practice of special attachment, our process of garnishment, or

12. Another name for the Hudson River.

trustee process, or our mode of extending execution upon land? And let me ask, at the same time, whether there be an individual of the profession, between this place and Maine, who is, at this moment, competent to the decision of questions arising under the peculiar system of land titles of Kentucky or Tennessee? If there be such a gentleman, I confess, I have not the honor of his acquaintance.

On the general question of the utility of constant occupation in perfecting the character of a judge, I do not mean now to enlarge. I am aware that men will differ on that subject, according to their different means or different habits of observation. To me it seems as clear as any moral proposition whatever. And I would ask the honorable member from Rhode Island [Tristam Burges], since he has referred to the judge of the first circuit,[13] and has spoken of him in terms of respect not undeserved, whether he supposes that that member of the court, if, fifteen years ago, on receiving his commission, he had removed to this city, and had remained here ever since, with no other connection with his profession than an annual session of six weeks in the Supreme Court, would have been the judge he now is? Sir, if this question were proposed to that distinguished person himself, and if he could overcome the reluctance which he would naturally feel to speak at all of his own judicial qualities, I am extremely mistaken if he would not refer to his connection with the Circuit Court, and the frequency and variety of his labors there, as efficient causes in the production of that eminent degree of ability with which he now discharges the duties of his station.

There is not, Sir, an entire revolution wrought in the mind of a professional man, by appointing him a judge. He is still a lawyer; and if he have but little to do as a judge, he is, in effect, a lawyer out of practice. And how is it, Sir, with lawyers who are not judges, and are yet out of practice? Let the opinion and the common practice of mankind decide this. If you require professional assistance in whatever relates to your reputation, your property, or your family, do you go to him who is retired from the bar, and who has uninterrupted leisure to pursue his readings and reflections; or do you address yourself to him, on the contrary, who is in the midst of affairs, busy every day, and every hour in the day, with professional pursuits? But I will not follow this topic farther, nor dwell on this part of the case.

I have already said, that, in my opinion, the present number of the court is more convenient than a larger number, for the hearing of a certain class of causes. This opinion I do not retract; for I believe it to be correct. But the question is, whether this inconvenience be not more than balanced by other advantages. I think it is.

It has been again and again urged, that this bill makes no provision

13. Joseph Story (1779–1845).

for clearing off the term business of the Supreme Court; and strange mistakes, as it appears to me, are committed, as to the amount of arrears in that court. I believe that the bill intended to remedy that evil will remedy it. I believe there is time enough for the court to go through its lists of causes here, without interfering with the sessions of the Circuit Courts; and, notwithstanding the mathematical calculations by which it has been proved that the proposed addition to the length of the term would enable the court to decide precisely nine additional causes, and no more, yet I have authority to say, that those who have the best means of knowing were of opinion, two years ago, that the proposed alteration of the term would enable the court, in two years, to go through all the causes before it ready for hearing.

It has been said, Sir, that this measure will injure the character of the Supreme Court; because, as we increase numbers, we lessen responsibility in the same proportion. Doubtless, as a general proposition, there is great truth in this remark. A court so numerous as to become a popular body would be unfit for the exercise of judicial functions. This is certain. But then this general truth, although admitted, does not enable us to fix with precision the point at which this evil either begins to be felt at all, or to become considerable; still less, where it is serious or intolerable. If seven be quite few enough, it may not be easy to show that ten must necessarily be a great deal too many. But there is another view of the case, connected with what I have said heretofore in this discussion, and which furnishes, in my mind, a complete answer to this part of the argument; and that is, that a judge who has various important individual duties to perform in the Circuit Court, and who sits in the appellate court with nine others, acts, on the whole, in a more conspicuous character, and under the pressure of more immediate and weighty responsibility, than if he performed no individual circuit duty, and sat on the appellate bench with six others only.

But again, it has been argued, that to increase the number of the Supreme Court is dangerous; because, with such a precedent, Congress may hereafter effect any purpose of its own, in regard to judicial decisions, by changing essentially the whole constitution of the court, and overthrowing its settled decisions, by augmenting the number of judges. Whenever Congress, it is said, may dislike the constitutional opinions and decisions of the court, it may mould it to its own views, upon the authority of the present example. But these abuses of power are not to be anticipated or supposed; and therefore no argument results from them.

If we were to be allowed to imagine that the legislature would act in entire disregard of its duty, there are ways enough, certainly, beside that supposed, in which it might destroy the judiciary, as well as any other

branch of the government. The judiciary power is conferred, and the Supreme Court established, by the Constitution; but then legislative acts are necessary to confer jurisdiction on inferior courts, and to regulate proceedings in all courts. If Congress should neglect the duty of passing such laws, the judicial power could not be efficiently exercised. If, for example, Congress were to repeal the twenty-fifth section of the judicial act of 1789, and make no substitute, there would be no mode by which the decisions of State tribunals, on questions arising under the Constitution and laws of the United States, could be revised in the Supreme Court. Of if they were to repeal the eleventh section of that act, the power of trying causes between citizens of different States, in the tribunals of this government, could not be exercised. All other branches of the government depend, in like manner, for their continuance in life and being, and for the proper exercise of their powers, on the presumption that the legislature will discharge its constitutional duties. If it were possible to adopt the opposite supposition, doubtless there are modes enough to which we may look, to see the subversion both of the courts and the whole Constitution.

Mr. Speaker, I will not detain you by further reply to the various objections which have been made to this bill. What has occurred to me as most important, I have noticed either now or heretofore; and I refer the whole to the dispassionate judgment of the House. Allow me, however, Sir, before I sit down, to disavow, on my own behalf and on behalf of the committee, all connection between this measure and any opinions or decisions, given or expected, in any causes, or classes of causes, by the Supreme Court. Of the merits of the case of which early mention was made in the debate, I know nothing. I presume it was rightly decided, because it was decided by sworn judges, composing a tribunal in which the Constitution and the laws have lodged the power of ultimate judgment. It would be unworthy, indeed, of the magnitude of this occasion, to bend our course a hair's breadth on the one side or the other, either to favor or to oppose what we might like, or dislike, in regard to particular questions. Surely we are not fit for this great work, if motives of that sort can possibly come near us. I have forborne, throughout this discussion, all expression of opinion on the manner in which the members of the Supreme Court have heretofore discharged, and still discharge, the responsible duties of their station. I should feel restraint and embarrassment, were I to make the attempt to express my sentiments on that point. Professional habits and pursuits connect me with the court, and I feel that it is not proper that I should speak here of the personal qualities of its members, either generally or individually. They shall not suffer, at least, from any ill-timed or clumsy eulogy of mine. I could not, if I would, make them better known than they are to their country; nor

could I either strengthen or shake the foundation of character and talent upon which they stand.

But of the judicial branch of the government, and of the institution of the Supreme Court, as the head of that branch, I beg to say that no man can regard it with more respect and attachment than myself. It may have friends more able, it has none more sincere. No conviction is deeper in my mind, than that the maintenance of the judicial power is essential and indispensable to the very being of this government. The Constitution without it would be no constitution; the government, no government. I am deeply sensible, too, and, as I think, every man must be whose eyes have been open to what has passed around him for the last twenty years, that the judicial power is the protecting power of the whole government. Its position is upon the outer wall. From the very nature of things and the frame of the Constitution, it forms the point at which our different systems of government meet in collision, when collision unhappily exists. By the absolute necessity of the case, the members of the Supreme Court become judges of the extent of constitutional powers. They are if I may so call them, the great arbitrators between contending sovereignties. Every man is able to see how delicate and how critical must be the exercise of such powers in free and popular governments. Suspicion and jealousy are easily excited, under such circumstances, against a body, necessarily few in number, and possessing by the Constitution a permanent tenure of office. While public men in more popular parts of the government may escape without rebuke, notwithstanding they may sometimes act upon opinions which are not acceptable, that impunity is not to be expected in behalf of judicial tribunals. It cannot but have attracted observation, that, in the history of our government, the courts have not been able to avoid severe, and sometimes angry complaint, for giving their sanction to those public measures which the representatives of the people had adopted without exciting particular disquietude. Members of this and the other house of Congress, acting voluntarily, and in the exercise of their general discretion, have enacted laws without incurring an uncommon degree of dislike or resentment; and yet, when those very laws have been brought before the court, and the question of their validity has been distinctly raised, and is necessarily to be determined, the judges affirming the constitutional validity of such acts, although the occasion was forced upon them, and they were absolutely bound to express the one opinion or the other, have, nevertheless, not escaped a severity of reproach bordering upon the very verge of denunciation. This experience, while it teaches us the dangers which environ this department, instructs us most persuasively in its importance. For its own security, and the security of the other branches of the government, it requires such an extraordinary union of discretion and

firmness, of ability and moderation, that nothing in the country is too distinguished for sober sense or too gifted with powerful talent, to fill the situations belonging to it.[14]

14. *Register of Debates*, 19th Cong., 1st sess., p. 1148, reports further concluding remarks as follows: "Sir, I will occupy the attention of the House no longer. I see no reason for postponing the bill. The subject has been thoroughly discussed, and fully considered. For myself, I expect no new lights, and feeling the necessity of doing something, I hope we may now give the form of law to the measure before us."

The Panama Mission, April 14, 1826

Early in 1825 Simon Bolivar, the South American Liberator, proposed a Congress of American States to meet at Panama the following year. His purpose was to unite Spanish America to resist any attempt by Spain to regain her lost colonies, and the United States was not included. Secretary of State Henry Clay, who had been one of the earliest champions of Latin American independence, heard about it from the United States minister in Lima. Clay saw in the proposed gathering something potentially much broader than Bolivar's intention: an approach to Western Hemisphere solidarity. He persuaded a reluctant Adams, and through South American diplomatic representatives in Washington secured an invitation. Adams accepted, and appointed two delegates to attend.

When the president submitted the names to the Senate for confirmation, however, the Panama Mission became a vehicle for galvanizing into a single opposition the various elements hostile each for its own reasons to the administration. The Jacksonians, who still felt they had been robbed of the presidency, took the lead, and the battle was on. After a bitter, name-calling fight the delegates were confirmed by a narrow margin. In the House the contest took a different twist when opponents sought to amend the appropriation for the expenses of the delegates so as sharply to curtail their authority. Webster, in the speech printed below, spoke against the amendments, and for the necessary appropriation. It was this debate that made him the acknowledged administration leader in the House, where Adams again won a narrow victory.

From the point of view of the National Republicans the whole episode was a blunder. It was a trivial issue on which to stake the prestige of a presidency, and one that aroused unnecessary hostility. Southern members opposed because they feared that slavery might be discussed, and that Negro delegates might attend from Haiti; Northern Jacksonians also opposed because Clay, who they charged had "sold" the presidency to Adams, was behind the mission; and many of the old Crawford men, still uncommitted, opposed because they saw the opposition as the long-term winner. For Adams the whole episode was a political disaster. Though he won the immediate battle he had definitely lost the war. He would not again command a majority in Congress.

Ironically, the blood-letting was in vain, for neither of the United

States delegates ever reached Panama. One died of fever on the way there, and the other, fearful of a similar fate, delayed his departure until the meeting was over.

Although delivered on April 14, Webster's speech on the Panama Mission was not published in the *National Intelligencer* until June 22. There appeared to be no great hurry, since Joseph Gales and William Winston Seaton, the proprietors of that paper, had issued the speech in pamphlet form before the end of April. Webster undoubtedly revised the reporter's transcript, according to the standard practice of the day. *Register of Debates*, 19th Cong., 1st sess., pp. 2254–2277, is simply a verbatim reprinting from the *Intelligencer*. The speech appeared four years later in *Speeches and Forensic Arguments*, 1: 322–350 with only trivial differences. This version was reprinted by Everett in *Works*, 3: 178–217, and thence without change in *Writings and Speeches*, 5: 178–217. It is from this last named source that the text below is taken.

> *Resolved,* That in the opinion of the House it is expedient to appropriate the funds necessary to enable the President of the United States to send ministers to the Congress of Panama;—

Mr. [Louis] McLane of Delaware submitted the following amendment thereto, viz.: —

> It being understood as the opinion of this House, that, as it has always been the settled policy of this government, in extending our commercial relations with foreign nations, to have with them as little political connection as possible, to preserve peace, commerce, and friendship with all nations, and to form entangling alliances with none; the ministers who may be sent shall attend at the said Congress in a diplomatic character merely, and ought not to be authorized to discuss, consider, or consult, upon any proposition of alliance, offensive or defensive, between this country and any of the Spanish American governments, or any stipulation, compact, or declaration, binding the United States in any way, or to any extent, to resist interference from abroad with the domestic concerns of the aforesaid governments; or any measure which shall commit the present or future neutral rights or duties of these United States, either as may regard European nations, or between the several states of Mexico and South America; leaving the United States free to adopt, in any event which may happen, affecting the relations of the South American governments with each other, or with foreign nations, such measures as the friendly disposition cherished by the American people towards the people of those states, and the honor and interest of this nation, may require;—

To which Mr. Rives of Virginia proposed to add, after the words "aforesaid governments," the following: —

> Or any compact or engagement by which the United States shall be pledged to the Spanish American states, to maintain, by force the principle that no part of the American continent is henceforward subject to colonization by any European power.

Mr. Chairman,—I am not ambitious of amplifying this discussion. On the contrary, it is my anxious wish to confine the debate, so far as I partake in it, to the real and material questions before us.

Our judgment of things is liable, doubtless, to be influenced by our opinions of men. It would be affectation in me, or in any one, to claim an exemption from this possibility of bias. I can say, however, that it has been my sincere purpose to consider and discuss the present subject with the single view of finding out what duty it devolves upon me, as a member of the House of Representatives. If any thing has diverted me from that sole aim, it has been against my intention.

I think, Sir, that there are two questions, and two only, for our decision. The first is, whether the House of Representatives will assume the responsibility of withholding the ordinary appropriation for carrying into effect an executive measure, which the executive department has constitutionally instituted. The second, whether, if it will not withhold the appropriation, it will yet take the responsibility of interposing, with its own opinions, directions, or instructions, as to the manner in which this particular executive measure shall be conducted.

I am, certainly, in the negative, on both these questions. I am neither willing to refuse the appropriation, nor am I willing to limit or restrain the discretion of the executive, beforehand, as to the manner in which it shall perform its own appropriate constitutional duties. And, Sir, those of us who hold these opinions have the advantage of being on the common highway of our national politics. We propose nothing new; we suggest no change; we adhere to the uniform practice of the government, as I understand it, from its origin. It is for those, on the other hand, who are in favor of either, or both, of the propositions, to show us the cogent reasons which recommend their adoption. It is their duty to satisfy the House and the country that there is something in the present occasion which calls for such an extraordinary and unprecedented interference.

The President and Senate have instituted a public mission, for the purpose of treating with foreign states. The Constitution gives to the President the power of appointing, with the consent of the Senate, ambassadors and other public ministers. Such appointment is, therefore, a

clear and unquestionable exercise of executive power. It is, indeed, less connected with the appropriate duties of this House, than almost any other executive act; because the office of a public minister is not created by any statute or law of our own government. It exists under the law of nations, and is recognized as existing by our Constitution. The acts of Congress, indeed, limit the salaries of public ministers; but they do no more. Every thing else in regard to the appointment of public ministers, —their numbers, the time of their appointment, and the negotiations contemplated in such appointments,—is matter for executive discretion. Every new appointment to supply vacancies in existing missions is under the same authority. There are, indeed, what we commonly term standing missions, so known in the practice of the government, but they are not made permanent by any law. All missions rest on the same ground. Now the question is, whether, the President and Senate having created this mission, or, in other words, having appointed the ministers, in the exercise of their undoubted constitutional power, this House will take upon itself the responsibility of defeating its objects, and rendering this exercise of executive power void?

By voting the salaries in the ordinary way, we assume, as it seems to me, no responsibility whatever. We merely empower another branch of the government to discharge its own appropriate duties, in that mode which seems to itself most conducive to the public interests. We are, by so voting, no more responsible for the manner in which the negotiation shall be conducted, than we are for the manner in which one of the heads of department may discharge the duties of his office.

On the other hand, if we withhold the ordinary means, we do[1] incur a heavy responsibility. We interfere, as it seems to me, to prevent the action of the government, according to constitutional forms and provisions. It ought constantly to be remembered, that our whole power in the case is merely incidental. It is only because public ministers must have salaries, like other officers, and because no salaries can be paid but by our vote, that the subject is referred to us at all. The Constitution vests the power of appointment in the President and Senate; the law gives to the President even the power of fixing the amount of salary, within certain limits; and the only question here is upon the appropriation. There is no doubt that we have the power, if we see fit to exercise it, to break up the mission, by withholding the salaries. We have power also to break up the court, by withholding the salaries of the judges, or to break up the office of President, by withholding the salary provided for it by law. All these things, it is true, we have the power to do, since we hold the keys of the treasury. But, then, can we rightfully exercise

1. *National Intelligencer* and *Register of Debates* read "do not," an error first corrected in *Speeches and Forensic Arguments*.

this power? The gentleman from Pennsylvania [James Buchanan] with whom I have great pleasure in concurring on this part of the case, while I regret that I differ with him on others, has placed this question in a point of view which cannot be improved. These officers do, indeed, already exist. They are public ministers. If they were to negotiate a treaty, and the Senate should ratify it, it would become a law of the land, whether we voted their salaries or not. This shows that the Constitution never contemplated that the House of Representatives should act a part in originating negotiations or concluding treaties.

I know, Sir, it is a useless labor to discuss the kind of power which this House incidentally holds in these cases. Men will differ in that particular; and as the forms of public business and of the Constitution are such that the power may be exercised by this House, there will always be some, or always may be some, who feel inclined to exercise it. For myself, I feel bound not to step out of my own sphere, and neither to exercise or control any authority, of which the Constitution has intended to lodge the free and unrestrained exercise in other hands. Cases of extreme necessity, in which a regard to public safety is to be the supreme law, or rather to take place of all law, must be allowed to provide for themselves when they arise. Arguments drawn from such possible cases will shed no light on the general path of our constitutional duty.

Mr. Chairman, I have an habitual and very sincere respect for the opinions of the gentleman from Delaware [Louis McLane]. And I can say with truth, that he is the last man in the House from whom I should have looked for this proposition of amendment, or from whom I should have expected to hear some of the reasons which he has given in its support. He says, that, in this matter, the source from which the measure springs should have no influence with us whatever. I do not comprehend this; and I cannot but think the honorable gentleman has been surprised into an expression which does not convey his meaning. This measure comes from the executive, and it is an appropriate exercise of executive power. How is it, then, that we are to consider it as entirely an open question for us,—as if it were a legislative measure originating with ourselves? In deciding whether we will enable the executive to exercise his own duties, are we to consider whether we should have exercised them in the same way ourselves? And if we differ in opinion with the President and Senate, are we on that account to refuse the ordinary means? I think not; unless we mean to say that we will ourselves exercise all the powers of the government.

But the gentleman argues, that, although generally such a course would not be proper, yet in the present case the President has especially referred the matter to our opinion; that he has thrown off, or attempted to throw off, his own constitutional responsibility; or at least, that he

proposes to divide it with us; that he requests our advice, and that we, having referred that request to the Committee on Foreign Affairs, have now received from that committee their report thereon.

Sir, this appears to me a very mistaken view of the subject; but if it were all so, if our advice and opinion had thus been asked, it would not alter the line of our duty. We cannot take, though it were offered, any share in executive duty. We cannot divide their own proper responsibility with other branches of the government. The President cannot properly ask, and we cannot properly give, our advice, as to the manner in which he shall discharge his duties. He cannot shift the responsibility from himself; and we cannot assume it. Such a course, Sir, would confound all that is distinct in our respective constitutional functions. It would break down all known divisions of power, and put an end to all just responsibility. If the President were to receive directions or advice from us, in things pertaining to the duties of his own office, what would become of his responsibility to us and to the Senate? We hold the impeaching power. We are to bring him to trial in any case of maladministration. The Senate are to judge him by the Constitution and laws; and it would be singular indeed, if, when such occasion should arise, the party accused should have the means of sheltering himself under the advice or opinions of his accusers. Nothing can be more incorrect or more dangerous than this pledging the House beforehand to any opinion as to the manner of discharging executive duties.

But, Sir, I see no evidence whatever that the President has asked us to take this measure upon ourselves, or to divide the responsibility of it with him. I see no such invitation or request. The Senate having concurred in the mission, the President has sent a message requesting the appropriation, in the usual and common form. In answer to a call of the House, another message is sent, communicating the correspondence, and setting forth the objects of the mission. It is contended, that by this message he asks our advice, or refers the subject to our opinion. I do not so understand it. Our concurrence, he says, by making the appropriation, is subject to our free determination. Doubtless it is so. If we determine at all, we shall determine freely; and the message does no more than leave to ourselves to decide how far we feel ourselves bound, either to support or to thwart the executive department, in the exercise of its duties. There is no message, no document, no communication to us, which asks for our concurrence, otherwise than as we shall manifest it by making the appropriation.

Undoubtedly, Sir, the President would be glad to know that the measure met the approbation of the House. He must be aware, unquestionably, that all leading measures mainly depend for success on the support of Congress. Still, there is no evidence that on this occasion he has

sought to throw off responsibility from himself, or that he desires us to be answerable for any thing beyond the discharge of our own constitutional duties. I have already said, Sir, that I know of no precedent for such a proceeding as the amendment proposed by the gentleman from Delaware. None which I think analogous has been cited. The resolution of the House, some years ago, on the subject of the slave-trade, is a precedent the other way. A committee had reported that, in order to put an end to the slave-trade, a mutual right of search might be admitted and arranged by negotiation. But this opinion was not incorporated, as the gentleman now proposes to incorporate his amendment, into the resolution of the House. The resolution only declared, in general terms, that the President be requested to enter upon such negotiations with other powers as he might deem expedient, for the effectual abolition of the African slave-trade. It is singular enough, and may serve as an admonition on the present occasion, that, a negotiation having been concluded, in conformity to the opinions expressed, not, indeed, by the House, but by the committee, the treaty, when laid before the Senate was rejected by that body.

The gentleman from Delaware himself says, that the Constitutional responsibility pertains alone to the executive department, and that none other has to do with it, as a public measure. These admissions seem to me to conclude the question; because, in the first place, if the constitutional responsibility appertains alone to the President, he cannot devolve it on us if he would; and because, in the second place, I see no proof of any intention on his part so to devolve it on us, even if he had the power.

Mr. Chairman, I will here take occasion, in order to prevent misapprehension, to observe, that no one is more convinced than I am, that it is the right of this House, and often its duty, to express its general opinion in regard to questions of foreign policy. Nothing, certainly, is more proper. I have concurred in such proceedings, and am ready to do so again. On those great subjects, for instance, which form the leading topics in this discussion, it is not only the right of the House to express its opinions, but I think it its duty to do so, if it should suppose the executive to be pursuing a general course of policy which the House itself will not ultimately approve. But that is something entirely different from the present suggestion. Here it is proposed to decide, by our vote, what shall be discussed by particular ministers, already appointed, when they shall meet the ministers of the other powers. This is not a general expression of opinion. It is a particular direction, or a special instruction. Its operation is limited to the conduct of particular men, on a particular occasion. Such a thing, Sir, is wholly unprecedented in our history. When the House proceeds in the accustomed way, by general resolution, its sentiments apply as far as expressed, to all public agents,

and on all occasions. They apply to the whole course of policy, and must necessarily be felt everywhere. But if we proceed by way of direction to particular ministers, we must direct them all. In short, we must take upon ourselves to furnish diplomatic instructions in all cases.

We now propose to prescribe what our ministers shall discuss, and what they shall not discuss, at Panama. But there is no subject coming up for discussion at Panama, which might not also be proposed for discussion either here, or at Mexico, or in the capital of Colombia. If we direct what our ministers at Panama shall or shall not say on the subject of Mr. Monroe's declaration, for example, why should we not proceed to say also what our other ministers abroad, or our Secretary at home, shall say on the same subject? There is precisely the same reason for the one as for the other. The course of the House hitherto, Sir, has not been such. It has expressed its opinions, when it deemed proper to express them at all, on great leading questions, by resolution, and in a general form. These general opinions, being thus made known, have doubtless always had, and such expressions of opinion doubtless always will have, their effect. This is the practice of the government. It is a salutary practice; but if we carry it further, or rather if we adopt a very different practice, and undertake to prescribe to our public ministers what they shall discuss, and what they shall not discuss, we take upon ourselves that which, in my judgment, does not at all belong to us. I see no more propriety in our deciding now in what manner these ministers shall discharge their duty, than there would have been in our prescribing to the President and Senate what persons ought to be appointed ministers.

An honorable member from Virginia [William Cabell Rives], who spoke some days ago, seems to go still further than the member from Delaware. He maintains, that we may distinguish between the various objects contemplated by the executive in the proposed negotiation, and adopt some and reject others. And this high, delicate, and important trust, the gentleman deduces simply from our power to withhold the ministers' salaries. The process of the gentleman's argument appears to me as singular as its conclusion. He founds himself on the legal maxim, that he who has the power to give may annex to the gift whatever condition or qualification he chooses. This maxim, Sir, would be applicable to the present case, if we were the sovereigns of the country; if all power were in our hands; if the public money were entirely our own; if our appropriation of it were mere grace and favor; and if there were no restraints upon us but our own sovereign will and pleasure. But the argument totally forgets that we are ourselves but public agents; that our power over the treasury is but that of stewards over a trust fund; that we have nothing to give, and therefore no gifts to limit or qualify; that it is as much our duty to appropriate to proper objects, as to withhold

appropriations from such as are improper; and that it is as much, and as clearly, our duty to appropriate in a proper and constitutional manner, as to appropriate at all.

The same honorable member advanced another idea, in which I cannot concur. He does not admit that confidence is to be reposed in the executive, on the present occasion, because confidence, he argues, implies only that, not knowing ourselves what will be done in a given case by others, we trust those who are to act in it, that they will act right; and as we know the course likely to be pursued in regard to this subject by the executive, confidence can have no place. This seems a singular notion of confidence, and certainly is not my notion of that confidence which the Constitution requires one branch of the government to repose in another. The President is not our agent, but, like ourselves, the agent of the people. They have trusted to his hands the proper duties of his office; and we are not to take those duties out of his hands, from any opinion of our own that we should execute them better ourselves. The confidence which is due from us to the executive, and from the excutive to us, is not personal, but official and constitutional. It has nothing to do with individual likings or dislikings; but results from that division of power among departments, and those limitations on the authority of each, which belong to the nature and frame of our government. It would be unfortunate indeed, if our line of constitutional action were to vibrate backward and forward, according to our opinions of persons, swerving this way to-day, from undue attachment, and the other way to-morrow, from distrust or dislike. This may sometimes happen from the weakness of our virtues, or the excitement of our passions; but I trust it will not be coolly recommended to us, as the rightful course of public conduct.

It is obvious to remark, Mr. Chairman, that the Senate have not undertaken to give directions or instructions in this case. That body is closely connected with the President in executive measures. Its consent to these very appointments is made absolutely necessary by the Constitution; yet it has not seen fit, in this or any other case, to take upon itself the responsibility of directing the mode in which the negotiations should be conducted.

For these reasons, Mr. Chairman, I am for giving no instructions, advice, or directions in the case. I prefer leaving it where, in my judgment, the Constitution has left it; to executive discretion and executive responsibility.

But, Sir, I think there are other objections to the amendment. There are parts of it which I could not agree to, if it were proper to attach any such condition to our vote. As to all that part of the amendment, indeed, which asserts the neutral policy of the United States, and the inexpediency of forming alliances, no man assents to those sentiments more read-

ily, or more entirely, than myself. On these points we are all agreed. Such is our opinion; such, the President assures us, in terms, is his opinion; such we know to be the opinion of the country. If it be thought necessary to affirm opinions which no one either denies or doubts, by a resolution of the House, I shall cheerfully concur in it. But there is one part of the proposed amendment to which I could not agree in any form. I wish to ask the gentleman from Delaware himself to reconsider it. I pray him to look at it again, and to see whether he means what it expresses or implies; for, on this occasion, I should be more gratified by seeing that the honorable gentleman himself had become sensible that he had fallen into some error in this respect, than by seeing the vote of the House against him by any majority whatever.

That part of the amendment to which I now object is that which requires, as a condition of the resolution before us, that the ministers shall not "be authorized to discuss, consider, or consult upon any measure which shall commit the present or future neutral rights or duties of these United States, either as may regard European nations, or between the several states of Mexico and South America."

I need hardly repeat, that this amounts to a precise instruction. It being understood that the ministers shall not be authorized to discuss particular subjects, is a mode of speech precisely equivalent to saying, "provided the ministers be instructed," or "the ministers being instructed, not to discuss those subjects." Notwithstanding all that has been said, or can be said, about this amendment being no more than a general expression of opinion, or an abstract proposition, this part of it is an exact and definite instruction. It prescribes to public ministers the precise manner in which they are to conduct a public negotiation; a duty manifestly and exclusively belonging, in my judgment, to the executive, and not to us.

But if we possessed the power to give instructions, this instruction would not be a proper one to give. Let us examine it. The ministers shall not "discuss, consider, or consult upon any measure which shall commit the present or future neutral rights or duties of these United States, either as may regard European nations, or between the several states of Mexico and South America."

Now, Sir, in the first place, it is to be observed that they are not only not to agree to any such measure, but they are not to discuss it. If proposed to them, they are not to give reasons for declining it. Indeed, they cannot reject it; they can only say they are not authorized to consider it. Would it not be better, Sir, to leave these agents at liberty to explain the policy of our government, fully and clearly, and to show the reasons which induce us to abstain, as far as possible, from foreign connections,

and to act in all things with a scrupulous regard to the duties of neutrality?

But again; they are to discuss no measure which may commit our neutral rights or duties. To commit is somewhat indefinite. May they not modify or in any degree alter our neutral rights and duties? If not, I hardly know whether a common treaty of commerce could be negotiated; because all such treaties affect or modify, more or less, the neutral rights or duties of the parties; especially all such treaties as our habitual policy leads us to form. But I suppose the author of the amendment uses the word in a larger and higher sense. He means that the ministers shall not discuss or consider any measure which may have a tendency, in any degree, to place us in a hostile attitude towards any foreign state. And here, again, one cannot help repeating, that the prohibition is, not against proposing or assenting to any such measure, but against considering it, against answering it if proposed, against resisting it with reasons.

But if this object were removed, still the instruction could not properly be given. What important or leading measure is there, connected with our foreign relations, which can be adopted without the possibility of committing us to the necessity of a hostile attitude? Any assertion of our plainest rights may, by possibility, have that effect. The author of the amendment seems to suppose that our pacific relations can never be changed but by our own option. He seems not to be aware that other states may compel us, in defence of our own rights, to measures which, in their ultimate tendency, may commit our neutrality. Let me ask, if the ministers of other powers, at Panama, should signify to our agents that it was in contemplation immediately to take some measure which these agents knew to be hostile to our policy, adverse to our rights, and such as we could not submit to; should they be left free to speak the sentiments of their government, to protest against the measure, and to declare that the United States would not see it carried into effect? Or should they, as this amendment proposes, be enjoined to silence, to let the measure proceed, in order that afterwards, when perhaps we have gone to war to redress the evil, we may learn that, if our objections had been fairly and frankly stated, the step would not have been taken? Look, Sir, to the very case of Cuba, the most delicate and vastly the most important point in all our foreign relations. Do gentlemen think they exhibit skill or statesmanship in laying such restraints as they propose on our ministers, in regard to this among other subjects? It has been made matter of complaint, that the executive has not used, already, a more decisive tone toward Mexico and Colombia, in regard to their designs on this island. Pray, Sir, what tone could be taken under these

instructions? Not one word, not one single word, could be said on the subject. If asked whether the United States would consent to the occupation of that island by these republics, or to its transfer by Spain to a European power, or whether we should resist such occupation or such transfer, what could they say? "That is a matter we cannot discuss, and cannot consider; it would commit our neutral relations; we are not at liberty to express the sentiments of our government on the subject; we have nothing at all to say." Is this, Sir, what the gentlemen wish, or what they would recommend?

If, Sir, we give these instructions, and they should be obeyed, and inconvenience or evil result, who is answerable? And I suppose it is expected they will be obeyed. Certainly it cannot be intended to give them, and not take the responsibility of the consequences, if they are followed. It cannot be intended to hold the President answerable both ways; first, to compel him to obey our instructions, and, secondly, to make him responsible if evil comes from obeying them.

Sir, events may change. If we had the power to give instructions, and if these proposed instructions were proper to be given, before we arrive at our own homes affairs may take a new direction, and the public interest require new and corresponding orders to our agents abroad.

This is said to be an extraordinary case, and, on that account, to justify our interference. If the fact were true, the consequence would not follow. If it be the exercise of a power assigned by the Constitution to the executive, it can make no difference whether the occasion be common or uncommon. But, in truth, there have been much stronger cases for the interference of the House, where, nevertheless, the House has not interfered. For example, in the negotiations for peace carried on at Ghent. In that case, Congress, by both houses, had declared war for certain alleged causes. After the war had lasted some years, the President, with the advice of the Senate, appointed ministers to treat of peace; and he gave them such instructions as he saw fit. Now, as the war was declared by Congress, and was waged to obtain certain ends, it would have been plausible to say that Congress ought to know the instructions under which peace was to be negotiated, that they might see whether the objects for which the war was declared had been abandoned. Yet no such claim was set up. The President gave instructions such as his judgment dictated, and neither house asserted any right of interference.

Sir, there are gentlemen in this House, opposed to this mission, who, I hope, will nevertheless consider this question of amendment on general constitutional grounds. They are gentlemen of much estimation in the community, likely, I hope, long to continue in the public service; and I trust they will well reflect on the effect of this amendment on the

separate powers and duties of the several departments of the government.

An honorable member from Pennsylvania [Joseph Hemphill] has alluded to a resolution introduced by me the session before the last.[2] I should not have referred to it myself, had he not invited the reference; but I am happy in the opportunity of showing how that resolution coincides with every thing which I say today. What was that resolution? When an interesting people were struggling for national existence against a barbarous despotism, when there were good hopes (hopes yet, I trust, to be fully realized) of their success, and when the Holy Alliance had pronounced against them certain false and abominable doctrines, I moved the House to resolve—what? Simply that provision ought to be made by law to defray the expense of an agent or commissioner to that country, whenever the President should deem it expedient to make such appointment. Did I propose any instruction to the President, or any limit on his discretion? None at all, Sir; none at all. What resemblance, then, can be found between that resolution and this amendment? Let those who think any such resemblance exists adopt, if they will, the words of the resolution as a substitute for this amendment. We shall gladly take them.

I am therefore, Mr. Chairman, against the amendment, not only as not being a proper manner of exercising any power belonging to this House, but also as not containing instructions fit to be given if we possessed the power of giving them. And as my vote will rest on these grounds, I might terminate my remarks here; but the discussion has extended over a broader surface, and, following where others have led, I will ask your indulgence to a few observations on the more general topics of the debate.

Mr. Chairman, it is our fortune to be called upon to act our part as public men at a most interesting era in human affairs. The short period of your life and of mine has been thick and crowded with the most important events. Not only new interests and new relations have sprung up among states, but new societies, new nations, and families of nations, have risen to take their places and perform their parts in the order and the intercourse of the world. Every man aspiring to the character of a statesman must endeavor to enlarge his views to meet this new state of things. He must aim at an adequate comprehension of it, and instead of being satisfied with that narrow political sagacity, which, like the power of minute vision, sees small things accurately, but can see nothing else, he must look to the far horizon, and embrace in his broad survey what-

2. See *Annals*, 18th Cong., 1st sess., p. 805.

ever the series of recent events has brought into connection, near or remote, with the country whose interests he studies to serve.

We have seen eight states, formed out of colonies on our own continent, assume the rank of nations.[3] This is a mighty revolution, and when we consider what an extent of the surface of the globe they cover, through what climates they extend, what population they contain, and what new impulses they must derive from this change of government, we cannot but perceive that great effects are likely to be produced on the intercourse and the interests of the civilized world. Indeed, it has been forcibly said, by the intelligent and distinguished statesman who conducts the foreign relations of England [George Canning] that when we now speak of Europe and the world, we mean Europe and America; and that the different systems of these two portions of the globe, and their several and various interests, must be thoroughly studied and nicely balanced by the statesmen of the times.

In many respects, Sir, the European and the American nations are alike. They are alike Christian states, civilized states, and commercial states. They have access to the same common fountains of intelligence; they all draw from those sources which belong to the whole civilized world. In knowledge and letters, in the arts of peace and war, they differ in degrees; but they bear, nevertheless, a general resemblance. On the other hand, in matters of government and social institutions, the nations on this continent are founded upon principles which never did prevail, to considerable extent, either at any other time or in any other place. There has never been presented to the mind of man a more interesting subject of contemplation than the establishment of so many nations in America, partaking in the civilization and in the arts of the Old World, but having left behind them those cumbrous institutions which had their origin in a dark and military age. Whatsoever European experience has developed favorable to the freedom and the happiness of man, whatever European genius has invented for his improvement or gratification, whatsoever of refinement or polish the culture of European society presents for his adoption and enjoyment,—all this is offered to man in America, with the additional advantage of the full power of erecting forms of government on free and simple principles, without overturning institutions suited to times long passed, but too strongly supported, either by interests or prejudices, to be shaken without convulsions. This un-

3. Webster is probably referring to Argentina, Bolivia, Brazil, the Central American Federation, Chile, Colombia, Mexico, and Peru. At this time Paraguay was a part of Argentina; the status of Uruguay was disputed; Ecuador, New Granada, and Venezuela were parts of Colombia; and the Central American Federation comprised the modern states of Guatemala, Honduras, El Salvador, Nicaragua, and Costa Rica.

precedented state of things presents the happiest of all occasions for an attempt to establish national intercourse upon improved principles, upon principles tending to peace and the mutual prosperity of nations. In this respect America, the whole of America, has a new career before her. If we look back on the history of Europe, we see for how great a portion of the last two centuries her states have been at war for interests connected mainly with her feudal monarchies. Wars for particular dynasties, wars to support or prevent particular successions, wars to enlarge or curtail the dominions of particular crowns, wars to support or to dissolve family alliances, wars to enforce or to resist religious intolerance,—what long and bloody chapters do not these fill in the history of European politics! Who does not see, and who does not rejoice to see, that America has a glorious chance of escaping at least these causes of contention? Who does not see, and who does not rejoice to see, that, on this continent, under other forms of government, we have before us the noble hope of being able, by the mere influence of civil liberty and religious toleration, to dry up these outpouring fountains of blood, and to extinguish these consuming fires of war. The general opinion of the age favors such hopes and such prospects. There is a growing disposition to treat the intercourse of nations more like the useful intercourse of friends; philosophy, just views of national advantage, good sense, the dictates of a common religion, and an increasing conviction that war is not the interest of the human race, all concur to magnify the importance of this new accession to the list of nations.

We have heard it said, Sir, that the topic of South American independence is worn out, and threadbare. Such it may be, Sir, to those who have contemplated it merely as an article of news, like the fluctuation of the markets, or the rise and fall of stocks. Such it may be to those who can see no consequences following from these great events. But whoever has either understood their present importance, or can at all estimate their future influence, whoever has reflected on the new relations they introduce with other states, whoever, among ourselves especially, has meditated on the new relations which we now bear to them, and the striking attitude in which we ourselves are now placed, as the oldest of the American nations, will feel that the topic can never be without interest; and will be sensible that, whether we are wise enough to perceive it or not, the establishment of South American independence will affect all nations, and ourselves perhaps more than any other, through all coming time.

But, Sir, although the independence of these new states seems effectually accomplished, yet a lingering and hopeless war is kept up against them by Spain. This is greatly to be regretted by all nations. To Spain it is, as every reasonable man sees, useless, and without hope. To the new

states themselves it is burdensome and afflictive. To the commerce of neutral nations it is annoying and vexatious. There seems to be something of the pertinacity of the Spanish character in holding on in such a desperate course. It reminds us of the seventy years during which Spain resisted the independence of Holland. I think, however, that there is some reason to believe that the war approaches its end. I believe that the measures adopted by our own government have had an effect in tending to produce that result. I understand, at least, that the question of recognition has been taken into consideration by the Spanish government; and it may be hoped that a war which Spain finds to be so expensive, which the whole world tells her is so hopeless, and which, if continued, now threatens her with new dangers, she may, ere long, have the prudence to terminate.

Our own course during this contest between Spain and her colonies is well known. Though entirely and strictly neutral, we were in favor of early recognition. Our opinions were known to the allied sovereigns when in congress at Aix-la-Chapelle in 1818, at which time the affairs of Spain and her colonies were under consideration; and probably the knowledge of those sentiments, together with the policy adopted by England, prevented any interference by other powers at that time. Yet we have treated Spain with scrupulous delicacy. We acted on the case as one of civil war. We treated with the new governments as governments *de facto*. Not questioning the right of Spain to reduce them to their old obedience, if she had the power, we yet held it to be our right to deal with them as with existing governments in fact, when the moment arrived at which it became apparent and manifest that the dominion of Spain over these, her ancient colonies, was at an end. Our right, our interest, and our duty, all concurred at that moment to recommend the recognition of their independence. We accordingly recognized it.

Now, Sir, the history of this proposed congress goes back to an earlier date than that of our recognition. It commences in 1821; and one of the treaties now before us, proposing such a meeting, that between Colombia and Chili, was concluded in July, 1822, a few months only after we had acknowledged the independence of the new states. The idea originated, doubtless, in the wish to strengthen the union among the new governments, and to promote the common cause of all, the effectual resistance to Spanish authority. As independence was at that time their leading object, it is natural to suppose that they contemplated this mode of mutual intercourse and mutual arrangement, as favorable to the concentration of purpose and of action necessary for the attainment of that object. But this purpose of the congress, or this leading idea, in which it may be supposed to have originated, has led, as it seems to me, to great misapprehensions as to its true character, and great mistakes in

regard to the danger to be apprehended from our sending ministers to the meeting. This meeting, Sir, is a congress; not a congress as the word is known to our Constitution and laws, for we use it in a peculiar sense; but as it is known to the law of nations. A congress, by the law of nations, is but an appointed meeting for the settlement of affairs between different nations, in which the representatives or agents of each treat and negotiate as they are instructed by their own government. In other words, this congress is a diplomatic meeting. We are asked to join no government, no legislature, no league, acting by votes. It is a congress, such as those of Westphalia, of Nimeguen, of Ryswick, or Utrecht; or such as those which have been held in Europe in our own time. No nation is a party to any thing done in such assemblies, to which it does not expressly make itself a party. No one's rights are put at the disposition of any of the rest, or of all the rest. What ministers agree to, being afterwards duly ratified at home, binds their government; and nothing else binds the government. Whatsoever is done, to which they do not assent, neither binds the ministers nor their government, any more than if they had not been present.

These truths, Sir, seem too plain and too commonplace to be stated. I find my apology only in those misapprehensions of the character of the meeting to which I have referred both now and formerly. It has been said that commercial treaties are not negotiated at such meetings. Far otherwise is the fact. Among the earliest of important stipulations made in favor of commerce and navigation, were those at Westphalia. What we call the treaty of Utrecht, was a bundle of treaties, negotiated at that congress; some of peace, some of boundary, and others of commerce. Again, it has been said, in order to prove that this meeting is a sort of confederacy, that such assemblies are out of the way of ordinary negotiation, and are always founded on, and provided for, by previous treaties. Pray Sir, what treaty preceded the congress at Utrecht? And the meeting of our plenipotentiaries with those of England at Ghent, what was that but a congress? and what treaty preceded it? It is said again, that there is no sovereign to whom our ministers can be accredited. Let me ask whether, in the case last cited, our ministers exhibited their credentials to the Mayor of Ghent? Sir, the practice of nations in these matters is well known, and is free from difficulty. If the government be not present, agents or plenipotentiaries interchange their credentials. And when it is said that our ministers at Panama will be, not ministers, but deputies, members of a deliberative body, not protected in their public character by the public law, propositions are advanced of which I see no evidence whatever, and which appear to me to be wholly without foundation.

It is contended that this congress, by virtue of the treaties which the

new states have entered into, will possess powers other than those of a diplomatic character, as between those new states themselves. If that were so, it would be unimportant to us. The real question here is, What will be our relation with those states, by sending ministers to this congress? Their arrangement among themselves will not affect us. Even if it were a government, like our old Confederation, yet, if its members had authority to treat with us in behalf of their respective nations on subjects on which we have a right to treat, the congress might still be a very proper occasion for such negotiations. Do gentlemen forget that the French minister was introduced to our old Congress, met it in its sessions, carried on oral discussions with it, and treated with it in behalf of the French king? All that did not make him a member of it, nor connect him at all with the relations which its members bore to each other. As he treated on the subject of carrying on the war against England, it was, doubtless, hostile towards that power; but this consequence followed from the object and nature of the stipulations, and not from the manner of the intercourse. The representatives of these South American states, it is said, will entertain belligerent counsels at this congress. Be it so; we shall not join in such counsels. At the moment of invitation, our government informed the ministers of those states, that we could not make ourselves a party to the war between them and Spain, nor to counsels for deliberating on the means of its further prosecution.

If, it is asked, we send ministers to a congress composed altogether of belligerents, is it not a breach of neutrality? Certainly not; no man can say it is. Suppose, Sir, that these ministers from the new states, instead of Panama, were to assemble at Bogota, where we already have a minister; their counsels at that place might be belligerent, while the war should last with Spain. But should we on that account recall our minister from Bogota? The whole argument rests on this; that because, at that same time and place, the agents of the South American governments may negotiate about their own relations with each other, in regard to their common war against Spain, therefore we cannot, at the same time and place, negotiate with them, or any of them, upon our own neutral and commercial relations. This proposition, Sir, cannot be maintained; and therefore all the inferences from it fail.

But, Sir, I see no proof that, as between themselves, the representatives of the South American states are to possess other than diplomatic powers. I refer to the treaties, which are essentially alike, and which have been often read.

With two exceptions, (which I will notice,) the articles of these treaties, describing the powers of the congress, are substantially like those of the treaty of Paris, in 1814, providing for the congress at Vienna. It was there stipulated that all the powers should send plenipotentiaries

to Vienna, to regulate, in general congress, the arrangements to complete the provisions of the present treaty. Now, it might have been here asked, how *regulate*? How regulate in general congress?—regulate by votes? Sir, nobody asked such questions; simply because it was to be a congress of plenipotentiaries. The two exceptions which I have mentioned are, that this congress is to act as a council, and to interpret treaties; but there is nothing in either of these to be done which may not be done diplomatically. What is more common than diplomatic intercourse, to explain and to interpret treaties? Or what more frequent than that nations, having a common object, interchange mutual counsels and advice, through the medium of their respective ministers? To bring this matter, Sir, to the test, let me ask, When these ministers assemble at Panama, can they do any thing but according to their instructions? Have they any organization, any power of action, or any rule of action, common to them all? No more, Sir, than the respective ministers at the congress of Vienna. Every thing is settled by the use of the word Plenipotentiary. That proves the meeting to be diplomatic, and nothing else. Who ever heard of a plenipotentiary member of the legislature? a plenipotentiary burgess of a city? or a plenipotentiary knight of the shire?

We may dismiss all fears, Sir, arising from the nature of this meeting. Our agents will go there, if they go at all, in the character of ministers, protected by the public law, negotiating only for ourselves, and not called on to violate any neutral duty of their own government. If it be that this meeting will have other powers, in consequence of other arrangements between other states, of which I see no proof, still we shall not be a party to these arrangements, nor can we be in any way affected by them. As far as this government is concerned, nothing can be done but by negotiation, as in other cases.

It has been affirmed, that this measure, and the sentiments expressed by the executive relative to its objects, are an acknowledged departure from the neutral policy of the United States. Sir, I deny that there is an acknowledged departure, or any departure at all, from the neutral policy of the country. What do we mean by our neutral policy? Not, I suppose, a blind and stupid indifference to whatever is passing around us; not a total disregard to approaching events, or approaching evils, till they meet us full in the face. Nor do we mean, by our neutral policy, that we intend never to assert our rights by force. No, Sir. We mean by our policy of neutrality, that the great objects of national pursuit with us are connected with peace. We covet no provinces; we desire no conquests; we entertain no ambitious projects of aggrandizement by war. This is our policy. But it does not follow from this, that we rely less than other nations on our own power to vindicate our own rights. We know that the last logic of kings is also our last logic; that our own interests must be

defended and maintained by our own arm; and that peace or war may not always be of our own choosing. Our neutral policy, therefore, not only justifies, but requires, our anxious attention to the political events which take place in the world, a skilful perception of their relation to our own concerns, and an early anticipation of their consequences, and firm and timely assertion of what we hold to be our own rights and our own interests. Our neutrality is not predetermined abstinence, either from remonstrances, or from force. Our neutral policy is a policy that protects neutrality, that defends neutrality, that takes up arms, if need be, for neutrality. When it is said, therefore, that this measure departs from our neutral policy, either that policy, or the measure itself, is misunderstood. It implies either that the object or the tendency of the measure is to involve us in the war of other states, which I think cannot be shown, or that the assertion of our own sentiments, on points affecting deeply our own interests, may place us in a hostile attitude toward other states, and that therefore we depart from neutrality; whereas the truth is, that the decisive assertion and the firm support of these sentiments may be most essential to the maintenance of neutrality.

An honorable member from Pennsylvania [James Buchanan] thinks this congress will bring a dark day over the United States. Doubtless, Sir, it is an interesting moment in our history; but I see no great proofs of thick-coming darkness. But the object of the remark seemed to be to show that the President himself saw difficulties on all sides, and, making a choice of evils, preferred rather to send ministers to this congress, than to run the risk of exciting the hostility of the states by refusing to send. In other words, the gentleman wished to prove that the President intended an alliance; although such intention is expressly disclaimed.

Much commentary has been bestowed on the letters of invitation from the ministers. I shall not go through with verbal criticisms on these letters. Their general import is plain enough. I shall not gather together small and minute quotations, taking a sentence here, a word there, and a syllable in a third place, dovetailing them into the course of remark, till the printed discourse bristles in every line with inverted commas.[4] I look to the general tenor of the invitations, and I find that we are asked to take part only in such things as concern ourselves. I look still more carefully to the answers, and I see every proper caution and proper guard. I look to the message, and I see that nothing is there contemplated likely to involve us in other men's quarrels, or that may justly give offence to any foreign state. With this I am satisfied.

I must now ask the indulgence of the committee to an important point

4. The *National Intelligencer*   harvest field."
version adds to this sentence "like a

in the discussion, I mean the delaration of the President in 1823.[5] Not only as a member of the House, but as a citizen of the country, I have an anxious desire that this part of our public history should stand in its proper light. The country has, in my judgment, a very high honor connected with that occurrence, which we may maintain, or which we may sacrifice. I look upon it as a part of its treasures of reputation; and, for one, I intend to guard it.

Sir, let us recur to the important political events which led to that declaration, or accompanied it. In the fall of 1822, the allied sovereigns held their congress at Verona. The great subject of consideration was the condition of Spain, that country then being under the government of the Cortes. The question was, whether Ferdinand should be reinstated in all his authority, by the intervention of foreign force. Russia, Prussia, France, and Austria were inclined to that measure; England dissented and protested; but the course was agreed on, and France, with the consent of these other Continental powers, took the conduct of the operation into her own hands. In the spring of 1823, a French army was sent into Spain. Its success was complete. The popular government was overthrown, and Ferdinand reestablished in all his power. This invasion, Sir, was determined on, and undertaken, precisely on the doctrines which

5. The Monroe Doctrine. Everett, in *Works*, 3: 200–201, adds a footnote quoting from Monroe's message to Congress of Dec. 2, 1823 as follows: "In the wars of the European powers, in matters relating to themselves, we have never taken any part, nor does it comport with our policy to do so. It is only when our rights are invaded, or seriously menaced, that we resent injuries or make preparations for defence. With the movements in this hemisphere we are of necessity more immediately connected, and by causes which must be obvious to all enlightened and impartial observers. The political system of the Allied Powers is essentially different, in this respect, from that of America. This difference proceeds from that which exists in their respective governments. And to the defence of our own, which has been achieved by the loss of so much blood and treasure, and matured by the wisdom of their most enlightened citizens, and under which we have enjoyed such unexampled felicity, this whole nation is devoted. We owe it, therefore, to candor, and to the amicable relations existing between the United States and those powers, to declare that we should consider any attempt on their part to extend their system to any portion of this hemisphere as dangerous to our peace and safety. With the existing colonies or dependencies of any European power, we have not interfered and shall not interfere. But with the governments who have declared their independence and maintained it, and whose independence we have on great consideration and on just principles acknowledged, we could not view any interposition for the purpose of oppressing them, or controlling in any other manner their destiny, in any other light than as the manifestation of an unfriendly disposition toward the United States." *Messages and Papers*, 2: 787.

the allied monarchs had proclaimed the year before, at Laybach; that is, that they had a right to interfere in the concerns of another state, and reform its government, in order to prevent the effects of its bad example; this bad example, be it remembered, always being the example of free government. Now, Sir, acting on this principle of supposed dangerous example, and having put down the example of the Cortes in Spain, it was natural to inquire with what eyes they would look on the colonies of Spain, that were following still worse examples. Would King Ferdinand and his allies be content with what had been done in Spain itself, or would he solicit their aid, and was it likely they would grant it, to subdue his rebellious American provinces?

Sir, it was in this posture of affairs, on an occasion which has already been alluded to, that I ventured to say, early in the session of December, 1823, that these allied monarchs might possibly turn their attention to America; that America came within their avowed doctrine, and that her examples might very possibly attract their notice. The doctrines of Laybach were not limited to any continent. Spain had colonies in America, and having reformed Spain herself to the true standard, it was not impossible that they might see fit to complete the work by reconciling, in their way, the colonies to the mother country. Now, Sir, it did so happen, that, as soon as the Spanish king was completely reëstablished, he invited the coöperation of his allies, in regard to South America. In the same month of December, of 1823, a formal invitation was addressed by Spain to the courts of St. Petersburg, Vienna, Berlin, and Paris, proposing to establish a conference at Paris, in order that the plenipotentiaries there assembled might aid Spain in adjusting the affairs of her revolted provinces. These affairs were proposed to be adjusted in such manner as should retain the sovereignty of Spain over them; and though the coöperation of the allies by force of arms was not directly solicited, such was evidently the object aimed at. The king of Spain, in making this request to the members of the Holy Alliance, argued as it has been seen he might argue. He quoted their own doctrines of Laybach; he pointed out the pernicious example of America; and he reminded them that their success in Spain itself had paved the way for successful operations against the spirit of liberty on this side of the Atlantic.

The proposed meeting, however, did not take place. England had already taken a decided course; for as early as October, Mr. Canning, in a conference with the French minister in London [François-Auguste Chateaubriand], informed him distinctly and expressly, that England would consider any foreign interference, by force or by menace, in the dispute between Spain and the colonies, as a motive for recognizing the latter without delay. It is probable this determination of the English government was known here at the commencement of the session of Congress;

and it was under these circumstances, it was in this crisis, that Mr. Monroe's declaration was made. It was not then ascertained whether a meeting of the allies would or would not take place, to concert with Spain the means of reëstablishing her power; but it was plain enough they would be pressed by Spain to aid her operations; and it was plain enough, also, that they had no particular liking to what was taking place on this side of the Atlantic, nor any great disinclination to interfere. This was the posture of affairs; and, Sir, I concur entirely in the sentiment expressed in the resolution of a gentleman from Pennsylvania [Philip S. Markley] that this declaration of Mr. Monroe was wise, seasonable, and patriotic.

It has been said, in the course of this debate, to have been a loose and vague declaration. It was, I believe, sufficiently studied. I have understood, from good authority, that it was considered, weighed, and distinctly and decidedly approved, by every one of the President's advisers at that time.[6] Our government could not adopt on that occasion precisely the course which England had taken. England threatened the immediate recognition of the provinces, if the Allies should take part with Spain against them. We had already recognized them. It remained, therefore, only for our government to say how we should consider a combination of the Allied Powers, to effect objects in America, as affecting ourselves; and the message was intended to say, what it does say, that we should regard such combination as dangerous to us. Sir, I agree with those who maintain the proposition, and I contend against those who deny it, that the message did mean something; that it meant much; and I maintain, against both, that the declaration effected much good, answered the end designed by it, did great honor to the foresight and the spirit of the government, and that it cannot now be taken back, retracted, or annulled, without disgrace. It met, Sir, with the entire concurrence and the hearty approbation of the country. The tone which it uttered found a corresponding response in the breasts of the free people of the United States. That people saw, and they rejoiced to see, that, on a fit occasion, our weight had been thrown into the right scale, and that, without departing from our duty, we had done something useful, and something effectual, for the cause of civil liberty. One general glow of exultation, one universal feeling of the gratified love of liberty, one conscious and proud perception of the consideration which the country possessed, and of the respect and honor which belonged to it, pervaded all bosoms. Possibly the public enthusiasm went too far; it certainly did go far. But, Sir, the sentiment which this declaration inspired was not confined to ourselves. Its force was felt everywhere, by all those who could understand its object and foresee its effect. In that very House of Commons of which the

6. Webster's source is probably John Quincy Adams. See Adams, *Memoirs*, 6: 178–210.

gentleman from South Carolina [James Hamilton, Jr.] has spoken with such commendation, how was it received? Not only, Sir, with approbation, but, I may say, with no little enthusiasm. While the leading minister [George Canning] expressed his entire concurrence in the sentiments and opinions of the American President, his distinguished competitor [Henry Peter Brougham] in that popular body, less restrained by official decorum, and more at liberty to give utterance to all the feeling of the occasion, declared that no event had ever created greater joy, exultation, and gratitude among all the free men in Europe; that he felt pride in being connected by blood and language with the people of the United States; that the policy disclosed by the message became a great, a free, and an independent nation; and that he hoped his own country would be prevented by no mean pride, or paltry jealousy, from following so noble and glorious an example.

It is doubtless true, as I took occasion to observe the other day, that this declaration must be considered as founded on our rights, and to spring mainly from a regard to their preservation. It did not commit us, at all events, to take up arms on any indication of hostile feeling by the powers of Europe towards South America. If, for example, all the states of Europe had refused to trade with South America until her states should return to their former allegiance, that would have furnished no cause of interference to us. Or if an armament had been furnished by the Allies to act against provinces the most remote from us, as Chili or Buenos Ayres, the distance of the scene of action diminishing our apprehension of danger, and diminishing also our means of effectual interposition, might still have left us to content ourselves with remonstrance. But a very different case would have arisen, if an army, equipped and maintained by these powers, had been landed on the shores of the Gulf of Mexico, and commenced the war in our own immediate neighborhood. Such an event might justly be regarded as dangerous to ourselves, and, on that ground, call for decided and immediate interference by us. The sentiments and the policy announced by the declaration, thus understood, were, therefore, in strict conformity to our duties and our interest.

Sir, I look on the message of December, 1823, as forming a bright page in our history. I will help neither to erase it nor tear it out; nor shall it be, by any act of mine, blurred or blotted. It did honor to the sagacity of the government, and I will not diminish that honor. It elevated the hopes, and gratified the patriotism, of the people. Over those hopes I will not bring a mildew; nor will I put that gratified patriotism to shame.

But how should it happen, Sir, that there should now be such a new-born fear on the subject of this declaration? The crisis is over; the danger is past. At the time it was made, there was real ground for apprehension; now there is none. It was then possible, perhaps not improbable, that the

Allied Powers might interfere with America. There is now no ground for any such fear. Most of the gentlemen who have now spoken on the subject were at that time here. They all heard the declaration. Not one of them complained. And yet now, when all danger is over, we are vehemently warned against the sentiments of the declaration.

To avoid this apparent inconsistency, it is, however, contended, that new force has been recently given to this declaration. But of this I see no evidence whatever. I see nothing in any instructions or communications from our government changing the character of that declaration in any degree. There is, as I have before said, in one of Mr. [Joel Roberts] Poinsett's[7] letters, an inaccuracy of expression. If he has recited correctly his conversation with the Mexican minister, he did go too far, farther than any instruction warranted. But, taking his whole correspondence together, it is quite manifest that he has deceived nobody, and that he has not committed the country. On the subject of a pledge, he put the Mexican minister entirely right. He stated to him distinctly, that this government had given no pledge which others could call upon it to redeem. What could be more explicit? Again, Sir, it is plain that Mexico thought us under no greater pledge than England; for the letters to the English and American ministers, requesting interference, were in precisely the same words. When this passage in Mr. Poinsett's letter was first noticed, we were assured there was and must be some other authority for it. It was confidently said he had instructions authorizing it in his pocket. It turns out otherwise. As little ground is there to complain of any thing in the Secretary's letter to Mr. Poinsett. It seems to me to be precisely what it should be. It does not, as has been alleged, propose any cöoperation between the government of Mexico and our own. Nothing like it. It instructs our ministers to bring to the notice of the Mexican government the line of policy which we have marked out for ourselves, acting on our own grounds, and for our own interests; and to suggest to that government, acting on its own ground, and for its own interests, the propriety of following a similar course. Here, Sir, is no alliance, nor even any cöoperation.

So, again, as to the correspondence which refers to the appearance of the French fleet in the West India seas. Be it remembered that our government was contending, in the course of this correspondence with Mexico, for an equality in matters of commerce. It insisted on being placed, in this respect, on the same footing as the other Spanish American states. To enforce this claim, our known friendly sentiments towards Mexico, as well as to the rest of the new states, were suggested, and properly suggested. Mexico was reminded of the timely declaration which had been made of these sentiments. She was reminded that she herself had been

7. U.S. Minister to Mexico, March 1825–Dec. 1829.

well inclined to claim the benefit resulting from that declaration, when a French fleet appeared in the neighboring seas; and she was referred to the course adopted by our government on that occasion, with an intimation that she might learn from it how the same government would have acted if other possible contingencies had happened. What is there in all this of any renewed pledge, or what is there of any thing beyond the true line of policy? Do gentlemen mean to say that the communication made to France, on this occasion, was improper? Do they mean to repel and repudiate that declaration? That declaration was, that we could not see Cuba transferred from Spain to another European power. If the House mean to contradict that, be it so. If it do not, then, as the government had acted properly in this case, it did furnish ground to believe it would act properly, also, in other cases, when they arose. And the reference to this incident or occurrence by the Secretary was pertinent to the argument which he was pressing on the Mexican government.

I have but a word to say on the subject of the declaration against European colonization in America. The late President seems to have thought the occasion used by him for that purpose to be a proper one for the open avowal of a principle which had already been acted on. Great and practical inconveniences, it was feared, might be apprehended from the establishment of new colonies in America, having a European orgin and a European connection. Attempts of that kind, it was obvious, might possibly be made, amidst the changes that were taking place in Mexico, as well as in the more southern states. Mexico bounds us, on a vast length of line, from the Gulf of Mexico to the Pacific Ocean. There are many reasons why it should not be desired by us, that an establishment, under the protection of a different power, should occupy any portion of that space. We have a general interest, that, through all the vast territories rescued from the dominion of Spain, our commerce may find its way, protected by treaties with governments existing on the spot. These views, and others of a similar character, rendered it highly desirable to us, that these new states should settle it, as a part of their policy, not to allow colonization within their respective territories. True, indeed, we did not need their aid to assist us in maintaining such a course for ourselves; but we had an interest in their assertion and support of the principle as applicable to their own territories.

I now proceed, Mr. Chairman, to a few remarks on the subject of Cuba, the most important point of our foreign relations. It is the hinge on which interesting events may possibly turn. I pray gentlemen to review their opinions on this subject before they fully commit themselves. I understood the honorable member from South Carolina [James Hamilton, Jr.] to say, that if Spain chose to transfer this island to any power in Europe, she had a right to do so, and we could not interfere to prevent it. Sir, this

is a delicate subject. I hardly feel competent to treat it as it deserves; and I am not quite willing to state here all that I think about it. I must, however, dissent from the opinion of the gentleman from South Carolina. The rights of nations, on subjects of this kind, are necessarily very much modified by circumstances. Because England or France could not rightfully complain of the transfer of Florida to us, it by no means follows, as the gentleman supposes, that we could not complain of the cession of Cuba to one of them. The plain difference is, that the transfer of Florida to us was not dangerous to the safety of either of those nations, nor fatal to any of their great and essential interests. Proximity of position, neighborhood, whatever augments the power of injuring and annoying, very properly belong to the consideration of all cases of this kind. The greater or less facility of access itself is of consideration in such questions, because it brings, or may bring, weighty consequences with it. It justifies, for these reasons and on these grounds, what otherwise might never be thought of. By negotiation with a foreign power, Mr. Jefferson obtained a province. Without any alteration of our Constitution, we have made it a part of the United States, and its Senators and Representatives, now coming from several States, are here among us. Now, Sir, if, instead of being Louisiana, this had been one of the provinces of Spain proper, or one of her South American colonies, he must have been a madman that should have proposed such an acquisition. A high conviction of its convenience, arising from proximity and from close natural connection, alone reconciled the country to the measure. Considerations of the same sort have weight in other cases.

An honorable member from Kentucky [Charles A. Wickliffe] argues, that although we might rightfully prevent another power from taking Cuba from Spain by force, yet, if Spain should choose to make the voluntary transfer, we should have no right whatever to interfere. Sir, this is a distinction without a difference. If we are likely to have contention about Cuba, let us first well consider what our rights are, and not commit ourselves. And, Sir, if we have any right to interfere at all, it applies as well to the case of a peaceable as to that of a forcible transfer. If nations be at war, we are not judges of the question of right in that war; we must acknowledge in both parties the mutual right of attack and the mutual right of conquest. It is not for us to set bounds to their belligerent operations so long as they do not affect ourselves. Our right to interfere in any such case is but the exercise of the right of reasonable and necessary self-defence. It is a high and delicate exercise of that right; one not to be made but on grounds of strong and manifest reason, justice, and necessity. The real question is, whether the possession of Cuba by a great maritime power of Europe would seriously endanger our own immediate security or our essential interests. I put the question, Sir, in the

language of some of the best considered state papers of modern times. The general rule of national law is, unquestionably, against interference in the transactions of other states. There are, however, acknowledged exceptions, growing out of circumstances and founded in those circumstances. These exceptions, it has been properly said, cannot without danger be reduced to previous rule, and incorporated into the ordinary diplomacy of nations. Nevertheless, they do exist, and must be judged of, when they arise, with a just regard to our own essential interests, but in a spirit of strict justice and delicacy also towards foreign states.

The ground of these exceptions is, as I have already stated, self-preservation. It is not a slight injury to our interest, it is not even a great inconvenience, that makes out a case. There must be danger to our security, or danger, manifest and imminent danger, to our essential rights and our essential interests. Now, Sir, let us look at Cuba. I need hardly refer to its present amount of commercial connection with the United States. Our statistical tables, I presume, would show us that our commerce with the Havana alone is more than our whole commercial intercourse with France and all her dependencies. But this is but one part of the case, and not the most important. Cuba, as is well said in the report of the Committee of Foreign Affairs, is placed in the mouth of the Mississippi. Its occupation by a strong maritime power would be felt, in the first moment of hostility, as far up the Mississippi and the Missouri as our population extends. It is the commanding point of the Gulf of Mexico. See, too, how it lies in the very line of our coastwise traffic; interposed in the very highway between New York and New Orleans.

Now, Sir, who has estimated, or who can estimate, the effect of a change which should place this island in other hands, subject it to new rules of commercial intercourse, or connect it with objects of a different and still more dangerous nature? Sir, I repeat that I feel no disposition to pursue this topic on the present occasion. My purpose is only to show its importance, and to beg gentlemen not to prejudice any rights of the country by assenting to propositions, which, perhaps, it may be necessary hereafter to review.

And here I differ again with the gentleman from Kentucky. He thinks, that, in this as in other cases, we should wait till the event comes, without any previous declaration of our sentiments upon subjects important to our own rights or our own interests. Sir, such declarations are often the appropriate means of preventing that which, if unprevented, it might be difficult to redress. A great object in holding diplomatic intercourse is frankly to expose the views and objects of nations, and to prevent, by candid explanation, collision and war. In this case, the government had said that we could not assent to the transfer of Cuba to another European state. Can we so assent? Do gentlemen think we can? If not, then it was

entirely proper that this intimation should be frankly and seasonably made. Candor required it; and it would have been unpardonable, it would have been injustice, as well as folly, to be silent while we might suppose the transaction to be contemplated, and then to complain of it afterwards. If we should have a subsequent right to complain, we have a previous right, equally clear, of protesting; and if the evil be one which, when it comes, would allow us to apply a remedy, it not only allows us, but it makes it our duty, also to apply prevention.

But, Sir, while some gentlemen have maintained that on the subject of a transfer to any of the European powers the President has said too much, others insist that on that of the occupation of the island by Mexico or Colombia he has said and done too little. I presume, Sir, for my own part, that the strongest language has been directed to the source of greatest danger. Heretofore that danger was, doubtless, greatest which was apprehended from a voluntary transfer. The other has been met as it arose; and, thus far adequately and sufficiently met.

And here, Sir, I cannot but say that I never knew a more extraordinary argument than we have heard on the conduct of the executive on this part of the case. The President is charged with inconsistency; and in order to make this out, public despatches are read, which, it is said, militate with one another.

Sir, what are the facts? This government saw fit to invite the Emperor of Russia to use his endeavors to bring Spain to treat of peace with her revolted colonies. Russia was addressed on this occasion as the friend of Spain; and, of course, every argument which it was thought might have influence, or ought to have influence, either on Russia or Spain, was suggested in the correspondence. Among other things, the probable loss to Spain of Cuba and Porto Rico was urged; and the question was asked, how it was or could be expected by Spain, that the United States should interfere to prevent Mexico and Colombia from taking those islands from her, since she was their enemy, in a public war, and since she pertinaciously, and unreasonably, as we think, insists on maintaining the war; and since these islands offered an obvious object of attack. Was not this, Sir, a very proper argument to be urged to Spain? A copy of this despatch, it seems, was sent to the Senate in confidence. It has not been published by the executive. Now, the alleged inconsistency is, that, notwithstanding this letter, the President has interfered to dissuade Mexico and Colombia from attacking Cuba; that, finding or thinking that those states meditated such a purpose, this government has urged them to desist from it. Sir, was ever any thing more unreasonable than this charge? Was it not proper, that, to produce the desired result of peace, our government should address different motives to the different parties in the war? Was it not its business to set before each party its dangers

and its difficulties in pursuing the war? And if now, by any thing unexpected, these respective correspondences have become public, are these different views, addressed thus to different parties and with different objects, to be relied on as proof of inconsistency? It is the strangest accusation ever heard of. No government not wholly destitute of common sense would have acted otherwise. We urged the proper motives to both parties. To Spain we urged the probable loss of Cuba; we showed her the dangers of its capture by the new states; and we asked her to inform us on what ground it was that we could interfere to prevent such capture, since she was at war with those states, and they had an unquestionable right to attack her in any of her territories; and, especially, she was asked how she could expect good offices from us on this occasion, since she fully understood our opinion to be that she was persisting in the war without or beyond all reason, and with a sort of desperation. This was the appeal made to the good sense of Spain, through Russia. But soon afterwards, having reason to suspect that Colombia and Mexico were actually preparing to attack Cuba, and knowing that such an event would most seriously affect us, our government remonstrated against such meditated attack, and to the present time it has not been made. In all this, who sees any thing either improper or inconsistent? For myself, I think that the course pursued showed a watchful regard to our own interest, and is wholly free from any imputation either of impropriety or inconsistency.

There are other subjects, Sir, in the President's message, which have been discussed in the debate, but on which I shall not long detain the committee.

It cannot be denied, that, from the commencement of our government, it has been its object to improve and simplify the principles of national intercourse. It may well be thought a fit occasion to urge these improved principles at a moment when so many new states are coming into existence, untrammelled, of course, with previous and long-established connections or habits. Some hopes of benefit connected with these topics are suggested in the message.

The abolition of private war on the ocean is also among the subjects of possible consideration. This is not the first time that that subject has been mentioned. The late President took occasion to enforce the considerations which he thought recommended it. For one, I am not prepared to say how far such abolition may be practicable, or how far it ought to be pursued; but there are views belonging to the subject which have not been, in any degree, answered or considered in this discussion. It is not always the party that has the power of employing the largest military marine that derives the greatest benefit from authorizing privateers in war. It is not enough that there are brave and gallant captors; there must

be something to be captured. Suppose, Sir, a war between ourselves and any one of the new states of South America were now existing, who would lose most by the practice of privateering in such a war? There would be nothing for us to attack, while the means of attacking us would flow to our enemies from every part of the world. Capital, ships, and men would be abundant in all their ports, and our commerce, spread over every sea, would be the destined prey. So, again, if war should unhappily spring up among those states themselves, might it not be for our interest, as being likely to be much connected by intercourse with all parties, that our commerce should be free from the visitation and search of private armed ships, one of the greatest vexations to neutral commerce in time of war? These, Sir, are some of the considerations belonging to this subject. I have mentioned them only to show that they well deserve serious attention.

I have not intended to reply to the many observations which have been submitted to us on the message of the President to this House, or that to the Senate. Certainly I am of opinion, that some of those observations merited an answer, and they have been answered by others. On two points only will I make a remark. It has been said, and often repeated, that the President, in his message to the Senate, has spoken of his own power in regard to missions in terms which the Constitution does not warrant. If gentlemen will turn to the message of President Washington relative to the mission to Lisbon,[8] they will see almost the exact form of expression used in this case. The other point on which I would make a remark is the allegation that an unfair use has been made, in the argument of the message, of General Washington's Farewell Address. There would be no end, Sir, to comments and criticisms of this sort if they were to be pursued. I only observe, that, as it appears to me, the argument of the message, and its use of the Farewell Address, are not fairly understood. It is not attempted to be inferred from the Farewell Address, that, according to the opinion of Washington, we ought now to have alliances with foreign states. No such thing. The Farewell Address recommends to us to abstain as much as possible from all sorts of political connection with the states of Europe, alleging as the reason for this advice, that Europe has a set of primary interests of her own, separate from ours, and with which we have no natural connection. Now the message argues, and argues truly, that, the new South American states not having a set of interests of their own, growing out of the balance of power, family alliances, and other similar causes, separate from ours, in the same manner and to the same degree as the primary interests of Europe were represented to be, this part of the Farewell Address, aimed at those separate

8. *Messages and Papers*, i : 97–98.

interests expressly, did not apply in this case. But does the message infer from this the propriety of alliances with these new states? Far from it. It infers no such thing. On the contrary, it disclaims all such purpose.

There is one other point, Sir, on which common justice requires a word to be said. It has been alleged that there are material differences as to the papers sent respectively to the two houses. All this, as it seems to me, may be easily and satisfactorily explained. In the first place, the instructions of May, 1823, which, it is said, were not sent to the Senate, were instructions on which a treaty had been already negotiated; which treaty had been subsequently ratified by the Senate. It may be presumed, that, when the treaty was sent to the Senate, the instructions accompanied it; and if so, they were actually already before the Senate; and this accounts for one of the alleged differences. In the next place, the letter to Mr. [Henry] Middleton,[9] in Russia, not sent to the House, but now published by the Senate, is such a paper as possibly the President might not think proper to make public. There is evident reason for such an inference. And, lastly, the correspondence of Mr. [James] Brown, sent here, but not to the Senate, appears from its date to have been received after the communication to the Senate.[10] Probably when sent to us, it was also sent, by another message, to that body.

These observations, Sir, are tedious and uninteresting. I am glad to be through with them. And here I might terminate my remarks, and relieve the patience, now long and heavily taxed, of the committee. But there is one part of the discussion, on which I must ask to be indulged with a few observations.

Pains, Sir, have been taken by the honorable member from Virginia [William Cabell Rives], to prove that the measure now in contemplation, and, indeed, the whole policy of the government respecting South America, is the unhappy result of the influence of a gentleman formerly filling the chair of this House.[11] To make out this, he has referred to certain speeches of that gentleman delivered here. He charges him with having become himself affected at an early day with what he is pleased to call the South American fever; and with having infused its baneful influence into the whole counsels of the country.

If, Sir, it be true that that gentleman, prompted by an ardent love of civil liberty, felt earlier than others a proper sympathy for the struggling colonies of South America; or that, acting on the maxim that revolutions

9. U.S. Minister to Russia, April 6, 1820–Aug. 3, 1830. For an explanation of Webster's allusion see *Register of Debates*, 19th Cong., 1st sess., pp. 2137–2138, 2148, 2178, 2214, 2246–2247, and Appendix, pp. 53–57, 74.

10. U.S. Minister to France, Dec. 10, 1823–June 28, 1829. For an explanation of this reference see *Register of Debates*, 19th Cong., 1st sess., Appendix, pp. 47, 61, 68, 69–73.

11. Henry Clay, now secretary of state.

do not go backward, he had the sagacity to foresee, earlier than others, the successful termination of those struggles; if, thus feeling, and thus perceiving, it fell to him to lead the willing or unwilling counsels of his country, in her manifestations of kindness to the new governments, and in her seasonable recognition of their independence,—if it be this which the honorable member imputes to him, if it be by this course of public conduct that he has identified his name with the cause of South American liberty, he ought to be esteemed one of the most fortunate men of the age. If all this be as is now represented, he has acquired fame enough. It is enough for any man thus to have connected himself with the greatest events of the age in which he lives, and to have been foremost in measures which reflect high honor on his country, in the judgment of mankind. Sir, it is always with great reluctance that I am drawn to speak, in my place here, of individuals; but I could not forbear what I have now said, when I hear, in the House of Representatives, and in this land of free spirits, that it is made matter of imputation and of reproach to have been first to reach forth the hand of welcome and of succor to new-born nations, struggling to obtain and to enjoy the blessings of liberty.

We are told that the country is deluded and deceived by cabalistic words. Cabalistic words! If we express an emotion of pleasure at the results of this great action of the spirit of political liberty; if we rejoice at the birth of new republican nations, and express our joy by the common terms of regard and sympathy; if we feel and signify high gratification that, throughout this whole continent, men are now likely to be blessed by free and popular institutions; and if, in the uttering of these sentiments, we happen to speak of sister republics, of the great American family of nations, or of the political system and forms of government of this hemisphere, then indeed, it seems, we deal in senseless jargon, or impose on the judgment and feeling of the community by cabalistic words! Sir, what is meant by this? Is it intended that the people of the United States ought to be totally indifferent to the fortunes of these new neighbors? Is no change in the lights in which we are to view them to be wrought, by their having thrown off foreign dominion, established independence, and instituted on our very borders republican governments essentially after our own example?

Sir, I do not wish to overrate, I do not overrate, the progress of these new states in the great work of establishing a well-secured popular liberty. I know that to be a great attainment, and I know they are but pupils in the school. But, thank God, they are in the school. They are called to meet difficulties such as neither we nor our fathers encountered. For these we ought to make large allowances. What have we ever known like the colonial vassalage of these states? When did we or our ancestors feel, like them, the weight of a political despotism that presses men to the

earth, or of that religious intolerance which would shut up heaven to all of a different creed?[12] Sir, we sprung from another stock. We belong to another race. We have known nothing, we have felt nothing, of the political despotism of Spain, nor of the heat of her fires of intolerance. No rational man expects that the South can run the same rapid career as the North; or that an insurgent province of Spain is in the same condition as the English colonies when they first asserted their independence. There is, doubtless, much more to be done in the first than in the last case. But on that account the honor of the attempt is not less; and if all difficulties shall be in time surmounted, it will be greater. The work may be more arduous, it is not less noble, because there may be more of ignorance to enlighten, more of bigotry to subdue, more of prejudice to eradicate. If it be a weakness to feel a strong interest in the success of these great revolutions, I confess myself guilty of that weakness. If it be weak *to feel that I am* an American, to think that recent events have not only opened new modes of intercourse, but have created also new grounds of regard and sympathy between ourselves and our neighbors; if it be weak to feel that the South, in her present state, is somewhat more emphatically a part of America than when she lay obscure, oppressed, and unknown, under the grinding bondage of a foreign power; if it be weak to rejoice when, even in any corner of the earth, human beings are able to rise from beneath oppression, to erect themselves, and to enjoy the proper happiness of their intelligent nature;—If this be weak; it is a weakness from which I claim no exemption.

A day of solemn retribution now visits the once proud monarchy of Spain. The prediction is fulfilled. The spirit of Montezuma and of the Incas might now well say,—

> "Art thou, too, fallen, Iberia? Do we see
> The robber and the murderer weak as we?
> Thou! that hast wasted earth and dared despise
> Alike the wrath and mercy of the skies,
> Thy pomp is in the grave; thy glory laid
> Low in the pits thine avarice has made."[13]

Mr. Chairman, I will only detain you with one more reflection on this subject. We cannot be so blind, we cannot so shut up our senses and smother our faculties, as not to see, that, in the progress and the establishment of South American liberty, our own example has been among the most stimulating causes.[14] In their emergencies, they have looked to

12. *National Intelligencer* reads "all but the bigoted." The softening of the language is Everett's, in *Works*, 3: 216.

13. "Charity," by William Cowper.

See Robert Southey, *The Life and Works of William Cowper* (London, 1854), 5: 182.

14. *National Intelligencer* inserts here the following: "That great light

our experience; in their political institutions, they have followed our models; in their deliberations, they have invoked the presiding spirit of our own liberty. They have looked steadily, in every adversity, to the *great Northern light.* In the hour of bloody conflict, they have remembered the fields which have been consecrated by the blood of our own fathers; and when they have fallen, they have wished only to be remembered with them, as men who had acted their parts bravely for the cause of liberty in the Western World.

Sir, I have done. If it be weakness to feel the sympathy of one's nature excited for such men, in such a cause, I am guilty of that weakness. If it be prudent to meet their proffered civility, not with reciprocal kindness, but with coldness or with insult, I choose still to follow where natural impulse leads, and to give up that false and mistaken prudence for the voluntary sentiments of my heart.

—a light which can never be hid— the light of our own glorious Revolution, has shone on the path of the South American Patriots, from the beginning of their course." The passage was dropped from *Speeches and Forensic Arguments,* 1: 349.

Adams and Jefferson, August 2, 1826

The simultaneous deaths of John Adams and Thomas Jefferson on July 4, 1826, the fiftieth birthday of the nation they had done so much to create, was greeted the country over with awed solemnity. It was as though God had spoken once more to His chosen people, to point again the way to the promised land. Everywhere, from the great cities to the rural hamlets, orators of sorts strove for words adequate to the occasion. The obvious and all but universal choice to deliver the Boston eulogy was Daniel Webster (Joseph Story to DW, July 11, 1826, *Correspondence*, 2: 126–127). He had already distinguished himself and enthralled audiences many times since he had taken up residence in Boston a decade earlier, most recently at the cornerstone laying of the Bunker Hill Monument only a year ago (*W & S*, 1: 235–254). As attorney, as representative in Congress, as public-spirited citizen, there was hardly a man or woman in Boston who did not know him, at least by sight and repute. He had, moreover, known personally both of the fabled statesmen now departed. With Adams he had worked in the Massachusetts Constitutional Convention of 1820; Jefferson he had visited at Monticello in December 1824, and had found all the partisan hostility of his Federalist days vanishing under the aged Virginian's charm and force of intellect.

The August 2 date set for the event left him little time for preparation, but it was enough. From Timothy Pickering, quartermaster general of the Revolutionary Army and secretary of state in Adams's cabinet, he received an exchange of letters in August 1822, giving the ex-president's recollection of the events of July 1776. He had in his own notes (*Correspondence*, 1: 375) something of Jefferson's memories of those stirring times. We may presume that he consulted the already formidable collections of the Massachusetts Historical Society, and talked to many whose memories went back farther than his own. Creative imagination did the rest.

The high point of the eulogy for most was the part where Adams answers at length the argument of one who opposes independence. As much as 20 years later Webster was still getting queries: Did Adams really say this? And always he answered "no." The hypothetical speech, worthy of Adams, to be sure, was written by Webster in the study of his

home on Summer Street (DW to Peter J. Becker, January 22, 1846, *W&S*, 1: 326).

The text of this much reworked eulogy is printed here from *Writings and Speeches*, 1: 289–324. We have in this case a manuscript in Webster's hand belonging to the New Hampshire Historical Society, which differs in many passages from the final published version. Variations that do not change the sense have been ignored; significant variations, generally omissions or additions, have been footnoted. Important additions have also been placed in brackets for the convenience of the reader. A pamphlet version appeared in Boston within two weeks of the delivery of the address. It embodies essentially all the changes that we may attribute to Webster's own careful editing. He deeply appreciated the honor conferred when the Boston council asked him to deliver the eulogy. He meant to make of it all the political capital inherent in the occasion. Some passages were amplified to drive home a point or to avoid any misconception; others were deleted lest some offense be taken where none was meant. Oratorical flourishes designed to please the ear were converted to sober narrative designed to catch the eye.

The pamphlet, published by Cummings, Hilliard & Company of Boston, under the title "A Discourse in Commemoration of the Lives and Services of John Adams and Thomas Jefferson, delivered in Faneuil Hall, Boston, on the 2nd of August, 1826," went through several editions, before it was incorporated in 1830 into the first volume of *Speeches and Forensic Arguments*, 1: 71–96. This text was followed in *Works*, 1: 113–148, from which it was reprinted verbatim in *Writings and Speeches*, 1: 289–324.

How far this declamation may have helped Webster's political career there is no way of knowing, but it certainly did him no harm. He was elected by the state legislature to the United States Senate less than a year later.

This is an unaccustomed spectacle. For the first time, fellow-citizens, badges of mourning shroud the columns and overhang the arches of this hall. These walls, which were consecrated, so long ago, to the cause of American liberty, which witnessed her infant struggles, and rung with the shouts of her earliest victories, proclaim, now, that distinguished friends and champions of that great cause have fallen. It is right that it should be thus.[1] The tears which flow, and the honors that are paid,

1. Manuscript adds: "Extraordinary occasions demand extraordinary notice. It is fit, that when all eyes see, & every heart feels, that occurrences have taken place, strangely blending peculiar sources of congratulation, with a deep sense of national loss; occurrences which wake, at

when the founders of the republic die, give hope that the republic itself may be immortal. It is fit that, by public assembly and solemn observance, by anthem and by eulogy, we commemorate the services of national benefactors, extol their virtues, and render thanks to God for eminent blessings, early given and long continued, through their agency, to our favored country.

ADAMS and JEFFERSON are no more; and we are assembled, fellow-citizens, the aged, the middle-aged and the young, by the spontaneous impulse of all, under the authority of the municipal government, with the presence of the chief magistrate of the Commonwealth, and others its official representatives, the University, and the learned societies, to bear our part in those manifestations of respect and gratitude which pervade the whole land. ADAMS and JEFFERSON are no more. On our fiftieth anniversary, the great day of national jubilee, in the very hour of public rejoicing, in the midst of echoing and reëchoing voices of thanksgiving, while their own names were on all tongues[2], they took their flight together to the world of spirits.

If it be true that no one can safely be pronounced happy while he lives, if that event which terminates life can alone crown its honors and its glory, what felicity is here! The great epic of their lives, how happily concluded! Poetry itself has hardly terminated illustrious lives, and finished the career of earthly renown, by such a consummation. If we had the power, we could not wish to reverse this dispensation of the Divine Providence. The great objects of life were accomplished, the drama was ready to be closed. It has closed; our patriots have fallen; but so fallen, at such age, with such coincidence, on such a day, that we cannot rationally lament that that end has come, which we knew could not be long deferred.

Neither of these great men, fellow-citizens, could have died, at any time, without leaving an immense void in our American society.[3] They have been so intimately, and for so long a time, blended with the history of the country, and especially so united, in our thoughts and recollections, with the events of the Revolution, that the death of either would have touched the chords of public sympathy. We should have felt that one great link, connecting us with former times, was broken; that we had lost something more, as it were, of the presence of the Revolution itself, and of the act of independence, and were driven on, by another

---

once, sorrow, gratitude, & wonder; we should manifest these strong and mixed emotions."

2. Manuscript adds: "& affection for their virtues swelling in all hearts."

3. Manuscript adds: "Whenever either might have bowed to the stroke, which terminates human existence, we should have been struck with a sense of great national loss."

great remove from the days of our country's early distinction, to meet posterity, and to mix with the future. Like the mariner, whom the currents of the ocean and the winds carry along, till he sees the stars which have directed his course and lighted his pathless way descend, one by one, beneath the rising horizon, we should have felt that the stream of time had borne us onward till another great luminary, whose light had cheered us and whose guidance we had followed, had sunk away from our sight.

But the concurrence of their death on the anniversary of Independence has naturally awakened stronger emotions. Both had been Presidents, both had lived to great age, both were early patriots, and both were distinguished and ever honored by their immediate agency in the act of independence. It cannot but seem striking and extraordinary, that these two should live to see the fiftieth year from the date of that act; that they should complete that year; and that then, on the day which had fast linked for ever their own fame with their country's glory, the heavens should open to receive them both at once. As their lives themselves were the gifts of Providence, who is not willing to recognize in their happy termination, as well as in their long continuance, proofs that our country and its benefactors are objects of His care?

ADAMS and JEFFERSON, I have said, are no more. As human beings, indeed, they are no more. They are no more, as in 1776, bold and fearless advocates of independence; no more, as at subsequent periods, the head of the government; no more, as we have recently seen them, aged and venerable objects of admiration and regard. They are no more. They are dead. But how little is there of the great and good which can die![4] To their country they yet live, and live for ever. They live in all that perpetuates the remembrance of men on earth; in the recorded proofs of their own great actions, in the offspring of their intellect, in the deep-engraved lines of public gratitude, and in the respect and homage of mankind. They live in their example; and they live, emphatically, and will live, in the influence which their lives and efforts, their principles and opinions, now exercise, and will continue to exercise, on the affairs of men, not only in their own country, but throughout the civilized world. A superior and commanding human intellect, a truly great man, when Heaven vouchsafes so rare a gift, is not a temporary flame, burning brightly for a while, and then giving place to returning darkness. It is rather a spark

4. Manuscript adds: "To them, it is not death, but renovation, & a new creation. Religion assures to all the good an immortality beyond the grave, and vain is that triumph of the king of terrors, which shuts the eye on earthly things, only that it may open to the visions of bliss above." The sentence following in the manuscript then begins with "And."

of fervent heat, as well as radiant light, with power to enkindle the common mass of human kind; so that when it glimmers in its own decay, and finally goes out in death, no night follows, but it leaves the world all light, all on fire, from the potent contact of its own spirit. Bacon died; but the human understanding, roused by the touch of his miraculous wand to a perception of the true philosophy and the just mode of inquiring after truth, has kept on its course successfully and gloriously. Newton died; yet the courses of the spheres are still known, and they yet move on by the laws which he discovered, and in the orbits which he saw, and described for them, in the infinity of space.

No two men now live, fellow-citizens, perhaps it may be doubted whether any two men have ever lived in one age, who, more than those we now commemorate, have impressed on mankind their own sentiments in regard to politics and government, infused their own opinions more deeply into the opinions of others, or given a more lasting direction to the current of human thought. Their work doth not perish with them. The tree which they assisted to plant will flourish, although they water it and protect it no longer; for it has struck its roots deep, it has sent them to the very centre; no storm, not of force to burst the orb, can overturn it; its branches spread wide; they stretch their protecting arms broader and broader, and its top is destined to reach the heavens. We are not deceived. There is no delusion here. No age will come in which the American Revolution will appear less than it is, one of the greatest events in human history. No age will come in which it shall cease to be seen and felt, on either continent, that a mighty step, a great advance, not only in American affairs, but in human affairs, was made on the 4th of July, 1776. And no age will come, we trust, so ignorant or so unjust as not to see and acknowledge the efficient agency of those we now honor in producing that momentous event.

We are not assembled, therefore, fellow-citizens, as men overwhelmed with calamity by the sudden disruption of the ties of friendship or affection, or as in despair for the republic by the untimely blighting of its hopes. Death has not surprised us by an unseasonable blow. We have, indeed, seen the tomb close, but it has closed only over mature years, over long-protracted public service, over the weakness of age, and over life itself only when the ends of living had been fulfilled. These suns, as they rose slowly and steadily, amidst clouds and storms, in their ascendant, so they have not rushed from their meridian to sink suddenly in the west. Like the mildness, the serenity, the continuing benignity of a summer's day, they have gone down with slow-descending, grateful, long-lingering light; and now that they are beyond the visible margin of the world, good omens cheer us from "the bright track of their fiery car"!

There were many points of similarity in the lives and fortunes of these

great men. They belonged to the same profession, and had pursued its studies and its practice, for unequal lengths of time indeed, but with diligence and effect. Both were learned and able lawyers. They were natives and inhabitants, respectively, of those two of the Colonies which at the Revolution were the largest and most powerful, and which naturally had a lead in the political affairs of the times. When the Colonies became in some degree united, by the assembling of a general Congress, they were brought to act together in its deliberations, not indeed at the same time, but both at early periods. Each had already manifested his attachment to the cause of the country, as well as his ability to maintain it, by printed addresses, public speeches, extensive correspondence, and whatever other mode could be adopted for the purpose of exposing the encroachments of the British Parliament, and animating the people to a manly resistance. Both were not only decided, but early, friends of Independence. While others yet doubted, they were resolved; where others hesitated, they pressed forward. They were both members of the committee for preparing the Declaration of Independence, and they constituted the sub-committee appointed by the other members to make the draft. They left their seats in Congress, being called to other public employments, at periods not remote from each other, although one of them returned to it afterwards for a short time. Neither of them was of the assembly of great men which formed the present Constitution, and neither was at any time a member of Congress under its provisions. Both have been public ministers abroad, both Vice-Presidents and both Presidents of the United States. These coincidences are now singularly crowned and completed. They have died together; and they died on the anniversary of liberty.

When many of us were last in this place, fellow-citizens, it was on the day of that anniversary. We were met to enjoy the festivities belonging to the occasion, and to manifest our grateful homage to our political fathers. We did not, we could not here, forget our venerable neighbor of Quincy. We knew that we were standing, at a time of high and palmy prosperity, where he had stood in the hour of utmost peril; that we saw nothing but liberty and security, where he had met the frown of power; that we were enjoying every thing, where he had hazarded every thing; and just and sincere plaudits rose to his name, from the crowds which filled this area, and hung over these galleries. He whose grateful duty it was to speak to us,[5] on that day, of the virtues of our fathers, had, indeed, admonished us that time and years were about to level his venerable frame with the dust. But he bade us hope that "the sound of a nation's joy, rushing from our cities, ringing from our valleys, echoing from our hills, might yet break the silence of his aged ear; that the rising blessings

5. Josiah Quincy (1772–1864), then mayor of Boston.

of grateful millions might yet visit with glad light his decaying vision."
Alas! that vision was then closing for ever. Alas! the silence which was
then settling on that aged ear was an everlasting silence! For, lo! in the
very moment of our festivities, his freed spirit ascended to God who gave
it! Human aid and human solace terminate at the grave; or we would
gladly have borne him upward, on a nation's outspread hands; we would
have accompanied him, and with the blessings of millions and the prayers
of millions, commended him to the Divine favor.

While still indulging our thoughts, on the coincidence of the death
of this venerable man with the anniversary of Independence, we learn
that Jefferson, too, has fallen; and that these aged patriots, these illustrious fellow-laborers, have left our world together. May not such events
raise the suggestion that they are not undesigned, and that Heaven does
so order things, as sometimes to attract strongly the attention and excite
the thoughts of men? The occurrence has added new interest to our anniversary, and will be remembered in all time to come.

The occasion, fellow-citizens, requires some account of the lives and
services of JOHN ADAMS and THOMAS JEFFERSON. This duty must necessarily be performed with great brevity, and in the discharge of it I shall
be obliged to confine myself, principally, to those parts of their history
and character which belonged to them as public men.

JOHN ADAMS was born at Quincy, then part of the ancient town of
Braintree, on the 19th day of October (old style), 1735. He was a de-
scendant of the Puritans, his ancestors having early emigrated from England, and settled in Massachusetts. Discovering in childhood a strong
love of reading and of knowledge, together with marks of great strength
and activity of mind, proper care was taken by his worthy father to provide for his education. He pursued his youthful studies in Braintree,
under Mr. [Joseph] Marsh, a teacher whose fortune it was that Josiah
Quincy, Jr., as well as the subject of these remarks, should receive from
him his instruction in the rudiments of classical literature. Having been
admitted, in 1751, a member of Harvard College, Mr. Adams was graduated, in course, in 1755; and on the catalogue of that institution, his
name, at the time of his death, was second among the living Alumni,
being preceded only by that of the venerable Holyoke.[6] With what degree
of reputation he left the University is not now precisely known.[7] We know
only that he was distinguished in a class which numbered Locke and
Hemmenway[8] among its members. Choosing the law for his profession,

6. Dr. Edward Augustus Holyoke,
(1728–1829), 98 at this time, would
live to pass 100.

7. Manuscript adds: ", but a mind
like his, with habits of application
like his, could hardly fail of distinguishing itself by the age of twenty."

8. Samuel Locke (1732–1778),
11th president of Harvard, 1770–
1773. Moses Hemmenway (1740–

he commenced and prosecuted its studies at Worcester, under the direction of Samuel Putnam, a gentleman whom he has himself described as an acute man, an able and learned lawyer, and as being in large professional practice at that time. In 1758 he was admitted to the bar, and entered upon the practice of the law in Braintree. He is understood to have made his first considerable effort, or to have attained his first signal success, at Plymouth, on one of those occasions which furnish the earliest opportunity for distinction to many young men of the profession, a jury trial, and a criminal cause. His business naturally grew with his reputation, and his residence in the vicinity afforded the opportunity, as his growing eminence gave the power, of entering on a larger field of practice in the capital. In 1766 he removed his residence to Boston, still continuing his attendance on the neighboring circuits, and not unfrequently called to remote parts of the Province. In 1770 his professional firmness was brought to a test of some severity, on the application of the British officers and soldiers to undertake their defence, on the trial of the indictments found against them on account of the transactions of the memorable 5th of March.[9] He seems to have thought, on this occasion, that a man can no more abandon the proper duties of his profession, than he can abandon other duties. The event proved, that as he judged well for his own reputation, so, too, he judged well for the interest and permanent fame of his country. The result of that trial proved, that, notwithstanding the high degree of excitement then existing in consequence of the measures of the British government, a jury of Massachusetts would not deprive the most reckless enemies, even the officers of that standing army quartered among them, which they so perfectly abhorred, of any part of that protection which the law, in its mildest and most indulgent interpretation, affords to persons accused of crimes.

Without following Mr. Adams's professional course further, suffice it to say, that on the first establishment of the judicial tribunals under the authority of the State, in 1776, he received an offer of the high and responsible station of Chief Justice of the Supreme Court of Massachusetts. But he was destined for another and a different career. From early life the bent of his mind was toward politics; a propensity which the state of the times, if it did not create, doubtless very much strengthened. Public subjects must have occupied the thoughts and filled up the conversation in the circles in which he then moved; and the interesting questions at that time just arising could not but seize on a mind like his, ardent, sanguine, and patriotic. A letter, fortunately preserved, written by him at

1824), minister of Wells, Maine for 51 years.

9. The Boston Massacre. See L.

Kinvin Wroth and Hiller B. Zobel, eds., *Legal Papers of John Adams* (3 vols., Cambridge, Mass. 1965), 3.

Worcester, so early as the 12th of October, 1755, is a proof of very comprehensive views, and uncommon depth of reflection, in a young man not yet quite twenty. In this letter he predicted the transfer of power, and the establishment of a new seat of empire in America; he predicted also, the increase of population in the Colonies; and anticipated their naval distinction, and foretold that all Europe combined could not subdue them. All this is said, not on a public occasion or for effect, but in the style of sober and friendly correspondence, as the result of his own thoughts. "I sometimes retire," said he, at the close of the letter, "and, laying things together, form some reflections pleasing to myself. The produce of one of these reveries you have read above." [10] This prognostication so early in his own life, so early in the history of the country, of independence, of vast increase of numbers, of naval force, of such augmented power as might defy all Europe, is remarkable. It is more remarkable that its author should live to see fulfilled to the letter what could have seemed to others, at the time, but the extravagance of youthful fancy. His earliest political feelings were thus strongly American, and from this ardent attachment to his native soil he never departed.

While still living at Quincy, and at the age of twenty-four, Mr. Adams was present, in this town, at the argument before the Supreme Court respecting *Writs of Assistance*, and heard the celebrated and patriotic speech of JAMES OTIS. Unquestionably, that was a masterly performance. No flighty declamation about liberty, no superficial discussion of popular topics, it was a learned, penetrating, convincing, constitutional argument, expressed in a strain of high and resolute patriotism. He grasped the question then pending between England and her Colonies with the

10. A note in the pamphlet version, presumably supplied by Webster himself, quotes from the letter of John Adams to Nathan Webb, Oct. 12, 1755, as follows: "Soon after the Reformation, a few people came over into this New World, for conscience' sake. Perhaps this apparently trivial incident may transfer the great seat of empire into America. It looks likely to me; for, if we can remove the turbulent Gallics, our people, according to the exactest computations, will, in another century, become more numerous than England itself. Should this be the case, since we have, I may say, all the naval stores of the nation in our hands, it will be easy to obtain a mastery of the seas; and then the united force of all Europe will not be able to subdue us. The only way to keep us from setting up for ourselves is to disunite us.

"Be not surprised that I am turned politician. This whole town is immersed in politics. The interests of nations, and all the *dira* of war, make the subject of every conversation. I sit and hear, and after having been led through a maze of sage observations, I sometimes retire, and, laying things together, form some reflections pleasing to myself. The produce of one of these reveries you have read above." See Robert J. Taylor and others, eds., *Papers of John Adams* (6 vols. to date, Cambridge and London, 1977–1983), 1: 5.

strength of a lion; and if he sometimes sported,[11] it was only because the lion himself is sometimes playful. Its success appears to have been as great as its merits, and its impression was widely felt. Mr. Adams himself seems never to have lost the feeling it produced, and to have entertained constantly the fullest conviction of its important effects. "I do say," he observes, "in the most solemn manner, that Mr. Otis's Oration against Writs of Assistance breathed into this nation the breath of life."[12]

In 1765 Mr. Adams laid before the public, anonymously, a series of essays, afterwards collected in a volume in London, under the title of A Dissertation on the Canon and Feudal Law.[13] The object of this work was to show that our New England ancestors, in consenting to exile themselves from their native land, were actuated mainly by the desire of delivering themselves from the power of the heirarchy, and from the monarchical and aristocratical systems of the other continent; and to make this truth bear with effect on the politics of the times. Its tone is uncommonly bold and animated for that period. He calls on the people, not only to defend, but to study and understand, their rights and privileges; urges earnestly the necessity of diffusing general knowledge; invokes the clergy and the bar, the colleges and academies, and all others who have the ability and the means to expose the insidious designs of arbitrary power, to resist its approaches, and to be persuaded that there is a settled design on foot to enslave all America. "Be it remembered," says the author, "that liberty must, at all hazards, be supported. We have a right to it, derived from our Maker. But if we had not, our fathers have earned and bought it for us, at the expense of their ease, their estates, their pleasure, and their blood. And liberty cannot be preserved without a general knowledge among the people, who have a right, from the frame of their nature, to knowledge, as their great Creator, who does nothing in vain, has given them understandings and a desire to know. But, besides this, they have

11. Manuscript adds: "with the broken fragments of his adversary's argument,".

12. The following note was supplied by Edward Everett in *Works*, 1: 121:

"Nearly all that was known of this celebrated argument, at the time the present Discourse was delivered, was derived from the recollections of John Adams, as preserved in Minot's History of Massachusetts, Vol II. p. 91. See Life and Works of John Adams, Vol. II. p. 124, published in the course of the past year (1850), in the Appendix to which, p. 521, will be found a paper hitherto unpublished, containing notes of the argument of Otis, 'which seem to be the foundation of the sketch published by Minot.' Tudor's Life of James Otis, p. 61." The quote in the text is from a letter of Adams to Henry Niles, Jan. 14, 1818, see Charles Francis Adams, ed. *The Life and Works of John Adams* (10 vols., Boston, 1856), 10: 276.

13. This note too was supplied by Everett, ibid.: "See Life and Works of John Adams, Vol. II. p. 447, and North American Review, Vol. LXXI. p. 430." See Taylor, *Adams*, 1: 103–128.

a right, an indisputable, unalienable indefeasible, divine right, to that most dreaded and envied kind of knowledge, I mean of the characters and conduct of their rulers. Rulers are no more than attorneys, agents, and trustees for the people; and if the cause, the interest and trust, is insidiously betrayed, or wantonly trifled away, the people have a right to revoke the authority that they themselves have deputed, and to constitute abler and better agents, attorneys, and trustees." [14]

The citizens of this town conferred on Mr. Adams his first political distinction, and clothed him with his first political trust, by electing him one of their representatives, in 1770. [Before [15] this time he had become extensively known throughout the Province, as well by the part he had acted in relation to public affairs, as by the exercise of his professional ability. He was among those who took the deepest interest in the controversy with England, and whether in or out of the legislature, his time and talents were alike devoted to the cause.] In the years 1773 and 1774 he was chosen a Councillor by the members of the General Court, but rejected by Governor Hutchinson in the former of those years, and by Governor Gage in the latter.

The time was now at hand, however, when the affairs of the Colonies urgently demanded united counsels throughout the country. An open rupture with the parent state appeared inevitable, and it was but the dictate of prudence that those who were united by a common interest and a common danger should protect that interest and guard against that danger by united efforts. A general Congress of Delegates from all the Colonies having been proposed and agreed to, the House of Representatives, on the 17th of June, 1774, elected James Bowdoin, Thomas Cushing, Samuel Adams, John Adams, and Robert Treat Paine, delegates from Massachusetts. [This [16] appointment was made at Salem, where the General Court had been convened by Governor Gage, in the last hour of the existence of a House of Representatives under the Provincial Charter. While engaged in this important business, the Governor, having been informed of what was passing, sent his secretary with a message dissolving the General Court. The secretary, finding the door locked, directed the messenger to go in and inform the Speaker that the secretary was at the door with a message from the Governor. The messenger returned, and informed the secretary that the orders of the House were that the doors should be kept fast; whereupon the secretary soon after read upon the stairs a proclamation dissolving the General Court. Thus terminated, for ever, the actual exercise of the political power of England in or over

14. Taylor, *Adams*, 1: 120–121.
15. Bracketed passage added in pamphlet version.

16. Bracketed passage added in pamphlet.

Massachusetts. The four last-named delegates accepted their appointments, and took their seats in Congress the first day of its meeting, the 5th of September, 1774, in Philadelphia.]

The proceedings of the first Congress are well known, and have been universally admired. [It[17] is in vain that we would look for superior proofs of wisdom, talent, and patriotism. Lord Chatham said, that, for himself, he must declare that he had studied and admired the free states of antiquity, the master states of the world, but that for solidity of reasoning, force of sagacity, and wisdom of conclusion, no body of men could stand in preference to this Congress. It is hardly inferior praise to say, that no production of that great man himself can be pronounced superior to several of the papers published as the proceedings of this most able, most firm, most patriotic assembly.] There is indeed, nothing superior to them in the range of political disquisition.[18] They not only embrace, illustrate, and enforce every thing which political philosophy, the love of liberty, and the spirit of free inquiry had antecedently produced, but they add new and striking views of their own, and apply the whole, with irrestible force, in support of the cause which had drawn them together.[19]

Mr. Adams was a constant attendant on the deliberations of this body, and bore an active part in its important measures. He was of the committee to state the rights of the Colonies, and of that also which reported the Address to the King.

As it was in the Continental Congress, fellow-citizens, that those whose deaths have given rise to this occasion were first brought together, and called upon to unite their industry and their ability in the service of the country, let us now turn to the other of these distinguished men, and take a brief notice of his life up to the period when he appeared within the walls of Congress.

THOMAS JEFFERSON, descended from ancestors who had been settled in Virginia for some generations, was born near the spot on which he died, in the county of Albemarle, on the 2d of April (old style), 1743. His youthful studies were pursued in the neighborhood of his father's

17. Bracketed passage added in pamphlet.

18. "There is indeed . . . political disquisition." The manuscript reads: "For myself, I confess, that having read them, as a boy, and having studied them, as a man, I know nothing superior to them in the whole range of political disquisition."

19. The manuscript adds: "If there be any thing, produced in the free states of antiquity, if there be any thing from the wisest & the best men of modern times, superior to the productions of the Congress of 1776, it has not fallen within the <course> sphere of my observation to be acquainted with them. A more patriotic, a more wise, a more enlightened body of public men never, in my judgment assembled on earth."

residence until he was removed to the College of William and Mary, the highest honors of which he in due time received. Having left the College with reputation, he applied himself to the study of the law under the tuition of George Wythe, one of the highest judicial names of which that State can boast. At an early age he was elected a member of the legislature, in which he had no sooner appeared than he distinguished himself by knowledge, capacity, and promptitude.[20]

Mr. Jefferson appears to have been imbued with an early love of letters and science, and to have cherished a strong disposition to pursue these objects. To the physical sciences, especially, and to ancient classic literature, he is understood to have had a warm attachment, and never entirely to have lost sight of them in the midst of the busiest occupations. But the times were times for action, rather than for contemplation. The country was to be defended, and to be saved, before it could be enjoyed. Philosophic leisure and literary pursuits, and even the objects of professional attention, were all necessarily postponed to the urgent calls of the public service. The exigency of the country made the same demand on Mr. Jefferson that it made on others who had the ability and the disposition to serve it; and he obeyed the call; thinking and feeling in this respect with the great Roman orator: "Quis enim est tam cupidus in perspicienda cognoscendaque rerum natura, ut, si ei tractanti contemplantique res cognitione dignissimas subito sit allatum periculum discrimenque patriæ, cui subvenire opitularique possit, non illa omnia relinquat atque abjiciat, etiam si dinumerare se stellas, aut metiri mundi magnitudinem posse arbitretur?"[21]

Entering with all his heart into the cause of liberty, his ability, patriotism, and power with the pen naturally drew upon him a large participation in the most important concerns. Wherever he was, there was found a soul devoted to the cause, power to defend and maintain it, and willingness to incur all its hazards. In 1774 he published a Summary View of the Rights of British America, a valuable production among those in-

20. "At an early age . . . and promptitude." Manuscript reads: "Almost as soon as he was of age, he was elected a member of the Legislature of that Colony, & he distinguished himself, in that body, as soon as he appeared in it; a body, too, in which distinction was not easy."

21. The Latin quotation, from Cicero, *De Officiis*, 1: 43, is absent from the manuscript. It has been translated by John Higginbotham, *Cicero on Moral Obligation* (Berkeley, 1967), p. 94, as follows: "Is there anyone so devoted to study and contemplation of the universe that if some sudden danger or crisis came upon his country while he was engaged in some study thoroughly worth while in itself, he would not throw everything aside and do what he could to help? Surely he would, even if he thought he was about to number the stars or measure the size of the earth."

tended to show the dangers which threatened the liberties of the country, and to encourage the people in their defence. In June, 1775, he was elected a member of the Continental Congress, as successor to Peyton Randolph, who had resigned his place on account of ill health, and took his seat in that body on the 21st of the same month.[22]

And now, fellow-citizens, without pursuing the biography of these illustrious men further, for the present, let us turn our attention to the most prominent act of their lives, their participation in the DECLARATION OF INDEPENDENCE.

Preparatory to the introduction of that important measure, a committee, at the head of which was Mr. Adams, had reported a resolution, which Congress adopted on the 10th of May, recommending, in substance, to all the Colonies which had not already established governments suited to the exigencies of their affairs, *to adopt such government as would, in the opinion of the representatives of the people, best conduce to the happiness and safety of their constituents in particular, and America in general.*

This significant vote was soon followed by the direct proposition which Richard Henry Lee had the honor to submit to Congress, by resolution, on the 7th day of June. [The [23] published journal does not expressly state it, but there is no doubt, I suppose, that this resolution was in the same words, when originally submitted by Mr. Lee, as when finally passed.] Having been discussed on Saturday, the 8th, and Monday, the 10th of June, this resolution was on the last mentioned day postponed for further consideration to the first day of July; and at the same time it was voted, that a committee be appointed to prepare a Declaration to the effect of the resolution. This committee was elected by ballot, on the following day, and consisted of Thomas Jefferson, John Adams, Benjamin Franklin, Roger Sherman, and Robert R. Livingston.

[It [24] is usual, when committees are elected by ballot, that their members should be arranged in order, according to the number of votes which each has received. Mr. Jefferson, therefore, had received the highest, and Mr. Adams the next highest number of votes. The difference is said to have been but a single vote.] Mr. Jefferson and Mr. Adams, standing thus at the head of the committee, were requested by the other members to act as a sub-committee to prepare the draft; and Mr. Jefferson drew

22. For the remainder of the paragraph, the manuscript reads "& took his seat in that Assembly on the 21st of the same month. In this August body he was the immediate successor of Peyton Randolph, & he remained in it, without intermission, till the summer of 177<7>8, when he retired from its service, to take upon himself the important situation of Governor of Virginia."

23. Bracketed passage absent from manuscript.

24. Bracketed passage absent from manuscript.

up the paper. The original draft, as brought by him from his study, and submitted to the other members of the committee, with interlineations in the handwriting of Dr. Franklin, and others in that of Mr. Adams, was in Mr. Jefferson's possession at the time of his death.[25] The merit of this paper is Mr. Jefferson's. Some changes were made in it at the suggestion of other members of the committee, and others by Congress while it was under discussion. But none of them altered the tone, the frame, the arrangement, or the general character of the instrument. As a composition, the Declaration is Mr. Jefferson's. It is the production of his mind, and the high honor of it belongs to him, clearly and absolutely.

It has sometimes been said, as if it were a derogation from the merits of this paper, that it contains nothing new; that it only states grounds of proceeding, and presses topics of argument, which had often been stated and pressed before. But [it[26] was not the object of the Declaration to produce any thing new. It was not to invent reasons for independence, but to state those which governed the Congress.] For great and sufficient causes, it was proposed to declare independence; and the proper business of the paper to be drawn was to set forth those causes, and justify the authors of the measure, in any event of fortune, to the country and to posterity. The cause of American independence, moreover, was now to be presented to the world in such manner; if it might so be, as to engage its sympathy, to command its respect, to attract its admiration; and in an assembly of most able and distinguished men, THOMAS JEFFERSON had the high honor of being the selected advocate of this cause. To say that he performed his great work well, would be doing him injustice. To say that he did excellently well, admirably well, would be inadequate and halting praise. Let us rather say, that he so discharged the duty assigned him, that all Americans may well rejoice that the work of drawing the title-deed of their liberties devolved upon him.

With all its merits, there are those who have thought that there was one thing in the Declaration to be regretted; and that is, the asperity and apparent anger with which it speaks of the person of the king; [the[27] industrious ability with which it accumulates and charges upon him all the injuries which the Colonies had suffered from the mother country.] Possibly some degree of injustice, now or hereafter, at home or abroad, may be done to the character of Mr. Jefferson, if this part of the Decla-

25. The following note was supplied by Everett in *Works*, 1: 126: "A facsimile of this ever-memorable state paper, as drafted by Mr. Jefferson, with the interlineations alluded to in the text, is contained in Mr. Jefferson's Writings, Vol. I. p. 146. See also, in reference to the history of the Declaration, the Life and Works of John Adams, Vol. II. p. 512 *et seq.*"

26. Bracketed passage absent from manuscript.

27. Bracketed passage absent from manuscript.

ration be not placed in its proper light. Anger or resentment, [certainly[28] much less personal reproach and invective,] could not properly find place in a composition of such high dignity, and of such lofty and permanent character.

A single reflection on the original ground of dispute between England and the Colonies is sufficient to remove any unfavorable impression in this respect.

The inhabitants of all the Colonies, while Colonies, admitted themselves bound by their allegiance to the king; but they disclaimed altogether the authority of Parliament; holding themselves, in this respect, to resemble the condition of Scotland and Ireland before the respective unions of those kingdoms with England, when they acknowledged allegiance to the same king, but had each its separate legislature. The tie, therefore, which our Revolution was to break did not subsist between us and the British Parliament, or between us and the British government in the aggregate, but directly between us and the king himself. The Colonies had never admitted themselves subject to Parliament. That was precisely the point of the original controversy. They had uniformly denied that Parliament had authority to make laws for them. There was, therefore, no subjection to Parliament to be thrown off.[29] But allegiance to the king did exist, and had been uniformly acknowledged; and down to 1775 the most solemn assurances had been given that it was not intended to break that allegiance, or to throw it off. Therefore, as the direct object and only effect of the Declaration, according to the principles on which the controversy had been maintained on our part, were to sever the tie of allegiance which bound us to the king, it was properly and necessarily founded on acts of the crown itself, as its justifying causes. Parliament is not so much as mentioned in the whole instrument. When odious and oppressive acts are referred to, it is done by charging the king

28. Bracketed passage absent from manuscript.

29. The following footnote was added in the pamphlet edition, presumably by Webster himself: "This question, of the power of Parliament over the Colonies, was discussed with singular ability, by Governor Hutchinson on the one side, and the House of Representatives of Massachusetts on the other, in 1773. The argument of the House is in the form of an answer to the Governor's Message, and was reported by Mr. Samuel Adams, Mr. Hancock, Mr. Hawley, Mr. Bowers, Mr. Hobson, Mr. Foster, Mr. Phillips, and Mr. Thayer. As the power of the Parliament had been acknowledged, so far at least as to affect us by laws of trade, it was not easy to settle the line of distinction. It was thought, however, to be very clear, that the charters of the Colonies had exempted them from the general legislation of the British Parliament. See Massachusetts State Papers, p. 351. The important assistance rendered by John Adams in the preparation of the answer of the House to the Message of the Governor may be learned from the Life and Works of John Adams, Vol. II, p. 311 *et seq.*"

with confederating with others "in pretended acts of legislation"; the object being constantly to hold the king himself directly responsible for those measures which were the grounds of separation. Even the precedent of the English Revolution was not overlooked, and in this case, as well as in that, occasion was found to say that the king had *abdicated* the government. Consistency with the principles upon which resistance began, and with all the previous state papers issues by Congress, required that the Declaration should be bottomed on the misgovernment of the king; and therefore it was properly framed with that aim and to that end. The king was known, indeed, to have acted, as in other cases, by his ministers, and with his Parliament; but as our ancestors had never admitted themselves subject either to ministers or to Parliament, there were no reasons to be given for now refusing obedience to thir authority. This clear and obvious necessity of founding the Declaration on the misconduct of the king himself, gives to that instrument its personal application, and its character of direct and pointed accusation.

The Declaration having been reported to Congress by the committee, the resolution itself was taken up and debated on the first day of July, and again on the second [on[30] which last day it was agreed to and adopted, in these words: —

["*Resolved*, That these united Colonies are, and of right ought to be, free and independent States; that they are absolved from all allegiance to the British crown, and that all political connection between them and the state of Great Britain is, and ought to be, totally dissolved."

[Having thus passed the main resolution, Congress proceeded to consider the reported draught of the Declaration. It was discussed on the second, and third, and FOURTH days of the month, in committee of the whole; and on the last of those days, being reported from that committee, it received the final approbation and sanction of Congress. It was ordered, at the same time, that copies be sent to the several States, and that it be proclaimed at the head of the army. The Declaration thus published did not bear the names of the members for as yet it had not been signed by them. It was authenticated, like other papers of the Congress, by the signatures of the President and Secretary. On the 19th of July, as appears by the secret journal, Congress "*Resolved*, That the Declaration, passed on the fourth, be fairly engrossed on parchment, with the title and style of THE UNANIMOUS DECLARATION OF THE THIRTEEN UNITED STATES OF AMERICA'; and that the same, when engrossed be signed by every member of Congress." And on the SECOND DAY OF AUGUST following, "the Declaration, being engrossed and compared at the table, was signed by the members." So that it happens, fellow-citizens, that we pay these honors to their memory on the anniversary of that day (2d of August) on which

30. The bracketed passages are absent from the manuscript.

these great men actually signed their names to the Declaration. The Declaration was thus made, that is, it passed and was adopted as an act of Congress, on the fourth of July; it was then signed, and certified by the President and Secretary, like other acts. The FOURTH OF JULY, therefore, is the ANNIVERSARY OF THE DECLARATION. But the signatures of the members present were made to it, being then engrossed on parchment, on the second day of August. Absent members afterwards signed, as they came in; and indeed it bears the names of some who were not chosen members of Congress until after the fourth of July. The interest belonging to the subject will be sufficient, I hope, to justify these details.][31]

The Congress of the Revolution, fellow-citizens, sat with closed doors, and no report of its debates was ever made. The discussion, therefore, which accompanied this great measure, has never been preserved, except in memory and by tradition.[32] But it is, I believe, doing no injustice to others to say, that the general opinion was, and uniformly has been, that in debate, on the side of independence, JOHN ADAMS had no equal. The great author of the Declaration himself has expressed that opinion uniformly and strongly. "JOHN ADAMS," said he, in the hearing of him who has now the honor to address you, "JOHN ADAMS was our colossus on the floor. Not graceful, not elegant, not always fluent, in his public addresses, he yet came out with a power, both of thought and of expression, which moved us from our seats."[33]

For the part which he was here to perform, Mr. Adams doubtless was eminently fitted. He possessed a bold spirit, which disregarded danger, and a sanguine reliance on the goodness of the cause, and the virtues of the people, which led him to overlook all obstacles. His character, too, had been formed in troubled times. He had been rocked in the early storms of the controversy, and had acquired a decision and a hardihood proportioned to the severity of the discipline which he had undergone.

He not only loved the American cause devoutly, but had studied and understood it. [It[34] was all familiar to him. He had tried his powers on the questions which it involved, often and in various ways; and had brought to their consideration whatever of argument or illustration the history of his own country, the history of England, or the stores of ancient or of legal learning could furnish. Every grievance enumerated in

31. Everett, in *Works*, 1: 130 adds this note: "The official copy of the Declaration, as engrossed and signed by the members of Congress, is framed and preserved in the Hall over the Patent-Office at Washington." The document is now in the National Archives.

32. Manuscript adds: "No man is now living who heard the Debate, the venerable Charles Carroll, sole survivor of the Assembly, having been absent, at the time, on public service."

33. Compare Webster's notes of his visit with Jefferson in December 1824, in *Correspondence*, 1: 375.

34. Bracketed passage absent from manuscript.

the long catalogue of the Declaration had been the subject of his discussion, and the object of his remonstrance and reprobation.] From 1760, the Colonies, the rights of the Colonies, the liberties of the Colonies, and the wrongs inflicted on the Colonies, had engaged his constant attention; and it has surprised those who have had the opportunity of witnessing it, with what full remembrance and with what prompt recollection he could refer, in his extreme old age, to every act of Parliament affecting the Colonies, distinguishing and stating their respective titles, sections, and provisions; and to all the Colonial memorials, remonstrances, and petitions, with whatever else belonged to the intimate and exact history of the times from that year to 1775. It was, in his own judgment, between these years that the American people came to a full understanding and thorough knowledge of their rights, and to a fixed resolution of maintaining them; and bearing himself an active part in all important transactions, the controversy with England being then in effect the business of his life, facts, dates, and particulars made an impression which was never effaced. He was prepared, therefore, by education and discipline, as well as by natural talent and natural temperament, for the part which he was now to act.

The eloquence of Mr. Adams resembled his general character, and formed, indeed, a part of it. It was bold, manly, and energetic; and such the crisis required. When public bodies are to be addressed on momentous occasions, when great interests are at stake, and strong passions excited, nothing is valuable in speech farther than as it is connected with high intellectual and moral endowments. Clearness, force, and earnestness are the qualities which produce conviction. True eloquence, indeed, does not consist in speech. It cannot be brought from far. Labor and learning may toil for it, but they will toil in vain. Words and phrases may be marshalled in every way, but they cannot compass it. It must exist in the man, in the subject, and in the occasion. Affected passion, intense expression, the pomp of declamation, all may aspire to it; they cannot reach it. It comes, if it comes at all, like the outbreaking of a fountain from the earth, or the bursting forth of volcanic fires, with spontaneous, original, native force. The graces taught in the schools, the costly ornaments and studied contrivances of speech, shock and disgust men, when their own lives, and the fate of their wives, their children, and their country, hang on the decision of the hour. Then words have lost their power, rhetoric is vain, and all elaborate oratory contemptible. Even genius itself then feels rebuked and subdued, as in the presence of higher qualities. Then patriotism is eloquent; then self-devotion is eloquent. The clear conception, outrunning the deductions of logic, the high purpose, the firm resolve, the dauntless spirit, speaking on the tongue, beaming from the eye, informing every feature, and urging the whole man on-

ward, right onward to his object,—this, this is eloquence; or rather it is something greater and higher than all eloquence, it is action, noble, sublime, godlike action.

In July, 1776, the controversy had passed the stage of argument. An appeal had been made to force, and opposing armies were in the field. Congress, then, was to decide whether the tie which had so long bound us to the parent state was to be severed at once, and severed for ever. [All [35] the Colonies had signified their resolution to abide by this decision,] and the people looked for it with the most intense anxiety. And surely, fellow-citizens, never, never, were men called to a more important political deliberation. [If [36] we contemplate it from the point where they then stood, no question could be more full of interest; if we look at it now, and judge of its importance by its effects, it appears of still greater magnitude.]

Let us, then, bring before us the assembly, which was about to decide a question thus big with the fate of empire. Let us open their doors and look in upon their deliberations. Let us survey the anxious and care-worn countenances, let us hear the firm-toned voices, of this band of patriots.

HANCOCK presides over the solemn sitting; and one of those not yet prepared to pronounce for absolute independence is on the floor, and is urging his reasons for dissenting from the declaration.

["Let [37] us pause! This step, once taken, cannot be retraced.] This resolution, once passed, will cut off all hope of reconciliation. [If [38] success attend the arms of England, we shall then be no longer Colonies, with charters and with privileges; these will all be forfeited by this act; and we shall be in the condition of other conquered people, at the mercy of the conquerors.] For ourselves, we may be ready to run the hazard; but are we ready to carry the country to that length? Is success so probable as to justify it? [Where [39] is the military, where the naval power, by which we are to resist the whole strength of the arm of England, for she will exert that strength to the utmost?] Can we rely on the constancy and perseverance of the people? or will they not act as the people of other countries have acted, and, wearied with a long war, submit, in the end, to a worse oppression? While we stand on our old ground, and insist on redress of grievances, we know we are right, and are not answerable for consequences. Nothing, then , can be imputed to us. But if we now change our object, carry our pretensions farther, and set up for absolute inde-

35. Bracketed passage absent from manuscript.

36. Bracketed passage absent from manuscript.

37. Bracketed passage absent from manuscript.

38. Bracketed passage absent from manuscript.

39. Bracketed passage absent from manuscript.

pendence, we shall lose the sympathy of mankind. [We[40] shall no longer be defending what we possess, but struggling for something which we never did possess, and which we have solemnly and uniformly disclaimed all intention of pursuing, from the very outset of the troubles. Abandoning thus our old ground, of resistance only to arbitrary acts of oppression, the nations will believe the whole to have been mere pretence, and they will look on us, not as injured, but as ambitious subjects. I shudder before this responsibility.] It will be on us, if, relinquishing the ground on which we have stood so long, and stood so safely, we now proclaim independence, and carry on the war for that object, while these cities burn, these pleasant fields whiten and bleach with the bones of their owners, and these streams run blood. It will be upon us, it will be upon us, if, failing to maintain this unseasonable and ill-judged declaration, a sterner despotism, maintained by military power, shall be established over our posterity, when we ourselves, given up by an exhausted, a harassed, misled people, shall have expiated our rashness and atoned for our presumption on the scaffold."

It was for Mr. Adams to reply to arguments like these. We know his opinions, and we know his character. He would commence with his accustomed directness and earnestness.

"Sink or swim, live or die, survive or perish, I give my hand and my heart to this vote. It is true, indeed, that in the beginning we aimed not at independence. But there's a Divinity which shapes our ends. The injustice of England has driven us to arms; and [blinded[41] to her own interest for our good, she has obstinately persisted, till] independence is now within our grasp. We have but to reach forth to it, and it is ours. Why, then, should we defer the Declaration? Is any man so weak as now to hope for a reconciliation with England, which shall leave either safety to the country and its liberties, or safety to his own life and his own honor? Are not you, Sir, who sit in that chair, is not he, our venerable colleague near you, are you not both already the proscribed and predestined objects of punishment and of vengeance? Cut off from all hope of royal clemency, what are you, what can you be, while the power of England remains, but outlaws? If we postpone independence, do we mean to carry on, or to give up, the war? Do we mean to submit to the measures of Parliament, Boston Port Bill and all? Do we mean to submit, and consent that we ourselves shall be ground to powder, and our country and its rights trodden down in the dust? I know we do not mean to submit. We never shall submit. Do we intend to violate that most solemn obligation ever entered into by men, that plighting, before God, of our sacred hon-

40. Bracketed passage absent from manuscript.

41. Bracketed passage absent from manuscript.

or to Washington, when, putting forth to incur the dangers of war, as well as the political hazards of the times, we promised to adhere to him, in every extremity, with our fortunes and our lives? I know there is not a man here, who would not rather see a general conflagration sweep over the land, or an earthquake sink it, than one jot or tittle of that plighted faith fall to the ground. [For[42] myself, having, twelve months ago, in this place, moved you, that George Washington be appointed commander of the forces raised, or to be raised, for defence of American liberty,[43] may my right hand forget her cunning, and my tongue cleave to the roof of my mouth, if I hesitate or waver in the support I give him.]

"The war, then, must go on. We must fight it through. And if the war must go on, why put off longer the Declaration of Independence? That measure will strengthen us. It will give us character abroad. The nations will then treat with us, which they can never can do while we acknowledge ourselves subjects, in arms against our sovereign. [Nay,[44] I maintain that England herself will sooner treat for peace with us on the footing of independence, than consent, by repealing her acts, to acknowledge that her whole conduct towards us has been a course of injustice and oppression. Her pride will be less wounded by submitting to that course of things which now predestinates our independence, than by yielding the points in controversy to her rebellious subjects. The former she would regard as the result of fortune; the latter she would feel as her own deep disgrace.] Why, then, why then, Sir, do we not as soon as possible change this from a civil to a national war? And since we must fight it through, why not put ourselves in a state to enjoy all the benefits of victory, if we gain the victory?

"If we fail, it can be no worse for us. But we shall not fail. [The[45] cause will raise up armies; the cause will create navies.] The people, the people, if we are true to them, will carry us and will carry themselves, gloriously, through this struggle. I care not how fickle other people have been found. I know the people of these Colonies, and I know that resistance to British aggression is deep and settled in their hearts and cannot be eradicated. Every Colony, indeed, has expressed its willingness to follow, if we but take the lead. Sir, the Declaration will inspire the people with increased courage. Instead of a long and bloody war for the restoration of privileges, for redress of grievances, for chartered immunities, held under a British king, set before them the glorious object of entire indepen-

42. Bracketed passage absent from manuscript.

43. Here Everett adds in *Works*, 1: 134, the citation "See Life and Works of John Adams, Vol. II. p. 417 *et seq.*"

44. Bracketed passage absent from manuscript.

45. Bracketed passage absent from manuscript.

dence, and it will breathe into them anew the breath of life. Read this Declaration at the head of the army; every sword will be drawn from its scabbard, and the solemn vow uttered, to maintain it, or to perish on the bed of honor. Publish it from the pulpit; religion will approve it, and the love of religious liberty will cling round it, resolved to stand with it, or fall with it. Send it to the public halls, proclaim it there;[46] let them hear it who heard the first roar of the enemy's cannon; let them see it who saw their brothers and their sons fall on the field of Bunker Hill, and in the streets of Lexington and Concord, and the very walls will cry out in its support.

Sir, I know the uncertainty of human affairs, but I see, I see clearly, through this day's business. You and I, indeed, may rue it. We may not live to the time when this Declaration shall be made good. We may die; die colonists; die slaves; die, it may be, ignominiously and on the scaffold. Be it so. Be it so. If it be the pleasure of Heaven that my country shall require the poor offering of my life, the victim shall be ready, at the appointed hour of sacrifice, come when that hour may. [But[47] while I do live, let me have a country, or at least the hope of a country, and that a free country.

["But whatever may be our fate, be assured, be assured that this Declaration will stand. It may cost treasure, and it may cost blood; but it will stand, and it will richly compensate for both.] Through the thick gloom of the present, I see the brightness of the future, as the sun in heaven. We shall make thus a glorious, an immortal day. When we are in our graves, our children will honor it. They will celebrate it with thanksgiving, with festivity, with bonfires, and illuminations. On its annual return they will shed tears, copious, gushing tears, not of subjection and slavery, not of agony and distress, but of exultation, of gratitude, and of joy. Sir, before God, I believe the hour is come. My judgment approves this measure, and my whole heart is in it. All that I have, and all that I am, and all that I hope, in this life, I am now ready here to stake upon it; and I leave off as I begun, that live or die, survive or perish, I am for the Declaration. It is my living sentiment, and by the blessing of God it shall be my dying sentiment, Independence, *now*, and INDEPENDENCE FOR EVER."[48]

And so that day shall be honored, illustrious prophet and patriot! so

46. Manuscript adds. "send it to the place where this great quarrel began".

47. Bracketed passage absent from manuscript.

48. Everett, in *Works*, 1: 136, refers the reader to a rather lengthy note following the speech which explains Webster composed these speeches himself. He had, however, drawn upon Timothy Pickering, a knowledgeable contemporary of Adams. See *Correspondence*, 2: 126–127.

that day shall be honored, and as often as it returns, thy renown shall come along with it, and the glory of thy life, like the day of thy death, shall not fail from the remembrance of men.

It would be unjust, fellow-citizens, on this occasion, while we express our veneration for him who is the immediate subject of these remarks, were we to omit a most respectful, affectionate, and grateful mention of those other great men, his colleagues, who stood with him, and with the same spirit, the same devotion, took part in the interesting transaction. [John] HANCOCK, the proscribed HANCOCK, exiled from his home by a military governor, cut off by proclamation from the mercy of the crown,— Heaven reserved for him the distinguished honor of putting this great question to the vote, and of writing his own name first, and most conspicuously, on that parchment which spoke defiance to the power of the crown of England. There, too, is the name of that other proscribed patriot, SAMUEL ADAMS, a man who hungered and thirsted for the independence of his country; who thought the Declaration halted and lingered, being himself not only ready, but eager, for it, long before it was proposed; a man of the deepest sagacity, the clearest foresight, and the profoundest judgment in men. And there is [Elbridge] GERRY, himself among the earliest and the foremost of the patriots, found, when the battle of Lexington summoned them to common counsels, by the side of [Joseph] WARREN[49]; a man who lived to serve his country at home and abroad, and to die in the second place in the government. There, too, is the inflexible, the upright, the Spartan character, ROBERT TREAT PAINE. He also lived to serve his country through the struggle, and then withdrew from her councils, only that he might give his labors and his life to his native State, in another relation. These names, fellow-citizens, are the treasures of the Commonwealth; and they are treasures which grow brighter by time.

It is now necessary to resume the narrative, and to finish with great brevity the notice of the lives of those whose virtues and services we have met to commemorate.

Mr. Adams remained in Congress from its first meeting till November, 1777, when he was appointed Minister to France. He proceeded on that service in the February following, embarking in the frigate Boston, from the shore of his native town, at the foot of Mount Wollaston.[50] The year following, he was appointed commissioner to treat of peace with England. Returning to the United States, he was a delegate from Braintree

49. Dr. Joseph Warren, although commissioned a major general, was president *pro tempore* of the provincial Congress of Massachusetts at the time of his death in the battle of Bunker Hill.

50. Manuscript adds: "While abroad he assisted to negotiate the Treaty with France."

in the Convention for framing the Constitution of this Commonwealth, in 1780.[51] At the latter end of the same year, he again went abroad in the diplomatic service of the country, and was employed at various courts, and occupied with various negotiations until 1788. [The[52] particulars of these interesting and important services this occasion does not allow time to relate. In 1782 he concluded our first treaty with Holland. His negotiations with that republic, his efforts to persuade the States-General to recognize our independence, his incessant and indefatigable exertions to represent the American cause favorably on the Continent, and to counteract the designs of its enemies, open and secret, and his successful undertaking to obtain loans, on the credit of a nation yet new and unknown, are among his most arduous, most useful, most honorable services. It was his fortune to bear a part in the negotiation for peace with England, and in something more than six years from the Declaration which he had so strenuously supported, he had the satisfaction of seeing the minister plenipotentiary of the crown subscribe his name to the instrument which declared that his "Britannic Majesty acknowledged the United States to be free, sovereign, and independent." In these important transactions, Mr. Adams's conduct received the marked approbation of Congress and of the country.

[While abroad, in 1787, he published his Defence of the American Constitutions; a work of merit and ability, though composed with haste, on the spur of a particular occasion, in the midst of other occupations, and under circumstances not admitting of careful revision. The immediate object of the work was to counteract the weight of opinions advanced by several popular European writers of that day, M. Turgot, the Abbé de Mably, and Dr. Price, at a time when the people of the United States were employed in forming and revising their systems of government.]

Returning to the United States in 1788, he found the new government about going into operation, and was himself elected the first Vice-President, a situation which he filled with reputation for eight years, at the expiration of which he was raised to the Presidential chair, as immediate successor to the immortal Washington. In this high station he was succeeded by Mr. Jefferson, after a memorable controversy between their re-

51. Note by Everett, *Works*, 1: 137: "In this Convention he served as chairman of the committee for preparing the draft of a constitution."

52. For the bracketed passages the manuscript reads: "He was the first minister to England, after the peace, & <how> he acquitted himself in all these important stations with entire approbation, of Congress & the Country <is known to all. His negotiations in Holland were extremely important, & his letters from the Court of that Government among our most valuable public papers>. While abroad he composed his work in Defense of the American Constitution." This final sentence is followed by a two-inch space in the manuscript.

spective friends, in 1801; and from that period his manner of life has been known to all who hear me. He has lived, for five-and-twenty years, with every enjoyment that could render old age happy. [Not[53] inattentive to the occurrences of the times, political cares have yet not materially, or for any long time, disturbed his repose. In 1820 he acted as elector of President and Vice-President, and in the same year we saw him, then at the age of eighty-five, a member of the Convention of this Commonwealth called to revise the Constitution. Forty years before, he had been one of those who formed that Constitution; and he had now the pleasure of witnessing that there was little which the people desired to change.][54] Possessing all his faculties to the end of his long life, with an unabated love of reading and contemplation, in the centre of interesting circles of friendship and affection, he was blessed in his retirement with whatever of repose and felicity the condition of man allows. He had, also, other enjoyments. He saw around him that prosperity and general happiness which had been the object of his public cares and labors. [No[55] man ever beheld more clearly, and for a longer time, the great and beneficial effects of the services rendered by himself to his country. That liberty which he so early defended, that independence of which he was so able an advocate and supporter, he saw, we trust, firmly and securely established. The population of the country thickened around him faster, and extended wider, than his own sanguine predictions had anticipated; and the wealth, respectability, and power of the nation sprang up to a magnitude which it is quite impossible he could have expected to witness in his day. He lived also to behold those principles of civil freedom which had been developed, established, and practically applied in America, attract attention, command respect, and awaken imitation, in other regions of the globe; and well might and well did, he exclaim, "Where will the consequences of the American Revolution end?"]

53. Bracketed passage absent from manuscript.

54. Note added by Everett in *Works*, 1: 138–139: "Upon the organization of this body, 15th November, 1820, John Adams was elected its President; an office which the infirmities of age compelled him to decline. For the interesting proceedings of the Convention on this occasion, the address of Chief Justice Parker, and the reply of Mr. Adams, see Journal of Debates and Proceedings in the Convention of Delegates chosen to revise the Constitution of Massachusetts, p. 8 *et seq.*"

55. For the bracketed passage the manuscript reads: "That Liberty, which he had done so much to establish, he saw firmly secured. He beheld the wonderful encrease & growth of the U. States, and sanguine as had been his own anticipations he saw them all realised. And he saw, too, the principles, which had been developed, established, & practically applied to America, begin to attract attention, to demand respect, to inspire admiration, & awaken imitation in other quarters of the Globe."

If any thing yet remain to fill this cup of happiness, let it be added, that he lived to see a great and intelligent people bestow the highest honor in their gift where he had bestowed his own kindest parental affections and lodged his fondest hopes. Thus honored in life, thus happy at death, he saw the JUBILEE, and he died; and with the last prayers which trembled on his lips was the fervent supplication for his country, "Independence for ever!"[56]

Mr. Jefferson, having been occupied in the years 1778 and 1779 in the important service of revising the laws of Virginia, was elected Governor of that State, as successor of Patrick Henry, and held the situation when the State was invaded by the British arms. In 1781 he published his Notes on Virginia, a work which attracted attention in Europe as well as America, dispelled many misconceptions respecting this continent, and gave its author a place among men distinguished for science. In November, 1783, he again took his seat in the Continental Congress, but in the May following was appointed Minister Plenipotentiary, to act abroad, in the negotiation of commercial treaties, with Dr. Franklin and Mr. Adams. He proceeded to France in execution of this mission, embarking at Boston; and that was the only occasion on which he ever visited this place. In 1785 he was appointed Minister to France, the duties of which situation he continued to perform until October, 1789 when he obtained leave to retire, just on the eve of that tremendous revolution which has so much agitated the world in our times. Mr. Jefferson's discharge of his diplomatic duties was marked by great ability, diligence, and patriotism; and while he resided at Paris, in one of the most interesting periods, his character for intelligence, his love of knowledge and of the society of learned men, distinguished him in the highest circles of the French capital. No court in Europe had at that time in Paris a representative commanding or enjoying higher regard, for political knowledge or for general attainments, than the minister of this then infant republic. Immediately on his return to his native country, at the organization of the government under the present Constitution, his talents and experience recommended him to President Washington for the first office in his gift. He was placed at the head of the Department of State. In this situation, also, he manifested conspicuous ability. His correspondence with the ministers of other powers residing here, and his instructions to our own diplomatic agents abroad, are among our ablest state papers. A thorough knowledge of the laws and usages of nations, perfect acquaintance with the immediate subject before him, great felicity, and still greater facility,

56. Everett, in Works, 1: 139, here refers the reader to Charles W. March's Reminiscences of Congress, (New York, 1850) p. 62, for "an account of Mr. Webster's last interview with Mr. Adams."

in writing, show themselves in whatever effort his official situation called on him to make. [It[57] is believed by competent judges, that the diplomatic intercourse of the government of the United States, from the first meeting of the Continental Congress in 1774 to the present time, taken together, would not suffer, in respect to the talent with which it has been conducted, by comparison with any thing which other and older governments can produce; and to the attainment of this respectability and distinction Mr. Jefferson has contributed his full part.]

On the retirement of General Washington from the Presidency, and the election of Mr. Adams to that office in 1797, he was chosen Vice-President. While presiding in this capacity over the deliberations of the Senate, he compiled and published a Manual of Parliamentary Practice, [a[58] work of more labor and more merit than is indicated by its size.] It is now received as the general standard by which proceedings are regulated, not only in both Houses of Congress, but in most of the other legislative bodies in the country. In 1801 he was elected President, in opposition to Mr. Adams, and reëlected in 1805, by a vote approaching unanimity.

From the time of his final retirement from public life, in 1808, Mr. Jefferson lived as became a wise man. Surrounded by affectionate friends, his ardor in the pursuit of knowledge undiminished,[59] with uncommon health and unbroken spirits, he was able to enjoy largely the rational pleasures of life, and to partake in that public prosperity which he had so much contributed to produce. His kindness and hospitality, the charm of his conversation, the ease of his manners, the extent of his acquirements, and, especially, the full store of Revolutionary incidents which he had treasured in his memory, and which he knew when and how to dispense, rendered his abode in a high degree attractive to his admiring countrymen, while his high public and scientific character drew towards him every intelligent and educated traveller from abroad. [Both[60] Mr. Adams and Mr. Jefferson had the pleasure of knowing that the respect which they so largely received was not paid to their official stations. They were not men made great by office; but great men, on whom the country for its own benefit had conferred office. There was that in them which office did not give, and which the relinquishment of office did not, and could not, take away. In their retirement, in the midst of their fellow-citizens, themselves private citizens, they enjoyed as high regard and esteem as when filling the most important places of public trust.]

57. Bracketed passage absent from manuscript.

58. Bracketed passage absent from manuscript.

59. Manuscript adds: ", his love of Country still glowing,".

60. Bracketed passage absent from manuscript.

There remained to Mr. Jefferson yet one other work of patriotism and beneficence, the establishment of a university in his native State. To this object he devoted years of incessant and anxious attention, and by the enlightened liberality of the Legislature of Virginia, and the coöperation of other able and zealous friends, he lived to see it accomplished. May all success attend this infant seminary; and may those who enjoy its advantages, as often as their eyes shall rest on the neighboring height, recollect what they owe to their disinterested and indefatigable benefactor; and may letters honor him who thus labored in the cause of letters! [61]

Thus useful, and thus respected, passed the old age of Thomas Jefferson. But time was on its ever-ceaseless wing, and was now bringing the last hour of this illustrious man. He saw its approach with undisturbed serenity. He counted the moments as they passed, and beheld that his last sands were falling. That day, too, was at hand which he had helped to make immortal. One wish, one hope, if it were not presumptuous, beat in his fainting breast. Could it be so, might it please God, he would desire once more to see the sun, once more to look abroad on the scene around him, on the great day of liberty. Heaven, in its mercy, fulfilled that prayer. He saw that sun, he enjoyed its sacred light, he thanked God for this mercy, and bowed his aged head to the grave. "Felix, non vitæ tantum claritate, sed etiam opportunitate mortis." [62]

[The [63] last public labor of Mr. Jefferson naturally suggests the expression of the high praise which is due, both to him and to Mr. Adams, for their uniform and zealous attachment to learning, and to the cause of general knowledge. Of the advantages of learning, indeed, and of literary accomplishments, their own characters were striking recommendations and illustrations. They were scholars, ripe and good scholars; widely acquainted with ancient, as well as modern literature, and not altogether uninstructed in the deeper sciences. Their acquirements, doubtless, were different, and so were the particular objects of their literary pursuits; as their tastes and characters, in these respects, differed like those of other

61. Note supplied by Everett, *Works*, 1: 142: "Mr. Jefferson himself considered his services in establishing the University of Virginia as among the most important rendered by him to the country. In Mr. Wirt's Eulogy, it is stated that a private memorandum was found among his papers, containing the following inscription to be placed on his monument: 'Here was buried Thomas Jefferson, Author of the Declaration of Independence, of the Statutes of Virginia for Religious Freedom, and Father of the University of Virginia.' Eulogies on Adams and Jefferson, p. 426."

62. Tacitus, *Agricola*, 45. "Happy indeed were you, Agricola, not only in your glorious life, but in your timely death." From *Tacitus, The Agricola and The Germania*, trans. H. Mattingly, revised by S.A. Handford (Harmondsworth, 1971), p. 98.

63. The following four bracketed paragraphs are absent from the manuscript.

men. Being, also, men of busy lives, with great objects requiring action constantly before them, their attainments in letters did not become showy or obtrusive. Yet I would hazard the opinion, that, if we could now ascertain all the causes which gave them eminence and distinction in the midst of the great men with whom they acted, we should find not among the least their early acquisitions in literature, the resources which it furnished, the promptitude and facility which it communicated, and the wide field it opened for analogy and illustration; giving them thus, on every subject, a larger view and a broader range, as well for discussion as for the government of their own conduct.

[Literature sometimes disgusts, and pretension to it much oftener disgusts, by appearing to hang loosely on the character, like something foreign or extraneous, not a part, but an ill-adjusted appendage; or by seeming to overload and weigh it down by its unsightly bulk, like the productions of bad taste in architecture, where there is massy and cumbrous ornament without strength or solidity of column. This has exposed learning, and especially classical learning, to reproach. Men have seen that it might exist without mental superiority, without vigor, without good taste, and without utility. But in such cases classical learning has only not inspired natural talent; or, at most, it has but made original feebleness of intellect, and natural bluntness of perception, something more conspicuous. The question, after all, if it be a question, is, whether literature, ancient as well as modern, does not assist a good understanding, improve natural good taste, add polished armor to native strength, and render its possessor, not only more capable of deriving private happiness from contemplation and reflection, but more accomplished also for action in the affairs of life, and especially for public action. Those whose memories we now honor were learned men; but their learning was kept in its proper place, and made subservient to the uses and objects of life. They were scholars, not common nor superficial; but their scholarship was so in keeping with their character, so blended and inwrought, that careless observers, or bad judges, not seeing an ostentatious display of it, might infer that it did not exist: forgetting, or not knowing, that classical learning in men who act in conspicuous public stations, perform duties which exercise the faculty of writing, or address popular, deliberative, or judicial bodies, is often felt where it is little seen, and sometimes felt more effectually because it is not seen at all.

[But the cause of knowledge, in a more enlarged sense, the cause of general knowledge and of popular education, had no warmer friends, nor more powerful advocates, than Mr. Adams and Mr. Jefferson. On this foundation they knew the whole republican system rested; and this great and all-important truth they strove to impress, by all the means in their power. In the early publication already referred to, Mr. Adams ex-

presses the strong and just sentiment, that the education of the poor is more important, even to the rich themselves, than all their own riches. On this great truth, indeed, is founded that unrivalled, that invaluable political and moral institution, our own blessing and the glory of our fathers, the New England system of free schools.

[As the promotion of knowledge had been the object of their regard through life, so these great men made it the subject of their testamentary bounty. Mr. Jefferson is understood to have bequeathed his library to the University of Virginia, and that of Mr. Adams is bestowed on the inhabitants of Quincy.]

Mr. Adams and Mr. Jefferson, fellow-citizens, were successively Presidents of the United States. The comparative merits of their respective administrations for a long time agitated and divided public opinion. They were rivals, each supported by numerous and powerful portions of the people, for the highest office.[64] This contest, partly the cause and partly the consequence of the long existence of two great political parties in the country, is now part of the history of our government. We may naturally regret that any thing should have occurred to create difference and discord between those who had acted harmoniously and efficiently in the great concerns of the Revolution. But this is not the time, nor this the occasion, for entering into the grounds of that difference, or for attempting to discuss the merits of the question which it involves. [As[65] practical questions, they were canvassed when the measures which they regarded were acted on and adopted; and as belonging to history, the time has not come for their consideration.]

It is, perhaps, not wonderful, that, when the Constitution of the United States first went into operation, different opinions should be entertained as to the extent of the powers conferred by it. [Here[66] was a natural source of diversity of sentiment.] It is still less wonderful, that that event, nearly contemporary with our government under the present Constitution, which so entirely shocked all Europe, and disturbed our relations with her leading powers, should be thought, by different men, to have different bearings on our own prosperity; and that the early measures adopted by the government of the United States, in consequence of this new state of things, should be seen in opposite lights. It is for the future historian, when what now remains of prejudice and misconception shall have passed away, to state these different opinions, and pronounce impartial judgment. In the mean time, all good men rejoice, and well may

64. Manuscript adds: "& one of them succeeded the other, in that place, before it had been holden so long as in the preceding, and in all subsequent instances."

65. Bracketed passage absent from manuscript.

66. Bracketed sentence absent from manuscript.

rejoice, that the sharpest differences sprung out of measures which, whether right or wrong, have ceased with the exigencies that gave them birth, and have left no permanent effect, either on the Constitution or on the general prosperity of the country. [This[67] remark, I am aware, may be supposed to have its exception in one measure, the alteration of the Constitution as to the mode of choosing President; but it is true in its general application.] Thus the course of policy pursued towards France in 1798, on the one hand, and the measures of commercial restriction commenced in 1807, on the other, both subjects of warm and severe opposition, have passed away and left nothing behind them. They were temporary, and whether wise or unwise, their consequences were limited to their respective occasions. It is equally clear, at the same time, and it is equally gratifying, that those measures of both administrations which were of durable importance, [and[68] which drew after them momentous and long remaining consequences,] have received general approbation. Such was the organization, or rather the creation, of the navy, in the administration of Mr. Adams; such the acquisition of Louisiana, in that of Mr. Jefferson. The country, it may safely be added, is not likely to be willing either to approve, or to reprobate, indiscriminately, and in the aggregate, all the measures of either, or of any administration. The dictate of reason and of justice is, that, holding each one his own sentiments on the points of difference, we imitate the great men themselves in the forbearance and moderation which they have cherished, and in the mutual respect and kindness which they have been so much inclined to feel and to reciprocate.

No men, fellow-citizens, ever served their country with more entire exemption from every imputation of selfish and mercenary motives, than those to whose memory we are paying these proofs of respect. A suspicion of any disposition to enrich themselves, or to profit by their public employments, never rested on either. No sordid motive approached them. [The[69] inheritance which they have left to their children is of their character and their fame.]

Fellow-citizens, I will detain you no longer by this faint and feeble tribute to the memory of the illustrious dead. Even in other hands, adequate justice could not be done to them, within the limits of this occasion.

---

67. Bracketed passage absent from manuscript.

68. Bracketed passage absent from manuscript.

69. Instead of the bracketed sentence, the manuscript reads: "Alas, it is almost the only circumstance, which now gives pain, that one of them should have <felt> experienced domestic pecuniary difficulty, in his old age. The topic is full both of delicacy & tenderness. The national honor is connected with it. I will not pursue it. The American Community, acting from natural impulse, & affectionate gratitude, will need no labored persuasion to the performance of the appropriate duty."

Their highest, their best praise, is your deep conviction of their merits, your affectionate gratitude for their labors and their services. [It[70] is not my voice, it is this cessation of ordinary pursuits, this arresting of all attention, these solemn ceremonies, and this crowded house, which speak their eulogy.] Their fame, indeed, is safe. That is now treasured up beyond the reach of accident. Although no sculptured marble should rise to their memory, nor engraved stone bear record of their deeds, yet will their remembrance be as lasting as the land they honored. Marble columns may, indeed, moulder into dust, time may erase all impress from the crumbling stone, but their fame remains; for with AMERICAN LIBERTY it rose, and with AMERICAN LIBERTY ONLY can it perish. [It[71] was the last swelling peal of yonder choir, "THEIR BODIES ARE BURIED IN PEACE, BUT THEIR NAME LIVETH EVERMORE." I catch that solemn song, I echo that lofty strain of funeral triumph, "THEIR NAME LIVETH EVERMORE."]

Of the illustrious signers of the Declaration of Independence there now remains only CHARLES CARROLL. He seems an aged oak, standing alone on the plain, which time has spared a little longer after all its contemporaries have been levelled with the dust. Venerable object! we delight to gather round its trunk, while yet it stands, and to dwell beneath its shadow. Sole survivor of an assembly of as great men as the world has witnessed, in a transaction one of the most important that history records, what thoughts, what interesting reflections, must fill his elevated and devout soul! If he dwell on the past, how touching its recollections; if he survey the present, how happy, how joyous, how full of the fruition of that hope, which his ardent patriotism indulged; if he glance at the future, how does the prospect of his country's advancement almost bewilder his weakened conception! Fortunate, distinguished patriot! Interesting relic of the past! Let him know that, while we honor the dead, we do not forget the living; and that there is not a heart here which does not fervently pray, that Heaven may keep him yet back from the society of his companions.

And now, fellow-citizens, let us not retire from this occasion without a deep and solemn conviction of the duties which have devolved upon us. This lovely land, this glorious liberty, these benign institutions, the dear purchase of our fathers, are ours; ours to enjoy, ours to preserve, ours to transmit. Generations past and generations to come hold us responsible for this sacred trust. Our fathers, from behind, admonish us, with their anxious paternal voices; posterity calls out to us, from the bosom of the future; the world turns hither its solicitous eyes; all, conjure us to act wisely, and faithfully, in the relation which we sustain.

70. Bracketed passage absent from manuscript.

71. Bracketed passage absent from manuscript.

We can never, indeed pay the debt which is upon us; but by virtue, by morality, by religion, by the cultivation of every good principle and every good habit, we may hope to enjoy the blessing, through our day, and to leave it unimpaired to our children. Let us feel deeply how much of what we are and of what we possess we owe to this liberty, and to these institutions of government. Nature has, indeed, given us a soil which yields bounteously to the hand of industry, the mighty and fruitful ocean is before us, and the skies over our heads shed health and vigor. But what are lands, and seas, and skies, to civilized man, without society, without knowledge, without morals, without religious culture; and how can these be enjoyed, in all their extent and all their excellence, but under the protection of wise institutions and a free government? Fellow-citizens, there is not one of us, there is not one of us here present, who does not, at this moment, and at every moment, experience, in his own condition, and in the condition of those most near and dear to him, the influence and the benefits, of this liberty and these institutions. Let us then acknowledge the blessing, [let[72] us feel it deeply and powerfully,] let us cherish a strong affection for it, and resolve to maintain and perpetuate it. The blood of our fathers, let it not have been shed in vain; the great hope of posterity, let it not be blasted.

The striking attitude, too, in which we stand to the world around us, a topic to which, I fear, I advert too often, and dwell on too long, cannot be altogether omitted here. Neither individuals nor nations can perform their part well, until they understand and feel its importance, and comprehend and justly appreciate all the duties belonging to it. [It[73] is not to inflate national vanity, nor to swell a light and empty feeling of self-importance, but it is that we may judge justly of our situation, and of our own duties, that I earnestly urge upon you this consideration of our position and our character among the nations of the earth.] It cannot be denied, but by those who would dispute against the sun, that with America, and in America, a new era commences in human affairs. This era is distinguished by free representative governments, by entire religious liberty, by improved systems of national intercourse, [by[74] a newly awakened and an unconquerable spirit of free inquiry, and by a diffusion of knowledge through the community, such as has been before altogether unknown and unheard of.] America, America, our country, fellow-citizens, our own dear and native land, is inseparably connected, fast bound up, in fortune and by fate, with these great interests. If they fall, we fall

72. Bracketed passage absent from manuscript.

73. Bracketed passage absent from manuscript.

74. For the bracketed passage the manuscript reads: "by equal protection of the law, by an unheard-of diffusion of knowledge, by a new spirit of inquiry, & unexampled enterprise, in private pursuits."

with them; if they stand, it will be because we have maintained them. Let us contemplate, then, this connection, which binds the prosperity of others to our own; and let us manfully discharge all the duties which it imposes. If we cherish the virtues and the principles of our fathers, Heaven will assist us to carry on the work of human liberty and human happiness. Auspicious omens cheer us. Great examples are before us. Our own firmament[75] now shines brightly upon our path. WASHINGTON is in the clear, upper sky. These other stars have now joined the American constellation; they circle round their centre, and the heavens beam with new light. Beneath this illumination let us walk the course of life, and at its close devoutly commend our beloved country, the common parent of us all, to the Divine Benignity.

75. Manuscript reads "hemisphere."

The Presidential Message on the Creek Indians, February 5, 1827

Climaxing a quarter century of steady pressure from the state of Georgia, the Creek Indians, still weakened by their terrible losses of 1814 in the bloody battle of Horseshoe Bend, ceded to the United States all of their remaining lands in Georgia by the treaty of Indian Springs, February 12, 1825. It quickly developed, however, that those who had made the treaty represented only eight of 56 Creek towns. The majority repudiated it, and the leader of those who made it, William McIntosh, was murdered. A new treaty was negotiated in Washington, signed January 25, 1826, which specifically rejected the earlier instrument and greatly curtailed its land cessions.

The state of Georgia, meanwhile, had begun surveying the Creek lands for sale and refused to be moved by the repudiation. The Creeks protested, and President John Quincy Adams, on February 5, 1827, laid the matter before Congress, pointing out that under the Indian Act of March 30, 1802, military force might be used to evict the unwelcome intruders. Since Georgia was already using her militia to protect the surveyors, a confrontation seemed in the making.

When the message was received in the House, John Forsyth of Georgia moved reference to the Committee of the Whole rather than to one of the standing committees—Indian Affairs, Military Affairs, Judiciary—thus bypassing normal channels to bring on immediate debate. In the course of his remarks he condemned the Federal Government for the continued existence of a problem which Georgia, he insisted, would long ago have resolved if she had been allowed to. Webster entered the chamber while Forsyth was speaking and rose to comment as soon as the Georgian had resumed his seat. His remarks were interrupted by a rejoinder from Forsyth, and by some caustic words from William Haile of Mississippi. Webster responded to Haile in kind before the House turned its attention to the order of the day.

The matter of Georgia and the Creeks was resumed on February 9, with some preliminary jockeying for position. Forsyth first moved to table the president's message, then withdrew the motion. Edward Everett followed, moving reference to the Judiciary Committee (of which Webster was chairman). Then Forsyth again moved reference to the Com-

mittee of the Whole, and there was some general debate participated in by Charles A. Wickliffe of Kentucky; George Washington Owen of Alabama, who wanted reference to a select committee; Haile, who concentrated his fire on Webster; and James Buchanan of Pennsylvania. Webster then resumed where he had left off a few days earlier and concluded what he had to say, though not without some further interruption.

The importance of this short speech, omitted by Everett (with Webster's concurrence) from *Works*, is twofold: it reveals Webster's early reactions to the growing controversy over Georgia's Indian lands; and it is one of the very few times in his career when he used sharp language toward a Congressional colleague. He understood as well as anyone the underlying states' rights aspect of the case: New England had not yet lived down the Hartford Convention; but more—much more—was still to come. The Georgia controversy would erupt in four or five years when the state would pointedly ignore the rulings of the Supreme Court in *Cherokee Nation* v. *Georgia* (1831) and *Worcester* v. *Georgia* (1832). The climax would come with Nullification in South Carolina in 1832.

Webster's own mature statement on state's rights would soon be made, in his Second Reply to Hayne of January, 1830; and in his Reply to Calhoun three years later. Both speeches are included in this volume.

The text here reproduced is from *Writings and Speeches*, 14: 107–118. The primary source is the *National Intelligencer*, February 6, 10, 1827, reprinted without change in *Register of Debates*, 19th Cong., 2d sess., pp. 936, 937–938; 1034–1036; 1046–1049. The various segments of the speech have been joined in *Writings and Speeches* to form a unit and we have left them that way, with only enough interpolation to carry the thread of argument.

Mr. Webster said, on rising, that he was not much concerned what course this communication should take, or whether it should be referred to one committee or another; but he was not contented that it should be supposed, either here or elsewhere, that there existed an entire unanimity of opinion with the gentleman from Georgia on this subject. The gentleman from Georgia must know that there were two sides to this question between Georgia and the United States; and he would tell the gentleman from Georgia that there existed two opinions also, not only on that question, but on the conduct which that gentleman had designated as "base and infamous."

This, Mr. Webster said, was strong language, but it was not argument. The gentleman had told the House that nothing had prevented everything going right in Georgia but the interference of the General Government. The gentleman denounced such interference, saying, in effect, "Hands

off for the present: leave the Indians to the remedy of the courts." But, Mr. Webster said, he would tell the gentleman, that if there were rights of the Indians, which the United States were bound to protect, that there were those in the House and in the country who would take their part. If we have bound ourselves by any treaty to do certain things, we must fulfil such obligation. High words will not terrify us—loud declamation will not deter us from the discharge of that duty. For myself, said Mr. Webster, the right of the parties in this question shall be fully and fairly examined, and none of them with more calmness than the rights of Georgia. In my own course in this matter, I shall not be dictated to by any State, or the Representative of any State on this floor. I shall not be frightened from my purpose, nor will I suffer harsh language to produce any reaction on my mind. I will examine with great and equal care all the rights of both parties. Occasion had been taken on the mere question of reference of this communication, he would not say for argument, but for the assumption of a position, as a matter of perfectly plain and indisputable, that the government had been all in the wrong in this question, and Georgia all in the right. For his own part, Mr. Webster said he did not care whether the communication did or did not go to a Committee of the Whole on the State of the Union, nor how soon it went there, and was there taken up for discussion. When he went into that committee, he should go there, not in a spirit of controversy, nor yet in a spirit of submission, but in a spirit of inquiry, calmly and deliberately to examine the circumstances of the case, and to investigate the rights of all parties concerned. But he had made these few remarks, to give the gentleman from Georgia to understand that it was not by bold denunciation, or by bold assumption, that the members of this House are to be influenced in the decision of high public concerns.

Forsyth disclaimed any wish to dictate to the House. He felt deeply on this question and would not conceal it. William Haile of Mississippi then placed his state beside Georgia, warning of "consequences likely to ensue" if the matter were not settled at this session.

["Mr. Webster[1] rose to make one remark in reply to the gentleman from Mississippi. That gentleman, he said, had reason to know that he (Mr. W.) was disposed to use all proper authority of the United States to extinguish Indian titles to lands within the States. But he must tell the gentleman from Mississippi that the States would act on their own responsibility and at their own peril, if they undertake to extend their legislation to lands where the Indian title has not been extinguished. If any such measure was contemplated in the State which the gentleman represented,

1. This passage, appearing in the *National Intelligencer*, Feb. 6, 1827, and in the *Register of Debates*, 19th Cong., 2nd sess., pp. 937–938, is omitted from *Writings and Speeches*.

Mr. W. hoped that gentleman would lose no time in warning his friends against making any such attempt. The relation which the United States held to these tribes, of parental guardianship over these remnants of mighty nations now no more, was a very delicate relation. Its general character was that of protection, and, while every facility was given to the extinguishment of Indian title, let not that circumstance be so far presumed on, that the States should attempt to exercise authority within the Indian limits. Any such course would be attempted at their own responsibility. Mr. W. concluded by saying that he was ready to do all that could be done to extinguish the Indian title in the States, and particularly in the States East of the Mississippi. But this disposition, common to all parts of the country, should not be so far presumed upon that any State should undertake, of its own mere notion, to exercise an authority over the lands to which the Indian title is guaranteed by treaties &c"].

The question was then tabled, to take up the Woollens Bill, which was the order of the day. The Georgia matter came up again on February 9, when, after some discussion involving various members, Mr. Webster observed, that the question before the House was a mere question respecting committees to which this communication was to be referred. He should confine his remarks to this question, and should not, therefore, without violating the proper order of debate, make any reply to the remarks which had fallen from the gentleman from Pennsylvania [Buchanan], on the general topics contained in the communication from the Executive. He thought the communication ought to go to some committee which might be competent to ascertain whether the whole matter was before the House, and whether any legislation would be necessary. He was not at all solicitous to send it to any particular committee; and certainly not to that committee with which he was himself connected. As one of that committee, he would say that they would neither seek the reference, nor shun it if it were made. But undoubtedly it ought to go to some committee, more especially as there was a proposition upon the table which looked to legislation on the subject. This was the ordinary and usual course in relation to executive communications, and, Mr. Webster said, he saw no reason why this should not follow the usual routine.

Mr. Webster agreed with the gentleman from Alabama (Mr. Owen), that the subject was both important and delicate. But he did not think that it was so very alarming a matter as that gentleman seemed to suppose. There were at least two sides to the question; and if there was a danger in denying the authority of any act of a State, so, on the other hand, it must be allowed there was danger in denying the validity of a treaty made under the authority of the United States, and duly ratified. The whole subject was one well worthy of mature deliberation. One word, said Mr. Webster, as to the honorable member from Mississippi [Haile]:

When any member of the House asks of me an explanation of anything personal as to himself, I am ready to make it; if any gentleman asks an explanation as to any facts, or any argument, or a clearer statement of any argument I have advanced, I am ready, at all times, to comply with his wishes. For all other purposes, I cannot submit to be catechized; and to some of the queries which that gentleman proposed to me, I shall, therefore, give no answer.

Mr. Webster went on to say, that he had menaced nobody; he had uttered no threats, as seemed to be supposed; but, on the contrary, the tone of menace seemed to him to come from the other side, and not from his side of the question; of that, however, the House would judge. What was this whole matter? Was it offensive to sovereign States for him to say that they acted, in any particular matter, on their own responsibility, and at their peril? Sir, those States do act at their peril; and if they undertake to extend their legislation in the manner referred to, they do so, on their responsibility, and at their peril. I shall not take back a syllable of what I said, either in manner or substance. I wish to be understood as repeating it, word for word, and syllable for syllable. Sir, what are the circumstances of the case? The lands over which these States claim to exercise exclusive jurisdiction have never been subject to State laws from the foundation of this Government; the control of those lands has always been with the Congress of the United States. We regulate the sale of those lands, or rather we forbid the purchase of them by individuals. We enact all general regulations concerning the Indian tribes who inhabit them. Their municipal concerns have hitherto been managed by themselves; they maintain their own peace and their own laws. It was now said, that the States of Alabama and Mississippi either had extended, or intended shortly to extend, their legislation to the lands and persons of these Indians. They will therein do what has never been done or attempted before, and what has at least a very doubtful aspect; and, when I said that they must do this on their responsibility and at their peril, I meant no more than that they would venture on the exercise of a power which they might be found not to possess. Does the gentleman call this language minatory, and come here a week afterwards, with a list of questions which he wishes to propound to me as to what I meant by the observations I made? I tell that gentleman that I mean what I say. I am told that the proposed measure will be the act of a sovereign State. Be it so. Is it not a possible thing that sovereign States may sometimes act in a manner which violates the Constitution? Are not conflicting laws of a State and of the United States to be discussed and settled, for or against a State, before the judicial tribunal? If I and my learned friends were in another part of this Capitol we could speak of these things without offence, and the judgment come upon them without offence. There,

at least, it is admitted to be very possible, that a sovereign State may be in the wrong.

It is not my intention now to discuss the general question, or to go into an extended reply to the observations which have been made upon it; but I am told by the honorable gentleman from Georgia (Mr. Forsyth), that the courts are open, and that this question may be settled by a judicial tribunal. This might have been a remarkably good argument to address to the State of Georgia before she took the remedy into her own hands. It is a new mode of settling a constitutional question, to seize the lands in dispute, and send out the Hancock troop of horse to defend the possession of them. But, at this stage of the affair, that appeal to the courts comes with rather an awkward grace. When a man advances a claim against the lands of his neighbor, he makes his appeal to the law; but, when he forcibly enters upon possession of them, he makes his appeal to something different from the law

Here [James] Hamilton of South Carolina called the gentleman to order; and, when called upon by the Chair to point out wherein Mr. Webster was out of order, he explained himself as wishing to prevent any course of remark which might tend to produce excitement. The Chair decided that Mr. Webster was in order.

Mr. Webster resumed: I have no intention to produce excitement on this subject, but I have my own opinions upon it. I believe them to be tenable, and, at a proper time I shall not forbear to express them in this House. I have been induced, on the present occasion, to make some re-Marks which I should not have made, had not the inquiries of the gentleman from Mississippi called me out. Mr. Webster concluded by expressing his hope, that the matter would be allowed to take the usual course of reference to a committee for examination. A general debate followed, involving especially Forsyth and Haile, after which Mr. Webster again rose.

He said [2] that he had been now for some years a member of this House; that, during that period, the course of argument had at different times placed him both for and against various members of it, and of various ages, and of various terms of service in the House, and he believed that gentlemen could bear witness that he had always treated them with becoming respect, and that he had always manifested this disposition in a special manner towards persons newly introduced into the House, and from whom the country had much to hope. He was not conscious of having departed from that line of conduct on the present occasion. He claimed for himself no privilege which he did not equally pertain to every other member. He stood on that floor in his own name, on the responsibility of his own character, connected with nobody, with a knowledge of

2. The text of this line follows the *Register*, p. 1046.

his own rights and disposed to use them temperately. He had used no menace to any gentleman in this House, or to any State represented in it, and he hardly expected—But, he said, he would not go out of the order of debate to follow a gentleman who had been pronounced out of order. He had been desirous of rising, that he might reply to some of the arguments of the gentleman from Georgia. That gentleman, not confining himself to the question before the House, had gone on to state his views of the general question pending between Georgia and the United States. Mr. Webster said he did not mean to have entered into that question; but, as the gentleman from Georgia had stated it, and brought his argument to bear upon it, he must be allowed to take the liberty of reviewing that statement. The gentleman had, with what he called great frankness, said that he (Mr. Webster), or the committee to which he belonged, were the adversaries of Georgia.

Here Mr. Forsyth explained, and stated what he had understood to be Mr. Webster's meaning when he had said that the language of menace had come from the other side.

Mr. Webster resumed: We sometimes hear those who have a cause at issue, especially when they have any reason to doubt the result, attempting to impeach the impartiality of the tribunal which is to decide it: sometimes, indeed, they challenge a trial, professing themselves willing to go with their cause anywhere before honorable men; that its justice is so clear as to admit of no mystification; and that nothing but integrity and common sense are requisite in order to a right decision. But in other cases, we hear the advocate of a cause declaring that the ordinary tribunals are not to be trusted—they are prejudiced—and they object to go there, lest a decision should be had against them. He need not say what was the usual inference from this contrast of language. Such arguments applied here amount to neither more nor less than this: that the committees of this House are not to be trusted. But if the committees of this House are to be supposed to be under such a prejudice as to render them unfit to decide the questions referred to them, there was an end to all reference of business to them.

The gentleman from Georgia, however, thinks that there are parties in the country, and in the House, and that the committees are so organized that one party is dominant in them all. For himself, Mr. Webster said, he believed that he rather thought there were some committees of the House not *exactly* so organized. But, said Mr. Webster, parting from this, let me answer the gentleman when he asks who I meant when I used the expression "on the other side." I tell the gentleman that I speak only for myself, and for nobody else. When I entered the House the other day, I heard that gentleman speaking, with excitement and warmth, and, as I thought, in a loud and menacing tone. What the subject was,

I did not know when I came in; but, on taking my seat, I found he was speaking on the Georgia question. The gentleman sits on that side of the House, and I sit on this side; and, when I subsequently observed that the tone and menace seemed rather to proceed from the other side, I referred to the gentleman from Georgia; for he and myself were the two sides, so far as this particular matter was concerned. This was all I meant when I said that I thought the threatening language came from the other side. If it is necessary to disclaim any thought of menace on my part in stronger terms, I do it in the strongest; and, since the gentleman from Georgia has condescended to ask me the question, I answer, that I represent on this floor nobody but myself. Does the gentleman suppose that the poor pittance of respect which *my* opinion is entitled to, is to be destroyed by the insinuation that I belong to the party of the Administration? Sir, I alone am answerable for my words or actions in this House. About this subject I know no more than others—no more than what is disclosed by the papers which are in possession of all. What my own weak judgment respecting it is, the House, in due time, shall know; but I wish it clearly understood, that I stand here for myself only, and that what I say implicates nobody but my humble self. It would be unjust to say that it implicates any other person.

Mr. Webster went on to say that the honorable gentleman from Georgia had not, in his opinion, stated the question between that State and the Government of the United States with perfect accuracy. What was the subject of the present debate? It was a message, with documents, the subject of which he would endeavor succinctly to state.

In the year 1825, a certain treaty was made by the United States with the Creek Indians, at a place called the Indian Springs, by which certain lands were ceded to the United States which lay within the territory of Georgia. Had nothing prevented this treaty from going into effect, in September, 1826, these lands, pursuant to an agreement between Georgia and the United States, would have become the territory of Georgia. But previous to the period assigned for this treaty's effect, for reasons which are known to all the House, and which consisted chiefly of the dissatisfaction of a large part of the Indian tribe which were one party to the treaty, and who complained that those who negotiated the treaty were not duly authorized so to do, a new treaty was formed, the very first article of which declares, that the former treaty, made at the Indian Springs, was entirely annulled, and done away.

This is the point which the gentleman, in his statement, seemed to Mr. Webster to have wholly omitted, and it was certainly a most important point in the case now. The claim now brought forward and insisted upon by Georgia, if he understood it, was, that this first treaty at the Indian Springs, being a valid treaty, had the operation to vest the title

to the lands then ceded in the State of Georgia, and that the nullification of this first treaty, which afterwards took place at Washington, and formed the first article in the treaty of Washington, could not, and did not, have the effect to divest Georgia of the title to those lands. That, said Mr. Webster, is the question. It may certainly be a very grave question—a question of great moment, respecting which I shall not be in any hurry to give my opinion.

Now, that is the Georgia side of the question. The United States side of the question is different. The United States Government, on its part, contends, that the second treaty does annul the first; that the parties who made it had the power to annul the first treaty; that, by express terms, it is annulled, in every section, clause, and article of it; and that, therefore, there is no title in Georgia to any lands not embraced within the new treaty. On this ground the Government of the United States was called upon to enforce this treaty, which was the law of the land, according to the pre-existing statute law. And what is that law? That whenever citizens of the United States shall interfere, whether as trespassers or as surveyors, to run lines on lands guaranteed to the Indian tribes by treaty, the United States shall resent such infractions of treaty stipulations, and shall punish such persons as offend against them. Now, by the last treaty with the Creeks, this protection of the United States was guaranteed to the Creek Indians, respecting all their lands lying beyond a certain line. The law of the United States, in so many words, provides distinctly for this case.

The State of Georgia, by its constituted authorities, acting on their ground of construction, and directly in the face of the second treaty (whether rightfully or not, I shall not now attempt to decide), sent their surveyors over that line, with orders to survey the land as pertaining to Georgia. The Creeks immediately called upon the United States to fulfil the guarantee of protection contained in the fourteenth article of the treaty of Washington. Georgia proposed to maintain her surveyors by military force, and the United States, on the other hand, is called upon by the Indians to maintain the faith of a treaty with them. This is a state of things deeply to be regretted; it is regretted by none more than me. But, regretted or not, that is the question at issue. It is plain that if Georgia considers herself called to maintain her surveyors by force, and the United States Government considers itself called upon to maintain the treaty by force, there must be a collision.

Now, under such a state of things, what objection can there be to give to the presidential communication the usual course—to refer it to a committee, when all the facts can be ascertained, the question deliberately examined, and by whom, perhaps, another measure may be reported as expedient—I mean the measure referred to in the joint resolution sub-

mitted by the gentleman from Georgia—an appropriation of money to buy out the Indian title. For myself (said Mr. Webster), even if I were ever so well satisfied that Georgia was wrong, I should still be opposed to going to extremes, if the matter could possibly be arranged in any other way. If, in the mean while, the whole subject can be arranged satisfactorily by a new treaty, for the purchase of the remaining land, certainly every honorable and fair man would wish that it should be. The amount of money necessary to accomplish such an object would be of comparatively little consequence. However, there did appear to Mr. Webster to be a great propriety in sending the subject to some committee. Far be it from me (said he) to desire to be among those to whom it is sent. I have no itching for the decision of such a subject.

But, to whomsoever it shall go, the gentleman from Georgia need be under no alarm as to the effect of their report. That report, whatever it shall be, will be subjected to the acute and deliberate examination of the gentleman himself, and of every other friend of the Georgia interpretation. If the report be adverse, gentlemen are here to reply to it. If there be a flaw in it, they will find it. They are not too unskilled to complain. Georgia is ably represented here, and any errors of a committee would no doubt be promptly exposed.

The gentleman from Georgia asks what I mean, when I say that, if the States attempt unauthorized legislation, they will attempt it on their own responsibility, and at their peril? Do I mean to drive them out of the Union, or that the other States shall make war against them? Sir, the gentleman has, in the alarm of his imagination, or from the love of effect, exaggerated and strained what is a very common phrase. When we say that, if an individual does a particular thing, he will do it at his peril, do we mean, that if he does it, he will be annihilated? If one man says of another, that if he does such a thing, he will do it on his responsibility, is it to be understood as meaning that, if the man does it, he must be pistolled? Sir, I stand by the expression. I say that a State, like an individual, must necessarily take the peril which necessarily follows a wrong action, if it commits one; which means no more than that it must incur the peril necessarily accruing from such a course of action. I mean that if it shall be found that these States, by extending their legislation over the Indian territory, come in collision with the United States, and with the provisions of treaties, they must be answerable for the consequences.

And, sir, is there no peril but on one side of this question? The Government of the United States incurs the same liability that a State incurs— the liability of having acted improperly, and violated the Constitution of the country. Sir, until I lose my own sense of self respect, I believe that I shall be incapable of using, toward any State, any language incom-

patible with the respect which I owe to myself, and the deep respect which I very sincerely feel toward all the States. Mr. Webster concluded by saying, that if this communication should not go to one of the standing committees of the House, he should then move that it go to a select committee, but most certainly with no wish that he should be one of that committee.

Second Reply to Hayne, January 26–27, 1830

The Tariff of 1828 left the South a hopeless minority. High duties on manufactured goods, primarily of British origin, enormously stimulated the growth of industry in New England and the middle states. The South, dependent as she was on the sale of her staple crop in England, enjoyed no such advantage. As import duties rose, the price of cotton fell, and southern leaders sought desperately for a way to avert disaster. In December 1828 Calhoun, already vice-president elect, prepared for the South Carolina legislature an *Exposition and Protest* in which he reasoned that in the last resort a state might invoke her original sovereignty and nullify within her own boundaries any act of the federal government that bore too heavily upon her.

By the end of 1829 another, less disruptive remedy had been conceived. The West wanted cheap public lands almost as much as the South wanted tariff reduction. Why should not the two sections combine forces to give each what it wanted? We do not know what discussions may have taken place in private, but the groundwork was already laid when the 21st Congress met in December 1829. The occasion was accidental. As the month ended, Senator Samuel A. Foot of Connecticut offered a resolution to "inquire into the expediency of limiting for a certain period the sales of the public lands to such lands only as have heretofore been offered for sale, and are subject to entry at the minimum price." In a word, do not sell new lands beyond the rim of settlement until poorer lands hitherto passed over by settlers had been sold.

Foot himself was quite unaware of the implications that would be read into his resolution, as southern and western leaders delayed discussion until they had prepared their strategy. Then, on January 18, 1830, the debate began. Senator Thomas Hart Benton of Missouri opened for the nascent alliance of South and West, denouncing the resolution as a device to slow down the settlement of the West, in order to keep at home a supply of cheap labor for tariff-fostered northern factories. The next day, after some sparring by New England senators, Robert Y. Hayne of South Carolina took the floor, proposing that the public lands be sold for a nominal sum to the states in which they lay. Webster, who had been arguing a case before the Supreme Court, entered the Senate chamber while Hayne was speaking. He rose to reply when the South Carolina

senator was done, then yielded to a motion to adjourn. What we know as the First Reply to Hayne was thus delivered on January 20, 1830.

The speech was in fact an adroit change of subject. Webster defended New England against Benton's charges, attributed the growth and prosperity of the Northwestern states to the exclusion of slavery, and drove a wedge between the new sectional partners by sharply attacking the South for a political doctrine he held little short of treasonous. He was answering not Hayne but Calhoun's *Exposition* of 1828. He did it, moreover, in deliberately provocative language, designed to draw more fire from Hayne. The latter, at white heat, began his reply on Thursday, January 21, concluding on Monday the 25th. Webster then began his Second Reply to Hayne on January 26, 1830, concluding the following day.

The debate on Foot's resolution, which continued intermittently for some four months, was thus converted by Webster from the public land issue to the nature and interpretation of the Constitution. It was such a debate as had not been heard before in either house of Congress, and its effects were incalculable. The United States of America entered the year 1830—the 41st under the Constitution—as a loosely-knit confederation of states, the division of power between them still unclear despite the valiant efforts of Chief Justice John Marshall. After January 27 the United States was a nation, no longer a plural but a singular noun.

Webster knew when Hayne so eagerly seized the bait and delivered his masterly defense of Calhoun's "South Carolina Doctrine" that his reply would be a watershed in his own career. He asked Joseph Gales of the *National Intelligencer*, the best shorthand reporter in the business but no longer active in that capacity, to report the speech personally. Gales read his shorthand record to his wife, who wrote it out in clear, readable script. The report then went to Webster, who spent the better part of a month revising it for publication. He was consciously converting the spoken words, embellished as they had been by gestures, modulations of voice, and changes of expression, into words that would be read without these accompaniments but would leave the reader as thrilled and awed as the listening audience had been.

The revised version of the Second Reply to Hayne was published in the *National Intelligencer* in three installments, February 23, 25, 27, 1830. It was issued by Gales and Seaton at the same time in pamphlet form, to be reprinted again and again by editors across the land. Within three months Gales and Seaton had printed and distributed 40,000 copies, and knew of at least 20 editions printed elsewhere. (*National Intelligencer*, May 21, 1830). The speech quickly became the most widely-read and most influential utterance of its time.

Webster's revision of February remained the classic version thereafter, being reprinted without change in *Speeches and Forensic Arguments*, 1: 358–433; in *Works*, 3: 270–355; and in *Writings and Speeches*, 6: 3–75.

Fortunately all three versions—Gales's shorthand, the transcription, and much of Webster's revision—have been preserved, bound together with a copy of the printed text. A handwritten inscription states:

> This volume was purchased by me of Mrs. Gales, in Washington, on the 26th of April, 1877, agreeably to the Subscription Paper herewith inclosed, & is now presented to The Public Library of Boston, —to be preserved forever in its archives,—in behalf of the Subscribers to that Paper.

The inscription is signed by Robert C. Winthrop, who had read law with Webster and in the 1840's had been Speaker of the House of Representatives. The accompanying paper lists twenty-three subscribers, each of whom contributed $25. (*Boston Transcript*, July 18, 1882. See also Robert C. Winthrop, "Webster's Reply to Hayne," *Scribner's Magazine*, 15 [January, 1894]: 118–128.)

The two texts are essentially the same in content, yet they differ so widely in form that it is impossible to collate the two, or even to match them for side-by-side reproduction. We have therefore published both versions below. The familiar, edited version is reprinted from *Writings and Speeches*; the reported text follows the manuscript in the Boston Public Library.

Mr. President,—When the mariner has been tossed for many days in thick weather, and on an unknown sea, he naturally avails himself of the first pause in the storm, the earliest glance of the sun, to take his latitude, and ascertain how far the elements have driven him from his true course. Let us imitate this prudence, and, before we float farther on the waves of this debate, refer to the point from which we departed, that we may at least be able to conjecture where we now are. I ask for the reading of the resolution before the Senate.

The Secretary read the resolution, as follows:—

> *Resolved,* That the Committee on Public Lands be instructed to inquire and report the quantity of public lands remaining unsold within each State and Territory, and whether it be expedient to limit for a certain period the sales of the public lands to such lands only as have heretofore been offered for sale, and are now subject to entry at the minimum price. And, also, whether the office of Surveyor-General, and some of the land offices, may not be abolished

without detriment to the public interest; or whether it be expedient to adopt measures to hasten the sales and extend more rapidly the surveys of the public lands.

We have thus heard, Sir, what the resolution is which is actually before us for consideration; and it will readily occur to every one, that it is almost the only subject about which something has not been said in the speech, running through two days, by which the Senate has been entertained by the gentleman from South Carolina. Every topic in the wide range of our public affairs, whether past or present,—every thing, general or local, whether belonging to national politics or party politics,—seems to have attracted more or less of the honorable member's attention, save only the resolution before the Senate. He has spoken of every thing but the public lands; they have escaped his notice. To that subject, in all his excursions, he has not paid even the cold respect of a passing glance.

When this debate, Sir, was to be resumed on Thursday morning, it so happened that it would have been convenient for me to be elsewhere. The honorable member, however, did not incline to put off the discussion to another day. He had a shot, he said, to return, and he wished to discharge it. That shot, Sir, which he thus kindly informed us was coming, that we might stand out of the way, or prepare ourselves to fall by it and die with decency, has now been received. Under all advantages, and with expectation awakened by the tone which preceded it, it has been discharged, and has spent its force. It may become me to say no more of its effect, than that, if nobody is found, after all, either killed or wounded, it is not the first time, in the history of human affairs, that the vigor and success of the war have not quite come up to the lofty and sounding phrase of the manifesto.

The gentleman, Sir, in declining to postpone the debate, told the Senate, with the emphasis of his hand upon his heart, that there was something rankling *here*, which he wished to relieve. [Mr. Hayne rose, and disclaimed having used the word *rankling*.] It would not, Mr. President, be safe for the honorable member to appeal to those around him, upon the question whether he did in fact make use of that word. But he may have been unconscious of it. At any rate, it is enough that he disclaims it. But still, with or without the use of that particular word, he had yet something *here*, he said, of which he wished to rid himself by an immediate reply. In this respect, Sir, I have a great advantage over the honorable gentleman. There is nothing *here*, Sir, which gives me the slightest uneasiness; neither fear, nor anger, nor that which is sometimes more troublesome than either, the consciousness of having been in the wrong. There is nothing, either originating *here*, or now received *here* by the gentleman's shot. Nothing originating here, for I had not the slightest feeling of unkindness towards the honorable member. Some passages,

it is true, had occurred since our acquaintance in this body, which I could have wished might have been otherwise; but I had used philosophy and forgotten them. I paid the honorable member the attention of listening with respect to his first speech; and when he sat down, though surprised, and I must even say astonished, at some of his opinions, nothing was farther from my intention than to commence any personal warfare. Through the whole of the few remarks I made in answer, I avoided, studiously and carefully, every thing which I thought possible to be construed into disrespect. And, Sir, while there is thus nothing originating *here* which I have wished at any time, or now wish, to discharge, I must repeat, also, that nothing has been received *here* which *rankles*, or in any way gives me annoyance. I will not accuse the honorable member of violating the rules of civilized war; I will not say, that he poisoned his arrows. But whether his shafts were, or were not, dipped in that which would have caused rankling if they had reached their destination, there was not, as it happened, quite strength enough in the bow to bring them to their mark. If he wishes now to gather up those shafts, he must look for them elsewhere; they will not be found fixed and quivering in the object at which they were aimed.

The honorable member complained that I had slept on his speech. I must have slept on it, or not slept at all. The moment the honorable member sat down, his friend from Missouri [Thomas Hart Benton] rose, and, with much honeyed commendation of the speech, suggested that the impressions which it had produced were too charming and delightful to be disturbed by other sentiments or other sounds, and proposed that the Senate should adjourn. Would it have been quite amiable in me, Sir, to interrupt this excellent good feeling? Must I not have been absolutely malicious, if I could have thrust myself forward, to destroy sensations thus pleasing? Was it not much better and kinder, both to sleep upon them myself, and to allow others also the pleasure of sleeping upon them? But if it be meant, by sleeping upon his speech, that I took time to prepare a reply to it, it is quite a mistake. Owing to other engagements, I could not employ even the interval between the adjournment of the Senate and its meeting the next morning, in attention to the subject of this debate. Nevertheless, Sir, the mere matter of fact is undoubtedly true. I did sleep on the gentleman's speech, and slept soundly. And I slept equally well on his speech of yesterday, to which I am now replying. It is quite possible that in this respect, also, I possess some advantage over the honorable member, attributable, doubtless, to a cooler temperament on my part; for, in truth, I slept upon his speeches remarkably well.

But the gentleman inquires why *he* was made the object of such a reply. Why was *he* singled out? If an attack has been made on the East, he, he assures us, did not begin it; it was made by the gentleman from

Missouri. Sir, I answered the gentleman's speech because I happened to hear it; and because, also, I chose to give an answer to that speech, which, if unanswered, I thought most likely to product injurious impressions. I did not stop to inquire who was the original drawer of the bill. I found a responsible indorser before me, and it was my purpose to hold him liable, and to bring him to his just responsibility, without delay. But, Sir, this interrogatory of the honorable member was only introductory to another. He proceeded to ask me whether I had turned upon him, in this debate, from the consciousness that I should find an overmatch, if I ventured on a contest with his friend from Missouri. If, Sir, the honorable member, *modestiæ gratia*, had chosen thus to defer to his friend, and to pay him a compliment, without intentional disparagement to others, it would have been quite according to the friendly courtesies of debate, and not at all ungrateful to my own feelings. I am not one of those, Sir, who esteem any tribute of regard, whether light and occasional, or more serious and deliberate, which may be bestowed on others, as so much unjustly withholden from themselves. But the tone and manner of the gentleman's question forbid me thus to interpret it. I am not at liberty to consider it as nothing more than a civility to his friend. It had an air of taunt and disparagement, something of the loftiness of asserted superiority, which does not allow me to pass it over without notice. It was put as a question for me to answer, and so put as if it were difficult for me to answer, whether I deemed the member from Missouri an overmatch for myself, in debate here. It seems to me, Sir, that this is extraordinary language, and an extraordinary tone, for the discussions of this body.

Matches and overmatches! Those terms are more applicable elsewhere than here, and fitter for other assemblies than this. Sir, the gentleman seems to forget where and what we are. This is a Senate, a Senate of equals, of men of individual honor and personal character, and of absolute independence. We know no masters, we acknowledge no dictators. This is a hall for mutual consultation and discussion; not an arena for the exhibition of champions. I offer myself, Sir, as a match for no man; I throw the challenge of debate at no man's feet. But then, Sir, since the honorable member has put the question in a manner that calls for an answer, I will give him an answer; and I tell him, that, holding myself to be the humblest of the members here, I yet know nothing in the arm of his friend from Missouri, either alone or when aided by the arm of *his* friend from South Carolina, that need deter even me from espousing whatever opinions I may choose to espouse, from debating whenever I may choose to debate, or from speaking whatever I may see fit to say, on the floor of the Senate. Sir, when uttered as matter of commendation or compliment, I should dissent from nothing which the honorable member might say of

his friend. Still less do I put forth any pretensions of my own. But when put to me as matter of taunt, I throw it back, and say to the gentleman, that he could possibly say nothing less likely than such a comparison to wound my pride of personal character. The anger of its tone rescued the remark from intentional irony, which otherwise, probably, would have been its general acceptation. But, Sir, if it be imagined that by this mutual quotation and commendation; if it be supposed that, by casting the characters of the drama, assigning to each his part, to one the attack, to another the cry of onset; or if it be thought that, by a loud and empty vaunt of anticipated victory, any laurels are to be won here; if it be imagined, especially, that any, or all these things will shake any purpose of mine, I can tell the honorable member, once for all, that he is greatly mistaken, and that he is dealing with one of whose temper and character he has yet much to learn. Sir, I shall not allow myself, on this occasion, I hope on no occasion, to be betrayed into any loss of temper; but if provoked, as I trust I never shall be, into crimination and recrimination, the honorable member may perhaps find that, in that contest, there will be blows to take as well as blows to give; that others can state comparisons as significant, at least, as his own, and that his impunity may possibly demand of him whatever powers of taunt and sarcasm he may possess. I commend him to a prudent husbandry of his resources.

But, Sir, the Coalition![1] The Coalition! Ay, "the murdered Coalition!" The gentleman asks, if I were led or frighted into this debate by the spectre of the Coalition. "Was it the ghost of the murdered Coalition," he exclaims, "which haunted the member from Massachusetts; and which, like the ghost of Banquo, would never down?" "The murdered Coalition!" Sir, this charge of a coalition, in reference to the late administration, is not original with the honorable member. It did not spring up in the Senate. Whether as a fact, as an argument, or as an embellishment, it is all borrowed. He adopts it, indeed, from a very low origin, and a still lower present condition. It is one of the thousand calumnies with which the press teemed, during an excited political canvass. It was a charge, of which there was not only no proof or probability, but which was in itself wholly impossible to be true. No man of common information ever believed a syllable of it. Yet it was of that class of falsehoods, which, by continued repetition, through all the organs of detraction and abuse, are capable of misleading those who are already far misled, and of further fanning passion already kindling into flame. Doubtless it served in its day, and in greater or less degree, the end designed by it. Having done that, it has sunk into the general mass of stale and loathed cal-

1. The Adams-Clay coalition of 1825 that had made the former president and the latter secretary of state.

umnies. It is the very cast-off slough of a polluted and shameless press. Incapable of further mischief, it lies in the sewer, lifeless and despised. It is not now, Sir, in the power of the honorable member to give it dignity or decency, by attempting to elevate it, and to introduce it into the Senate. He cannot change it from what it is, an object of general disgust and scorn. On the contrary, the contact, if he choose to touch it, is more likely to drag him down, down, to the place where it lies itself.

But, Sir, the honorable member was not, for other reasons, entirely happy in his allusion to the story of Banquo's murder and Banquo's ghost. It was not, I think, the friends, but the enemies of the murdered Banquo, at whose bidding his spirit would not *down*. The honorable gentleman is fresh in his reading of the English classics, and can put me right if I am wrong; but according to my poor recollection, it was at those who had begun with caresses and ended with foul and treacherous murder that the gory locks were shaven. The ghost of Banquo, like that of Hamlet, was an honest ghost. It disturbed no innocent man. It knew where its appearance would strike terror, and who would cry out, A ghost! It made itself visible in the right quarter, and compelled the guilty and the conscience-smitten, and none others, to start, with,

> "Pr'ythee, see there! behold!—look! lo
> If I stand here, I saw him!"

Their eyeballs were seared (was it not so, Sir?) who had thought to shield themselves by concealing their own hand, and laying the imputation of the crime on a low and hireling agency in wickedness; who had vainly attempted to stifle the workings of their own coward consciences by ejaculating through white lips and chattering teeth, "Thou canst not say I did it!" I have misread the great poet if those who had no way partaken in the deed of the death, either found that they were, or *feared that they should be*, pushed from their stools by the ghost of the slain, or exclaimed to a spectre created by their own fears and their own remorse, "Avaunt! and quit our sight!"

There is another particular, Sir, in which the honorable member's quick perception of resemblances might, I should think, have seen something in the story of Banquo, making it not altogether a subject of the most pleasant contemplation. Those who murdered Banquo, what did they win by it? Substantial good? Permanent power? Or disappointment, rather, and sore mortification; dust and ashes, the common fate of vaulting ambition overleaping itself? Did not even-handed justice ere long commend the poisoned chalice to their own lips? Did they not soon find that for another they had "filed their mind"? that their ambition, though apparently for the moment successful, had but put a barren sceptre in their grasp? Ay, Sir,

"a barren sceptre in their gripe,
Thence to be wrenched with an unlineal hand,
No son of theirs succeeding."

Sir, I need pursue the allusion no farther. I leave the honorable gentleman to run it out at his leisure, and to derive from it all the gratification
it is calculated to administer. If he finds himself pleased with the associations, and prepared to be quite satisfied, though the parallel should be
entirely completed, I had almost said, I am satisfied also; but that I shall
think of. Yes, Sir, I will think of that.

In the course of my observations the other day, Mr. President, I paid
a passing tribute of respect to a very worthy man, Mr. [Nathan] Dane
of Massachusetts. It so happened that he drew the Ordinance of 1787,
for the government of the Northwestern Territory. A man of so much
ability, and so little pretence; of so great a capacity to do good, and so
unmixed a disposition to do it for its own sake; a gentleman who had
acted an important part, forty years ago, in a measure the influence of
which is still deeply felt in the very matter which was the subject of debate, might, I thought, receive from me a commendatory recognition.
But the honorable member was inclined to be facetious on the subject.
He was rather disposed to make it matter of ridicule, that I had introduced into the debate the name of one Nathan Dane, of whom he assures
us he had never before heard. Sir, if the honorable member had never
before heard of Mr. Dane, I am sorry for it. It shows him less acquainted
with the public men of the country than I had supposed. Let me tell him,
however, that a sneer from him at the mention of the name of Mr. Dane
is in bad taste. It may well be a high mark of ambition, Sir, either with
the honorable gentleman or myself, to accomplish as much to make our
names known to advantage, and remembered with gratitude, as Mr.
Dane has accomplished. But the truth is, Sir, I suspect, that Mr. Dane
lives a little too far north. He is of Massachusetts, and too near the north
star to be reached by the honorable gentleman's telescope. If his sphere
had happened to range south of Mason and Dixon's line, he might, probably, have come within the scope of his vision.

I spoke, Sir, of the Ordinance of 1787, which prohibits slavery, in all
future times, northwest of the Ohio, as a measure of great wisdom and
foresight, and one which had been attended with highly beneficial and
permanent consequences. I suppose that, on this point, no two gentlemen
in the Senate could entertain different opinions. But the simple expression of this sentiment has led the gentleman, not only into a labored defence of slavery, in the abstract, and on principle, but also into a warm
accusation against me, as having attacked the system of domestic slavery
now existing in the Southern States. For all this, there was not the slight-

est foundation, in any thing said or intimated by me. I did not utter a single word which any ingenuity could torture into an attack on the slavery of the South. I said, only, that it was highly wise and useful, in legislating for the Northwestern country while it was yet a wilderness, to prohibit the introduction of slaves; and I added, that I presumed there was no reflecting and intelligent person, in the neighboring State of Kentucky, who would doubt that, if the same prohibition had been extended, at the same early period, over that commonwealth, her strength and population would, at this day, have been far greater than they are. If these opinions be thought doubtful, they are nevertheless, I trust, neither extraordinary nor disrespectful. They attack nobody and menace nobody. And yet, Sir, the gentleman's optics have discovered, even in the mere expression of this sentiment, what he calls the very spirit of the Missouri question! He represents me as making an onset on the whole South, and manifesting a spirit which would interfere with, and disturb, their domestic condition!

Sir, this injustice no otherwise surprises me, than as it is committed here, and committed without the slightest pretence of ground for it. I say it only surprises me as being done here; for I know full well, that it is, and has been, the settled policy of some persons in the South, for years, to represent the people of the North as disposed to interfere with them in their own exclusive and peculiar concerns. This is a delicate and sensitive point in Southern feeling; and of late years it has always been touched, and generally with effect, whenever the object has been to unite the whole South against Northern men or Northern measures. This feeling, always carefully kept alive, and maintained at too intense a heat to admit discrimination or reflection, is a lever of great power in our political machine. It moves vast bodies, and gives to them one and the same direction. But it is without adequate cause, and the suspicion which exists is wholly groundless. There is not, and never has been, a disposition in the North to interfere with these interests of the South. Such interference has never been supposed to be within the power of government; nor has it been in any way attempted. The slavery of the South has always been regarded as a matter of domestic policy, left with the States themselves, and with which the federal government had nothing to do. Certainly, Sir, I am, and ever have been, of that opinion. The gentleman, indeed, argues that slavery, in the abstract, is no evil. Most assuredly I need not say I differ with him, altogether and most widely, on that point. I regard domestic slavery as one of the greatest evils, both moral and political. But whether it be a malady, and whether it be curable, and if so, by what means; or, on the other hand, whether it be the *vulnus immedicabile* of the social system, I leave it to those whose right and duty it is to inquire and to decide. And this I believe, Sir, is, and uniformly has been, the sentiment of the North. Let us look a little at the history of this matter.

When the present Constitution was submitted for the ratification of the people, there were those who imagined that the powers of the government which it proposed to establish might, in some possible mode, be exerted in measures tending to the abolition of slavery. This suggestion would of course attract much attention in the Southern conventions. In that of Virginia, Governor [Edmund] Randolph said: —

> I hope there is none here, who, considering the subject in the calm light of philosophy, will make an objection dishonorable to Virginia; that, at the moment they are securing the rights of their citizens, an objection is started, that there is a spark of hope that those unfortunate men now held in bondage may, by the operation of the general government, be made free.[2]

At the very first Congress, petitions on the subject were presented, if I mistake not, from different States. The Pennsylvania society for promoting the abolition of slavery took a lead, and laid before Congress a memorial, praying Congress to promote the abolition by such powers as it possessed. This memorial was referred, in the House of Representatives, to a select committee, consisting of Mr. [Abiel] Foster, of New Hampshire, Mr. [Elbridge] Gerry of Massachusetts, Mr. [Benjamin] Huntington of Connecticut, Mr. [John] Lawrence of New York, Mr. [Thomas] Sinnickson of New Jersey, Mr. [Thomas] Hartley of Pennsylvania, and Mr. [Josiah] Parker of Virginia; all of them, Sir, as you will observe, Northern men but the last. This committee made a report, which was referred to a committee of the whole House, and there considered and discussed for several days; and being amended, although without material alteration, it was made to express three distinct propositions, on the subject of slavery and the slave-trade. First, in the words of the Constitution, that Congress could not, prior to the year 1808, prohibit the migration or importation of such persons as any of the States then existing should think proper to admit; and secondly, that Congress had authority to restrain the citizens of the United States from carrying on the African slave-trade, for the purpose of supplying foreign countries. On this proposition, our early laws against those who engage in that traffic are founded. The third proposition, and that which bears on the present question, was expressed in the following terms: —

> Resolved, That Congress have no authority to interfere in the emancipation of slaves, or in the treatment of them in any of the States; it remaining with the several States alone to provide rules and regulations therein which humanity and true policy may require.

2. Elliot, Debates, 3:598.

This resolution received the sanction of the House of Representatives so early as March, 1790. And now, Sir, the honorable member will allow me to remind him, that not only were the select committee who reported the resolution, with a single exception, all Northern men, but also that, of the members then composing the House of Representatives, a large majority, I believe nearly two thirds, were Northern men also.

The House agreed to insert these resolutions in its journal, and from that day to this it has never been maintained or contended at the North, that Congress had any authority to regulate or interfere with the condition of slaves in the several States. No Northern gentleman, to my knowledge, has moved any such question in either House of Congress.

The fears of the South, whatever fears they might have entertained, were allayed and quieted by this early decision; and so remained till they were excited afresh, without cause, but for collateral and indirect purposes. When it became necessary, or was thought so, by some political persons, to find an unvarying ground for the exclusion of Northern men from confidence and from lead in the affairs of the republic, then, and not till then, the cry was raised, and the feeling industriously excited, that the influence of Northern men in the public counsels would endanger the relation of master and slave. For myself, I claim no other merit than that this gross and enormous injustice towards the whole North has not wrought upon me to change my opinions or my political conduct. I hope I am above violating my principles, even under the smart of injury and false imputations. Unjust suspicions and undeserved reproach, whatever pain I may experience from them, will not induce me, I trust, to overstep the limits of constitutional duty, or to encroach on the rights of others. The domestic slavery of the Southern States I leave where I find it,—in the hands of their own governments. It is their affair, not mine. Nor do I complain of the peculiar effect which the magnitude of that population has had in the distribution of power under this federal government. We know, Sir, that the representation of the States in the other house is not equal. We know that great advantage in that respect is enjoyed by the slave-holding States; and we know, too, that the intended equivalent for that advantage, that is to say, the imposition of direct taxes in the same ratio, has become merely nominal, the habit of the government being almost invariably to collect its revenue from other sources and in other modes. Nevertheless, I do not complain; nor would I countenance any movement to alter this arrangement of representation. It is the original bargain, the compact; let it stand; let the advantage of it be fully enjoyed. The Union itself is too full of benefit to be hazarded in propositions for changing its original basis. I go for the Constitution as it is, and for the Union as it is. But I am resolved not to submit in silence to accusations, either against myself individually or against the North,

wholly unfounded and unjust; accusations which impute to us a disposition to evade the constitutional compact, and to extend the power of the government over the internal laws and domestic condition of the States. All such accusations, wherever and whenever made, all insinuations of the existence of any such purposes, I know and feel to be groundless and injurious. And we must confide in Southern gentlemen themselves; we must trust to those whose integrity of heart and magnanimity of feeling will lead them to a desire to maintain and disseminate truth, and who possess the means of its diffusion with the Southern public; we must leave it to them to disabuse that public of its prejudices. But in the mean time, for my own part, I shall continue to act justly, whether those towards whom justice is exercised receive it with candor or with contumely.

Having had occasion to recur to the Ordinance of 1787, in order to defend myself against the inferences which the honorable member has chosen to draw from my former observations on that subject, I am not willing now entirely to take leave of it without another remark. It need hardly be said, that that paper expresses just sentiments on the great subject of civil and religious liberty. Such sentiments were common, and abound in all our state papers of that day. But this Ordinance did that which was not so common, and which is not even now universal; that is, it set forth and declared it to be a high and binding duty of government itself to support schools and advance the means of education, on the plain reason that religion, morality, and knowledge are necessary to good government, and to the happiness of mankind. One observation further. The important provision incorporated into the Constitution of the United States, and into several of those of the States, and recently, as we have seen, adopted into the reformed constitution of Virginia, restraining legislative power in questions of private right, and from impairing the obligation of contracts, is first introduced and established, as far as I am informed, as matter of express written constitutional law, in this Ordinance of 1787. And I must add, also, in regard to the author of the Ordinance, who has not had the happiness to attract the gentleman's notice heretofore, nor to avoid his sarcasm now, that he was chairman of that select committee of the old Congress, whose report first expressed the strong sense of that body, that the old Confederation was not adequate to the exigencies of the country and recommended to the States to send delegates to the convention which formed the present Constitution.[3]

An attempt has been made to transfer from the North to the South the

3. Webster here refers to Note A, one of several following the text of the speech, quoting a passage from the "Journal of the Congress of the Confederation," see *Journals of the Continental Congress* (34 vols., Washington, D.C., 1904–1937), 32: 71–72.

honor of this exclusion of slavery from the Northwestern Territory. The journal, without argument or comment, refutes such attempts. The cession by Virginia was made in March, 1784. On the 19th of April following, a committee, consisting of Messrs. [Thomas] Jefferson, [Jeremiah Townley] Chase, and [David] Howell, reported a plan for a temporary government of the territory, in which was this article: "That, after the year 1800, there shall be neither slavery nor involuntary servitude in any of the said States, otherwise than in punishment of crimes, whereof the party shall have been convicted." Mr. [Richard Dobbs] Spaight of North Carolina moved to strike out this paragraph. The question was put, according to the form then practised, "Shall these words stand as a part of the plan?" New Hampshire, Massachusetts, Rhode Island, Connecticut, New York, New Jersey, and Pennsylvania, seven States, voted in the affirmative; Maryland, Virginia, and South Carolina, in the negative. North Carolina was divided. As the consent of nine States was necessary, the words could not stand, and were struck out accordingly. Mr. Jefferson voted for the clause, but was overruled by his colleagues.

In March of the next year (1785), Mr. [Rufus] King of Massachusetts, seconded by Mr. [William] Ellery of Rhode Island, proposed the formerly rejected article, with this addition: "And that this regulation shall be an article of compact, and remain a fundamental principle of the constitutions between the thirteen original States, and each of the States described in the resolve." On this clause, which provided the adequate and thorough security, the eight Northern States at that time voted affirmatively, and the four Southern States negatively. The votes of nine States were not yet obtained, and thus the provision was again rejected by the Southern States. The perseverance of the North held out, and two years afterwards the object was attained. It is no derogation from the credit, whatever that may be, of drawing the Ordinance, that its principles had before been prepared and discussed, in the form of resolutions. If one should reason in that way, what would become of the distinguished honor of the author of the Declaration of Independence? There is not a sentiment in that paper which had not been voted and resolved in the assemblies, and other popular bodies in the country, over and over again.

But the honorable member has now found out that this gentleman, Mr. Dane, was a member of the Hartford Convention. However uninformed the honorable member may be of characters and occurrences at the North, it would seem that he has at his elbow, on this occasion, some high-minded and lofty spirit, some magnanimous and true-hearted monitor, possessing the means of local knowledge, and ready to supply the honorable member with every thing, down even to forgotten and moth-eaten two-penny pamphlets, which may be used to the disadvantage of his own country. But as to the Hartford Convention, Sir, allow me to say,

that the proceedings of that body seem now to be less read and studied in New England than farther South. They appear to be looked to, not in New England, but elsewhere, for the purpose of seeing how far they may serve as a precedent. But they will not answer the purpose, they are quite too tame. The latitude in which they originated was too cold. Other conventions, of more recent existence, have gone a whole bar's length beyond it. The learned doctors of Colleton and Abbeville have pushed their commentaries on the Hartford collect so far, that the original text-writers are thrown entirely into the shade. I have nothing to do, Sir, with the Hartford Convention. Its journal, which the gentleman has quoted, I never read. So far as the honorable member may discover in its proceedings a spirit in any degree resembling that which was avowed and justified in those other conventions to which I have alluded, or so far as those proceedings can be shown to be disloyal to the Constitution, or tending to disunion, so far I shall be as ready as any one to bestow on them reprehension and censure.

Having dwelt long on this convention, and other occurrences of that day, in the hope, probably, (which will not be gratified,) that I should leave the course of this debate to follow him at length in those excursions, the honorable member returned, and attempted another object. He referred to a speech of mine in the other house,[4] the same which I had occasion to allude to myself, the other day; and has quoted a passage or two from it, with a bold, though uneasy and laboring, air of confidence, as if he had detected in me an inconsistency. Judging from the gentleman's manner, a stranger to the course of the debate and to the point in discussion would have imagined, from so triumphant a tone, that the honorable member was about to overwhelm me with a manifest contradiction. Any one who heard him, and who had not heard what I had, in fact, previously said, must have thought me routed and discomfited, as the gentleman had promised. Sir, a breath blows all this triumph away. There is not the slightest difference in the purport of my remarks on the two occasions. What I said here on Wednesday is in exact accordance with the opinion expressed by me in the other house in 1825. Though the gentleman had the metaphysics of Hudibras, though he were able

> "to sever and divide
> A hair twixt north and northwest side,"

he yet could not insert his metaphysical scissors between the fair reading of my remarks in 1825, and what I said here last week. There is not only no contradiction, no difference, but, in truth, too exact a similarity, both

4. Webster's speech on the Cumberland Road, Jan. 18, 1825, pp. 161– 168, above.

in thought and language, to be entirely in just taste. I had myself quoted the same speech; had recurred to it, and spoke with it open before me; and much of what I said was little more than a repetition from it. In order to make finishing work with this alleged contradiction, permit me to recur to the origin of this debate, and review its course. This seems expedient, and may be done as well now as at any time.

Well, then, its history is this. The honorable member from Connecticut [Samuel A. Foot] moved a resolution, which constitutes the first branch of that which is now before us; that is to say, a resolution, instructing the committee on public lands to inquire into the expediency of limiting, for a certain period, the sales of the public lands, to such as have heretofore been offered for sale; and whether sundry offices connected with the sales of the lands might not be abolished without detriment to the public service. In the progress of the discussion which arose on this resolution, an honorable member from New Hampshire [Levi Woodbury] moved to amend the resolution, so as entirely to reverse its object; that is, to strike it all out, and insert a direction to the committee to inquire into the expediency of adopting measures to hasten the sales, and extend more rapidly the surveys, of the lands.

The honorable member from Maine [Peleg Sprague] suggested that both those propositions might well enough go for consideration to the committee; and in this state of the question, the member from South Carolina addressed the Senate in his first speech. He rose, he said, to give us his own free thoughts on the public lands. I saw him rise with pleasure, and listened with expectation, though before he concluded I was filled with surprise. Certainly, I was never more surprised, than to find him following up, to the extent he did, the sentiments and opinions which the gentleman from Missouri had put forth, and which it is known he has long entertained.

I need not repeat at large the general topics of the honorable gentleman's speech. When he said yesterday that he did not attack the Eastern States, he certainly must have forgotten, not only particular remarks, but the whole drift and tenor of his speech; unless he means by not attacking, that he did not commence hostilities, but that another had preceded him in the attack. He, in the first place, disapproved of the whole course of the government, for forty years, in regard to its disposition of the public lands; and then, turning northward and eastward, and fancying he had found a cause for alleged narrowness and niggardliness in the "accursed policy" of the tariff, to which he represented the people of New England as wedded, he went on for a full hour with remarks, the whole scope of which was to exhibit the results of this policy, in feelings and in measures unfavorable to the West. I thought his opinions unfounded and

erroneous, as to the general course of the government, and ventured to reply to them.

The gentleman had remarked on the analogy of other cases, and quoted the conduct of European governments towards their own subjects settling on this continent, as in point, to show that we had been harsh and rigid in selling, when we should have given the public lands to settlers without price. I thought the honorable member had suffered his judgment to be betrayed by a false analogy; that he was struck with an appearance of resemblance where there was no real similitude. I think so still. The first settlers of North America were enterprising spirits, engaged in private adventure, or fleeing from tyranny at home. When arrived here, they were forgotten by the mother country, or remembered only to be oppressed. Carried away again by the appearance of analogy, or struck with the eloquence of the passage, the honorable member yesterday observed, that the conduct of government towards the Western emigrants, or my representation of it, brought to his mind a celebrated speech in the British Parliament. It was, Sir, the speech of Colonel Barre. On the question of the stamp act, or tea tax, I forget which, Colonel Barre had heard a member on the treasury bench argue, that the people of the United States, being British colonists, planted by the maternal care, nourished by the indulgence, and protected by the arms of England, would not grudge their mite to relieve the mother country from the heavy burden under which she groaned. The language of Colonel Barre, in reply to this, was,—"They planted by your care? Your oppression planted them in America. They fled from your tyranny, and grew by your neglect of them. So soon as you began to care for them, you showed your care by sending persons to spy out their liberties, misrepresent their character, prey upon them, and eat out their substance."[5]

And how does the honorable gentleman mean to maintain, that language like this is applicable to the conduct of the government of the United States towards the Western emigrants, or to any representation given by me of that conduct? Were the settlers in the West driven thither by our oppression? Have they flourished only by our neglect of them? Has the government done nothing but prey upon them, and eat out their substance? Sir, this fervid eloquence of the British speaker, just when and where it was uttered, and fit to remain an exercise for the schools, is not a little out of place, when it is brought thence to be applied here, to the conduct of our own country towards her own citizens. From America to

5. Col. Isaac Barré (1726–1802) was a staunch defender of the rights of the American colonists. The quote is taken from the debate on the Stamp Act, Feb. 13, 1765, William Cobbett, ed., *The Parliamentary History of England* (36 vols., London, 1806–1820), 16: 38–39.

England, it may be true; from Americans to their own government, it would be strange language. Let us leave it, to be recited and declaimed by our boys against a foreign nation; not introduce it here, to recite and declaim ourselves against our own.

But I come to the point of the alleged contradiction. In my remarks on Wednesday, I contended that we could not give away gratuitously all the public lands; that we held them in trust; that the government had solemnly pledged itself to dispose of them as a common fund for the common benefit, and to sell and settle them as its discretion should dictate. Now, Sir, what contradiction does the gentleman find to this sentiment in the speech of 1825? He quotes me as having then said, that we ought not to hug these lands as a very great treasure. Very well, Sir, supposing me to be accurately reported in that expression, what is the contradiction? I have not now said, that we should hug these lands as a favorite source of pecuniary income. No such thing. It is not my view. What I have said, and what I do say, is, that they are a common fund, to be disposed of for the common benefit, to be sold at low prices for the accommodation of settlers, keeping the object of settling the lands as much in view as that of raising money from them. This I say now, and this I have always said. Is this hugging them as a favorite treasure? Is there no difference between hugging and hoarding this fund, on the one hand, as a great treasure, and, on the other, of disposing of it at low prices, placing the proceeds in the general treasury of the Union? My opinion is, that as much is to be made of the land as fairly and reasonably may be, selling it all the while at such rates as to give the fullest effect to settlement. This is not giving it all away to the States, as the gentleman would propose; nor is it hugging the fund closely and tenaciously, as a favorite treasure; but it is, in my judgment, a just and wise policy, perfectly according with all the various duties which rest in government. So much for my contradiction. And what is it? Where is the ground of the gentleman's triumph? What inconsistency in word or doctrine has he been able to detect? Sir, if this be a sample of that discomfiture with which the honorable gentleman threatened me, commend me to the word *discomfiture* for the rest of my life.

But, after all, this is not the point of the debate; and I must now bring the gentleman back to what is the point.

The real question between me and him is, Has the doctrine been advanced at the South or the East, that the population of the West should be retarded, or at least need not be hastened, on account of its effect to drain off the people from the Atlantic States? Is this doctrine, as has been alleged, of Eastern origin? That is the question. Has the gentleman found any thing by which he can make good his accusation? I submit to the Senate, that he has entirely failed; and, as far as this debate has

shown, the only person who has advanced such sentiments is a gentleman from South Carolina, and a friend of the honorable member himself. The honorable gentleman has given no answer to this; there is none which can be given. The simple fact, while it requires no comment to enforce it, defies all argument to refute it. I could refer to the speeches of another Southern gentleman, in years before, of the same general character, and to the same effect, as that which has been quoted; but I will not consume the time of the Senate by the reading of them.

So then, Sir, New England is guiltless of the policy of retarding Western population, and of all envy and jealousy of the growth of the new States. Whatever there be of that policy in the country, no part of it is hers. If it has a local habitation, the honorable member has probably seen by this time where to look for it; and if it now has received a name, he has himself christened it.

We approach, at length, Sir, to a more important part of the honorable gentleman's observations. Since it does not accord with my views of justice and policy to give away the public lands altogether, as a mere matter of gratuity, I am asked by the honorable gentleman on what ground it is that I consent to vote them away in particular instances. How, he inquires, do I reconcile with these professed sentiments, my support of measures appropriating portions of the lands to particular roads, particular canals, particular rivers, and particular institutions of education in the West? This leads, Sir, to the real and wide difference in political opinion between the honorable gentleman and myself. On my part, I look upon all these objects as connected with the common good, fairly embraced in its object and its terms; he, on the contrary, deems them all, if good at all, only local good. This is our difference. The interrogatory which he proceeded to put, at once explains this difference. "What interest," asks he, "has South Carolina in a canal in Ohio?" Sir, this very question is full of significance. It develops the gentleman's whole political system; and its answer expounds mine. Here we differ. I look upon a road over the Alleghanies, a canal round the falls of the Ohio, or a canal or railway from the Atlantic to the Western waters, as being an object large and extensive enough to be fairly said to be for the common benefit. The gentleman thinks otherwise, and this is the key to his construction of the powers of the government. He may well ask what interest has South Carolina in a canal in Ohio. On his system, it is true, she has no interest. On that system, Ohio and Carolina are different governments, and different countries; connected here, it is true, by some slight and ill-defined bond of union, but in all main respects separate and diverse. On that system, Carolina has no more interest in a canal in Ohio than in Mexico. The gentleman, therefore, only follows out his own principles; he does no more than arrive at the natural conclusions of his own doc-

trines; he only announces the true results of that creed which he has adopted himself, and would persuade others to adopt, when he thus declares that South Carolina has no interest in a public work in Ohio.

Sir, we narrow-minded people of New England do not reason thus. Our *notion* of things is entirely different. We look upon the States, not as separated, but as united. We love to dwell on that union, and on the mutual happiness which it has so much promoted, and the common renown which it has so greatly contributed to acquire. In our contemplation, Carolina and Ohio are parts of the same country; States, united under the same general government, having interests, common, associated, intermingled. In whatever is within the proper sphere of the constitutional power of this government, we look upon the States as one. We do not impose geographical limits to our patriotic feeling or regard; we do not follow rivers and mountains, and lines of latitude, to find boundaries, beyond which public improvements do not benefit us. We who come here, as agents and representatives of these narrow-minded and selfish men of New England, consider ourselves as bound to regard with an equal eye the good of the whole, in whatever is within our powers of legislation. Sir, if a railroad or canal, beginning in South Carolina and ending in South Carolina, appeared to me to be of national importance and national magnitude, believing, as I do that the power of government extends to the encouragement of works of that description, if I were to stand up here and ask, What interest has Massachusetts in a railroad in South Carolina? I should not be willing to face my constituents. These same narrow-minded men would tell me, that they had sent me to act for the whole country, and that one who possessed too little comprehension, either of intellect or feeling, one who was not large enough, both in mind and in heart, to embrace the whole, was not fit to be intrusted with the interest of any part.

Sir, I do not desire to enlarge the powers of the government by unjustifiable construction, nor to exercise any not within a fair interpretation. But when it is believed that a power does exist, then it is, in my judgment, to be exercised for the general benefit of the whole. So far as respects the exercise of such a power, the States are one. It was the very object of the Constitution to create unity of interests to the extent of the powers of the general government. In war and peace we are one; in commerce, one; because the authority of the general government reaches to war and peace, and to the regulation of commerce. I have never seen any more difficulty in erecting lighthouses on the lakes, than on the ocean; in improving the harbors of inland seas, than if they were within the ebb and flow of the tide; or in removing obstructions in the vast streams of the West, more than in any work to facilitate commerce on

the Atlantic coast. If there be any power for one, there is power also for the other; and they are all and equally for the common good of the country.

There are other objects, apparently more local, or the benefit of which is less general, towards which, nevertheless, I have concurred with others, to give aid by donations of land. It is proposed to construct a road, in or through one of the new States, in which this government possesses large quantities of land. Have the United States no right, or, as a great and untaxed proprietor, are they under no obligation to contribute to an object thus calculated to promote the common good of all the proprietors, themselves included? And even with respect to education, which is the extreme case, let the question be considered. In the first place, as we have seen, it was made matter of compact with these States, that they should do their part to promote education. In the next place, our whole system of land laws proceeds on the idea that education is for the common good; because, in every division, a certain portion is uniformly reserved and appropriated for the use of schools. And, finally, have not these new States singularly strong claims, founded on the ground already stated, that the government is a great untaxed proprietor, in the ownership of the soil? It is a consideration of great importance, that probably there is in no part of the country, or of the world, so great call for the means of education, as in these new States, owing to the vast numbers of persons within those ages in which education and instruction are usually received, if received at all. This is the natural consequence of recency of settlement and rapid increase. The census of these States shows how great a proportion of the whole population occupies the classes between infancy and manhood. These are the wide fields, and here is the deep and quick soil for the seeds of knowledge and virtue; and this is the favored season, the very spring-time for sowing them. Let them be disseminated without stint. Let them be scattered with a bountiful hand, broadcast. Whatever the government can fairly do towards these objects, in my opinion, ought to be done.

These, Sir, are the grounds, succinctly stated, on which my votes for grants of lands for particular objects rest; while I maintain, at the same time, that it is all a common fund, for the common benefit. And reasons like these, I presume, have influenced the votes of other gentlemen from New England. Those who have a different view of the powers of the government, of course, come to different conclusions, on these, as on other questions. I observed, when speaking on this subject before, that if we looked to any measure, whether for a road, a canal, or any thing else, intended for the impovement of the West, it would be found that, if the New England *ayes* were struck out of the lists of votes, the South-

ern *noes* would always have rejected the measure. The truth of this has not been denied, and cannot be denied. In stating this, I thought it just to ascribe it to the constitutional scruples of the South, rather than to any other less favorable or less charitable cause. But no sooner had I done this, than the honorable gentleman asks if I reproach him and his friends with their constitutional scruples. Sir, I reproach nobody. I stated a fact, and gave the most respectful reason for it that occurred to me. The gentleman cannot deny the fact; he may, if he choose, disclaim the reason. It is not long since I had occasion, in presenting a petition from his own State, to account for its being intrusted to my hands, by saying, that the constitutional opinions of the gentleman and his worthy colleague prevented them from supporting it. Sir, did I state this as matter of reproach? Far from it. Did I attempt to find any other cause than an honest one for these scruples? Sir, I did not. It did not become me to doubt or to insinuate that the gentleman had either changed his sentiments, or that he had made up a set of constitutional opinions accommodated to any particular combination of political occurrences. Had I done so, I should have felt, that, while I was entitled to little credit in thus questioning other people's motives, I justified the whole world in suspecting my own. But how has the gentleman returned this respect for others' opinions? His own candor and justice, how have they been exhibited towards the motives of others, while he has been at so much pains to maintain, what nobody has disputed, the purity of his own? Why, Sir, he has asked *when*, and *how*, and *why* New England votes were found going for measures favorable to the West. He has demanded to be informed whether all this did not begin in 1825, and while the election of President was still pending.

Sir, to these questions retort would be justified; and it is both cogent and at hand. Nevertheless, I will answer the inquiry, not by retort, but by facts. I will tell the gentleman *when*, and *how*, and *why* New England has supported measures favorable to the West. I have already referred to the early history of the government, to the first acquisition of the lands, to the original laws for disposing of them, and for governing the territories where they lie; and have shown the influence of New England men and New England principles in all these leading measures. I should not be pardoned were I to go over that ground again. Coming to more recent times, and to measures of a less general character, I have endeavored to prove that every thing of this kind, designed for Western improvement, has depended on the votes of New England; all this is true beyond the power of contradiction. And now, Sir, there are two measures to which I will refer, not so ancient as to belong to the early history of the public lands, and not so recent as to be on this side of the period when

the gentleman charitably imagines a new direction may have been given to New England feeling and New England votes. These measures, and the New England votes in support of them, may be taken as samples and specimens of all the rest.

In 1820 (observe, Mr. President, in 1820) the people of the West besought Congress for a reduction in the price of lands. In favor of that reduction, New England, with a delegation of forty members in the other house, gave thirty-three votes, and one only against it. The four Southern States, with more than fifty members, gave thirty-two votes for it, and seven against it. Again, in 1821 (observe again, Sir, the time), the law passed for the relief of the purchasers of the public lands. This was a measure of vital importance to the West, and more especially to the Southwest. It authorized the relinquishment of contracts for lands which had been entered into at high prices, and a reduction in other cases of not less than thirty-seven and a half per cent. on the purchase-money. Many millions of dollars, six or seven, I believe, probably much more, were relinquished by this law. On this bill, New England, with her forty members, gave more affirmative votes than the four Southern States, with their fifty-two or fifty-three members. These two are far the most important general measures respecting the public lands which have been adopted within the last twenty years. They took place in 1820 and 1821. That is the time *when*.

As to the manner *how*, the gentleman already sees that it was by voting in solid column for the required relief; and, lastly, as to the cause *why*, I tell the gentleman it was because the members from New England thought the measures just and salutary; because they entertained towards the West neither envy, hatred, nor malice; because they deemed it becoming them, as just and enlightened public men, to meet the exigency which had arisen in the West with the appropriate measure of relief; because they felt it due to their own characters, and the characters of their New England predecessors in this government, to act towards the new States in the spirit of a liberal, patronizing, magnanimous policy. So much, Sir, for the cause *why*; and I hope that by this time, Sir, the honorable gentleman is satisfied; if not, I do not know *when*, or *how*, or *why* he ever will be.

Having recurred to these two important measures, in answer to the gentleman's inquiries, I must now beg permission to go back to a period somewhat earlier, for the purpose of still further showing how much, or rather how little, reason there is for the gentleman's insinuation that political hopes or fears, or party associations, were the grounds of these New England votes. And after what has been said, I hope it may be forgiven me if I allude to some political opinions and votes of my own, of

very little public importance certainly, but which, from the time at which they were given and expressed, may pass for good witnesses on this occasion.

This government, Mr. President, from its origin to the peace of 1815, had been too much engrossed with various other important concerns to be able to turn its thoughts inward, and look to the development of its vast internal resources. In the early part of President Washington's administration, it was fully occupied with completing its own organization, providing for the public debt, defending the frontiers, and maintaining domestic peace. Before the termination of that administration, the fires of the French Revolution blazed forth, as from a new-opened volcano, and the whole breadth of the ocean did not secure us from its effects. The smoke and the cinders reached us, though not the burning lava. Difficult and agitating questions, embarrassing to government and dividing public opinion, sprung out of the new state of our foreign relations, and were succeeded by others, and yet again by others, equally embarrassing and equally exciting division and discord, through the long series of twenty years, till they finally issued in the war with England. Down to the close of that war, no distinct, marked, and deliberate attention had been given, or could have been given, to the internal condition of the country, its capacities of improvement, or the constitutional power of the government in regard to objects connected with such improvement.

The peace, Mr. President, brought about an entirely new and a most interesting state of things; it opened to us other prospects and suggested other duties. We ourselves were changed, and the whole world was changed. The pacification of Europe, after June, 1815, assumed a firm and permanent aspect. The nations evidently manifested that they were disposed for peace. Some agitation of the waves might be expected, even after the storm had subsided, but the tendency was, strongly and rapidly, towards settled repose.

It so happened, Sir, that I was at that time a member of Congress, and, like others, naturally turned my thoughts to the contemplation of the recently altered condition of the country and of the world. It appeared plainly enough to me, as well as to wiser and more experienced men, that the policy of the government would naturally take a start in a new direction; because new directions would necessarily be given to the pursuits and occupations of the people. We had pushed our commerce far and fast, under the advantage of a neutral flag. But there were now no longer flags, either neutral or belligerent. The harvest of neutrality had been great, but we had gathered it all. With the peace of Europe, it was obvious there would spring up in her circle of nations a revived and invigorated spirit of trade, and a new activity in all the business and objects of civilized life. Hereafter, our commercial gains were to be earned

only by success in a close and intense competition. Other nations would produce for themselves, and carry for themselves, and manufacture for themselves, to the full extent of their abilities. The crops of our plains would no longer sustain European armies, nor our ships longer supply those whom war had rendered unable to supply themselves. It was obvious, that, under these circumstances, the country would begin to survey itself, and to estimate its own capacity of improvement.

And this improvement,—how was it to be accomplished, and who was to accomplish it? We were ten or twelve millions of people, spread over almost half a world. We were more than twenty States, some stretching along the same seaboard, some along the same line of inland frontier, and others on opposite banks of the same vast rivers. Two considerations at once presented themselves with great force, in looking at this state of things. One was, that that great branch of improvement which consisted in furnishing new facilities of intercourse necessarily ran into different States in every leading instance, and would benefit the citizens of all such States. No one State, therefore, in such cases, would assume the whole expense, nor was the coöperation of several States to be expected. Take the instance of the Delaware breakwater. It will cost several millions of money. Would Pennsylvania alone ever have constructed it? Certainly never, while this Union lasts, because it is not for her sole benefit. Would Pennsylvania, New Jersey, and Delaware have united to accomplish it at their joint expense? Certainly not, for the same reason. It could not be done, therefore, but by the general government. The same may be said of the large inland undertakings, except that, in them, government, instead of bearing the whole expense, coöperates with others who bear a part. The other consideration is, that the United States have the means. They enjoy the revenues derived from commerce, and the States have no abundant and easy sources of public income. The custom-houses fill the general treasury, while the States have scanty resources, except by resort to heavy direct taxes.

Under this view of things, I thought it necessary to settle, at least for myself, some definite notions with respect to the powers of the government in regard to internal affairs. It may not savor too much of self-commendation to remark, that, with this object, I considered the Constitution, its judicial construction, its contemporaneous exposition, and the whole history of the legislation of Congress under it; and I arrived at the conclusion, that government had power to accomplish sundry objects, or aid in their accomplishment, which are now commonly spoken of as INTERNAL IMPROVEMENTS. That conclusion, Sir, may have been right, or it may have been wrong. I am not about to argue the grounds of it at large. I say only, that it was adopted and acted on even so early as in 1816. Yes, Mr. President, I made up my opinion, and determined on

my intended course of political conduct, on these subjects, in the Fourteenth Congress, in 1816. And now, Mr. President, I have further to say,
that I made up these opinions, and entered on this course of political
conduct, *Teucro duce*.[6] Yes, Sir, I pursued in all this a South Carolina
track on the doctrines of internal improvement. South Carolina, as she
was then represented in the other house, set forth in 1816 under a fresh
and leading breeze, and I was among the followers. But if my leader sees
new lights and turns a sharp corner, unless I see new lights also, I keep
straight on in the same path. I repeat, that leading gentlemen from South
Carolina were first and foremost in behalf of the doctrines of internal
improvements, when those doctrines came first to be considered and
acted upon in Congress. The debate on the bank question, on the tariff of
1816, and on the direct tax, will show who was who, and what was what,
at that time.

The tariff of 1816, (one of the plain cases of oppression and usurpation, from which, if the government does not recede, individual States
may justly secede from the government,) is, Sir, in truth, a South Carolina tariff, supported by South Carolina votes. But for those votes, it
could not have passed in the form in which it did pass; whereas, if it had
depended on Massachusetts votes, it would have been lost. Does not the
honorable gentleman well know all this? There are certainly those who
do, full well, know it all. I do not say this to reproach South Carolina. I
only state the fact; and I think it will appear to be true, that among the
earliest and boldest advocates of the tariff, as a measure of protection,
and on the express ground of protection, were leading gentlemen of South
Carolina in Congress. I did not then, and cannot now, understand their
language in any other sense. While this tariff of 1816 was under discussion in the House of Representatives, an honorable gentleman from
Georgia [John Forsyth], now of this house, moved to reduce the proposed
duty on cotton. He failed, by four votes, South Carolina giving three votes
(enough to have turned the scale) against his motion. The act, Sir, then
passed, and received on its passage the support of a majority of the Representatives of South Carolina present and voting. This act is the first
in the order of those now denounced as plain usurpations. We see it daily
in the list, by the side of those of 1824 and 1828, as a case of manifest
oppression, justifying disunion. I put it home to the honorable member
from South Carolina, that his own State was not only "art and part" in
this measure, but the *causa causans*. Without her aid, this seminal prin-

6. The reference is to John C. Calhoun, then vice-president of the
United States, and presiding over the
Senate when this speech was delivered. In the 14th Congress, although belonging to different parties,
Calhoun and Webster were often on
the same side in debates.

ciple of mischief, this root of Upas, could not have been planted. I have already said, and it is true, that this act proceeded on the ground of protection. It interfered directly with existing interests of great value and amount. It cut up the Calcutta cotton trade by the roots, but it passed, nevertheless, and it passed on the principle of protecting manufactures, on the principle against free trade, on the principle opposed to that *which lets us alone*.[7]

Such, Mr. President, were the opinions of important and leading gentlemen from South Carolina, on the subject of internal improvement, in 1816. I went out of Congress the next year, and, returning again in 1823, thought I found South Carolina where I had left her. I really supposed that all things remained as they were, and that the South Carolina doctrine of internal improvements would be defended by the same eloquent voices, and the same strong arms, as formerly. In the lapse of these six years, it is true, political associations had assumed a new aspect and new divisions. A strong party had arisen in the South hostile to the doctrine of internal improvements. Anticonsolidation was the flag under which this party fought; and its supporters inveighed against internal improvements, much after the manner in which the honorable gentleman has now inveighed against them, as part and parcel of the system of consolidation. Whether this party arose in South Carolina itself, or in the neighborhood, is more than I know. I think the latter. However that may have been, there were those found in South Carolina ready to make war upon it, and who did make intrepid war upon it. Names being regarded as things in such controversies, they bestowed on the anti-improvement gentlemen the appellation of Radicals. Yes, Sir, the appellation of Radicals, as a term of distinction applicable and applied to those who denied the liberal doctrines of internal improvement, originated, according to the best of my recollection, somewhere between North Carolina and Georgia. Well, Sir, these mischievous Radicals were to be put down, and the strong arm of South Carolina was stretched out to put them down. About this time I returned to Congress. The battle with the Radicals had been fought, and our South Carolina champions of the doctrines of internal improvement had nobly maintained their ground, and were understood to have achieved a victory. We looked upon them as conquerors. They had driven back the enemy with discomfiture, a thing, by the way, Sir, which is not always performed when it is prom-

7. Webster here refers to his appended Note B, which gives lengthy excerpts from speeches by Calhoun on the tariff of 1816, on the direct tax, and from his report on roads and canals while secretary of war. See *Annals*, 14th Cong., 1st sess., pp. 837, 1335–1336; *Reports of Committees*, 17th Cong., 1st sess., Serial No. 70, Report No. 8, p. 89.

ised. A gentleman to whom I have already referred in this debate had come into Congress, during my absence from it, from South Carolina, and had brought with him a high reputation for ability. He came from a school with which we had been acquainted, *et noscitur a sociis.* I hold in my hand, Sir, a printed speech of this distinguished gentleman [George McDuffie], "ON INTERNAL IMPROVEMENTS," delivered about the period to which I now refer, and printed with a few introductory remarks upon *consolidation*; in which, Sir, I think he quite consolidated the arguments of his opponents, the Radicals, if to *crush* be to consolidate. I give you a short but significant quotation from these remarks. He is speaking of a pamphlet, then recently published, entitled "Consolidation"; and having alluded to the question of renewing the charter of the former Bank of the United States, he says: —

> Moreover, in the early history of parties, and when Mr. [William H.] Crawford advocated a renewal of the old charter, it was considered a Federal measure; which internal improvement *never was*, as this author erroneously states. This latter measure originated in the administration of Mr. Jefferson, with the appropriation for the Cumberland Road; and was first proposed, *as a system*, by Mr. Calhoun, and carried through the House of Representatives by a large majority of the Republicans, including almost every one of the leading men who carried us through the late war.[8]

So, then, internal improvement is not one of the Federal heresies. One paragraph more, Sir: —

> The author in question, not content with denouncing as Federalists, General Jackson, Mr. Adams, Mr. Calhoun, and the majority of the South Carolina delegation in Congress, modestly extends the denunciation to Mr. Monroe and the whole Republican party. Here are his words: — 'During the administration of Mr. Monroe much has passed which the Republican party would be glad to approve if they could!! But the principal feature, and that which has chiefly elicited these observations, is the renewal of the SYSTEM OF INTERNAL IMPROVEMENTS.' Now this measure was adopted by a vote of 115 to 86 of a Republican Congress, and sanctioned by a Republican President. Who, then, is this author, who assumes the high prerogative of denouncing, in the name of the Republican party, the Republican administration of the country? A denunciation including within its sweep *Calhoun*, [William] *Lowndes*, and [Langdon] *Cheves*, men who will be regarded as the brightest ornaments of South Carolina, and the strongest pillars of the Republican party, as

8. *Speech of Mr. McDuffie on Internal Improvements, With a Few Introductory Remarks in Answer to a*   *Pamphlet Entitled "Consolidation"* (Columbia, S.C., 1824), p. 4.

long as the late war shall be remembered, and talents and patriotism shall be regarded as the proper objects of the admiration and gratitude of a free people!![9]

Such are the opinions, Sir, which were maintained by South Carolina gentlemen, in the House of Representatives, on the subject of internal improvements, when I took my seat there as a member from Massachusetts in 1823. But this is not all. We had a bill before us, and passed it in that house, entitled, "An Act to procure the necessary surveys, plans, and estimates upon the subject of roads and canals." It authorized the President to cause surveys and estimates to be made of the routes of such roads and canals as he might deem of national importance in a commercial or military point of view, or for the transportation of the mail, and appropriated thirty thousand dollars out of the treasury to defray the expense. This act, though preliminary in its nature, covered the whole ground. It took for granted the complete power of internal improvement, as far as any of its advocates had ever contended for it. Having passed the other house, the bill came up to the Senate, and was here considered and debated in April, 1824. The honorable member from South Carolina was a member of the Senate at that time. While the bill was under consideration here, a motion was made to add the following proviso:—"*Provided*, That nothing herein contained shall be construed to affirm *or admit* a power in Congress, on their own authority, to make roads or canals within any of the States of the Union." The yeas and nays were taken on this proviso, and the honorable member voted *in the negative!* The proviso failed.

A motion was then made to add this proviso, viz.:—"*Provided*, That the faith of the United States is hereby pledged, that no money shall ever be expended for roads or canals, except it shall be among the several States, and in the same proportion as direct taxes are laid and assessed by the provisions of the Constitution." The honorable member voted *against this proviso* also, and it failed. The bill was then put on its passage, and the honorable member voted *for it*, and it passed, and became a law.

Now it strikes me, Sir, that there is no maintaining these votes, but upon the power of internal improvement, in its broadest sense. In truth, these bills for surveys and estimates have always been considered as test questions; they show who is for and who against internal improvement. This law itself went the whole length, and assumed the full and complete power. The gentleman's votes sustained that power, in every form in which the various propositions to amend presented it. He went for the entire and unrestrained authority, without consulting the States, and

9. Ibid., p. 6.

without agreeing to any proportionate distribution. And now suffer me to remind you, Mr. President, that it is this very same power, thus sanctioned, in every form, by the gentleman's own opinion, which is so plain and manifest a usurpation, that the State of South Carolina is supposed to be justified in refusing submission to any laws carrying the power into effect. Truly, Sir, is not this a little too hard? May we not crave some mercy, under favor and protection of the gentleman's own authority? Admitting that a road, or a canal, must be written down flat usurpation as was ever committed, may we find no mitigation in our respect for his place, and his vote, as one that knows the law?

The tariff, which South Carolina had an efficient hand in establishing, in 1816, and this asserted power of internal improvement, advanced by her in the same year, and, as we have seen, approved and sanctioned by her Representatives in 1824, these two measures are the great grounds on which she is now thought to be justified in breaking up the Union, if she sees fit to break it up!

I may now safely say, I think, that we have had the authority of leading and distinguished gentlemen from South Carolina in support of the doctrine of internal improvement. I repeat, that, up to 1824, I for one followed South Carolina; but when that star, in its ascension, veered off in an unexpected direction, I relied on its light no longer. [Here the Vice-President said, "Does the chair understand the gentleman from Massachusetts to say that the person now occupying the chair of the Senate has changed his opinions on the subject of internal improvements?"]

From nothing ever said to me, Sir, have I had reason to know of any change in the opinions of the person filling the chair of the Senate. If such change has taken place, I regret it. I speak generally of the State of South Carolina. Individuals we know there are, who hold opinions favorable to the power. An application for its exercise, in behalf of a public work in South Carolina itself, is now pending, I believe, in the other house, presented by members from that State.

I have thus, Sir, perhaps not without some tediousness of detail, shown, if I am in error on the subject of internal improvement, how, and in what company, I fell into that error. If I am wrong, it is apparent who misled me.

I go to other remarks of the honorable member; and I have to complain of an entire misapprehension of what I said on the subject of the national debt, though I can hardly perceive how any one could misunderstand me. What I said was, not that I wished to put off the payment of the debt, but, on the contrary, that I had always voted for every measure for its reduction, as uniformly as the gentleman himself. He seems to claim the exclusive merit of a disposition to reduce the public charge. I do not allow it to him. As a debt, I was, I am for paying it, because it

is a charge on our finances, and on the industry of the country. But I observed, that I thought I perceived a morbid fervor on that subject, an excessive anxiety to pay off the debt, not so much because it is a debt simply, as because, while it lasts, it furnishes one objection to disunion. It is, while it continues, a tie of common interest. I did not impute such motives to the honorable member himself, but that there is such a feeling in existence I have not a particle of doubt. The most I said was, that if one effect of the debt was to strengthen our Union, that effect itself was not regretted by me, however much others might regret it. The gentleman has not seen how to reply to this, otherwise than by supposing me to have advanced the doctrine that a national debt is a national blessing. Others, I must hope, will find much less difficulty in understanding me. I distinctly and pointedly cautioned the honorable member not to understand me as expressing an opinion favorable to the continuance of the debt. I repeated this caution, and repeated it more than once; but it was thrown away.

On yet another point, I was still more unaccountably misunderstood. The gentleman had harangued against "consolidation." I told him, in reply, that there was one kind of consolidation to which I was attached, and that was the consolidation of our Union; that this was precisely that consolidation to which I feared others were not attached, and that such consolidation was the very end of the Constitution, the leading object, as they had informed us themselves, which its framers had kept in view. I turned to their communication,[10] and read their very words, "the consolidation of the Union," and expressed my devotion to this sort of consolidation. I said, in terms, that I wished not in the slightest degree to augment the powers of this government; that my object was to preserve, not to enlarge; and that by consolidating the Union I understood no more than the strengthening of the Union, and perpetuating it. Having been thus explicit, having thus read from the printed book the precise words which I adopted, as expressing my own sentiments, it passes comprehension how any man could understand me as contending for an extension of the powers of the government, or for consolidation in that odious sense in which it means an accumulation, in the federal government, of the powers properly belonging to the States.

I repeat, Sir, that, in adopting the sentiment of the framers of the Constitution, I read their language audibly, and word for word; and I pointed out the distinction, just as fully as I have now done, between the consolidation of the Union and that other obnoxious consolidation which I disclaimed. And yet the honorable member misunderstood me. The

10. The letter of the Federal Convention to the Congress of the Confederation, Sept. 17, 1787 transmitting the plan of the Constitution. *Journals of the Continental Congress*, 33: 502.

gentleman had said that he wished for no fixed revenue,—not a shilling. If by a word he could convert the Capitol into gold, he would not do it. Why all this fear of revenue? Why, Sir, because, as the gentleman told us, it tends to consolidation. Now this can mean neither more nor less than that a common revenue is a common interest, and that all common interests tend to preserve the union of the States. I confess I like that tendency; if the gentleman dislikes it, he is right in deprecating a shilling of fixed revenue. So much, Sir, for consolidation.

As well as I recollect the course of his remarks, the honorable gentleman next recurred to the subject of the tariff. He did not doubt the word must be of unpleasant sound to me, and proceeded, with an effort neither new nor attended with new success, to involve me and my votes in inconsistency and contradiction. I am happy the honorable gentleman has furnished me an opportunity of a timely remark or two on that subject. I was glad he approached it, for it is a question I enter upon without fear from any body. The strenuous toil of the gentleman has been to raise an inconsistency between my dissent to the tariff in 1824, and my vote in 1828. It is labor lost. He pays undeserved compliment to my speech in 1824; but this is to raise me high, that my fall, as he would have it, in 1828, may be more signal. Sir, there was no fall. Between the ground I stood on in 1824 and that I took in 1828, there was not only no precipice, but no declivity. It was a change of position to meet new circumstances, but on the same level. A plain tale explains the whole matter. In 1816 I had not acquiesced in the tariff, then supported by South Carolina. To some parts of it, especially, I felt and expressed great repugnance. I held the same opinions in 1820, at the meeting in Faneuil Hall, to which the gentleman has alluded. I said then, and say now, that, as an original question, the authority of Congress to exercise the revenue power, with direct reference to the protection of manufactures, is a questionable authority, far more questionable, in my judgment, than the power of internal improvements. I must confess, Sir, that in one respect some impression has been made on my opinions lately. Mr. Madison's publication[11] has put the power in a very strong light. He has placed it, I must acknowledge, upon grounds of construction and argument which seem impregnable. But even if the power were doubtful, on the face of the Constitution itself, it had been assumed and asserted in the first revenue law ever passed under that same Constitution; and on this ground, as a matter settled by contemporaneous practice, I had refrained from expressing the opinion that the tariff laws transcended constitutional

11. James Madison, *Letters on the Constitutionality of the Power in Congress to Impose a Tariff for the Protection of Manufactures* (Washington, 1828). Two more editions were published in 1829 under slightly different titles.

limits, as the gentleman supposes. What I did say at Faneuil Hall, as far as I now remember, was, that this was originally matter of doubtful construction. The gentleman himself, I suppose, thinks there is no doubt about it, and that the laws are plainly against the Constitution. Mr. Madison's letters, already referred to, contain, in my judgment, by far the most able exposition extant of this part of the Constitution. He has satisfied me, so far as the practice of the government had left it an open question.

With a great majority of the Representatives of Massachusetts, I voted against the tariff of 1824. My reasons were then given, and I will not now repeat them. But, notwithstanding our dissent, the great States of New York, Pennsylvania, Ohio, and Kentucky went for the bill, in almost unbroken column, and it passed. Congress and the President sanctioned it, and it became the law of the land. What, then, were we to do? Our only option was, either to fall in with this settled course of public policy, and accommodate ourselves to it as well as we could, or to embrace the South Carolina doctrine, and talk of nullifying the statute by State interference.

This last alternative did not suit our principles, and of course we adopted the former. In 1827, the subject came again before Congress, on a proposition to afford some relief to the branch of wool and woollens. We looked upon the system of protection as being fixed and settled. The law of 1824 remained. It had gone into full operation, and, in regard to some objects intended by it, perhaps most of them, had produced all its expected effects. No man proposed to repeal it; no man attempted to renew the general contest on its principle. But, owing to subsequent and unforeseen occurrences, the benefit intended by it to wool and woollen fabrics had not been realized. Events not known here when the law passed had taken place, which defeated its object in that particular respect. A measure was accordingly brought forward to meet this precise deficiency, to remedy this particular defect. It was limited to wool and woollens. Was ever any thing more reasonable? If the policy of the tariff laws had become established in principle, as the permanent policy of the government, should they not be revised and amended, and made equal, like other laws, as exigencies should arise, or justice require? Because we had doubted about adopting the system, were we to refuse to cure its manifest defects, after it had been adopted, and when no one attempted its repeal? And this, Sir, is the inconsistency so much bruited. I had voted against the tariff of 1824, but it passed; and in 1827 and 1828, I voted to amend it, in a point essential to the interest of my constituents. Where is the inconsistency? Could I do otherwise? Sir, does political consistency consist in always giving negative votes? Does it require of a public man to refuse to concur in amending laws, because they passed

against his consent? Having voted against the tariff originally, does consistency demand that I should do all in my power to maintain an unequal tariff, burdensome to my own constituents in many respects, favorable in none? To consistency of that sort, I lay no claim. And there is another sort to which I lay as little, and that is, a kind of consistency by which persons feel themselves as much bound to oppose a proposition after it has become a law of the land as before.

The bill of 1827, limited, as I have said, to the single object in which the tariff of 1824 had manifestly failed in its effect, passed the House of Representatives, but was lost here. We had then the act of 1828. I need not recur to the history of a measure so recent. Its enemies spiced it with whatsoever they thought would render it distasteful; its friends took it, drugged as it was. Vast amounts of property, many millions, had been invested in manufactures, under the inducements of the act of 1824. Events called loudly, as I thought, for further regulation to secure the degree of protection intended by that act. I was disposed to vote for such regulation, and desired nothing more; but certainly was not to be bantered out of my purpose by a threatened augmentation of duty on molasses, put into the bill for the avowed purpose of making it obnoxious. The vote may have been right or wrong, wise or unwise; but it is little less than absurd to allege against it an inconsistency with opposition to the former law.

Sir, as to the general subject of the tariff, I have little now to say. Another opportunity may be presented. I remarked the other day, that this policy did not begin with us in New England; and yet, Sir, New England is charged with vehemence as being favorable, or charged with equal vehemence as being unfavorable, to the tariff policy, just as best suits the time, place, and occasion for making some charge against her. The credulity of the public has been put to its extreme capacity of false impression relative to her conduct in this particular. Through all the South, during the late contest, it was New England policy and a New England administration that were afflicting the country with a tariff beyond all endurance; while on the other side of the Alleghanies even the act of 1828 itself, the very sublimated essence of oppression, according to Southern opinions, was pronounced to be one of those blessings for which the West was indebted to the "generous South."

With large investments in manufacturing establishments, and many and various interests connected with and dependent on them, it is not to be expected that New England, any more than other portions of the country, will now consent to any measure destructive or highly dangerous. The duty of the government, at the present moment, would seem to be to preserve, not to destroy; to maintain the position which it has assumed; and, for one, I shall feel it an indispensable obligation to hold

it steady, as far as in my power, to that degree of protection which it has undertaken to bestow. No more of the tariff.

Professing to be provoked by what he chose to consider a charge made by me against South Carolina, the honorable member, Mr. President, has taken up a new crusade against New England. Leaving altogether the subject of the public lands, in which his success, perhaps, had been neither distinguished nor satisfactory, and letting go, also, of the topic of the tariff, he sallied forth in a general assault on the opinions, politics, and parties of New England, as they have been exhibited in the last thirty years. This is natural. The "narrow policy" of the public lands had proved a legal settlement in South Carolina, and was not to be removed. The "accursed policy" of the tariff, also, had established the fact of its birth and parentage in the same State. No wonder, therefore, the gentleman wished to carry the war, as he expressed it, into the enemy's country. Prudently willing to quit these subjects, he was, doubtless, desirous of fastening on others, which could not be transferred south of Mason and Dixon's line. The politics of New England became his theme; and it was in this part of his speech, I think, that he menaced me with such sore discomfiture. Discomfiture! Why, Sir, when he attacks any thing which I maintain, and overthrows it, when he turns the right or left of any position which I take up, when he drives me from any ground I choose to occupy, he may then talk of discomfiture, but not till that distant day. What has he done? Has he maintained his own charges? Has he proved what he alleged? Has he sustained himself in his attack on the government, and on the history of the North, in the matter of the public lands? Has he disproved a fact, refuted a proposition, weakened an argument, maintained by me? Has he come within beat of drum of any position of mine? O, no; but he has "carried the war into the enemy's country"! Carried the war into the enemy's country! Yes, Sir, and what sort of a war has he made of it? Why, Sir, he has stretched a drag-net over the whole surface of perished pamphlets, indiscreet sermons, frothy paragraphs, and fuming popular addresses; over whatever the pulpit in its moments of alarm, the press in its heats, and parties in their extravagance, have severally thrown off in times of general excitement and violence. He has thus swept together a mass of such things as, but that they are now old and cold, the public health would have required him rather to leave in their state of dispersion. For a good long hour or two, we had the unbroken pleasure of listening to the honorable member, while he recited with his usual grace and spirit, and with evident high gusto, speeches, pamphlets, addresses, and all the *et cæteras* of the political press, such as warm heads produce in warm times; and such as it would be "discomfiture" indeed for any one, whose taste did not delight in that sort of reading, to be obliged to peruse. This is his war. This it is to carry

war into the enemy's country. It is in an invasion of this sort, that he flatters himself with the expectation of gaining laurels fit to adorn a Senator's brow!

Mr. President, I shall not, it will not, I trust, be expected that I should, either now or at any time, separate this farrago into parts, and answer and examine its components. I shall barely bestow upon it all a general remark or two. In the run of forty years, Sir, under this Constitution, we have experienced sundry successive violent party contests. Party arose, indeed, with the Constitution itself, and, in some form or other, has attended it through the greater part of its history. Whether any other constitution than the old Articles of Confederation was desirable, was itself a question on which parties divided; if a new constitution were framed, what powers should be given to it was another question; and when it had been formed, what was, in fact, the just extent of the powers actually conferred was a third. Parties, as we know, existed under the first administration, as distinctly marked as those which have manifested themselves at any subsequent period. The contest immediately preceding the political change in 1801, and that, again, which existed at the commencement of the late war, are other instances of party excitement, of something more than usual strength and intensity. In all these conflicts there was, no doubt, much of violence on both and all sides. It would be impossible, if one had a fancy for such employment, to adjust the relative *quantum* of violence between these contending parties. There was enough in each, as must always be expected in popular governments. With a great deal of popular and decorous discussion, there was mingled a great deal, also, of declamation, virulence, crimination, and abuse. In regard to any party, probably, at one of the leading epochs in the history of parties, enough may be found to make out another inflamed exhibition, not unlike that with which the honorable member has edified us. For myself, Sir, I shall not rake among the rubbish of bygone times, to see what I can find, or whether I cannot find something by which I can fix a blot on the escutcheon of any State, any party, or any part of the country. General Washington's administration was steadily and zealously maintained, as we all know, by New England. It was violently opposed elsewhere. We know in what quarter he had the most earnest, constant, and persevering support, in all his great and leading measures. We know where his private and personal character was held in the highest degree of attachment and veneration; and we know, too, where his measures were opposed, his services slighted, and his character vilified. We know, or we might know, if we turned to the journals, who expressed respect, gratitude, and regret, when he retired from the chief magistracy, and who refused to express either respect, gratitude, or regret. I shall not open those journals. Publications more abusive or scurrilous never saw

the light, than were sent forth against Washington, and all his leading measures, from presses south of New England. But I shall not look them up. I employ no scavengers, no one is in attendance on me, furnishing such means of retaliation; and if there were, with an ass's load of them, with a bulk as huge as that which the gentleman himself has produced, I would not touch one of them. I see enough of the violence of our own times, to be no way anxious to rescue from forgetfulness the extravagances of times past.

Besides, what is all this to the present purpose? It has nothing to do with the public lands, in regard to which the attack was begun; and it has nothing to do with those sentiments and opinions which, I have thought, tend to disunion, and all of which the honorable member seems to have adopted himself, and undertaken to defend. New England has, at times, so argues the gentleman, held opinions as dangerous as those which he now holds. Suppose this were so; why should *he* therefore abuse New England? If he finds himself countenanced by acts of hers, how is it that, while he relies on these acts, he covers, or seeks to cover, their authors with reproach? But, Sir, if, in the course of forty years, there have been undue effervescences of party in New England, has the same thing happened nowhere else? Party animosity and party outrage, not in New England, but elsewhere, denounced President Washington, not only as a Federalist, but as a Tory, a British agent, a man who in his high office sanctioned corruption. But does the honorable member suppose, if I had a tender here who should put such an effusion of wickedness and folly into my hand, that I would stand up and read it against the South? Parties ran into great heats again in 1799 and 1800. What was said, Sir, or rather what was not said, in those years, against John Adams, one of the committee that drafted the Declaration of Independence, and its admitted ablest defender on the floor of Congress? If the gentleman wishes to increase his stores of party abuse and frothy violence, if he has a determined proclivity to such pursuits, there are treasures of that sort south of the Potomac, much to his taste, yet untouched. I shall not touch them.

The parties which divided the country at the commencement of the late war were violent. But then there was violence on both sides, and violence in every State. Minorities and majorities were equally violent. There was no more violence against the war in New England, than in other States; nor any more appearance of violence, except that, owing to a dense population, greater facility of assembling, and more presses, there may have been more in quantity spoken and printed there than in some other places. In the article of sermons, too, New England is somewhat more abundant than South Carolina; and for that reason the chance of finding here and there an exceptionable one may be greater. I

hope, too, there are more good ones. Opposition may have been more formidable in New England, as it embraced a larger portion of the whole population; but it was no more unrestrained in principle, or violent in manner. The minorities dealt quite as harshly with their own State governments as the majorities dealt with the administration here. There were presses on both sides, popular meetings on both sides, ay, and pulpits on both sides also. The gentleman's purveyors have only catered for him among the productions of one side. I certainly shall not supply the deficiency by furnishing samples of the other. I leave to him, and to them, the whole concern.

It is enough for me to say, that if, in any part of this their grateful occupation, if, in all their researches, they find any thing in the history of Massachusetts, or New England, or in the proceedings of any legislative or other public body, disloyal to the Union, speaking slightingly of its value, proposing to break it up, or recommending non-intercourse with neighboring States, on account of difference of political opinion, then, Sir, I give them all up to the honorable gentleman's unrestrained rebuke; expecting, however, that he will extend his buffetings in like manner *to all similar proceedings, wherever else found.*

The gentleman, Sir, has spoken at large of former parties, now no longer in being, by their received appellations, and has undertaken to instruct us, not only in the knowledge of their principles, but of their respective pedigrees also. He has ascended to their origin, and run out their genealogies. With most exemplary modesty, he speaks of the party to which he professes to have himself belonged, as the true Pure, the only honest, patriotic party, derived by regular descent, from father to son, from the time of the virtuous Romans! Spreading before us the *family tree* of political parties, he takes especial care to show himself snugly perched on a popular bough! He is wakeful to the expediency of adopting such rules of descent as shall bring him in, to the exclusion of others, as an heir to the inheritance of all public virtue and all true political principle. His party and his opinions are sure to be orthodox; heterodoxy is confined to his opponents. He spoke, Sir, of the Federalists, and I thought I saw some eyes begin to open and stare a little, when he ventured on that ground. I expected he would draw his sketches rather lightly, when he looked on the circle round him, and especially if he should cast his thoughts to the high places out of the Senate. Nevertheless, he went back to Rome, *ad annum urbis conditæ*, and found the fathers of the Federalists in the primeval aristocrats of that renowned city! He traced the flow of Federal blood down through successive ages and centuries, till he brought it into the veins of the American Tories, of whom, by the way, there were twenty in the Carolinas for one in Massachusetts. From the Tories he followed it to the Federalists; and, as the Federal party was

broken up, and there was no possibility of transmitting it further on this side the Atlantic, he seems to have discovered that it has gone off collaterally, though against all the canons of descent, into the Ultras of France, and finally become extinguished, like exploded gas, among the adherents of Don Miguel! This, Sir, is an abstract of the gentleman's history of Federalism. I am not about to controvert it. It is not, at present, worth the pains of refutation; because, Sir, if at this day any one feels the sin of Federalism lying heavily on his conscience, he can easily procure remission. He may even obtain an indulgence, if he be desirous of repeating the same transgression. It is an affair of no difficulty to get into this same right line of patriotic descent. A man now-a-days is at liberty to choose his political parentage. He may elect his own father. Federalist or not, he may, if he choose, claim to belong to the favored stock, and his claim will be allowed. He may carry back his pretensions just as far as the honorable gentleman himself; nay, he may make himself out the honorable gentleman's cousin, and prove, satisfactorily, that he is descended from the same political great-grandfather. All this is allowable. We all know a process, Sir, by which the whole Essex Junto could, in one hour, be all washed white from their ancient Federalism, and come out, every one of them, original Democrats, dyed in the wool! Some of them have actually undergone the operation, and they say it is quite easy. The only inconvenience it occasions, as they tell us, is a slight tendency of the blood to the face, a soft suffusion, which, however, is very transient, since nothing is said by those whom they join calculated to deepen the red on the cheek, but a prudent silence is observed in regard to all the past. Indeed, Sir, some smiles of approbation have been bestowed, and some crumbs of comfort have fallen, not a thousand miles from the door of the Hartford Convention itself. And if the author of the Ordinance of 1787 possessed the other requisite qualifications, there is no knowing, notwithstanding his Federalism, to what heights of favor he might not yet attain.

Mr. President, in carrying his warfare, such as it is, into New England, the honorable gentleman all along professes to be acting on the defensive. He chooses to consider me as having assailed South Carolina, and insists that he comes forth only as her champion, and in her defence. Sir, I do not admit that I made any attack whatever on South Carolina. Nothing like it. The honorable member, in his first speech, expressed opinions, in regard to revenue and some other topics, which I heard both with pain and with surprise. I told the gentleman I was aware that such sentiments were entertained *out* of the government, but had not expected to find them advanced in it; that I knew there were persons in the South who speak of our Union with indifference or doubt, taking pains to magnify its evils, and to say nothing of its benefits; that the honorable member

himself, I was sure, could never be one of these; and I regretted the expression of such opinions as he had avowed, because I thought their obvious tendency was to encourage feelings of disrespect to the Union, and to impair its strength. This, Sir, is the sum and substance of all I said on the subject. And this constitutes the attack which called on the chivalry of the gentleman, in his own opinion, to harry us with such a foray among the party pamphlets and party proceedings of Massachusetts! If he means that I spoke with dissatisfaction or disrespect of the ebullitions of individuals in South Carolina, it is true. But if he means that I assailed the character of the State, her honor, or patriotism, that I reflected on her history or her conduct, he has not the slightest ground for any such assumption. I did not even refer, I think, in my observations, to any collection of individuals. I said nothing of the recent conventions. I spoke in the most guarded and careful manner, and only expressed my regret for the publication of opinions, which I presumed the honorable member disapproved as much as myself. In this, it seems, I was mistaken. I do not remember that the gentleman has disclaimed any sentiment, or any opinion, of a supposed anti-union tendency, which on all or any of the recent occasions has been expressed. The whole drift of his speech has been rather to prove, that, in divers times and manners, sentiments equally liable to my objection have been avowed in New England. And one would suppose that his object, in this reference to Massachusetts, was to find a precedent to justify proceedings in the South, were it not for the reproach and contumely with which he labors, all along, to load these his own chosen precedents. By way of defending South Carolina from what he chooses to think an attack on her, he first quotes the example of Massachusetts, and then denounces that example in good set terms. This twofold purpose, not very consistent, one would think, with itself, was exhibited more than once in the course of his speech. He referred, for instance, to the Hartford Convention. Did he do this for authority, or for a topic of reproach? Apparently for both, for he told us that he should find no fault with the mere fact of holding such a convention, and considering and discussing such questions as he supposes were then and there discussed; but what rendered it obnoxious was its being held at the time, and under the circumstances of the country then existing. We were in a war, he said, and the country needed all our aid; the hand of government required to be strengthened, not weakened; and patriotism should have postponed such proceedings to another day. The thing itself, then, is a precedent; the time and manner of it only, a subject of censure.

Now, Sir, I go much further, on this point, than the honorable member. Supposing, as the gentleman seems to do, that the Hartford Convention assembled for any such purpose as breaking up the Union, because they

thought unconstitutional laws had been passed, or to consult on that subject, or *to calculate the value of the Union*; supposing this to be their purpose, or any part of it, then I say the meeting itself was disloyal, and was obnoxious to censure, whether held in time of peace or time of war, or under whatever circumstances. The material question is the *object*. Is dissolution the *object*? If it be, external circumstances may make it a more or less aggravated case, but cannot affect the principle. I do not hold, therefore, Sir, that the Hartford Convention was pardonable, even to the extent of the gentleman's admission, if its objects were really such as have been imputed to it. Sir, there never was a time, under any degree of excitement, in which the Hartford Convention, or any other convention, could have maintained itself one moment in New England, if assembled for any such purpose as the gentleman says would have been an allowable purpose. To hold conventions to decide constitutional law! To try the binding validity of statutes by votes in a convention! Sir, the Hartford Convention, I presume, would not desire that the honorable gentleman should be their defender or advocate, if he puts their case upon such untenable and extravagant grounds.

Then, Sir, the gentleman has no fault to find with these recently promulgated South Carolina opinions. And certainly he need have none; for his own sentiments, as now advanced, and advanced on reflection, as far as I have been able to comprehend them, go the full length of all these opinions. I propose, Sir, to say something on these, and to consider how far they are just and constitutional. Before doing that, however, let me observe that the eulogium pronounced by the honorable gentleman on the character of the State of South Carolina, for her Revolutionary and other merits, meets my hearty concurrence. I shall not acknowledge that the honorable member goes before me in regard for whatever of distinguished talent, or distinguished character, South Carolina has produced. I claim part of the honor, I partake in the pride, of her great names. I claim them for countrymen, one and all, the Laurenses, the Rutledges, the Pinckneys, the Sumpters, the Marions, Americans all, whose fame is no more to be hemmed in by State lines, than their talents and patriotism were capable of being circumscribed within the same narrow limits. In their day and generation, they served and honored the country, and the whole country; and their renown is of the treasures of the whole country. Him whose honored name the gentleman himself bears,—does he esteem me less capable of gratitude for his patriotism, or sympathy for his sufferings, than if his eyes had first opened upon the light of Massachusetts, instead of South Carolina? Sir, does he suppose it in his power to exhibit a Carolina name so bright, as to produce envy in my bosom? No, Sir, increased gratification and delight, rather. I thank God, that, if I am gifted with little of the spirit which is able to raise mortals

to the skies, I have yet none, as I trust, of that other spirit, which would drag angels down. When I shall be found, Sir, in my place here in the Senate, or elsewhere, to sneer at public merit, because it happens to spring up beyond the little limits of my own State or neighborhood; when I refuse, for any such cause, or for any cause, the homage due to American talent, to elevated patriotism, to sincere devotion to liberty and the country; or, if I see an uncommon endowment of Heaven, if I see extraordinary capacity and virtue, in any of the South, and if, moved by local prejudice or gangrened by State jealousy, I get up here to abate the tithe of a hair from his just character and just fame, may my tongue cleave to the roof of my mouth!

Sir, let me recur to pleasing recollections; let me indulge in refreshing remembrance of the past; let me remind you that, in early times, no States cherished greater harmony, both of principle and feeling, than Massachusetts and South Carolina. Would to God that harmony might again return! Shoulder to shoulder they went through the Revolution, hand in hand they stood round the administration of Washington, and felt his own great arm lean on them for support. Unkind feeling, if it exist, alienation, and distrust are the growth, unnatural to such soils, of false principles since sown. They are weeds, the seeds of which that same great arm never scattered.

Mr. President, I shall enter on no encomium upon Massachusetts; she needs none. There she is. Behold her, and judge for yourselves. There is her history; the world knows it by heart. The past, at least, is secure. There is Boston, and Concord, and Lexington, and Bunker Hill; and there they will remain for ever. The bones of her sons, falling in the great struggle for Independence, now lie mingled with the soil of every State from New England to Georgia; and there they will lie for ever. And Sir, where American Liberty raised its first voice, and where its youth was nurtured and sustained, there it still lives, in the strength of its manhood and full of its original spirit. If discord and disunion shall wound it, if party strife and blind ambition shall hawk at and tear it, if folly and madness, if uneasiness under salutary and necessary restraint, shall succeed in separating it from that Union, by which alone its existence is made sure, it will stand, in the end, by the side of that cradle in which its infancy was rocked; it will stretch forth its arm with whatever of vigor it may still retain over the friends who gather round it; and it will fall at last, if fall it must, amidst the proudest monuments of its own glory, and on the very spot of its origin.

There yet remains to be performed, Mr. President, by far the most grave and important duty, which I feel to be devolved on me by this occasion. It is to state, and to defend, what I conceive to be the true principles of the Constitution under which we are here assembled. I might

well have desired that so weighty a task should have fallen into other and abler hands. I could have wished that it should have been executed by those whose character and experience give weight and influence to their opinions, such as cannot possibly belong to mine. But, Sir, I have met the occasion, not sought it; and I shall proceed to state my own sentiments, without challenging for them any particular regard, with studied plainness, and as much precision as possible.

I understand the honorable gentleman from South Carolina to maintain, that it is a right of the State legislatures to interfere, whenever, in their judgment, this government transcends its constitutional limits, and to arrest the operation of its laws.

I understand him to maintain this right, as a right existing *under* the Constitution, not as a right to overthrow it on the ground of extreme necessity, such as would justify violent revolution.

I understand him to maintain an authority, on the part of the States, thus to interfere, for the purpose of correcting the exercise of power by the general government, of checking it, and of compelling it to conform to their opinion of the extent of its powers.

I understand him to maintain, that the ultimate power of judging of the constitutional extent of its own authority is not lodged exclusively in the general government, or any branch of it; but that, on the contrary, the States may lawfully decide for themselves, and each State for itself, whether, in a given case, the act of the general government transcends its power.

I understand him to insist, that, if the exigency of the case, in the opinion of any State government, require it, such State government may, by its own sovereign authority, annul an act of the general government which it deems plainly and palpably unconstitutional.

This is the sum of what I understand from him to be the South Carolina doctrine, and the doctrine which he maintains. I propose to consider it, and compare it with the Constitution. Allow me to say, as a preliminary remark, that I call this the South Carolina doctrine only because the gentleman himself has so denominated it. I do not feel at liberty to say that South Carolina, as a State, has ever advanced these sentiments. I hope she has not, and never may. That a great majority of her people are opposed to the tariff laws, is doubtless true. That a majority, somewhat less than that just mentioned, conscientiously believe these laws unconstitutional, may probably also be true. But that any majority holds to the right of direct State interference at State discretion, the right of nullifying acts of Congress by acts of State legislation, is more than I know, and what I shall be slow to believe.

That there are individuals besides the honorable gentleman who do maintain these opinions, is quite certain. I recollect the recent expression

of a sentiment, which circumstances attending its utterance and publication justify us in supposing was not unpremeditated. "The sovereignty of the State,— never to be controlled, construed, or decided on but by her own feelings of honorable justice." [12]

[Mr. Hayne here rose and said, that, for the purpose of being clearly understood, he would state that his proposition was in the words of the Virginia resolution, as follows: —

> [That this assembly doth explicitly and peremptorily declare, that it views the powers of the federal government, as resulting from the compact to which the States are parties, as limited by the plain sense and intention of the instrument constituting that compact, as no farther valid than they are authorized by the grants enumerated in that compact; and that, in case of a deliberate, palpable, and dangerous exercise of other powers, not granted by the said compact, the States who are parties thereto have the right, and are in duty bound, to interpose, for arresting the progress of the evil, and for maintaining within their respective limits the authorities, rights, and liberties appertaining to them. [13]

[Mr. Webster resumed: —]

I am quite aware, Mr. President, of the existence of the resolution which the gentleman read, and has now repeated, and that he relies on it as his authority. I know the source, too, from which it is understood to have proceeded. I need not say that I have much respect for the constitutional opinions of Mr. Madison; they would weigh greatly with me always. But before the authority of his opinion be vouched for the gentleman's proposition, it will be proper to consider what is the fair interpretation of that resolution, to which Mr. Madison is understood to have given his sanction. As the gentleman construes it, it is an authority for him. Possibly, he may not have adopted the right construction. That resolution declares, that, *in the case of the dangerous exercise of powers not granted by the general government, the States may interpose to arrest the progress of the evil.* But how interpose, and what does this declaration purport? Does it mean no more than that there may be extreme cases, in which the people, in any mode of assembling, may resist usurpation, and relieve themselves from a tyrannical government? No one will deny this. Such resistance is not only acknowledged to be just in America, but in England also. Blackstone admits as much, in the theory,

12. This toast was made by Dr. Thomas Cooper (1759–1839), president of South Carolina College, at a dinner for Langdon Cheves in Columbia, S.C., Dec. 9, 1829. *Niles' Register*, 37 (Jan. 2, 1830): 315.

13. The Virginia resolution on the Alien and Sedition Acts was adopted on Dec. 21, 1798. *Resolutions of Virginia and Kentucky* (Richmond, 1835), p. 209.

and practice, too, of the English constitution. We, Sir, who oppose the Carolina doctrine, do not deny that the people may, if they choose, throw off any government when it becomes oppressive and intolerable, and erect a better in its stead. We all know that civil institutions are established for the public benefit, and that when they cease to answer the ends of their existence they may be changed. But I do not understand the doctrine now contended for to be that, which, for the sake of distinction, we may call the right of revolution. I understand the gentleman to maintain, that, without revolution, without civil commotion, without rebellion, a remedy for supposed abuse and transgression of the powers of the general government lies in a direct appeal to the interference of the State governments.

[Mr. Hayne here rose and said: He did not contend for the mere right of revolution, but for the right of constitutional resistance. What he maintained was, that in case of a plain, palpable violation of the Constitution by the general government, a State may interpose; and that this interposition is constitutional.

Mr. Webster resumed: —]

So, Sir, I understood the gentleman, and am happy to find that I did not misunderstand him. What he contends for is, that it is constitutional to interrupt the administration of the Constitution itself, in the hands of those who are chosen and sworn to administer it, by the direct interference, in form of law, of the States, in virtue of their sovereign capacity. The inherent right in the people to reform their government I do not deny; and they have another right, and that is, to resist unconstitutional laws, without overturning the government. It is no doctrine of mine that unconstitutional laws bind the people. The great question is, Whose prerogative is it to decide on the constitutionality or unconstitutionality of the laws? On that, the main debate hinges. The proposition, that, in case of a supposed violation of the Constitution by Congress, the States have a constitutional right to interfere and annul the law of Congress, is the proposition of the gentleman. I do not admit it. If the gentleman had intended no more than to assert the right of revolution for justifiable cause, he would have said only what all agree to. But I cannot conceive that there can be a middle course, between submission to the laws, when regularly pronounced constitutional, on the one hand, and open resistance, which is revolution or rebellion, on the other. I say, the right of a State to annul a law of Congress cannot be maintained, but on the ground of the inalienable right of man to resist oppression; that is to say, upon the ground of revolution. I admit that there is an ultimate violent remedy, above the Constitution and in defiance of the Constitution, which may be resorted to when a revolution is to be justified. But I do not admit, that, under the Constitution and in conformity with it, there is any mode

in which a State government, as a member of the Union, can interfere and stop the progress of the general government, by force of her own laws, under any circumstances whatever.

This leads us to inquire into the origin of this government and the source of its power. Whose agent is it? Is it the creature of the State legislatures, or the creature of the people? If the government of the United States be the agent of the State governments, then they may control it, provided they can agree in the manner of controlling it; if it be the agent of the people, then the people alone can control it, restrain it, modify, or reform it. It is observable enough, that the doctrine for which the honorable gentleman contends leads him to the necessity of maintaining, not only that this general government is the creature of the States, but that it is the creature of each of the States severally, so that each may assert the power for itself of determining whether it acts within the limits of its authority. It is the servant of four-and-twenty masters, of different wills and different purposes, and yet bound to obey all. This absurdity (for it seems no less) arises from a misconception as to the origin of this government and its true character. It is, Sir, the people's Constitution, the people's government, made for the people, made by the people, and answerable to the people. The people of the United States have declared that the Constitution shall be the supreme law. We must either admit the proposition, or dispute their authority. The States are, unquestionably, sovereign, so far as their sovereignty is not affected by this supreme law. But the State legislatures, as political bodies, however sovereign, are yet not sovereign over the people. So far as the people have given power to the general government, so far the grant is unquestionably good, and the government holds of the people, and not of the State governments. We are all agents of the same supreme power, the people. The general government and the State governments derive their authority from the same source. Neither can, in relation to the other, be called primary, though one is definite and restricted, and the other general and residuary. The national government possesses those powers which it can be shown the people have conferred on it, and no more. All the rest belongs to the State governments, or to the people themselves. So far as the people have restrained State sovereignty, by the expression of their will, in the Constitution of the United States, so far, it must be admitted, State sovereignty is effectually controlled. I do not contend that it is, or ought to be, controlled farther. The sentiment to which I have referred propounds that State sovereignty is only to be controlled by its own "feeling of justice"; that is to say, it is not to be controlled at all, for one who is to follow his own feelings is under no legal control. Now, however men may think this ought to be, the fact is, that the people of the United States have chosen to impose control on State sovereignties.

There are those, doubtless, who wish they had been left without restraint; but the Constitution has ordered the matter differently. To make war, for instance, is an exercise of sovereignty; but the Constitution declares that no State shall make war. To coin money is another exercise of sovereign power, but no State is at liberty to coin money. Again, the Constitution says that no sovereign State shall be so sovereign as to make a treaty. These prohibitions, it must be confessed, are a control on the State sovereignty of South Carolina, as well as of the other States, which does not arise "from her own feelings of honorable justice." The opinion referred to, therefore, is in defiance of the plainest provisions of the Constitution.

There are other proceedings of public bodies which have already been alluded to, and to which I refer again, for the purpose of ascertaining more fully what is the length and breadth of that doctrine, denominated the Carolina doctrine, which the honorable member has now stood up on this floor to maintain. In one of them I find it resolved, that "the tariff of 1828, and every other tariff designed to promote one branch of industry at the expense of others, is contrary to the meaning and intention of the federal compact; and such a dangerous, palpable, and deliberate usurpation of power, by a determined majority, wielding the general government beyond the limits of its delegated powers, as calls upon the States which compose the suffering minority, in their sovereign capacity, to exercise the powers which, as sovereigns, necessarily devolve upon them, when their compact is violated."[14]

Observe, Sir, that this resolution holds the tariff of 1828, and every other tariff designed to promote one branch of industry at the expense of another, to be such a dangerous, palpable, and deliberate usurpation of power, as calls upon the States, in their sovereign capacity, to interfere by their own authority. This denunciation, Mr. President, you will please to observe, includes our old tariff of 1816, as well as all others; because that was established to promote the interest of the manufacturers of cotton, to the manifest and admitted injury of the Calcutta cotton trade. Observe, again, that all the qualifications are here rehearsed and charged upon the tariff, which are necessary to bring the case within the gentleman's proposition. The tariff is a usurpation; it is a dangerous usurpation; it is a palpable usurpation; it is a deliberate usurpation. It is such a usurpation, therefore, as calls upon the States to exercise their right of interference. Here is a case, then, within the gentleman's principles, and all his qualifications of his principles. It is a case for action. The Constitution is plainly, dangerously, palpably, and deliberately violated; and the States must interpose their own authority to arrest the law. Let us sup-

[14] This resolution was adopted by a public meeting at Abbeville, on Sept. 25, 1828. *Niles' Register*, 35 (Oct. 25, 1828): 141–142.

pose the State of South Carolina to express this same opinion, by the voice of her legislature. That would be very imposing; but what then? Is the voice of one State conclusive? It so happens that, at the very moment when South Carolina resolves that the tariff laws are unconstitutional, Pennsylvania and Kentucky resolve exactly the reverse. *They* hold those laws to be both highly proper and strictly constitutional. And now, Sir, how does the honorable member propose to deal with this case? How does he relieve us from this difficulty, upon any principle of his? His construction gets us into it; how does he propose to get us out?

In Carolina, the tariff is a palpable, deliberate usurpation; Carolina, therefore, may nullify it, and refuse to pay the duties. In Pennsylvania, it is both clearly constitutional and highly expedient; and there the duties are to be paid. And yet we live under a government of uniform laws, and under a Constitution too, which contains an express provision, as it happens, that all duties shall be equal in all the States. Does not this approach absurdity?

If there be no power to settle such questions, independent of either of the States, is not the whole Union a rope of sand? Are we not thrown back again, precisely, upon the old Confederation?

It is too plain to be argued. Four-and-twenty interpreters of constitutional law, each with a power to decide for itself, and none with authority to bind any body else, and this constitutional law the only bond of their union! What is such a state of things but a mere connection during pleasure, or, to use the phraseology of the times, *during feeling*? And that feeling, too, not the feeling of the people, who established the Constitution, but the feeling of the State governments.

In another of the South Carolina addresses, having premised that the crisis requires "all the concentrated energy of passion,"[15] an attitude of open resistance to the laws of the Union is advised. Open resistance to the laws, then, is the constitutional remedy, the conservative power of the State, which the South Carolina doctrines teach for the redress of political evils, real or imaginary. And its authors further say, that, appealing with confidence to the Constitution itself, to justify their opinions, they cannot consent to try their accuracy by the courts of justice. In one sense, indeed, Sir, this is assuming an attitude of open resistance in favor of liberty. But what sort of liberty? The liberty of establishing their own opinions, in defiance of the opinions of all others; the liberty of judging and of deciding exclusively themselves, in a matter in which others have as much right to judge and decide as they; the liberty of placing their own opinions above the judgment of all others, above the

15. Robert Barnwell Rhett (1800–1876), addressing a public meeting at Walterborough, S.C., June 12, 1828. *Niles' Register*, 34 (June 28, 1828): 288.

laws, and above the Constitution. This is their liberty, and this is the fair result of the proposition contended for by the honorable gentleman. Or, it may be more properly said, it is identical with it rather than a result from it.

In the same publication we find the following: —"Previously to our Revolution, when the arm of oppression was stretched over New England, where did our Northern brethren meet with a braver sympathy than that which sprung from the bosoms of Carolinians? We had no extortion, no oppression, no collision with the king's ministers, no navigation interests springing up, in envious rivalry of England."[16]

This seems extraordinary language. South Carolina no collision with the king's ministers in 1775! No extortion! No oppression! But, Sir, it is also most significant language. Does any man doubt the purpose for which it was penned? Can any one fail to see that it was designed to raise in the reader's mind the question, whether, *at this time,*—that is to say, in 1828,—South Carolina has any collision with the king's ministers, any oppression, or extortion, to fear from England? whether, in short, England is not as naturally the friend of South Carolina as New England, with her navigation interests springing up in envious rivalry of England?

Is it not strange, Sir, that an intelligent man in South Carolina, in 1828, should thus labor to prove that, in 1775, there was no hostility, no cause of war, between South Carolina and England? That she had no occasion, in reference to her own interest, or from a regard to her own welfare, to take up arms in the Revolutionary contest? Can any one account for the expression of such strange sentiments, and their circulation through the State, otherwise than by supposing the object to be what I have already intimated, to raise the question, if they had no *"collision"* (mark the expression) with the ministers of King George the Third, in 1775, what *collision* have they, in 1828, with the ministers of King George the Fourth? What is there now in the existing state of things, to separate Carolina from *Old,* more, or rather, than from *New England?*

Resolutions, Sir, have been recently passed by the legislature of South Carolina.[17] I need not refer to them; they go no farther than the honorable gentleman himself has gone, and I hope not so far. I content myself, therefore, with debating the matter with him.

And now, Sir, what I have first to say on this subject is, that at no time, and under no circumstances, has New England, or any State in

16. Ibid., p. 289.

17. According to *Niles' Register,* 37 (Jan. 2, 1830): 294, the South Carolina legislature adopted a report insisting upon the repeal of the tariff laws and the abandonment of their principle.

New England, or any respectable body of persons in New England, or any public man of standing in New England, put forth such a doctrine as this Carolina doctrine.

The gentleman has found no case, he can find none, to support his own opinions by New England authority. New England has studied the Constitution in other schools, and under other teachers. She looks upon it with other regards, and deems more highly and reverently both of its just authority and its utility and excellence. The history of her legislative proceedings may be traced. The ephemeral effusions of temporary bodies, called together by the excitement of the occasion, may be hunted up; they have been hunted up. The opinions and votes of her public men, in and out of Congress, may be explored. It will all be in vain. The Carolina doctrine can derive from her neither countenance nor support. She rejects it now; she always did reject it; and till she loses her senses, she always will reject it. The honorable member has referred to expressions on the subject of the embargo law, made in this place, by an honorable and venerable gentleman,[18] now favoring us with his presence. He quotes that distinguished Senator as saying, that, in his judgment, the embargo law was unconstitutional, and that therefore, in his opinion, the people were not bound to obey it. That, Sir, is perfectly constitutional language. An unconstitutional law is not binding; *but then it does not rest with a resolution or a law of a State legislature to decide whether an act of Congress be or be not constitutional.* An unconstitutional act of Congress would not bind the people of this District, although they have no legislature to interfere in their behalf; and, on the other hand, a constitutional law of Congress does bind the citizens of every State, although all their legislatures should undertake to annul it by act or resolution. The venerable Connecticut Senator is a constitutional lawyer, of sound principles and enlarged knowledge; a statesman practised and experienced, bred in the company of Washington, and holding just views upon the nature of our governments. He believed the embargo unconstitutional, and so did others; but what then? Who did he suppose was to decide that question? The State legislatures? Certainly not. No such sentiment ever escaped his lips.

Let us follow up, Sir, this New England opposition to the embargo laws; let us trace it, till we discern the principle which controlled and governed New England throughout the whole course of that opposition. We shall then see what similarity there is between the New England school of constitutional opinions, and this modern Carolina school. The gentleman, I think, read a petition from some single individual addressed to the legislature of Massachusetts, asserting the Carolina doc-

18. James Hillhouse (1754–1832), former representative and senator from Connecticut, was in the Senate gallery.

trine; that is, the right of State interference to arrest the laws of the Union. The fate of that petition shows the sentiment of the legislature. It met no favor. The opinions of Massachusetts were very different. They had been expressed in 1798, in answer to the resolutions of Virginia, and she did not depart from them, nor bend them to the times. Misgoverned, wronged, oppressed, as she felt herself to be, she still held fast her integrity to the Union. The gentleman may find in her proceedings much evidence of dissatisfaction with the measures of government, and great and deep dislike to the embargo; all this makes the case so much the stronger for her; for, notwithstanding all this dissatisfaction and dislike, she still claimed no right to sever the bonds of the Union. There was heat, and there was anger in her political feeling. Be it so; but neither her heat nor her anger betrayed her into infidelity to the government. The gentleman labors to prove that she disliked the embargo as much as South Carolina dislikes the tariff, and expressed her dislike as strongly. Be it so; but did she propose the Carolina remedy? did she threaten to interfere, by State authority, to annul the laws of the Union? That is the question for the gentleman's consideration.

No doubt, Sir, a great majority of the people of New England conscientiously believed the embargo law of 1807 unconstitutional; as conscientiously, certainly, as the people of South Carolina hold that opinion of the tariff. They reasoned thus: Congress has power to regulate commerce; but here is a law, they said, stopping all commerce, and stopping it indefinitely. The law is perpetual; that is, it is not limited in point of time, and must of course continue until it shall be repealed by some other law. It is as perpetual, therefore, as the law against treason or murder. Now, is this regulating commerce, or destroying it? Is it guiding, controlling, giving the rule to commerce, as a subsisting thing, or is it putting an end to it altogether? Nothing is more certain, than that a majority in New England deemed this law a violation of the Constitution. The very case required by the gentleman to justify State interference had then arisen. Massachusetts believed this law to be "a deliberate, palpable, and dangerous exercise of a power not granted by the Constitution." Deliberate it was, for it was long continued; palpable she thought it, as no words in the Constitution gave the power, and only a construction, in her opinion most violent, raised it; dangerous it was, since it threatened utter ruin to her most important interests. Here, then, was a Carolina case. How did Massachusetts deal with it? It was, as she thought, a plain, manifest, palpable violation of the Constitution, and it brought ruin to her doors. Thousands of families, and hundreds of thousands of individuals, were beggared by it. While she saw and felt all this, she saw and felt also, that, as a measure of national policy, it was perfectly futile; that the country was no way benefited by that

which caused so much individual distress; that it was efficient only for the production of evil, and all that evil inflicted on ourselves. In such a case, under such circumstances, how did Massachusetts demean herself? Sir, she remonstrated, she memorialized, she addressed herself to the general government, not exactly "with the concentrated energy of passion," but with her own strong sense, and the energy of sober conviction. But she did not interpose the arm of her own power to arrest the law, and break the embargo. Far from it. Her principles bound her to two things; and she followed her principles, lead where they might. First, to submit to every constitutional law of Congress, and secondly, if the constitutional validity of the law be doubted, to refer that question to the decision of the proper tribunals. The first principle is vain and ineffectual without the second. A majority of us in New England believed the embargo law unconstitutional; but the great question was, and always will be in such cases, Who is to decide this? Who is to judge between the people and the government? And, Sir, it is quite plain, that the Constitution of the United States confers on the government itself, to be exercised by its appropriate department, and under its own responsibility to the people, this power of deciding ultimately and conclusively upon the just extent of its own authority. If this had not been done, we should not have advanced a single step beyond the old Confederation.

Being fully of opinion that the embargo law was unconstitutional, the people of New England were yet equally clear in the opinion, (it was a matter they did doubt upon,) that the question, after all, must be decided by the judicial tribunals of the United States. Before those tribunals, therefore, they brought the question.[19] Under the provisions of the law, they had given bonds to millions in amount, and which were alleged to be forfeited. They suffered the bonds to be sued, and thus raised the question. In the old-fashioned way of settling disputes, they went to law. The case came to hearing, and solemn argument; and he who espoused their cause, and stood up for them against the validity of the embargo act, was none other than that great man, of whom the gentleman has made honorable mention, Samuel Dexter. He was then, Sir, in the fulness of his knowledge, and the maturity of his strength. He had retired from long and distinguished public service here, to the renewed pursuit of professional duties, carrying with him all that enlargement and expansion, all the new strength and force, which an acquaintance with the more general subjects discussed in the national councils is capable of adding to professional attainment, in a mind of true greatness and compre-

19. *United States* v. *Brigantine William* was argued before the U.S. District Court for the District of Massachusetts in September 1808. 28 *Federal Cases* 614 (1808).

hension. He was a lawyer, and he was also a statesman. He had studied the Constitution, when he filled public station, that he might defend it; he had examined its principles that he might maintain them. More than all men, or at least as much as any man, he was attached to the general government and to the union of the States. His feelings and opinions all ran in that direction. A question of constitutional law, too, was, of all subjects, that one which was best suited to his talents and learning. Aloof from technicality, and unfettered by artificial rule, such a question gave opportunity for that deep and clear analysis, that mighty grasp of principle, which so much distinguished his higher efforts. His very statement was argument; his inference seemed demonstration. The earnestness of his own conviction wrought conviction in others. One was convinced, and believed, and assented, because it was gratifying, delightful, to think, and feel, and believe, in unison with an intellect of such evident superiority.

Mr. Dexter, Sir, such as I have described him, argued the New England cause. He put into his effort his whole heart, as well as all the powers of his understanding; for he had avowed, in the most public manner, his entire concurrence with his neighbors on the point in dispute. He argued the cause; it was lost, and New England submitted. The established tribunals pronounced the law constitutional, and New England acquiesced. Now, Sir, is not this the exact opposite of the doctrine of the gentleman from South Carolina? According to him, instead of referring to the judicial tribunals, we should have broken up the embargo by laws of our own; we should have repealed it, *quoad* New England; for we had a strong, palpable, and oppressive case. Sir, we believed the embargo unconstitutional; but still that was matter of opinion, and who was to decide it? We thought it a clear case; but, nevertheless, we did not take the law into our own hands, because we did not wish to bring about a revolution, nor to break up the Union; for I maintain, that between submission to the decision of the constituted tribunals, and revolution, or disunion, there is no middle ground; there is no ambiguous condition, half allegiance and half rebellion. And, Sir, how futile, how very futile it is, to admit the right of State interference, and then attempt to save it from the character of unlawful resistance, by adding terms of qualification to the causes and occasions, leaving all these qualifications, like the case itself, in the discretion of the State governments. It must be a clear case, it is said, a deliberate case, a palpable case, a dangerous case. But then the State is still left at liberty to decide for herself what is clear, what is deliberate, what is palpable, what is dangerous. Do adjectives and epithets avail any thing?

Sir, the human mind is so constituted, that the merits of both sides of a controversy appear very clear, and very palpable, to those who re-

spectively espouse them; and both sides usually grow clearer as the controversy advances. South Carolina sees unconstitutionality in the tariff; she sees oppression there also, and she sees danger. Pennsylvania, with a vision not less sharp, looks at the same tariff, and sees no such thing in it; she sees it all constitutional, all useful, all safe. The faith of South Carolina is strengthened by opposition, and she now not only sees, but *resolves*, that the tariff is palpably unconstitutional, oppressive, and dangerous; but Pennsylvania, not to be behind her neighbors, and equally willing to strengthen her own faith by a confident asseveration, *resolves*, also, and gives to every warm affirmative of South Carolina, a plain, downright, Pennsylvania negative. South Carolina, to show the strength and unity of her opinion, brings her assembly to a unanimity, within seven voices; Pennsylvania, not to be outdone in this respect any more than in others, reduces her dissentient fraction to a single vote. Now, Sir, again, I ask the gentleman, What is to be done? Are these States both right? Is he bound to consider them both right? If not, which is in the wrong? or rather, which has the best right to decide? And if he, and if I, are not to know what the Constitution means, and what it is, till those two State legislatures, and the twenty-two others, shall agree in its construction, what have we sworn to, when we have sworn to maintain it? I was forcibly struck, Sir, with one reflection, as the gentleman went on in his speech. He quoted Mr. Madison's resolutions, to prove that a State may interfere, in a case of deliberate, palpable, and dangerous exercise of a power not granted. The honorable member supposes the tariff law to be such an exercise of power; and that consequently a case has arisen in which the State may, if it see fit, interfere by its own law. Now it so happens, nevertheless, that Mr. Madison deems this same tariff law quite constitutional. Instead of a clear and palpable violation, it is, in his judgment, no violation at all. So that, while they use his authority for a hypothetical case, they reject it in the very case before them. All this, Sir, shows the inherent futility, I had almost used a stronger word, of conceding this power of interference to the State, and then attempting to secure it from abuse by imposing qualifications of which the States themselves are to judge. One of two things is true; either the laws of the Union are beyond the discretion and beyond the control of the States; or else we have no constitution of general government, and are thrust back again to the days of the Confederation.

Let me here say, Sir, that if the gentleman's doctrine had been received and acted upon in New England, in the times of the embargo and nonintercourse, we should probably not now have been here. The government would very likely have gone to pieces, and crumbled into dust. No stronger case can ever arise than existed under those laws; no States can ever entertain a clearer conviction than the New England States then

entertained; and if they had been under the influence of that heresy of opinion, as I must call it, which the honorable member espouses, this Union would, in all probability, have been scattered to the four winds. I ask the gentleman, therefore, to apply his principles to that case; I ask him to come forth and declare, whether, in his opinion, the New England States would have been justified in interfering to break up the embargo system under the conscientious opinions which they held upon it? Had they a right to annul that law? Does he admit or deny? If what is thought palpably unconstitutional in South Carolina justifies that State in arresting the progress of the law, tell me whether that which was thought palpably unconstitutional also in Massachusetts would have justified her in doing the same thing. Sir, I deny the whole doctrine. It has not a foot of ground in the Constitution to stand on. No public man of reputation ever advanced it in Massachusetts in the warmest times, or could maintain himself upon it there at any time.

I wish now, Sir, to make a remark upon the Virginia resolutions of 1798. I cannot undertake to say how these resolutions were understood by those who passed them. Their language is not a little indefinite. In the case of the exercise by Congress of a dangerous power not granted to them, the resolutions assert the right, on the part of the State, to interfere and arrest the progress of the evil. This is susceptible of more than one interpretation. It may mean no more than that the States may interfere by complaint and remonstrance, or by proposing to the people an alteration of the Federal Constitution. This would all be quite unobjectionable. Or it may be that no more is meant than to assert the general right of revolution, as against all governments, in cases of intolerable oppression. This no one doubts, and this, in my opinion, is all that he who framed the resolutions could have meant by it; for I shall not readily believe that he was ever of opinion that a State, under the Constitution and in conformity with it, could, upon the ground of her own opinion of its unconstitutionality, however clear and palpable she might think the case, annul a law of Congress, so far as it should operate on herself, by her own legislative power.

I must now beg to ask, Sir, Whence is this supposed right of the States derived? Where do they find the power to interfere with the laws of the Union? Sir, the opinion which the honorable gentleman maintains is a notion founded in a total misapprehension, in my judgment, of the origin of this government, and of the foundation on which it stands. I hold it to be a popular government, erected by the people; those who administer it, responsible to the people; and itself capable of being amended and modified, just as the people may choose it should be. It is as popular, just as truly emanating from the people, as the State governments. It is created for one purpose; the State governments for an-

other. It has its own powers; they have theirs. There is no more authority with them to arrest the operation of a law of Congress, than with
Congress to arrest the operation of their laws. We are here to administer a Constitution emanating immediately from the people, and trusted
by them to our administration. It is not the creature of the State governments. It is of no moment to the argument, that certain acts of the State
legislatures are necessary to fill our seats in this body. That is not one of
their original State powers, a part of the sovereignty of the State. It is a
duty which the people, by the Constitution itself, have imposed on the
State legislatures; and which they might have left to be performed elsewhere, if they had seen fit. So they have left the choice of President
with electors; but all this does not affect the proposition that this whole
government, President, Senate, and House of Representatives, is a popular government. It leaves it still all its popular character. The governor
of a State (in some of the States) is chosen, not directly by the people,
but by those who are chosen by the people, for the purpose of performing, among other duties, that of electing a governor. Is the government
of the State, on that account, not a popular government? This government, Sir, is the independent offspring of the popular will. It is not the
creature of State legislatures; nay, more, if the whole truth must be
told, the people brought it into existence, established it, and have hitherto supported it, for the very purpose, amongst others, of imposing certain salutary restraints on State sovereignties. The States cannot now
make war; they cannot contract alliances; they cannot make, each for
itself, separate regulations of commerce; they cannot lay imposts; they
cannot coin money. If this Constitution, Sir, be the creature of State
legislatures, it must be admitted that it has obtained a strange control
over the volitions of its creators.

The people, then, Sir, erected this government. They gave it a Constitution, and in that Constitution they have enumerated the powers which
they bestow on it. They have made it a limited government. They have
defined its authority. They have restrained it to the exercise of such
powers as are granted; and all others, they declare, are reserved to the
States or the people. But, Sir, they have not stopped here. If they had,
they would have accomplished but half their work. No definition can be
so clear, as to avoid possibility of doubt; no limitation so precise, as to
exclude all uncertainty. Who, then, shall construe this grant of the
people? Who shall interpret their will, where it may be supposed they
have left it doubtful? With whom do they repose this ultimate right of
deciding on the powers of the government? Sir, they have settled all this
in the fullest manner. They have left it with the government itself, in
its appropriate branches. Sir, the very chief end, the main design, for
which the whole Constitution was framed and adopted, was to establish

a government that should not be obliged to act through State agency, or depend on State opinion and State discretion. The people had had quite enough of that kind of government under the Confederation. Under that system, the legal action, the application of law to individuals, belonged exclusively to the States. Congress could only recommend; their acts were not of binding force, till the States had adopted and sanctioned them. Are we in that condition still? Are we yet at the mercy of State discretion and State construction? Sir, if we are, then vain will be our attempt to maintain the Constitution under which we sit.

But, Sir, the people have wisely provided, in the Constitution itself, a proper, suitable mode and tribunal for settling questions of constitutional law. There are in the Constitution grants of powers to Congress, and restrictions on these powers. There are, also, prohibitions on the States. Some authority must, therefore, necessarily exist, having the ultimate jurisdiction to fix and ascertain the interpretation of these grants, restrictions, and prohibitions. The Constitution has itself pointed out, ordained, and established that authority. How has it accomplished this great and essential end? By declaring, Sir, that *"the Constitution, and the laws of the United States made in pursuance thereof, shall be the supreme law of the land, any thing in the constitution or laws of any State to the contrary notwithstanding."*

This, Sir, was the first great step. By this the supremacy of the Constitution and laws of the United States is declared. The people so will it. No State law is to be valid which comes in conflict with the Constitution, or any law of the United States passed in pursuance of it. But who shall decide this question of interference? To whom lies the last appeal? This, Sir, the Constitution itself decides also, by declaring, *"that the judicial power shall extend to all cases arising under the Constitution and laws of the United States."* These two provisions cover the whole ground. They are, in truth, the keystone of the arch! With these it is a government; without them it is a confederation. In pursuance of these clear and express provisions, Congress established, at its very first session, in the judicial act, a mode for carrying them into full effect, and for bringing all questions of constitutional power to the final decision of the Supreme Court. It then, Sir, became a government. It then had the means of self-protection; and but for this, it would, in all probability, have been now among things which are past. Having constituted the government, and declared its powers, the people have further said, that, since somebody must decide on the extent of these powers, the government shall itself decide; subject, always, like other popular governments, to its responsibility to the people. And now, Sir, I repeat, how is it that a State legislature acquires any power to interfere? Who, or what, gives them the right to say to the people, "We, who are your agents and servants for one

purpose, will undertake to decide, that your other agents and servants, appointed by you for another purpose, have transcended the authority you gave them!" The reply would be, I think, not impertinent,—"Who made you a judge over another's servants? To their own masters they stand or fall."

Sir, I deny this power of State legislatures altogether. It cannot stand the test of examination. Gentlemen may say, that, in an extreme case, a State government might protect the people from intolerable oppression. Sir, in such a case, the people might protect themselves, without the aid of the State governments. Such a case warrants revolution. It must make, when it comes, a law for itself. A nullifying act of a State legislature cannot alter the case, nor make resistance any more lawful. In maintaining these sentiments, Sir, I am but asserting the rights of the people. I state what they have declared, and insist on their right to declare it. They have chosen to repose this power in the general government, and I think it my duty to support it, like other constitutional powers.

For myself, Sir, I do not admit the competency of South Carolina, or any other State, to prescribe my constitutional duty; or to settle, between me and the people, the validity of laws of Congress, for which I have voted. I decline her umpirage. I have not sworn to support the Constitution according to her construction of its clauses. I have not stipulated, by my oath of office or otherwise, to come under any responsibility, except to the people, and those whom they have appointed to pass upon the question, whether laws, supported by my votes, conform to the Constitution of the country. And, Sir, if we look to the general nature of the case, could any thing have been more preposterous, than to make a government for the whole Union, and yet leave its powers subject, not to one interpretation, but to thirteen or twenty-four interpretations? Instead of one tribunal, established by all, responsible to all, with power to decide for all, shall constitutional questions be left to four-and-twenty popular bodies, each at liberty to decide for itself, and none bound to respect the decisions of others; and each at liberty, too, to give a new construction on every new election of its own members? Would any thing, with such a principle in it, or rather with such a destitution of all principle, be fit to be called a government? No, Sir. It should not be denominated a Constitution. It should be called, rather, a collection of topics for everlasting controversy; heads of debate for a disputatious people. It would not be a government. It would not be adequate to any practical good, or fit for any country to live under.

To avoid all possibility of being misunderstood, allow me to repeat again, in the fullest manner, that I claim no powers for the government by forced or unfair construction. I admit that it is a government of strictly limited powers; of enumerated, specified, and particularized

powers; and that whatsoever is not granted, is withheld. But notwithstanding all this, and however the grant of powers may be expressed, its limit and extent may yet, in some cases, admit of doubt; and the general government would be good for nothing, it would be incapable of long existing, if some mode had not been provided in which those doubts, as they should arise, might be peaceably, but authoritatively, solved.

And now, Mr. President, let me run the honorable gentleman's doctrine a little into its practical application. Let us look at his probable *modus operandi*. If a thing can be done, an ingenious man can tell *how* it is to be done, and I wish to be informed *how* this State interference is to be put in practice, without violence, bloodshed, and rebellion. We will take the existing case of the tariff law. South Carolina is said to have made up her opinion upon it. If we do not repeal it (as we probably shall not), she will then apply to the case the remedy of her doctrine. She will, we must suppose, pass a law of her legislature, declaring the several acts of Congress, usually called the tariff laws, null and void, so far as they respect South Carolina, or the citizens thereof. So far, all is a paper transaction, and easy enough. But the collector at Charleston is collecting the duties imposed by these tariff laws. He, therefore, must be stopped. The collector will seize the goods if the tariff duties are not paid. The State authorities will undertake their rescue, the marshal, with his posse, will come to the collector's aid, and here the contest begins. The militia of the State will be called out to sustain the nullifying act. They will march, Sir, under a very gallant leader; for I believe the honorable member himself commands the militia of that part of the State. He will raise the NULLIFYING ACT on his standard, and spread it out as his banner! It will have a preamble, setting forth, that the tariff laws are palpable, deliberate, and dangerous violations of the Constitution! He will proceed, with this banner flying, to the custom-house in Charleston,

"All the while,
Sonorous metal blowing martial sounds."[20]

Arrived at the custom-house, he will tell the collector that he must collect no more duties under any of the tariff laws. This he will be somewhat puzzled to say, by the way, with a grave countenance, considering what hand South Carolina herself had in that of 1816. But, Sir, the collector would not, probably, desist, at his bidding. He would show him the law of Congress, the treasury instruction, and his own oath of office. He would say, he should perform his duty, come what come might.

Here would ensue a pause; for they say that a certain stillness pre-

20. Milton, *Paradise Lost*, Book 1, lines 539–540.

cedes the tempest. The trumpeter would hold his breath awhile, and before all this military array should fall on the custom-house, collector, clerks, and all, it is very probable some of those composing it would request of their gallant commander-in-chief to be informed a little upon the point of law; for they have, doubtless, a just respect for his opinions as a lawyer, as well as for his bravery as a soldier. They know he has read Blackstone and the Constitution, as well as Turenne and Vauban. They would ask him, therefore, something concerning their rights in this matter. They would inquire, whether it was not somewhat danger-ous to resist a law of the United States. What would be the nature of their offence, they would wish to learn, if they, by military force and array, resisted the execution in Carolina of a law of the United States, and it should turn out, after all, that the law *was constitutional*? He would answer, of course, Treason. No lawyer could give any other an-swer. John Fries,[21] he would tell them, had learned that, some years ago. How, then, they would ask, do you propose to defend us? We are not afraid of bullets, but treason has a way of taking people off that we do not much relish. How do you propose to defend us? "Look at my floating banner," he would reply; "see there the *nullifying law!*" Is it your opinion, gallant commander, they would then say, that, if we should be indicted for treason, that same floating banner of yours would make a good plea in bar? "South Carolina is a sovereign State," he would reply. That is true; but would the judge admit our plea? "These tariff laws," he would repeat, "are unconstitutional, palpably, deliber-ately, dangerously." That may all be so; but if the tribunal should not happen to be of that opinion, shall we swing for it? We are ready to die for our country, but it is rather an awkward business, this dying with-out touching the ground! After all, that is a sort of hemp tax worse than any part of the tariff.

Mr. President, the honorable gentleman would be in a dilemma, like that of another great general. He would have a knot before him which he could not untie. He must cut it with his sword. He must say to his followers, "Defend yourselves with your bayonets"; and this is war,—civil war.

Direct collision, therefore, between force and force, is the unavoidable result of that remedy for the revision of unconstitutional laws which the gentleman contends for. It must happen in the very first case to which it is applied. Is not this the plain result? To resist by force the execution of a law, generally, is treason. Can the courts of the United States take notice of the indulgence of a State to commit treason? The

21. John Fries (c. 1750–1818) led a rebellion in early 1799 against the direct federal property tax enacted by Congress in 1798.

common saying, that a State cannot commit treason herself, is nothing to the purpose. Can she authorize others to do it? If John Fries had produced an act of Pennsylvania, annulling the law of Congress, would it have helped his case? Talk about it as we will, these doctrines go the length of revolution. They are incompatible with any peaceable administration of the government. They lead directly to disunion and civil commotion; and therefore it is, that at their commencement, when they are first found to be maintained by respectable men, and in a tangible form, I enter my public protest against them all.

The honorable gentleman argues, that if this government be the sole judge of the extent of its own powers, whether that right of judging be in Congress or the Supreme Court, it equally subverts State sovereignty. This the gentleman sees, or thinks he sees, although he cannot perceive how the right of judging, in this matter, if left to the exercise of State legislatures, has any tendency to subvert the government of the Union. The gentleman's opinion may be, that the right *ought not* to have been lodged with the general government; he may like better such a constitution as we should have under the right of State interference; but I ask him to meet me on the plain matter of fact. I ask him to meet me on the Constitution itself. I ask him if the power is not found there, clearly and visibly found there?[22]

But, Sir, what is this danger, and what are the grounds of it? Let it be remembered, that the Constitution of the United States is not unalterable. It is to continue in its present form no longer than the people who established it shall choose to continue it. If they shall become convinced that they have made an injudicious or inexpedient partition and distribution of power between the State governments and the general government, they can alter that distribution at will.

If any thing be found in the national Constitution, either by original provision or subsequent interpretation, which ought not to be in it, the people know how to get rid of it. If any construction, unacceptable to them, be established, so as to become practically a part of the Constitution, they will amend it, at their own sovereign pleasure. But while the people choose to maintain it as it is, while they are satisfied with it, and refuse to change it, who has given, or who can give, to the State legislatures a right to alter it, either by interference, construction, or otherwise? Gentlemen do not seem to recollect that the people have any power to do any thing for themselves. They imagine there is no safety for them, any longer than they are under the close guardianship of the State legis-

22. Webster's appendix Note C, to which he here refers, reproduces various resolutions of the Virginia legis- lature of 1809–1810. See *W & S*, 6: 85–88.

latures. Sir, the people have not trusted their safety, in regard to the general Constitution, to these hands. They have required other security, and taken other bonds. They have chosen to trust themselves, first, to the plain words of the instrument, and to such construction as the government themselves, in doubtful cases, should put on their own powers, under their oaths of office, and subject to their responsibility to them; just as the people of a State trust their own State governments with a similar power. Secondly, they have reposed their trust in the efficacy of frequent elections, and in their own power to remove their own servants and agents whenever they see cause. Thirdly, they have reposed trust in the judicial power, which, in order that it might be trustworthy, they have made as respectable, as disinterested, and as independent as was practicable. Fourthly, they have seen fit to rely, in case of necessity, or high expediency, on their known and admitted power to alter or amend the Constitution, peaceably and quietly, whenever experience shall point out defects or imperfections. And, finally, the people of the United States have at no time, in no way, directly or indirectly, authorized any State legislature to construe or interpret *their* high instrument of government; much less, to interfere, by their own power, to arrest its course and operation.

If, Sir, the people in these respects had done otherwise than they have done, their constitution could neither have been preserved, nor would it have been worth preserving. And if its plain provisions shall now be disregarded, and these new doctrines interpolated in it, it will become as feeble and helpless a being as its enemies, whether early or more recent, could possibly desire. It will exist in every State but as a poor dependent on State permission. It must borrow leave to be; and will be, no longer than State pleasure, or State discretion, sees fit to grant the indulgence, and to prolong its poor existence.

But, Sir, although there are fears, there are hopes also. The people have preserved this, their own chosen Constitution, for forty years, and have seen their happiness, prosperity, and renown grow with its growth, and strengthen with its strength. They are now, generally strongly attached to it. Overthrown by direct assault, it cannot be; evaded, undermined, NULLIFIED, it will not be, if we, and those who shall succeed us here, as agents and representatives of the people, shall conscientiously and vigilantly discharge the two great branches of our public trust, faithfully to preserve, and wisely to administer it.

Mr. President, I have thus stated the reasons of my dissent to the doctrines which have been advanced and maintained. I am conscious of having detained you and the Senate much too long. I was drawn into the debate with no previous deliberation, such as is suited to the discussion

of so grave and important a subject. But it is a subject of which my heart is full, and I have not been willing to suppress the utterance of its spontaneous sentiments. I cannot, even now, persuade myself to relinquish it, without expressing once more my deep conviction, that since it respects nothing less than the Union of the States, it is of most vital and essential importance to the public happiness. I profess, Sir, in my career hitherto, to have kept steadily in view the prosperity and honor of the whole country, and the preservation of our Federal Union. It is to that Union we owe our safety at home, and our consideration and dignity abroad. It is to that Union that we are chiefly indebted for whatever makes us most proud of our country. That Union we reached only by the discipline of our virtues in the severe school of adversity. It had its origin in the necessities of disordered finance, prostrate commerce, and ruined credit. Under its benign influences, these great interests immediately awoke, as from the dead, and sprang forth with newness of life. Every year of its duration has teemed with fresh proofs of its utility and its blessings; and although our territory has stretched out wider and wider, and our population spread farther and farther, they have not outrun its protection or its benefits. It has been to us all a copious fountain of national, social, and personal happiness.

I have not allowed myself, Sir, to look beyond the Union, to see what might lie hidden in the dark recess behind. I have not coolly weighed the chances of preserving liberty when the bonds that unite us together shall be broken asunder. I have not accustomed myself to hang over the precipice of disunion, to see whether, with my short sight, I can fathom the depth of the abyss below; nor could I regard him as a safe counsellor in the affairs of this government, whose thoughts should be mainly bent on considering, not how the Union may be best preserved, but how tolerable might be the condition of the people when it should be broken up and destroyed. While the Union lasts, we have high, exciting, gratifying prospects spread out before us, for us and our children. Beyond that I seek not to penetrate the veil. God grant that in my day, at least, that curtain may not rise! God grant that on my vision never may be opened what lies behind! When my eyes shall be turned to behold for the last time the sun in heaven, may I not see him shining on the broken and dishonored fragments of a once glorious Union; on States dissevered, discordant, belligerent; on a land rent with civil feuds, or drenched, it may be, in fraternal blood! Let their last feeble and lingering glance rather behold the gorgeous ensign of the republic, now known and honored throughout the earth, still full high advanced, its arms and trophies streaming in their original lustre, not a stripe erased or polluted, nor a single star obscured, bearing for its motto, no such miserable interrog-

atory as "What is all this worth?" nor those other words of delusion and folly, "Liberty first and Union afterwards"; but everywhere, spread all over in characters of living light, blazing on all its ample folds, as they float over the sea and over the land, and in every wind under the whole heavens, that other sentiment, dear to every true American heart,—Liberty *and* Union, now and for ever, one and inseparable!

Reported Version

Mr. Webster, when our Reporter entered the room, was speaking of the circumstances of the debate which preceded Mr. Haynes last speech, disclaiming any intention to have roused that gentleman's ire, or having the least unkind feeling towards him, &c. This debate was not sought by him, and he had been called to the floor only by the speech of the gentleman from South Carolina. In reply to the complaint of Mr. Hayne, that, before replying to his first speech, he had "slept upon it," Mr. W. said he must have done so, or he should not have slept at all; for the House had adjourned upon Mr. Hayne's Speech upon the motion of the gentleman from Missouri [Thomas Hart Benton], who intimated that the sensations which it had produced were too delightful to be disturbed that day by any votes discordant to it. And as to his reply being "studied," Mr. W. said, he had, from the pressure of circumstances had no time to study it; fifteen or twenty minutes examination of documents being all that he had bestowed upon it. 'Twas true, he had slept upon it. He had done the same last night: and if the gentleman's speech had not produced so vivid an impression on his mind as to disturb his repose, Mr. W. said it was probably owing to something more of phlegm in his constitution. But the gentleman from SoCa. [South Carolina] why was his Speech directed at him? He had not commenced the war—he had not *invited* the discussion. Mr. W. said he had answered the gentleman's Speech because he heard it, and because he chose to answer that Speech which, if unanswered, was likely to be most injurious in its effects. I did not stop to inquire (said Mr. W.) who drew the bill which I found before me: I saw that it had a responsible endorser, and I took it on his responsibility.

The gentleman from SoCa further asked me (said Mr. W.) whether I had turned upon him in this debate because experience had taught me that I had an overmatch in the gentleman from Missouri. When the gentleman chuses *en gratia* to compliment his friend from Missouri upon his superior ability, the courtesies of the place where we stand would reprehend a contradiction of him. But there was something in the tone & manner in which he alluded to me which I confess I was not prepared to expect from him. He put it as a serious taunt to me, whether upon the whole I did not feel that I was overmatched. If the

gentleman thought by this to move my pride of character, I will admit, as a point of complaisance, that I am not superior to the member from Missouri, or to the humblest member on this floor. But put it as a matter of taunt, and I tell the gentleman from South Carolina that I know nothing of the strength of the gentleman from Missouri, which with the aid of the Member from South Carolina, could deter me from the expression of my opinions here. These expressions "match" and "over-match" rather belong to another arena than to this. On the floor of this Senate, we are all equal: men of honor, character, & independence, we are all equal. We know no inferiors—we acknowledge no superior—we witness the exhibition of no championship. Is it supposed that by this parade of strength—by this sort of challenge to the attack—by the empty vaunt of anticipated victory, that any thing is to be accomplished? Sir, if it be supposed by the gentleman from South Carolina that any one or all of these things can have any effect on me, he has a person to deal with, of whose temper & character he has much to learn. Disclaiming any anger on this occasion, Mr. W. said he could not [but?] be conscious of some feeling. He would say to the gentleman from South Carolina that this was a conflict in which blows were to be taken as well as to be given, and in which other honorable gentlemen besides himself would make comparisons. For I myself (said Mr. W.) it becomes me to say, once for all, these things move me not.

The honorable member in the next place undertook to find out what motive it was that induced me to engage in this debate, and said, with great emphasis, that I saw "the ghost of the murdered Coalition," like Banquo's ghost, &c. Yes, sir, the Coalition! The murdered Coalition! This charge of a "coalition," Sir, was not originally made in the Senate: it was one of those thousand false and slanderous calumnies with which the press teems in every warm political canvass. It was a thing in itself wholly impossible, and which no man of common intelligence believed in: and yet it was one of those falsehoods which, by continual repetition by the hired organs of detraction, served the purpose of the occasion. As it has become useless, it is cast off by its original owners —a mere slough not worth raking from the kennel. Nor can the gentleman from South Carolina give it either respect or dignity by bringing it into the Senate. He is in much more danger of being drawn down by it—down, down, down, to the depth where it lies rotting.

It appeared also to Mr. W. that the honorable member from South Carolina was not as felicitous as usual in his reference to Banquo's ghost. To the best of my poor recollection (said Mr. W.) it was none other than the murderer whose senses were appalled by Banquo's ghost —one, who having cherished him as a friend, had betrayed him & robbed him of his life—foresaw the future destiny of his race, &c. And

if the measures of the late Administration are to be considered its progeny & issue (said Mr. W.) I am not one of those to whom the future prospect, in reference to them, gives any distress at all.

There is another circumstance in which, too, I think the gentleman was rather unhappy in his allusion. Does it not occur to him, in regard to those whose ambition led them thus to betray & murder Banquo, that they rather missed their golden road? That they derived, from their success, no gratification, but bitter dust & ashes? Does it not occur to them, that, after being [lured?] by the weird sisters (their own bad passions) to the commission of crime in the pursuit of power, they found, when it was achieved, a barren sceptre in their grasp, next to be wielded by an unlineal hand, no son of theirs succeeding to the throne?

So much for Banquo's ghost, Sir, and if the gentleman from South Carolina is satisfied with the association [of] ideas it suggests, so am I —I was going to say, but I will not. That is a matter for the gentleman himself to adjust with his own consciousness [conscience].

For the sake of perspicuity, Mr. W. then proceeded to re-state a little of the debate of Thursday.

In the course of my remarks on that day I took occasion to compliment Mr. Dane, of Massachusetts, for the agency which I supposed him to have had in the establishment of the ordinance of 1787 for the govt. of the North Western territory. He was a man of so much ability & so little pretense—so much capacity to do good, and so much disposition to do good for the sake of it, that the tribute was due to him from me. But the gentleman had never heard of him before! He spoke of him as *one of the name of Dane,* whom he had never heard of before. I am sorry for it, Sir. I am sorry that his knowledge of our public men is not more extensive. I went on to say, then, that I knew of no measure which was impressed with stronger marks of wisdom than that section of the ordinance of 1787 which prohibited involuntary servitude in the territory North West of the Ohio. I certainly did not imagine that any one could infer from this remark that I meant any reflection upon the South. Yet that single remark, and one other equally unexceptionable the gent[lema]n took occasion, in a discourse of two hours, to represent as having been made in the spirit of the Missouri question, &c. The Senate will bear me out, said Mr. W. in saying that there was not the least reason for this construction put upon my language. I expressed it as matter of opinion, that it was the good fortune of the territory North-West of the Ohio, that slavery was prohibited there. Does the gentleman think differently? If so, that is a matter of opinion, between us, which has nothing to do with the question with Slavery where it now exists. With *that* matter I am as far as any one

from meddling. God knows I am. Whether it be the *vulnus immedi-cabile* or not, I am not the person to disturb it. But, Sir, why should I be reproached for having expressed, as a general impression, that it is not desirable that Slavery should exist in the Territory North West of the Ohio? Does the gentleman think it is? How does he thence infer that I mean to reflect on the weakness of the South? If the gentleman chuses to defend Slavery as being a good in the abstract, I have no objection. But let him not impute to me motives which are not in my breast. I say that, when up before on this subject, I made no reflection upon the South, in reference to this matter. I made not the slightest allusion to it. Not a word escaped my lips which had any bearing upon the subject whatever.

I will now refer to a document of some importance to show that other persons South as well as North of Mason & Dixon's line, enter-tained the same opinion as I have expressed of this feature in the ordi-nance of 1787. It would be recollected by many gentlemen, that about the year 1803, Indiana preferred her petition to Congress to release her from the operation of the ordinance, so far as to allow for a limited time the admission of Slaves into that Territory. That petition was referred to a com[mitt]ee of the House of Reps, of which Mr. Randolph was the Chairman, & that com[mitt]ee made a report, in which it is stated, in substance, that Indiana will have to wait but a little time before she will be herself convinced that, in this interdiction of slavery, she will have been relieved from great affliction. If that could be said, without offence, in 1803, by the gentleman who is at the head of that committee, it may be said by me now without subjecting me to the imputation of being a heretic. On this subject of slavery, Sir, allow me to say, in reference to a partial effort that has been made to induce the South to believe in the disposition of the people of the North to inter-fere with their domestic relations, that I know of no such intention, or wish. I know of no Northern man in public life that has ever pro-posed such a thing, or hinted at, or meditated such a purpose.

Look back to history, in reference to this topic. When the constitution of the United States was adopted, gentlemen in the public councils were not as sensitive on the subject of slavery, and on every proposition to relieve its evils, as they now are. It was a question, in the Convention which framed the Constitution whether it did become proper for Congress to interfere with the relation of Slavery. There were some persons who thought that it did. It will be found in the Speech of Governor Randolph.

He said, we ought not to like it less, because, by the agency of the General govt, we should get rid of a great & terrible calamity. The Con-stitution having gone into operation, many people supposed that, some way or other (though they could not very well see how) Congress had

power on this subject, & Congress was immediately petitioned to abolish Slavery. At first & second Sessions of the First Congress, they were petitioned, from various parts of the country, to take the subject of Slavery into consideration, and provide a remedy for it, Pennsylvania taking the lead in the whole of it. Congress took up the matter. A committee, consisting principally of New-England men, was appointed. The committee was instructed to inquire & report on the subject of the power of Congress in regard to this matter of Domestic Slavery. It is well known that committee made a report, which was referred to a committee of the whole house, debated, amended, & adopted as amended. And that report contains three distinct resolutions, which I well remember, though it is now some years since I have seen it. The first of these resolutions was, that Congress had no power to prevent the importation of Slavery into the United States earlier than the year 1808. The third was, that Congress had power before 1808 to restrain the Slave Trade from abroad. The second was, that Congress possessed no power under the Constitution of the U[nited] States to interfere with emancipation or treatment of Slaves in the several States, but that it was reserved to the States themselves, &c. Since the year 1790, no man has doubted that is the true construction of the Constitution. No man has disturbed, or attempted to disturb, it from that day to this. That, Sir, is my doctrine on the subject, and it is the doctrine of the New England States. Gentlemen will not find, if they think proper to examine, that, on the whole course of my life, I ever reproached the Southern States on this subject, or ever complained of the power through this means, acquired & retained by the South. We have seen, in the operation of the Constitution, how far one side of the bargain has been wholly useless; but we do not complain of that. For the foundation of the bargain was the principle of direct Taxation, which, it was then supposed, would be the main source of revenue to the country. But, whilst in the forty years practice of the govt. we have had but three or four years of direct tax, the other influence has been in full operation the whole time. Do we complain of it? Not at all: it was a fair arrangement, to obtain a constitution. To attain that object I would, as at present impressed, had I been a Member of the Convention, have made almost any sacrifice. I must therefore say, Sir, that any thing which imputes to me any unkindness towards the South, or any disposition to interfere with their treatment of their own Concerns, is wholly unfounded.

A passing remark, Mr. W. said he would further make in regard to the ordinance already referred to, as being the fruit of the wisdom of Mr. Dane. The best principles, civil & religious, said Mr. W. are to be found in this Ordinance. One of these principles was theretofore new in this govt, and new in the world. It is a principle now running through our whole of law. That great & invaluable principle, that the Legislative

power cannot interfere to impair the obligation of contracts, is first on earth to be found in that Ordinance, and from that Ordinance was transferred into the Constitution of the U[nited] States. Again, said, Mr. W. this same Mr. Dane—this "one Nathan Dane" according to the gentleman from South Carolina, was Chairman of the first committee in Congress, when sitting at Annapolis, that reported in favor of a Convention for framing this Constitution.

But the honorable Member from South Carolina, who either knows very much about our local politics & electioneering squabbles in New-England, or is very easily taught all about them, has found out that Mr. Dane was a Member of the Hartford Convention: and the gentleman told us much about the proceedings of that Convention. I incline to think, Sir, that the Proceedings of that Convention have been more studied else where than in the East: they seemed to be wanted as what we at the bar call a precedent. But other Conventions, since held, have thrown the Hartford Convention quite into the shade. The text of that Convention has been carried so much farther by the proceedings at Colleton & Edgefield, that no one now looks to the original, but to the copy. As to the Hartford Convention really, Sir, until I heard it on this floor, I have not heard its name for months; though I have heard something about *other* Conventions, of which I shall have occasion to say something more before I conclude. I was not sent here, Sir, to defend the Hartford Convention. To the best of my recollection I have never read either its proceeding or its journal. I mean to keep myself clear from all necessity of defending it. All the responsibility, &c. (Here the Latin quotation which the Reporter lost.)

But the gentleman, referring to a former Speech of mine (said Mr. W.) the gentleman has made quotations from it with all the air of triumphant refutation of what I said the other day, as if there was something in that Speech so contradictory of what I have now said, that I should not be able, after hearing it to hold my head: and I dare say that any gentleman who heard him, and did not hear what I said before, taking all from the gentleman's manner, would suppose that he had convicted me of the most palpable contradiction. Sir, fairly compared there is not a hair's breadth difference between the sentiments of the two Speeches. A man, who like the hero of Hudibras could split a hair between the North & the South side of it, could not find a place for his scissors between the true version of what I said on the floor of the other House in 1825, and what I said here last week. Recurring to the content, it will be seen that there is not only no difference between them—not only no contradiction, but an extraordinary similarity of language. And this, Sir, seems as proper a time as any to recur to the origin of this discussion.

Well, then: the Member from Conn[ecticu]t (Mr. Foot) moved a resolution which comprizes the first branch of the proposition before the
Senate. Some debate took place upon it. In the progress of that debate,
an honorable Member from Tennessee[1] moved to amend the resolution
so as to reverse its object. A gentleman from Maine [Peleg Sprague] suggested that both propositions should be referred to a committee. In this
state of the question, the honorable member from South Carolina rose
to give us his own free thoughts on the subject of the Public Lands. I saw
him rise as I always do, with pleasure; though I was never in my life more
surprised than at the sentiments which he advanced, though I knew
they were sentiments which the gentleman from Missouri had expressed
before him. The gentleman began by saying that he might vote for or
against the proposition before the Senate. He went on, however, to say,
that there were two different opinions as to the manner in which the
Atlantic States had treated the Western States: that one set of opinion
was, that the Western States had been treated as spoiled children. He
then went on to speak of what he often calls the accursed policy of the
Tariff—and when the gentleman said, yesterday, that he did not in this
allude to the Eastern States, he must have forgotten what he did say,
viz: that the Manufacturing States were disposed to keep their population at home that they might surround themselves with paupers to carry
their manufactures on. The gentleman went on to say what *his* opinions
were as to the general course of the govt. as to the Western States: that
from the beginning it had been too severe, exacting payment for the
public lands, whereas the govt. should have referred to the policy of other
States: that he never asked to see the govt. possess one shilling of the
proceeds of these sales of the public lands: that if it was possible to turn
this capital of land into gold he would not do it: that such an administration of the revenue had only the two-fold effect of consolidating the
govt. and corrupting the people: and the gentleman then stated what his
views were for the future. I agree (said Mr. W.) that the gentleman's
views were not digested—were not reduced to definite form & shape;
but they were in substance what I have stated. I undertook to reply to
all these arguments of the honorable gentleman. I undertook to say that
it was an unfounded imputation on the United States to say that they
had dealt hardly or harshly with the West, and I questioned the correctness of the gentleman's reasoning from analogy. I ventured to suggest that the idea of analogy had misled the gentleman entirely: for that
the original settlers in this country were persons from the old country,
who came here at great expense; who fled from tyranny at home and
came here as outlaws, and who fought their way to possession of the soil
or peacefully extinguished the Indian title to it. They were forgotten by

1. The revised speech says New Hampshire. See p. 300, above.

the mother country, or remembered only to be persecuted, instead of being cherished & protected as the settlers of the West have been. Again, on Thursday last, carried away by analogy, he said that my representation brought to his mind a specimen of eloquence in the British Senate; and he proceeded to quote a speech of Colonel Barre! That natural orator heard, in the British House of Commons, some member arguing that the people of the Colonies would be willing to relieve Great Britain of some part of her debt, in return for the protection which they had received from the mother country &c. Col. Barre replied, in language, which I dare say, Sir, you & I have both recited from our school books, exclaiming "(Here insert the quotation")[2] Does the gentleman maintain that that language is appropriate language for the Western States, or for any body for them, to address to us on this floor? Did the settlers on the Ohio flee from the oppression of our laws and the cruelty of our govt.? Have they felt no protection from our arm—no guardianship from our paternal care? Is that the analogy which any gentleman on this floor will make between the case of the pilgrims and that of the settlers of the West? And I reminded the gentleman that much blood & treasure was spent in sustaining those settlements; that two or three armies sent out from the Atlantic States were annihilated there, & that their places had been supplied by others. During the five or six years of Washington's administration, the great object was to protect the frontiers.

But, that is not all, Sir. We have received these grants of lands from the States with solemn conditions. I rehearsed to the gentleman what those conditions were: that these lands should be held as a common fund, to be expended for the common benefit of all the States: that the cession of these lands was made in consequence of a previous vote of Congress soliciting the grant, &c. And then I argued that it was not in the power of Congress to regard the land so granted as valueless and give [it] away; for that they not only held it, by compact, as a common fund for the benefit of all the States, but they took it as a trust to be executed— one condition of which restrained the govt. from selling it in large quantities, either to States or individuals; and another of which was that the territory so ceded should become a State as soon as its population would allow. And I then endeavored to show that there was nothing in the charge (proceed whence it might) of hostility on the part of the Eastern States against the West.

Mr. W. said he had, the other day, denied the fact that the Tariff was the policy of the New England States; and he denied it still. I then said (continued Mr. W.) that the majority of the Representatives of

2. Isaac Barré, in William Cobbett, ed., *The Parliamentary History of England* (36 vols., London, 1806–1820), 16: 38–39. See above, p. 301, for the quotation.

the New England States in Congress had resisted the Tariff policy as long as they could: and, speaking of the act which may be considered as settling the policy of the govt. in this particular—the act of 1824— I said that even Virginia herself lent more aid to that act than the reproached Commonwealth of Massachusetts. No man, examining the words of the govt. looking where the votes come from, but must, I said, see and admit that the States of the East have been the steady friends of Western interests. I did not mean to say that they had in this respect transcended the proper line; but I do say that the Eastern States have been ready at all times to do whatever had a tendency to favor the progress in population, prosperity, and general happiness of the Western States.

The gentleman from South Carolina quoted a passage from the report of the late Secretary of the Treasury,[3] in which the Tariff policy was recommended, on the ground of one of its tendencies being to restrain migration to the West. I looked at that passage, and made such observations as it seemed to me to call for, not feeling myself under any particular obligation to defend it. But I said, as the cheapness of land in the West operated as a palpable bounty to agriculture, it seemed no more than just that Manufacturers should have some protection, or else that emigration Westward will increase too much for the interest either of the West or of the East. I said that a report, made in the other House, by an eminent gentleman from South Carolina[4] first advanced the idea. He goes upon the ground that he would not make roads & canals for the purpose of facilitating the population of the West; that he would not adopt measures which would tend to withdraw the present population from the part of the country, which, he said, was already scourged by the Tariff policy. I stated that, with regard to the Public Lands, it was to be understood that we hold them as a common fund for the common benefit. I said that we did not wish to hug the public lands as a great source of revenue. I alluded to the same ideas in a Speech I delivered in 1825 on this subject, being identically the same which I now express. I said that the progress of p[op]ulation of the Western States made a great drain—I did *not* say "to a foreign land"—I alluded to the known disposition in human nature to invest money in land where it is cheap and good. Now, Sir, if any man can understand the difference between *giving away* and hugging as public treasure, then he will see that I have always taken

3. Annual report by Secretary of the Treasury Richard Rush, Dec. 8, 1827, *Senate Documents*, 20th Cong., 1st sess., Serial No. 163, Doc. No. 4, pp. 24–26.

4. George McDuffie, in debate on the Cumberland Road, Jan. 18, 1825. *Register of Debates*, 18th Cong., 2d sess., p. 254.

the medium course for my rule of conduct: then will he acknowledge that there is *no* contradiction between what I have said on one occasion on this subject, and what I have said upon another. The country enjoys a benefit as well in the sale of the lands as in what it receives from the sale. And, though I have said that the public lands are held by us as a common fund for the common benefit, yet I have always considered that the sale of the land was also a common benefit. The sale of the land is itself a good. The money received from the sale is also good, because it is so much in the Treasury. My view in 1825 was, and now is, that the land should be brought into market as it is needed and sold at prices so low as to secure, to every man who is able to cultivate it, a comfortable and sufficient farm, but not so low as to throw it into the hands of speculators. In reducing its sales, by division of sections, to tracts as small as eighty acres, the govt. has taken care that every able-bodied man in the country should be able, if willing to buy himself a freehold.

The real question between me and the gent[lema]n now is, where does the doctrine arise, (in the East or in the South?) that the population of the West should be retarded lest there should be a drain of population from East to West. Does the gentleman find that that doctrine, which he has charged upon the East, is of Eastern manufacture? Does it originate there? Has he, in producing his authorities, found any thing to make good that assertion? Sir, he has not. I am not in the habit, on these occasions, of looking up old Speeches. But I can find strong speeches here from South[er]n gent[leme]n in the volume of the Reg[iste]r of Debates, which lay on Mr. W's desk ag[ains]t Internal Improvement, and ag[ains]t facilities for improving intercourse between the Atlantic States & the West, &c.

But, the gentleman has said, that we internal improvement men still refuse to give away the Public Lands, and asks us how we can justify our plan for refusing to do so. This part of the case, Sir, leads to the opining of the whole crux of the difference between the honorable Member & myself. Here is the point upon which we differ *toto caelo*. This is the point upon which I have felt myself bound to rise and defend the ground I have occupied, &c. I call the making a Road to Ohio, a Canal at the Falls of the Ohio, a Canal or Rail Road from the Chesapeake to the Ohio, all, measures for the public good. The honorable gent[lema]n from So. Ca. asked a most significant question; the Key of the whole system of construction of the Constitution of the United States, which opens the door to a full view of the whole difference between us. He asks me, what interest has South Carolina in a Canal to the Ohio? The answer to that question expounds the whole diversity of sentiment between that gentleman & me. According to *his* understanding, and doctrine, she has no

interest in it. According to his doctrine, Ohio is one country, one State, and one government, and South Carolina is another Country, another State, another government, connected it is true, in some sort, for the purpose of conducting their foreign relations, but substantially different States & rival sovereignties. And, thus considering them, the gent[le-ma]n asks, what interest has So Carolina in a Canal in Ohio? I know that in his view of the matter, SoCa has no more interest in a Canal or Road in Missouri [Ohio?] than it has in similar improvements in Missouri. I, sir, take a different view of the whole matter. I look upon the Ohio and the Chesapeake to be parts of one whole—parts of the same country—and that country is my country; and that both of them are, in reference to this matter, under the influence of the beneficent action of this government. And, wherever, therefore, an act of this government is useful to one part of the country, it is an axiom in my politics that it is useful to the whole. It might as well be asked of me, in my own State, if a Canal were proposed through Suffolk or Middlesex, what interest it was of Barnstable or Plymouth, as to ask me what interest Massachusetts has in a Canal in Ohio or a Rail-Road in South Carolina. Sir, this geographical reasoning will not do. I come here to legislate for the whole interest of the country; not to consider that I will do this for one distinct part of it, and that for another; but, to the rightful extent of the authority of Congress, to legislate for the whole, and apply that legislation where it is most for the benefit of the whole. That, Sir, is *my* doctrine, and I am much oftener the advocate of it elsewhere than here. If support be asked from Congress for a Rail-road in South Carolina, shall I inquire what *interest* Massachusetts has in it? Sir, were I to do so, I should act contrary to the whole tenor of my political life, and I should be ashamed to shew my face in public after it, because it would be so. If I am asked whether it be national &c. [Two lines largely blank in manuscript.]

This power of Internal Improvement in the General Government, if exercised at all, must be exercised on liberal views. We must survey with an enlarged view the whole United States: we must go for the country, and the whole country. We must look to the character & capacity, of the country, and adapt our legislation accordingly. We cannot make Rivers where Nature has denied them: nor can we make Canals where there is no water or seaports where there is no salt water. But if we have any power whatever in regard to Internal Improvement, it is as beneficial to the interior as to the sea board: it is not dependent on the flux or reflux of the tide. I know of no principle upon which a lighthouse or a pier or a harbour (every day actions of the govt.) by which we cannot do identically the same thing on Lake Erie on Lake Ontario, or by which we cannot improve, in any expedient manner, the navigation of the Ohio or the Mississippi. I will not go into

the question at large, however. I have stated the general ground I stand upon in reference to this power. That is my doctrine, Sir: the doctrine of the gentleman from South Carolina is different. I claim no power for the general govt which I do not think clearly conferred by the express grants of power properly construed: but, when I have come to the conclusion that the govt does possess certain powers, I say we must exercise them upon the conviction that the States are one; and, for myself, I go for the benefit of THE WHOLE.

Now, Sir, the grounds on which I go for these Roads and Canals in the Western States, or any other States, are susceptible of very easy & plain statement.

The Congress of the U[nited] States, under the fundamental law, has as much power over matters of commerce on land as on the borders of the ocean. When I look into the Constitution, Sir, I am desirous to find there as well the benefits and blessings in peace, as strength and security in war. Is not a road through the State of Ohio, which conducts to a great mass of the property of the govt, a matter of some importance? The United States—is she not (for wise reasons) an *untaxed* proprietor in that country? Is she not a large proprietor? And is it not fairly within the scope of powers which are to be exercised for the common benefit, that we assist, with our means, to open roads & make canals for internal improvement and intercourse with that country, every step in whose improvements is to redound to our advantage? So, Sir, on the subject of public schools, and of Kenyon College:[5] Education is admitted to be one of the great objects of civilized govt. I do not say that the powers of this govt. apply in all cases to the promotion of education, but there are some cases in which they do: in the case, for example, where the govt. is the great untaxed proprietor of the Soil. Suppose it to be true, as I believe it to be, that in no part of this country, or perhaps of the world, is there a greater call for provision for education than in the Western and North Western States, young and growing as they are, where between the ages of infancy & manhood a greater number than in any other country call for education. I think that in that case there is an extraordinary call on the U[nited] States, as the untaxed great proprietor, to do their duty cautiously, but liberally, in the prosecution of the great object of public education. These are the general grounds on which my views of Roads & Canals, and

5. In February 1828, Kenyon College petitioned Congress for a grant of 20,000 acres of land. The bill passed the Senate but died in the House of Representatives. The petition was renewed in December 1829, but was again rejected by Congress, a victim of the controversy over Foot's Resolution.

Education, within the powers of the General Govt, must stand or fall.

Having made these remarks, I now proceed to answer another question of the gentleman from South Carolina. In endeavoring, Sir, in my poor way, to defend my country against the charge of hostility to the West, I did say, the other day, that if you take up any one measure, Road or Canal, or anything else, proposed in Congress for the benefit of the West, if you look to the Yeas & Nays upon it, the searcher of the record will find that in every case where he meets a New England *Aye*, the claim has been voted down, or at least voted against, by a Southern *No*. Not one measure, I repeat, has been proposed for the benefit of the West, the success of which did not depend upon the Eastern votes outnumbering the Southern votes. It is very lately I had occasion to remark that the gentlemen from the South have had constitutional scruples on the subject: and the gentleman from South Carolina thereupon asks me if I would have them violate their oaths, or reproach their withholding principles which they believe to be those of the constitution, and which they have therefore sworn to support. Sir, I stated this, not as a reproach, but as a fact. The gentleman has not found me imputing it, as matter of reproach to him or his colleagues, that they could not vote for Internal Improvement. Far from it. But, Sir, what question did the gent[lema]n from South Carolina put to *me* on this subject, and what respect did he show to *my* political opinions? He asked me, when, and how, and why, New England votes were found going for measures favorable to the West and he asked me, if [it] was not in the year 1825, before the Presidential Election was determined? Here again I might re-introduce on the stage the ghost of the murdered Banquo: but I forbear. And now I will answer the honorable gentleman why, and how, and when, the Eastern States sustained measures in Congress beneficial to the West.

Departing from measures of occasional relief such as have found their way to notice in debate, let us look to other questions, of infinite magnitude to the West, which have been agitated within the walls of this House since 1815, and especially to two of them, one in 1820 and the other in 1821. In the first of these cases, the People of the West applied for a reduction in the minimum price of the Public Lands. The minimum price had been two dollars per acre: they wished it reduced to one dollar and twenty-five cents. They made out a fair case. The law passed for reducing the minimum price. And how did it pass? Was New England behind the South on that occasion? No, Sir: New England, the country that had been charged in this debate with a disposition to restrain emigration, was in favor of it. In the New England delegation in this House, consisting of forty members, there was a greater proportion for it than in the four larger Southern States with fifty members. The New England

Representatives gave all but an unanimous vote in favor of it—33 votes to one: the Southern States gave 32 to 7. Their support was a generous and a proper one, but not quite up to that of the narrow-minded New Englanders. In 1821, the relinquishment bill came up for consideration; it was a measure of most vital importance to the West. Upon this bill, for discharging the purchasers of public lands from a debt of Six Millions of dollars, were the New England States tenacious of their bargains, from the narrowness of their views and their tenacious policy? Great changes had taken place in the value of the public lands since they had been bought by the purchasers: gentlemen who fear to know, that if Congress had not interfered, ruin and desolation would have over taken the settlers of the West to a great extent. On that bill, New England, with forty Members in this house, gave more votes in its favor than the South, with its fifty-two or fifty three Members. I hope, Sir, that the gentleman from South Carolina will now remember that it was not in 1825, but in 1820 & 1821, that decisive evidences were given of the friendliness of the Eastern States to the interest of the West. That, Sir, in answer to one branch of the gentleman's question, was *the time when.*

The next branch of his question is as to the *How,* the Eastern States have shown their friendliness to the West. I answer, by voting on different occasions, in solid column, for what the West supposed its interests to require. They moved in close phalanx on these questions. And that, Sir, is the *how* they showed their attachment to the West.

And, Sir, as to the *Why* they did go in solid column for what the interests of the West appeared to them to require, they did so because they found it to be their duty, as liberal men, to go for their country, and for the whole country. They believed it due to their own character as statesmen; to the character of the patriots their predecessors, from whom they <derived> inherited their authority to act here; to the magnanimity & justice which they have shown in all their dealings with their Western brethren, to relieve these settlers from the burthens under which they labored. That, Sir, is the *Why* they did it.

Now that the gentleman from South Carolina is answered, I hope he will be satisfied. If he be not, I do not know how, when or why he will be so.

But, sir, on the present occasion, as the gentleman from South Carolina has asked me when the Eastern States showed a disposition favorable to the interests of the West, having referred him to two great measures in which this disposition was manifested, I must be allowed to go back a little farther into the history of the country, at least to show that "the Coalition" did not seduce me into the policy of Internal Improvements.

This government, Sir, up to the period of 1815 had too much to do

with various other matters to turn its thoughts inward, and look to the development of its vast internal resources. In the early part of the Administration of Washington, it was occupied in settling the accounts & providing for paying off the debt of the Revolution, and in resisting & curbing the Western Indians. Almost before the termination of his own administration, and during the whole of the succeeding Administration, questions of the most delicate in regard to our foreign relations almost entirely engrossed the attention of the government. The effects of the French Revolution began to be felt even here, and questions of great difficulty sprung out of it. The great volcano threw its smoke and cinders, if not its burning lava also, on our shores. We became involved in questions concerning our foreign relations, which occupied mainly the attention of both Congress and the People, and which finally terminated in the war of 1812. Up to the close of that war there was no attention—no marked distinct attention, paid to the internal condition of this country, or to its capability of improvement under the constitutional action of the general government.

The Peace of 1815 brought about an entire change in our prospects. The war in Europe had terminated before our War. In 1815 we found ourselves at peace, and we found the whole world at peace, and the whole world so tired of scenes of war, that peace for a long time to come was anticipated. This was an entire change. All the occupations of the govt growing out of our foreign relations terminated in the general peace. I must say that, in my humble judgment, that Peace found Congress assembled, embracing as much talent, and as high character, as any Congress that has assembled since my knowledge of it. Well, Sir: it then appeared to me, in common with much wiser & abler heads, that the policy of the govt should take a different course from what it had heretofore done: that it should now turn its attention inward: that it should be the disposition of the govt. to do in peace the works of peace. For it was quite obvious, in regard to our commerce & navigation which had been reaping such a rich harvest of neutrality, that this source of prosperity would be in a great measure dried up, because every nation would be at liberty to build up its own trade, and to sustain its own marine, to exchange its own commodities for those of other countries.

It was under this state of things, Sir, that I had to settle for myself some views with respect to the powers of the general govt. I took the several questions up succinctly; I read the arguments concerning these powers; I made myself acquainted with the history of the legislation of the govt: and I came to the conclusion, that the govt possessed the power of Internal Improvement. Yes, Mr President, [in] the Session of 1816–17, I made up my mind on that subject, *to duce*. I voted therefore

in favor of the bill sent [setting] aside the Bank bonus as a fund for Internal Improvement.[6] I was then about to retire from service in Congress, without any expectation of returning to it. I then, and under those circumstances entered into the doctrine of Internal Improvement, and I entered it under a South Carolina lead. I followed an able leader. But, Sir, if my leader sees new lights, and turns a sharp angle, and I am not able to see them, it is not surprising that I should go straight on, & hold the same doctrine now that I did then. The debate on the Bank question, the Debate on the Tariff question, and the Debate on the continuance of the Direct Tax shew who was who, and what was what, at that time.

You, Sir, know that the Direct Tax was continued a year or two after the Peace, and the gent[lema]n from South Carolina will find, on examination, that honorable and leading men from the South of Mason & Dixon's Line were then for keeping up the system of internal taxes, for the purpose, *inter alia*, of prosecuting Internal Improvements. And the Tariff of 1816, that is now one of those plain cases, that, if the U[nited] States do not recede from it, a State may recede from the Union—may leave her P.P.C. for Uncle Sam, & be off; this Tariff of 1816 was a South Carolina Tariff—& was carried by South Carolina votes against Massachusetts votes. Without those votes it would not have gone. If it could not have gone without the Massachusetts' votes, it would not have budged. Does not the gentleman know of this? I mention this as no demerit in the State of South Carolina; but I say that the very boldest men that ever stood up to advocate the Tariff as a measure of protection, were the able and talented Sons of South Carolina: and I say that *they* carried the Tariff of 1817 [1816]. I say, that when the question was upon the proposed duty on cotton, a member from Georgia now in my eye (Mr. Forsyth) moved to reduce it: he failed by two votes, and South Carolina gave those votes against it. This act then passed, Sir, was the seminal principle of the Tariff as it now exists. It was the Tariff of 1816 that put an end to the Calcutta Trade. Did not the Tariff give a bounty of things which interfere with other pursuits? At the time it did. It cut up the great Salem trade. South Carolina went for it, and it succeeded. I do not mean to say that *all* South Carolina voted for it; but certainly a portion, and a sufficient portion to decide the motion which I refer to, did vote for it. On the principle of protection; the principle against free trade, and against letting things take their own course, South Carolina, South Carolina votes turned the doubtful scale. A leading gentleman from that State, in debate expressed himself as follows:

"The question of manufactures," (Insert A)[7]

6. This was Calhoun's bill, vetoed by President Madison.

7. John C. Calhoun, Jan. 31, 1816, *Annals*, 14th Cong., 1st sess., p. 837.

That, Sir, was the let-us-alone principle. Again, Sir, the same gentleman said—

"Let us make great public roads," (Insert B)[8]

Again, Sir (and here comes the question of consolidation) the same gentleman said—

"To bind together," &c. (Insert C)[9]

That, Sir, was the code of leading gentlemen from South Carolina in 1816–17.

Well, Sir: in the year 1823 I came back to Congress, and I really thought to have found the South Carolina doctrine where I left it. I thought to have found the South Carolina doctrine defended by the same strong arms and the same eloquent voice as when I first embraced it. But, in the mean time, political parties had assumed a new aspect. A party had arisen in the South hostile to the doctrine of Internal Improvements and had attacked it. A sort of anti-consolidation was the flag they raised, and they denounced these doctrines. That flag was not raised *in* South Carolina, but near South Carolina. Some gentlemen from the State of South Carolina attacked this anti-orthodox party, and called them, in derision, Radicals. All the party, indeed, which, being opposed to the exercise of constructive powers by the government, were called Radicals, got their name some where between North Carolina & Georgia. This every man knows, Sir, who is not blessed with a very short memory. Well, Sir, these mischievous Radicals were to be put down, & the chivalrous arm of South Carolina was ready to put them down. How was it done? About that time, as I have said, Sir, I returned to Congress. Our champions had maintained their ground: they had driven back their opponents with discomfiture—a thing, by the way, Sir, that is not always done when it is threatened.

I had occasion, in the early part of this debate, to refer to the language of a gentleman from South Carolina of extraordinary talent, with whom in my day I have had some passages in debate; who is almost always right in his judgment, & expresses himself upon all subjects with a plainess, directness & vigor, &c. This gentleman had come into Congress during my absence from it, and he was from a good school on this subject. *Ex pede Herculem*. If I may be indulged with another quotation, *Noscitur a [ex] sociis*—he was known from the company he had been keeping. I hold in my hand. Sir, the printed Speech of Mr. [George] McDuffie, to whom I refer, made about that time, with a few introductory remarks upon Consolidation, and in which, Sir, I think he consolidated the argument, if crushing may be called consolidation. These remarks are

8. Ibid., p. 837.
9. Calhoun's speech of April 4, 1816, *Annals*, 14th Cong., 1st sess., pp. 1335–1336.

few. The days of men are said to be few and full of evil: and full of evil these few remarks are to the cause of consolidation. I will quote from them. The writer is replying to the charge of Consolidation by the Radicals: (Insert the quotation)[10]

These, Sir, I found, on my return, were the doctrines of South Carolina, which, I suppose, have not changed to this day. If he has, I have no reason to know it; and, if he has, I have no doubt he can give very good reasons for it. Seeing then this Speech, and other indications of a like nature, I thought that we stood on the old platform on which we stood when I last parted. I do not know that this is all the proof that I have, but it is all that I shall trouble the Senate with at present, that the doctrines of South Carolina, as late as 1823, were those of Internal Improvement, which is now termed Consolidation—internal improvement, that [illegible] power.

When I returned, Sir, I found here also the gent[lema]n from South Carolina to whom I am opposed in this debate: and I will say that I rejoiced to meet him, to hear that he was spoken of as a man of national politics here, and of talent, consideration, & character at home.

Well, Sir: referring [to] the Journal of the Senate I find that there was before us, in April, 1823, a bill to authorize the President of the United States to procure the necessary surveys, plans & estimates, for Roads & Canals. What was the act? That the President of the U[nited] States should cause to be made such surveys of Roads & Canals, &c. as should in his opinion, be of importance in a national point of view, &c. In the view which I take of this record, I may be mistaken: if so, I may be put right. But, if I am right, it is of some importance. When this bill was under debate in the Senate, an honorable Member, who doubted the power of Congress, in regard to Internal Improvements, moved an amendment, that nothing therein contained should be taken to affirm or deny the power in Congress. I may be mistaken in my inference; but if I find the name of a Member in the negative on that proposition, that is to me a pretty strong indication that the doctrine of Internal Improvement was not, in his opinion, a very great heresy. Amongst those who voted in the negative on that question I find the name of the gentleman from South Carolina. But, Sir, that is not all. Another member moved, that, previous to the making of such surveys, the assent of the States in which they were to be made should be obtained; and the honorable Member voted in the Negative also on that proposition. If that vote means any thing, it is that such surveys would be made, and such Internal Improvement prosecuted, without the consent of the States. Another amendment proposed a pledge that all the moneys appropriated for this purpose should

10. *Speech of Mr. McDuffie on Internal Improvements* . . . (Columbia,   S.C., 1824), pp. 4–6.

be appropriated among the several States according to their representation in Congress; and the gentleman voted against that. And, when the bill was on its passage, after refusing all these amendments, the gentleman voted for it; which according to my apprehension, was pretty much going the whole for Internal Improvements. If I was misled, it was by very great authority—by no less than that of the gentleman himself, who, notwithstanding this bill proposed measures of that now offensive character, "national importance," still voted for it throughout.

Now, Sir, I do not think that one who followed in the wake of such high authority, and who held onto his leader as long as a hair was left by which he could hold on; I do not think that he is to be denounced as an unforgiven & unforgiveable Federalist, because he has yielded his opinion to such authorities.

But when the great leading star among them moved off upon another track—[Here The *Vice President* (Mr *Calhoun*, the Presiding Officer of the Senate) addressing Mr. Webster, said, does the Chair understand the gentleman from Massachusetts to mean that the person who now occupies the Chair of the Senate has changed his opinion on the subject of Internal Improvement?]

By no means, Sir, replied Mr. *Webster*. I am to say, Sir, that I have had no reason to know that he has. It would give me great pain to know that he had. I am anxious not to misrepresent any one, and especially not one so situated as not to be able to respond on the floor. I would, on the contrary, do him all possible justice; and to that end I state that I believe his opinion to be that there ought to be something like a systematic arrangement for the development of this system, with a view to the proper and impartial exercise of the power by the General Government. I presume, Sir, from other circumstances, whatever be the prevailing sentiment in South Carolina, that *all* South Carolina has not changed its opinion on this subject. It is not long since, that the gentleman who represents the City of Charleston [William Drayton] in the other House presented a resolution, inviting the action of the govt on that principle, from a portion of his constituents.

I have to complain, Sir, of a misconception, by the honorable gentleman from South Carolina, of what I said on another occasion—on the subject of the public debt. I said that I was surprized & that I regretted to find the gent[lema]n throwing out ideas that would have the effect to do away whatever by its own force holds the country together. He wants, he says, no permanent revenue, because it will consolidate the country. I said, in reply, that the feeling of anxiety to get rid of the public debt was too strong some times to be easily accounted for, and that there seemed to be something at the bottom of it more than the public debt. But, Sir, the gentlemen seem to claim the exclusive merit of a disposition

to pay off the public debt. Sir, I do not yield that merit to them. It cannot be shown that I, or those with whom I act have now, or at any time, resisted the discharge of the public debt. I have said that I would go as far as any man in paying off that debt, because its annual charge was a burthen on the finances of the country, of which I wished them to be relieved. I respectfully called on the gentleman from South Carolina not to infer that I was in favor of paying off the public debt, not even for the collateral benefit, as I repeated again and again, of weakening the ties which hold the Union together. And now the gentleman comes out and says, that I am for keeping on the public debt! Now, by what extraordinary construction he can come here and charge me with doctrines which I took care, in every possible way to guard against the imputation of, is to me most marvellous. On the subject of Consolidation, I profess that I did not think it was within the power of man to misapprehend me; and yet I was misapprehended. I cannot now account, unless by supposing I was not heard.

A fixed revenue, he said, tends to consolidation. Well, Sir, what did I say? That the consolidation of the affections of the People towards the Union, which he considered dangerous, I considered the contrary. I told him that I go for the consolidation of *the Union*. I told him so expressly, and in terms. I said and repeated that I was for drawing to the government no new powers on the federal head. I repeated it again & again. I read the Constitution, audibly, word for word. I said that there *is* a consolidation which I am a friend of, ever have been and ever will be a friend of: that sort of consolidation which the framers of the Constitution said, in their address to the People accompanying the Constitution, had been the great object of their care & labor. I then opened and read what I will now open and read again. Mr. W. then read as follows: I said, I regretted the remarks of the gentleman from South Carolina, because they gave too much countenance to the suggestion that the union was to be considered as a temporary thing—a matter of expediency. I said that we were not to consider this union as a deep fountain of govt. never to be frozen up. I said that there [is] a sense in which consolidation was near and dear to my heart: that was, in the sense of strengthening or corroborating *the union* of the States. I opened the book as I now open it; I read the passage, as I shall now read it, and told the gentleman that that was my consolidation. Mr. W. then read the passage as follows:

"In all our deliberations" (Insert D)[11]

11. Webster read this quotation in his First Reply to Hayne, Jan. 20, 1830, *Register of Debates*, 21st Cong., 1st sess., p. 38. The passage is from a letter of the Federal Convention to the Congress of the Confederation submitting the Constitution to the consideration of the people, Sept. 17,

How, Sir, after this, could I be mistaken to say, that I was for a con-solidation of the Federal powers of the government to the Federal head. I spoke my view of this matter as plainly as I could, and, as clinching it beyond the possibility of warping. I read the passage which I just quoted, and said that was my consolidation—that the doctrine of General *Wash-ington* and his patriotic associates in forming the Constitution was my doctrine. For, I think that the strengthening the cord of the union, not by inferring new powers from the Constitution, but the exercise of ex-isting powers kindly and usefully over all parts of the United States, tends to hold together its various parts, and that every thing which thus strengthens the union is of vital importance, so long as the union is deemed to be of any value.

In the course of my remarks, I said that we heard, on every subject, constant allusions to the Tariff. The gent[lema]n says that I quoted dog-grel rhymes upon it. I quoted none, Sir, either doggrel or [manuscript blank for approximately one line]

and know not what I should have quoted

He said, it was no wonder that I should be so displeased with the sound of the word Tariff, and he then alluded to the effort made by me, in the House, against the Tariff of 1824. Sir, I did oppose that Tariff—most zealously and conscientiously oppose it. As I had not in the year 1816 acquiesced in this Tariff policy, then sustained by the eloquence and influence of South Carolina, so I had not brought my mind to approve it in 1823–24. The gentleman from S.C. praises my speech on that occa-sion, he raises me so high that he thinks I shall break my neck in the fall he is about to give me—and indeed he said, that he had prostrated me quite too low to recover. Sir, I can state, as [to] reconcile, entirely to my own satisfaction at least, the grounds on which I acted in regard to the Tariff of 1824 and to the Tariff of 1828.

In 1824, I was opposed to what is now called the Tariff policy. The gentleman alludes to the part which I took at a previous public meeting in 1821. He says that I advanced an opinion that a Tariff for the pro-tection of Manufactures was utterly unconstitutional. I said, on that occasion, perhaps, that there were doubts upon that question; for there certainly were; or, probably that, as an original question, this question of exercising the revenue powers with an intention to protect manufac-tures, was a debateable one. I have said, I know, that the power is by no means as clear a one as the power of Internal Improvement. Between the two propositions, I have thought it much more clear that these mea-

sures of Internal Improvement, which have been objected to, are within the power of regulating commerce, than that the Tariff policy is within the power of raising revenue. I must confess that the recent publication by Mr. Madison[12] on that subject which had never before been imparted to me and when I found that in the Preamble to the first art[ic]le[?] under this govt for raising a revenue, the protection of manufactures was stated as one of the objects of it; when I found the Constitution thus construed by its fathers and contemporaries, I changed my views of the subject somewhat. My reasons for doing so are on the record. I wish that the gentleman who has been searching for what Mr. Webster said before he went out of Congress in 1817 had found for me the report of my Speech which contains them—I cannot find it myself, and it is not worth any other person's searching for—I said in that Speech, among other things, that if the Tariff policy was adopted, we should see the Representatives of different interests debating the matter before the Reps of the People in the other part of the Capitol; and in that particular I have not been mistaken. When, after the act of 1824 had gone fully into operation, what was then the state of things? There was an option presented to New England, as it was to South Carolina, and to other States: that was, either to act on the settled policy of the country, and fall in with it, or to hold off, and quarrel with it. The people of New England did not, thus situated, propose to call the attention of their Legislatures to the enquiry whether or not they could nullify the act. They considered it as settled principle, and they acted upon that ground. When, after the act of 1824 had been for some time in operation, the subject of the Tariff came into the House again, that act had failed to answer the object of the Manufacturers, at whose instance it was passed. Then, what was proposed? We said to ourselves, we have now a system fixed upon and in operation; no one proposes to repeal it: but, without amendment, it is useless, and therefore oppressive. The amendment deemed necessary to make the policy effective for good was proposed: and I voted for it. This, Sir, has been the head, and front, and substance, of my offending. Finding that, without any agency of mine, this had become the settled policy of the country, and that the capital of my constituents had been devoted to this channel, was it not my duty to acquiesce in the decision of the govt., and to take care of the interests of my constituents, many of whom had embarked their all on this [bottom?] Mr. W. here illustrated his situation by that of his going a journey (say to Georgetown) with another person —they differing as to the mode of travelling, he preferring to walk and the other to ride, and he yielding to his companion—suppose a wheel was to run off the carriage, was he to persist in attempting to go on with

12. *Letters on the Constitutionality of the Power in Congress to Impose a* *Tariff for the Protection of Manufactures* (1828).

three wheels because he had been opposed to going on at all? Or was he to lend a hand to repair the defect, that they might at least go safely on? [End of 1st day.]

Wednesday Jan. 27.

Mr Webster resumed his argument. Recurring to the defects pointed out by experience in the Tariff act of 1824, requiring that that act should be either repealed or amended, he denied the inconsistency of the efforts subsequently made to amend it. He ran over the history of the effects of the law of 1824, and of the efforts made to amend it. A bill for that purpose, he said, had been proposed, in which the care commenced just where the wound was—the remedy proposing to go just to the extent of the mischief, and no farther. That bill passed the House of Representatives in 1827, and was rejected in the Senate. In 1828, another bill was brought in on the same subject, which had been christened by a gentleman who sat before him by the name of a bill of abominations.[13] Mr. W. reviewed the history of that bill. Provisions, he said, were put into it which were expected at that time to lean with peculiar hardship on New England, and with the assumed motive to render the bill odious. We were obliged (said Mr. W.) to take that bill or nothing. Perceiving that my own constituents had deeply ventured their property on the faith of the law of 1824, and that, owing to the subsequent events, what was intended for their benefit by the act of 1824 failed of its effect as to them, whilst as to other parts of the country it had its full effect, I thought it my duty, as far as in me lay, that what was intended for the benefit of my constituents should be carried into effect for their benefit.

As to the general question of the Tariff Policy, Sir, New England has been charged as being favorable to it or unfavorable to it, just as the particular time and the particular place of such representation of it, one way or the other, would make the most impression against her. That has been the true history of the practice upon public credulity in relation to this subject. In the South, the Tariff has been represented as the New England measure, whilst in the West New York & Pennsylvania had been represented as forming the great phalanx in support of it. Yes, Sir, whilst in the South, all the enormity of this measure has been laid at the door of New England, in the part of the country where the Tariff policy has been a little more acceptable, it has been represented that the New England States have been opposed to the Tariff policy, and that the Western States are indebted for it to "the generous South." Yes, Sir, I remember

13. According to Webster this phrase originated with Senator Samuel Smith of Maryland. See *Register of Debates*, 20th Cong., 1st sess., p.

756. Smith apparently made the remark in debate on May 7, 1828, but no text of his speech has been found.

a Circular from a gentleman recently distinguished in this govt.—more recently very particularly distinguished,[14] in which he congratulated his constituents, that, thanks to the generous South, we have a Tariff. Thanks to the generous South!

The gentleman from South Carolina, Mr. W. said, had indulged, in the course of his Speech, in a wide range of historical remarks, and a long enumeration of facts and occurrences to prove positions which he seemed to have it very much at heart to establish. Now, Sir, said Mr. W. it will be well to premise, here, that in the early history of our govt, a great difference of opinion existed in regard to the necessity of this govt— or of any constitution or form of govt beyond the old confederation. If any thing further was necessary, there was a difference of opinion as to what that govt should be, and whether this was the proper form of government. A difference existed, also and still continues to exist as to what are the powers conferred by the government. Differences, many & fearful, have likewise arisen out of our foreign relations. In 1790, 1797 & 1798, public opinion was much excited as to the course of the Administration, and the excitement did not cease until after the political revolution of 1801. In the year 1807, the Embargo produced an excitement, which continued with the succeeding nonintercourse system, and arrived at its height about the time of the Declaration of War in 1812. In these various epochs of our history, the country saw, what I suppose will always be seen in popular government, a great deal of proper and decorous discussion, but also a great deal of declamation, of virulence, of violence, and of unjust abuse & crimination. In regard to any party or any one of these crises, much matter may be found capable of very inflamed exhibition & exaggeration now. If, Sir, we go back to the period of Washington's administration, was any Chief Magistrate we have had more vilified than he? Where I ask, was he most vilified? Where did his Administration obtain the most, and where did it obtain the least, support? Where were his character and services held at the highest repute, and where at the lowest? If there be evidence on the Journals of Congress to show, that on his retirement, there were persons desirous to withhold approbation of his public course, I will not stop to ask whether those who desired to oppose it were of the North or of the South. If his personal & private as well as public character were attacked just as grossly as those of his successors have been, I shall [go] no further than the instructive fact. I shall not go to the South & the West to show what vio-

14. According to *Niles' Register*, 35 (Sept. 20, 1828): 52, "we see it also published, as having been lately said by Mr. [Thomas P.] Moore, of Kentucky, that but for southern support, no tariff bill would have passed." Moore (1797–1853) served in the House until March, 1829, when he was appointed by President Jackson as minister to New Grenada.

lence was done to the Administration of Mr. Adams. I shall not rake in the rubbish of those times for all that they produced most exceptionable. I shall not do it myself, and Sir, I have no scavenger to do it for me. I see enough of the violence of my own times to disgust me, without rescuing from their own oblivion the evanescent &c. In all these contests, Sir, some part of the people, in every part of the country, dissents from the predominant sentiment. The People are never unanimous, for or against any measure, or for or against any administration. Washington, though principally supported in the East, had firm and honorable friends in the South. His Administration numbered among its friends the best names of South Carolina. The administrations of Jefferson & Madison found firm supporters also there; and it never happened in any State, opposed to the course of the General Govt that the authorities of that State were not grossly abused &c. The gentleman, Sir, has read us quotations from what he calls the organ of the Federal party in New Engl[an]d: he read them from some book or collect of that kind of light reading, which seemed to have been carefully prepared. He read them to show the sentiment of New England at the time they were published. The gentleman, Sir, has this advantage of me, in any comparison of this sort, that, as we publish much *more* in New England than is published in the South, it is natural that we should publish more that is unsound. Sir, we are much more in the habit of printing our foolish thoughts, as well as our wise ones, than the people of the South. We have a longer time to be assailed upon, in the proportion of forty to their ten. If more violence can therefore be quoted upon us, this is one way in which it can be accounted for. While the gentleman from S. Carolina was searching among the federal organs and federal the Lord knows what, for evidences of political violence, he might, if he had continued his search further South, have found on record effusions in that quarter quite as violent. The opposition to the war in the South was as decided, firm, and unmeasured in its principles, as far as it went, as in the East. On the other hand, if the gentleman will look among the records of the party supporting the war, he will find as much violence as could possibly have been exhibited on the other side. Sir, I shall undertake no controversy of this nature. I have no collects, I invoke the sympathies of no party. I have been furnished with no extracts from party papers, and, if I *had* been furnished with them, I could not use them. It is enough for me to say, that, if, in any of these researches of his, he finds any thing in the history of Massachusetts or of New England, or in the proceedings of any public body therein, disloyal to the Union, or manifesting a disposition to recede from it, or to break up this confederation; whatever it is, wherever it is found, I set upon it my distinct mark of reprobation.

The gentleman, Sir, entertained us with a pretty considerably exten-

sive history of parties. He found out a way, by geneology, to trace the history of parties to the commencement of Govt. He says that the federal party is the Tory party of the Revolution, and that it is the ultra party of this day, &c. & that the democratic party—that is *our* party—for, Sir, orthodoxy is my doxy, heterodoxy is y[ou]r doxy—the party, Sir, is the good old whig party of the revolution. This composition of the gentleman strikes me, Sir, as a work of entire supererogation at the present day. If there is any member of this body on whose conscience it weighs that he has ever been a Federalist, it remains now obvious to him how he may escape the reproach of that sin. I thought, Sir, the gentleman would have been very careful how he touched on that point. The sin of federalism, Sir! We all know the process by which in one hour—aye, Sir, in one short hour the most obnoxious Essex-Junto-man could be washed clean of this sin and converted into an original Jackson democrat, dyed in the wool; by which he would become just as good a democrat, carrying back his patent just as far, as the honourable member himself or his honourable grandfather. Sir, some smiles have been bestowed, of late, as well as frowns, on that [three or four words illegible] at the door of the Hartford convention itself. If other qualifications were united in him, I do not know what power even Nathan Dane himself might not hope for from the gentleman and his party, so truly is it said that politics, like misery, does bring people into very strange company.

The honourable member, in going along, under the mistaken idea that I was the invader of his Territory, and that it was his duty to drive me from its frontier, took some pains to defend S. Carolina. Yes Sir, I who had taken extraordinary care to avoid saying any thing which, by any deflexion of expression, could be considered disrespectful to the South, being nevertheless considered its assailant, the gentleman goes on to bestow a high and merited eulogism on the revolutionary character of S. Carolina. Sir the time was—would to god it was again—that the poor praises bestowed by the citizen of Mass[achuse]tts, whose name the honourable member never heard before today upon the Statesmen of S. Carolina, filled me with admiration of them. I have heard him discourse of the Laurens, the Rutledges, the Pinkneys, the Sumters, the Marians, and of him who nobly sustained the honoured name which the honourable gentleman himself bears, until my heart warmed towards them, filled with sentiments of the most profound gratitude and respect. There is no gentleman of S. Carolina, who has served in the Councils of his Country or distinguished himself in the field, whom I do not know something of and feel a proper respect for. In our revolutionary struggle, Sir, S. Carolina and Mass[achuse]tts went hand in hand. They stood side by side, and hand in hand they supported the administration of the first President: Shoulder to shoulder they breasted the storm of the French rev-

olution and carried us through it—and without their mutual support we could not have been carried through it as we were. Sir, can I forget these things? *Shall* I forget them? Is there a man in South Carolina to whom I would not measure with a liberal hand his due merit? No, Sir, not a man. The treasures of S. Carolina are those of *my country*. Whatever she possesses that is great and good, whatever of that character high heaven has sent down and planted in the rich soil of S. C[arolina] it belongs to *my country*, and I participate in the pride that it inspires. Do I envy it? God forbid that I should envy it. Let me see character, candour, devotion to the cause of public liberty, elevation of sentiment to the highest pitch of patriotism, I will emulate it. If, Sir, stimulated by State jealousy, I ever touch a hair of it in the way of detraction from its merit, may my tongue cleave to the roof of my mouth!

Sir, I shall be led, on this occasion, into no eulogium on Mass[achuse]tts. I shall paint no portraiture of her merits, original, ancient, or modern. Yet, Sir, I cannot but remember that Boston *was* the cradle of liberty. That in Massachusetts (the parent of this accursed policy so eternally narrow to the west) &c. &c. &c. I cannot forget that Lexington, Concord, and Bunker Hill *are* in Mass[achuse]tts—and that, in men, and means, and money, she did contribute more than any other State to carry on the revolutionary war. There was not a State in the union whose soil was not wetted with Mass[achuse]tts blood in the revolutionary war: and it is to be remembered, that of the army to which Cornwallis surrendered at York town; a majority consisted of New England Troops. It is painful for me to recur to these recollections even for purposes of self defence. And even for that end, Sir, I will not extol the intelligence, the character, and the virtues of the people of New England. I leave the theme to itself, here and every where, now and forever.

But, Sir, suppose all the mass of matters which the gentleman has introduced to criminate the New England States—Suppose it all to be in the nature of official documents, and worthy of being received as evidence: What does it prove? Why, he says, it proves that, under the influence of a spirit of opposition to Govt. the people carried their opposition to the late war to a point which menaced the Union; and that the proceedings in the Hartford Convention went to break up the Govt. and withhold the resources for carrying on the war. *En gratia*, yield all this. The question then arises whether it is a transaction to be cemented forever, or to be considered as a precedent on which other similar transactions are now to [be] justified. If there be any thing tending to disunion in the proceedings of the Hartford Convention, there are other portions of the Country in which proceedings have taken place equally obnoxious to censure. If I suppose, for example, that the declaration of the S.C. doctrine is likely to break up the govt., is it any answer for me to say that

similar sentiments, held else where fifteen years ago, brought the govt. to the verge of dissolution? That, Sir, is the point between the honourable member and myself: and that it is which has brought on this discussion. In my remarks I avoided scrupulously every thing personal towards the gentleman. I said that I lamented his doctrine on the evils of a fixed revenue, and the wish that he expressed that this govt. should never have a shilling of permanent revenue, because those sentiments I consider essentially hostile to the continuance of the Union of the States. I did say, and in saying it I quoted an expression of a distinguished gentleman of his own State, that those persons would find an encouragement in his doctrines who had said that "it was time to calculate the value of the Union."[15] I went out of my way to say that I imputed no such sentiments to him. Now, Sir, in saying this, I might be right or I may be wrong. In the first place there may be no tendency in his doctrine to encourage such sentiments. If not, I am clearly wrong. In the next place, if the tendency of his doctrines be such as to encourage such sentiments, and no such sentiments are any where entertained, still I may be wrong. But how does it answer that remark, on my part, to say that he thinks my remark is an attack upon S. Carolina? And then the gentleman told me that he would drive me the next day beyond that frontier: and to tell the truth he was all the way to Boston, in this enterprise before I had sight of him again, when I beheld him enveloped in a cloud of the ghosts of pamphlets which died from memory at the end of the war. Was this right? I have not invited this discussion. I have said nothing which justifies the gentleman to go back and bring up this waste paper, this poor stuff the offspring of poorer minds in by-gone times. I feel it my duty to go back to this starting point of debate. I feel it my duty to call in question the soundness of the argument by which the gentleman justifies what has been done in one part of the Country by what has been done in the other. And the gentleman when he opened the book of the Hartford Convention made the remark that he did not complain of the assembling of the Convention, but of the time, and circumstances of it: That it was in time of war, and of pressure from abroad when all the talents and energy of the Country were required to defend the Country from a foreign enemy. We must sir in matters of this sort decide between what is substantial and what is circumstantial. Now, Sir, I say that if there was any thing in the Hartford Convention tending to discriminate or tending to break the cord that binds us together, it deserved reprehension, not because it was in time of war, but because it took place at all. It may have been more unpatriotic at that time in a state of war

15. The quotation is from a speech delivered at Columbia, S.C., on July 2, 1827, by Dr. Thomas Cooper, then president of South Carolina College. *Niles' Register*, 33 (Sept. 8, 1827): 28–32.

than it would have been in time of general peace such as we now enjoy. But the right is the same in either case: for I deny the right as matter of right both in the one case and in the other. I say that neither the Hartford Convention, nor any other set of men assembled wherever they be, have the right to express opinions unfavorable to the Union of the States. I do not speak of those cases of extremity in which govts. may be dissolved on account of their oppression of the people. But whenever there is disloyalty to the Govt. whether under the depression of embargo or war effecting the New England States or, of a Tariff in S. Carolina a just and reasonable opposition never ought to go to the extent of recommending a remedy which the gentleman from part of his reasoning seemed to think a practicable remedy in the shape of the resistance of the authority of the general govt. If therefore there be a tendency to disunion in such proceedings as those of the Hartford Convention or in similar proceedings in other parts of the Country—if there be such a tendency whether in the one case or the other both are according to my doctrine subjects of legal reproof.

There is a wide difference Sir, between the Honorable gentleman's doctrine and my own. He labored to prove that the object of the Hartford Convention was to break up the Union and yet, he founded his main allegation on the time and circumstances of its meeting. I found my objection to the doctrines which he supposes it to have avowed, on the ideas themselves, which, whenever, or wherever avowed in all times and in all circumstances I deem inconceivable with the permanence of the Union and the true interests of the Country.

Having arrayed his host of proof against the New England States: having read the most violent phrases out of the most violent books of the most violent men from which he drew the most violent inference— the law speaks of violent presumption: his was a perfect tempest of presumption: a whirlwind of passion—but having carried it to the full extent, his argument was felonious to itself because he turned about and justified the proceedings in S. C. on a principle vastly more dangerous than that of the proceedings of the Hartford Convention. Speaking with disapprobation of the proceedings of the Legislature of Massachusetts and of every one of the New England States, the gentleman advanced a principle more dangerous to the permanence of this Union than any doctrine ever hinted at by the Legislature of any one of these States. I say it Sir, and I say it with grief. I am going to consider what that proposition is to collate it with some of the acts which I rather hinted at than described in my former remarks to see whether such a doctrine can be maintained by any sound politician or constitutional lawm[an?]. I have spoken of this doctrine as the doctrine of S. Carolina only because the gentleman calls it the Carolina doctrine. I supposed that a majority of

the people of S. C. are opposed to the Tariff: a majority not large however, may be of opinion that it is not warranted by the Constitution: but whether a majority of people of S. C. are ready to maintain the ground that has been taken by the honourable member, I entertain a very great doubt.

Now Sir if I understand the doctrine of the Hon. gentleman to which I refer, it is this: That if the exigency of the case in the opinion of any State govt. may require it, a State may by its own sovereign authority nullify an act of the general Govt. which it holds to be clearly & palpably unconstitutional. I believe Sir that I lay down the doctrine correctly with all its qualifications. This proposition is one to which I mean to give some attention. I suppose I do not mistake the gentleman for any thing tend[ing] to show that that is the doctrine of S. C. in proof of which Mr. W. quoted a sentiment delivered in the shape of a toast at a public dinner by a distinguished citizen of that state, to the following effect. "The sovereignty of the State never to be controuled, construed, or decided upon but by her own feelings."[16]

[Mr. Hayne said that to avoid misapprehension he would state that his proposition was in the words of the Virginia resolutions, substantially affirmed by the report of Mr. Madison, as follows (here insert them).[17]]

Mr. Webster resumed I am quite aware Sir of these authorities, in the course of this discussion. I shall not quote them to reproach them with their errors, nor, shall I follow them in their opinions because they are theirs. Whether the doctrine maintained by the gentleman from S. C. be the same as that of the Virginia resolution is a matter which depends on interpretation. That resolution says there may be extreme cases &c &c &c. This is no more than the assertion of the original and inalienable right of man to throw off any Govt. which he finds intolerable and oppressive. This is the theory of our Govt. and Blackstone says as much under the Theory of the English Govt. We sir, who oppose the S. C. doctrine do not say that a people may not throw off any form of Govt. and adopt another peaceably, forcibly if they must. We all know that civil Institutions are made for the public benefit and when a case is plainly made out to justify it let those who made any form of Govt. dissolve it and take up another more likely to comport with their habits and their feelings. But if the Gentleman means that the people of the United States

16. Dr. Thomas Cooper, at a dinner for Langdon Cheves in Columbia, S.C., Dec. 9, 1829. *Niles' Register*, 37 (Jan. 2, 1830): 315.

17. The reference is to a document known as "Madison's Report" or the "Virginia Report of 1799–1800 Touch-ing the Alien and Sedition Laws." See *Resolutions of Virginia and Kentucky* (1835), pp. 25–63. Hayne's quotation from the Virginia Resolutions is contained in the *W & S* version, p. 328, above.

have any authority more than any other men to resist the operation of the laws there is an end of the argument for there is nothing to be argued. The sentiment however, attributed to South Carolina is as I understand it, that the remedy for any abuse or supposed abuse lies in an appeal to the State Govt.

[Mr. Hayne here explained. He did not contend he said for the right of revolution but for the right of Constitutional resistance. What he maintained was, that in case of a plain palpable violation of the Constitution by the General government, a State may interpose, and that this interpretation is constitutional. This, Mr. H[ayne] said, was the doctrine of the celebrated Kentucky Resolutions, drawn up by Mr. Jefferson in which that State, by a vote of great unanimity called upon all the other States to stand by it in maintaining their natural rights.]

Mr. Webster resumed: When the gentleman from South Carolina says that there exists the right of Revolution; when he says that *the People* have a right to resist unconstitutional laws, I agree with him. It is no doctrine of mine, that the people have no right to resist an unconstitutional law. But, Sir, on the plain proposition that in case of a supposed palpable violation of the Constitution by the Federal government the citizen has a right of redress by calling upon the State authorities to nullify an act of Congress, I say Quaere de hoc; and long shall I query it. If the gentleman goes back to the natural rights of man, and to the revolutionary ground, it is very well: but I protest against this middle state, which is neither to be an assertion of natural rights or a submission to the laws. I protest against it. I say that the right of a State to resist a law of the U[nited] States must rest (and, Sir, the gentleman's argument admits it) on the inalienable right of man to resist oppression. I admit that there is a violent remedy <for> which may be pursued when the extremity of the case justifies a recurrence to it—the remedy and the right of Revolution. But there is no way in which a State, as a member of the union, can interfere and stop the progress of the govt. on any pretence whatever. The enquiry into this matter could lead us to the source of the Federal Govt. Who was it, Sir, that constituted the Congress of the U[nited] States, and gave them power? Do they not derive their authority from the same fountain as the Legislatures of the States?

Mr. W. here repeated the Toast, &c. Is that, Sir, the S. Carolina sentiment as to what is meant by the Sovereignty of a State? If so, it would be pretty difficult to reconcile it with the Constitution of the U[nited] States. The Constitution had decided the matter very differently. As "Sovereign States," the individual States might make war: but the Constitution says they shall not make war. As Sovereign States, they might make Treaties & form alliances: but the Constitution has said that they shall not, as Sovereign States they might coin moneys: but the Constitution

says the contrary. The Constitution says that no Sovereign State shall be so sovereign as to make a Treaty: it says, further, that no Sovereign State shall be so Sovereign as to coin money. This at least must be allowed to be a control upon the Sovereignty of the State of Carolina, as of every other State, which does not arise from her own "feelings of honorable justice." These Proceedings of South Carolina, Sir, I do not use to show the inflamed state of public feeling in that quarter; I do not lay an emphasis on any part of them; I do not impose them by any parade; I do not know that I shall read even the non-intercourse clauses. I mean merely to see what are the *principles* of these Proceedings, & then to see what is the Constitution of the Country. Without referring more minutely to them, I believe it will be sufficient briefly to state them. Mr. W. here read some public proceedings in South Carolina, which advise "active open resistance." This, Mr. W. said, was following up the principle of the Declaration of Independence, very properly put forth by our Fathers when they were about to resort to the natural right of revolution. The proceedings conclude, he said, with some propositions of general truth, but from which very lame conclusions were drawn. Mr. W. then quoted further as follows:

(Insert extract.)[18]

Sir, said Mr. W. names are things. Why should an intelligent man in South Carolina, in 1828, labor to show that, in 1775, there was no competition, no rivalry of interests between Great Britain & South Carolina? That she had no occasion, in reference to her own interests, or from a regard to her own welfare, to be at war with England in 1775? Can any man fail to see, that the reading of that paragraph draws after it this question: If we had no collusion with the Ministers of King George in 1775; if we had no rivalship with England in 1775; if there were nothing which should withdraw us from our connection with Great Britain in 1775; what is there now, in the existing state of things, to separate us from *Old* England rather than from New? Resolutions, in reference to these questions of State Sovereignty & Federal usurpation have been passed by the Legislature of South Carolina: I will not comment upon them, because they go no further than the doctrines of the honorable gentleman. He stands upon the right of the States to interfere, as States, when in their opinion there has taken place any palpable violation of the Constitution. This principle has never been advanced before, in any part & any State, *upon consideration.* If it has, it has not been by any Legislature of any New England State—certainly not by the Legislature of Massachusetts. I think that the gentleman read a petition addressed to

18. The quote is from a speech delivered by Robert Barnwell Rhett at Walterborough, S.C., on June 12, 1828. *Niles' Register*, 34 (June 28, 1828): 288. See pp. 332–333, above.

the Legislature of Massachusetts, showing that they had a right to interfere and oppose the execution of the Laws of the U[nited] States. Sir, the
Legislature of Massachusetts thought differently, & did not so interfere.
The gentleman quoted also the remarks of a venerable gentleman (Mr.
Hillhouse) then a Member of the Senate of the U[nited] States, and now
present, in reference to the Embargo laws. That Senator said, that he
thought those laws were unconstitutional, and that it was his opinion
that the People were not bound to obey them. Right or wrong, Sir, those
were *constitutional* opinions. But it would not have been a constitutional
opinion, had he said that the States were to take it upon themselves to
resist those laws. The People, the honorable Senator said, were not bound
to obey them; nor would they have been any more bound had there been
no such thing as a State govt. The People of this District, who have no
local Legislature, are not bound to submit to an unconstitutional law.
Following up that question of the gentleman, what did take place ex-
emplifies the question of the right interference by a State Legislature to
resist the acts of Congress. What did take place then, in Massachusetts,
and in New England, on the occasion referred to? A decided majority
of the People supposed the Embargo laws to be unconstitutional. They
reasoned thus: Congress has the right to regulate commerce; but here
is a law stopping all commerce, which is the exercise of a power, not to
regulate, but to destroy. It is not a regulation, which causes to stop the
watch which is sent to be regulated. This was believed, fully believed,
by a large majority of the People of Massachusetts. Now, Sir, observe
the course which those who were opposed to it took to be relieved from
what they believed to be an unconstitutional law. Did they assert the
right of the State govt. to interfere? Did any State undertake to say, this
is a plain and palpable departure from the Constitution, to the last degree
oppressive and ruinous, and we by our act will nullify it? Did the State
of Massachusetts do this? Far from it. They did no such thing. They felt
bound to two things, both equally indispensable, if we mean to have a
Constitution at all: first, to submit to every exercise of power by the
general govt.; and, secondly, in every case of doubt, to refer the decision
of the question to the proper tribunals. We believe the laws to be constitutional: but the question then was, and in these matters the great question always is, who is to judge between the People & the Govt.? The
Constitution confers, necessarily, and expressly, upon the Judiciary the
power to decide on the extent & limit of the powers granted by it to
Congress. If that had not been done, Sir, the govt. would not have advanced one step beyond that poor & feeble thing the Old Confederation.
It being the opinion of the People that the law was unconstitutional, they
entertained the opinion also that the question as to its constitutionality
must be settled by the Judiciary of the U[nited] States, and they preferred

these bonds given under those laws to be sued upon. The matter came in due course to a solemn hearing & argument before the Supreme Court of the U[nited] States. That great and good man, to whom the gentleman from S. C. alluded, and whose steps he wished me to follow—I might, Sir, in zeal; but follow him in comparison of talent is beyond my presumption—that great & good man came forth to the argument with a most settled conviction, freely & openly expressed every where, that the Embargo Law was unconstitutional. He who was made, formed by nature, for his profession; who saw through forms how to grasp the substance on all questions of Constitutional law, whose inferences were demonstrable; Yes, Sir, *Samuel Dexter*, in public and in private, on the responsibility of his character as a lawyer & a citizen, held the embargo law to be unconstitutional. Well, what did we do, in regard to a law the unconstitutionality of which was sustained by the authority of so great a name? *We went to law;* we took the old fashioned course: we tried the right: we went where only we could go to with the question: we went to the Supreme Court,[19] with Mr. Dexter at our head; and never was there a greater exhibition of talent and learning than he displayed on that occasion. We were cast, Sir, and *we paid our bonds*— bonds covering millions of money, involving the ruin of families not to be counted. The fate of men, women & children by thousands—not their opulence, or competence, but their means of procuring the very necessities of life were depending on it. The law took its course. The Judges decided the cause. They held the law to be constitutional; *and we acquiesced in the decision.* That, Sir, is *our* mode of trying the constitutionality of an Act of Congress.

The doctrine of the gentleman from South Carolina leads to a different remedy. He agrees that there may be a strong, palpable & oppressive case of revocation of the Constitution. That was exactly our case in reference to the Embargo; for we could not then see (and we have never since got any light upon the subject) how in any degree the public good was to be promoted by such an enormous oppression as we suffered under the operation of that measure. Of the oppressiveness of the law there was no doubt, nor any difference of opinion. But its constitutionality or unconstitutionality was matter of opinion. Who was to decide it? We thought it a clear case, but we did not therefore take the law into our own hands; we were not ripe for Revolution. Who then was to

19. Either Webster's recollection is mistaken, or he is deliberately distorting the truth for the purpose of effect. The case did not reach the Supreme Court; rather, it was argued before the U.S. District Court for Massachusetts in September 1808. *United States* v. *Brigantine William*, 28 *Federal Cases* 614 (1808). See how Webster changed his language for the printed edition of the speech, pp. 334–337, above.

decide it? The human mind is so construed, Sir, that in proportion as a question is brought into controversy, in that very proportion those who are on the two sides see their way perfectly clear, becoming obstinate as the question becomes doubtful. Nothing sharpens the optics of an impassioned arguer more than opposition: what perhaps before appeared doubtful to him is then seen perfectly clear. This is true in metaphysics, in religion & in law. So that if a case once is said to be a clear & palpable case, on one side, it will always be so; for it is a matter of opinion; and it will be thought just as clear, plain & palpable, on the opposite side, by others. Every man thinks his own case clear, and that he can put his finger upon: but, after all, it is but *his* opinion of the matter. Perhaps the gentleman from South Carolina—certainly some gentlemen of South Carolina, think this question concerning the Tariff to be clear, plain & palpable—so much so that if all the Courts in the world were to decide differently, it would not affect their opinion. Well, Sir, what is that case? Mr. Madison has been quoted here as authority for the doctrine of the gentleman: but Mr. Madison certainly does not sustain the gentleman's side of the question; for he, instead of considering the Tariff law as a plain, clear and palpable violation of the Constitution, says that the law *is Constitutional*. What is the inference, then? That, if the Legislature of a State *thinks* that [a] case has occurred of violation of the Constitution, though such thinking on its part be against all authority & the settled practice of the government, it has the right to interfere and arrest the execution of the law. This, Sir, I say is unconstitutional doctrine.

Before I go further, let me here say, that, if the States of New England, had acted upon this principle, in reference to your laws of Embargo, non-intercourse, & war, this glorious govt. would have crumbled into dust. This fabric would not have reared its dome. This Capitol would have been now empty. What one of those States did not think, in regard to the Embargo, as South Carolina does in regard to the Tariff? No stronger case can arise than that was. And if any one of those States hold any such doctrine, heresy as I must call it [,] as that of the gentleman of S. Carolina, and would have maintained that opinion by force, there would have been an end to the Union. Can the gentleman produce in any form, an opinion of S. C. against the Tariff, stronger than the feelings of Massachusetts against the embargo? I ask him whether it would have been justifiable in Massachusetts to have broken up the govt. And I take care not to touch the subject of patriotism but to present the abstract question: whether they had a right if they were fully convinced that this was a case accompanied with all the circumstances of the gentleman's proposition, to nullify the embargo law within the State of Massachusetts! I deny the proposition altogether. It en-

tered into the head of no public man in Massachusetts and no public man could stand to it for a moment.

Sir, whence is this supposed right derived of the State authorities to interfere with the action of this govt.? It has its foundation, in my opinion, in a total mistake of the origin of this govt. I hold it to be a popular govt. coming from the people, created by the people, responsible to the people, capable of [being] amended and modified in such manner as the people may prescribe; just as popular, just as much emanating from the people as the State govts. and there is no more authority in the State govts. to interfere and arrest the action of any law of Congress because they think it unconstitutional, than Congress has to arrest the action of any law of any State because it is contrary to the Constitution of that State. Sir, I go the whole length. This Govt. has no dependence on the State govts. We the People of the United States made this Govt. It is as pure an emanation of popular opinion as any State Govt. whatever. It is no answer to this to say that the action of the State govts. is required in appointing us to Seats in this Hall. The people might delegate that power to the State legislatures just as they did to electors the power to appoint a President and Vice President of the United States. Their doing so did not take away from the govt. its popular basis. This Senate is not less popular because it was chosen by the legislatures of the States any more than the election of President is less popular because the electors interpose in it. In case of a Govt. of a State being chosen by its legislature is the govt. of the State therefore not a popular govt.? This govt. came from the people, is responsible to them, and is an independent fruit of the popular [will?]. How is it then that the State Govts. have a right to interfere in the action of this govt.? The right cannot be found any where short of the doctrine of revolution. A State undertakes to say that the Govt. of the United States is exercising an unconstitutional power and they will interfere to stop it. Where do they get the power to do so! and that sir is the *crux* of this argument. If the people of the United States, in delegating the power by which we sit here, and receiving this Constitution, have, by express provision, or by reasonable construction, vested the States with power to interfere, then I grant that it follows that they may interfere, when they find us transgressing. But how is that matter? Where is the power lodged to determine on the constitutionality or unconstitutionality of the acts of Congress? Is it in the State Govts.? or in the general Government? Why Sir you must see at once that if it be not lodged in the general govt., but be left to the judgment or discretion of the State legislatures, we have not advanced one step beyond the confederation. What then did the constitution of 1787 do for us? nothing at all, absolutely nothing. It left us where we were—a rope of sand. It was to

settle that very question—to provide for the Govt. such powers for executing its own will as should be effectual over all the States—for that purpose and for that purpose only, that this Constitution was established. The very design of this Constitution was to establish a mode of Govt. which should act directly from and upon the people without the intervention of the State Govts. Under the old confederation the general Govt. acted only by *recommendation* to the States. The legal action—the application of law to the individual man emanated from the State legislatures. It originated there. The taxes recommended by the general govt. were collected under their authority and of course under their discretion; and they were collected or not collected accordingly. And the consequence was that the general govt. could not get along etc. Now if the people, establishing this Constitution, had not provided some general power which should act over all the States, and decide, for all, whether an act of Congress be constitutional or not, then they would have left us just where they found us. Must it not be so? Take a case. Suppose that a state may interfere to nullify an act of Congress within its limits. Suppose it to be the tariff act, and that it may be nullified by the State of S. Carolina that is, the tax created by it be not collected in S. Carolina. How would it be in the State of New York? She holds the act to be constitutional, and the taxes collected within her limits. Then we have one State paying and another refusing to pay its just proportion of taxation. Is not the same old confederation come again? It is stated strongly in the Pamphlet from Carolina which I alluded to the other day, that whoever holds the doctrine of the right of a state to nullify a law of the general govt. forgets the Confederation —Aye Sir, and forgets the contents of the Constitution itself.

The people of the United States in framing this Constitution were too well instructed by experience not to perceive the necessity of making provision for giving to it its full effect. They were too wise to leave it to the States to judge of the constitutional exercise of powers of Congress. They provided by the Constitution itself a proper mode of settling questions of Constitutional law. Having granted to Congress certain powers, which, I agree, are limited powers—restricted powers—was it not obvious, as long as man is the fallible being that he is, as long as there was much imperfection in language, questions might and naturally would arise in the interpretations of these powers, however express and particular the terms in which they were granted? There are in this Constitution restrictions on the State govts. as well as grants of power to the general govts. The next question was to provide some authority to give the law its true interpretation. The sentiment which I have quoted says that the laws are to be construed only by the sense of justice entertained by the States. I hold otherwise. The people saw

the necessity of a common tribunal which should give the laws to Massachusetts and to S. Carolina, to New York & to Delaware; that it was necessary to the very idea of a federal govt. the people went on, and, having stated whatsoever should be conferred on the general govt., and divided them into the common partition of legislative, executive, and judicial, they proceeded to make that govt. the constitutional, the only Constitutional, the paramount judge of is own power. If they had not done this they would have done nothing. The key stone of this arch is the principle that the Constitutional authority shall decide what is the true construction of the parts of this instrument.

Well, Sir, how has the constitution attained this great end of making the govt. of the U[nited] States the interpreter of its own powers? By a manifest and plain provision. It says that "this Constitution, and the laws of the U[nited] States which shall be made in pursuance thereof, shall be the supreme law of the land; any thing in Constitution or laws of any state to the contrary notwithstanding." Thus establishing the paramount authority of the laws of the United States. This was one step. The people had said that no state law should be valid in conflict with the Constitution or laws of the U[nited] States, but they had not said who should decide that question when it arose. If they had stopped here, that question would still have gone back to the State judges and we should have had no common rule of property, no common rule of duty, no common rule of right. Therefore, having declared the paramount authority of the Constitution and laws of the U[nited] States, they put the key stone in this arch by declaring that on this question the judiciary of the U[nited] States shall decide. Authority to dwell on all cases involving the constitutionality of acts of Congress is given by the express language of the Constitution to "the judicial power."

And accordingly at the first session of Congress under the Constitution the law was passed establishing a judicial system of the U[nited] States and referring all questions ultimately to the Supreme Court of the U[nited] States. This was decisive of a govt. [making] it competent by giving it the power of self protection; and nothing else would have made it effective. This Govt. would have been among forgotten things long ago but for this ultimate power. But for that, the Govt. of this union would have been as short lived as its predecessors. Look at the idea just referred to. The people of Massachusetts believe the Embargo law to be unconstitutional: such would have been the decision of the Courts of that State had the question been referred to them. What would have been the consequence? The Constitution would have crumbled into dust but for the provision which it contains that on this matter of the constitutionality of the laws of Congress State Courts shall not judge, but our own judges shall. I should like to know, on this case, how it is, that

the State legislatures can undertake to act? *The People* have constituted this govt.; the People have conferred upon us these powers. The People have said that since some body must decide on the true interpretation of these powers, our will is that you shall decide it yourself. How does a State legislature get the power to decide on this point? Who gave them the right to say, to the People, we, who are your servants for one purpose, will undertake to decide that your other servants have transgressed their authority? Sir, I deny this power altogether. It cannot stand for a moment the test of examination. Gentlemen may say that in an extreme case a State Govt. may protect the People from oppression by the laws of the Union. That Sir is the revolutionary principle, just as much as if the People instead of the State Govt. were to resist the law. Such a nullifying act neither makes nor proves a law to be unconstitutional. Sir, I stand up for the People—for this is the govt. of the People. This Constitution is the expressed will of the People; and this People have said in it, that to the judicature of the general Govt. shall be reserved the ultimate power of construing its provisions. Then Sir I say that the construction of the Constitution of the law cannot be made to depend upon the honourable feelings of justice of any State legislature.

For myself, Sir, I decline the umpirage which is tendered to me by the State of South Carolina between the Constitution and the law. I have not sworn to support the Constitution according to the construction of the State of South Carolina. I have not stipulated, by my oath of office, to come under any responsibility but to my own conscience & to my constituents. I hold myself bound by the Constitution as I interpret it, and as those interpret it who are placed by it over my head. The gentlemen who composed the meeting to which I have referred, say, that if all the Courts of the world were decided against them, they might submit to it as power, but they would not acquiesce to it as justice. In all these cases Sir somebody must decide. If we mean to have a govt. fit for, or capable of any thing but eternal discord and laxity; a government which will answer the ends of the people in instituting it, some questions must be decided at sometimes: and there must be somebody to decide them: and, when they are decided, they must be acquiesced in. On that subject, nothing can be more just, Statesmanlike and sound, than the remarks of Mr. Madison when Pres[ident] of the U[nited] States in returning to Congress the act for establishing a Bank of the U[nited] States. [Here Mr. W. quoted Mr. Madison's message.] [20]

20. Webster omitted this quote from the printed speech, so it is not clear exactly what he said. It is likely that the passage he read was the last paragraph of Madison's veto message of January 30, 1815:

In discharging this painful duty of stating objections to a measure which has

And are the Gentlemen of Colleton right sir in say[ing] that so long as *they* believe a law to be unconstitutional they will not acquiesce in it? How long can this govt. go on—how long could any govt. go on under the influence of such doctrines?

Let me be understood, all along, as drawing no powers from the Constitution by construction. I admit that this is a government of strictly limited powers; that any power not granted is withheld. I agree, that the object of those who framed this Constitution was to confer some powers, and to restrain the exercise of some powers; that this govt. is a government of special, delegated, and particularized powers, and that it is nothing more. What of that? I say, that, however the grant of power may be expressed, in whatever terms it may be framed, its exact extent and limit might be a question of doubt; and that this govt. would be good for nothing if the Constitution had not provided some way in which this government could maintain its own authority. Let us consider whether this is not necessarily so.

If a thing can be done well, an ingenious man can tell *how* it can be done. I then ask, how is this nullifying act, when passed, to operate in S. C. upon an act of Congress. I wish to know something of the *modus operandi.* What will be the course of things? We will begin with the Tariff law, which is said to be unconstitutional to every man's apprehension. To remedy this grievance there is to be an act passed declaring it null and void so far as it affects S. Carolina. Suppose that S. C. passes such an act. The Tax is to be collected in Charleston. The act makes it the duty of the State officers to stop this collection in Charleston. The proper officer must go in some force or, being forbidden by law the people will not pay over the money. The Collector then will call upon the Marshal to call out the Militia. The nullifying People must come out with their force; and then the Civil War begins. If gentlemen say, this is all *in terrorem;* we propose to pass a nullifying act which is a nullity itself, which amounts to nothing, then, &c. But if it is to be an act which is to be acted upon, let us pursue it to its consequences. The Collector will be resisted: he will be resisted by force—a very respectable force for what I know, and probably is so, for the honorable Member himself commands it, and if the Militia is to be called out, it could not be under a more gallant leader—they carry on these banners the nullifying act. They tell your Collector, he shall collect no tax under

undergone the deliberations and received the sanction of the two Houses of the National Legislature, I console myself with the reflection that if they have not the weight which I attach to them they can be constitutionally overruled, and with a confidence that in a contrary event the wisdom of Congress will hasten to substitute a more commensurate and certain provision for the public exigencies.

Messages and Papers, I: 555–557.

the Tariff law: they will be puzzled though, to do so with a grave countenance, for they themselves made the Tariff law of 1816. But they
would tell the Collector he should collect no revenue. The Collector
would not depart at their bidding. They would then come to a pause.
They would go to the Member from South Carolina, their chivalrous
Commander, and enquire of him—for they have doubtless a just respect
for his acquirements as a lawyer, as well as for his gallantry as a soldier—they would want to learn something from him of Coke & Littleton
as well as of Turenne and Vauban—they would ask him for something
of their rights in this matter. They would ask him if it was not rather
dangerous to resist a law of the U[nited] States? He would be asked
by them, Suppose we say that this Tariff law is an unconstitutional law,
and that we will oppose by force its execution in South Carolina—Is
not that Treason? Certainly: John Fries learnt that by sore experience
some time ago. His history should warn them in time that to resist a law
of the U[nited] States by force is Treason. What advice, Sir, would the
gentleman give them to help them out of that danger? He would tell
them, here is the act of the State of S. C. They would probably ask him
of what avail are the acts of S. Carolina against the laws of the U[nited]
States? Can they help us to a plea in bar of an inditement for Treason?
Who is to determine what is a plea in bar in such a case? If we are
taken from this collection District before a Court of the U[nited] States,
will the Court hold this law to be a plea in bar? Will they hold it to be
a constitutional act? if not, how are we to be protected? The gentleman
may answer I will show the judge my bayonets. That Sir would be another offense. What then? The Court comes: it passes upon the case. If
it holds the law to be unconstitutional, what then? Why, then, the Court
must be stopped. And we thought in New England, that we were pretty
near revolution. We thought we had passed the rubicon, when, some
fifty odd years ago, we stopped the Kings Court. This leads to war. What
possible effect, short of this, can a nullifying act of the State of S. Carolina have? When a man is arraigned for resistance of the laws of the
U. S. what possible justification can he set up in the opinion of his
State, which amounts to no more than an opinion, that the law is void?
[Take?] the case of John Fries.[21] Would it have bettered his case, if he
could have produced from the Legislature of Penn[sylvania] a nullifying act? Would that have made him a plea in bar? So, disguise it as
you will, these doctrines go to the extreme length of revolution. The
only remedy they propose is a remedy which goes to break up the foundation of the Govt. and would explode it to atoms.

The People have not thus dealt with the Constitution. Let it be taken

21. Fries (c. 1750–1818) led a rebellion in early 1799 against the direct federal property tax enacted by
Congress in 1798.

into consideration that this Constitution is not like the laws of the
Medes and Persians, unalterable. If there be any thing in it which, either
by express grant, or by subsequent interpretation, ought not to be in
it, the People of the U[nited] States have a right to amend it. And I
say, if the construction of the Constitution be established so that it
becomes a part of the Constitution, contrary to their opinion, it is in the
power of the People to erase it. But, while the People submit to the Constitution as construed—whilst they choose to have it as it is there is
no power elsewhere to alter it. It is their instrument. They have the right
to alter it: but they see no occasion to do so. The interference of any
State with the right thus reserved to the People is an interference with
what the State has nothing to do with. The People have chosen to trust
themselves. First, to such construction as the Govt. itself shall put on
its own power. Secondly, to choosing their public servants by frequent
Elections, and holding them to their responsibility. Thirdly, as a further
caution, to the power of amending the Constitution whenever they shall
think it requires amendment. On these three principles the People of
the U[nited] States have chosen to be governed by this Constitution;
& they have at no time, directly or indirectly authorised a State Legislature to interfere in the question whether we have exercised these
powers constitutionally or unconstitutionally. All proceedings of that
nature by a State Legislature are *coram non judice*.

Well, Sir, If the supposed power of the States be vain and illusory,
as I have shown it to be, in the matter of the Tariff, how would it be
in the case of their interfering to prevent the appropriation of money
for the purposes of internal improvement, the constitutionality of which
has also been questioned. We have no right to expend the public money
but within the limit of our Constitutional power. We think we have a
right to construct a rail road in South Carolina. Suppose, instead of
making a rail road in S. C. as proposed, we were to undertake to make
a rail road in Ohio. She will not go to war with us to prevent it Sir;
but still, if it be unconstitutional, it is as much an injury to S. C. as if
it had been undertaken within her limits. I do not say that the arguments against this power would prevent my voting for an appropriation
for the rail road supposed to be in South C., no Sir, notwithstanding all
the Colleton protests and all the Collects of the gentleman from South
C., I shall do just the same for that road as I would for one in Ohio:
that is, I shall have pleasure in voting for it. But, to return to the
argument if part of the money appropriated for internal improvement
is to be expended in the State of Ohio, how is the State of S. Carolina
to interfere to prevent it? How is she to nullify, within her boundaries a
law which takes effect, not there, but within the boundaries of another
State? The answer to this question shows that it never could have been

contemplated that this power of resistance of the laws should be vested in the States, because they could make nothing of the power if they had it. They could not exercise it to restrain the power of Congress as established by the Constitution. Last of all let me say, that this being after all but mere matter of opinion on the construction of written instrument, it became a matter of necessity to say *whose* opinion should finally and conclusively decide it. If this be not done this Govt. is holden in every State a poor dependent on State permission. It has no independent existence at all. Because, if all its powers are subject to the control of the States, you must so exercise your powers as that no State can take exception to your acts, or else your acts are perfectly nugatory.

These Sir are the reasons which induce me not to subscribe to the doctrine of the right of a State to decide upon the constitutionality of a Law of the U[nited] States: That the power contended for is incompatible with the existence of this Govt.; that there is no more power in a State Legislature to this end than in any equal number of other citizens; that there is no more power in the citizens of a State to interfere as against this govt. than as against their State Govt.; but that, in any one and all of these cases the resort is to the inalienable right of man, the right of revolution. I admit that if the People see fit to make a revolution they may do it. All that I mean to maintain is that they have not constituted State governments their revolutionary Heads. They have not given *them* the power of deciding what and where this confederacy shall be broken up. That power they have reserved to themselves. Whether wisely or not is a question which I will not enter into. If any man doubts it, he draws into question the relative merits of the present Constitution and the old confederation. On that subject it is only necessary to say, that I entertain the opinion, which I presume is universal, that the happiness, the prosperity, and the glory of our Country have taken root and grown up since the adoption of the parent Constitution.

To return Sir to the propositions, with which I entered this debate that there was no ground for charging the U[nited] States with unkind feelings toward the western States; That there was, especially, [none?] for charging the Eastern States with hostility to the West; and thirdly, (to which I suppose I owe the lecture the gentleman gave me,) that I heard with regret the doctrine maintained by him of the right of a State to sit in judgment on the Laws of the United States. Perhaps, in the attempt which I have made to sustain these positions I am to be "discomfited," as the gentleman promised the Senate I should be. I submit to the discomfiture, if it be so, and, under the views I have taken I shall not be offended by being reminded of it as long as I live. I do not mean to say any thing to touch the feelings of the gentleman from S. Car-

olina. I neither intended it in putting on the harness, nor do I mean to do it in taking it off. If he has not effected the discomfiture, it is not fault of his. He promised it only with the blessing of God, and, if he has not accomplished it as well as he expected, it has been God's will that he should not.

Mr. W. here recapitulated. When the Govt. of the U[nited] States began the sale of the public lands, the Government was very weak and the Indians were very strong: and there was a double object in selling this Land—defence as well as revenue. In the first instance, a proposition was made that it should be sold at public auction in the City of New York, where Congress then sat. At the same time it was known to have been a favorite policy of Washington to keep the settlements close together until the Country should become more populous. The Government at that time did not command protection to the frontier. The settlers, even on this side of the Ohio, were not safe from the Indians, and, when they began their improvements on the other side of the Ohio, they came back of nights to this side of the river for safe repose. After Wayne's victory, the frontier having become comparatively safer, the Government went on to sell the land. Soon after was passed the ordinance of 1787 so often referred to. I understood the member to say that the merit of the authorship of that ordinance had all been taken away by the suggestion of the gentleman from Missouri, who had discovered some one else to be entitled to it. As I understood the blow that he struck, it was that certain articles had been submitted in Congress before the date of that ordinance. I have looked into that matter Sir and will state shortly how it is, with this remark: Suppose it to be all true that he says—what of that? Mr. Jefferson drew up the Declaration of Independence. There is nothing new in it, nor is there a proposition in it which had not long before exhausted argument by repeated discussions. What of that? Mr. Jefferson drew up that paper and he was fully entitled to the credit which posterity has awarded him for the authorship of it.

The session of the Lands north west of the Ohio was made in March 1784. In April 1784 a committee of Congress was appointed

[Here insert a statement of facts *et cetera*.][22]

Sir, I am sorry to detain the Senate so long. I have been drawn into this debate without the least premeditation. But I do not wish to leave it, even now, without stating that the question, upon which I have been this morning addressing the Senate, is one of deep and vital importance to the People of the U[nited] States. I profess through the whole of my

22. This statement of facts, etc., comes from the *Journals of the Continental Congress*, 26: 246–247; 28: 164–165. See Webster's description of these events, pp. 297–298, above.

latter political career, to have had mainly in view the prosperity and glory of the Country, and the Union of the States. I have felt that I had no wish to look beyond this Union to see what might be hidden in the dark recess behind. I have not made the enquiry whether Liberty herself would survive the rupture of its bonds. I believe that all that we have in prosperity and safety at home and in consideration and dignity abroad, has its source in that copious fountain of national, social, and personal felicity, the Union of the States. I profess myself a devotee to this object of my admiration and profound veneration: While the Union lasts, we have a great prospect of prosperity before us: and, when this Union breaks up, there is nothing in prospect, for me to look at, but what I regard with horror and despair. God forbid! Yes, Sir, God forbid, that I should live to see this cord broken; to behold that state of things which carries us back to disunion, calamity, and civil war! When my eyes shall be turned for the last time on the meridian sun, I hope I may see him shining brightly upon my united, free and happy Country. I hope I shall not live to see his beams falling upon the dispersed fragments of the structure of this once glorious Union. I hope that I may not see the flag of my Country, with its stars separated or obliterated, torn by commotion, smoking with the blood of civil war. I hope I may not see the standard raised of separate State rights, star against star, and stripe against stripe; but that the flag of the Union may keep its stars and its stripes corded and bound together in indissoluble ties. I hope I shall not see written, as its motto, *First* Liberty, and *then* Union. I hope I shall see no such delusive and deluded motto on the flag of that Country. I hope to see spread all over it, blazoned in letters of light, and proudly floating over Land and Sea that other sentiment, dear to my heart, "Union *and* Liberty, now and forever, one and inseparable."

The Salem Murder Trial, August 1830

During the night of April 6, 1830, in Salem, 82-year old Joseph White, merchant, shipowner, and retired sea captain, was murdered as he slept. He was wealthy, but no money or other valuables were taken. The town of some 14,000 souls reacted in panic. A vigilance committee of 27 prominent citizens was created, and took to itself the task of finding the murderer. Captain White's nearest relatives were a nephew, Stephen White, whose wife was a sister of Supreme Court Justice Joseph Story; and a niece, Mrs. Beckford, who was the old man's housekeeper. Mrs. Beckford's daughter Mary had also lived in the house until lately. She had married Joseph J. Knapp, Jr., master of one of Captain White's ships, but not regarded by White as a suitable husband for his grandniece. Knapp had been discharged and Mary evicted from the house. The young Knapps then went to live on Mrs. Beckford's farm at Wenham, where they were enjoying a visit from Mrs. Beckford on the night of the murder. Knapp's father, Joseph J., Sr., also a retired sea captain, was well and favorably known in Salem as a merchant. There were two other Knapp boys: Phippen who had recently been admitted to the Salem bar; and John Francis, known as Frank, whose reputation was somewhat less savory.

Also residents of the area were the brothers Richard and George Crowninshield, black sheep of a wealthy and public-spirited New England family. Their uncle Benjamin had been secretary of the navy under presidents Madison and Monroe; their uncle Jacob had served three terms in Congress. At this time the brothers were operating a machine shop in nearby Danvers. Frank Knapp and Dick Crowninshield were frequent companions; they had even been in jail together.

The vigilance committee, financed by Stephen White, began its investigation at Charleston prison, where several inmates were interviewed. Vague allusions and gossipy half-memories involved others, no longer in prison. An old plot, never carried out, to steal Captain White's "chest," supposed to contain substantial sums of money, was uncovered; then overheard conversations in which the old man's murder seemed to be an object. Parties to those conversations, according to the eavesdroppers, were the Crowninshields. The vigilance committee, des-

perate for action, had the brothers arrested on May 2. Three days later, largely on hearsay evidence, they were indicted by a grand jury.

The next break in the case came on May 14 when Captain Joseph Knapp, Sr. received a cryptic blackmail letter, posted from Belfast, Maine, and signed "Charles Grant." Baffled, Knapp showed the letter to Joseph, Jr. (for whom it was in fact intended), who called it "trash" and recommended it be turned over to the vigilance committee. The committee promptly dispatched a reply—and an agent to watch the Belfast post office. The man who called for the letter was arrested and brought in irons to Salem, but not before he had mailed two letters to the committee, charging Stephen White with responsibility for the crime. "Grant" turned out to be John C. R. Palmer, friend and former intimate of Dick Crowninshield. On the strength of Palmer's disclosures, Joe and Frank Knapp and two other alleged conspirators were arrested.

As the sordid tale now unfolded, Joe had conceived the plot, the purpose of which was to destroy Captain White's will. It was generally believed in Salem that the bulk of the considerable estate had been left to Stephen White and his children. Even so exact an observer as Joseph Story believed this (Story to DW, April 17, 1830, *Correspondence*, 3: 56), and apparently Joe Knapp never questioned it. He reasoned that if the will could be destroyed, and the old man should die intestate, his mother-in-law would share the estate equally with Stephen. He discussed it with his brother Frank, who arranged with his friend Dick Crowninshield to do the deed, for $1000. Joe opened a window for Dick's later use, then went home to Wenham. Dick sent Frank home to bed, but Frank could not wait for the word that all was well. He returned in time to be seen in neighboring Brown Street by several witnesses. George Crowninshield spent the evening with two women of easy virtue who would later so testify.

Joe had earlier removed and destroyed the will, but it proved to be an older instrument, later superseded. The will that was actually filed for probate in May divided the estate among many legatees.

On May 28 the Reverend Henry Colman injected himself into the case. The Knapps and the Whites were his parishioners. He had married Joe and Mary. But he was now a member of the vigilance committee and he believed his duty to be plain. He undertook to persuade Joe to confess. Ultimately he succeeded, even getting Frank's reluctant consent, by promising immunity in return for Joe's testimony at the trial. He had no authority to make any such promise, but hastily secured it from the attorney general. The fact that Joe had confessed could hardly have been concealed, even if the triumphant vigilance committee had not released a summary of it to the papers. Dated May 29, 1830, the confession is in the handwriting of the Reverend Colman, who

signed it along with Joseph Knapp, Jr. It is included in the pamphlet *Report of the Trial*, cited below, and with minor omissions is reprinted in Howard A. Bradley and James A. Winans, *Daniel Webster and the Salem Murder* (Columbia, Mo., 1956), pp. 222–224.

Phippen Knapp retained as counsel for his brothers two distinguished Boston attorneys, Franklin Dexter and William Howard Gardiner, who were to be assisted by young Robert Rantoul, Jr., of Salem, friend and Harvard classmate of Phippen's. Perhaps two weeks after Joe's confession, Dexter was visiting his clients at the Salem jail when Dick Crowninshield sent word he would like to see him. The Crowninshields were to be defended by Samuel Hoar of Concord, assisted by Ebenezer Shillaber and John Walsh of Salem, but Dexter obliged, since the request seemed urgent. Dick wanted to know if it was true that an accessory to a crime could not be tried unless a principal had first been convicted. He was assured that under Massachusetts law as it then stood such was the case. The next morning Crowninshield was found dead in his cell, hanged from a window bar with two silk handkerchiefs. As Dick understood the law he had thus saved the lives and freedom of his brother George and the two Knapps.

The Massachusetts legislature, meanwhile, had directed the supreme judicial court to hold a special session in Salem on the third Tuesday in July. On that day, the 20th, Chief Justice Isaac Parker presided over a grand jury. Summoned as a witness, Joe Knapp refused to testify. Without his testimony, or his confession which became inadmissible, the case for the prosecution was much weakened. By the same token Joe gave up his immunity, and prepared to stand trial with the others. Separate trials having been granted, the prosecution selected Frank for the first test of strength. Whoever stood first in the dock would now have to be tried as a principal, and Frank was the only one who could be placed anywhere near the scene at the appropriate time. Proving the case would be difficult at best—especially so for the attorney general, Perez Morton, who would have to overcome the infirmities of his 79 years, the heat of midsummer, and the efforts of unusually able defense counsel. On July 27, however—the day Frank's trial was to begin—proceedings were halted by announcement of the sudden death of the chief justice. The court adjourned for a week, which gave the state time to summon reinforcements.

It was probably Joseph Story's idea to seek Webster's aid, though the invitation came from Stephen White, accompanied by the offer of a $1000 fee. The attorney general added his weight to the invitation, and Webster reluctantly left the cool comfort of Marshfield to take charge of the prosecution. Fresh from the triumph of his debate with Hayne, he had little to gain and perhaps much to lose by thus accommodating

his friends. With the trial date now set for August 3, Webster had less than a week to master the intricate details of the case, and prepare for his unaccustomed role.

The first trial of Frank Knapp lasted ten days and ended in a hung jury. With Joe's confession now inadmissible, the prosecution had only the memory of Reverend Colman for many of the details. Hesitant witnesses would not say positively it had been Frank they saw loitering in Brown Street on that night, nor did they agree on what he had been wearing. The jury was discharged, a new jury impaneled and the second trial began the day after the first trial ended. This time the business took only six days. On August 20, 1830, John Francis Knapp was found guilty of conspiracy to murder Joseph White. He was sentenced to death by hanging and was executed on September 28.

The speech reproduced below is Webster's summation for the jury in the second trial. It has been called the greatest ever delivered to an American jury, and has been placed by connoisseurs of such things a notch above Demosthenes's Oration on the Crown. Granted these extravagances are a century and upwards in the past, they still contain more than a kernel of reality.

In November Joseph Jenkins Knapp, Jr. was tried as an accessory before the fact, with Webster again appearing for the prosecution, this time associated only with solicitor-general Daniel Davis. Joe was easily convicted and like his younger brother was hanged. In a subsequent trial George Crowninshield was acquitted, having proved an alibi. In this last of the Salem trials, Webster did not take part.

The text here reproduced is that included in the first volume of Webster's *Speeches and Forensic Arguments*, pp. 450–489. This version follows that published in the *Appendix to the Report of the Trial of John Francis Knapp, on an Indictment for Murder*, Salem, 1830. The "Appendix" version was a revision, undoubtedly improved, from one or more of the contemporary reports. The Boston *Daily Evening Transcript* devoted its entire issue of August 28 to Webster's summation, which might well have been the basis for his revision, but other publishers also reported the trial. It is probable that *Speeches and Forensic Arguments*, edited by Webster's nephew Charles Brickett Haddock, professor of rhetoric at Dartmouth, was in fact delayed to include this speech. The volume bears a copyright date of November 29, 1830, although we know from the correspondence that much of the work was done in the spring. (See DW to Haddock, March 4, 1830, *Correspondence*, 3: 22–24.) The speech is also published in John D. Lawson, ed., *American State Trials* (17 vols., St. Louis, 1914–1936), 7: 395–670.

The version that passed through Edward Everett's hands into *Works*,

6: 41–105 included various changes, most of them minor. Those regarded as of some significance are footnoted. The Everett version reappears in *Writings and Speeches,* 11: 41–105. The detailed work of Bradley and Winans, *Daniel Webster and the Salem Murder* (Columbia, Mo., 1956), reprints the text from the appendix to the trial report, essentially the same text that we have used here.

Gentlemen of the Jury:

I am little accustomed, gentlemen, to the part which I am now attempting to perform. Hardly more than once or twice has it happened to me to be concerned on the side of the government in any criminal prosecution whatever; and never, until the present occasion, in any case affecting life.

But I very much regret that it should have been thought necessary to suggest to you that I am brought here to "hurry you against the law and beyond the evidence."[1] I hope I have too much regard for justice, and too much respect for my own character, to attempt either; and were I to make such attempt, I am sure that in this court nothing can be carried against the law, and that gentlemen intelligent and just as you are, are not, by any power, to be hurried against the evidence. Though I could well have wished to shun this occasion, I have not felt at liberty to withhold my professional assistance, when it is supposed that I might be in some degree useful in investigating and discussing the truth respecting this most extraordinary murder. It has seemed to be a duty incumbent on me, as on every other citizen, to do my best and my utmost to bring to light the perpetrators of this crime. Against the prisoner at the bar, as an individual, I cannot have the slightest prejudice. I would not do him the smallest injury or injustice. But I do not affect to be indifferent to the discovery and the punishment of this deep guilt. I cheerfully share in the opprobrium, how much soever it may be, which is cast on those who feel and manifest an anxious concern that all who had a part in planning, or a hand in executing, this deed of midnight assassination, may be brought to answer for their enormous crime at the bar of public justice.

Gentlemen, it is a most extraordinary case. In some respects it has hardly a precedent anywhere; certainly none in our New England his-

1. Apparently an assertion made by Franklin Dexter, counsel for the defense. Bradley and Winans, p. 96, print an extract from Webster's summation at the first trial of John Francis Knapp, in which he exclaims, "It was . . . with some regret that I heard the learned counsel for the prisoner assert that I was brought here to hurry the jury beyond the evidence and against the law."

tory. This bloody drama exhibited no suddenly excited, ungovernable rage. The actors in it were not surprised by any lion-like temptation springing upon their virtue, and overcoming it, and overcoming it before resistance could begin. Nor did they do the deed to glut savage vengeance, or satiate long-settled and deadly hate. It was a cool, calculating, money-making murder. It was all "hire and salary, not revenge." It was the weighing of money against life; the counting out of so many pieces of silver against so many ounces of blood.

An aged man, without an enemy in the world, in his own house, and in his own bed, is made the victim of a butcherly murder for mere pay. Truly, here is a new lesson for painters and poets. Whoever shall hereafter draw the portrait of murder, if he will show it as it has been exhibited in an example where such example was last to have been looked for—in the very bosom of our New England society—let him not give it the grim visage of Moloch, the brow knitted by revenge, the face black with settled hate, and the bloodshot eye emitting livid fires of malice. Let him draw, rather, a decorous, smooth-faced, bloodless demon; a picture in *repose*, rather, than in *action*; not so much an example of human nature in its depravity, and in its paroxysms of *crime*, as an infernal nature, a fiend in the ordinary display and development of his character.

The deed was executed with a degree of self-possession and steadiness equal to the wickedness with which it was planned. The circumstances now clearly in evidence spread out the whole scene before us. Deep sleep had fallen on the destined victim, and on all beneath his roof. A healthful old man, to whom sleep was sweet, the first sound slumbers of the night held him in their soft but strong embrace. The assassin enters, through the window already prepared, into an unoccupied apartment. With noiseless foot he paces the lonely hall, half lighted by the moon. He winds up the ascent of the stairs and reaches the door of the chamber. Of this he moves the lock, by soft and continued pressure, till it turns on hinges, and he enters, and beholds his victim before him. The room was uncommonly open to the admission of light. The face of the innocent sleeper was turned from the murderer, and the beams of the moon, resting on the locks of his aged temple, showed him where to strike. The fatal blow is given, and the victim passes, without a struggle or a motion, from the repose of sleep to the repose of death! It is the assassin's purpose to make sure work, and he yet plies the dagger, though it was obvious that life had been destroyed by the blow of the bludgeon. He even raises the aged arm, that he may not fail in his aim at the heart, and replaces it again over the wounds of the poniard! To finish the picture, he explores the wrist for the pulse! He feels it, and ascertains that it beats no longer! It is accomplished. The deed is done. He retreats, retraces his steps to the window, passes out through it as he

came in, and escapes. He had done the murder. No eye has seen him; no ear has heard him. The *secret* is his own, and it is safe!

Ah, gentlemen, that was a dreadful mistake! Such a secret can be safe nowhere. The whole creation of God has neither nook nor corner where the guilty can bestow it and say it is safe. Not to speak of that eye which glances through all disguises, and beholds everything as in the splendor of noon, such secrets of guilt are never safe from detection, even by men. True it is, generally speaking, that "murder will out." True it is that Providence hath so ordained, and doth so govern things, that those who break the great law of Heaven by shedding man's blood seldom succeed in avoiding discovery. Especially in a case exciting so much attention as this, discovery must come, and will come, sooner or later. A thousand eyes turn at once to explore every man, every thing, every circumstance connected with the time and place; a thousand ears catch every whisper; a thousand excited minds intensely dwell on the scene, shedding all their light, and ready to kindle the slightest circumstance into a blaze of discovery. Meantime the guilty soul cannot keep its own secret. It is false to itself, or, rather, it feels an irresistible impulse of conscience to be true to itself. It labors under its guilty possession, and knows not what to do with it. The human heart was not made for the residence of such an inhabitant. It finds itself preyed on by a torment which it does not acknowledge to God or man. A vulture is devouring it, and it can ask no sympathy or assistance, either from heaven or earth. The secret which the murderer possesses soon comes to possess him, and, like the evil spirits of which we read, it overcomes him, and leads him whithersoever it will. He feels it beating at his heart, rising to his throat, and demanding disclosure. He thinks the whole world sees it in his face, reads it in his eyes, and almost hears its workings in the very silence of his thoughts. It has become his master. It betrays his discretion, it breaks down his courage, it conquers his prudence. When suspicions from without begin to embarrass him, and the net of circumstance to entangle him, the fatal *secret* struggles with still greater violence to burst forth. It must be confessed, *it will be* confessed; there is no refuge from confession but suicide, and suicide is confession.

Much has been said on this occasion, of the excitement which has existed and still exists, and of the extraordinary measures taken to discover and punish the guilty. No doubt there has been, and is, much excitement, and strange indeed were it, had it been otherwise. Should not all the peaceable and well-disposed naturally feel concerned, and naturally exert themselves to bring to punishment the authors of this secret assassination? Was it a thing to be slept upon or forgotten? Did you, gentlemen, sleep quite as quietly in your beds after this murder

as before? Was it not a case for rewards, for meetings, for committees, for the united efforts of all the good to find out a band of murderous conspirators, of midnight ruffians, and to bring them to the bar of justice and law? If this be excitement, is it an unnatural or an improper excitement?

It seems to me, gentlemen, that there are appearances of another feeling of a very different nature and character, not very extensive, I should hope, but still there is too much evidence of its existence. Such is human nature that some persons lose their abhorrence of crime in their admiration of its magnificent exhibitions. Ordinary vice is reprobated by them; but extraordinary guilt, exquisite wickedness, the high flights and poetry of crime seize on the imagination, and lead them to forget the depths of the guilt in admiration of the excellence of the performance, or the unequaled atrocity of the purpose. There are those in our day who have made great use of this infirmity of our nature, and by means of it done infinite injury to the cause of good morals. They have affected not only the taste, but I fear also the principles, of the young, the heedless and the imaginative, by the exhibition of interesting and beautiful monsters. They render depravity attractive, sometimes by the polish of its manners, and sometimes by its very extravagance, and study to show off crime under all the advantages of cleverness and dexterity. Gentlemen, this is an extraordinary murder, but it is still a murder. We are not to lose ourselves in wonder at its origin, or in gazing on its cool and skillful execution. We are to detect and to punish it; and while we proceed with caution against the prisoner, and are to be sure that we do not visit on his head the offenses of others, we are yet to consider that we are dealing with a case of most atrocious crime, which has not the slightest circumstance about it to soften its enormity. It is murder; deliberate, concerted, malicious murder.

Although the interest of this case may have diminished by the repeated investigation of the facts, still the additional labor which it imposes upon all concerned is not to be regretted if it should result in removing all doubts of the guilt of the prisoner.

The learned counsel for the prisoner has said truly that it is your individual duty to judge the prisoner; that it is your individual duty to determine his guilt or innocence; and that you are to weigh the testimony with candor and fairness. But much, at the same time, has been said, which, although it would seem to have no distinct bearing on the trial, cannot be passed over without some notice.

A tone of complaint so peculiar has been indulged as would almost lead us to doubt whether the prisoner at the bar, or the managers of this prosecution, are now on trial. Great pains have been taken to com-

plain of the *manner* of the prosecution.[2] We hear of getting up a case; of setting in motion trains of machinery; of foul testimony; of combinations to overwhelm the prisoner; of private prosecutors; that the prisoner is hunted, persecuted, driven to his trial; that everybody is against him; and various other complaints, as if those who would bring to punishment the authors of this murder were almost as bad as they who committed it.

In the course of my whole life, I have never heard before so much said about the particular counsel who happen to be employed; as if it were extraordinary that other counsel than the usual officers of the government should be assisting in the conducting of a case on the part of the government. In one of the last capital trials in this county, that of Jackman for the "Goodridge robbery"[3] (so called), I remember that the learned head of the Suffolk bar, Mr. [William] Prescott, came down in aid of the officers of the government. This was regarded as neither strange nor improper. The counsel for the prisoner in that case contented themselves with answering his arguments, as far as they were able, instead of carping at his presence.

Complaint is made that rewards were offered in this case, and temptations held out, to obtain testimony. Are not rewards always offered when great and secret offenses are committed? Rewards were offered in the case to which I alluded, and every other means taken to discover the offenders that ingenuity or the most persevering vigilance could suggest. The learned counsel have suffered their zeal to lead them to a strain of complaint at the manner in which the perpetrators of this crime were detected, almost indicating that they regard it as a positive injury to them to have found out their guilt. Since no man witnesses it, since they do not now confess it, attempts to discover it are half esteemed as officious intermeddling and impertinent inquiry.

It is said that here even a committee of vigilance was appointed. This is a subject of reiterated remark. The committee are pointed at as though they had been officiously intermeddling with the administration of justice. They are said to have been "laboring for months" against the prisoner. Gentlemen, what must we do in such a case? Are people to be dumb and still, through fear of overdoing? Is it come to this: that an effort cannot be made, a hand cannot be lifted, to discover the guilty, without its being said there is a combination to overwhelm innocence? Has the

2. Webster is referring to comments made by William H. Gardiner during the first trial, and Dexter during the second. See the Salem, 1830 edition of the *Report of the Trial of John Francis Knapp*, pp. 53–54; and the *Appendix*, pp. 9–10.

3. Webster acted as counsel for the defense in this case, argued in April, 1817. See "Defense of the Kennistons," *W & S*, 10: 173–193.

community lost all moral sense? Certainly, a community that would not be roused to action upon an occasion such as this was—a community which should not deny sleep to their eyes, and slumber to their eyelids, till they had exhausted all the means of discovery and detection—must indeed be lost to all moral sense, and would scarcely deserve protection from the laws. The learned counsel have endeavored to persuade you that there exists a prejudice against the persons accused of this murder. They would have you understand that it is not confined to this vicinity alone, but that even the legislature have caught this spirit; that, through the procurement of the gentleman here styled "private prosecutor," who is a member of the senate, a special session of this court was appointed for the trial of these offenders; that the ordinary movements of the wheels of justice were too slow for the purposes devised. But does not everybody see and know that it was a matter of absolute necessity to have a special session of the court? When or how could the prisoners have been tried without a special session? In the ordinary arrangement of the courts, but one week in a year is allotted for the whole court to sit in this county. In the trial of all capital offenses, a majority of the court, at least, is required to be present. In the trial of the present case alone, three weeks have already been taken up. Without such special session, then, three years would not have been sufficient for the purpose. It is answer sufficient to all complaints on this subject to say that the law was drawn by the late chief justice himself, to enable the court to accomplish its duties, and to afford the persons accused an opportunity for trial without delay.

Again, it is said that it was not thought of making Francis Knapp, the prisoner at the bar, a *principal* till after the death of Richard Crown-inshield, Jr.; that the present indictment is an afterthought; that "testimony was got up" for the occasion. It is not so. There is no authority for this suggestion. The case of the Knapps had not then been before the grand jury. The officers of the government did not know what the testimony would be against them. They could not, therefore, have determined what course they should pursue. They intended to arraign all as principals who should appear to have been principals, and all as accessories who should appear to have been accessories. All this could be known only when the evidence should be produced.

But the learned counsel for the defendant take a somewhat loftier flight still. They are more concerned, they assure us, for the law itself, than even for their client. Your decision in this case, they say, will stand as a precedent. Gentlemen, we hope it will. We hope it will be a precedent both of candor and intelligence, of fairness and of firmness; a precedent of good sense and honest purpose pursuing their investigation

discretely, rejecting loose generalities, exploring all the circumstances, weighing each, in search of truth, and embracing and declaring the truth when found.

It is said that "laws are made, not for the punishment of the guilty but for the protection of the innocent." This is not quite accurate, perhaps, but, if so, we hope they will be so administered as to give that protection. But who are the innocent whom the law would protect? Gentlemen, Joseph White was innocent. They are innocent who, having lived in the fear of God through the day, wish to sleep in His peace through the night, in their own beds. The law is established that those who live quietly may sleep quietly; that they who do no harm may feel none. The gentlemen can think of none that are innocent except the prisoner at the bar, not yet convicted. Is a proved conspirator to murder innocent? Are the Crowninshields and the Knapps innocent? What is innocence? How deep stained with blood, how reckless in crime, how deep in depravity may it be, and yet remain innocence? The law is made, if we would speak with entire accuracy, to protect the innocent by punishing the guilty. But there are those innocent out of court, as well as in; innocent citizens not suspected of crime, as well as innocent prisoners at the bar.

The criminal law is not founded in a principle of vengeance. It does not punish that it may inflict suffering. The humanity of the law feels and regrets every pain it causes, every hour of restraint it imposes, and, more deeply still, every life it forfeits. But it uses evil as the means of preventing greater evil. It seeks to deter from crime by the example of punishment. This is its true, main object. It restrains the liberty of the few offenders, that the many who do not offend may enjoy their own liberty. It forfeits the life of the murderer, that other murders may not be committed. The law might open the jails, and at once set free all persons accused of offenses, and it ought to do so if it could be made certain that no other offenses would hereafter be committed; because it punishes, not to satisfy any desire to inflict pain, but simply to prevent the repetition of crimes. When the guilty, therefore, are not punished, the law has so far failed of its purpose; the safety of the innocent is so far endangered. Every unpunished murder takes away something from the security of every man's life. And whenever a jury, through whimsical and ill-founded scruples, suffer the guilty to escape, they make themselves answerable for the augmented danger of the innocent.

We wish nothing to be strained against this defendant. Why, then, all this alarm? Why all this complaint against the manner in which crime is discovered? The prisoner's counsel catch at supposed flaws of evidence, or bad character of witnesses, without meeting the case. Do they

mean to deny the conspiracy? Do they mean to deny that the two Crown-inshields and the two Knapps were conspirators? Why do they rail against Palmer, while they do not disprove, and hardly dispute, the truth of any one fact sworn to by him? Instead of this, it is made a matter of sentimentality that Palmer has been prevailed upon to betray his bosom companions, and to violate the sanctity of friendship. Again I ask, why do they not meet the case? If the fact is out, why not meet it? Do they mean to deny that Captain White is dead? One should have almost supposed even that, from some of the remarks that have been made. Do they mean to deny the conspiracy? Or, admitting a conspiracy, do they mean to deny only that Frank Knapp, the prisoner at the bar, was abetting in the murder, being present, and so deny that he was a principal? If a conspiracy is proved, it bears closely upon every subsequent subject of inquiry. Why don't they come to the fact? Here the defense is wholly indistinct. The counsel neither take ground nor abandon it. They neither fly nor light—they hover. But they must come to a closer mode of contest. They must meet the facts, and either deny or admit them. Had the prisoner at the bar, then, a knowledge of this conspiracy or not? This is the question. Instead of laying out their strength in complaining of the *manner* in which the deed is discovered, of the extraordinary pains taken to bring the prisoner's guilt to light, would it not be better to show there was no guilt? Would it not be better to show that he had committed no crime? They say, and they complain, that the community feel a great desire that he should be punished for his crimes. Would it not be better to convince you that he has committed no crime?

Gentlemen, let us now come to the case. Your first inquiry on the evidence will be, was Captain White murdered in pursuance of a conspiracy, and was the defendant one of this conspiracy? If so, the second inquiry is, was he so connected with the murder itself as that he is liable to be convicted as a *principal*? The defendant is indicted as a *principal*. If not guilty, *as such*, you cannot convict him. The indictment contains three distinct classes of counts. In the *first*, he is charged as having done the deed with his own hand; in the *second*, as an aider and abettor to Richard Crowninshield, Jr., who did the deed; in the *third*, as an aider and abettor to some person unknown. If you believe him guilty on either of these counts, or in either of these ways, you must convict him.

It may be proper to say, as a preliminary remark, that there are two remarkable circumstances attending this trial. One is that Richard Crowninshield, Jr., the supposed immediate *perpetrator* of the murder, since his arrest, has committed suicide. He has gone to answer before a tribunal of perfect infallibility. The other is that Joseph Knapp, the supposed origin and planner of the murder, having once made a full

disclosure of the facts under a promise of indemnity, is, neverthless, not now a witness. Notwithstanding his disclosure and his promise of indemnity, he now refuses to testify. He chooses his original state, and now stands answerable himself when the time shall come for his trial. These circumstances it is fit you should remember in your investigation of the case.

Your decision may affect more than the life of this defendant. If he be not convicted as principal, no one can be. Nor can anyone be convicted of a participation in the crime as accessory. The Knapps and George Crowninshield will be again on the community. This shows the importance of the duty you have to perform, and to remind you of the care and wisdom necessary to be exercised in its performance. But certainly these considerations do not render the prisoner's guilt any clearer, nor enhance the weight of the evidence against him. No one desires you to regard consequences in that light. No one wishes anything to be strained or too far pressed against the prisoner. Still, it is fit you should see the full importance of the duty devolved upon you.

And now, gentlemen, in examining this evidence, let us begin at the beginning, and see, first, what we know independent of disputed testimony. This is a case of circumstantial evidence; and these circumstances, we think, are full and satisfactory. The case mainly depends upon them, and it is common that offenses of this kind must be proved in this way. Midnight assassins take no witnesses. The evidence of the *facts* relied on has been somewhat sneeringly denominated by the learned counsel "*circumstantial stuff*," but it is not such *stuff* as dreams are made of. Why does he not rend this *stuff*? Why does he not tear it away with the crush of his hand? He dismisses it a little too summarily. It shall be my business to examine this *stuff*, and try its cohesion.

The letter from Palmer at Belfast, is that no more than flimsy *stuff*?

The fabricated letters from Knapp to the committee and Mr. White, are nothing but *stuff*?

The circumstance that the housekeeper was away at the time the murder was committed, as it was agreed that she would be, is that, too, a useless piece of the same *stuff*?

The facts that the key of the chamber door was taken out and secreted, that the window was unbarred and unbolted, are these to be so slightly and so easily disposed of?

It is necessary, gentlemen, now to settle, at the commencement, the great question of a *conspiracy*. If there was none, or the defendant was not a party, then there is no evidence here to convict him. If there was a conspiracy, and he is proved to have been a party, then these two facts have a strong bearing on others, and all the great points of inquiry. The defendant's counsel take no distinct ground, as I have already said,

on this point, neither to admit nor to deny. They choose to confine themselves to a hypothetical mode of speech. They say, supposing there *was* a conspiracy, *non sequitur* that the prisoner is guilty as *principal*. Be it so. But still, if there was a conspiracy, and if he was a conspirator, and helped to plan the murder, this may shed much light on the evidence which goes to charge him with the execution of that plan.

We mean to make out the conspiracy, and that the defendant was a party to it, and then to draw all just inferences from these facts.

Let me ask your attention, then, in the first place, to those appearances, on the morning after the murder, which have a tendency to show that it was done in pursuance of a preconcerted plan of operation. What are they? A man was found murdered in his bed. No stranger had done the deed; no one unacquainted with the house had done it. It was apparent that somebody from within had opened, and somebody from without had entered. There had been there, obviously and certainly, concert and cooperation. The inmates of the house were not alarmed when the murder was perpetrated. The assassin had entered without any riot or any violence. He had found the way prepared for him. The house had been opened. The window was unbarred from within, and its fastening unscrewed. There was a lock on the door of the chamber in which Mr. White slept, but the key was gone. It had been taken away and secreted. The footsteps of the murderer were visible, out doors, tending towards the window. The plank by which he entered the window still remained. The road he pursued had been prepared for him. The victim was slain, and the murderer had escaped. Everything indicated that somebody *within* had cooperated with somebody *without*. Everything proclaimed that some of the inmates, or somebody having access to the house, had had a hand in the murder. On the face of the circumstances, it was apparent, therefore, that this was a premeditated, concerted, conspired murder. Who, then, were the conspirators? If not now found out, we are still groping in the dark, and the whole tragedy is still a mystery.

If the Knapps and the Crowninshields were not the conspirators in this murder, then there is a whole set of conspirators not yet discovered. Because, independent of the testimony of Palmer and Leighton, independent of all disputed evidence, we know from uncontroverted facts, that this murder was, and must have been, the result of concert and cooperation between two or more. We know it was not done without plan and deliberation. We see that whoever entered the house to strike the blow was favored and aided by someone who had been previously in the house, without suspicion, and who had prepared the way. This is concert; this is cooperation; this is conspiracy. If the Knapps and the Crowninshields, then, were not the conspirators, who were? Joseph

Knapp had a motive to desire the death of Mr. White, and that motive has been shown.

He was connected by marriage with the family of Mr. White. His wife was the daughter of Mrs. Beckford, who was the only child of a sister of the deceased. The deceased was more than eighty years old, and he had no children. His only heirs were nephews and nieces. He was expected to be possessed of a very large fortune, which would have descended, by law, to his several nephews and nieces in equal shares, or, if there was a will, then according to the will; but as Captain White had but two branches of heirs—the children of his brother, Henry White, and of Mrs. Beckford—according to the common idea each of these branches would have shared one-half of his property.

This popular idea is not legally correct; but it is common, and very probably was entertained by the parties. According to this, Mrs. Beckford, on Mr. White's death without a will, would have been entitled to one-half of Mr. White's ample fortune, and Joseph Knapp had married one of her three children. There was a will, and this will gave the bulk of the property to others; and we learn from Palmer that one part of the design was to destroy the will before the murder was committed. There had been a previous will, and that previous will was known or believed to have been more favorable than the other to the Beckford family; so that, by destroying the last will and destroying the life of the testator at the same time, either the first and more favorable will would be set up, or the deceased would have no will, which would be, as was supposed, still more favorable. But the conspirators not having succeeded in obtaining and destroying the last will, though they accomplished murder, but the last will being found in existence and safe, and that will bequeathing the mass of the property to others, it seemed at the time impossible for Joseph Knapp, as for anyone else, indeed, but the principal devisee, to have any motive which should lead to the murder. The key which unlocks the whole mystery is the knowledge of the intention of the conspirators to steal the will. This is derived from Palmer, and it explains all. It solves the whole marvel. It shows the motive actuating those against whom there is much evidence, but who, without the knowledge of this intention, were not seen to have had a motive. This intention is proved, as I have said, by Palmer; and it is so congruous with all the rest of the case—it agrees so well with all facts and circumstances—that no man could well withhold his belief, though the facts were stated by a still less credible witness. If one desirous of opening a lock turns over and tries a bunch of keys till he finds one that will open it, he naturally supposes he has found *the* key of *that* lock. So, in explaining circumstances of evidence which are apparently irreconcil-

able or unaccountable, if a fact be suggested which at once accounts for all and reconciles all, by whomsoever it may be stated, it is still difficult not to believe that such fact is the true fact belonging to the case. In this respect, Palmer's testimony is singularly confirmed. If he were false, then his ingenuity could not furnish us such clear exposition of strange appearing circumstances. Some truth not known before can alone do that.

When we look back, then, to the state of things immediately on the discovery of the murder, we see that suspicion would naturally turn at once, not to the heirs at law, but to those principally benefited by the will. They, and they alone, would be supposed or seem to have a direct object for wishing Mr. White's life to be terminated. And, strange as it may seem, we find counsel now insisting that, if no apology, it is yet mitigation of the atrocity of the Knapps' conduct in attempting to charge this foul murder on Mr. White, the nephew and principal devisee, that public suspicion was already so directed. As if assassination of character were excusable in proportion as circumstances may render it easy! Their endeavors, when they knew they were suspected themselves, to fix the charge on others, by foul means and by falsehood, is fair and strong proof of their own guilt. But more of that hereafter.

The counsel say that they might safely admit that Richard Crowninshield, Jr., was the perpetrator of this murder.

But how could they safely admit that? If that were admitted, everything else would follow. For why should Richard Crowninshield, Jr., kill Mr. White? He was not his heir nor his devisee; nor was he his enemy. What could be his motive? If Richard Crowninshield, Jr., killed Mr. White, he did it at someone's procurement, who himself had a motive; and who, having any motive, is shown to have had any intercourse with Richard Crowninshield, Jr., but Joseph Knapp, and this principally through the agency of the prisoner at the bar? It is the infirmity, the distressing difficulty, of the prisoner's case, that his counsel cannot and dare not admit what they yet cannot disprove, and what all must believe. He who believes, on this evidence, that Richard Crowninshield, Jr., was the immediate murderer, cannot doubt that both the Knapps were conspirators in that murder. The counsel, therefore, are wrong, I think, in saying they might safely admit this. The admission of so important and so connected a fact would render it impossible to contend further against the proof of the entire conspiracy, as we state it.

What, then, was this conspiracy? J. J. Knapp, Jr., desirous of destroying the will, and of taking the life of the deceased, hired a ruffian, who, with the aid of other ruffians, was to enter the house and murder him in his own bed.

As far back as January this conspiracy began. Endicott testifies to

a conversation with J. J. Knapp at that time, in which Knapp told him that Captain White had made a will, and given the principal part of his property to Stephen White. When asked how he knew, he said, "Black and white don't lie." When asked if the will was not locked up, he said, "There is such a thing as two keys to the same lock." And, speaking of the then late illness of Captain White, he said that Stephen White would not have been sent for if he had been there.

Hence it appears that, as early as January, Knapp had a knowledge of the will, and that he had access to it by means of false keys. The knowledge of the will, and an intent to destroy it, appear also from Palmer's testimony, a fact disclosed to him by the other conspirators. He says that he was informed of this by the Crowninshields on the 2d of April. But then it is said that Palmer is not to be credited; that, by his own confession, he is a felon; that he has been in the state prison in Maine; and, above all, that he was an inmate and associate with these conspirators themselves. Let us admit these facts; let us admit him to be as bad as they would represent him to be; still, in law, he is a competent witness. How else are the secret designs of the wicked to be proved but by their wicked companions, to whom they have disclosed them? The government does not select its witnesses. The conspirators themselves have chosen Palmer. He was the confidant of the prisoners. The fact, however, does not depend on his testimony alone. It is corroborated by other proof, and, taken in connection with the other circumstances, it has strong probability. In regard to the testimony of Palmer, generally, it may be said that it is less contradicted, in all parts of it, either by himself or others, than that of any other material witness, and that everything he has told has been corroborated by other evidence, so far as it was susceptible of confirmation. An attempt has been made to impair his testimony as to his being at the Halfway House on the night of the murder; you have seen with what success. Mr. Babb is called to contradict him. You have seen how little he knows, and even that not certainly; for he himself is proved to have been in an error by supposing him to have been at the Halfway House on the evening of the 9th of April. At that time he is proved to have been in Dustin's, in Danvers. If, then, Palmer, bad as he is, has disclosed the secrets of the conspiracy, and has told the truth, there is no reason why it should not be believed. Truth is truth, come whence it may, though it were even from the bottom of the bottomless pit.

The facts show that this murder had been long in agitation; that it was not a new proposition on the 2d of April; that it had been contemplated for five or six weeks before. Richard Crowninshield was at Wenham in the latter part of March, as testified by Starrett. Frank Knapp was at Danvers in the latter part of February, as testified by Allen.

Richard Crowninshield inquired whether Captain Knapp was about home when at Wenham. The probability is that they would open the case to Palmer as a new project. There are other circumstances that show it to have been some weeks in agitation. Palmer's testimony as to the transactions on the 2d of April is corroborated by Allen, and by Osborn's books. He says that Frank Knapp came there in the afternoon, and again in the evening. So the book shows. He says that Captain White had gone out to his farm on that day. So others prove. How could this fact, or these facts have been known to Palmer, unless Frank Knapp had brought the knowledge? And was it not the special object of this visit to give information of this fact, that they might meet him and execute their purpose on his return from the farm? The letter of Palmer, written at Belfast, has intrinsic marks of genuineness.[4] It was mailed at Belfast, May 13th. It states facts that he could not have known unless his testimony be true. This letter was not an afterthought; it is a genuine narrative. In fact, it says, "I know the business your brother Frank was transacting on the 2d of April." How could he have possibly known this unless he had been there? The "one thousand dollars that was to be paid"—where could he have obtained this knowledge? The testimony of Endicott, of Palmer, and these facts are to be taken together; and they most clearly show that the death of Captain White must have been caused by *somebody interested* in putting an end to his life.

As to the testimony of Leighton, as far as manner of testifying goes, he is a bad witness; but it does not follow from this that he is not to be believed. There are some strange things about him. It is strange that he should make up a story against Captain Knapp, the person with whom he lived; that he never voluntarily told anything;—all that he said is screwed out of him. But the story could not have been invented by him; his character for truth is unimpeached; and he intimated to another witness, soon after the murder happened, that he knew something he should not tell. There is not the least contradiction in his testimony, though he gives a poor account of withholding it. He says that he was extremely *bothered* by those who questioned him. In the main story that he relates he is universally consistent with himself. Some things are for him, and some against him. Examine the intrinsic probability of what he says. See if some allowance is not to be made for him on account of

4. Bradley and Winans' note here reads: "Dexter had the better of the argument as to the corroborative force of this letter. Palmer was right about the thousand dollars, as we learn from Joe's confession, but that confession was not evidence in this trial. There are several places in Webster's argument where he rests on the assumption that it was familiar to the jury."

his ignorance with things of this kind. It is said to be extraordinary that he should have heard just so much of the conversation, and no more; that he should have heard just what was necessary to be proved, nothing else. Admit that this is extraordinary; still, this does not prove it is not true. It is extraordinary that you twelve gentlemen should be called upon, out of all the men in the county to decide this case.[5] No one could have foretold this three weeks since. It is extraordinary that the first clue to this conspiracy should have been derived from information given by the father of the prisoner at the bar. And in every case that comes to trial there are many things extraordinary. The murder itself in this case is a most extraordinary one; but still we do not doubt its reality.

It is argued that this conversation between Joseph and Frank could not have been as Leighton testified, because they had been together for several hours before; this subject must have been uppermost in their minds, whereas this appears to have been the commencement of their conversation upon it. Now this depends altogether upon the tone and manner of the expression; upon the particular word in the sentence which was emphatically spoken. If he had said, "When did you *see* Dick, Frank?" this would not seem to be the beginning of the conversation.[6] With what emphasis it was uttered it is not possible to learn, and nothing therefore can be made of this argument. If this boy's testimony stood alone, it should be received with caution. And the same may be said of the testimony of Palmer. But they do not stand alone. They furnish a clue to numerous other circumstances, which, when known, react in corroborating what would have been received with caution until thus corroborated. How could Leighton have made up this conversation? "When did you see Dick?" "I saw him this morning." "When is he going to kill the old man?" "I don't know." "Tell him, if he don't do it soon, I won't pay him." Here is a vast amount in a few words. Had he wit enough to invent this? There is nothing so powerful as truth, and often

5. Bradley and Winans' note here reads: "It is certainly not remarkable that *some* twelve men should be made jurors. Walter's report on this point is more reasonable than Webster's revision." Walter is Lynde M. Walter (1799–1842), editor of the Boston *Daily Evening Transcript*.

6. Bradley and Winans' note here reads: "In the résumé of the first two hours of the speech printed in the Salem *Gazette*, appears a passage found neither in the *Transcript* version nor in Webster's revision: 'With regard to this dialogue, abrupt as it seemed upon repetition, Mr. Webster was not by any means sure that these words were the commencement. The jury well knew that it was by means of intonation alone that that point could be decided, and the witness was evidently incapable of transmitting that. By emphasizing thus: "When *is* Dick going to kill the old man?" it is plainly seen that it is but the repetition of an idea before expressed; and so it may be varied in half a dozen ways.' "

nothing so strange. It is not even suggested that the story was made for him. There is nothing so extraordinary in the whole matter as it would have been for this country boy to invent this story.

The acts of the parties themselves furnish strong presumption of their guilt. What was done on the receipt of the letter from Maine? This letter was signed by Charles Grant, Jr., a person not known to either of the Knapps, nor was it known to them that any other person besides the Crowninshields knew of the conspiracy. This letter, by the accidental omission of the word "Jr," fell into the hands of the father, when intended for the son. The father carried it to Wenham, where both the sons were. They both read it. Fix your eyes steadily on this part of the *"circumstantial stuff"* which is in the case, and see what can be made of it. This was shown to the two brothers on Saturday, the 15th of May. They, neither one of them, knew Palmer. And, if they had known him, they could not have known him to have been the writer of this letter. It was mysterious to them how anyone at Belfast could have had knowledge of this affair. Their conscious guilt prevented due circumspection. They did not see the bearing of its publication. They advised their father to carry it to the committee of vigilance, and it was so carried. On the Sunday following, Joseph began to think there might be something in it. Perhaps, in the meantime, he had seen one of the Crowninshields. He was apprehensive that they might be suspected. He was anxious to turn attention from their family. What course did he adopt to effect this? He addressed one letter, with a false name, to Mr. White, and another to the committee, and, to complete the climax of his folly, he signed the letter addressed to the committee, "Grant," the same name as that signed to the letter they then had from Belfast addressed to Knapp. It was in the knowledge of the committee that no person but the Knapps had seen this letter from Belfast, and that no other person knew its signature. It therefore must have been irresistibly plain to them that one of the Knapps must have been the writer of the letter received by the committee, charging the murder on Mr. White. Add to this the fact of its having been dated at Lynn, and mailed at Salem four days after it was dated, and who could doubt respecting it? Have you ever read or known of folly equal to this? Can you conceive of crime more odious and abominable? Merely to explain the apparent mysteries of the letter from Palmer, they excite the basest suspicions of a man who, if they were innocent, they had no reason to believe guilty, and who if they were guilty, they most certainly knew to be innocent. Could they have adopted a more direct method of exposing their own infamy? The letter to the committee has intrinsic marks of a knowledge of this transaction. It tells the *time* and the *manner* in which the murder was committed. Every line speaks the writer's condemnation. In attempting to divert

attention from his family, and to charge the guilt upon another, he indelibly fixes it upon himself.

Joseph Knapp requested Allen to put these letters into the post office, because, said he, "I wish to nip this silly affair in the bud." If this were not the order of an overruling Providence, I should say that it was the silliest piece of folly that was ever practiced. Mark the destiny of crime. It is ever obliged to resort to such subterfuges; it trembles in the broad light; it betrays itself in seeking concealment. He alone walks safely who walks uprightly. Who for a moment can read these letters and doubt of Joseph Knapp's guilt? The constitution of nature is made to inform against him. There is no corner dark enough to conceal him. There is no turnpike broad enough or smooth enough for a man so guilty to walk in without stumbling. Every step proclaims his secret to every passenger. His own acts come out to fix his guilt. In attempting to charge another with his *own crime*, he writes his *own confession*. To do away with the effect of Palmer's letter, signed "Grant," he writes his own letter and affixes to it the name of Grant. He writes in a disguised hand. But how could it happen that the same Grant should be in Salem that was in Belfast? This has brought the whole thing out. Evidently he did it, because he has adopted the same style. Evidently he did it, because he speaks of the price of blood, and of other circumstances connected with the murder, that no one but a conspirator could have known.[7]

Palmer says he made a visit to the Crowninshields on the 9th of April. George then asked him whether he had heard of the *murder*. Richard inquired whether he had heard the *music at Salem*. They said that *they were suspected*, that a committee had been appointed to search houses, and that they had melted up the dagger the day after the murder, because it would be a suspicious circumstance to have it found in their possession. Now, this committee was not appointed, in fact, until Friday evening. But this proves nothing against Palmer; it does not prove that George *did not tell him so;* it only proves that he gave a false reason for a fact. They had heard that they were suspected. How could they have heard this unless it were from the whisperings of their own consciences? Surely this rumor was not thus public.

About the 27th of April, another attempt is made by the Knapps to give a direction to public suspicion. They reported themselves to have been *robbed*, in passing from Salem to Wenham, near Wenham pond. They came to Salem and stated the particulars of the adventure. They described persons, their dress, size, and appearance, who had been *sus-*

7. According to Bradley and Winans, "At this point the court adjourned. The *Transcript* was the only paper that reported the remainder of Webster's speech."

pected of the murder. They would have it understood that the community was infested by a band of ruffians, and that *they* themselves were the particular objects of their vengeance. Now, this turns out to be all fictitious, all false.[8] Can you conceive of anything more enormous—any wickedness greater—than the circulation of such reports, than the allegation of crimes, if committed, capital? If no such thing—thus it reacts with double force upon themselves, and goes very far to show their guilt. How did they conduct on this occasion? Did they give information that they had been assaulted that night at Wenham? No such thing. They rested quietly on that night; they waited to be called on for the particulars of their adventure; they made no attempt to arrest the offenders—this was not their object. They were content to fill the thousand mouths of rumor, to spread abroad false reports, to divert the attention of the public from themselves; for they thought every man suspected them, because they knew they ought to be suspected.

The manner in which the compensation for this murder was paid is a circumstance worthy of consideration. By examining the facts and dates it will satisfactorily appear that Joseph Knapp paid a sum of money to Richard Crowninshield, in five-franc pieces, on the 24th of April.[9] On the 21st of April, Joseph Knapp received five hundred five-franc pieces as the proceeds of an adventure at sea. The remainder of this species of currency that came home in the vessel was deposited in a bank at Salem. On Saturday, the 24th of April, Frank and Richard rode to Wenham. They were there with Joseph an hour or more—appeared to be negotiating private business. Richard continued in the chaise. Joseph came to the chaise and conversed with him. These facts are proved by Hart and Leighton, and by Osborn's books. On Saturday evening, about this time, Richard Crowninshield is proved to have been at Wenham with another person, whose appearance corresponds with Frank, by Lummus. Can anyone doubt this being the same evening? What had Richard Crowninshield to do at Wenham with Joseph, unless it were business? He was there before the murder; he was there after the murder; he was there clandestinely, unwilling to be seen. If it were not upon this business, let it be told what it was for. Joseph Knapp could explain it. Frank Knapp might explain it. But they do not explain it, and the inference is against them.

Immediately after this, Richard passes five-franc pieces—on the same

8. Here Bradley and Winans note that "No evidence had been presented to support this assertion. Webster is resting again on the excluded confession of Joe."

9. A bit of editorializing creeps in- to Bradley and Winans' note here: "It will be seen that this is plain bluff if one scans the evidence. Webster is again making use of the jury's knowledge of Joe's confession."

evening, *one* to Lummus, *five* to Palmer—and, near this time, George passes *three* or *four* in Salem. This is extraordinary. It is an unusual currency. In ordinary business, few men would pass nine such pieces in the course of a year. If they were not received in this way, why not explain how they came by them? Money was not so flush in their pockets that they could not tell whence it came, if it honestly came there. It is extremely important to them to explain whence this money came, and they would do it if they could. If, then, the price of blood was paid at this time, in the presence and with the knowledge of this defendant, does not this prove him to have been connected with this conspiracy?

Observe, also, the effect on the mind of Richard of Palmer's being arrested and committed to prison; the various efforts he makes to discover the fact; the lowering, through the crevices of the rock, the pencil and paper for him to write upon; the sending two lines of poetry, with the request that he would return the corresponding lines; the shrill and peculiar whistle; the inimitable exclamations of "Palmer! Palmer! Palmer!" All these things prove how great was his alarm. They corroborate Palmer's story, and tend to establish the conspiracy. [10]

Joseph Knapp had a part to act in this matter. He must have opened the window, and secreted the key. He had free access to every part of the house; he was accustomed to visit there; he went in and out at his pleasure; he could do this without being suspected. He is proved to have been there the Saturday preceding.

If all these things, taken in connection, do not prove that Captain White was murdered in pursuance of a conspiracy, then the case is at an end.

Savary's testimony is wholly unexpected. He was called for a different purpose. When asked who the person was that he saw come out of Captain White's yard between three and four o'clock in the morning, he answered *Frank Knapp*. I am not clear this is not true. There may be many circumstances of importance connected with this, though we believe the murder to have been committed between ten and eleven o'clock. The letter to Dr. Barstow states it to have been done about *eleven o'clock*; it states it to have been done *with a blow on the head*, from a weapon loaded with lead. Here is too great a correspondence with reality not to have some meaning to it. Dr. Peirson was always of the opinion that the two classes of wounds were made with different instruments, and by different hands. It is possible that one class was inflicted at one time, and the other at another. It is possible that, on the last visit, the pulse might not have entirely ceased to beat, and then the finishing

10. Bradley and Winans think "it is difficult to see corroboration" for Palmer's story. They state their sus- picion that Webster added this story to the evidence for its dramatic effect.

stroke was given. It is said, when the body was discovered, some of the wounds weeped, while others did not. They may have been inflicted from mere wantonness. It was known that Captain White was accustomed to keep specie by him in his chamber. This perhaps may explain the last visit. It is proved that this defendant was in the habit of retiring to bed, and leaving it afterwards, without the knowledge of his family. Perhaps he did so on this occasion. We see no reason to doubt the fact; and it does not shake our belief that the murder was committed early in the night.

What are the probabilities as to the time of the murder? Mr. White was an aged man. He usually retired to bed at about half-past nine. He slept soundest in the early part of the night; usually awoke in the middle and latter parts; and his habits were perfectly well known. When would persons, with a knowledge of these facts, be most likely to approach him? Most certainly in the first hour of his sleep. This would be the safest time. If seen then going to or from the house, the appearance would be least suspicious. The earlier hour would, then, have been most probably selected.

Gentlemen, I shall dwell no longer on the evidence which tends to prove that there was a conspiracy, and that the prisoner was a conspirator. All the circumstances concur to make out this point. Not only Palmer swears to it, in effect, and Leighton, but Allen mainly supports Palmer, and Osborn's books lend confirmation, so far as possible from such a source. Palmer is contradicted in nothing, either by any other witness or any proved circumstance or occurrence. Whatever could be expected to support him does support him. All the evidence clearly manifests, I think, that there was a conspiracy; that it originated with Joseph Knapp; that defendant became a party to it, and was one of its conductors, from first to last. One of the most powerful circumstances is Palmer's letter from Belfast. The amount of this was a direct charge on the Knapps of the authorship of this murder. How did they treat this charge—like honest men, or like guilty men? We have seen how it was treated. Joseph Knapp fabricated letters, charging another person, and caused them to be put into the post office.

I shall now proceed on the supposition that it is proved that there was a conspiracy to murder Mr. White, and that the prisoner was party to it.

The second and the material inquiry is, *was the prisoner present at the murder, aiding and abetting therein*?

This leads to the legal question in the case. What does the law mean when it says, in order to charge him as a principal, "he must be present, aiding and abetting in the murder"?

In the language of the late chief justice: "It is not required that the abettor shall be actually upon the spot when the murder is committed, or even in sight of the more immediate perpetrator of the victim, to make him a principal. If he be at a distance, cooperating in the act, by watching to prevent relief, or to give an alarm, or to assist his confederate in escape, *having knowledge of the purpose and object of the assassin,* this, in the eye of the law, is being present, aiding and abetting, so as to make him a principal in the murder."[11]

"If he be at a *distance,* cooperating." This is not a *distance* to be measured by feet or rods. If the intent to lend aid combine with a knowledge that the murder is to be committed, and the person so intending be so situate that he can by any possibility lend this aid in any manner, then he is *present* in legal contemplation. He need not lend any actual aid,— to be ready to assist is assisting.

There are two sorts of murder. The distinction between them is of essential importance to bear in mind: (1) Murder in an affray, or upon sudden and unexpected provocation; (2) murder secretly, with a deliberate, predetermined intention to commit murder. Under the first class, the question usually is whether the offense be murder or manslaughter in the person who commits the deed. Under the second class, it is often a question whether others than he who actually did the deed were present, aiding and assisting thereto. Offenses of this kind ordinarily happen when there is nobody present except those who go on the same design. If a riot should happen in the court house, and one should kill another, this may be murder, or it may not, according to the intention with which it was done, which is always matter of fact, to be collected from the circumstances at the time. But in secret murders, premeditated and determined on, there can be no doubt of the murderous intention. There can be no doubt, if a person be present, knowing a murder is to be done, of his concurring in the act. His being there is a proof of his intent to aid and abet, else why is he there?

It has been contended that proof must be given that the person accused did actually afford aid,—did lend a hand in the murder itself,—and without this proof, although he may be near by, he may be presumed to be there for an innocent purpose; he may have crept silently there to hear the news, or from mere curiosity to see what was going on. Preposterous! Absurd! Such an idea shocks all common sense. A man is found to be a conspirator to do a murder; he has planned it; he has assisted in arranging the time, the place, and the means; and he is found in the place, and at the time, and yet it is suggested that he might

11. Parker made this statement in his address to the grand jury at the beginning of the trial. See the *Report of the Trial* (Salem, 1830), p. 6.

have been there, not for cooperation and concurrence, but from curiosity! Such an argument deserves no answer. It would be difficult to give it one in decorous terms. Is it not to be taken for granted that a man seeks to accomplish his own purposes? When he has planned a murder, and is present at its execution, is he there to forward or to thwart his own design? Is he there to assist, or there to prevent? But "curiosity!" He may be there from mere "curiosity!" Curiosity to witness the success of the execution of his own plan of murder! The very walls of a court house ought not to stand, the plowshare should run through the ground it stands on, where such an argument could find toleration.

It is not necessary that the abettor should actually lend a hand,—that he should take a part in the act itself. If he be present ready to assist, that is assisting. Some of the doctrines advanced would acquit the defendant, though he had gone to the bedchamber of the deceased, though he had been standing by when the assassin gave the blow. This is the argument we have heard today.

[The court here said they did not so understand the argument of the counsel for defendant. Mr. Dexter said, The intent and power alone must cooperate.]

No doubt the law is that being ready to assist is assisting, if he has the power to assist, in case of need. It is so stated by Foster, who is a high authority. "If A. happeneth to be present at a murder, for instance, and taketh no part in it, nor endeavoreth to prevent it, nor apprehendeth the murderer, nor levyeth hue and cry after him, this strange behavior of his, though highly criminal, will not of itself render him either principal or accessory." "But if a fact amounting to murder should be committed in prosecution of some unlawful purpose, *though it were but a bare trespass*, to which A., in the case last stated, had consented, and he had gone in order to give assistance, if need were, for carrying it into execution, this would have amounted to murder in him, and in every person present and joining with him." "If the fact was committed in prosecution of the original purpose, *which was unlawful*, the whole party will be involved in the guilt of him who gave the blow; for in combinations of this kind, the mortal stroke, though given by one of the party, is considered in the eye of the law, and of sound reason too, as given by every individual present and abetting. The person actually giving the stroke is no more than the hand or instrument by which the others strike." [12] The author, in speaking of being present, means actual presence; not *actual* in opposition to *constructive*, for the law knows

12. Sir Michael Foster, *Report of Some Proceedings on the Commission . . . for the Trial of the Rebels in the Year 1746 . . . and of Other Crown Cases* (Oxford, 1762), Discourse 3, Ch. 1, section 5, 6, pp. 350–351.

no such distinction. There is but one presence, and this is the situation from which aid, or supposed aid, may be rendered. The law does not say where he is to go, or how near he is to go, but somewhere he may give assistance, or where the perpetrator may suppose that he may be assisted by him. Suppose that he is acquainted with the design of the murderer, and has a knowledge of the time when it is to be carried into effect, and goes out with a view to render assistance, if need be; why, then, even though the murderer does not know of this, the person so going out will be an abettor in the murder.

It is contended that the prisoner at the bar could not be a principal, he being in Brown Street, because he could not there render assistance; and you are called upon to determine this case, according as you may be of opinion whether Brown Street was or was not a suitable, convenient, well-chosen place to aid in this murder. This is not the true question. The inquiry is not whether you would have selected this place in preference to all others, or whether you would have selected it at all. If they chose it, why should we doubt about it? How do we know the use they intended to make of it, or the kind of aid that he was to afford by being there? The question for you to consider is, did the defendant go into Brown Street *in aid of this murder*? Did he go there by agreement, —by appointment with the perpetrator? If so, everything else follows. The main thing—indeed the only thing—is to inquire whether he was in Brown Street by appointment with Richard Crowninshield. It might be to keep general watch; to observe the lights, and advise as to time of access; to meet the prisoner on his return, to advise him as to his escape; to examine his clothes, to see if any marks of blood; to furnish exchange of clothes, or new disguise, if necessary; to tell him through what streets he could safely retreat, or whether he could deposit the club in the place designed; or it might be without any distinct object, but merely to afford that encouragement which would be afforded from Richard Crowninshield's consciousness that he was near. It is of no consequence whether, in your opinion, the place was well chosen, or not, to afford aid. If it was so chosen—if it was by appointment that he was there—it is enough. Suppose Richard Crowninshield, when applied to to commit the murder, had said, "I won't do it unless there can be someone near by to favor my escape. I won't go unless you will stay in Brown Street. Upon the gentleman's argument, he would not be an aider and abettor in the murder, because the place was not well chosen, though it is apparent that the being in the place chosen was a condition without which the murder would never have happened.

You are to consider the defendant as one in the league, in the combination, to commit the murder. If he was there by appointment with

the perpetrator, he is an abettor. The concurrence of the perpetrator in his being there is proved by the previous evidence of the conspiracy. If

The perpetrator would derive courage and strength and confidence from the knowledge of the fact that one of his associates was near by. Richard Crowninshield, for any purpose whatsoever, made it a condition of the agreement that Frank Knapp should stand as *backer*, then Frank Knapp was an aider and abettor, no matter what the aid was, or what sort it was or degree, be it ever so little, even if it were to judge of the hour when it was best to go, or to see when the lights were extinguished, or to give an alarm if anyone approached. Who better calculated to judge of these things than the murderer himself? And, if he so determined them, that is sufficient.

Now as to the facts. Frank Knapp knew that the murder was that night to be committed. He was one of the conspirators; he knew the object; he knew the time. He had that day been to Wenham to see Joseph, and probably to Danvers to see Richard Crowninshield, for he kept his motions secret. He had that day hired a horse and chaise of Osborn and attempted to conceal the purpose for which it was used. He had intentionally left the *place* and the *price* blank on Osborn's books. He went to Wenham by the way of Danvers. He had been told the week before to hasten Dick. He had seen the Crowninshields several times within a few days. He had a saddle horse the Saturday night before. He had seen Mrs. Beckford at Wenham, and knew she would not return that night. She had not been away before for six weeks, and probably would not soon be again. He had just come from there. Every day, for the week previous, he had visited one or other of these conspirators, save Sunday, and then probably he saw them in town. When he saw Joseph on the 6th, Joseph had prepared the house, and would naturally tell him of it. There were constant communications between them; daily and nightly visitations; too much knowledge of these parties and this transaction to leave a particle of doubt on the mind of anyone that Frank knew that the murder was to be committed this night. The hour was come, and he knew it. If so, and he was in Brown Street without explaining why he was there, can the jury for a moment doubt whether he was there to countenance, aid, or support, or for curiosity alone, or to learn how the wages of sin and death were earned by the perpetrator?

[Here Mr. Webster read the law from Hawkins,—1 Hawk. 204, lib. 1, c. 32, sec. 7.] [13]

13. William Hawkins, *A Treatise of the Pleas of the Crown* (1788). The correct citation here is actually chapter 32, section 6. In discussing the case of a wife who procures someone to murder her husband, the passage states that "if the wife . . . be either actually present . . . or present only

If he was in Brown Street, he could have been there for no other purpose. If there for this purpose, then he was, in the language of the law, *present,* aiding and abetting in the murder.

His interest lay in being somewhere else. If he had nothing to do with the murder, no part to act, why not stay at home? Why should he jeopard his own life if it was not agreed that he should be there? He would not voluntarily go where the very place would probably cause him to swing if detected. We would not voluntarily assume the place of danger. His taking this place proves that he went to give aid. His staying away would have made an alibi. If he had nothing to do with the murder, he would be at home, where he could prove his alibi. He knew he was in danger, because he was guilty of the conspiracy, and, if he had nothing to do, would not expose himself to suspicion or detection.

Did the prisoner at the bar countenance this murder? Did he concur, or did he nonconcur, in what the perpetrator was about to do? Would he have tried to shield him? Would he have furnished his cloak for protection? Would he have pointed out a safe way of retreat? As you would answer these questions, so you should answer the general question whether he was there *consenting to the murder*, or whether he was there *a spectator only.*

One word more on this *presence*, called *constructive presence*. What aid is to be rendered? Where is the line to be drawn between acting and omitting to act? Suppose he had been in the house, suppose he had followed the perpetrator to the chamber, what could he have done? This was to be a murder by stealth. It was to be a secret assassination. It was not their purpose to have an open combat; they were to approach their victim unawares, and silently give the fatal blow. But if he had been in the chamber, no one can doubt that he would have been an abettor, because of his presence and ability to render services, if needed. What service could he have rendered if there? Could he have helped him fly? Could he have facilitated his retreat on the first alarm? Surely this was a case where there was more safety in going alone than with another; where company would only embarrass. Richard Crowninshield would prefer to go alone. He knew his errand too well. His nerves needed no collateral support. He was not the man to take with him a trembling companion. He would prefer to have his aid at a distance. He would not wish to be embarrassed by his presence. He would prefer to have him out of the house. He would prefer that he should be in Brown Street. But whether in the chamber, in the house, in the garden, or in

---

in judgment of law," and her presence "encourages or emboldens the murderer to commit the fact," then she is a principal as much as the murderer.

the street, whatsoever is aiding in *immediate presence* is aiding in *constructive presence;* anything that is aid in one case is aid in the other.

[Here Mr. Webster read the law from Hawkins,—4 Hawk. 201, lib. 4, c. 29, sec. 8.] [14]

If, then, the aid be anywhere, that emboldens the perpetrator, that affords him hope or confidence in his enterprise, it is the same as though the person stood at his elbow with his sword drawn. His being there ready to act, with the power to act—that is what makes him an abettor.

[Here Mr. Webster referred to the cases of Kelly, of Hyde, and others, cited by the counsel for the defendant, and showed that they did not militate with the doctrine for which he contended. The difference is, in those cases there was open violence. This was a case of secret assassination. The aid must meet the occasion. Here no *acting* was necessary, but watching concealment of escape, management.]

What are the facts in relation to his presence? Frank Knapp is proved a conspirator; proved to have known that the deed was now to be done. Is it not probable that he was in Brown Street to concur in the murder? There were four conspirators. It was natural that some of them would go with the perpetrator. Richard Crowninshield was to be the perpetrator; he was to give the blow. No evidence of any casting of the parts for the others. The defendant would probably be the man to take the second part. He was fond of exploits; he was accustomed to the use of sword canes and dirks. If any aid was required, he was the man to give it. At least there is no evidence to the contrary of this.

Aid could not have been received from Joseph Knapp or from George Crowninshield. Joseph Knapp was at Wenham, and took good care to prove that he was there. George Crowninshield has proved satisfactorily where he was,—that he was in other company, such as it was, until eleven o'clock. This narrows the inquiry. This demands of the prisoner to show that if he was not in this place, where he was. It calls on him loudly to show this, and to show it truly. If he could show it, he would do it. If he don't tell, and that truly, it is against him. The defense of an alibi is a double-edged sword. He knew that he was in a situation that he might be called upon to account for himself. If he had had no particular appointment or business to attend to, he would have taken care to have been able so to account. He would have been out of town,

---

14. This passage states that an abettor may be considered a principal to a felony if the perpetrator of the crime is encouraged and emboldened by the hope of the abettor's presence and assistance. It also states that if people have combined together to commit a murder, all of the company are equally principals, even though at the time some of them may have been distant from the scene of the crime.

or in some good company. Has he accounted for himself on that night to your satisfaction?

The prisoner has attempted to prove an alibi in two ways: In the first place, by four young men with whom he says he was in company, on the evening of the murder, from seven o'clock till near ten o'clock. This depends upon the *certainty of the night*. In the second place, by his family, from ten o'clock afterwards. This depends upon the *certainty of the time of the night*. These two classes of proof have no connection with each other. One may be true, and the other false; or they may both be true, or both be false. I shall examine this testimony with some attention, because, on a former trial, it made more impression on the minds of the court than on my mind. I think, when carefully sifted and compared, it will be found to have in it more *plausibility* than *reality*.

Mr. Page testifies that, on the evening of the 6th of April, he was in company with Burchmore, Balch, and Forrester, and that he met the defendant about seven o'clock, near the Salem Hotel; that he afterwards met him at Remond's, about nine o'clock, and that he was in company with him a considerable part of the evening. This young gentleman is a member of college, and says that he came in town the Saturday evening previous; that he is now able to say that it was the night of the murder when he walked with Frank Knapp, from the recollection of the fact that he called himself to an account, on the morning after the murder, as was natural for men to do when an extraordinary occurrence happens. Gentlemen, this kind of evidence is not satisfactory; general impressions as to time are not to be relied on. If I were called upon to state the particular day on which any witness testified in this cause, I could not do it. Every man will notice the same thing in his own mind. There is no one of these young men that could give an account of himself for any *other* day in the month of April. They are made to remember the fact, and then they think they remember the time. He has no means of knowing it was Tuesday, more than any other time. He did not know it at first; he could not know it afterwards. He says he called himself to an account. This has no more to do with the murder than with the man in the moon. Such testimony is not worthy to be relied on in any forty-shilling case. What occasion had he to call himself to an account? Did he suppose that he should be suspected? Had he an intimation of this conspiracy?

Suppose, gentlemen, you were either of you asked where you were, or what you were doing, on the fifteenth day of June. You could not answer that question without calling to mind some event to make it certain. Just as well may you remember on what you dined on each day of the year past. Time is identical. Its subdivisions are all alike. No man knows

one day from another, or one hour from another, but by some fact connected with it. Days and hours are not visible to the senses, nor to be apprehended and distinguished by the understanding. The flow of time known only by something which marks it; and he who speaks of the date of occurrences with nothing to guide his recollection speaks at random, and is not to be relied on. This young gentleman remembers the facts and occurrences; he knows nothing why they should not have happened on the evening of the 6th; but he knows no more. All the rest is evidently conjecture or impression.

Mr. White informs you that he told him he could not tell what night it was. The first thoughts are all that are valuable in such case. They miss the mark by taking second aim.

Mr. Balch believes, but is not sure, that he was with Frank Knapp on the evening of the murder. He has given different accounts of the time. He has no means of making it certain. All he knows is that it was some evening before Fast but whether Monday, Tuesday, or Saturday, he cannot tell.

Mr. Burchmore says, to the best of his belief, it was the evening of the murder. Afterwards he attempts to speak positively, from recollecting that he mentioned the circumstances to William Peirce as he went to the Mineral Spring on Fast Day. Last Monday morning he told Colonel Putnam he could not fix the time. This witness stands in a much worse plight than either of the others. It is difficult to reconcile all he has said with any belief in the accuracy of his recollections.

Mr. Forrester does not speak with any certainty as to the night, and it is very certain that he told Mr. Loring and others that he did not know what night it was.

Now, what does the testimony of these four young men amount to? The only circumstances by which they approximate to an identifying of the night is that three of them say it was cloudy. They think their walk was either on Monday or Tuesday evening, and it is admitted that Monday evening was clear, whence they draw the inference that it must have been Tuesday.

But, fortunately, there is one *fact* disclosed in their testimony that settles the question. Balch says that on the evening, whenever it was that he saw the prisoner, the prisoner told him he was going out of town on horseback for a distance of about twenty minutes' ride, and that he was going to get a horse at Osborn's. This was about seven o'clock. At about nine, Balch says he saw the prisoner again, and was then told by him that he had had his ride, and had returned. Now it appears by Osborn's books that the prisoner had a saddle horse from his stable, not on Tuesday evening, the night of the murder, but on the Saturday evening previous. This fixes the time about which these young

men testify, and is a complete answer and refutation of the attempted alibi on Tuesday evening.

I come now to speak of the testimony adduced by the defendant to explain where he was after ten o'clock on the night of the murder. This comes chiefly from members of the family—from his father and brothers.

It is agreed that the affidavit of the prisoner should be received as evidence of what his brother, Samuel H. Knapp, would testify if present. Samuel H. Knapp says that, about ten minutes past ten o'clock, his brother, Frank Knapp, on his way to bed, opened his chamber door, made some remarks, closed the door, and went to his chamber, and that he did not hear him leave it afterwards. How is this witness able to fix the time at ten minutes past ten? There is no circumstance mentioned by which he fixes it. He had been in bed, probably asleep, and was aroused from his sleep by the opening of the door. Was he in a situation to speak of time with precision? Could he know, under such circumstances, whether it was ten minutes past ten or ten minutes before eleven when his brother spoke to him? What would be the natural result in such a case? But we are not left to conjecture this result. We have positive testimony on this point. Mr. Webb tells you that Samuel told him, on the 8th of June, "that he did not know what time his brother Frank came home, and that he was not at home when *he* went to bed." You will consider the testimony of Mr. Webb as indorsed upon this affidavit, and, with this indorsement upon it, you will give it its due weight. This statement was made to him after Frank was arrested.

I come to the testimony of the father.[15] I find myself incapable of speaking of him or his testimony with severity. Unfortunate old man! Another Lear, in the conduct of his children; another Lear, I fear, in the effect of his distress upon his mind and understanding. He is brought here to testify, under circumstances that disarm severity, and call loudly for sympathy. Though it is impossible not to see that his story cannot be

15. Bradley and Winans' note here reads: "In both his cross-examination and in his summation, Webster deals gently with Frank's father. Plainly he wishes to avoid the appearance of severity with this unfortunate man (although Walter's report of Webster's speech in the Boston *Transcript* does suggest perjury more plainly). Probably Webster was genuinely sorry for a man ruined in business and with two sons in the shadow of the gallows, and he probably realized that a ruthless attack might turn sympathy the wrong way. Webster prefers to say in elegant language that Mr. Knapp is soft in the head. Knapp, whose age Webster stresses, was fifty-seven years old—eight years older than Webster. It is difficult to find any evidence of mental degeneration in his testimony." According to the *Transcript* Webster actually says "I will not cast a doubt over the integrity of this poor old man, but gentlemen it is impossible to believe that what he says is true."

credited, yet I am not able to speak of him otherwise than in sorrow and grief. Unhappy father! he strives to remember, perhaps persuades himself that he does remember, that on the evening of the murder he was himself at home at ten o'clock. He thinks, or seems to think, that his son came in at about five minutes past ten. He fancies that he remembers his conversation; he thinks he spoke of bolting the door; he thinks he asked the time of night; he seems to remember his then going to his bed. Alas! these are but the swimming fancies of an agitated and distressed mind. Alas! they are but the dreams of hope, its uncertain lights, flickering on the thick darkness of parental distress. Alas! the miserable father knows nothing, in reality, of all these things.

Mr. Shepard says that the first conversation he had with Mr. Knapp was soon after the murder, and *before* the arrest of his sons. Mr. Knapp says it *was after* the arrest of his sons. His own fears led him to say to Mr. Shepard that his "son Frank was at home that night, and so Phippen told him," or "as Phippen told him." Mr. Shepard says that he was struck with the remark at the time; that it made an unfavorable impression on his mind. He does not tell you what that impression was, but when you connect it with the previous inquiry he had made, whether Frank had continued to associate with the Crowninshields, and recollect that the Crowninshields were then known to be suspected of this crime, can you doubt what this impression was? Can you doubt as to the fears he then had?

This poor old man tells you that he was greatly perplexed at the time; that he found himself in embarrassed circumstances; that on this very night he was engaged in making an assignment of his property to his friend, Mr. Shepard. If ever charity should furnish a mantle for error, it should be here. Imagination cannot picture a more deplorable, distressed condition.

The same general remarks may be applied to his conversation with Mr. Treadwell as have been made upon that with Mr. Shepard. He told him that he believed Frank was at home about the usual time. In his conversations with either of these persons, he did not pretend to know, of his own knowledge, the time that he came home. He now tells you positively that he recollects the time, and that he so told Mr. Shepard. He is directly contradicted by both these witnesses, as respectable men as Salem affords.

This idea of an alibi is of recent orgin. Would Samuel Knapp have gone to sea if it were then thought of? His testimony, if true, was too important to be lost. If there be any truth in this part of the alibi, it is so near in point of time that it cannot be relied on. The mere variation of half an hour would avoid it. The mere variations of different timepieces would explain it.

Has the defendant proved where he was on that night? If you doubt about it, there is an end of it. The burden is upon him to satisfy you beyond all reasonable doubt.[16] Osborn's books, in connection with what the young men state, are conclusive, I think, on this point. He has not, then, accounted for himself. He has attempted it, and has failed. I pray you to remember, gentlemen, that this is a case in which the prisoner would, more than any other, be rationally able to account for himself on the night of the murder if he could do so. He was in the conspiracy, he knew the murder was then to be committed, and, if he himself was to have no hand in its actual execution, he would of course, as a matter of safety and precaution, be somewhere else, and be able to prove afterwards that he had been somewhere else. Having this motive to prove himself elsewhere, and the power to do it if he were elsewhere, his failing in such proof must necessarily leave a strong inference against him.

But, gentlemen, let us now consider what is the evidence produced on the part of the government to prove that John Francis Knapp, the prisoner at the bar, was in Brown Street on the night of the murder. This is a point of vital importance in this cause. Unless this be made out, beyond reasonable doubt, the law of *presence* does not apply to the case. The government undertakes to prove that he was present, aiding in the murder, by proving that he was in Brown Street for this purpose. Now, what are the undoubted facts? They are that two persons were seen in that street, at several times during that evening, under suspicious circumstances,—under such circumstances as induced those who saw them to watch their movements. Of this there can be no doubt. Mirick saw a man standing at the post opposite his store from fifteen minutes before nine until twenty minutes after, dressed in a full frock coat, glazed cap, and so forth, in size and general appearance answering to the prisoner at the bar. This person was waiting there, and, whenever any one approached him, he moved to and from the corner, as though he would avoid being suspected or recognized. Afterwards, two persons were seen by Webster walking in Howard Street with a slow, deliberate movement that attracted his attention. This was about half-past nine. One of these he took to be the prisoner at the bar; the other he did not know.

16. Bradley and Winans' note here reads: "The burden is never on the prisoner to prove anything beyond all reasonable doubt. *Commonwealth* v. *York,* 9 Met. (Mass.) 95, 116–117. The burden is upon the prosecution to prove beyond a reasonable doubt every 'constituent element of the crime,' and in this case presence is a constituent element. In *Massachusetts Trial Evidence,* Norman and Houghton, section 959, we read: 'In the case of an alibi, if the evidence of the defendant is such that, taken with the other evidence, the jury have reasonable doubt that the defendant was present, they must acquit him.' "

About half-past ten a person is seen sitting on the ropewalk steps, wrapped in a cloak. He drops his head when passed, to avoid being known. Shortly after, two persons are seen to meet in this street, without ceremony or salutation, and in a hurried manner to converse for a short time, then to separate, and run off with great speed. Now, on this same night, a gentleman is slain—murdered in his bed—his house being entered by stealth from without, and his house situated within three hundred feet of this street. The windows of his chamber were in plain sight from this street. A weapon of death is afterwards found in a place where these persons were seen to pass, in a retired place, around which they had been seen lingering. It is now known that this murder was committed by a conspiracy of four persons, conspiring together for this purpose. No account is given who these suspicious persons thus seen in Brown Street and its neighborhood were. Now I ask you gentlemen, whether you or any man can doubt that this murder was committed by the persons who were thus in and about Brown Street. Can any person doubt that they were there for purposes connected with this murder? If not for this purpose, what were they there for? When there is a cause so near at hand, why wander into conjecture for an explanation? Common sense requires you to take the nearest adequate cause for a known effect. Who were these suspicious persons in Brown Street? There was something extraordinary about them; something noticeable, and noticed at the time; something in their appearance that aroused suspicion. And a man is found the next morning murdered in the near vicinity.

Now, so long as no other account shall be given of those suspicious persons, so long the inference must remain irresistible that they were the murderers. Let it be remembered that it is already shown that this murder was the result of conspiracy and of concert; let it be remembered that the house, having been opened from within, was entered by stealth from without; let it be remembered that Brown Street, where these persons were repeatedly seen under such suspicious circumstances, was a place from which every occupied room in Mr. White's house is clearly seen; let it be remembered that the place, though thus very near to Mr. White's house, was a retired and lonely place; and let it be remembered that the instrument of death was afterwards found concealed very near the same spot. Must not every man come to the conclusion that these persons thus seen in Brown Street were the murderers? Every man's own judgment, I think, must satisfy him that this must be so. It is a plain deduction of common sense. It is a point on which each one of you may reason like a Hale or a Mansfield. The two occurrences explain each other. The murder shows why these persons were thus lurking, at that hour, in Brown Street, and their lurking in Brown Street shows who committed the murder.

If, then, the persons in and about Brown Street were the plotters and executers of the murder of Captain White, we know who they were, and you know that *there* is one of them.

This fearful concatenation of circumstances puts him to an account. He was a conspirator. He had entered into this plan of murder. The murder is committed, and he is known to have been within three minutes' walk of the place. He must account for himself. He has attempted this, and failed. Then, with all these general reasons to show he was actually in Brown Street, and his failures in his alibi, let us see what is the direct proof of his being there. But first let me ask, is it not very remarkable that there is no attempt to show where Richard Crowninshield, Jr., was on that night? We hear nothing of him. He was seen in none of his usual haunts about the town. Yet, if he was the actual perpetrator of the murder, which nobody doubts, he was in the town somewhere. Can you therefore entertain a doubt that he was one of the prisoners seen in Brown Street? And as to the prisoner, you will recollect that, since the testimony of the young men has failed to show where he was that evening, the last we hear or know of him on the day preceding the murder is that at four o'clock P.M. he was at his brother's in Wenham. He had left home, after dinner, in a manner doubtless designed to avoid observation, and had gone to Wenham, probably by way of Danvers. As we hear nothing of him after four o'clock P.M. for the remainder of the day and evening; as he was one of the conspirators; as Richard Crowninshield, Jr., was another; as Richard Crowninshield, Jr., was in town in the evening, and yet seen in no usual place of resort—the inference is very fair that Richard Crowninshield, Jr., and the prisoner were together, acting in execution of their conspiracy. Of the four conspirators, J. J. Knapp, Jr., was at Wenham, and George Crowninshield has been accounted for, so that, if the persons seen in Brown Street were the murderers, one of them must have been Richard Crowninshield, Jr., and the other must have been the prisoner at the bar.

Now as to the proof of his identity with one of the persons seen in Brown Street.

Mr. Mirick, a cautious witness, examined the person he saw closely, in a light night, and says that he thinks the prisoner at the bar is the person, and that he should not hesitate at all if he were seen in the same dress. His opinion is formed partly from his own observation, and partly from the description of others; but this description turns out to be only in regard to the dress. It is said that he is now more confident than on the former trial. If he has varied in his testimony, make such allowance as you may think proper. I do not perceive any material variance. He thought him the same person when he was first brought to court, and as he saw him get out of the chaise. This is one of the cases

in which a witness is permitted to give an opinion. This witness is as honest as yourselves—neither willing nor swift; but he says he believes it was the man—"this is my opinion," and this is proper for him to give. If partly founded on what he has *heard,* then his opinion is not to be taken; but *if* on what he *saw,* then you can have no better evidence. I lay no stress on similarity of dress. No man will ever be hanged by my voice on such evidence. But then it is proper to notice that no inferences drawn from any *dissimilarity* of dress can be given in the prisoner's favor, because, in fact, the person seen by Mirick was dressed like the prisoner.

The description of the person seen by Mirick answers to that of the prisoner at the bar. In regard to the supposed discrepancy of statements, before and now, there would be no end to such minute inquiries. It would not be strange if witnesses should vary. I do not think much of slight shades of variation. If I believe the witness is honest, that is enough. If he has expressed himself more strongly now than then, this does not prove him false.

Peter E. Webster saw the prisoner at the bar, as he then thought, and still thinks, walking in Howard Street at half-past nine o'clock. He then thought it was Frank Knapp, and has not altered his opinion since. He knew him well; he had long known him. If he then thought it was he, this goes far to prove it. He observed him the more, as it was unusual to see gentlemen walk there at that hour. It was a very retired, lonely street. Now, is there reasonable doubt that Mr. Webster did see him there that night? How can you have more proof than this? He judged by his walk, by his general appearance, by his deportment. We all judge in this manner. If you believe he is right, it goes a great way in this case. But then this person, it is said, had a cloak on, and that he could not, therefore, be the same person that Mirick saw. If we were treating of men that had no occasion to disguise themselves or their conduct, there might be something in this argument. But as it is, there is little in it. It may be presumed that they would change their dress. This would help their disguise. What is easier than to throw off a cloak, and again put it on? Perhaps he was less fearful of being known when alone than when with the perpetrator.

Mr. Southwick swears all that a man can swear. He has the best means of judging that could be had at the time. He tells you that he left his father's house at half-past ten o'clock, and, as he passed to his own house in Brown Street, he saw a man sitting on the steps of the ropewalk; that he passed him three times, and each time he held down his head, so that he did not see his face; that the man had on a cloak, which was not wrapped around him, and a glazed cap; that he took the man to be Frank Knapp at the time; that, when he went into his house,

he told his wife that he thought it was Frank Knapp; that he knew him well, having known him from a boy. And his wife swears that he did so tell her at the time. What could mislead this witness at the time? He was not then suspecting Frank Knapp of anything. He could not then be influenced by any prejudice. If you believe that the witness saw Frank Knapp in this position at this time, it proves the case. Whether you believe it or not depends upon the credit of the witness. He swears it. If true, it is solid evidence. Mrs. Southwick supports her husband. Are they true? Are they worthy of belief? If he deserves the epithets applied to him, then he ought not to be believed. In this fact they cannot be mistaken; they are right, or they are perjured. As to his not speaking to Frank Knapp, that depends upon their intimacy. But a very good reason is, Frank chose to disguise himself. This makes nothing against his credit. But it is said that he should not be believed. And why? Because, it is said, he himself now tells you that, when he testified before the grand jury at Ipswich, he did not then say that he thought the person he saw in Brown Street was Frank Knapp, but that "the person was about the size of Selman." The means of attacking him, therefore, come from himself. If he is a false man, why should he tell truths against himself? They rely on his veracity to prove that he is a liar. Before you can come to this conclusion, you will consider whether all the circumstances are now known that should have a bearing on this point. Suppose that, when he was before the grand jury, he was asked by the attorney this question. "Was the person you saw in Brown Street about the size of Selman?" and he answered, "Yes." This was all true. Suppose, also, that he expected to be inquired of further, and no further questions were put to him. Would it not be extremely hard to impute to him perjury for this? It is not uncommon for witnesses to think that they have done all their duty when they have answered the questions put to them. But suppose that we admit that he did not then tell all he knew, this does not alter the *fact* at all, because he did tell, at the time, in the hearing of others, that the person he saw was Frank Knapp. There is not the slightest suggestion against the veracity or accuracy of Mrs. Southwick. Now, she swears positively that her husband came into the house and told her that he had seen a person on the ropewalk steps, and believed it was Frank Knapp.

It is said that Mr. Southwick is contradicted, also, by Mr. Shillaber. I do not understand Mr. Shillaber's testimony. I think what they both testify is reconcilable and consistent. My learned brother said, on a similar occasion, that there is more probability, in such cases, that the persons hearing should misunderstand, than that the person speaking should contradict himself. I think the same remark applicable here.

You have all witnessed the uncertainty of testimony when witnesses

are called to testify what other witnesses said. Several respectable coun-
selors have been called on, on this occasion, to give testimony of that
sort. They have, every one of them, given different versions. They all
took minutes at the time, and without doubt intended to state the truth.
But still they differ. Mr. Shillaber's version is different from everything
that Southwick has stated elsewhere. But little reliance is to be placed on
slight variations in testimony, unless they are manifestly intentional.
I think that Mr. Shillaber must be satisfied that he did not rightly understand Mr. Southwick. I confess I misunderstood Mr. Shillaber on the
former trial, if I now rightly understand him. I therefore did not then
recall Mr. Southwick to the stand. Mr. Southwick, as I read it, understood Mr. Shillaber as asking him about a person coming out of Newbury
Street, and whether, for aught he knew, it might not be Richard Crowninshield, Jr. He answered that he could not tell. He did not understand
Mr. Shillaber as questioning him as to the person whom he saw sitting
on the steps of the ropewalk. Southwick, on this trial, having heard Mr.
Shillaber, has been recalled to the stand, and states that Mr. Shillaber entirely misunderstood him. This is certainly most probable, because the
controlling fact in the case is not controverted,—that is, that Southwick
did tell his wife, at the very moment he entered his house, that he had
seen a person on the ropewalk steps, whom he believed to be Frank
Knapp. Nothing can prove with more certainty than this: that Southwick, at the time, *thought* the person whom he thus saw to be the prisoner at the bar.

Mr. Bray is an acknowledged accurate and intelligent witness. He was
highly complimented by my brother on the former trial, although he
now charges him with varying his testimony. What could be his motive?
You will be slow in imputing to him any design of this kind. I deny
altogether that there is any contradiction. There may be differences,
but no contradiction. These arise from the difference in the questions
put; the difference between *believing* and *knowing*. On the first trial, he
said he did not *know* the person, and now says the same. Then, we did
not do all we had a right to do. We did not ask him who he *thought* it
was. Now, when so asked, he says he *believes* it was the prisoner at the
bar. If he had then been asked this question, he would have given the
same answer. That he has expressed himself stronger I admit; but he has
not contradicted himself. He is more confident now, and that is all. A
man may not assert a thing, and still not have any doubt upon it. Cannot
every man see this distinction to be consistent? I leave him in that attitude; that only is the difference. On questions of identity, opinion is
evidence. We may ask the witness, either if he *knew* who the person
seen was, or who he *thinks* he was. And he may well answer, as Captain

Bray has answered, that he does not *know* who it was, but that he *thinks* it was the prisoner.

We have offered to produce witnesses to prove that, as soon as Bray saw the prisoner, he pronounced him the same person. We are not at liberty to call them to corroborate our own witness. How, then, could this fact of the prisoner's being in Brown Street be better proved? If ten witnesses had testified to it, it would be no better. Two men, who knew him well, took it to be Frank Knapp, and one of them so said, when there was nothing to mislead them. Two others that examined him closely, now swear to their opinion that he is the man.

Miss Jaqueth saw three persons pass by the ropewalk several evenings before the murder. She saw one of them pointing towards Mr. White's house. She noticed that another had something which appeared to be like an instrument of music; that he put it behind him, and attempted to conceal it. Who were these persons? This was but a few steps from the place where this apparent instrument of music (of *music* such as Richard Crowninshield, Jr., spoke of to Palmer) was afterwards found. These facts prove this a point of rendezvous for these parties. They show Brown Street to have been the place for consultation and observation, and to this purpose it was well suited.

Mr. Burns' testimony is also important. What was the defendant's object in his private conversation with Burns? He knew that Burns was out that night; that he lived near Brown Street, and that he had probably seen him, and he wished him to say nothing. He said to Burns, "If you saw any of your friends out that night, say nothing about it; my brother Joe and I are your friends." This is plain proof that he wished to say to him, if you saw me in Brown Street that night, say nothing about it.

But it is said that Burns ought not to be believed because he mistook the color of the dagger, and because he has varied in his description of it. These are slight circumstances, if his general character be good. To my mind they are of no importance. It is for you to make what deduction you may think proper, on this account, from the weight of his evidence. His conversation with Burns, if Burns is believed, shows two things: First, that he desired Burns not to mention it, if he had seen him on the night of the murder; second, that he wished to fix the charge of murder on Mr. Stephen White. Both of these prove his own guilt.

I think you will be of opinion that Brown Street was a *probable place* for the conspirators to assemble, and for an aid to be. If we knew their whole plan, and if we were skilled to judge in such a case, then we could perhaps determine on this point better. But it is a retired place, and still commands a full view of the house; a lonely place, but still a place of observation; not so lonely that a person would excite suspicion to be

seen walking there in an ordinary manner; not so public as to be noticed by many. It is near enough to the scene of action in point of law. It was their point of *centrality*. The club was found near the spot, in a place provided for it, in a place that had been previously hunted out, in a concerted place of concealment. *Here was their point of rendezvous;* here might the lights be seen; here might an aid be secreted; here was he within call; here might he be aroused by the sound of the *whistle;* here might he carry the weapon; here might he receive the murderer after the murder.

Then, gentlemen, the general question occurs, is it satisfactorily proved, by all these facts and circumstances, that the defendant was in and about Brown Street on the night of the murder? Considering that the murder was effected by a conspiracy; considering that he was one of the four conspirators; considering that two of the conspirators have accounted for themselves on the night of the murder, and were not in Brown Street; considering that the prisoner does not account for himself, nor show where he was; considering that Richard Crowninshield, the other conspirator and the perpetrator, is not accounted for, nor shown to be elsewhere; considering that it is now past all doubt that two persons were seen in and about Brown Street at different times, lurking, avoiding observation, and exciting so much suspicion that the neighbors actually watched them; considering that, if these persons thus lurking in Brown Street at that hour were not murderers, it remains to this day wholly unknown who they were or what their business was; considering the testimony of Miss Jaqueth, and that the club was afterwards found near this place; considering, finally, that Webster and Southwick saw these persons, and then took one of them for the defendant, and that Southwick then told his wife so, and that Bray and Mirick examined them closely, and now swear to their belief that the prisoner was one of them—it is for you to say, putting these considerations together, whether you believe the prisoner was actually in Brown Street at the time of the murder.

By the counsel for the defendant, much stress has been laid upon the question whether Brown Street was a place in which aid could be given —a place in which actual assistance could be rendered in this transaction. This must be mainly decided by their own opinion who selected the place; by what they thought at the time, according to their plan of operation.

If it was agreed that the prisoner should be there to assist, it is enough. If they thought the place proper for their purpose, according to their plan, it is sufficient.

Suppose we could prove expressly that they agreed that Frank should be there, and he was there, and you should think it not a well-chosen

place for aiding and abetting, must he be acquitted? No! It is not what *I* think or *you* think of the appropriateness of the place; it is what *they* thought *at the time*.

If the prisoner was in Brown Street by appointment and agreement with the perpetrator, for the purpose of giving assistance if assistance should be needed, it may safely be presumed that the place was suited to such assistance as it was supposed by the parties might chance to become requisite.

If, in Brown Street, was he there by appointment? Was he there to aid, if aid were necessary? Was he there for or against the murderer? to concur, or to oppose? to favor, or to thwart? Did the perpetrator know he was there—waiting? If so, then it follows, he was there by appointment. He was at the post half an hour. He was waiting for somebody. This proves *appointment, arrangement, previous agreement;* then it follows he was there to aid, to encourage, to embolden the perpetrator, and that is enough. If he were in such a situation as to afford aid, or that he was relied upon for aid, then he was aiding and abetting. It is enough that the conspirator desired to have him there. Besides, it may be well said that he could afford just as much aid there as if he had been in Essex Street—as if he had been standing even at the gate or at the window. It was not an act of power against power that was to be done; it was a secret act, to be done by stealth. The aid was to be placed in a position secure from observation. It was important to the security of both that he should be in a lonely place. Now, it is obvious that there are many purposes for which he might be in Brown Street.

1. Richard Crowninshield might have been secreted in the garden, and waiting for a signal;

2. Or he might be in Brown Street to advise him as to the time of making his entry into the house;

3. Or to favor his escape;

4. Or to see if the street was clear when he came out;

5. Or to conceal the weapon or the clothes;

6. To be ready for any other unforeseen contingency.

Richard Crowninshield lived in Danvers. He would retire by the most secret way. Brown Street is that way. If you find him there, can you doubt why he was there!

If, gentlemen, the prisoner went into Brown Street, by appointment with the perpetrator, to render aid or encouragement in any of these ways, he was *present*, in legal contemplation, aiding and abetting in this murder. It is not necessary that he should have done anything; it is enough that he was ready to act, and in a place to act. If his being in Brown Street, by appointment, at the time of the murder, emboldened the purpose and encouraged the heart of the murderer by the hope of

instant aid if aid should become necessary, then, without doubt, he was present, aiding and abetting, and was a principal in the murder.

I now proceed, gentlemen, to the consideration of the testimony of Mr. Colman. Although this evidence bears on every material part of the cause, I have purposely avoided every comment on it till the present moment, when I have done with the other evidence in the case. As to the admission of this evidence, there has been a great struggle, and its importance demanded it. The general rule of law is that confessions are to be received as evidence. They are entitled to great or to little consideration, according to the circumstances under which they are made. Voluntary, deliberate confessions are the most important and satisfactory evidence; but confessions hastily made, or improperly obtained, are entitled to little or no consideration. It is always to be inquired whether they were purely voluntary, or were made under any undue influence of *hope* or *fear*; for, in general, if any influence were exerted on the mind of the person confessing, such confessions are not to be submitted to a jury.

Who is Mr. Colman? He is an intelligent, accurate, and cautious witness; a gentleman of high and well known character, and of unquestionable veracity; as a clergyman, highly respectable; as a man, of fair name and fame.

Why was Mr. Colman with the prisoner? Joseph J. Knapp was his parishioner; he was the head of a family, and had been married by Mr. Colman. The interests of his family were dear to him. He felt for their afflictions, and was anxious to alleviate their sufferings. He went from the purest and best of motives to visit Joseph Knapp. He came to save, not to destroy; to rescue, not to take away life. In this family he thought there might be a chance to save one. It is a misconstruction of Mr. Colman's motives, at once the most strange and the most uncharitable—a perversion of all just views of his conduct and intentions the most unaccountable—to represent him as acting, on this occasion, in hostility to anyone, or as desirous of injuring or endangering anyone. He has stated his own motives and his own conduct in a manner to command universal belief and universal respect. For intelligence, for consistency, for accuracy, for caution, for candor, never did witness acquit himself better, or stand fairer. In all that he did as a man, and all he has said as a witness, he has shown himself worthy of entire regard.

Now, gentlemen, very important confessions made by the prisoner are sworn to by Mr. Colman. They were made in the prisoner's cell, where Mr. Colman had gone with the prisoner's brother, N. Phippen Knapp. Whatever conversation took place was in the presence of N. P. Knapp. Now, on the part of the prisoner, two things are asserted: First, that such inducements were suggested to the prisoner, in this interview, that any confessions made by him ought not to be received; second, that in point

of fact, he made no such confession as Mr. Colman testifies to, nor, indeed, any confessions at all. These two propositions are attempted to be supported by the testimony of N. P. Knapp. These two witnesses, Mr. Colman and N. P. Knapp, differ entirely. There is no possibility of reconciling them. No charity can cover both. One or the other has sworn falsely. If N. P. Knapp be believed, Mr. Colman's testimony must be wholly disregarded. It is, then, a question of credit—a question of belief between the two witnesses. As you decide between these, so you will decide on all this part of the case.

Mr. Colman has given you a plain narrative, a consistent account, and has uniformly stated the same things. He is not contradicted by anything in the case except Phippen Knapp. He is influenced, as far as we can see, by no bias or prejudice, any more than other men, except so far as his character is now at stake. He has feelings on this point doubtless, and ought to have. If what he has stated be not true, I cannot see any ground for his escape. If he be a true man, he must have heard what he testifies. No treachery of memory brings to memory things that never took place. There is no reconciling his evidence with good intentions if the facts are not as he states them. He is on trial as to his veracity.

The relation in which the other witness stands deserves your careful consideration. He is a member of the family. He has the lives of two brothers depending, as he may think, on the effect of his evidence; depending on every word he speaks. I hope he has not another responsibility resting upon him. By the advice of a friend, and that friend Mr. Colman, J. Knapp made a full and free confession, and obtained a promise of pardon. He has since, as you know, probably by the advice of other friends, retracted that confession, and rejected the offered pardon. Events will show who of these friends and advisers advised him best and befriended him most. In the meantime, if this brother, the witness, be one of these advisers, and advised the retraction, he has, most emphatically, the lives of his brothers resting upon his evidence and upon his conduct. Compare the situation of these two witnesses. Do you not see mighty motive enough on the one side, and want of all motive on the other? I would gladly find an apology for that witness in his agonized feelings, in his distressed situation; in the agitation of that hour, or of this. I would gladly impute it to error, or to want of recollection, to confusion of mind, or disturbance of feeling. I would gladly impute [it] to any pardonable source which cannot be reconciled to facts and to truth; but, even in a case calling for so much sympathy, justice must yet prevail, and we must come to the conclusion, however reluctantly, which that demands from us.

It is said Phippen Knapp was probably correct, because he knew he should be called as a witness. Witness to what? When he says there was

no confession, what could he expect to bear witness of? But I do not put it on the ground that he did not hear. I am compelled to put it on the other ground, that he did hear, and does not now truly tell what he heard.

If Mr. Colman were out of the case, there are other reasons why the story of Phippen Knapp should not be believed. It has in it inherent improbabilities. It is unnatural, and inconsistent with the accompanying circumstances. He tells you that they went "to the cell of Frank, to see if he had any objection to taking a trial, and suffering his brother to accept the offer of pardon,"—in other words, to obtain Frank's consent to Joseph's making a confession,—and, in case this consent was not obtained, that the pardon would be offered to Frank. Did they bandy about the chance of life, between these two, in this way? Did Mr. Colman, after having given this pledge to Joseph, after having received a disclosure from Joseph, go to the cell of Frank for such a purpose as this? It is impossible; it cannot be so.

Again, we know that Mr. Colman found the club the next day; that he went directly to the place of deposit, and found it at the first attempt, exactly where he says he had been informed it was. Now, Phippen Knapp says that Frank stated nothing respecting the club; that it was not mentioned in that conversation. He says, also, that he was present in the cell of Joseph all the time that Mr. Colman was there; that he believes he heard all that was said in Joseph's cell; and that he did not himself know where the club was, and never had known where it was, until he heard it stated in court. Now, it is certain that Mr. Colman says he did not learn the particular place of deposit of the club from Joseph; that he only learned from him that it was deposited under the steps of the Howard Street meeting house, without defining the particular steps. It is certain, also, that he had more knowledge of the position of the club than this; else how could he have placed his hand on it so readily? and where else could he have obtained this knowledge, except from Frank?

[Here Mr. Dexter said that Mr. Colman had had other interviews with Joseph, and might have derived the information from him at previous visits. Mr. Webster replied, that Mr. Colman had testified that he learned nothing in relation to the club until this visit. Mr. Dexter denied there being any such testimony. Mr. Colman's evidence was read, from the notes of the judges, and several other persons, and Mr. Webster then proceeded.]

My point is to show that Phippen Knapp's story is not true—is not consistent with itself; that, taking it for granted, as he says, that he heard all that was said to Mr. Colman in both cells, by Joseph and by Frank, and that Joseph did not state particularly where the club was de-

posited, and that he knew as much about the place of deposit of the club as Mr. Colman knew, why then, Mr. Colman must either have been miraculously informed respecting the club, or Phippen Knapp has not told you the whole truth. There is no reconciling this without supposing that Mr. Colman has misrepresented what took place in Joseph's cell, as well as what took place in Frank's cell.

Again, Phippen Knapp is directly contradicted by Mr. Wheatland. Mr. Wheatland tells the same story as coming from Phippen Knapp, as Colman now tells. Here there are two against one. Phippen Knapp says that Frank made no confessions, and that he said he had none to make. In this he is contradicted by Wheatland. He, Phippen Knapp, told Wheatland that Mr. Colman did ask Frank some questions, and that Frank answered them. He told him also what these answers were. Wheatland does not recollect the questions or answers, but recollects his reply, which was: "Is not this *premature*? I think this answer is sufficient to make Frank a principal." Here Phippen Knapp opposes himself to Wheatland, as well as to Mr. Colman.

Do you believe Phippen Knapp against these two respectable witnesses, or them against him?

Is not Mr. Colman's testimony credible, natural, and proper? To judge of this, you must go back to that scene.

The murder had been committed. The two Knapps were now arrested. Four persons were already in jail supposed to be concerned in it—the Crowninshields, and Selman, and Chase. Another person at the eastward was supposed to be in the plot. It was important to learn the facts. To do this, some one of those suspected must be admitted to turn state's witness. The contest was, *who should have this privilege?* It was understood that it was about to be offered to Palmer, then in Maine. There was no good reason why he should have the preference. Mr. Colman felt interested for the family of the Knapps, and particularly for Joseph. He was a young man who had hitherto sustained a fair standing in society. He was a husband. Mr. Colman was particularly intimate with his family. With these views he went to the prison. He believed that he might safely converse with the prisoner, because he thought confessions made to a clergyman were sacred, and that he could not be called upon to disclose them. He went, the first time, in the morning, and was requested to come again. He went again at three o'clock, and was requested to call again at five o'clock. In the meantime he saw the father and Phippen, and they wished he would not go again, because it would be said the prisoners were making confession. He said he had engaged to go again at five o'clock, but would not, if Phippen would excuse him to Joseph. Phippen engaged to do this, and to meet him at his office at five o'clock. Mr. Colman went to the office at the time, and waited; but, as Phippen

was not there he walked down street, and saw him coming from the jail. He met him, and while in conversation near the church, he saw Mrs. Beckford and Mrs. Knapp going in a chaise towards the jail. He hastened to meet them, as he thought it not proper for them to go in at that time. While conversing with them near the jail, he received two distinct messages from Joseph that he wished to see him. He thought it proper to go; he then went to Joseph's cell, and while there it was that the disclosures were made. Before Joseph had finished his statement, Phippen came to the door. He was soon after admitted. A short interval ensued, and they went together to the cell of Frank. Mr. Colman went in by invitation of Phippen. He had come directly from the cell of Joseph, where he had for the first time learned the incidents of the tragedy. He was incredulous as to some of the facts which he had learned, they were so different from his previous impressions. He was desirous of knowing whether he could place confidence in what Joseph had told him. He therefore put the questions to Frank as he has testified before you, in answer to which Frank Knapp informed him:

1. That the murder took place between ten and eleven o'clock.

2. That Richard Crowninshield was alone in the house.

3. That he, Frank Knapp, went home afterwards.

4. That the club was deposited under the steps of the Howard Street meeting house, and under the part nearest the burying ground, in a rathole.

5. That the dagger or daggers had been worked up at the factory.

It is said that these five answers just fit the case; that they are just what was wanted, and neither more or less. True, they are; but the reason is because truth always fits. Truth is always congruous, and agrees with itself. Every truth in the universe agrees with every other truth in the universe; whereas falsehoods not only disagree with truths, but usually quarrel among themselves. Surely Mr. Colman is influenced by no bias, no prejudice. He has no feelings to warp him, except now, he is contradicted, he may feel an interest to be believed.

If you believe Mr. Colman, then the evidence is fairly in the case.

I shall now proceed on the ground that you do believe Mr. Colman.

When told that Joseph had determined to confess, the defendant said: "It is hard or unfair that Joseph should have the benefit of confessing, since the thing was done for his benefit." What thing was done for his benefit? Does not this carry an implication of the guilt of the defendant? Does it not show that he had a knowledge of the object and history of the murder?

The defendant said: "I told Joseph, when he proposed it, that it was a silly business, and would get us into trouble." He knew, then, what this business was. He knew that Joseph proposed it, and that he agreed to it,

else it could not get us into trouble. He understood its bearings and its consequences. Thus much was said, under circumstances that make it clearly evidence against him, before there is any pretense of an inducement held out. And does not this prove him to have had a knowledge of the conspiracy?

He knew the daggers had been destroyed, and he knew who committed the murder. How could he have innocently known these facts? Why, if by Richard's story, this shows him guilty of a knowledge of the murder and of the conspiracy. More than all, he knew *when* the deed was done, and that he went home *afterwards*. This shows his participation in that deed. "Went home afterwards!" Home *from what scene?* home *from what fact?* home *from what transaction?* home *from what place?* This confirms the supposition that the prisoner was in Brown Street for the purposes ascribed to him. These questions were directly put, and directly answered. He does not intimate that he received the information from another. Now, if he knows the time, and went home afterwards, and does not excuse himself, is not this an admission that he had a hand in this murder? Already proved to be a conspirator in the murder, he now confesses that he knew who did it, at what time it was done, that he was himself out of his own house at the time, and went home afterwards. Is not this conclusive, if not explained? Then comes the club. He told where it was. This is like possession of stolen goods. He is charged with the guilty knowledge of this concealment. He must *show*, not *say*, how he came by this knowledge. If a man be found with stolen goods, he must *prove* how he came by them. The place of deposit of the club was premeditated and selected, and he knew where it was.

Joseph Knapp was an accessory, and an accessory only; he knew only what was told him. But the prisoner knew the particular spot in which the club might be found. This shows his knowledge something more than that of an accessory.

This presumption must be rebutted by evidence, or it stands strong against him. He has too much knowledge of this transaction to have come innocently by it. It must stand against him until he explains it.

The testimony of Mr. Colman is represented as new matter, and therefore an attempt has been made to excite a prejudice against it. It is not so. How little is there in it, after all, that did not appear from other sources. It is mainly confirmatory. Compare what you learn from this confession with what you before knew;

As to its being proposed by Joseph, was not that true?

As to Richard's being alone in the house, was not that true?

As to the daggers, was that not true?

As to the time of the murder, was not that true?

As to his being out that night, was not that true?

As to his returning afterwards, was not that true?

As to the club, was not that true?

So this information confirms what was known before, and fully confirms it.

One word as to the interview between Mr. Colman and Phippen Knapp on the turnpike. It is said that Mr. Colman's conduct in this matter is inconsistent with his testimony. There does not appear to me to be any inconsistency. He tells you that his object was to save Joseph, and to hurt no one, and least of all the prisoner at the bar. He had probably told Mr. White the substance of what he heard at the prison. He had probably told him that Frank *confirmed* what Joseph had *confessed*. He was unwilling to be the instrument of harm to Frank. He therefore, at the request of Phippen Knapp, wrote a note to Mr. White, requesting him to consider Joseph as authority for the information he had received. He tells you that this is the only thing he has to regret, as it may seem to be an evasion, as he doubts whether it was entirely correct. If it was an evasion, if it was a deviation, if it was an error, it was an error of mercy, an error of kindness—an error that proves he had no hostility to the prisoner at the bar. It does not in the least vary his testimony or affect its correctness. Gentlemen, I look on the evidence of Mr. Colman as highly important, not as bringing into the cause new facts, but as confirming, in a very satisfactory manner, other evidence. It is incredible that he can be false, and that he is seeking the prisoner's life through false swearing. If he is true, it is incredible that the prisoner can be innocent.

Gentlemen, I have gone through with the evidence in this case, and have endeavored to state it plainly and fairly before you. I think there are conclusions to be drawn from it, which you cannot doubt. I think you cannot doubt that there was a conspiracy formed for the purpose of committing this murder, and who the conspirators were.

That you cannot doubt that the Crowninshields and the Knapps were parties in this conspiracy.

That you cannot doubt that the prisoner at the bar knew that the murder was to be done on the night of the 6th of April.

That you cannot doubt that the murderers of Captain White were the suspicious persons seen in and about Brown Street on that night.

That you cannot doubt that Richard Crowninshield was the perpetrator of that crime.

That you cannot doubt that the prisoner at the bar was in Brown Street on that night.

If there, then it must be by arrangement, to countenance, to aid, the perpetrator, and, if so, then he is guilty as *principal*.

Gentlemen, your whole concern should be to do your duty, and leave consequences to take care of themselves. You will receive the law from the court. Your verdict, it is true, may endanger the prisoner's life, but then it is to save other lives. If the prisoner's guilt has been shown and proved beyond all reasonable doubt, you will convict him. If such reasonable doubt of guilt still remain, you will acquit him. You are the judges of the whole case. You owe a duty to the public, as well as to the prisoner at the bar. You cannot presume to be wiser than the law. Your duty is a plain, straightforward one. Doubtless we would all judge him in mercy. Towards him, as an individual, the law inculcates no hostility; but towards him, if proved to be a murderer, the law, and the oaths you have taken, and public justice demand that you do your duty.

With consciences satisfied with the discharge of duty, no consequences can harm you. There is no evil that we cannot either face or fly from but the consciousness of duty disregarded.

A sense of duty pursues us ever. It is omnipresent, like the Deity. If we take to ourselves the wings of the morning, and dwell in the uttermost parts of the sea, duty performed or duty violated is still with us, for our happiness or our misery. If we say the darkness shall cover us, in the darkness, as in the light, our obligations are yet with us. We cannot escape their power, nor fly from their presence. They are with us in this life, will be with us at its close; and in that scene of inconceivable solemnity, which lies yet farther onward, we shall still find ourselves surrounded by the consciousness of duty, to pain us wherever it has been violated, and to console us so far as God may have given us grace to perform it.

Public Dinner at New York, March 24, 1831

After the debate with Hayne, Webster's stature as a national statesman was unchallenged. His name had become a household word. The great and the near-great of the political and commercial worlds vied with each other to do him honor. Such was the purpose of a public dinner in New York, March 24, 1831. The event differed from others of a similar cast only in the prestige of its 250 guests and in the nature of Webster's remarks, reproduced below. New York's Chancellor James Kent presided, setting the tone for the occasion.

As a consequence of the great debate of the previous year, Kent declared, constitutional law was no longer the private domain of the lawyers. "Socrates was said to have drawn down philosophy from the skies, and scattered it among the schools. It may with equal truth be said that constitutional law, by means of those Senatorial discussions, and the master genius that guided them, was rescued from the archives of our tribunals and the libraries of lawyers, and placed under the eye and submitted to the judgment of the American people. Their verdict is with us, and from it there is no appeal." He then offered the toast required by the occasion: "Our guest Daniel Webster—to his talents we owe a most triumphant vindication of the great principles of the Constitution."

Webster's reply was at once a tribute to New York's role in the creation of that document and a capsuled restatement of his own nationalistic interpretation of it.

The dinner, according to the New York *Evening Post* and to the contemporary pamphlet issued in Boston "from N. Hale's steam-powered press," was held on March 24, 1831. Philip Hone, who was among the guests, records the event in his diary entry for that day.* The March 10 date given in volume 2 of Webster's *Speeches and Forensic Arguments*, published in 1835 by Perkins & Marvin of Boston, is clearly in error. It is repeated in *Works*, 1: 193, and in *Writings and Speeches*,

---

*In a selective edition of this famous diary (Allan Nevins, ed., *The Diary of Philip Hone: 1828–1851* [2 vols., New York, 1927], 1: 38–39), the entry is transcribed as "Tuesday, March 22," but the manuscript in the New York Historical Society leaves no doubt.

2: 43. Further evidence of the correct date is Webster's letter to Chancellor Kent, Morgan Lewis, and others, dated March 1, 1831, whereby he accepts their invitation to speak and proposes March 24 (*W&S*, 16: 207). Again, in a letter to Warren Dutton, written from New York "Friday 4 o'clock" and postmarked at Providence March 27 (mDW 10771), he refers to a dinner and speech of the preceding day. The March 10 date of *Speeches and Forensic Arguments* can only have been erroneously supplied by the editor, in this case Edward Everett.

The text here reproduced is that of *Works*, 1: 195–215 and of *Writings and Speeches*, 2: 45–65, with significant variations from the contemporary pamphlet noted. The pamphlet, *Speeches of Chancellor Kent and the Hon. Daniel Webster at a Public Dinner Given to the Latter at the City Hall in New York, March 24, 1831*, provided the text for *Speeches and Forensic Arguments*. One can only assume that the dated cover was missing from the copy used by the editor. This text, in turn, became the basis of the edited version of the *Works*.

I owe the honor of this occasion, Gentlemen, to your patriotic and affectionate attachment to the Constitution of our country. For an effort, well intended, however otherwise of unpretending character, made in the discharge of public duty, and designed to maintain the Constitution and vindicate its just powers, you have been pleased to tender me this token of your respect. It would be idle affectation to deny that it gives me singular gratification. Every public man must naturally desire the approbation of his fellow-citizens; and though it may be supposed that I should be anxious, in the first place, not to disappoint the expectations of those whose immediate representative I am, it is not possible but that I should feel, nevertheless, the high value of such a mark of esteem as is here offered. But, Gentlemen, I am conscious that the main purpose of this occasion is higher than mere manifestation of personal regard. It is to evince your devotion to the Constitution, your sense of its transcendent value,[1] and your just alarm at whatever threatens to weaken its proper authority, or endanger its existence.

Gentlemen, this could hardly be otherwise. It would be strange, indeed, if the members of this vast commercial community should not be first and foremost to rally for the Constitution, whenever opinions and doctrines are advanced hostile to its principles. Where sooner than here, where louder than here, may we expect a patriotic voice to be raised, when the union of the States is threatened? In this great empo-

---

1. This clause is not in the pamphlet version.

rium, at this central point of the united commerce of the United States, of all places, we may expect the warmest, the most determined and universal feeling of attachment to the national government. Gentlemen, no one can estimate more highly than I do the natural advantages of your city. No one entertains a higher opinion than myself, also, of that spirit of wise and liberal policy, which has actuated the government of your own great State[2] in the accomplishment of high objects, important to the growth and prosperity both of the State and the city. But all these local advantages, and all this enlightened state policy, could never have made your city what it now is, without the aid and protection of a general government, extending over all the States, and establishing for all a common and uniform system of commercial regulation. Without national character, without public credit, without systematic finance, without uniformity of commercial laws, all other advantages possessed by this city would have decayed and perished, like unripe fruit. A general government was, for years before it was instituted, the great object of desire to the inhabitants of this city. New York, at a very early day, was conscious of her local advantages for commerce; she saw her destiny, and was eager to embrace it; but nothing else than a general government could make free her path before her, and set her forward on her brilliant career. She early saw all this, and to the accomplishment of this great and indispensable object she bent every faculty, and exerted every effort. She was not mistaken. She formed no false judgment. At the moment of the adoption of the Constitution, New York was the capital of one State, and contained thirty-two or three thousand people. It now contains more than two hundred thousand people, and is justly regarded as the commercial capital, not only of all the United States, but of the whole continent also, from the pole to the South Sea. Every page of her history, for the last forty years, bears high and irresistible testimony to the benefits and blessings of the general government. Her astonishing growth is referred to, and quoted, all the world over, as one of the most striking proofs of the effects of our Federal Union. To suppose her now to be easy and indifferent, when notions are advanced tending to its dissolution, would be to suppose her equally forgetful of the past and blind to the present, alike ignorant of her own history and her own interest, metamorphosed, from all that she has been, into a being tired of its prosperity, sick of its own growth and greatness, and infatuated for its own destruction. Every blow aimed at the union of the States strikes on the tenderest nerve of her interest and her happiness. To bring the Union into debate is to bring her own future prosperity into debate also. To speak of arresting the laws of the Union, of inter-

2. "of the state" in pamphlet.

posing State power in matters of commerce and revenue, of weakening the full and just authority of the general government, would be, in regard to this city, but another mode of speaking of commercial ruin, of abandoned wharfs, of vacated houses, of diminished and dispersing population, of bankrupt merchants, of mechanics without employment, and laborers without bread. The growth of this city and the Constitution of the United States are coevals and contemporaries. They began together, they have flourished together, and if rashness and folly destroy one, the other will follow it to the tomb.

Gentlemen, it is true, indeed, that the growth of this city is extraordinary, and almost unexplained. It is now, I believe, sixteen or seventeen years since I first saw it. Within that comparatively short period, it has added to its number three times the whole amount of its population when the Constitution was adopted. Of all things having power to check this prosperity, of all things potent to blight and blast it, of all things capable of compelling this city to recede as fast as she has advanced, a disturbed government, an enfeebled public authority, a broken or a weakened union of the States, would be most efficacious.[3] This would be cause efficient enough. Every thing else, in the common fortune of communities, she may hope to resist or to prevent; but this would be fatal as the arrow of death.

Gentlemen, you have personal recollections and associations, connected with the establishment and adoption of the Constitution, which are necessarily called up on an occasion like this. It is impossible to forget the prominent agency exercised by eminent citizens of your own, in regard to that great measure. Those great men are now recorded among the illustrious dead; but they have left names never to be forgotten, and never to be remembered without respect and veneration. Least of all can they be forgotten by you, when assembled here for the purpose of signifying your attachment to the Constitution, and your sense of its inestimable importance to the happiness of the people.

I should do violence to my own feelings, Gentlemen, I think I should offend yours, if I omitted respectful mention of distinguished names yet fresh in your recollections. How can I stand here, to speak of the Constitution of the United States, of the wisdom of its provisions, of the difficulties attending its adoption, of the evils from which it rescued the country, and of the prosperity and power to which it has raised it, and yet pay no tribute to those who were highly instrumental in accomplishing the work? While we are here to rejoice that it yet stands firm and strong, while we congratulate one another that we live under its benign influence, and cherish hopes of its long duration, we cannot

3. For "most efficacious" pamphlet reads "sovereign."

forget who they were that, in the day of our national infancy, in the times of despondency and despair, mainly assisted to work out our deliverance. I should feel that I was unfaithful to[4] the strong recollections which the occasion presses upon us, that I was not true to gratitude, not true to patriotism, not true to the living or the dead, not true to your feelings or my own, if I should forbear to make mention of ALEXANDER HAMILTON.

Coming from the military service of the country yet a youth, but with knowledge and maturity, even in civil affairs, far beyond his years, he made this city the place of his adoption; and he gave the whole powers of his mind to the contemplation of the weak and distracted condition of the country. Daily increasing in acquaintance and confidence with the people of New York, he saw, what they also saw, the absolute necessity of some closer bond of union for the States. This was the great object of desire. He never appears to have lost sight of it, but was found in the lead whenever any thing was to be attempted for its accomplishment. One experiment after another, as is well known, was tried, and all failed. The States were urgently called on to confer such further powers on the old Congress as would enable it to redeem the public faith, or to adopt, themselves, some general and common principle of commercial regulation. But the States had not agreed, and were not likely to agree. In this posture of affairs, so full of public difficulty and public distress, commissioners from five or six of the States met, on the request of Virginia, at Annapolis, in September, 1786. The precise object of their appointment was to take into consideration the trade of the United States; to examine the relative situations and trade of the several States; and to consider how far a uniform system of commercial regulations was necessary to their common interest and permanent harmony. Mr. Hamilton was one of those commissioners; and I have understood, though I cannot assert the fact, that their report was drawn by him. His associate from this State was the venerable Judge [Egbert] Benson, who has lived long, and still lives, to see the happy results of the counsels which originated in this meeting. Of its members, he and Mr. Madison are, I believe, now the only survivors. These commissioners recommended, what took place the next year, a general Convention of all the States, to take into serious deliberation the condition of the country, and devise such provisions as should render the constitution of the federal government adequate to the exigencies of the Union. I need not remind you, that of this Convention Mr. Hamilton was an active and efficient member. The Constitution was framed, and submitted to the country. And then another great work was to be undertaken. The Con-

4. For "was unfaithful to" pamphlet reads "disregarded."

stitution would naturally find, and did find, enemies and opposers. Objections to it were numerous, and powerful, and spirited. They were to be answered; and they were effectually answered. The writers of the numbers of the Federalist, Mr. Hamilton, Mr. Madison, and Mr. Jay, so greatly distinguished themselves in their discussions of the Constitution, that those numbers are generally received as important commentaries on the text, and accurate expositions, in general, of its objects and purposes. Those papers were all written and published in this city. Mr. Hamilton was elected one of the distinguished delegation from the city to the State Convention at Poughkeepsie, called to ratify the new Constitution. Its debates are published. Mr. Hamilton appears to have exerted, on this occasion, to the utmost, every power and faculty of his mind.

The whole question was likely to depend on the decision of New York. He felt the full importance of the crisis; and the reports of his speeches, imperfect as they probably are, are yet lasting monuments to his genius and patriotism. He saw at last his hopes fulfilled; he saw the Constitution adopted, and the government under it established and organized. The discerning eye of Washington immediately called him to that post, which was far the most important in the administration of the new system. He was made Secretary of the Treasury; and how he fulfilled the duties of such a place, at such a time, the whole country perceived with delight and the whole world saw with admiration. He smote the rock of the national resources, and abundant streams of revenue gushed forth. He touched the dead corpse of the Public Credit, and it sprung upon its feet. The fabled birth of Minerva, from the brain of Jove, was hardly more sudden or more perfect than the financial system of the United States, as it burst forth from the conceptions of ALEXANDER HAMILTON.

Your recollections, Gentlemen, your respect, and your affections, all conspire to bring before you, at such a time as this, another great man, now too numbered with the dead. I mean the pure, the disinterested, the patriotic JOHN JAY. His character is a brilliant jewel in the sacred treasures of national reputation. Leaving his profession at an early period, yet not before he had singularly distinguished himself in it, his whole life, from the commencement of the Revolution until his final retirement, was a life of public service. A member of the first Congress, he was the author of that political paper which is generally acknowledged to stand first among the incomparable productions of that body;[5] productions which called forth that decisive strain of commendation from the great Lord Chatham, in which he pronounced them not inferior to the finest productions of the master statesmen of the world. Mr. Jay

5. John Jay, "Address to the People of Great Britain," October 21, 1774, see *Journals of the Continental Congress* (34 vols., Washington, D.C., 1904–1937), 1: 82–90.

had been abroad, and he had also been long intrusted with the difficult duties of our foreign correspondence at home. He had seen and felt, in the fullest measures and to the greatest possible extent, the difficulty of conducting our foreign affairs honorably and usefully, without a stronger and more perfect domestic union. Though not a member of the Convention which framed the Constitution, he was yet present while it was in session, and looked anxiously for its result. By the choice of this city, he had a seat in the State Convention, and took an active and zealous part for the adoption of the Constitution. On the organization of the new government he was selected by Washington to be the first Chief Justice of the Supreme Court of the United States; and surely the high and most responsible duties of that station could not have been trusted to abler or safer hands. It is the duty of that tribunal, one of equal importance and delicacy, to decide constitutional questions, occasionally arising on State laws. The general learning and ability, and especially the prudence, the mildness, and the firmness of his character, eminently fitted Mr. Jay to be the head of such a court. When the spotless ermine of the judicial robe fell on John Jay, it touched nothing less spotless than itself.

These eminent men, Gentlemen, the contemporaries of some of you, known to most, and revered by all, were so conspicuous in the framing and adopting of the Constitution, and called so early to important stations under it, that a tribute, better, indeed, than I have given, or am able to give, seemed due to them from us, on this occasion.

There was yet another, of whom mention is to be made. In the Revolutionary history of the country, the name of CHANCELLOR [Robert] LIVINGSTON became early prominent. He was a member of that Congress which declared Independence; and a member, too, of the committee which drew and reported the immortal Declaration. At the period of the adoption of the Constitution, he was its firm friend and able advocate. He was a member of the State Convention, being one of that list of distinguished and gifted men who represented this city in that body; and he threw the whole weight of his talents and influence into the doubtful scale of the Constitution.

Gentlemen, as connected with the Constitution, you have also local recollections which must bind it still closer to your attachment and affection. It commenced its being and its blessings here. It was in this city, in the midst of friends, anxious, hopeful, and devoted, that the new government started in its course. To us, Gentlemen, who are younger, it has come down by tradition; but some around me are old enough to have witnessed, and did witness, the interesting scene of the first inauguration. They remember what voices of gratified patriotism, what shouts of enthusiastic hope, what acclamations rent the air, how many

eyes were suffused with tears of joy, how cordially each man pressed the hand of him who was next to him, when, standing in the open air, in the centre of the city, in the view of assembled thousands, the first President of the United States was heard solemnly to pronounce the words of his official oath, repeating them from the lips of Chancellor Livingston. You then thought, Gentlemen, that the great work of the Revolution was accomplished. You then felt that you had a government; that the United States were then, indeed, united. Every benignant star seemed to shed its selectest influence on that auspicious hour. Here were heroes of the Revolution; here were sages of the Convention; here were minds, disciplined and schooled in all the various fortunes of the country, acting now in several relations, but all coöperating to the same great end, the successful administration of the new and untried Constitution. And he,—how shall I speak of him?—he was at the head, who was already first in war, who was already first in the hearts of his countrymen, and who was now shown also, by the unanimous suffrage of the country, to be first in peace.

Gentlemen, how gloriously have the hopes then indulged been fulfilled! Whose expectation was then so sanguine, I may almost ask, whose imagination then so extravagant, as to run forward, and contemplate as probable, the one half of what has been accomplished in forty years? Who among you can go back to 1789, and see what this city, and this country, too, then were; and, beholding what they now are, can be ready to consent that the Constitution of the United States shall be weakened,—dishonored,—*nullified?* [6]

Gentlemen, before I leave these pleasant recollections, I feel it an irresistible impulse of duty to pay a tribute of respect to another distinguished person, not, indeed, a fellow-citizen of your own, but associated with those I have already mentioned in important labors, and an early and indefatigable friend and advocate in the great cause of the Constitution. I refer to MR. MADISON. I am aware, Gentlemen, that a tribute of regard from me to him is of little importance; but if it shall receive your approbation and sanction, it will become of value. Mr. Madison, thanks to a kind Providence, is yet among the living, and there is certainly no other individual living, to whom the country is so much indebted for the blessings of the Constitution. He was one of the commissioners who met at Annapolis, in 1786, to which meeting I have already referred, and which, to the great credit of Virginia, had its origin in a proceeding of that State. He was a member of the Convention of 1787,[7] and of that of Virginia in the following year. He was thus intimately acquainted with the whole progress of the formation

6. Pamphlet reads "weakened, nullified, or dishonored."

7. Pamphlet reads "1789."

of the Constitution, from its very first step to its final adoption. If ever man had the means of understanding a written instrument, Mr. Madison has the means of understanding the Constitution. If it be possible to know what was designed by it, he can tell us. It was in this city, that, in conjunction with Mr. Hamilton and Mr. Jay, he wrote the numbers of the Federalist; and it was in this city that he commenced his brilliant career under the new Constitution, having been elected into the House of Representatives of the first Congress. The recorded votes and debates of those times show his active and efficient agency in every important measure of that Congress. The necessary organization of the government, the arrangement of the departments, and especially the paramount subject of revenue, engaged his attention, and divided his labors.

The legislative history of the first two or three years of the government is full of instruction. It presents, in striking light, the evils intended to be remedied by the Constitution, and the provisions which were deemed essential to the remedy of those evils. It exhibits the country, in the moment of its change from a weak and ill-defined confederacy of States, into a general, efficient, but still restrained and limited government. It shows the first working of our peculiar system, moved, as it then was, by master hands.

Gentlemen, for one, I confess I like to dwell on this part of our history. It is good for us to be here. It is good for us to study the situation of the country at this period, to survey its difficulties, to look at the conduct of its public men, to see how they struggled with obstacles, real and formidable, and how gloriously they brought the Union [8] out of its state of depression and distress. Truly, Gentlemen, these founders and fathers of the Constitution were great men, and thoroughly furnished for every good work. All that reading and learning could do; all that talent and intelligence could do; and, what perhaps is still more, all that long experience in difficult and troubled times and a deep and intimate practical knowledge of the condition of the country could do, —conspired to fit them for the great business of forming a general, but limited government, embracing common objects, extending over all the States, and yet touching the power of the States no further than those common objects require. I confess I love to linger around these original fountains, and to drink deep of their waters. I love to imbibe, in as full measure as I may, the spirit of those who laid the foundations of the government, and so wisely and skilfully balanced and adjusted its bearings and proportions.

Having been afterwards, for eight years, Secretary of State, and as

8. For "Union" pamphlet reads "country."

long President, Mr. Madison has had an experience in the affairs of the Constitution, certainly second to no man. More than any other man living, and perhaps more than any other who has lived, his whole public life has been incorporated, as it were, into the Constitution; in the original conception and project of attempting to form it, in its actual framing, in explaining and recommending it, by speaking and writing, in assisting at the first organization of the government under it, and in a long administration of its executive powers,—in these various ways he has lived near the Constitution, and with the power of imbibing its true spirit, and inhaling its very breath, from its first pulsation of life. Again, therefore, I ask, If he cannot tell us what the Constitution is, and what it means, who can? He had retired with the respect and regard of the community, and might naturally be supposed not willing to interfere again in matters of political concern. He has, nevertheless, not withholden his opinions on the vital question discussed on that occasion, which has caused this meeting. He has stated, with an accuracy almost peculiar to himself, and so stated as, in my opinion, to place almost beyond further controversy, the true doctrines of the Constitution. He has stated, not notions too loose and irregular to be called even a theory, not ideas struck out by the feeling of present inconvenience or supposed maladministration, not suggestions of expediency, or evasions of fair and straightforward construction, but elementary principles, clear and sound distinctions, and indisputable truths. I am sure, Gentlemen, that I speak your sentiments, as well as my own, when I say, that, for making public so clearly and distinctly as he has done his own opinions on these vital questions of constitutional law, Mr. Madison has founded a new and strong claim on the gratitude of a grateful country. You will think, with me, that, at his advanced age, and in the enjoyment of general respect and approbation for a long career of public services, it was an act of distinguished patriotism, when he saw notions promulgated and maintained which he deemed unsound and dangerous, not to hesitate to come forward and to place the weight of his own opinion in what he deemed the right scale, come what come might. I am sure, Gentlemen, it cannot be doubted,—the manifestation is clear,—that the country feels deeply the force of this new obligation.[9]

Gentlemen, what I have said of the benefits of the Constitution to your city might be said, with little change, in respect to every other part of the country. Its benefits are not exclusive. What has it left undone, which any government could do, for the whole country? In what condition has it placed us? Where do we now stand? Are we elevated, or degraded, by its operation? What is our condition under its influence,

9. James Madison to the editor of the *North American Review*, August, 1830, in *North American Review*, 31 (October, 1830): 537–546.

at the very moment when some talk of arresting its power and breaking its unity? Do we not feel ourselves on an eminence? Do we not challenge the respect of the whole world? What has placed us thus high? What has given us this just pride? What else is it, but the unrestrained and free operation of that same Federal Constitution, which it has been proposed now to hamper, and manacle, and nullify? Who is there among us, that, should he find himself on any spot of the earth where human beings exist, and where the existence of other nations is known, would not be proud to say, I am an American? I am a countryman of Washington? I am a citizen of that republic, which, although it has suddenly sprung up, yet there are none on the globe who have ears to hear, and have not heard of it; who have eyes to see, and have not read of it; who know any thing, and yet do not know of its existence and its glory? And, Gentlemen, let me now reverse the picture. Let me ask, who there is among us, if he were to be found to-morrow in one of the civilized countries of Europe, and were there to learn that this goodly form of government had been overthrown, that the United States were no longer united, that a death-blow had been struck upon their bond of union, that they themselves had destroyed their chief good and their chief honor,—who is there whose heart would not sink within him? Who is there who would not cover his face for very shame?

At this very moment, Gentlemen, our country is a general refuge for the distressed and the persecuted of other nations. Whoever is in affliction from political occurrences in his own country looks here for shelter. Whether he be republican, flying from the oppression of thrones, or whether he be monarch or monarchist, flying from thrones that crumble and fall under or around him, he feels equal assurance, that, if he get foothold on our soil, his person will be safe, and his rights will be respected.

And who will venture to say, that, in any government now existing in the world, there is greater security for persons or property than in that of the United States? We have tried these popular institutions in times of great excitement and commotion, and they have stood, substantially, firm and steady, while the fountains of the great political deep have been elsewhere broken up; while thrones, resting on ages of proscription, have tottered and fallen; and while, in other countries, the earthquake of unrestrained popular commotion has swallowed up all law, and all liberty, and all right together. Our government has been tried in peace, and it has been tried in war, and has proved itself fit for both. It has been assailed from without, and it has successfully resisted the shock; it has been disturbed within, and it has effectually quieted the disturbance. It can stand trial, it can stand assault, it can stand adversity, it can stand every thing, but the marring of its own

beauty, and the weakening of its own strength. It can stand every thing but the effects of our own rashness and our own folly. It can stand every thing but disorganization, disunion, and nullification.

It is a striking fact, and as true as it is striking, that at this very moment, among all the principal civilized states of the world, *that* government is most secure against the danger of popular commotion which is itself entirely popular. It seems, indeed, that the submission of every thing to the public will, under constitutional restraints, imposed by the people themselves, furnishes itself security that they will desire nothing wrong.

Certain it is, that popular, constitutional liberty, as we enjoy it, appears, in the present state of the world, as sure and stable a basis for government to rest upon, as any government of enlightened states can find, or does find. Certain it is, that, in these times of so much popular knowledge, and so much popular activity, those governments which do not admit the people to partake in their administration, but keep them under and beneath, sit on materials for an explosion, which may take place at any moment, and blow them into a thousand atoms.

Gentlemen, let any man who would degrade and enfeeble the national Constitution, let any man who would nullify its laws, stand forth and tell us what he would wish. What does he propose? Whatever he may be, and whatever substitute he may hold forth, I am sure the people of this country will decline his kind interference, and hold on by the Constitution which they possess. Any one who would willingly destroy it, I rejoice to know, would be looked upon with abhorrence. It is deeply intrenched in the regards of the people. Doubtless it may be undermined by artful and long-continued hostility; it may be imperceptibly weakened by secret attack; it may be insidiously shorn of its powers by slow degrees; the public vigilance may be lulled, and when it awakes, it may find the Constitution frittered away. In these modes, or some of them, it is possible that the union of the States may be dissolved.

But if the general attention of the people be kept alive, if they see the intended mischief before it is effected, they will prevent it by their own sovereign power. They will interpose themselves between the meditated blow and the object of their regard and attachment. Next to the controlling authority of the people themselves, the preservation of the government is mainly committed to those who administer it. If conducted in wisdom, it cannot but stand strong. Its genuine, original spirit is a patriotic, liberal, and generous spirit; a spirit of conciliation, of moderation, of candor, and charity; a spirit of friendship, and not a spirit of hostility toward the States; a spirit careful not to exceed, and equally careful not to relinquish, its just powers. While no interest can or ought to feel itself shut out from the benefits of the Constitution, none should consider

those benefits as exclusively its own. The interests of all must be consulted, and reconciled, and provided for, as far as possible, that all may perceive the benefits of a united government.

Among other things, we are to remember that new States have arisen, possessing already an immense population, spreading and thickening over vast regions which were a wilderness when the Constitution was adopted. Those States are not, like New York, directly connected with maritime commerce. They are entirely agricultural, and need markets for consumption; and they need, too, access to those markets. It is the duty of the government to bring the interests of these new States into the Union, and incorporate them closely in the family compact. Gentlemen, it is not impracticable to reconcile these various interests, and so to administer the government as to make it useful to all. It was never easier to administer the government than it is now. We are beset with none, or with few, of its original difficulties; and it is a time of great general prosperity and happiness. Shall we admit ourselves incompetent to carry on the government, so as to be satisfactory to the whole country? Shall we admit that there has so little descended to us of the wisdom and prudence of our fathers? If the government could be administered in Washington's time, when it was yet new, when the country was heavily in debt, when foreign relations were in a threatening condition, and when Indian wars pressed on the frontiers, can it not be administered now? Let us not acknowledge ourselves so unequal to our duties.

Gentlemen, on the occasion referred to by the chair,[10] it became necessary to consider the judicial power, and its proper functions under the Constitution. In every free and balanced government, this is a most essential and important power. Indeed, I think it is a remark of Mr. Hume, that the administration of justice seems to be the leading object of institutions of government; that legislatures assemble, that armies are embodied, that both war and peace are made, with a sort of ultimate reference to the proper administration of laws, and the judicial protection of private rights. The judicial power comes home to every man. If the legislature passes incorrect or unjust general laws, its members bear the evil as well as others. But judicature acts on individuals. It touches every private right, every private interest, and almost every private feeling. What we possess is hardly fit to be called our own, unless we feel secure in its possession; and this security, this feeling of perfect safety, cannot exist under a wicked, or even under a weak and ignorant, administration of the laws. There is no happiness, there is no liberty, there is no enjoyment of life, unless a man can say

10. The reference is to the Webster-Hayne debate of the previous year.

when he rises in the morning, I shall be subject to the decision of no unjust judge to-day.

But, Gentlemen, the judicial department, under the Constitution of the United States, possesses still higher duties. It is true, that it may be called on, and is occasionally called on, to decide questions which are, in one sense, of a political nature. The general and State governments, both established by the people, are established for different purposes, and with different powers. Between those powers questions may arise; and who shall decide them? Some provision for this end is absolutely necessary. What shall it be? This was the question before the Convention; and various schemes were suggested. It was foreseen that the States might inadvertently pass laws inconsistent with the Constitution of the United States, or with acts of Congress. At least, laws might be passed which would be charged with such inconsistency. How should these questions be disposed of? Where shall the power of judging, in cases of alleged interference, be lodged? One suggestion in the Convention was, to make it an executive power, and to lodge it in the hands of the President, by requiring all State laws to be submitted to him, that he might negative such as he thought appeared repugnant to the general Constitution. This idea, perhaps, may have been borrowed from the power exercised by the crown over the laws of the Colonies. It would evidently have been, not only an inconvenient and troublesome proceeding, but dangerous also to the powers of the States. It was not pressed. It was thought wiser and safer, on the whole, to require State legislatures and State judges to take an oath to support the Constitution of the United States, and then leave the States at liberty to pass whatever laws they pleased, and if interference, in point of fact, should arise, to refer the question to judicial decision. To this end, the judicial power, under the Constitution of the United States, was made coextensive with the legislative power. It was extended to all cases arising under the Constitution and the laws of Congress. The judiciary became thus possessed of the authority of deciding, in the last resort, in all cases of alleged interference, between State laws and the Constitution and laws of Congress.

Gentlemen, this is the actual Constitution, this is the law of the land. There may be those who think it unnecessary, or who would prefer a different mode of deciding such questions. But this is the established mode, and, till it be altered, the courts can no more decline their duty on these occasions than on other occasions. But can any reasonable man doubt the expediency of this provision, or suggest a better? Is it not absolutely essential to the peace of the country that this power should exist somewhere? Where can it exist, better than where it now does exist? The national judiciary is the common tribunal of the whole

country. It is organized by the common authority, and its places filled by the common agent. This is a plain and practical provision. It was framed by no bunglers, nor by any wild theorists. And who can say that it has failed? Who can find substantial fault with its operation or its results? The great question is, whether we shall provide for the peaceable decision of cases of collision. Shall they be decided by law, or by force? Shall the decisions be decisions of peace, or decisions of war?

On the occasion which has given rise to this meeting, the proposition contended for in opposition to the doctrine just stated was, that every State, under certain supposed exigencies, and in certain supposed cases, might decide for itself, and act for itself, and oppose its own force to the execution of the laws. By what argument, do you imagine, Gentlemen, was such a proposition maintained? I should call it metaphysical and subtle; but these terms would imply at least ingenuity, and some degree of plausibility; whereas the argument appears to me plain assumption, mere perverse construction of plain language in the body of the Constitution itself. As I understand it, when put forth in its revised and most authentic shape, it is this: that the Constitution provides that any amendments may be made to it which shall be agreed to by three fourths of the States; there is, therefore, to be nothing in the Constitution to which three fourths of the States have not agreed. All this is true; but then comes this inference, namely, that, when one State denies the constitutionality of any law of Congress, she may arrest its execution as to herself, and keep it arrested, till the States can all be consulted by their conventions, and three fourths of them shall have decided that the law is constitutional. Indeed, the inference is still stranger than this; for State conventions have no authority to construe the Constitution, though they have authority to amend it; therefore the argument must prove, if it prove any thing, that, when any one State denies that any particular power is included in the Constitution, it is to be considered as not included, and cannot be found there till three fourths of the States agree to insert it. In short, the result of the whole is, that, though it requires three fourths of the States to insert any thing in the Constitution, yet any one State can strike any thing out of it. For the power to strike out, and the power of deciding, without appeal, upon the construction of what is already in, are substantially and practically the same.

And, Gentlemen, what a spectacle should we have exhibited under the actual operation of notions like these! At the very moment when our government was quoted, praised, and commended all over the world, when the friends of republican liberty everywhere were gazing at it with delight, and were in perfect admiration at the harmony of its movements, one State steps forth, and, by the power of nullification,

breaks up the whole system, and scatters the bright chain of the Union into as many sundered links as there are separate States!

Seeing the true grounds of the Constitution thus attacked, I raised my voice in its favor, I must confess with no preparation or previous intention. I can hardly say that I embarked in the contest from a sense of duty. It was an instantaneous impulse of inclination, not acting against duty, I trust, but hardly waiting for its suggestions. I felt it to be a contest for the integrity of the Constitution, and I was ready to enter into it, not thinking, or caring, personally, how I might come out.

Gentlemen, I have true pleasure in saying that I trust the crisis has in some measure passed by. The doctrines of nullification have received a severe and stern rebuke from public opinion. The general reprobation of the country has been cast upon them. Recent expressions of the most numerous branch of the national legislature are decisive and imposing. Everywhere, the general tone of public feeling is for the Constitution. While much will be yielded—every thing, almost, but the integrity of the Constitution, and the essential interests of the country—to the cause of mutual harmony and mutual conciliation, no ground can be granted, not an inch, to menace and bluster. Indeed, menace and bluster, and the putting forth of daring, unconstitutional doctrines, are, at this very moment, the chief obstacles to mutual harmony and satisfactory accommodation. Men cannot well reason, and confer, and take counsel together, about the discreet exercise of a power, with those who deny that any such power rightfully exists, and who threaten to blow up the whole Constitution if they cannot otherwise get rid of its operation. It is a matter of sincere gratification, Gentlemen, that the voice of this great State has been so clear and strong, and her vote all but unanimous, on the most interesting of these occasions, in the House of Representatives. Certainly, such respect to the Union becomes New York. It is consistent with her interests and her character. That singularly prosperous State, which now is, and is likely to continue to be, the greatest link in the chain of the Union, will ever be, I am sure,[11] the strongest link also. The great States which lie in her neighborhood agreed with her fully in this matter. Pennsylvania, I believe, was loyal to the Union, to a man; and Ohio raises her voice, like that of a lion, against whatsoever threatens disunion and dismemberment. This harmony of sentiment is truly gratifying. It is not to be gainsaid, that the union of opinion in this great central mass of our population, on this momentous point of the Constitution, augurs well for our future prosperity and security.

I have said, Gentlemen, what I verily believe to be true, that there is

11. For "I am sure" pamphlet reads "it is to be hoped."

no danger to the Union from open and avowed attacks on its essential principles. Nothing is to be feared from those who will march up boldly to their own propositions, and tell us that they mean to annihilate powers exercised by Congress. But, certainly, there are dangers to the Constitution, and we ought not to shut our eyes to them. We know the importance of a firm and intelligent judiciary; but how shall we secure the continuance of a firm and intelligent judiciary? Gentlemen, the judiciary is in the appointment of the executive power. It cannot continue or renew itself. Its vacancies are to be filled in the ordinary modes of executive appointment. If the time shall ever come (which Heaven avert), when men shall be placed in the supreme tribunal of the country, who entertain opinions hostile to the just powers of the Constitution, we shall then be visited by an evil defying all remedy. Our case will be past surgery. From that moment the Constitution is at an end. If they who are appointed to defend the castle shall betray it, woe betide those within! If I live to see that day come, I shall despair of the country. I shall be prepared to give it back to all its former afflictions, in the days of the Confederation. I know no security against the possibility of this evil, but an awakened public vigilance. I know no safety, but in that state of public opinion which shall lead it to rebuke and put down every attempt, either to gratify party by judicial appointments, or to dilute the Constitution by creating a court which shall construe away its provisions. If members of Congress betray their trust, the people will find it out before they are ruined. If the President should at any time violate his duty, his term of office is short, and popular elections may supply a seasonable remedy. But the judges of the Supreme Court possess, for very good reasons, an independent tenure of office. No election reaches them. If, with this tenure, they betray their trusts, Heaven save us! Let us hope for better results. The past, certainly, may encourage us. Let us hope that we shall never see the time when there shall exist such an awkward posture of affairs, as that the government shall be found in opposition to the Constitution, and when the guardians of the Union shall become its betrayers.

Gentlemen, our country stands, at the present time, on commanding ground. Older nations, with different systems of government, may be somewhat slow to acknowledge all that justly belongs to us. But we may feel without vanity, that America is doing her part in the great work of improving human affairs. There are two principles, Gentlemen, strictly and purely American, which are now likely to prevail through-out[12] the civilized world. Indeed, they seem the necessary result of the progress of civilization and knowledge. These are, first, popular govern-

12. For "prevail throughout" pamphlet reads "overrun."

ments, restrained by written constitutions; and secondly, universal education. Popular governments and general education, acting and reacting, mutually producing and reproducing each other, are the mighty agencies which in our days appear to be exciting, stimulating, and changing civilized societies. Man, everywhere, is now found demanding a participation in government,—and he will not be refused; and he demands knowledge as necessary to self-government. On the basis of these two principles, liberty and knowledge, our own American systems rest. Thus far we have not been disappointed in their results. Our existing institutions, raised on these foundations, have conferred on us almost unmixed happiness. Do we hope to better our condition by change? When we shall have nullified the present Constitution, what are we to receive in its place? As fathers, do we wish for our children better government, or better laws? As members of society, as lovers of our country, is there any thing we can desire for it better than that, as ages and centuries roll over it, it may possess the same invaluable institutions which it now enjoys? For my part, Gentlemen, I can only say, that I desire to thank the beneficent Author of all good for being born *where* I was born, and *when* I was born; that the portion of human existence allotted to me has been meted out to me in this goodly land, and at this interesting period. I rejoice that I have lived to see so much development of truth, so much progress of liberty, so much diffusion of virtue and happiness. And, through good report and evil report, it will be my consolation to be a citizen of a republic unequalled in the annals of the world for the freedom of its institutions, its high prosperity, and the prospects of good which yet lie before it. Our course, Gentlemen, is onward, straight onward, and forward. Let us not turn to the right hand, not to the left. Our path is marked out for us, clear, plain, bright, distinctly defined, like the milky way across the heavens. If we are true to our country, in our day and generation, and those who come after us shall be true to it also, assuredly, assuredly, we shall elevate her to a pitch of prosperity and happiness, of honor and power, never yet reached by any nation beneath the sun.

Gentlemen, before I resume my seat, a highly gratifying duty remains to be performed. In signifying your sentiments of regard, you have kindly chosen to select as your organ for expressing them the eminent person[13] near whom I stand. I feel, I cannot well say how sensibly, the manner in which he has seen fit to speak on this occasion. Gentlemen, if I may be supposed to have made any attainment in the knowledge

13. New York State Chancellor James Kent, whose *Commentaries on American Law,* completed less than a year earlier, was the most authoritative and already the most widely used work of its kind. Joseph Story's *Commentaries on the Constitution* did not appear until 1833.

of constitutional law, he is among the masters in whose schools I have been taught. You see near him a distinguished magistrate,[14] long associated with him in judicial labors, which have conferred lasting benefits and lasting character, not only on the State, but on the whole country. Gentlemen, I acknowledge myself much their debtor. While yet a youth, unknown, and with little expectation of becoming known beyond a very limited circle, I have passed days and nights, not of tedious, but of happy and gratified labor, in the study of the judicature of the State of New York. I am most happy to have this public opportunity of acknowledging the obligation, and of repaying it as far as it can be repaid, by the poor tribute of my profound regard, and the earnest expression of my sincere respect.[15]

Gentlemen, I will no longer detain you than to propose a toast: —

The City of New York; herself the noblest eulogy on the Union of the States.

14. Ambrose Spencer, (1765–1848) former chief justice of the New York Supreme Court.

15. Pamphlet reads ". . . my profound regard and most sincere good wishes."

The Nomination of Van Buren, January 24–25, 1832

By the middle of Andrew Jackson's first term in office his administration was torn by political and social dissension. The aristocratic wife of Vice-President John C. Calhoun refused social amenities with the wife of Jackson's old friend and comrade-in-arms, now secretary of war, John H. Eaton. Peggy Eaton's father ran a tavern where Peggy herself had once been a barmaid. Other cabinet wives followed Mrs. Calhoun's lead. The cabinet could not meet because the two factions would not sit down together. Only Secretary of State Martin Van Buren, a widower with sons but no daughters, supported Eaton, thereby endearing himself to the president.

Deeper and far more important was the not-unrelated political cleavage over the presidential succession. Calhoun, who had also been vice-president under the preceding administration of John Quincy Adams, had allowed his name to go on the Jackson ticket because he believed that Jackson, also a southern slaveholder, was committed to a reduction of the tariff. So much the better that the strong-willed Tennessean had also made it known that he would serve one term only. Calhoun saw himself as the natural successor, and behaved accordingly. The Jackson inner circle, and the president himself, saw things differently, and the friction beginning with the Eaton affair was soon blown up into a major quarrel based now on General Jackson's unauthorized activities in pursuit of the Seminole Indians in 1818 while Calhoun was secretary of war. The crisis came in April 1831, Ostensibly to give the president a free hand to reorganize the cabinet, Van Buren and Eaton resigned. The secretaries of Treasury and Navy, and the attorney general declined to follow suit and were removed. Within days Louis McLane, the American minister in London, was recalled to become secretary of the treasury, and incidentally to make a place for Van Buren. The former secretary of state was commissioned as minister to Great Britain on August 1, 1831; the appointment was announced on the twelfth and Van Buren sailed for England on August 16. He had been performing his official duties for almost three months before the 22nd Congress met the first week in December, and his appointment was submitted for ratification to the Senate.

Some three weeks passed before the nomination was referred to the

Committee on Foreign Relations, which did not report until January 10, 1832. During this interval political lines were forming. Calhoun held Van Buren responsible for the sudden resurfacing of the Seminole controversy, now turned to the vice-president's detriment. Clay and his National Republican following still seethed over instructions Van Buren had sent to McLane in London—instructions that seemed not only to repudiate but to condemn the foreign policy of the Adams administration. With Calhoun's following joined to Clay's the Senate came near to an even division.

When the nomination reached the floor, in executive session on January 17, a move to table it was carried by the casting vote of the vice-president, after Webster had created a tie by leaving the Senate chamber as the vote was called. A week later, again in executive session, debate began. Webster spoke in opposition, adding further remarks the following day, January 25. The question then came to a vote, Webster voting in the negative. A 23–23 tie was broken by Calhoun against the nomination. Webster's argument, including remarks on both days, is reproduced below.

The strategy of this episode may be, and often has been, questioned. By thus making a martyr of the New Yorker, his opponents were in fact aiding in his political advancement, for Jackson, who had already decided to accept a second term after all, was now certain to tap Van Buren for his vice-president and eventual successor. So obvious was this outcome to Van Buren's personal following that they privately rejoiced in his defeat. This first incipient union of Calhoun, Clay and Webster foreshadowed the birth of the Whig Party two years later.

The text followed here is that published first in 1835 in the second volume of *Speeches and Forensic Arguments*, pp. 48–59, reprinted without change in *Works*, 3: 356–368, and in *Writings and Speeches*, 6: 89–101. The contemporary report in the *National Intelligencer* for January 28 and 31, 1832, after the injunction of secrecy was lifted, is the source for the official report in the *Register of Debates*, 22d Cong., 1st sess., pp. 1329–1333; 1365–1367. The speeches in this debate, according to the *Register* (1310), "were furnished by the respective speakers." Minor variations between this version, and that published here, are footnoted.

Mr. President, as it is highly probable that our proceedings on this nomination will be published, I deem it proper to state shortly the considerations which have influenced my opinion, and will decide my vote.

I regard this as a very important and delicate question. It is full of responsibility; and I feel the whole force of that responsibility. While

I have been in the Senate, I have opposed no nomination of the President, except for cause; and I have at all times thought that such cause should be plain and sufficient; that it should be real and substantial, not unfounded or fanciful.

I have never desired, and do not now desire, to encroach in the slightest degree on the constitutional powers of the chief magistrate of the nation. I have heretofore gone far, very far, in assenting to nominations which have been submitted to us. I voted for the appointment of all the gentlemen who composed the first cabinet; I have opposed no nomination of a foreign minister; and I have not opposed the nominations recently before us, for the reorganization of the administration. I have always been especially anxious, that, in all matters relating to our intercourse with other nations, the utmost harmony, the greatest unity of purpose, should exist between the President and the Senate. I know how much of usefulness to the public service[1] such harmony and union are calculated to produce.

I am now fully aware, Sir, that it is a serious, a very serious matter, to vote against the confirmation of a minister to a foreign court, who has already gone abroad, and has been received and accredited by the government to which he is sent. I am aware that the rejection of this nomination, and the necessary recall of the minister, will be regarded by foreign states, at the first blush, as not in the highest degree favorable to the character of our government. I know, moreover, to what injurious reflections one may subject himself, especially in times of party excitement, by giving a negative vote on such a nomination. But, after all, I am placed here to discharge *a duty*. I am not to go through a formality; I am to perform a substantial and responsible *duty*. I am to *advise* the President in matters of appointment. This is my constitutional obligation; and I shall perform it conscientiously and fearlessly. I am bound to say, then, Sir, that, for one, I do not advise nor consent to this nomination. I do not think it a fit and proper nomination; and my reasons are found in the letter of instructions written by Mr. Van Buren, on the 20th of July, 1829, to Mr. McLane, then going to the court of England, as American Minister.[2] I think these instructions derogatory, in a high degree, to the character and honor of the country. I think they show a manifest disposition in the writer of them to establish a distinction between his country and his party; to place that party above the country; to make interest at a foreign court for that party rather than for the country; to persuade the English ministry, and the English monarch, that *they* have an interest in maintaining in the

1. "to the public service" absent from *Register*.

2. No. 2, Van Buren to McLane, July 30, 1829. DNA, RG 59, Instructions, Great Britain, M–77, Roll No. 73.

United States the ascendency of the party to which the writer belongs. Thinking thus of the purpose and object of these instructions, I cannot be of opinion that their author is a proper representative of the United States at that court. Therefore it is, that I propose to vote against his nomination. It is the first time, I believe, in modern diplomacy, it is certainly the first time in our history, in which a minister to a foreign court has sought to make favor for one party at home against another, or has stooped from being the representative of the whole country to be the representative of a party. And as this is the first instance in our history of any such transaction, so I intend to do all in my power to make it the last. For one, I set my mark of disapprobation upon it; I contribute my voice and my vote to make it a negative example, to be shunned and avoided by all future ministers of the United States. If, in a deliberate and formal letter of instructions, admonitions and directions are given to a minister, and repeated, once and again, to urge these mere party considerations on the foreign government, to what extent is it probable the writer himself will be disposed to urge them, in his thousand opportunities of informal intercourse with the agents of that government?

I propose, Sir, to refer to some particular parts of these instructions; but before I do that, allow me to state, very generally, the posture of the subject to which those particulars relate. That subject is the state of our trade with the British West India colonies. I do not deem it necessary to go minutely into all the history of that trade. The occasion does not call for it. All know, that, by the convention of 1815, a reciprocity of intercourse was established between us and Great Britain. The ships of both countries were allowed to pass to and from each other respectively, with the same cargoes, and subject to the same duties. But this arrangement did not extend to the British West Indies. There our intercourse was cut off. Various discriminating and retaliatory acts were passed by England and by the United States. Eventually, in the summer of 1825, the English Parliament passed an act, offering reciprocity, *so far as the mere carrying trade was concerned*, to all nations who might choose, within one year, to accept that offer.

Mr. Adams's administration did not accept that offer; first, because it was never officially communicated to it; secondly, because, only a few months before, a negotiation on the very same subject had been suspended, with an understanding that it might be resumed; and thirdly, because it was very desirable to arrange the whole matter, if possible, by treaty, in order to secure, if we could, *the admission of our products into the British islands for consumption*, as well as the admission of our vessels. This object had been earnestly pursued ever since the peace of 1815. It was insisted on, as every body knows, through the

whole of Mr. Monroe's administration. He would not treat at all, without treating of this object. He thought the existing state of things better than any arrangement which, while it admitted our *vessels* into West India ports, still left our *productions* subject to such duties there, that they could not be carried.

Now, Sir, Mr. Adams's administration was not the first to take this ground. It only occupied the same position which its predecessor had taken. It saw no important objects to be gained by changing the state of things, unless that change was to admit our products into the British West Indies directly from our ports, and not burdened with excessive duties. The direct trade, by English enactments and American enactments, had become closed. No British ship came here from the British West Indies. No American ship went hence to those places. A circuitous trade took place through the islands of third powers; and that circuitous trade was, in many respects, not disadvantageous to us.

In this state of things, Sir, Mr. McLane was sent to England; and he received his instructions from the Secretary of State. In these instructions, and in relation to this subject of the colonial trade, are found the sentiments of which I complain. What are they? Let us examine and see.

Mr. Van Buren tells Mr. McLane, "The opportunities which you have derived from a participation in our public counsels, as well as other sources of information, will enable you to speak with confidence (as far as you may deem it proper and useful so to do) of the respective parts taken by those to whom the administration of this government is now committed, in relation to the course heretofore pursued upon the subject of the colonial trade."

Now, this is neither more nor less than saying, "You will be able to tell the British minister, whenever you think proper, that you, and I, and the leading persons in this administration, have opposed the course heretofore pursued by the government, and the country, on the subject of the colonial trade. Be sure to let him know, that, on that subject, we have held with England, and not with our own government." Now, I ask you, Sir, if this be dignified diplomacy. Is this statesmanship? Is it patriotism, or is it mere party? Is it a proof of a high regard to the honor and renown of the whole country, or is it evidence of a disposition to make a merit of belonging to one of its political divisions?

The Secretary proceeds: "Their views" (that is, the views of the present administration) "upon that point have been submitted to the people of the United States; and the counsels by which your conduct is now directed are the result of the judgment expressed by the only earthly tribunal to which the late administration was amenable for its acts."

Now, Sir, in the first place, there is very little reason to suppose that the *first* part of this paragraph is true, in point of fact; I mean that part

which intimates that the change of administration was brought about by public disapprobation of Mr. Adams's conduct respecting the subject of the colonial trade. Possibly so much was then said on a subject which so few understood, that some degree of impression may have been produced by it. But be assured, Sir, another cause will be found, by future historians, for this change; and that cause will be the popularity of a successful soldier, united with a feeling, made to be considerably extensive, that the preferences of the people in his behalf had not been justly regarded on a previous occasion. There is, Sir, very little ground to say that "the only tribunal to which the late administration was amenable" has pronounced any judgment against it for its conduct on the whole subject of the colonial trade.

But, however this may be, the *other* assertion in the paragraph is manifestly quite wide of the facts. Mr. Adams's administration did not bring forward this claim. I have stated, already, that it had been a subject both of negotiation and legislation through the whole eight years of Mr. Monroe's administration. This the Secretary knew, or was bound to know. Why, then, does he speak of it as set up by the late administration, and afterwards abandoned by them, and not now revived?

But the most humiliating part of the whole follows:—"To set up the acts of the late administration as the cause of forfeiture of privileges which would otherwise be extended to the people of the United States, would, under existing circumstances, be unjust in itself, and could not fail to excite their deepest sensibility."

So, then, Mr. President, we are reduced, are we, to the poor condition, that we see a minister of this great republic instructed to argue, or to intercede, with the British minister, lest he should find us to have forfeited our privileges; and lest these privileges should no longer be extended to us! And we have forfeited those privileges by our misbehavior in choosing rulers, who thought better of our own claim than of the British! Why, Sir, this is patiently submitting to the domineering tone of the British minister, I believe Mr. Huskisson—[Mr. Clay said, "No, Mr. Canning."]—Mr. Canning, then, Sir, who told us that all our trade with the West Indies was a boon, granted to us by the indulgence of England. The British minister calls it a boon, and our minister admits it as a privilege, and hopes that his Majesty[3] will be gracious to decide that we have forfeited this privilege, by our misbehavior in the choice of our rulers! Sir, for one, I reject all idea of holding any right of trade, or any other rights, as a privilege or a boon from the British government, or any other government.

3. *Register* reads "royal Majesty."

At the conclusion of the paragraph, the Secretary says, "You cannot press this view of the subject too earnestly upon the consideration of the British ministry. It has bearings and relations that reach beyond the immediate question under discussion."

Adverting again to the same subject, towards the close of the despatch, he says, "I will add nothing as to the impropriety of suffering any feelings that find their origin in the past pretensions of this government to have an adverse influence upon the present condition of Great Britain."

I ask again, Mr. President, if this be statesmanship? if this be dignity? if this be elevated regard for country? Can any man read this whole despatch with candor, and not admit that it is plainly and manifestly the writer's intention to promote the interests of his party at the expense of those of the country?[4]

Lest I should do the Secretary injustice, I will read all that I find, in this letter, upon this obnoxious point. These are the paragraphs:—

> Such is the present state of our commercial relations with the British colonies; and such the steps by which we have arrived at it. In reviewing the events which have preceded, and more or less contributed to, a result so much to be regretted, there will be found three grounds upon which we are most assailable;—1st. In our too long and too tenaciously resisting the right of Great Britain to impose protecting duties in her colonies; 2d, &c.
>
> The opportunities which you have derived from a participation in our public counsels, as well as other sources of information, will enable you to speak with confidence (as far as you may deem it proper and useful so to do) of the respective parts taken by those to whom the administration of this government is now committed, in relation to the course heretofore pursued upon the subject of the colonial trade. Their views upon that point have been submitted to the people of the United States; and the counsels by which your conduct is now directed are the result of the judgment expressed by the only earthly tribunal to which the late administration was amenable for its acts. It should be sufficient that the claims set up by them, and which caused the interruption of the trade in question, have been explicitly abandoned by those who first asserted them, and are not revived by their successors. If Great Britain deems it adverse to her interests to allow us to participate in the trade with her colonies, and finds nothing in the extension of it to others to induce her to apply the same rule to us, she will, we hope, be sensible of the propriety of placing her re-

4. For "the writer's intention" to the end of the paragraph, *Register* substitutes "the writer's object, to gain credit, with the British Ministry, for the present Administration, at the expense of the past? Certainly this object appears to me as plain and visible as the sun at noon."

fusal on those grounds. To set up the acts of the late administration as the cause of forfeiture of privileges which would otherwise be extended to the people of the United States, would, under existing circumstances, be unjust in itself, and could not fail to excite their deepest sensibility. The tone of feeling which a course so unwise and untenable is calculated to produce, would doubtless be greatly aggravated by the consciousness that Great Britain has, by order in council, opened her colonial ports to Russia and France, notwithstanding a similar omission on their part to accept the terms offered by the act of July, 1825. You cannot press this view of the subject too earnestly upon the consideration of the British ministry. It has bearings and relations that reach beyond the immediate question under discussion.

I will add nothing as to the impropriety of suffering any feelings that find their origin in the past pretensions of this government to have an adverse influence upon the present conduct of Great Britain.

Sir, I submit to you, and to the candor of all just men, if I am not right in saying that the pervading topic, through the whole, is, not American rights, not American interests, not American defence, but denunciation of past pretensions of our own country, reflections on the past administration, and exultation and a loud claim of merit for the administration now in power. Sir, I would forgive mistakes; I would pardon the want of information; I would pardon almost any thing, where I saw true patriotism and sound American feeling; but I cannot forgive the sacrifice of this feeling to mere party. I cannot concur in sending abroad a public agent, who has not conceptions so large and liberal as to feel, that, in the presence of foreign courts, amidst the monarchies of Europe, he is to stand up for his country, and his whole country; that no jot nor tittle of her honor is to suffer in his hands; that he is not to allow others to reproach either his government or his country, and far less is he himself to reproach either; that he is to have no objects in his eye but American objects, and no heart in his bosom but an American heart; and that he is to forget self, and forget party, to forget every sinister and narrow feeling, in his proud and lofty attachment to the republic whose commission he bears.

Mr. President, I have discharged an exceedingly unpleasant duty, the most unpleasant of my public life. But I have looked upon it *as a duty*, and it was not to be shunned. And, Sir, however unimportant may be the opinion of so humble an individual as myself, I now only wish that I might be heard by every independent freeman in the United States, by the British minister and the British king, and by every minister and every crowned head in Europe, while, standing here in my place, I pronounce my rebuke, as solemnly and as decisively as I can, upon this

first instance in which an American minister has been sent abroad as the representative of his party, and not as the representative of his country.

[The Senate did not resume its debates on the Van Buren nomination until Thursday, January 26, when it again went into executive session, following brief discussion of the Bank question. Forsyth continued to be spokesman for the Jackson administration, and it was in reply to some remarks by the Georgia senator that Webster took the floor to pick up the threads of his earlier argument.]

It is, in my judgment, a great mistake to suppose that what is now called the American "pretension" originated with Mr. Adams, either as President or Secretary of State. By the way, it is singular enough that the American side of this question is called, in the instructions before us, a pretension too long persisted in; while the British side of it is called a right, too long and too tenaciously resisted by us. This courteous mode of speaking of the claims of a foreign government, and this reproachful mode of speaking of the claims of our own, is certainly somewhat novel in diplomacy. But whether it be called, respectfully, a claim, or, reproachfully, a pretension, it did not originate with Mr. Adams. It had a much earlier origin. This "pretension," now abandoned with so much scorn, or this claim, said, reproachfully, to have been first set up by the late administration, originated with George Washington. He put his own hand to it. He insisted on it; and he would not treat with England on the subject of the colonial trade without considering it.

In his instructions to Mr. Morris, under his own hand, in October, 1789, President Washington says: —

> Let it be strongly impressed on your mind, that the privilege of carrying our productions in our vessels to their islands, and bringing in return the productions of those islands to our own ports and markets, is regarded here as of the highest importance; and you will be careful not to countenance any idea of our dispensing with it in a treaty. Ascertain, if possible, their views on this subject; for it would not be expedient to commence negotiations without previously having good reasons to expect a satisfactory termination of them.[5]

Observe, Sir, that President Washington, in these instructions, is not speaking of the empty and futile right of sending our own vessels without cargoes to the British West Indies; but he is speaking of the substantial right of carrying our own products to the islands, for sale and for consumption there. And whether these products were shut out by a

5. Washington to Gouverneur Morris, Oct. 13, 1789. Walter Lowrie and Matthew St. Clair, eds., *American* *State Papers: Foreign Relations* (6 vols., Washington, D.C., 1832–1859), 1: 122.

positive act of Parliament, or by a tariff of duties absolutely and necessarily prohibitory, could make no difference. The object was to provide by treaty, if it could be done, that our products should find their way, effectually and profitably, into the markets of the British West Indies. This was General Washington's object. This was the "pretension" which *he* set up.

It is well known, Sir, that no satisfactory arrangement was made in General Washington's time respecting our trade with the British West Indies. But the breaking out of the French Revolution, and the wars which it occasioned, were causes which of themselves opened the ports of the West Indies. During the long continuance of those wars, our vessels, with cargoes of our own products, found their way into the British West India Islands, under a practical relaxation of the British colonial system. While this condition of things lasted, we did very well without a particular treaty. But on the general restoration of peace, in 1815,[6] Great Britain returned to her former system; then the islands were shut against us; and then it became necessary to treat on the subject,[7] and our ministers were, successively, instructed to treat, from that time forward. And, Sir, I undertake to say, that neither Mr. Madison, who was then President, nor his successor, Mr. Monroe, gave any authority or permission to any American minister to abandon this pretension,[8] or even to waive it or postpone it, and make a treaty without providing for it. No such thing. On the contrary, it will appear, I think, if we look through papers which have been sent to the Senate, that, under Mr. Madison's administration, our minister in England was fully instructed on this subject, and expected to press it. As to Mr. Monroe, I have means of being informed, in a manner not liable to mistake, that he was on this subject always immovable. He would not negotiate without treating on this branch of the trade; nor did I ever understand, that, in regard to this matter, there was any difference of opinion whatever among the gentlemen who composed Mr. Monroe's cabinet. Mr. Adams, as Secretary of State, wrote the despatches and the instructions; but the policy was the policy of the whole administration, as far as I ever understood. Certain it is, it was the settled and determined policy of Mr. Monroe himself. Indeed, Sir, so far is it from being true that this *pretension* originated with Mr. Adams, that it was in his administration that, for the first time, permission was given, under very peculiar circumstances, and with instructions,[9] to negotiate a

6. For this clause *Register* reads: "But when the European wars, and our war, all ceased, then . . ."

7. *Register* puts a period after "subject" and adds: "And, sir, we proposed to treat; our ministers . . ."

8. After "pretension" *Register* inserts "and give it up."

9. For "instructions" *Register* reads "restrictions."

treaty, waiving this part of the question. This has been already alluded to, and fully explained, by the honorable member from Kentucky. [10]

So, then, Sir, this *pretension*, asserted in the instructions to have been first set up by the late administration, is shown to have had President Washington for its author, and to have received the countenance of every President who had occasion to act on the subject, from 1789 down to the time of the present administration.

But this is not all. Congress itself sanctioned the same "pretension." The act of the 1st of March, 1823, makes it an express condition upon which, and upon which alone, our ports shall be opened to British vessels and cargoes from the West Indies on paying the same duties as our vessels and cargoes, *that our products shall be admitted into these islands without paying any other or higher duties than shall be paid on similar productions coming from elsewhere.* All this will be seen by reference to the third section of that act. Now remember, Sir, that this act of Congress passed in March, 1823, two years before the commencement of Mr. Adams's administration. The act originated in the Senate. The honorable Senator from Maryland [Samuel Smith], who has spoken on this subject to-day, was then a member of the Senate, and took part in the discussion of this very bill, and he supported it, and voted for it. It passed both houses, without material opposition in either. How is it possible, after referring to this law of 1823, to find any apology for the assertion contained in these instructions, that this claim is a pretension first set up by Mr. Adams's administration? [11] How is it possible that this law could have been overlooked or not remembered? In short, Sir, with any tolerable acquaintance with the history of the negotiations of the United States or their legislation, how are we to account for it that such an assertion as these instructions contain should have found its way into them?

But the honorable member from Georgia [John Forsyth] asks why we lay all this to the charge of the Secretary, and not to the charge of the President. The answer is, the President's conduct is not before us. We

10. Clay's remarks were generally defensive of the Adams administration, in which he himself had been secretary of state. He does not fail to note the problems created for foreign intercourse by a hostile Congress.

11. The following footnote appears in the *Register* at this point: "The circumstances did not occur to Mr. Webster's recollection at the moment he was speaking, but the truth is, that Mr. Van Buren was himself a member of the Senate at the very time of the passing of the law of 1823, and Mr. McLane was at the same time a member of the House of Representatives. So that Mr. Van Buren did himself certainly concur in 'setting up the pretension,' two years before Mr. Adams became President." In *Speeches and Forensic Arguments*, 2: 49–59, *Works*, 3: 356–368, and *W&S*, 5: 89–101, the note is transposed to the end of the speech.

are not, and cannot become, his accusers, even if we thought there were any thing in his conduct which gave cause for accusation. But the Secretary *is* before us. Not brought before us by any act of ours, but placed before us by the President's nomination. On that nomination we cannot decline to act. We must either confirm or reject it. As to the notion that the Secretary of State was but the instrument of the President, and so not responsible for these instructions, I reject at once all such defence, excuse, or apology, or whatever else it may be called. If there be any thing in a public despatch derogatory to the honor of the country, as I think there is in this, it is enough for me that I see whose hand is to it. If it be said, that the signer was only an instrument in the hands of others, I reply, that I cannot concur in conferring a high public diplomatic trust on any one who has consented, under any circumstances, to be an instrument in such a case.

The honorable member from Georgia asks, also, why we have slept on this subject, and why, at this late day, we bring forward complaints. Sir, nobody has slept upon it. Since these instructions have been made public, there has been no previous opportunity to discuss them. The honorable member will recollect, that the whole arrangement with England was made and completed before these instructions saw the light. The President opened the trade by his proclamation, in October, 1830; but these instructions were not publicly sent to Congress till long[12] afterwards, that is, till January, 1831. They were not then sent with any view that either house should act upon the subject, for the whole business was already settled. For one, I never saw the instructions, nor heard them read, till January, 1831; nor did I ever hear them spoken of as containing these obnoxious passages. This, then, is the first opportunity for considering these instructions.

That they have been subjects of complaint out doors since they were made public, and of much severe animadversion, is certainly true. But, until now, there never has been an opportunity naturally calling for their discussion here. The honorable gentleman may be assured, that, if such occasion had presented itself, it would have been embraced.

I entirely forbear, Mr. President, from going into the merits of the late arrangement with England, as a measure of commercial policy. Another time will come, I trust, more suitable for that discussion. For the present, I confine myself strictly to such parts of the instructions as I think plainly objectionable, whatever may be the character of the agreement between us and England, as a matter of policy. I repeat, Sir, that I place the justification of my vote on the *party* tone and *party* character of these instructions. Let us[13] ask, If such considerations as

12. *Register* omits "long."   13. *Register* reads "me."

these are to be addressed to a foreign government, what is that foreign government to expect in return? The ministers of foreign courts will not bestow gratuitous favors, nor even gratuitous smiles, on American parties. What, then, I repeat, is to be the return? What is party to do[14] for that foreign government which has done, is expected to do, or is asked to do, something for party[15]? What is to be the consideration paid for this foreign favor? Sir, must not every man see, that any mixture of such causes or motives of action in our foreign intercourse is as full of danger as it is of dishonor?

I will not pursue the subject. I am anxious only to make my own ground fully and clearly understood; and willingly leave every other gentleman to his own opinions. And I cheerfully submit my own vote to the opinions of the country. I willingly leave it to the people of the United States to say, whether I am acting a factious and unworthy part, or the part of a true-hearted American, in withholding my approbation from the nomination of a gentleman as minister to England, who has already, as it appears to me, instructed his predecessor at the same court to carry party considerations, to argue party merits, and solicit party favors, at the foot of the British throne.

14. *Register* inserts "here."   15. *Register* inserts "here."

Report on Apportionment, April 5, 1832

The constitutional provision for apportionment of representatives after each decennial census is stated in general terms. Representation is to be in proportion to population, with two qualifications: the base for representation must be not less than 30,000 persons, but each state must have at least one representative. It is left to Congress to decide every ten years how many representatives there shall be and how large a population each shall serve. The ambiguity appeared with the first census. The House divided the population of each state by 30,000, disregarded remainders (which would necessarily be less than the prescribed minimum), and sent to the Senate a bill providing for 112 representatives. The Senate divided the total population by 30,000 and came up with 120. The extra eight representatives were assigned to states having the largest fractions. The House accepted this arrangement, but the president did not. Washington vetoed the bill on the ground that representation of fractions violated the Constitution. A new bill, rejecting fractions, was substituted and became the precedent for succeeding censuses.

A bill to apportion representatives under the 5th Census passed the House early in February 1832, embodying the same provisions as in previous apportionments. A base figure was selected, divided into the total population of each state (including three-fifths of the slaves), and the quotient became the number of representatives to which the state was entitled. The leftovers, or fractions, were disregarded. By this time the always politically sensitive problem was aggravated by rising tension between North and South, and by the rapid growth of the West where the balance of power now lodged. The House bill, using a ratio of 47,700, would increase New York's representation by 6 and Pennsylvania's by 2; the slave states would receive an aggregate of 6 additional representatives, while the West gained 11. But in New England a gain of one seat in Maine was less than enough to offset losses of one each in New Hampshire and Massachusetts.

The Massachusetts delegation was outraged. The day before the new apportionment passed the House, John Quincy Adams spoke to Webster, who assured the ex-president that he "would make a dead set against the bill in the Senate." The morning of the 17th, before Congress met at noon, the entire Massachusetts delegation, senators as well

as representatives, met at Adams's call to discuss their problem. Webster promised to ask reference to a select committee in the Senate, in hopes of reducing the ratio to 44,000 (Adams, *Memoirs*, 8: 472–474) but he well knew that would not be enough. When the House apportionment bill reached the Senate that afternoon Webster duly moved that it be referred to a select committee of seven members, and it was so ordered. Webster, by custom, was named chairman, the others being Alexander Buckner of Missouri, George M. Dallas of Pennsylvania, John Forsyth of Georgia, Robert Y. Hayne of South Carolina, William L. Marcy of New York, and John Tipton of Indiana. It was not such a committee as would be likely to follow Webster's lead in the matter at hand, and it did not. The House bill was reported without amendment on February 21. (For the parliamentary record see *Senate Journal*, 22d Cong., 1st sess., Feb. 17–Apr. 26, *passim.*)

Webster was not ready to accept such a verdict. On February 27 he laid on the table an amendment which he intended to propose when the House bill came up for consideration. The amendment was a substitute, offering a ratio of 47,000 but providing "one additional member for each State whose fractional numbers, remaining after dividing its whole numbers by forty-seven thousand as aforesaid, shall exceed twenty-five thousand persons, the said number of representatives in any State not exceeding one for every thirty thousand persons." (*Register of Debates*, 22d Cong., 1st sess., p. 487.) New England's losses were made up and the region gained two representatives. In explanation of his amendment Webster "made an eloquent speech" according to John Quincy Adams, who had left his seat in the House to sit in the Senate gallery. Debate continued over the next four weeks during which different ratios and combinations were discussed, each Senator having an eye to his own state. On March 27 John M. Clayton of Delaware moved reference to another select committee, this time of five members, again to be chaired by Webster. Forsyth and Hayne remained from the old committee, with Clayton and Willie P. Mangum of North Carolina added. On April 5 Webster, for his new committee, offered the Report printed below.

Debate continued until April 26, when a modified version of Webster's bill passed, 20 to 18. In the major debate on April 25, Webster said little. Dallas led the opposition, while Clayton carried the chief burden of defending the bill. As finally passed the size of the House was fixed at 251 and the ratio, as sent up from the House, at 47,700. New England gained two seats; but more important for Webster was the principle of representing major fractions. The triumph was short-lived. The House refused to concur in the amendments, and on May 19 the Senate receded, 26–19. The apportionment under the 5th Census

remained as the House had provided, but Webster's more equitable distribution of representatives would be taken up at another census. (See Walter F. Willcox, "The Apportionment Problem and the Size of the House: A Return to Webster," *Cornell Law Quarterly*, 35 (Winter, 1950): 367–389. See also *Correspondence*, 3: 151–153, 155–157, 168; and Edward Everett to Joseph Story, May 19, 1832, Massachusetts Historical Society *Proceedings*, 2d series, 15: 206–207.)

The text of Webster's *Report*, as reproduced below, is from *Writings and Speeches*, 6: 102–121, identical with *Works*, 3: 369–388. The *Report* first appeared in the *National Intelligencer*, April 12, 1832. It reached official publication as Senate Document No. 119, 22d Cong., 1st sess., in Serial 214. The Senate Document appears to have been the text followed in *Speeches and Forensic Arguments*, 2: 60–75, which in turn became the text for *Works*. Differences are very minor, but are identified in footnotes.

The Select Committee, to whom was referred, on the 27th of March, the bill from the House of Representatives, entitled, "An Act for the Apportionment of Representatives among the several States according to the Fifth Census," have had the subject under consideration, and now ask leave to report:

This bill, like all laws on the same subject, must be regarded as of an interesting and delicate nature. It respects the distribution of political power among the States of the Union. It is to determine the number of voices which, for ten years to come, each State is to possess in the popular branch of the legislature. In the opinion of the committee, there can be few or no questions which it is more desirable to settle on just, fair, and satisfactory principles, than this; and, availing themselves of the benefit of the discussion which the bill has already undergone in the Senate, they have given to it a renewed and anxious consideration. The result is, that, in their opinion, the bill ought to be amended. Seeing the difficulties which belong to the whole subject, they are fully convinced that the bill has been framed and passed in the other House with the sincerest desire to overcome these difficulties, and to enact a law which should do as much justice as possible to all the States. But the committee are constrained to say, that this object appears to them not to have been attained. The unequal operation of the bill on some of the States, should it become a law, seems to the committee most manifest; and they cannot but express a doubt whether its actual apportionment of the representative power among the several States can be considered as conformable to the spirit of the Constitution.

The bill provides, that from and after the 3d of March, 1833, the House of Representatives shall be composed of members elected agreeably to a ratio of one Representative for every forty-seven thousand and seven hundred persons in each State, computed according to the rule prescribed by the Constitution. The addition of the seven hundred to the forty-seven thousand, in the composition of this ratio, produces no effect whatever in regard to the constitution of the House. It neither adds to nor takes from the number of members assigned to any State. Its only effect is a reduction of the apparent amount of the fractions, as they are usually called, or residuary numbers, after the application of the ratio. For all other purposes, the result is precisely the same as if the ratio had been forty-seven thousand.

As it seems generally admitted that inequalities do exist in this bill, and that injurious consequences will arise from its operation, which it would be desirable to avert, if any proper means of averting them, without producing others equally injurious, could be found, the committee do not think it necessary to go into a full and particular statement of these consequences. They will content themselves with presenting a few examples only of these results, and such as they find it most difficult to reconcile with justice and the spirit of the Constitution.

In exhibiting these examples, the committee must necessarily speak of particular States; but it is hardly necessary to say, that they speak of them as examples only, and with the most perfect respect, not only for the States themselves, but for all those who represent them here.

Although the bill does not commence by fixing the whole number of the proposed House of Representatives, yet the process adopted by it brings out the number of two hundred and forty members. Of these two hundred and forty members, forty are assigned to the State of New York; that is to say, precisely one sixth part of the whole. This assignment would seem to require that New York should contain one sixth part of the whole population of the United States, and should be bound to pay one sixth part of all direct taxes. Yet neither of these is the case. The whole representative population of the United States is 11,929,005; that of New York is 1,918,623, which is less than one sixth of the whole, by nearly 70,000. Of a direct tax of two hundred and forty thousand dollars, New York would pay only $38.59.

But if, instead of comparing the numbers assigned to New York with the whole numbers of the House, we compare her with other States, the inequality is still more evident and striking. To the State of Vermont the bill assigns five members. It gives, therefore, eight times as many Representatives to New York as to Vermont; but the population of New York is not equal to eight times the population of Vermont, by more than three hundred thousand. Vermont has five members only for 280,-

657 persons. If the same proportion were to be applied to New York, it would reduce the number of her members from forty to *thirty-four*, making a difference more than equal to the whole representation of Vermont, and more than sufficient to overcome her whole power in the House of Representatives.

A disproportion almost equally striking is manifested, if we compare New York with Alabama. The population of Alabama is 262,203[1]; for this she is allowed five members. The rule of proportion which gives to her but five members for her number, would give to New York but thirty-six for her number. Yet New York receives forty. As compared with Alabama, then, New York has an excess of representation equal to four fifths of the whole representation of Alabama; and this excess itself will give her, of course, as much weight in the House as the whole delegation of Alabama, within a single vote. Can it be said, then, that Representatives are apportioned to these States according to their respective numbers?

The ratio assumed by the bill, it will be perceived, leaves large fractions, so called, or residuary numbers, in several of the small States, to the manifest loss of a great part[2] of their just proportion of representative power. Such is the operation of the ratio, in this respect, that New York, with a population less than that of New England by thirty or thirty-five thousand, has yet two more members than all the New England States; and there are seven States in the Union, represented, according to the bill, by one hundred and twenty-three members, being a clear majority of the whole House, whose aggregate fractions, all together, amount to fifty-three thousand; while Vermont and New Jersey, having together but eleven members, have a joint fraction of seventy-five thousand.

Pennsylvania, by the bill, will have, as it happens, just as many members as Vermont, New Hampshire, Massachusetts, and New Jersey; but her population is not equal to theirs by a hundred and thirty thousand; and the reason of this advantage, derived to her from the provision of the bill, is, that her fraction, or residuum, is twelve thousand only, while theirs is a hundred and forty-four thousand.

But the subject is capable of being presented in a more exact and mathematical form. The House is to consist of two hundred and forty members. Now, the precise portion of power, out of the whole mass presented by the number of two hundred and forty,[3] to which New York would be entitled according to her population, is 38.59; that is to say,

1. This same figure appears in the Senate Document, but all charts and tables appended to the latter version give 262,508.

2. Senate Document deletes "great."

3. Senate Document reads "represented" instead of "presented"; also deletes "of" following.

she would be entitled to thirty-eight members, and would have a residuum or fraction; and even if a member were given her for that fraction, she would still have but thirty-nine. But the bill gives her forty.

These are a part, and but a part, of those results, produced by the bill in its present form, which the committee cannot bring themselves to approve. While it is not to be denied, that, under any rule of apportionment, some degree of relative inequality must always exist, the committee cannot believe that the Senate will sanction inequality and injustice to the extent in which they exist in this bill, if it can be avoided. But, recollecting the opinions which had been expressed in the discussions of the Senate, the committee have diligently sought to learn whether there was not some other number which might be taken for a ratio, the application of which would produce more justice and equality. In this pursuit, the committee have not been successful. There are, it is true, other numbers, the adoption of which would relieve many of the States which suffer under the present; but this relief would be obtained only by shifting the pressure to other States, thus creating new grounds of complaint in other quarters. The number 44,000 has been generally spoken of as the most acceptable substitute for 47,700; but should this be adopted, great relative inequality would fall on several States, and, among them, on some of the new and growing States, whose relative disproportion, thus already great, would be constantly increasing.

The committee, therefore, are of opinion that the bill should be altered in the mode of apportionment. They think that the process which begins by assuming a ratio should be abandoned, and that the bill ought to be framed on the principle of the amendment which has been the main subject of discussion before the Senate. The fairness of the principle of this amendment, and the general equity of its results, compared with those which flow from the other process, seem plain and undeniable. The main question has been, whether the principle itself be constitutional, and this question the committee proceed[4] to examine, respectfully asking of those who have doubted its constitutional propriety to consider the question of so much importance as to justify a second reflection.

The words of the Constitution are,—

> Representatives and direct taxes shall be apportioned among the several States, which may be included within this Union, according to their respective numbers, which shall be determined by adding to the whole number of free persons, including those bound to service for a term of years, and excluding Indians, three

4. Senate Document reads "proceeded."

fifths of all other persons. The actual enumeration shall be made within three years after the first meeting of the Congress of the United States, and within every subsequent term of ten years, in such manner as they shall by law direct. The number of Representatives shall not exceed one for every thirty thousand, but each State shall have at least one Representative.

There would seem to be little difficulty in understanding these provisions. The terms used are designed, doubtless, to be received in no peculiar or technical sense, but according to their common and popular acceptation. To *apportion* is to distribute by right measure, to set off in just parts, to assign in due and proper proportion. These clauses of the Constitution respect not only the portions of power, but the portions of the public burden, also, which should fall to the several States; and the same language is applied to both. Representatives are to be apportioned among the States according to their respective numbers, and direct taxes are to be apportioned by the same rule. The end aimed at is, that representation and taxation should go hand in hand; that each State should be represented in the same extent to which it is made subject to the public charges by direct taxation. But between the apportionment of Representatives and the apportionment of taxes, there necessarily exists one essential difference. Representation founded on numbers must have some limit, and being, from its nature, a thing not capable of indefinite subdivision, it cannot be made precisely equal. A tax, indeed, cannot always, or often, be apportioned with perfect exactness; as in other matters of account, there will be fractional parts of the smallest coins, and the smallest denomination of money of account; yet, by the usual subdivisions of the coin, and of the denominations of money, the apportionment of taxes is capable of being made so exact, that the inequality becomes minute and invisible. But representation cannot be thus divided. Of representation, there can be nothing less than one Representative; nor, by our Constitution, more Representatives than one for every thirty thousand. It is quite obvious, therefore, that the apportionment of representative power can never be precise and perfect. There must always exist some degree of inequality. Those who framed and those who adopted the Constitution were, of course, fully acquainted with this necessary operation of the provision. In the Senate, the States are entitled to a fixed number of Senators; and therefore, in regard to their representation in that body, there is no consequential or incidental inequality. But, being represented in the House of Representatives according to their respective numbers of people, it is unavoidable that, in assigning to each State its number of members, the exact proportion of each, out of a given number, cannot always or often be expressed in whole numbers; that is to say, it will not often

be found that there belongs to a State exactly one tenth, or one twentieth, or one thirtieth of the whole House; and therefore no number of Representatives will exactly correspond with the right of such State, or the precise share of representation which belongs to it, according to its population.

The Constitution, therefore, must be understood, not as enjoining an absolute relative equality, because that would be demanding an impossibility, but as requiring of Congress to make the apportionment of Representatives among the several States according to their respective numbers, *as near as may be.* That which cannot be done perfectly must be done in a manner as near perfection as can be. If exactness cannot, from the nature of things, be attained, then the nearest practicable approach to exactness ought to be made.

Congress is not absolved from all rule merely because the rule of perfect justice cannot be applied. In such a case, approximation becomes a rule; it takes the place of that other rule, which would be preferable, but which is found inapplicable, and becomes itself an obligation of binding force. The nearest approximation to exact truth or exact right, when that exact truth or that exact right cannot itself be reached, prevails in other cases, not as matter of discretion, but as an intelligible and definite rule, dictated by justice and conforming to the common sense of mankind; a rule of no less binding force in cases to which it is applicable, and no more to be departed from, than any other rule or obligation.

The committee understand the Constitution as they would have understood it if it had said, in so many words, that Representatives should be apportioned among the States according to their respective numbers, *as near as may be.* If this be not its true meaning, then it has either given, on this most delicate and important subject, a rule which is always impracticable, or else it has given no rule at all; because, if the rule be that Representatives shall be apportioned *exactly* according to numbers, it is impracticable in every case; and if, for this reason, that cannot be the rule, then there is no rule whatever, unless the rule be that they shall be apportioned *as near as may be.*

This construction, indeed, which the committee adopt, has not, to their knowledge, been denied; and they proceed in the discussion of the question before the Senate, taking for granted that such is the true and undeniable meaning of the Constitution.

The next thing to be observed is, that the Constitution prescribes no particular process by which this apportionment is to be wrought out. It has plainly described the end to be accomplished, namely, the nearest approach to relative equality of representation among the States; and whatever accomplishes this end, and nothing else, is the true process.

In truth, if, without any process whatever, whether elaborate or easy, Congress could perceive the exact proportion of representative power rightfully belonging to each State, it would perfectly fulfil its duty by conferring that portion on each, without reference to any process whatever. It would be enough that the proper end had been attained. And it is to be remarked, further, that, whether this end be attained best by one process or by another, becomes, when each process has been carried through, not matter of opinion, but matter of mathematical certainty. If the whole population of the United States, the population of each State, and the proposed number of the House of Representatives, be all given, then, between two bills apportioning the members among the several States, it can be told with absolute certainty which bill assigns to any and every State the number nearest to the exact proportion of that State; in other words, which of the two bills, if either, apportions the Representatives according to the numbers in the States,[5] respectively, *as near as may be*. If, therefore, a particular process of apportionment be adopted, and objection be made to the injustice or inequality of its result, it is surely no answer to such objection to say, that the inequality necessarily results from the nature of the process. Before such answer could avail, it would be necessary to show, either that the Constitution prescribes such process, and makes it necessary, or that there is no other mode of proceeding which would produce less inequality and less injustice. If inequality, which might have otherwise been avoided, be produced by a given process, then that process is a wrong one. It is not suited to the case, and should be rejected.

Nor do the committee perceive how it can be matter of constitutional propriety or validity, or in any way a constitutional question, whether the process which may be applied to the case be simple or compound, one process or many processes; since, in the end, it may always be seen whether the result be that which has been aimed at, namely, the nearest practicable approach to precise justice and relative equality. The committee, indeed, are of opinion, in this case, that the simplest and most obvious way of proceeding is also the true and constitutional way. To them it appears, that, in carrying into effect this part of the Constitution, the first thing naturally to be done is to decide on the whole number of which the House is to be composed; as when, under the same clause of the Constitution, a tax is to be apportioned among the States, the amount of the whole tax is, in the first place, to be settled.

When the whole number of the proposed House is thus ascertained and fixed, it becomes the entire representative power of all the people in the Union. It is then a very simple matter to ascertain how much of

5. Senate Document reads "number of the States."

this representative power each State is entitled to by its numbers. If, for example, the House is to contain two hundred and forty members, then the number 240 expresses the representative power of all the States; and a plain calculation readily shows how much of this power belongs to each State. This portion, it is true, will not always, nor often, be expressed in whole numbers, but it may always be precisely exhibited by a decimal form of expression. If the portion of any State be seldom or never one exact tenth, one exact fifteenth, or one exact twentieth, it will still always be capable of precise decimal expression, as one tenth and two hundredths, one twelfth and four hundredths, one fifteenth and six hundredths, and so on. And the exact portion of the State, being thus decimally expressed, will always show, to mathematical certainty, what integral number comes nearest to such exact portion. For example, in a House consisting of 240 members, the exact mathematical proportion to which her numbers entitle the State of New York is 38.59; it is certain, therefore, that 39 is the integral or whole number nearest to her exact proportion of the representative power of the Union. Why, then, should she not have thirty-nine? and why should she have forty? She is not quite entitled to thirty-nine; that number is something more than her right. But allowing her thirty-nine, from the necessity of giving her whole numbers, and because that is the nearest whole number, is not the Constitution fully obeyed when she has received the thirty-ninth member? Is not her proper number of Representatives then apportioned to her, as near as may be? And is not the Constitution disregarded when the bill goes further, and gives her a fortieth member? For what is such a fortieth member given? Not for her absolute numbers, for her absolute numbers do not entitle her to thirty-nine. Not for the sake of apportioning her members to her numbers as near as may be because thirty-nine is a nearer apportionment of members to numbers than forty. But it is given, say the advocates of the bill, because the *process* which has been adopted gives it. The answer is, No such process is enjoined by the Constitution.

The case of New York may be compared, or contrasted, with that of Missouri. The exact proportion of Missouri, in a general representation of 240, is two and six tenths; that is to say, it comes nearer to three members than to two, yet it is confined to two. But why is not Missouri entitled to that number of Representatives which comes nearest to her exact proportion? Is the Constitution fulfilled as to her, while that number is withheld, and while, at the same time, in another State, not only is that nearest number given, but an additional member given also? Is it an answer with which the people of Missouri ought to be satisfied, when it is said that this obvious injustice is the necessary result of the process adopted by the bill? May they not say with propriety, that, since

three is the nearest whole number to their exact right, to that number they are entitled, and the process which deprives them of it must be a wrong process? A similar comparison might be made between New York and Vermont. The exact proportion to which Vermont is entitled, in a representation of 240, is 5.646. Her nearest whole number, therefore, would be six. Now two things are undeniably true; first, that to take away the fortieth member from New York would bring her representation nearer to her exact proportion than it stands by leaving her that fortieth member; second, that giving the member thus taken from New York to Vermont would bring her representation nearer to her exact right than it is by the bill. And both these propositions are equally true of a transfer to Delaware of the twenty-eighth member assigned by the bill to Pennsylvania, and to Missouri of the thirteenth member assigned to Kentucky. In other words, Vermont has, by her numbers, more right to six members than New York has to forty; Delaware, by her numbers, has more right to two members than Pennsylvania has to twenty-eight; and Missouri, by her numbers, has more right to three members than Kentucky has to thirteen. Without disturbing the proposed number of the House, the mere changing of these three members from and to the six States, respectively, would bring the representation of the whole six[6] nearer to their due proportion, according to their respective numbers, than the bill in its present form makes it. In the face of this indisputable truth, how can it be said that the bill apportions members of Congress among those States according to their respective numbers, *as near as may be*?

The principle on which the proposed amendment is founded is an effectual corrective for these and all other equally great inequalities. It may be applied at all times, and in all cases, and its result will always be the nearest approach to perfect justice. It is equally simple and impartial. As a rule of apportionment, it is little other than a transcript of the words of the Constitution, and its results are mathematically certain. The Constitution, as the committee understand it, says, Representatives shall be apportioned among the States according to their respective numbers of people, as near as may be. The rule adopted by the committee says, out of the whole number of the House, that number shall be apportioned to each State which comes nearest to its exact right according to its number of people.

Where is the repugnancy between the Constitution and the rule? The arguments against the rule seem to assume, that there is a necessity of instituting some process, adopting some number as the ratio, or as that number of people which each member shall be understood to represent.

6. Senate Document reads "each of the whole six." *Speeches and Fo-* *rensic Arguments* here follows Senate Document.

But the committee see no occasion for any other process whatever, than simply the ascertainment of that *quantum,* out of the whole mass of the representative power, which each State may claim.

But it is said that, although a State may receive a number of Representatives which is something less than its exact proportion of representation, yet that it can in no case constitutionally receive more. How is this proposition proved? How is it shown that the Constitution is less perfectly fulfilled by allowing a State a small excess, than by subjecting her to a large deficiency? What the Constitution requires is the nearest practicable approach to precise justice. The rule is approximation; and we ought to approach, therefore, on whichever side we can approach nearest.

But there is a still more conclusive answer to be given to this suggestion. The whole number of Representatives of which the House is to be composed is, of necessity, limited. This number, whatever it is, is that which is to be apportioned, and nothing else can be apportioned. This is the whole sum to be distributed. If, therefore, in making the apportionment, some States receive less than their just share, it must necessarily follow that some other States have received more than their just share. If there be one State in the Union with less than its right, some other State has more than its right; so that the argument, whatever be its force, applies to the bill in its present form, as strongly as it can ever apply to any bill.

But the objection most usually urged against the principle of the proposed amendment is, that it provides for the representation of fractions. Let this objection be examined and considered. Let it be ascertained, in the first place, what these fractions, or fractional numbers, or residuary numbers, really are, which it is said will be represented, should the amendment prevail.

A fraction is the broken part of some integral number. It is, therefore, a relative or derivative idea. It implies the previous existence of some fixed number, of which it is but a part or remainder. If there be no necessity for fixing or establishing such previous number, then the fraction resulting from it is itself not matter of necessity, but matter of choice or accident. Now, the argument which considers the plan proposed in the amendment as a representation of fractions, and therefore unconstitutional, assumes as its basis, that, according to the Constitution, every member of the House of Representatives represents, or ought to represent, the same, or nearly the same, number of constituents; that this number is to be regarded as an integer; and any thing less than this is therefore called a fraction, or a residuum, and cannot be entitled to a Representative. But nothing of this is prescribed

by[7] the Constitution of the United States. That Constitution contemplates no integer, or any common number for the constituents of a member of the House of Representatives. It goes not at all into these subdivisions of the population of a State. It provides for the apportionment of Representatives *among the several States*, according to their respective numbers, and stops there. It makes no provision for the representation of districts of States, or for the representation of any portion of the people of a State less than the whole. It says nothing of ratios or of constituent numbers. All these things it leaves to State legislation. The right which each State possesses to its own due portion of the representative power is a State right, strictly. It belongs to the State, as a State; and it is to be used and exercised as the State may see fit, subject only to the constitutional qualifications of electors. In fact, the States do make, and always have made, different provisions for the exercise of this power. In some, a single member is chosen for a certain defined district; in others, two or three members are chosen for the same district; and in some, again, as New Hamsphire, Rhode Island, Connecticut, New Jersey, and Georgia, the entire representation of the State is a joint and undivided representation.[8] In each of these last-mentioned States, every member of the House of Representatives has for his constituents all the people of the State; and all the people of those States are consequently represented in that branch of Congress.

If the bill before the Senate should pass into a law, in its present form, whatever injustice it might do to any of those States, it would not be correct to say to them, nevertheless, that any portion of their people was unrepresented. The well-founded objection would be, as to some of them at least, that they were not adequately, competently, fairly represented; that they had not as many voices and as many votes in the House of Representatives as they were entitled to. This would be the objection. There would be no unrepresented fraction; but the State, as a State, as a whole, would be deprived of some part of its just rights.

On the other hand, if the bill should pass as it is now proposed to be amended, there would be no representation of fractions in any State; for a fraction supposes a division and a remainder. All that could justly be said would be, that some of these States, as States, possessed a portion of legislative power a little larger than their exact right; as it must be admitted, that, should the bill pass unamended, they would possess of that power much less than their exact right. The same remarks are

7. Senate Document and *Speeches* read "But all this is not the provision of."

8. Senate Document and *Speeches* read "the whole representation of the State is exerted as a joint undivided representation."

substantially true, if applied to those States which adopt the district system, as most of them do. In Missouri, for example there will be no fraction unrepresented, should the bill become a law in its present form; nor any member for a fraction, should the amendment prevail. Because the mode of apportionment which is nearest to its exact right[9] applies no assumed ratios, makes no subdivisions, and, of course, produces no fractions. In the one case, or in the other, the State, as a State, will have something more, or something less, than its exact proportion of representative power; but she will part out this power among her own people, in either case, in such mode as she may choose, or exercise it altogether as an entire representation of the people of the State.

Whether the subdivision of the representative power within any State, if there be a subdivision, be equal or unequal, or fairly or unfairly made, Congress cannot know, and has no authority to inquire. It is enough that the State presents her own representation on the floor of Congress in the mode she chooses to present it. If a State were to give to one portion of her territory a Representative for every twenty-five thousand persons, and to the rest a Representative only for every fifty thousand, it would be an act of unjust legislation, doubtless; but it would be wholly beyond redress by any power in Congress, because the Constitution has left all this to the State itself.

These considerations, it is thought, may show that the Constitution has not, by any implication or necessary construction, enjoined that which it certainly has not ordained in terms, namely, that every member of the House should be supposed to represent the same number of constituents; and therefore, that the assumption of a ratio, as representing the common number of constituents, is not called for by the Constitution. All that Congress is at liberty to do, as it would seem, is to divide the whole representative power of the Union into twenty-four parts, assigning one part to each State, as near as practicable according to its right, and leaving all subsequent arrangement, and all subdivisions, to the State itself.

If the view thus taken of the rights of the States and the duties of Congress be the correct view, then the plan proposed in the amendment is in no just sense a representation of fractions. But suppose it was otherwise; suppose a direct provision were made for allowing a Representative to every State in whose population, it being first divided by a common ratio, there should be found a fraction exceeding half the amount of that ratio, what constitutional objection could be fairly urged against such a provision? Let it always be remembered, that the case

9. Senate Document reads "Because the mode of apportionment which assigns to each State that number which is nearest to its exact right."

here supposed provides only for a fraction exceeding the moiety of the ratio; for the committee admit at once that the representation of fractions less than a moiety is unconstitutional; because, should a member be allowed to a State for such a fraction, it would be certain that her representation would not be so near her exact right as it was before. But the allowance of a member for a major fraction is a direct approximation towards justice and equality. There appears to the committee to be nothing, either in the letter or the spirit of the Constitution, opposed to such a mode of apportionment. On the contrary, it seems entirely consistent with the very object which the Constitution contemplated, and well calculated to accomplish it. The argument commonly urged against it is, that it is necessary to apply some one common divisor, and to abide by its results.

If by this it be meant that there must be some common rule, or common measure, applicable, and applied impartially, to all the States, it is quite true. But if that which is intended be, that the population of each State must be divided by a fixed ratio, and all resulting fractions, great or small, disregarded, this is but to take for granted the very thing in controversy. The question is, whether it be unconstitutional to make approximation to equality by allowing Representatives for major fractions. The affirmative of this question is, indeed, denied, but it is not disproved, by saying that we must abide by the operation of division by an assumed ratio, and disregard fractions. The question still remains as it was before, and it is still to be shown what there is in the Constitution which rejects approximation as the rule of apportionment.

But suppose it to be necessary to find a divisor, and to abide its results. What is a divisor? Not necessarily a simple number. It may be composed of a whole number and a fraction; it may itself be the result of a previous process; it may be any thing, in short, which produces accurate and uniform division. Whatever does this is a common rule, a common standard, or, if the word be important, a common divisor. The committee refer, on this part of the case, to some observations by Professor Dean, with a table, both of which accompany this report.[10]

As it is not improbable that opinion has been a good deal influenced on this subject by what took place on the passing of the first act making an apportionment of Representatives among the States, the committee have examined and considered that precedent. If it be in point to the present case, it is certainly entitled to very great weight; but if it be of questionable application, the text of the Constitution, even if it were doubtful, cannot be explained by a doubtful commentary. In the opinion of the committee, it is only necessary that what was said on this

10. Appendixes not included. See Senate Document.

occasion should be understood in connection with the subject-matter then under consideration; and in order to see what that subject-matter really was, the committee think it necessary shortly to state the case.

The two houses of Congress passed a bill, after the first enumeration of the people, providing for a House of Representatives which should consist of 120 members.[11] The bill expressed no rule or principle by which these members were assigned to the several States. It merely said that New Hampshire should have five members, Massachusetts ten, and so on; going through all the States, and assigning the whole number of one hundred and twenty. Now, by the census then recently taken, it appeared that the whole representative population of the United States was 3,615,920; and it was evidently the wish of Congress to make the House as numerous as the Constitution would allow. But the Constitution provides that there shall not be more than one member for every thirty thousand persons.

This prohibition was, of course, to be obeyed; but did the Constitution mean that no State should have more than one member for every thirty thousand persons? Or did it only mean that the whole House, as compared with the whole population of the United States, should not contain more than one member for every thirty thousand persons? If this last were the true construction, then the bill, in that particular, was right; if the first were the true construction, then it was wrong; because so many members could not be assigned to the States, without giving to some of them more members than one for every thirty thousand. In fact, the bill did propose to do this in regard to several States.

President Washington adopted that construction of the Constitution which applied its prohibition to each State individually. He thought that no State could constitutionally receive more than one member for every thirty thousand of her population. On this, therefore, his main objection to the bill was founded. That objection he states in these words: —

> "The Constitution has also provided that the number of Representatives shall not exceed one for every thirty thousand; which restriction is, by the context, and by fair and obvious construction, to be applied to the separate and respective numbers of the States; and the bill has allotted to eight of the States more than one for every thirty thousand."[12]

It is now necessary to see what there was further objectionable in this bill. The number of one hundred and twelve members was all that

11. The House passed this bill on Nov. 24, 1791. The Senate passed its version on March 19, 1792, and the House agreed to the Senate bill on March 23. See *Annals*, 2d Cong., 1st sess., pp. 109, 111–112, 119, 210, 482–483.

12. Washington's veto message of April 5, 1792. See *Messages and Papers*, 1: 124.

could be divided among the States, without giving to some of them more than one member for thirty thousand inhabitants. Therefore, having allotted these one hundred and twelve, there still remained eight of the one hundred and twenty to be assigned; and these eight the bill assigned to the States having the largest fractions. Some of these fractions were large, and some were small. No regard was paid to fractions over a moiety of the ratio, any more than to fractions under it. There was no rule laid down, stating what fractions should entitle the States to whom they might happen to fall, or in whose population they might happen to be found, to a Representative therefor. The assignment was not made on the principle that each State should have a member for a fraction greater than half the ratio; or that all the States should have a member for a fraction, in all cases where the allowance of such member would bring her representation nearer to its exact proportion than its disallowance. There was no common measure or common rule adopted, but the assignment was matter of arbitrary discretion. A member was allowed to New Hampshire, for example, for a fraction of less than one half the ratio; thus placing her representation farther from her exact proportion than it was without such additional member; while a member was refused to Georgia, whose case closely resembled that of New Hampshire, both having what were thought large fractions, but both still under a moiety of the ratio, and distinguished from each other only by a very slight difference of absolute numbers. The committee have already fully expressed their opinion on such a mode of apportionment.

In regard to this character of the bill, President Washington said: "The Constitution has prescribed that Representatives shall be apportioned among the several States according to their respective numbers; and there is no one proportion or divisor, which, applied to the respective numbers of the States, will yield the number and allotment of Representatives proposed by the bill."[13]

This was all undoubtedly true, and was, in the judgment of the committee, a decisive objection against the bill. It is, nevertheless, to be observed, that the other objection completely covered the whole ground. *There could, in that bill, be no allowance for a fraction, great or small;* because Congress had taken for the ratio the lowest number allowed by the Constitution, viz. thirty thousand. Whatever fraction a State might have less than that ratio, no member could be allowed for it. It is scarcely necessary to observe, that no such objection applies to the amendment now proposed. No State, should the amendment prevail, will have a greater number of members than one for every thirty thou-

13. Ibid.

sand; nor is it likely that the objection will ever again occur. The whole force of the precedent, whatever it be, in its application to the present case, is drawn from the other objection. And what is the true import of that objection? Does it mean any thing more than that the apportionment was not made on a common rule or principle, applicable and applied to all the States?

President Washington's words are: "There is no one proportion or divisor, which, applied to the respective numbers of the States, will yield the number and allotment of Representatives proposed by the bill."

If, then, he could have found a common proportion, it would have removed this objection. He required a proportion or divisor. These words he evidently uses as explanatory of each other. He meant by *divisor*, therefore, no more than by *proportion*. What he sought was some common and equal rule, by which the allotment had been made among the several States; he did not find such common rule; and, on that ground, he thought the bill objectionable.

In the opinion of the committee, no such objection applies to the amendment recommended by them. That amendment gives a rule, plain, simple, just, uniform, and of universal application. The rule has been frequently stated. It may be clearly expressed in either of two ways. Let the rule be, that *the whole number of the proposed House shall be apportioned among the several States according to their respective numbers, giving to each State that number of members which comes nearest to her exact mathematical part or proportion;* or let the rule be, that *the population of each State shall be divided by a common divisor, and, in addition to the number of members resulting from such division, a member shall be allowed to each State whose fraction exceeds a moiety of the divisor.*

Either of these is, it seems to the committee, a fair and just rule, capable of uniform application, and operating with entire impartiality. There is no want of a common proportion, or a common divisor; there is nothing left to arbitrary discretion. If the rule, in either of these forms, be adopted, it can never be doubtful how every member of any proposed number for a House of Representatives ought to be assigned. Nothing will be left in the discretion of Congress; the right of each State will be a mathematical right, easily ascertained, about which there can be neither doubt nor difficulty; and, in the application of the rule, there will be no room for preference, partiality, or injustice. In any case, in all time to come, it will do all that human means can do to allot to every State in the Union its proper and just proportion of representative power. And it is because of this, its capability of constant application, as well as because of its impartiality and justice, that the committee are earnest in recommending its adoption by Congress. If it shall

be adopted, they believe it will remove a cause of uneasiness and dis-satisfaction, recurring, or liable to recur, with every new census, and place the rights of the States, in this respect, on a fixed basis, of which none can with reason complain. It is true, that there may be some num-bers assumed for the composition of the House of Representatives, to which, if the rule were applied, the result might give a member to the House more than was proposed. But it will be always easy to correct this by altering the proposed number by adding one to it, or taking one from it; so that this can be considered no objection to the rule.

The committee, in conclusion, cannot admit that it is sufficient rea-son for rejecting this mode of apportionment, that a different process has heretofore prevailed. The truth is, the errors and inequalities of that process were at first not obvious and startling. But they have gone on increasing; they are greatly augmented and accumulated at every new census; and it is of the very nature of the process itself, that its unjust results must grow greater and greater in proportion as the population of the country enlarges. What was objectionable, though tolerable, yes-terday, becomes intolerable to-morrow. A change, the committee are persuaded, must come, or the whole just balance and proportion of representative power among the States will be disturbed and broken up.

Veto of the Bank Bill, July 11, 1832

The Second Bank of the United States, like its predecessor, was controversial even before it opened its doors. Established in 1816 to serve a nation on the verge of post-war bankruptcy, the BUS as it soon came to be called represented a compromise between political factions, unable to agree even upon the functions the bank was to perform. (See Webster's speech of April 26, 1816 on the Legal Currency, pages 33–43, above). Its early history was chaotic and scandal-ridden. It was saved from destruction at the hands of the states only by the timely intervention of the Supreme Court in *McCulloch* v. *Maryland*, a case in which Webster argued for the bank. Mismanagement, defects in its organization, and the outright dishonesty of some of its officers, especially in the Baltimore branch, came very close to provoking the revocation of its charter. It was saved only by a rigorous reorganization and a retrenchment so drastic that many of its debtors were forced into bankruptcy. The bank was solvent but friendless when Nicholas Biddle became its president in 1822.

Over the next decade the Bank of the United States functioned as smoothly and efficiently as any central bank in the world. It handled without a hitch the complex financial transactions of the government. It served the needs of a far-flung merchant constituency whose ships carried American products to trading ports the world over. It provided capital for a growing industrial empire. Above all it provided the stable currency so essential to commerce, by rejecting in payment of taxes the notes of state and local banks that did not redeem their own paper in specie or Treasury issues on demand. In performing these functions, the bank became a powerful engine, able at will to promote or to curtail the activities of the business community. It was not a sufficient safeguard, many believed, that the bank operated under a charter granted by Congress for a term of years, or that 5 of its 25 directors were appointed by the president of the United States. It exercised a power too great to be vested in private hands.

Among those who shared this reservation was Andrew Jackson, who was inclined to distrust all banks, who remembered only too well the effects in Tennessee of the contraction of 1819–1821, and who had no doubt that the influence of the BUS had been used against his election.

In his first annual message, December 8, 1829, Jackson noted that the bank's charter would expire in 1836. He accused the institution of dereliction, and suggested that it might not be too early to consider the question of renewal. Biddle sought to placate the president with his appointments to branch bank directorates and through an easing of credit in the West. By 1832, with Jackson seeking a second term, Biddle and his political advisors decided on a showdown. Although the bank's charter still had four years to run, a bill to renew was introduced in the Senate, backed by Clay who was already the National Republican nominee for president, and by Webster who served as one of the bank's attorneys. The reasoning was that Jackson could not veto it without losing his supporters in the business community, nor could he sign it without alienating the radical wing of his party. Most of the cabinet, including treasury secretary Louis McLane, favored renewal, and the bill incorporated modifications which Biddle had been assured would make the recharter acceptable to the president.

The bill passed both houses of Congress easily but without sufficient margin to override the veto Jackson promptly applied. The veto message, presumed to have been written by Attorney General Roger B. Taney, pronounced the Bank unconstitutional, and it was to this point that Webster largely addressed himself in the accompanying speech.

For this speech, with its often caustic criticism of President Jackson, there are no significant variant texts. The reproduction below follows *Writings and Speeches*, 6: 149–180, which in turn duplicates *Works*, 3: 416–447. The original source was the *National Intelligencer* for September 22, 1832, a time lag which seems to imply that the speech was to be used as a campaign document. The *Intelligencer's* report contains an unusual number of errors for that generally meticulous journal. This text, errors and all, is carried over into the official record in *Register of Debates*, 22d Cong., 1st sess., pp. 1221–1258, published in 1833. In the interval a number of pamphlet editions appeared, all based on the *Intelligencer* text. The speech also appears in *Speeches and Forensic Arguments*, 2: 98–124. Edward Everett, who edited both this volume and the *Works* of 1851, corrected some errors here and others in the later edition.

Significant variations between the text below and that of the *Intelligencer* as reproduced in the *Register of Debates* are footnoted, but are in fact minor. Various contemporary comments on the speech are to be found in *Correspondence*, 3.

Mr. President, no one will deny the high importance of the subject now before us. Congress, after full deliberation and discussion, has passed a

bill, by decisive majorities, in both houses, for extending the duration of the Bank of the United States. It has not adopted this measure until its attention had been called to the subject, in three successive annual messages of the President. The bill having been thus passed by both houses, and having been duly presented to the President, instead of signing and approving it, he has returned it with objections. These objections go against the whole substance of the law originally creating the bank. They deny, in effect, that the bank is constitutional; they deny that it is expedient; they deny that it is necessary for the public service.

It is not to be doubted, that the Constitution gives the President the power which he has now exercised; but while the power is admitted, the grounds upon which it has been exerted become fit subjects of examination. The Constitution makes it the duty of Congress, in cases like this, to reconsider the measure which they have passed, to weigh the force of the President's objections to that measure, and to take a new vote upon the question.

Before the Senate proceeds to this second vote, I propose to make some remarks upon those objections. And, in the first place, it is to be observed, that they are such as to extinguish all hope that the present bank, or any bank at all resembling it, or resembling any known similar institution, can ever receive his approbation. He states no terms, no qualifications, no conditions, no modifications, which can reconcile him to the essential provisions of the existing charter. He is against the bank, and against any bank constituted in a manner known either to this or any other country. One advantage, therefore, is certainly obtained by presenting him the bill. It has caused the President's sentiments to be made known. There is no longer any mystery, no longer a contest between hope and fear, or between those prophets who predicted a *veto* and those who foretold an approval. The bill is negatived; the President has assumed the responsibility of putting an end to the bank; and the country must prepare itself to meet that change in its concerns which the expiration of the charter will produce. Mr. President, I will not conceal my opinion that the affairs of the country are approaching an important and dangerous crisis. At the very moment of almost unparalleled general prosperity, there appears an unaccountable disposition to destroy the most useful and most approved institutions of the government. Indeed, it seems to be in the midst of all this national happiness that some are found openly to question the advantages of the Constitution itself; and many more ready to embarrass the exercise of its just power, weaken its authority, and undermine its foundations. How far these notions may be carried, it is impossible yet to say. We have before us the practical result of one of them. The bank has fallen, or is to fall.

It is now certain, that, without a change in our public counsels, this bank will not be continued, nor will any other be established, which, according to the general sense and language of mankind, can be entitled to the name. Within three years and nine months from the present moment, the charter of the bank expires; within that period, therefore, it must wind up its concerns. It must call in its debts, withdraw its bills from circulation, and cease from all its ordinary operations. All this is to be done in three years and nine months; because, although there is a provision in the charter rendering it lawful to use the corporate name for two years after the expiration of the charter, yet this is allowed only for the purpose of suits and for the sale of the estate belonging to the bank, and for no other purpose whatever. The whole active business of the bank, its custody of public deposits, its transfer of public moneys, its dealing in exchange, all its loans and discounts, and all its issues of bills for circulation, must cease and determine on or before the third day of March, 1836; and within the same period its debts must be collected, as no new contract can be made with it, as a corporation, for the renewal of loans, or discount of notes or bills, after that time.

The President is of opinion, that this time is long enough to close the concerns of the institution without inconvenience. His language is, "The time allowed the bank to close its concerns is ample, and if it has been well managed, its pressure will be light, and heavy only in case its management has been bad. If, therefore, it shall produce distress, the fault will be its own."[1] Sir, this is all no more than general statement, without fact or argument to support it. We know what the management of the bank has been, and we know the present state of its affairs. We can judge, therefore, whether it be probable that its capital can be all called in, and the circulation of its bills withdrawn, in three years and nine months, by any discretion or prudence in management, without producing distress. The bank has discounted liberally, in compliance with the wants of the community. The amount due to it on loans and discounts, in certain large divisions of the country, is great; so great, that I do not perceive how any man can believe that it can be paid, within the time now limited, without distress. Let us look at known facts. Thirty millions of the capital of the bank are now out, on loans and discounts, in the States on the Mississippi and its waters; ten millions of which are loaned on the discount of bills of exchange, foreign and domestic, and twenty millions on promissory notes. Now, Sir, how is it possible that this vast amount can be collected in so short a period without suffering, by any management whatever? We are to remember, that, when the collection of this debt begins, at that same time, the

1. Jackson's veto message, July 10, 576–591.
1832. See *Messages and Papers*, 2:

existing medium of payment, that is, the circulation of the bills of the bank, will begin also to be restrained and withdrawn; and thus the means of payment must be limited just when the necessity of making payment becomes pressing. The whole debt is to be paid, and within the same time the whole circulation withdrawn.

The local banks, where there are such, will be able to afford little assistance; because they themselves will feel a full share of the pressure. They will not be in a condition to extend their discounts, but, in all probability, obliged to curtail them. Whence, then, are the means to come for paying this debt? and in what medium is payment to be made? If all this may be done with but slight pressure on the community, what course of conduct is to accomplish it? How is it to be done? What other thirty millions are to supply the place of these thirty millions now to be called in? What other circulation or medium of payment is to be adopted in the place of the bills of the bank? The message, following a singular train of argument, which had been used in this house, has a loud lamentation upon the suffering of the Western States on account of their being obliged to pay even interest on this debt. This payment of interest is itself represented as exhausting their means and ruinous to their prosperity. But if the interest cannot be paid without pressure, can both interest and principal be paid in four years without pressure? The truth is, the interest has been paid, is paid, and may continue to be paid, without any pressure at all; because the money borrowed is profitably employed by those who borrow it, and the rate of interest which they pay is at least two per cent. lower than the actual value of money in that part of the country. But to pay the whole principal in less than four years, losing, at the same time, the existing and accustomed means and facilities of payment created by the bank itself, and to do this without extreme embarrassment, without absolute distress, is, in my judgment, impossible. I hesitate not to say, that, as this *veto* travels to the West, it will depreciate the value of every man's property from the Atlantic States to the capital of Missouri. Its effects will be felt in the price of lands, the great and leading article of Western property, in the price of crops, in the products of labor, in the repression of enterprise, and in embarrassment to every kind of business and occupation. I state this opinion strongly, because I have no doubt of its truth, and am willing its correctness should be judged by the event. Without personal acquaintance with the Western States, I know enough of their condition to be satisfied that what I have predicted must happen. The people of the West are rich, but their riches consist in their immense quantities of excellent land, in the products of these lands, and in their spirit of enterprise. The actual value of money, or rate of interest, with them is high, because their pecuniary capital bears little

proportion to their landed interest. At an average rate, money is not worth less than eight per cent. per annum throughout the whole Western country, notwithstanding that it has now a loan or an advance from the bank of thirty millions, at six per cent. To call in this loan, at the rate of eight millions a year, in addition to the interest on the whole, and to take away, at the same time, that circulation which constitutes so great a portion of the medium of payment throughout that whole region, is an operation, which, however wisely conducted, cannot but inflict a blow on the community of tremendous force and frightful consequences. The thing cannot be done without distress, bankruptcy, and ruin, to many. If the President had seen any practical manner in which this change might be effected without producing these consequences, he would have rendered infinite service to the community by pointing it out. But he has pointed out nothing, he has suggested nothing; he contents himself with saying, without giving any reason, that, if the pressure be heavy, the fault will be the bank's. I hope this is not merely an attempt to forestall opinion, and to throw on the bank the responsibility of those evils which threaten the country, for the sake of removing it from himself.

The responsibility justly lies with him, and there it ought to remain. A great majority of the people are satisfied with the bank as it is, and desirous that it should be continued. They wished no change. The strength of this public sentiment has carried the bill through Congress, against all the influence of the administration, and all the power of organized party. But the President has undertaken, on his own responsibility, to arrest the measure, by refusing his assent to the bill. He is answerable for the consequences, therefore, which necessarily follow the change which the expiration of the bank charter may produce; and if these consequences shall prove disastrous, they can fairly be ascribed to his policy only, and the policy of his administration.

Although, Sir, I have spoken of the effects of this *veto* in the Western country, it has not been because I considered that part of the United States exclusively affected by it. Some of the Atlantic States may feel its consequences, perhaps, as sensibly as those of the West, though not for the same reasons. The concern manifested by Pennsylvania for the renewal of the charter shows her sense of the importance of the bank to her own interest, and that of the nation. That great and enterprising State has entered into an extensive system of internal improvements, which necessarily makes heavy demands on her credit and her resources; and by the sound and acceptable currency which the bank affords, by the stability which it gives to private credit, and by occasional advances, made in anticipation of her revenues, and in aid of her great objects, she has found herself benefitted, doubtless, in no in-

considerable degree. Her legislature has instructed her Senators here to advocate the renewal of the charter, at this session. They have obeyed her voice, and yet they have the misfortune to find that, in the judgment of the President, *the measure is unconstitutional, unnecessary, dangerous to liberty, and is, moreover, ill-timed.*

But, Mr. President, it is not the local interest of the West, nor the particular interest of Pennsylvania, or any other State, which has influenced Congress in passing this bill. It has been governed by a wise foresight, and by a desire to avoid embarrassment in the pecuniary concerns of the country, to secure the safe collection and convenient transmission of public moneys, to maintain the circulation of the country, sound and safe as it now happily is, against the possible effects of a wild spirit of speculation. Finding the bank highly useful, Congress has thought fit to provide for its continuance.

As to the *time* of passing this bill, it would seem to be the last thing to be thought of, as a ground of objection, by the President; since, from the date of his first message to the present time, he has never failed to call our attention to the subject with all possible apparent earnestness. So early as December, 1829, in his message to the two houses, he declares, that he "cannot, in justice to the parties interested, too soon present the subject to the deliberate consideration of the legislature, in order to avoid the evils resulting from precipitancy, in a measure involving such important principles and such deep pecuniary interests."[2] Aware of this early invitation given to Congress to take up the subject, by the President himself, the writer of the message seems to vary the ground of objection, and, instead of complaining that the time of bringing forward this measure was premature, to insist, rather, that, after the report of the committee of the other house, the bank should have withdrawn its application for the present! But that report offers no just ground, surely, for such withdrawal. The subject was before Congress; it was for Congress to decide upon it, with all the light shed by the report; and the question of postponement, having been made in both houses, was lost, by clear majorities, in each. Under such circumstances, it would have been somewhat singular, to say the least, if the bank itself had withdrawn its application. It is indeed known to every body, that neither the report of the committee, nor any thing contained in that report, was relied on by the opposers of the renewal. If it has been discovered elsewhere, that that report contained matter important in itself, or which should have led to further inquiry, this may be proof of superior sagacity; for certainly no such thing was discerned by either House of Congress.

2. Jackson's first annual message,   2: 462.
Dec. 8, 1829, *Messages and Papers,*

But, Sir, do we not now see that it was time, and high time, to press this bill, and to send it to the President? Does not the event teach us, that the measure was not brought forward one moment too early? The time had come when the people wished to know the decision of the administration on the question of the bank. Why conceal it, or postpone its declaration? Why, as in regard to the tariff, give out one set of opinions for the North, and another for the South.

An important election is at hand, and the renewal of the bank charter is a pending object of great interest, and some excitement. Should not the opinions of men high in office, and candidates for reëlection, be known, on this, as on other important public questions? Certainly, it is to be hoped that the people of the United States are not yet mere man-worshippers, that they do not choose their rulers without some regard to their political principles, or political opinions. Were they to do this, it would be to subject themselves voluntarily to the evils which the hereditary transmission of power, independent of all personal qualifications, inflicts on other nations. They will judge their public servants by their acts, and continue or withhold their confidence, as they shall think it merited, or as they shall think it forfeited. In every point of view, therefore, the moment had arrived, when it became the duty of Congress to come to a result, in regard to this highly important measure. The interests of the government, the interests of the people, the clear and indisputable voice of public opinion, all called upon Congress to act without further loss of time. It has acted, and its act has been negatived by the President; and this result of the proceedings here places the question, with all its connections and all its incidents, fully before the people.

Before proceeding to the constitutional question, there are some other topics, treated in the message, which ought to be noticed. It commences by an inflamed statement of what it calls the "favor" bestowed upon the original bank by the government, or, indeed, as it is phrased, the "monopoly of its favor and support"; and through the whole message all possible changes are rung on the "gratuity," the "exclusive privileges," and "monopoly," of the bank charter. Now, Sir, the truth is, that the powers conferred on the bank are such, and no others, as are usually conferred on similar institutions. They constitute no monopoly, although some of them are of necessity, and with propriety, exclusive privileges. "The original act," says the message, "operated as a gratuity of many millions to the stockholders." What fair foundation is there for this remark? The stockholders received their charter, not gratuitously, but for a valuable consideration in money, prescribed by Congress, and actually paid. At some times the stock has been above *par*, at other times below *par*, according to prudence in management, or according to commercial occurrences.

But if, by a judicious administration of its affairs, it had kept its stock always above *par*, what pretence would there be, nevertheless, for saying that such augmentation of its value was a "gratuity" from government? The message proceeds to declare, that the present act proposes another donation, another gratuity, to the same men, of at least seven millions more. It seems to me that this is an extraordinary statement, and an extraordinary style of argument, for such a subject and on such an occasion. In the first place, the facts are all assumed; they are taken for true without evidence. There are no proofs that any benefit to that amount will accrue to the stockholders, nor any experience to justify the expectation of it. It rests on random estimates, or mere conjecture. But suppose the continuance of the charter should prove beneficial to the stockholders; do they not pay for it? They give twice as much for a charter of fifteen years, as was given before for one of twenty. And if the proposed *bonus*, or premium, be not, in the President's judgment, large enough, would he, nevertheless, on such a mere matter of opinion as that, negative the whole bill? May not Congress be trusted to decide even on such a subject as the amount of the money premium to be received by government for a charter of this kind?

But, Sir, there is a larger and a much more just view of this subject. The bill was not passed for the purpose of benefiting the present stockholders. Their benefit, if any, is incidental and collateral. Nor was it passed on any idea that they had a *right* to a renewed charter, although the message argues against such right, as if it had been somewhere set up and asserted. No such right has been asserted by any body. Congress passed the bill, not as a bounty or a favor to the present stockholders, nor to comply with any demand of right on their part; but to promote great public interests, for great public objects. Every bank must have some stockholders, unless it be such a bank as the President has recommended, and in regard to which he seems not likely to find much concurrence of other men's opinions; and if the stockholders, whoever they may be, conduct the affairs of the bank prudently, the expectation is always, of course, that they will make it profitable to themselves, as well as useful to the public. If a bank charter is not to be granted, because, to some extent, it may be profitable to the stockholders, no charter can be granted. The objection lies against all banks.

Sir, the object aimed at by such institutions is to connect the public safety and convenience with private interests. It has been found by experience, that banks are safest under private management, and that government banks are among the most dangerous of all inventions. Now, Sir, the whole drift of the message is to reverse the settled judgment of all the civilized world, and to set up government banks, independent of private interest or private control. For this purpose the mes-

sage labors, even beyond the measure of all its other labors, to create jealousies and prejudices, on the ground of the alleged benefit which individuals will derive from the renewal of this charter. Much less effort is made to show that government, or the public, will be injured by the bill, than that individuals will profit by it. Following up the impulses of the same spirit, the message goes on gravely to allege, that the act, as passed by Congress, proposes to make a *present* of some millions of dollars to foreigners because a portion of the stock is held by foreigners. Sir, how would this sort of argument apply to other cases? The President has shown himself not only willing, but anxious, to pay off the three per cent. stock of the United States at *par*, notwithstanding that it is notorious that foreigners are owners of the greater part of it. Why should he not call that a donation to foreigners of many millions?

I will not dwell particularly on this part of the message. Its tone and its arguments are all in the same strain. It speaks of the certain gain of the present stockholders, of the value of the monopoly; it says that all monopolies are granted at the expense of the public; that the many millions which this bill bestows on the stockholders come out of the earnings of the people; that, if government sells monopolies, it ought to sell them in open market; that it is an erroneous idea, that the present stockholders have a prescriptive right either to the favor or the bounty of government; that the stock is in the hands of a few, and that the whole American people are excluded from competition in the purchase of the monopoly. To all this I say, again, that much of it is assumption without proof; much of it is an argument against that which nobody has maintained or asserted; and the rest of it would be equally strong against any charter, at any time. These objections existed in their full strength, whatever that was, against the first bank. They existed, in like manner, against the present bank at its creation, and will always exist against all banks. Indeed, all the fault found with the bill now before us is, that it proposes to continue the bank substantially as it now exists. "All the objectionable principles of the existing corporation," says the message, "and most of its odious features, are retained without alleviation"; so that the message[3] is aimed against the bank, as it has existed from the first, and against any and all others resembling it in its general features.

Allow me, now, Sir, to take notice of an argument founded on the practical operation of the bank. That argument is this. Little of the stock of the bank is held in the West, the capital being chiefly owned by citizens of the Southern and Eastern States, and by foreigners. But the Western and Southwestern States owe the bank a heavy debt, so heavy

8. *Register of Debates* reads "measure."

that the interest amounts to a million six hundred thousand a year. This interest is carried to the Eastern States, or to Europe, annually, and its payment is a burden on the people of the West, and a drain of their currency, which no country can bear without inconvenience and distress. The true character and the whole value of this argument are manifest by the mere statement of it. The people of the West are, from their situation, necessarily large borrowers. They need money, capital, and they borrow it, because they can derive a benefit from its use, much beyond the interest which they pay. They borrow at six per cent. of the bank, although the value of money with them is at least as high as eight. Nevertheless, although they borrow at this low rate of interest, and although they use all they borrow thus profitably, yet they cannot pay the interest without "inconvenience and distress"; and then, Sir, follows the logical conclusion, that, although they cannot pay even the interest without inconvenience and distress, yet less than four years is ample time for the bank to call in the whole, both principal and interest, without causing more than a light pressure. This is the argument.

Then follows another, which may be thus stated. It is competent to the States to tax the property of their citizens vested in the stock of this bank; but the power is denied of taxing the stock of foreigners; therefore the stock will be worth ten or fifteen per cent. more to foreigners than to residents, and will of course inevitably leave the country, and make the American people debtors to aliens in nearly the whole amount due the bank, and send across the Atlantic from two to five millions of specie every year, to pay the bank dividends.

Mr. President, arguments like these might be more readily disposed of, were it not that the high and official source from which they proceed imposes the necessity of treating them with respect. In the first place, it may safely be denied that the stock of the bank is any more valuable to foreigners than to our own citizens, or an object of greater desire to them, except in so far as capital may be more abundant in the foreign country, and therefore its owners more in want of opportunity of investment. The foreign stockholder enjoys no exemption from taxation. He is, of course, taxed by his own government for his incomes, derived from this as well as other property; and this is a full answer to the whole statement. But it may be added, in the second place, that it is not the practice of civilized states to tax the property of foreigners under such circumstances. Do we tax, or did we ever tax, the foreign holders of our public debt? Does Pennsylvania, New York, or Ohio tax the foreign holders of stock in the loans contracted by either of these states? Certainly not. Sir, I must confess I had little expected to see, on such an occasion as the present, a labored and repeated attempt to produce an impression on the public opinion unfavorable to the bank, from the cir-

cumstance that foreigners are among its stockholders. I have no hesitation in saying, that I deem such a train of remark as the message contains on this point, coming from the President of the United States, to be injurious to the credit and character of the country abroad; because it manifests a jealousy, a lurking disposition not to respect the property, of foreigners invited hither by our own laws. And, Sir, what is its tendency but to excite this jealousy, and create groundless prejudices?

From the commencement of the government, it has been thought desirable to invite, rather than to repel, the introduction of foreign capital. Our stocks have all been open to foreign subscriptions; and the State banks, in like manner, are free to foreign ownership. Whatever State has created a debt has been willing that foreigners should become purchasers, and desirous of it. How long is it, Sir, since Congress itself passed a law vesting new powers in the President of the United States over the cities in this District, for the very purpose of increasing their credit abroad, the better to enable them to borrow money to pay their subscriptions to the Chesapeake and Ohio Canal?[4] It is easy to say that there is danger to liberty, danger to independence, in a bank open to foreign stockholders, because it is easy to say any thing. But neither reason nor experience proves any such danger. The foreign stockholder cannot be a director. He has no voice even in the choice of directors. His money is placed entirely in the management of the directors appointed by the President and Senate and by the American stockholders. So far as there is dependence or influence either way, it is to the disadvantage of the foreign stockholder. He has parted with the control over his own property, instead of exercising control over the property or over the actions of others. And, Sir, let it now be added, in further answer to this class of objections, that experience has abundantly confuted them all. This government has existed forty-three years, and has maintained, in full being and operation, a bank, such as is now proposed to be renewed, for thirty-six years out of the forty-three. We have never for a moment had a bank not subject to every one of these objections. Always, foreigners might be stockholders; always, foreign stock has been exempt from State taxation, as much as at present; always, the same power and privileges; always, all that which is now called a "monopoly," a "gratuity," a "present," have been possessed by the bank. And yet there has been found no danger to liberty, no introduction of foreign influence, and no accumulation of irresponsible power in a few hands. I cannot but hope, therefore, that the people of the United States will not now yield up their judgment to those notions which would reverse all our best[5] experience, and persuade us to discontinue a useful institution from the influence of

4. Act of May 24, 1828. 4 U.S.
Stat. 294–297.

5. *Register* reads "past."

vague and unfounded declamation against its danger to the public liberties. Our liberties, indeed, must stand upon very frail foundations, if the government cannot, without endangering them, avail itself of those common facilities, in the collection of its revenues and the management of its finances, which all other governments, in commercial countries, find useful and necessary.

In order to justify its alarm for the security of our independence, the message supposes a case. It supposes that the bank should pass principally into the hands of the subjects of a foreign country, and that we should be involved in war with that country, and then it exclaims, "What would be our condition?" Why, Sir, it is plain that all the advantages would be on our side. The bank would still be our institution, subject to our own laws, and all its directors elected by ourselves; and our means would be enhanced, not by the confiscation and plunder, but by the proper use, of the foreign capital in our hands. And, Sir, it is singular enough, that this very state of war, from which this argument against a bank is drawn, is the very thing which, more than all others, convinced the country and the government of the necessity of a national bank. So much was the want of such an institution felt in the late war, that the subject engaged the attention of Congress, constantly, from the declaration of that war down to the time when the existing bank was actually established; so that in this respect, as well as in others, the argument of the message is directly opposed to the whole experience of the government, and to the general and long-settled convictions of the country.

I now proceed, Sir, to a few remarks upon the President's constitutional objections to the bank; and I cannot forbear to say, in regard to them, that he appears to me to have assumed very extraordinary grounds of reasoning. He denies that the constitutionality of the bank is a settled question. If it be not, will it ever become so, or what disputed question ever can be settled? I have already observed, that for thirty-six years out of the forty-three during which the government has been in being, a bank has existed, such as is now proposed to be continued.

As early as 1791, after great deliberation, the first bank charter was passed by Congress, and approved by President Washington. It established an institution, resembling, in all things now objected to, the present bank. That bank, like this, could take lands in payment of its debts; that charter, like the present, gave the States no power of taxation; it allowed foreigners to hold stock; it restrained Congress from creating other banks. It gave also exclusive privileges, and in all particulars it was, according to the doctrine of the message, as objectionable as that now existing. That bank continued twenty years. In 1816,

the present institution was established, and has been ever since in full operation. Now, Sir, the question of the power of Congress to create such institutions has been contested in every manner known to our Constitution and laws. The forms of the government furnish no new mode in which to try this question. It has been discussed over and over again, in Congress; it has been argued and solemnly adjudged in the Supreme Court; every President, except the present, has considered it a settled question; many of the State legislatures have instructed their Senators to vote for the bank; the tribunals of the States, in every instance, have supported its constitutionality; and, beyond all doubt and dispute, the general public opinion of the country has at all times given, and does now give, its full sanction and approbation to the exercise of this power, as being a constitutional power. There has been no opinion questioning the power expressed or intimated, at any time, by either house of Congress, by any President, or by any respectable judicial tribunal. Now, Sir, if this practice of near forty years, if these repeated exercises[6] of the power, if this solemn adjudication of the Supreme Court, with the concurrence and approbation of public opinion, do not settle the question, how is any question ever to be settled, about which any one may choose to raise a doubt?

The argument of the message upon the Congressional precedents is either a bold and gross fallacy, or else it is an assertion without proofs, and against known facts. The message admits, that, in 1791, Congress decided in favor of a bank; but it adds, that another Congress, in 1811, decided against it. Now, if it be meant that, in 1811, Congress decided against the bank on constitutional ground, then the assertion is wholly incorrect, and against notorious fact. It is perfectly well known, that members, in both houses, voted against the bank in 1811, who had no doubt at all of the constitutional power of Congress. They were entirely governed by other reasons given at the time. I appeal, Sir, to the honorable member from Maryland, who was then a member of the Senate, and voted against the bank, whether he, and others who were on the same side, did not give those votes on other well-known grounds, and not at all on constitutional ground?

[General Samuel Smith here rose, and said, that he voted against the bank in 1811, but not at all on constitutional grounds, and had no doubt such was the case with other members.]

We all know, Sir, the fact to be as the gentleman from Maryland has stated it. Every man who recollects, or who has read, the political occurrences of that day, knows it. Therefore, if the message intends to say, that in 1811 Congress denied the existence of any such constitutional

6. *Register* reads "exertions."

power, the declaration is unwarranted, and altogether at variance with the facts. If, on the other hand, it only intends to say, that Congress decided against the proposition then before it on some other grounds, then it alleges that which is nothing at all to the purpose. The argument, then, either assumes for truth that which is not true, or else the whole statement is immaterial and futile.

But whatever value others may attach to this argument, the message thinks so highly of it, that it proceeds to repeat it. "One Congress," it says, "in 1815, decided against a bank; another, in 1816, decided in its favor. There is nothing in precedent, therefore, which, if its authority were admitted, ought to weigh in favor of the act before me." Now, Sir, since it is known to the whole country, one cannot but wonder how it should remain unknown to the President, that Congress *did not* decide against a bank in 1815. On the contrary, that very Congress passed a bill for erecting a bank, by very large majorities. In one form, it is true, the bill failed in the House of Representatives; but the vote was reconsidered, the bill recommitted, and finally passed by a vote of one hundred and twenty to thirty-nine. There is, therefore, not only no solid ground, but not even any plausible pretence, for the assertion, that Congress in 1815 decided against the bank. That very Congress passed a bill to create a bank, and its decision, therefore, is precisely the other way, and is a direct practical precedent in favor of the constitutional power. What are we to think of a constitutional argument which deals in this way with historical facts? When the message declares, as it does declare, that there is nothing in precedent which ought to weigh in favor of the power, it sets at naught repeated acts of Congress affirming the power, and it also states other acts, which were in fact, and which are well known to have been, directly the reverse of what the message represents them. There is not, Sir, the slightest reason to think that any Senate or any House of Representatives, ever assembled under the Constitution, contained a majority that doubted the constitutional existence of the power of Congress to establish a bank. Whenever the question has arisen, and has been decided, it has always been decided one way. The legislative precedents all assert and maintain the power; and these legislative precedents have been the law of the land for almost forty years. They settle the construction of the Constitution, and sanction the exercise of the power in question, so far as these effects can ever be produced[7] by any legislative precedents whatever.

But the President does not admit the authority of precedent. Sir, I have always found, that those who habitually deny most vehemently the general force of precedent, and assert most strongly the supremacy of

7. *Register* reads "accomplished."

private opinion, are yet, of all men, most tenacious of that very authority of precedent, whenever it happens to be in their favor. I beg leave to ask, Sir, upon what ground, except that of precedent, and precedent alone, the President's friends have placed his power of removal from office. No such power is given by the Constitution, in terms, nor anywhere intimated, throughout the whole of it; no paragraph or clause of that instrument recognizes such a power. To say the least, it is as questionable, and has been as often questioned, as the power of Congress to create a bank; and, enlightened by what has passed under our own observation, we now see that it is of all powers the most capable of flagrant abuse. Now, Sir, I ask again, What becomes of this power, if the authority of precedent be taken away? It has all along been denied to exist; it is nowhere found in the Constitution; and its recent exercise, or, to call things by their right names, its recent abuse, has, more than any other single cause, rendered good men either cool in their affections toward the government of their country, or doubtful of its long continuance. Yet there is *precedent* in favor of this power, and the President exercises it. We know, Sir, that, without the aid of that *precedent,* his acts could never have received the sanction of this body, even at a time when his voice was somewhat more potential here than it now is, or, as I trust, ever again will be. Does the President, then, reject the authority of all precedent except what it is suitable to his own purpose to use? And does he use, without stint or measure, all precedents which may augment his own power, or gratify his own wishes?

But if the President thinks lightly of the authority of Congress in construing the Constitution, he thinks still more lightly of the authority of the Supreme Court. He asserts a right of individual judgment on constitutional questions, which is totally inconsistent with any proper administration of the government, or any regular execution of the laws. Social disorder, entire uncertainty in regard to individual rights and individual duties, the cessation of legal authority, confusion, the dissolution of free government,—all these are the inevitable consequences of the principles adopted by the message, whenever they shall be carried to their full extent. Hitherto it has been thought that the final decision of constitutional questions belonged to the supreme judicial tribunal. The very nature of free government, it has been supposed, enjoins this; and our Constitution, moreover, has been understood so to provide, clearly and expressly. It is true, that each branch of the legislature has an undoubted right, in the exercise of its functions, to consider the constitutionality of a law proposed to be passed. This is naturally a part of its duty; and neither branch can be compelled to pass any law, or do any other act, which it deems to be beyond the reach of its constitutional power. The President has the same right, when a bill is presented

for his approval, for he is, doubtless, bound to consider, in all cases, whether such bill be compatible with the Constitution, and whether he can approve it consistently with his oath of office. But when a law has been passed by Congress, and approved by the President, it is now no longer in the power, either of the same President, or his successors, to say whether the law is constitutional or not. He is not at liberty to disregard it; he is not at liberty to feel or to affect "constitutional scruples," and to sit in judgment himself on the validity of a statute of the government, and to nullify it, if he so chooses. After a law has passed through all the requisite forms; after it has received the requisite legislative sanction and the executive approval, the question of its constitutionality then becomes a judicial question, and a judicial question alone. In the courts that question may be raised, argued, and adjudged; it can be adjudged nowhere else.

The President is as much bound by the law as any private citizen, and can no more contest its validity than any private citizen. He may refuse to obey the law, and so may a private citizen; but both do it at their own peril, and neither of them can settle the question of its validity. The President may *say* a law is unconstitutional, but he is not the judge. Who is to decide that question? The judiciary alone possesses this unquestionable and hitherto unquestioned right. The judiciary is the constitutional tribunal of appeal for the citizens, against both Congress and the executive, in regard to the constitutionality of laws. It has this jurisdiction expressly conferred upon it, and when it has decided the question, its judgment must, from the very nature of all judgments that are final, and from which there is no appeal, be conclusive. Hitherto, this opinion, and a correspondent practice, have prevailed, in America, with all wise and considerate men. If it were otherwise, there would be no government of laws; but we should all live under the government, the rule, the caprices, of individuals. If we depart from the observance of these salutary principles, the executive power becomes at once purely despotic; for the President, if the principle and the reasoning of the message be sound, may either execute or not execute the laws of the land, according to his sovereign pleasure. He may refuse to put into execution one law, pronounced valid by all branches of the government, and yet execute another, which may have been by constitutional authority pronounced void.

On the argument of the message, the President of the United States holds, under a new pretence and a new name,[8] a *dispensing power* over the laws as absolute as was claimed by James the Second of England, a month before he was compelled to fly the kingdom. That which is

8. *Register* omits "and a new name."

now claimed by the President is in truth nothing less, and nothing else, than the old dispensing power asserted by the kings of England in the worst of times; the very climax, indeed, of all the preposterous pretensions of the Tudor and the Stuart races. According to the doctrines put forth by the President, although Congress may have passed a law, and although the Supreme Court may have pronounced it constitutional, yet it is nevertheless, no law at all, if he, in his good pleasure, sees fit to deny it effect; in other words, to repeal and annul it. Sir, no President and no public man ever before advanced such doctrines in the face of the nation. There never was a moment in which any President would have been tolerated in asserting such a claim to despotic power. After Congress has passed the law, and after the Supreme Court has pronounced its judgment on the very point in controversy, the President has set up his own private judgment against its constitutional interpretation. It is to be remembered, Sir, that it is the present law, it is the act of 1816, it is the present charter of the bank, which the President pronounces to be unconstitutional. It is no bank *to be created*, it is no law proposed to be passed, which he denounces; it is the *law now existing*, passed by Congress, approved by President Madison, and sanctioned by a solemn judgment of the Supreme Court, which he now declares unconstitutional, and which, of course, so far as it may depend on him, cannot be executed. If these opinions of the President be maintained, there is an end of all law and all judicial authority. Statutes are but recommendations, judgments no more than opinions. Both are equally destitute of binding force. Such a universal power as is now claimed for him, a power of judging over the laws and over the decisions of the judiciary, is nothing else but pure despotism. If conceded to him, it makes him at once what Louis the Fourteenth proclaimed himself to be when he said, "I am the State."

The Supreme Court has unanimously declared and adjudged that the existing bank *is* created by a constitutional law of Congress. As has been before observed, this bank, so far as the present question is concerned, is like that which was established in 1791 by Washington, and sanctioned by the great men of that day. In every form, therefore, in which the question can be raised, it has been raised and has been settled. Every process and every mode of trial known to the Constitution and laws have been exhausted, and always and without exception the decision has been in favor of the validity of the law. But all this practice, all this precedent, all this public approbation, all this solemn adjudication directly on the point, is to be disregarded and rejected, and the constitutional power flatly denied. And, Sir, if we are startled at this conclusion, our surprise will not be lessened when we examine the argument by which it is maintained.

By the Constitution, Congress is authorized to pass all laws "necessary and proper" for carrying its own legislative powers into effect. Congress has deemed a bank to be "necessary and proper" for these purposes, and it has therefore established a bank. But although the law has been passed, and the bank established, and the constitutional validity of its charter solemnly adjudged, yet the President pronounces it unconstitutional, because some of the powers bestowed on the bank are, in his opinion, not necessary or proper. It would appear that powers which in 1791 and in 1816, in the time of Washington and in the time of Madison, were deemed "necessary and proper," are no longer to be so regarded, and therefore the bank is unconstitutional. It has really come to this, that the constitutionality of a bank is to depend upon the opinion which one particular man may form of the utility or necessity of some of the clauses in its charter! If that individual chooses to think that a particular power contained in the charter is not necessary to the proper constitution of the bank, then the act is unconstitutional!

Hitherto it has always been supposed that the question was of a very different nature. It has been thought that the policy of granting a particular charter may be materially dependent on the structure and organization and powers of the proposed institution. But its general constitutionality has never before been understood to turn on such points. This would be making its constitutionality depend on subordinate questions; on questions of expediency and questions of detail; upon that which one man may think necessary, and another may not. If the constitutional question were made to hinge on matters of this kind, how could it ever be decided? All would depend on conjecture; on the complexional feeling, on the predjudices, on the passions, of individuals; on more or less practical skill or correct judgment in regard to banking operations among those who should be the judges; on the impulse of momentary interests, party objects, or personal purposes. Put the question in this manner to a court of seven judges, to decide whether a particular bank was constitutional, and it might be doubtful whether they could come to any result, as they might well hold very various opinions on the practical utility of many clauses of the charter.

The question in that case would be, not whether the bank, in its general frame, character, and objects, was a proper instrument to carry into effect the powers of the government, but whether the particular powers, direct or incidental, conferred on a particular bank, were better calculated than all others to give success to its operations. For if not, then the charter, according to this sort of reasoning, would be unwarranted by the Constitution. This mode of construing the Constitution is certainly a novel discovery. Its merits belong entirely to the Pres-

ident and his advisers. According to this rule of interpretation, if the President should be of opinion, that the capital of the bank was larger, by a thousand dollars, than it ought to be; or that the time for the continuance of the charter was a year too long; or that it was unnecessary to require it, under penalty, to pay specie; or needless to provide for punishing, as forgery, the counterfeiting of its bills,—either of these reasons would be sufficient to render the charter, in his opinion, unconstitutional, invalid, and nugatory. This is a legitimate conclusion from the argument. Such a view of the subject has certainly never before been taken. This train of reasoning has hitherto not been heard within the halls of Congress, nor has any one ventured upon it before the tribunals of justice. The first exhibition, its first appearance, as an argument, is in a message of the President of the United States.

According to that mode of construing the Constitution which was adopted by Congress in 1791, and approved by Washington, and which has been sanctioned by the judgment of the Supreme Court, and affirmed by the practice of nearly forty years, the question upon the constitutionality of the bank involves two inquiries. First, whether a bank, in its general character, and with regard to the general objects with which banks are usually connected, be, in itself, a fit means, a suitable instrument, to carry into effect the powers granted to the government. If it be so, then the second, and the only other question is, whether the powers given in a particular charter are appropriate for a bank. If they are powers which are appropriate for a bank, powers which Congress may fairly consider to be useful to the bank or the country, then Congress may confer these powers; because the discretion to be exercised in framing the constitution of the bank belongs to Congress. One man may think the granted powers not indispensable to the particular bank; another may suppose them injudicious, or injurious; a third may imagine that other powers, if granted in their stead, would be more beneficial; but all these are matters of expediency, about which men may differ; and the power of deciding upon them belongs to Congress.

I again repeat, Sir, that if, for reasons of this kind, the President sees fit to negative a bill, on the ground of its being inexpedient or impolitic, he has a right to do so. But remember, Sir, that we are now on the constitutional question; remember, that the argument of the President is, that, because powers were given to the bank by the charter of 1816 which he thinks unnecessary, that charter is unconstitutional. Now, Sir, it will hardly be denied, or rather it was not denied or doubted before this message came to us, that, if there was to be a bank, the powers and duties of that bank must be prescribed in the law creating it. Nobody but Congress, it has been thought, could grant these powers and privileges, or prescribe their limitations. It is true, indeed, that the

message pretty plainly intimates, that the President should have been *first* consulted, and that he should have had the framing of the bill; but we are not yet accustomed to that order of things in enacting laws, nor do I know a parallel to this claim, thus now brought forward, except that, in some peculiar cases in England, highly affecting the royal prerogative, the assent of the monarch is necessary, before either the House of Peers, or his Majesty's faithful Commons, are permitted to act upon the subject, or to entertain its consideration. But supposing, Sir, that our accustomed forms and our republican principles are to be followed, and that a law creating a bank is, like all other laws, to originate with Congress, and that the President has nothing to do with it till it is presented for his approval, then it is clear that the powers and duties of a proposed bank, and all the terms and conditions annexed to it, must, in the first place be settled by Congress.

This power, if constitutional at all, is only constitutional in the hands of Congress. Anywhere else, its exercise would be plain usurpation. If, then, the authority to decide what powers ought to be granted to a bank belong to Congress, and Congress shall have exercised that power, it would seem little better than absurd to say, that its act, nevertheless, would be unconstitutional and invalid, if, in the opinion of a third party, it had misjudged, on a question of expediency, in the arrangement of details. According to such a mode of reasoning, a mistake in the exercise of jurisdiction takes away the jurisdiction. If Congress decide right, its decision may stand; if it decide wrong, its decision is nugatory; and whether its decision be right or wrong another is to judge, although the original power of making the decision must be allowed to be exclusively in Congress. This is the end to which the argument of the message will conduct its followers.

Sir, in considering the authority of Congress to invest the bank with the particular powers granted to it, the inquiry is not, and cannot be, how appropriate these powers are, but whether they be at all appropriate; whether they come within the range of a just and honest discretion; whether Congress may fairly esteem them to be necessary. The question is not, Are they the fittest means, the best means? or whether the bank might not be established without them; but the question is, Are they such as Congress, *bonâ fide*, may have regarded as appropriate to the end? If any other rule were to be adopted, nothing could ever be settled. A law would be constitutional to-day and unconstitutional to-morrow. Its constitutionality would altogether depend upon individual opinion on a matter of mere expediency. Indeed, such a case as that is now actually before us. Mr. Madison deemed the powers given to the bank, in its present charter, proper and necessary. He held the bank, therefore, to be constitutional. But the present President, not acknowl-

edging that the power of deciding on these points rests with Congress, nor with Congress and the then President, but setting up his own opinion as the standard, declares the law now in being unconstitutional, because the powers granted by it are, in his estimation, not necessary and proper. I pray to be informed, Sir, whether, upon similar grounds of reasoning, the President's own scheme for a bank, if Congress should do so unlikely a thing as to adopt it, would not become unconstitutional also, if it should so happen that his successor should hold his bank in as light esteem as he holds those established under the auspices of Washington and Madison?

If the reasoning of the message be well founded, it is clear that the charter of the existing bank is not a law. The bank has no legal existence; it is not responsible to government; it has no authority to act; it is incapable of being an agent; the President may treat it as a nullity to-morrow, withdraw from it all the public deposits, and set afloat all the existing national arrangements of revenue and finance. It is enough to state these monstrous consequences, to show that the doctrine, principles, and pretensions of the message are entirely inconsistent with a government of laws. If that which Congress has enacted, and the Supreme Court has sanctioned,[9] be not the law of the land, then the reign of law has ceased, and the reign of individual opinion has already begun.

The President, in his commentary on the details of the existing bank charter, undertakes to prove that one provision, and another provision, is not necessary and proper; because, as he thinks, the same objects proposed to be accomplished by them might have been better attained in another mode; and therefore such provisions are not necessary, and so not warranted by the Constitution. Does not this show, that, according to his own mode of reasoning, his *own* scheme would not be constitutional, since another scheme, which probably most people would think a better one, might be substituted for it? Perhaps, in any bank charter, there may be no provisions which may be justly regarded as absolutely indispensable; since it is probable that for any of them some others might be substituted. No bank, therefore, ever could be established; because there never has been, and never could be, any charter, of which every provision should appear to be indispensable, or necessary and proper, in the judgment of every individual. To admit, therefore, that there may be a constitutional bank, and yet to contend for such a mode of judging of its provisions and details as the message adopts, involves an absurdity. Any charter which may be framed may be taken up, and each power conferred by it successively denied, on

9. *Register* omits "and the Supreme Court has sanctioned."

the ground, that, in regard to each, either no such power is "necessary or proper" in a bank, or, which is the same thing in effect, some other power might be substituted for it, and supply its place. That can never be necessary, in the sense in which the message understands that term, which may be dispensed with; and it cannot be said that any power may not be dispensed with, if there be some other which might be substituted for it, and which would accomplish the same end. Therefore, no bank could ever be constitutional, because none could be established which should not contain some provisions which might have been omitted, and their place supplied by others.

Mr. President, I have understood the true and well-established doctrine to be, that, after it has been decided that it is competent for Congress to establish a bank, then it follows, that it may create such a bank as it judges, in its discretion, to be best, and invest it with all such power as it may deem fit and suitable; with this limitation, always, that all is to be done in the *bonâ fide* execution of the power to create a bank. If the granted powers are appropriate to the professed end, so that the granting of them cannot be regarded as usurpation of authority by Congress, or an evasion of constitutional restrictions, under color of establishing a bank, then the charter is constitutional, whether these powers be thought indispensable by others or not, or whether even Congress itself deemed them absolutely indispensable, or only thought them fit and suitable, or whether they are more or less appropriate to their end. It is enough that they are appropriate; it is enough that they are suited to produce the effects designed; and no comparison is to be instituted, in order to try their constitutionality, between them and others which may be suggested. A case analogous to the present is found in the constitutional power of Congress over the mail. The Constitution says no more than that "Congress shall have power to establish post-offices and post-roads"; and, in the general clause, "all powers necessary and proper" to give effect to this. In the execution of this power, Congress has protected the mail, by providing that robbery of it shall be punished with death. Is this infliction of capital punishment constitutional?[10] Certainly it is not, unless it be both "proper and necessary." The President may not think it necessary or proper; the law, then, according to the system of reasoning enforced by the message, is of no binding force, and the President may disobey it, and refuse to see it executed.

The truth is, Mr. President, that if the general object, the subject-matter, properly belong to Congress, all its incidents belong to Congress also. If Congress is to establish post-offices and post-roads, it may, for that end, adopt one set of regulations or another; and either would be

10. *Register* reads "unconstitutional."

constitutional. So the details of one bank are as constitutional as those of another, if they are confined fairly and honestly to the purpose of organizing the institution, and rendering it useful. One *bank* is as constitutional as another *bank*. If Congress possesses the power to make a bank, it possesses the power to make it efficient, and competent to produce the good expected from it. It may clothe it with all such power and privileges, not otherwise inconsistent with the Constitution, as may be necessary, in its own judgment, to make it what government deems it should be. It may confer on it such immunities as may induce individuals to become stockholders, and to furnish the capital; and since the extent of these immunities and privileges is matter of discretion, and matter of opinion, Congress only can decide it, because Congress alone can frame or grant the charter. A charter, thus granted to individuals, becomes a contract with them, upon their compliance with its terms. The bank becomes an agent, bound to perform certain duties, and entitled to certain stipulated rights and privileges, in compensation for the proper discharge of these duties; and all these stipulations, so long as they are appropriate to the object professed, and not repugnant to any other constitutional injunction, are entirely within the competency of Congress. And yet, Sir, the message of the President toils through all the commonplace topics of monopoly, the right of taxation, the suffering of the poor, and the arrogance of the rich, with as much painful effort, as if one, or another, or all of them, had something to do with the constitutional question.

What is called the "monopoly" is made the subject of repeated rehearsal, in terms of special complaint. By this "monopoly," I suppose, is understood the restriction contained in the charter, that Congress shall not, during the twenty years, create another bank. Now, Sir, let me ask, Who would think of creating a bank, inviting stockholders into it, with large investments, imposing upon it heavy duties, as connected with the government, receiving some millions of dollars as a *bonus* or premium, and yet retaining the power of granting, the next day, another charter, which would destroy the whole value of the first? If this be an unconstitutional restraint on Congress, the Constitution must be strangely at variance with the dictates both of good sense and sound morals. Did not the first Bank of the United States contain a similar restriction? And have not the States granted bank charters with a condition, that, if the charter should be accepted, they would not grant others? States have certainly done so; and, in some instances, where no *bonus* or premium was paid at all; but from the mere desire to give effect to the charter, by inducing individuals to accept it and organize the institution. The President declares that this restriction is not necessary to the efficiency of the bank; but that is the very thing which Con-

gress and his predecessor in office were called on to decide, and which they did decide, when the one passed and the other approved the act. And he has now no more authority to pronounce his judgment on that act than any other individual in society. It is not his province to decide on the constitutionality of statutes which Congress has passed, and his predecessors approved.

There is another sentiment in this part of the message, which we should hardly have expected to find in a paper which is supposed, whoever may have drawn it up, to have passed under the review of professional characters. The message declares, that this limitation to create no other bank is unconstitutional, because, although Congress may use the discretion vested in them, "they may not limit the discretion of their successors." This reason is almost too superficial to require an answer. Every one at all accustomed to the consideration of such subjects knows that every Congress can bind its successors to the same extent that it can bind itself. The power of Congress is always the same; the authority of law always the same. It is true, we speak of the Twentieth Congress and the Twenty-first Congress; but this is only to denote the period of time, or to mark the successive organizations of the House of Representatives under the successive periodical election of its members. As a politic body, as the legislative power of the government, Congress is always continuous, always identical. A particular Congress, as we speak of it, for instance, the present Congress, can no farther restrain itself from doing what it may choose to do at the next session, than it can restrain any succeeding Congress from doing what it may choose. Any Congress may repeal the act or law of its predecessor, if in its nature it be repealable, just as it may repeal its own act; and if a law or an act be irrepealable in its nature, it can no more be repealed by a subsequent Congress than by that which passed it. All this is familiar to every body. And Congress, like every other legislature, often passes acts which, being in the nature of grants or contracts, are irrepealable ever afterwards. The message, in a strain of argument which it is difficult to treat with ordinary respect, declares that this restriction on the power of Congress, as to the establishment of other banks, is a palpable attempt to amend the Constitution by an act of legislation. The reason on which this observation purports to be founded is, that Congress, by the Constitution, is to have exclusive legislation over the District of Columbia; and when the bank charter declares that Congress will create no new bank within the District, it annuls this power of exclusive legislation! I must say, that this reasoning hardly rises high enough to entitle it to a passing notice. It would be doing it too much credit to call it plausible. No one needs to be informed that exclusive power of legislation is not unlimited power of legislation; and if it were,

how can that legislative power be unlimited that cannot restrain itself, that cannot bind itself by contract? Whether as a government or as an individual, that being is fettered and restrained which is not capable of binding itself by ordinary obligation. Every legislature binds itself, whenever it makes a grant, enters into a contract, bestows an office, or does any other act or thing which is in its nature irrepealable. And this, instead of detracting from its legislative power, is one of the modes of exercising that power. The legislative power of Congress over the District of Columbia would not be full and complete, if it might not make just such a stipulation as the bank charter contains.

As to the taxing power of the States, about which the message says so much, the proper answer to all it says is, that the States possess no power to tax any instrument of the government of the United States. It was no part of their power before the Constitution, and they derive no such power from any of its provisions. It is nowhere given to them. Could a State tax the *coin* of the United States at the mint? Could a State lay a stamp tax on the process of the courts of the United States, and on custom-house papers? Could it tax the transportation of the mail, or the ships of war, or the ordnance, or the muniments[11] of war, of the United States? The reason that these cannot be taxed by a State is, that they are means and instruments of the government of the United States. The establishment of a bank exempt from State taxation takes away no existing right in a State. It leaves it all it ever possessed. But the complaint is, that the bank charter does not *confer* the power of taxation. This, certainly, though not a new (for the same argument was urged here), appears to me to be a strange mode of asserting and maintaining State rights. The power of taxation is a sovereign power; and the President and those who think with him are of opinion, in a given case, that this sovereign power[12] should be conferred on the States by an act of Congress. There is, if I mistake not, Sir, as little compliment to State sovereignty in this idea, as there is of sound constitutional doctrine. Sovereign rights held under the grant of an act of Congress present a proposition quite new in constitutional law.

The President himself even admits that an instrument of the government of the United States ought not, as such, to be taxed by the States; yet he contends for such a power of taxing property connected with this instrument, and essential to its very being, as places its whole existence in the pleasure of the States. It is not enough that the States may tax all the property of all their own citizens, wherever invested or however employed. The complaint is, that the power of State taxation does not reach so far as to take cognizance over persons out of the State, and

11. *Register* reads "munitions."   12. *Register* reads "right."

to tax them for a franchise lawfully exercised under the authority of the United States. Sir, when did the power of the States, or indeed of any government, go to such an extent as that? Clearly never. The taxing power of all communities is necessarily and justly limited to the property of its own citizens, and to the property of others, having a distinct local existence as property, within its jurisdiction; it does not[13] extend to rights and franchises, rightly exercised, under the authority of other governments, nor to persons beyond its jurisdiction. As the Constitution has left the taxing power of the States, so the bank charter leaves it. Congress has not undertaken either to take away, or to confer, a taxing power; nor to enlarge, or to restrain it; if it were to do either, I hardly know which of the two would be the least excusable.

I beg leave to repeat, Mr. President, that what I have now been considering are the President's objections, not to the policy or expediency, but to the constitutionality of the bank; and not to the constitutionality of any new or proposed bank, but of the bank as it now is, and as it has long existed. If the President had declined to approve this bill because he thought the original charter unwisely granted, and the bank, in point of policy and expediency, objectionable or mischievous, and in that view only had suggested the reasons now urged by him, his argument, however inconclusive, would have been intelligible, and not, in its whole frame and scope, inconsistent with all well-established first principles. His rejection of the bill, in that case, would have been, no doubt, an extraordinary exercise of power; but it would have been, nevertheless, the exercise of a power belonging to his office, and trusted by the Constitution to his discretion. But when he puts forth an array of arguments such as the message employs, not against the expediency of the bank, but against its constitutional existence, he confounds all distinctions, mixes questions of policy and questions of right together, and turns all constitutional restraints into mere matters of opinion. As far as its power extends, either in its direct effects or as a precedent, the message not only unsettles every thing which has been settled under the Constitution, but would show, also, that the Constitution itself is utterly incapable of any fixed construction or definite interpretation, and that there is no possibility of establishing, by its authority, any practical limitations on the powers of the respective branches of the government.

When the message denies, as it does, the authority of the Supreme Court to decide on constitutional questions, it effects, so far as the opinion of the President and his authority can effect it, a complete change in our government. It does two things; first, it converts constitutional

13. *Register* omits "not."

limitations of power into mere matters of opinion, and then it strikes the judicial department, as an efficient department, out of our system. But the message by no means stops even at this point. Having denied to Congress the authority of judging what powers may be constitutionally conferred on a bank, and having erected the judgment of the President himself into a standard by which to try the constitutional character of such powers, and having denounced the authority of the Supreme Court to decide finally on constitutional questions, the message proceeds to claim for the President, not the power of approval, but the primary power, the power of originating laws. The President informs Congress, that *he* would have sent them such a charter, if it had been properly asked for, as they ought to confer.[14] He very plainly intimates, that, in his opinion, the establishment of all laws, of this nature at least, belongs to the functions of the executive government; and that Congress ought to have waited for the manifestation of the executive will, before it presumed to touch the subject. Such, Mr. President, stripped of their disguises, are the real pretences set up in behalf of the executive power in this most extraordinary paper.

Mr. President, we have arrived at a new epoch. We are entering on experiments, with the government and the Constitution of the country, hitherto untried, and of fearful and appalling aspect. This message calls us to the contemplation of a future which little resembles the past. Its principles are at war with all that public opinion has sustained, and all which the experience of the government has sanctioned. It denies first principles; it contradicts truths, heretofore received as indisputable. It denies to the judiciary the interpretation of law, and claims to divide with Congress the power of originating statutes. It extends the grasp of executive pretension over every power of the government. But this is not all. It presents the chief magistrate of the Union in the attitude of arguing away the powers of that government over which he has been chosen to preside; and adopting for this purpose modes of reasoning which, even under the influence of all proper feeling towards high official station, it is difficult to regard as respectable. It appeals to every prejudice which may betray men into a mistaken view of their own interests, and to every passion which may lead them to disobey the impulses of their understanding. It urges all the specious topics of State rights and national encroachment against that which a great majority of the States have affirmed to be rightful, and in which all of them have acquiesced. It sows, in an unsparing manner, the seeds of jealously and ill-will against that government of which its author is the official head. It raises a cry, that liberty is in danger, at the very moment when it puts

14. *Register* reads "to possess."

forth claims to powers heretofore unknown and unheard of. It affects alarm for the public freedom, when nothing endangers that freedom so much as its own unparalleled pretences. This, even, is not all. It manifestly seeks to inflame[15] the poor against the rich; it wantonly attacks whole classes of the people, for the purpose of turning against them the prejudices and the resentments of other classes. It is a state paper which finds no topic too exciting for its use, no passion too inflammable for its address and its solicitation.

Such is this message. It remains now for the people of the United States to choose between the principles here avowed and their government. These cannot subsist together. The one or the other must be rejected. If the sentiments of the message shall receive general approbation, the Constitution will have perished even earlier than the moment which its enemies originally allowed for the termination of its existence. It will not have survived to its fiftieth year.

15. *Register* reads "influence."

National Republican Convention at Worcester, October 12, 1832

The National Republicans of Massachusetts assembled at Worcester on October 11, 1832, with Webster's friend and financial backer, Stephen White of Salem, in the chair. The purpose of the gathering was to choose electors for the party ticket—Henry Clay of Kentucky for president and John Sergeant of Pennsylvania for vice-president—and to nominate candidates for governor and lieutenant governor. The first day was devoted to routine matters: the selection of Nathaniel Silsbee of Salem, Webster's Senate colleague, as president of the convention, and the appointment of numerous committees through which the scheduled business would be accomplished. The next day, October 12, electors were duly chosen; Levi Lincoln, the incumbent, was nominated for governor with Samuel P. Armstrong as his running mate; and an "Address to the People of Massachusetts," prepared by a committee chaired by Edward Everett, was adopted. (*Journal of the Proceedings of the National Republican Convention, held at Worcester, October 11, 1832* [Boston, Stimpson & Clapp, 1832].)

The assembled delegates then settled back to listen while Webster, himself a delegate, delivered what we would call today the party keynote for the upcoming election. According to *Niles' Register* it was "perhaps the most powerful, as well as most splendid effort that he ever made." It was also the only speech delivered at the convention. Everett spoke for them all when he presumed no one would attempt "to add perfume to the violet, strength to the oak, or majesty to the thunder." (*Niles' Register*, 43 [Oct. 27, 1832]: 133.)

The presidential election of 1832 offered many issues—the bank, the tariff, the public lands, the removal of the Indians to the unsettled West —but overriding them all was Andrew Jackson himself. Never before had a president aroused such wild enthusiasm among his followers, or such bitter hostility in the opposition. He had been swept into office in 1828 on a wave of popular rejection of the too-intellectual Adams, and a widespread belief, encouraged if not actually conceived by Jackson's managers, that the colorful general had been the victim four years earlier of a "corrupt bargain" between Adams and Clay. He had been carefully non-committed on the major issues of the day, so that states as

diverse in their economies as Pennsylvania, Missouri, and South Carolina could give him their allegiance. He came to the presidency with no political debts to pay, save to those he called "the people" who had elected him.

The course of the administration thereafter, as it appeared to leaders of the opposition, may be followed in the speech reproduced below, which needs no commentary here. Webster's admirers lamented only that it had not come in time to be read the country over before the election. "It must have settled thousands and thousands of votes," wrote Philip Fendall, "unless the Devil himself has got as deeply into the minds of the people as he has into the heart of Jackson." (Fendall to DW, Oct. 26, 1832, NhHi, mDW 10309.) The president, as was his custom, used from Webster's attack what suited his own purposes. According to Van Buren there were those who believed that Jackson's Proclamation Against the Nullifiers of December 10, 1832, was "taken altogether from Webster's speech at Worcester," (*Autobiography of Martin Van Buren* [Washington, 1920], p. 680).

The text here reproduced is taken from *Writings and Speeches*, 2: 87–128, which is reprinted in turn from *Works*, 1: 237–278. The original source is the Boston *Columbian Centinel* for October 17, 20, and 24, 1832. The Worcester *Massachusetts Spy* published the speech on October 24, and the Washington *National Intelligencer* reprinted it in two installments on October 23 and 25. There were also no less than four pamphlet versions distributed from Boston alone, at least one of which must have preceded the last installment in the *Centinel*. Philip R. Fendall, writing to Webster from Washington on October 26, acknowledges the pamphlet, "received this morning," adding that he "had before read every word of it in the newspapers." For a detailed analysis of the pamphlets, see Clifford Blake Clapp, "Analytical Methods in Bibliography, Applied to Daniel Webster's Speech at Worcester in 1832," *Bibliographical Essays; a tribute to Wilberforce Eames* (Cambridge, 1924), pp. 211–219. The text is also included in *Speeches and Forensic Arguments*, 2: 125–159, where it shows minor variations from the *Columbian Centinel*. These editorial "improvements" are carried over into *Works*, in which still other changes, also minor in nature, are made. It should be noted that Edward Everett was the editor both of volume two of *Speeches*, and of the *Works*. The changes are undoubtedly his.

The version here published may be called "official" or "definitive" since the *Works*, first published in 1851, carried Webster's own stamp of approval. This text has been compared with that of the *Columbian Centinel*, and variations regarded as having any significance have been footnoted.

Mr. President,—I offer no apology for addressing the meeting. Holding, by the favor of the people of this Commonwealth, an important public situation, I deem it no less than a part of my duty, at this interesting moment, to make known my opinions on the state of public affairs, and, however I may have performed other duties, this, at least, it is my purpose, on the present occasion, fully to discharge. Not intending to comment at length on all the subjects which now attract public attention, nor to discuss any thing in detail, I wish, nevertheless, before an assembly so large and respectable as the present, and through them before the whole people of the State, to lay open, without reserve, my own sentiments, hopes, and fears respecting the state and the prospects[1] of our common country.

The resolutions which have been read from the chair express the opinion, that the public good requires an effectual change, in the administration of the general government, both of measures and of men. In this opinion I heartily concur.

Mr. President, there is no citizen of the State, who, in principle and by habitual sentiment, is less disposed than myself to general opposition to government, or less desirous of frequent changes in its administration. I entertain this feeling strongly, and at all times, towards the government of the United States; because I have ever regarded the Federal Constitution as a frame of government so peculiar, and so delicate in its relations to the State governments, that it might be in danger of overthrow, as well from an indiscriminate and wanton opposition, as from a weak or a wicked administration. But a case may arise in which the government is no longer safe in the hands to which it has been intrusted. It may come to be a question, not so much in what particular manner, or according to what particular political opinions, the government shall be administered, as whether the Constitution itself shall be preserved and maintained. Now, Sir, in my judgment, just such a case and just such a question are at this moment before the American people. Entertaining this sentiment, and thoroughly and entirely convinced of its truth, I wish, as far as my humble power extends, to produce in the people a more earnest attention to their public concerns. With the people, and the people alone, lies any remedy for the past or any security for the future. No delegated power is equal to the exigency of the present crisis. No public servants, however able or faithful, have ability to check or to stop the fearful tendency of things. It is a case for sovereign interposition. The rescue, if it come at all, must come from that power which no other on earth can resist. I earnestly wish, therefore, unimportant as my own opinions may be, and entitled, as I know they

1. *Columbian Centinel* reads "fate."

are, to no considerable regard, yet, since they are honest and sincere, and since they respect nothing less than dangers which appear to me to threaten the government and Constitution of the country, I fervently wish that I could now make them known, not only to this meeting and to this State, but to every man in the Union. I take the hazard of the reputation of an alarmist; I cheerfully submit to the imputation of over-excited apprehension; I discard all fear of the cry of false prophecy, and I declare, that, in my judgment, not only the great interests of the country, but the Constitution itself, are in imminent peril, and that nothing can save either the one or the other but that voice which has authority to say to the evils of misrule and misgovernment, "Hitherto shall ye come, but no further."

It is true, Sir, that it is the natural effect of a good constitution to protect the people. But who shall protect the constitution? Who shall guard the guardian? What arm but the mighty arm of the people itself is able, in a popular government, to uphold public institutions? The constitution itself is but the creature of the public will; and in every crisis which threatens it, it must owe its security to the same power to which it owes its origin.

The appeal, therefore, is to the people; not to party nor to partisans, not to professed politicians, not to those who have an interest in office and place greater than their stake in the country, but to the people, and the whole people; to those who, in regard to political affairs, have no wish but for a good government, and who have power to accomplish their own wishes.

Mr. President, are the principles and leading measures of the administration hostile to the great interests of the country?

Are they dangerous to the Constitution, and to the union of the States?

Is there any prospect of a beneficial change of principles and measures, without a change of men?

Is there reasonable ground to hope for such a change of men?

On these several questions, I desire to state my own convictions fully, though as briefly as possible.

As government is intended to be a practical institution, if it be wisely formed, the first and most natural test of its administration is the effect produced by it. Let us look, then, to the actual state of our affairs. Is it such as should follow a good administration of a good constitution?

Sir, we see one State openly threatening to arrest the execution of the revenue laws of the Union, by acts of her own.[2] This proceeding is

2. South Carolina was preparing to nullify the tariff. For Webster's views see *Correspondence*, 3: 195.

threatened, not by irresponsible persons, but by those who fill her chief places of power and trust.

In another State, free citizens of the country are imprisoned, and held in prison, in defiance of a judgment of the Supreme Court, pronounced for their deliverance.[3] Immured in a dungeon, marked and patched as subjects of penitentiary punishment, these free citizens pass their days in counting the slow-revolving hours of their miserable captivity, and their nights in feverish and delusive dreams of their own homes and their own families; while the Constitution stands adjudged to be violated, a law of Congress is effectually repealed by the act of a State, and a judgment of deliverance by the Supreme Court is set at naught and contemned.

Treaties, importing the most solemn and sacred obligations, are denied to have binding force.[4]

A feeling that there is great insecurity for property, and the stability of the means of living, extensively prevails.

The whole subject of the tariff, acted on for the moment, is at the same moment declared not to be at rest, but liable to be again moved, and with greater effect, just so soon as power for that purpose shall be obtained.

The currency of the country, hitherto safe, sound, and universally satisfactory, is threatened with a violent change; and an embarrassment in pecuniary affairs, equally distressing and unnecessary, hangs over all the trading and active classes of society.

A long-used and long-approved legislative instrument for the collection of revenue, well secured against abuse, and always responsible to Congress and to the laws, is denied further existence; and its place is proposed to be supplied by a new branch of the executive department, with a money power controlled and conducted solely by executive agency.

3. Samuel Worcester, missionary to the Cherokees, remained in a Georgia jail, although the Supreme Court had declared unconstitutional the state law under which he had been convicted. *Worcester* v. *Georgia,* 6 Peters 515 (1832). See pp. 561–562, below.

4. Webster is referring to treaties negotiated between the United States and the Cherokee Indians from 1785 up to 1828. These treaties recognized the Cherokees as a sovereign nation.

Jackson, however, believed that Indians were subjects of the U.S., and held the treaties to be subordinate to state law. During the conflict between Georgia and the Cherokees which erupted in 1828 Jackson refused to exercise the obligation of the Federal government to protect the Indians. See Jackson's annual message of Dec. 8, 1829, and his special message of Feb. 22, 1831, *Messages and Papers,* 2: 456–459, 536–541.

The power of the VETO is exercised, not as an extraordinary, but as an ordinary power; as a common mode of defeating acts of Congress not acceptable to the executive. We hear, one day, that the President needs the advice of no cabinet; that a few secretaries, or clerks, are enough for him. The next, we are informed that the Supreme Court is but an obstacle to the popular will, and the whole judicial department but an encumbrance to government. And while, on one side, the judicial power is thus derided and denounced, on the other arises the cry, "Cut down the Senate!" and over the whole, at the same time, prevails the loud avowal, shouted with all the lungs of conscious party strength and party triumph, that the spoils of the enemy belongs to the victors. This condition of things, Sir, this general and obvious aspect of affairs, is the result of three years' administration, such as the country has experienced.

But, not resting on this general view of results, let me inquire what[5] the principles and policy of the administration are, on the leading interests of the country, subordinate to the Constitution itself. And first, what are its principles, and what its policy, respecting the tariff? Is this great question settled, or unsettled? And is the present administration for, or against, the tariff?

Sir, the question is wholly unsettled, and the principles of the administration, according to its most recent avowal of those principles, are adverse to the protective policy, decidedly hostile to the whole system, root and branch; and this on permanent and alleged constitutional grounds.

In the first place, nothing has been done to settle the tariff question. The anti-tariff members of Congress[6] who voted for the late law have, none of them, said they would adhere to it. On the contrary, they supported it, because, as far as it went, it was reduction, and that was what they wished; and if they obtained this degree of reduction now, it would be easier to obtain a greater degree hereafter; and they frankly declared, that their intent and purpose was to insist on reduction, and to pursue reduction, unremittingly, till all duties on imports should be brought down to one general and equal percentage, and that regulated by the mere wants of the revenue; or, if different rates of duty should remain on different articles, still, that the whole should be laid for revenue, and revenue only; and that they would, to the utmost of their power, push this course, till protection by duties, as a special object of national policy, should be abandoned altogether in the national councils. It is a delusion, therefore, Sir, to imagine that the present tariff

5. *Columbian Centinel* reads 'whether."

6. *Centinel* reads "gentlemen."

stands, safely, on conceded ground. It covers not an inch that has not been fought for, and must not be again fought for. It stands while its friends can protect it, and not an hour longer.

In the next place, in that compend of executive opinion contained in the veto message, the whole principle of the protective policy is plainly and pointedly denounced.

Having gone through its argument against the bank charter, as it now exists, and as it has existed, either under the present or a former law,[7] for near forty years, and having added to the well-doubted logic of that argument the still more doubtful aid of a large array of opprobrious epithets, the message, in unveiled allusion to the protective policy of the country, holds this language: —

> Most of the difficulties our government now encounters, and most of the dangers which impend over our Union, have sprung from an abandonment of the legitimate objects of government by our national legislation, and the adoption of such principles as are embodied in this act. Many of our rich men have been content with equal protection and equal benefits, but have besought us to make them richer by act of Congress. By attempting to gratify their desires, we have, in the results of our legislation, arrayed section against section, interest against interest, and man against man, in a fearful commotion which threatens to shake the foundations of our Union. It is time to pause in our career, to review our principles, and, if possible, revive that devoted patriotism and spirit of compromise which distinguished the sages of the Revolution and the fathers of our Union. If we cannot at once, in justice to interests vested under improvident legislation, make our government what it ought to be, we can at least take a stand against all new grants of monopolies and exclusive privileges, against any prostitution of our government to the advancement of the few at the expense of the many, and in favor of compromise and gradual reform in our code of laws and system of political economy.[8]

Here, then, we have the whole creed. Our national legislation has abandoned the legitimate objects of government. It has adopted such principles as are embodied in the bank charter; and these principles are elsewhere called objectionable, odious, and unconstitutional. All this has been done, because rich men have besought the government to render them richer by acts of Congress. It is time to pause in our career. It is time *to review these principles*. And if we cannot at once MAKE

7. Passage absent from *Centinel*. Webster means to include the statute chartering the first Bank of the United States in 1791. See 1 *U.S.*

8. Veto message of July 10, 1832, *Messages and Papers*, 2: 590–591. *Stat.* 191–196.

OUR GOVERNMENT WHAT IT OUGHT TO BE, we can, at least, take a stand against new grants of power and privilege.

The plain meaning of all this is, that our protecting laws are founded in an abandonment of the legitimate objects of government; that this is the great source of our difficulties; that it is time to stop in our career, to review the principles of these laws, and, as soon as we can, MAKE OUR GOVERNMENT WHAT IT OUGHT TO BE.

No one can question, Mr. President, that these paragraphs, from the last official publication of the President, show that, *in his opinion, the tariff, as a system designed for protection, is not only impolitic, but unconstitutional also.* They are quite incapable of any other version or interpretation. They defy all explanation, and all glosses.

Sir, however we may differ from the principles or the policy of the administration, it would, nevertheless, somewhat satisfy our pride of country, if we could ascribe to it the character of consistency. It would be grateful if we could contemplate the President of the United States as an identical idea. But even this secondary pleasure is denied to us. In looking to the published records of executive opinions, sentiments favorable to protection and sentiments against protection either come confusedly before us, at the same moment, or else follow each other in rapid succession, like the shadows of a phantasmagoria.

Having read an extract from the veto message, containing the statement of *present opinions*, allow me to read another extract from the annual message of 1830. It will be perceived, that in that message both the clear constitutionality of the tariff laws, and their indispensable policy, are maintained in the fullest and strongest manner. The argument on the constitutional point is stated with more than common ability; and the policy of the laws is affirmed in terms importing the deepest and most settled conviction. We hear in this message nothing of improvident[9] legislation; nothing of the abandonment of the legitimate objects of government; nothing of the necessity of pausing in our career and reviewing our principles; nothing of the necessity of changing our government, *till it shall be made what it ought to be.* But let the message speak for itself.

> The power to impose duties on imports originally belonged to the several States. The right to adjust those duties with a view to the encouragement of domestic branches of industry is so completely incidental to that power, that it is difficult to suppose the existence of the one without the other. The States have delegated their whole authority over imports to the general government, without limitation or restriction, saving the very inconsiderable reservation relating to their inspection laws. This authority having

9. *Columbian Centinel* reads "independent."

thus entirely passed from the States, the right to exercise it for the purpose of protection does not exist in them; and consequently, if it be not possessed by the general government, it must be extinct. Our political system would thus present the anomaly of a people stripped of the right to foster their own industry, and to counteract the most selfish and destructive policy which might be adopted by foreign nations. This surely cannot be the case; this indispensable power, thus surrendered by the States, must be within the scope of the authority on the subject expressly delegated to Congress.

In this conclusion I am confirmed, as well by the opinions of Presidents Washington, Jefferson, Madison, and Monroe, who have each repeatedly recommended the exercise of this right under the Constitution, as by the uniform practice of Congress, the continued acquiescence of the States, and the general understanding of the people.

I am well aware that this is a subject of so much delicacy, on account of the extended interests it involves, as to require that it should be touched with the utmost caution; and that, while an abandonment of the policy in which it originated, a policy coeval with our government, pursued through successive administrations, is neither to be expected nor desired, the people have a right to demand, and have demanded, that it be so modified as to correct abuses and obviate injustice.[10]

Mr. President, no one needs to point out inconsistencies plain and striking as these. The message of 1830 is a well-written paper; it proceeded, probably, from the cabinet proper. Whence the veto message of 1832 proceeded, I know not; perhaps from the cabinet improper.

But, Sir, there is an important record of an earlier date than 1830.[11] If, as the President avers, we have been guilty of improvident legislation, what act of Congress is the most striking instance of that improvidence? Certainly it is the act of 1824. The principle of protection, repeatedly recognized before that time, was, by that act, carried to a new and great extent; so new and so great, that the act was considered as the foundation of the system. That law it was which conferred on the distinguished citizen, whose nomination for President this meeting has received with so much enthusiasm, (Mr. Clay,) the appellation of the "Author of the American System." Accordingly, the act of 1824 has been the particular object of attack, in all the warfare waged against the protective policy. If Congress ever abandoned legitimate objects of legislation in favor of protection, it did so by that law. If any laws now on

10. Second annual message, Dec. 6, 1830, *Messages and Papers*, 2: 523, 525. The last paragraph of the quota-tion is omitted in the *Columbian Centinel*.

11. *Centinel* reads "1832."

the statute-book, or which ever were there, show, by their character as laws of protection, that our government is not what it ought to be, and that it ought to be altered, and, in the language of the veto message, *made* what it ought to be, the law of 1824 is the very law which, more than any and more than all others, makes good that assertion.[12] And yet, Sir, the President of the United States, then a Senator in Congress, voted for that law! And, though I have not recurred to the journal, my recollection is, that, as to some of its provisions, his support was essential to their success. It will be found, I think, that some of its enactments, and those now most loudly complained of, would have failed, but for his own personal support of them by his own vote.

After all this, it might have been hoped that there would be, in 1832, some tolerance of opinion toward those who cannot think that improvidence, abandonment of all the legitimate objects of legislation, a desire to gratify the rich, who have besought Congress to make them still richer, and the adoption of principles unequal, oppressive, and odious, are the true characteristics to be ascribed to the system of protection.

But, Sir, it is but a small part of my object to show inconsistencies in executive opinions. My main purpose is different, and tends to more practical ends. It is, to call the attention of the meeting, and of the people, to the principles avowed in the late message as being the President's *present opinions,* and proofs of his *present purposes,* and to the consequences, if they shall be maintained by the country. These principles are there expressed in language which needs no commentary. They go, with a point-blank aim, against the fundamental stone of the protective system; that is to say, against the constitutional power of Congress to establish and maintain that system, in whole or in part. The question, therefore, of the tariff, the question of every tariff, the question between maintaining our agricultural and manufacturing interests where they now are, and breaking up the entire system, and erasing every vestige of it from the statute-book, is a question materially to be affected by the pending election.

The President has exercised his NEGATIVE power on the law for continuing the bank charter. Here, too, he denies both the constitutionality and the policy of an existing law of the land. It is true that the law, or a similar one, has been in operation nearly forty years. Previous Presidents and previous Congresses have, all along, sanctioned and upheld it. The highest courts, and indeed all the courts, have pronounced it constitutional. A majority of the people, greater than exists on almost any other question, agrees with all the Presidents, all the Congresses, and all the courts of law. Yet, against all this weight of authority, the

12. *Centinel* reads "shows that truth."

President puts forth his own individual opinion, and has negatived the bill for continuing the law. Which of the members of his administration, or whether any one of them, concur in his sentiments, we know not. Some of them, we know, have recently advanced precisely the opposite opinions, and in the strongest manner recommended to Congress the continuation of the bank charter. Having himself urgently and repeatedly called the attention of Congress to the subject, and his Secretary of the Treasury—who, and all the other secretaries, as the President's friends say, are but so many pens in his hand—having, in his communication to Congress, at this very session, insisted both on the constitutionality and necessity of the bank, the President nevertheless saw fit to negative the bill, passed, as it had been, by strong majorities in both Houses, and passed, without doubt or question, in compliance with the wishes of a vast majority of the American people.

The question respecting the constitutional power of Congress to establish a bank, I shall not here discuss. On that, as well as on the general expediency of renewing the charter, my opinions have been elsewhere expressed.[13] They are before the public, and the experience of every day confirms me in their truth. All that has been said of the embarrassment and distress which will be felt from discontinuing the bank falls far short of an adequate representation. What was prophecy only two months ago is already history.

In this part of the country, indeed, we experience this distress and embarrassment in a mitigated degree. The loans of the bank are not so highly important, or at least not so absolutely necessary, to the present operations of our commerce; yet we ourselves have a deep interest in the subject, as it is connected with the general currency of the country, and with the cheapness and facility of exchange.

The country, generally speaking, was well satisfied with the bank. Why not let it alone? No evil had been felt from it in thirty-six years. Why conjure up a troop of fancied mischiefs, as a pretence to put it down? The message struggles to excite prejudices, from the circumstance that foreigners are stockholders; and on this ground it raises a loud cry against a moneyed aristocracy. Can any thing, Sir, be conceived more inconsistent than this? any thing more remote from sound policy and good statesmanship? In the United States the rate of interest is high, compared with the rates abroad. In Holland and England, the actual value of money is no more than three, or perhaps three and a half, per cent. In our Atlantic States, it is as high as five or six, taking the whole length of the seaboard; in the Northwestern States, it is eight or ten, and in the Southwestern ten or twelve. If the introduction, then,

13. See Webster's speech on the Bank veto, pp. 501–529, above.

of foreign capital be discountenanced and discouraged, the American moneylender may fix his own rate anywhere from five to twelve per cent. per annum. On the other hand, if the introduction of foreign capital be countenanced and encouraged, its effect is to keep down the rate of interest, and to bring the value of money in the United States so much the nearer to its value in older and richer countries. Every dollar brought from abroad, and put into the mass of active capital at home, by so much diminishes the rate of interest; and by so much, therefore, benefits all the active and trading classes of society, at the expense of the American capitalist. Yet the President's invention, for such it deserves to be called, that which is to secure us against the possibility of being oppressed by a moneyed aristocracy, is to shut the door and bar it safely against all introduction of foreign capital!

Mr. President, what is it that has made England a sort of general banker for the civilized world? Why is it that capital from all quarters of the globe accumulates at the centre of her empire, and is thence again distributed? Doubtless, Sir, it is because she invites it, and solicits it. She sees the advantage of this;[14] and no British minister ever yet did a thing so rash, so inconsiderate, so startling, as to exhibit a groundless feeling of dissatisfaction at the introduction or employment of foreign capital.

Sir, of all the classes of society, the larger stockholders of the bank are among those least likely to suffer from its discontinuance. There are, indeed, on the list of stockholders many charitable institutions, many widows and orphans, holding small amounts. To these, and other proprietors of a like character, the breaking up of the bank will, no doubt, be seriously inconvenient. But the capitalist, he who has invested money in the bank merely for the sake of the security and the interest, has nothing to fear. The refusal to renew the charter will, it is true, diminish the value of the stock; but, then, the same refusal will create a scarcity of money; and this[15] will reduce the price of all other stocks; so that the stockholders in the bank, receiving, on its dissolution, their portion respectively of its capital, will have opportunities of new and advantageous[16] investment.

The truth is, Sir, the great loss, the sore embarrassment, the severe distress, arising from this VETO, will fall on the public, and especially on the more active and industrious portion of the public. It will inevitably create a scarcity of money; in the Western States, it will most materially depress the value of property; it will greatly enhance, every-

---

14. *Columbian Centinel* has a period here, then inserts the following: "She manifests no weak or pretended jealousy of foreign influence, from the freest intercourse with the commercial world;".

15. *Centinel* reads 'in time."

16. *Centinel* reads "cheap."

where, the price of domestic exchange; it threatens, everywhere, fluctuations of the currency; and it drives all our well-settled and safe operations of revenue and finance out of their accustomed channels. All this is to be suffered on the pretended ground of a constitutional scruple, which no respect for the opinion of others, no deference to legislative precedent, no decent regard to judicial decision, no homage to public opinion, expressed and maintained for forty years, have power to overcome. An idle apprehension of danger is set up against the experience of almost half a century; loose and flimsy theories are asserted against facts of general notoriety; and arguments are urged against continuing the charter, so superficial and frivolous, and yet so evidently addressed to those of the community who have never had occasion to be conversant with objects of this sort, that an intelligent reader, who wishes to avoid imputing obliquity of motive, is obliged to content himself with ascribing to the source of the message, whatever and wherever that source may have been, no very distinguished share of the endowments of intellect.

Mr. President, as early as December, 1829, the President called the attention of Congress to the subject of the bank, in the most earnest manner. Look to his annual message of that date. You will find that he then felt constrained, by an irresistible sense of duty to the various interests concerned, not to delay beyond that moment his urgent invitation to Congress to take up the subject. He brought forward the same topic again, in all his subsequent annual messages; yet when Congress *did* act upon it, and, on the fourth of July, EIGHTEEN HUNDRED AND THIRTY-TWO, *did* send him a bill, he returned it with his objections; and among these objections, he not only complained *that the executive was not consulted on the propriety of present action*, but affirmed also, in so many words, *that present action was deemed premature by the executive department.*

Let me ask, Mr. President, if it be possible that the same President, the same chief magistrate, the same mind, could have composed these two messages? Certainly they much more resemble the production of *two* minds, holding, on this point, precisely opposite opinions. The message of December, 1829, asserts that the time had *then* come for Congress to consider the bank subject; the message of 1832 declares, that, even then, the action of Congress on the same subject was *premature*; and both these messages were sent to Congress by the President of the United States. Sir, I leave these two messages to be compared and considered by the people.

Mr. President, I will here take notice of but one other suggestion of the President, relative to the time and manner of passing the late bill. A decent respect for the legislature of the country has hitherto been ob-

served by all who have had occasion to hold official intercourse with it, and especially by all other branches of the government. The purity of the motives of Congress, in regard to any measure, has never been assailed from any respectable quarter. But in the veto message there is one expression, which, as it seems to me, no American can read without some feeling. There is an expression, evidently not casual or accidental, but inserted with design and composed with care, which does carry a direct imputation of the possibility of the effect of *private interest* and *private influence* on the deliberations of the two Houses of Congress. I quote the passage, and shall leave it without a single remark: —"Whatever interest or influence, whether public or private, has given birth to this act, it cannot be found either in the wishes or necessities of the executive department, by which present action is deemed premature."[17]

Among the great interests of the country, Mr. President, there is one which appears to me not to have attracted from the people of this Commonwealth a degree of attention altogether equal to its magnitude. I mean the public lands.

If we run our eye over the map of the country, and view the regions, almost boundless, which now constitute the public domain, and over which an active population is rapidly spreading itself, and if we recollect the amount of annual revenue derived from this source, we shall hardly fail to be convinced that few branches of national interest are of more extensive and lasting importance. So large a territory, belonging to the public, forms a subject of national concern of a very delicate nature, especially in popular governments. We know, in the history of other countries, with what views and designs the public lands have been granted. Either in the form of gifts and largesses, or in that of reduction of prices to amounts merely nominal, or as compensation for services, real or imagined, the public domain, in other countries and other times, has not only been diverted from its just use and destination, but has been the occasion, also, of introducing into the state and into the public counsels no small portion both of distraction and corruption.

Happily, our own system of administering this great interest has hitherto been both safe and successful. Nothing under the government has been better devised than our land system; and nothing, thus far, more beneficially conducted. But the time seems to have arrived, in the progress of our growth and prosperity, when it has become necessary to reflect, not on any new mode of sale, for that can hardly be improved, but on some disposition of the proceeds such as shall be just and equal to the whole country, and shall insure also a constant and vigilant attention to this important subject from the people of all the States. It is

17. Jackson's bank veto, *Messages and Papers*, 2: 590.

not to be denied or disguised, that sentiments have recently sprung up, in some places, of a very extraordinary character, respecting the ownership, the just proprietary interest, in these lands. The lands are well known to have been obtained by the United States, either by grants from individual States, or by treaties with foreign powers. In both cases, and in all cases, the grants and cessions were to the United States, for the interest of the whole Union; and the grants from individual States contain express limitations and conditions, binding up the whole property to the common use of all the States for ever. Yet, of late years, an idea has been suggested, indeed seriously advanced, *that these lands, of right, belong to the States respectively in which they happen to lie.* This doctrine, Sir, which, I perceive, strikes this assembly as being somewhat extravagant, is founded on an argument derived, as is supposed,[18] from the nature of State sovereignty. It has been openly espoused, by candidates for office, in some of the new States, and, indeed, has been announced in the Senate of the United States.

To the credit of the country, it should be stated, that, up to the present moment, these notions have not spread widely; and they will be repudiated, undoubtedly, by the power of general opinion, so soon as that opinion shall be awakened and expressed. But there is another tendency more likely, perhaps, to run to injurious excess; and that is, a constant effort to reduce the price of land to sums almost nominal, on the ground of facilitating settlement. The sound policy of the government has been, uniformly, to keep the prices of the public lands low; so low that every actual settler might easily obtain a farm; but yet not so low as to tempt individual capitalists to buy up large quantities to hold for speculation. The object has been to meet, at all times, the whole actual demand, at a cheap rate; and this object has been attained. It is obviously of the greatest importance to keep the prices of the public lands from all influences, except the single one of the desire of supplying the whole actual demand at a cheap rate. The present minimum price is one dollar and a quarter per acre; and millions of acres of land, much of it of an excellent quality, are now in the market at this rate. Yet every year there are propositions to reduce the price, and propositions to graduate the price; that is to say, to provide that all lands having been offered for sale for a certain length of time at the established rate, if not then sold, shall be offered at a less rate; and again reduced, if not sold, to one still less. I have myself thought, that, in some of the oldest districts, some mode might usefully be adopted of disposing of the remainder of the unsold lands, and closing the offices; but a universal system of graduation, lowering prices at short intervals,

18. *Centinel* omits "as is supposed."

and by large degrees, could have no other effect than a general depression of price in regard to the whole mass, and would evidently be great mismanagement of the public property. This convention, Sir, will think it singular enough, that a reduction of prices of the public lands should have been demanded on the ground *that other impositions for revenue, such as the duty on tea and coffee, have been removed*; thus considering and treating the sums received for lands sold as a *tax*, a *burden*, an *imposition*, and a great *drain* on the means and the industry of the new States. A man goes from New England to one of the Western States, buys a hundred acres of the best land in the world for one hundred and twenty-five dollars, pays his money, and receives an indisputable title; and immediately some one stands up in Congress to call this operation the laying of a *tax*, the imposition of a *burden*; and the whole of these purchases and payments, taken together, are represented as an intolerable *drain* on the money and the industry of the new States. I know not, Sir, which deserves to pass for the original, and which for the copy; but this reasoning is not unlike that which maintains that the trading community of the West will be exhausted and ruined by the privilege of borrowing money of the Bank of the United States at six per cent. interest; this interest being, as is said in the veto message, a burden upon their industry, and a drain of their currency, which no country can bear without inconvenience and distress!

It was in a forced connection with the reduction of duties of impost, that the subject of the public lands was referred to the Committee of Manufactures in the Senate, at the late session of Congress. This was a legislative movement, calculated to throw on Mr. Clay, who was acting a leading part on the subject of the tariff and the reduction of duties, a new and delicate responsibility. From this responsibility, however, Mr. Clay did not shrink. He took up the subject, and his report upon it, and his speech delivered afterwards in defence of the report, are, in my opinion, among the very ablest of the efforts which have distinguished his long public life.[19] I desire to commend their perusal to every citizen of Massachusetts. They will show him the deep interest of all the States, his own among the rest, in the security, and proper management, and disposal, of the public domain. Founded on the report of the committee, Mr. Clay introduced a bill, providing for the distribution among all the States, according to population, of the proceeds of the sales of the public lands for five years, first making a deduction of a considerable percentage in favor of the new States; the sums thus

19. Clay's "Report on the Public Lands" of April 16, 1832 is published in the *Register of Debates,* 22d Cong., 1st sess., Appendix, pp. 112–118. The speech was delivered on June 20, 1832; see *Register of Debates,* 22d Cong., 1st sess., pp. 1096–1119.

Maine of a very large sum of money, justly due to them. It is now fifteen or sixteen years since the money was advanced; and it was advanced for the most necessary and praiseworthy public purposes. The interest on the sum already refunded, and on that which may reasonably be expected to be hereafter refunded, is not less than *five hundred thousand dollars*. But for the President's refusal, in this unusual mode, to give his approbation to a bill which had passed Congress almost unanimously, these two States would already have been in the receipt of a very considerable portion of this money, and the residue, to be received in due season, would have been made sure to them.

Mr. President, I do not desire to raise mere pecuniary interests to an undue importance in political matters. I admit there are principles and objects of paramount obligation and importance. I would not oppose the President merely because he has refused to the State what I thought her entitled to, in a matter of money, provided he had made known his reasons, and they had appeared to be such as might fairly influence an intelligent and honest mind. But in a matter of such great and direct importance to a State, where the justice of this case is so plain, that men agree in it who agree in hardly any thing else, where her claim has passed Congress without considerable opposition in either House, a refusal to approve the bill without giving the slightest reason, the taking advantage of the rising of Congress to give it a silent go-by, *is* an act that may well awaken the attention of the people in the States concerned. It *is* an act requiring close examination. It *is* an act which calls loudly for justification by its author. And now, Sir, I will close what I have to say on this particular subject by stating, that, on the 22d of March, 1832, the President did actually approve and sign a bill,[23] in favor of South Carolina, by which it was enacted that her claim *for interest upon money actually expended* by her for military stores during the late war should be settled and paid; *the money so expended having been drawn by the State from a fund upon which she was receiving interest.* This was precisely the case of Massachusetts.

Mr. President, I now approach an inquiry of a far deeper and more affecting interest. Are the principles and measures of the administration dangerous to the Constitution and to the union of States? Sir, I believe them to be so, and I shall state the grounds of that belief.

In the first place, any administration is dangerous to the Constitution and to the union of the States, which denies the essential powers of the Constitution, and thus strips it of the capacity to do the good intended by it.

The principles embraced by the administration, and expressed in the

23. 4 *U.S. Stat.* 499–500.

veto message, are evidently hostile to the whole system of protection by duties of impost, *on constitutional grounds*. Here, then, is *one* great power struck at once out of the Constitution, and one great end of its adoption defeated. And while this power is thus struck out of the Constitution, it is clear that it exists nowhere else, since the Constitution expressly takes it away from all the States.

The veto message denies the constitutional power of creating or continuing such an institution as our whole experience has approved, for maintaining a sound, uniform, national currency, and for the safe collection of revenue. Here is *another* power, long used, and now lopped off. And *this* power, too, thus lopped off from the Constitution, is evidently not within the power of any of the individual States. No State can maintain a national currency; no State institution can render to the revenue the services performed by a national institution.

The principles of the administration are hostile to internal improvements. Here is another power, heretofore exercised in many instances, now denied. The administration denies the power, except with qualifications which cast an air of ridicule over the whole subject; being founded on such distinctions as between salt water and fresh water, places above custom-houses and places below, and others equally extraordinary.

Now, Sir, in all these respects, as well as in others, I think the principles of the administration are at war with the true principles of the Constitution; and that, by the zeal and industry which it exerts to support its own principles, it does daily weaken the Constitution, and does put in doubt its long continuance. The inroad of to-day opens the way for an easier inroad to-morrow. When any one essential part is rent away, or, what is nearer the truth, when many essential parts are rent away, who is there to tell us *how long any other part is to remain?*

Sir, our condition is singularly paradoxical. We have an administration opposed to the Constitution; we have an opposition which is the main support of the government and the laws. We have an administration denying to the very government which it administers powers that have been exercised for forty years; it denies the protective power, the bank power, and the power of internal improvement. The great and leading measures of the national legislature are all resisted by it. These, strange as it may seem, depend on the *opposition* for support. We have, in truth, an opposition, without which it would be difficult for the government to get along at all. I appeal to every member of Congress present, (and I am happy to see many here,) to say what would now become of the government, if all the members of the opposition were withdrawn from Congress. For myself, I declare my own conviction that its continuance would probably be very short. Take away the opposition from Congress, and let us see what would probably be done, the first

session. The TARIFF would be entirely *repealed*. Every enactment having protection by duties as its main object would be struck from the statute-book. This would be the first thing done. Every work of internal improvement would be stopped. This would follow, as matter of course. The bank would go down, and a *treasury money agency* would take its place. The Judiciary Act of 1789 would be repealed, so that the Supreme Court should exercise no power of revision over State decisions. And who would resist the doctrines of NULLIFICATION? Look, Sir, to the votes of Congress for the last three years, and you will see that each of these things would, in all human probability, take place at the next session, if the opposition were to be withdrawn. The Constitution is threatened, therefore, imminently threatened, by the very fact that those intrusted with its administration are hostile to its essential powers.

But, Sir, in my opinion, a yet greater danger threatens the Constitution and the government; and that is from the attempt *to extend the power of the executive at the expense of all the other branches of the government, and of the people themselves*. Whatever accustomed power is denied to the Constitution, whatever accustomed power is denied to Congress, or to the judiciary, *none is denied to the executive*. Here there is no retrenchment; here no apprehension is felt for the liberties of the people; here it is not thought necessary to erect barriers against corruption.

I begin, Sir, with the subject of removals from office for opinion's sake, one of the most signal instances, as I think, of the attempt to extend executive power. This has been a leading measure, a cardinal point, in the course of the administration. It has proceeded, from the first, on a settled proscription for political opinions; and this system it has carried into operation to the full extent of its ability. The President has not only filled all vacancies with his own friends, generally those most distinguished as personal partisans, but he has turned out political opponents, and thus created vacancies, in order that he might fill them with his own friends. I think the number of removals and appointments is said to be *two thousand*. While the administration and its friends have been attempting to circumscribe and to decry the powers belonging to other branches, it has thus seized into its own hands a patronage most pernicious and corrupting, an authority over men's means of living most tyrannical and odious, and a power to punish free men for political opinions altogether intolerable.

You will remember, Sir, that the Constitution says not one word about the President's power of removal from office. It is a power raised entirely by construction. It is a constructive power, introduced at first to meet cases of extreme public necessity. It has now become coextensive with the executive will, calling for no necessity, requiring no exi-

gency for its exercise; to be employed at all times, without control, without question, without responsibility. When the question of the President's power of removal was debated in the first Congress, those who argued for it limited it to *extreme cases*. Cases, they said, might arise, in which it would be *absolutely necessary* to remove an officer before the Senate could be assembled. An officer might become insane; he might abscond; and from these and other supposable cases, it was said, the public service might materially suffer if the President could not remove the incumbent. And it was further said, that there was little or no danger of the abuse of the power for party or personal objects. No President, it was thought, would ever commit such an outrage on public opinion. Mr. Madison, who thought the power ought to exist, and to be exercised in cases of high necessity, declared, nevertheless, that if a President should resort to the power when not required by any public exigency, and merely for personal objects, *he would deserve to be impeached*. By a very small majority,—I think, in the Senate, by the casting vote of the Vice-President,—Congress decided in favor of the existence of the power of removal, upon the grounds which I have mentioned; granting the power in a case of clear and absolute necessity; and denying its existence everywhere else.

Mr. President, we should recollect that this question was discussed, and thus decided, when Washington was in the executive chair. Men knew that in his hands the power would not be abused; nor did they conceive it possible that any of his successors could so far depart from his great and bright example, as, by abuse of the power, and by carrying that abuse to its utmost extent, to change the essential character of the executive from that of an impartial guardian and executor of the laws into that of the chief dispenser of party rewards. Three or four instances of removal occurred in the first twelve years of the government. At the commencement of Mr. Jefferson's administration, he made several others, not without producing much dissatisfaction; so much so, that he thought it expedient to give reasons to the people, in a public paper, for even the limited extent to which he had exercised the power. He rested his justification on particular circumstances and peculiar grounds; which, whether substantial or not, showed, at least, that he did not regard the power of removal as an ordinary power, still less as a mere arbitrary one, to be used as he pleased, for whatever ends he pleased, and without responsibility. As far as I remember, Sir, after the early part of Mr. Jefferson's administration, hardly an instance occurred for near thirty years. If there were any instances, they were few. But at the commencement of the present administration, the precedent of these previous cases was seized on, and a *system*, a regular *plan of government*, a well-considered scheme for the maintenance of party power

by the patronage of office, and this patronage to be created by general removal, was adopted, and has been carried into full operation. Indeed, before General Jackson's inauguration, the party put the system into practice. In the last session of Mr. Adams's administration, the friends of General Jackson constituted a majority in the Senate; and nominations, made by Mr. Adams to fill vacancies which had occurred in the ordinary way, were postponed, by this majority, beyond the 3d of March, *for the purpose, openly avowed, of giving the nominations to General Jackson.* A nomination for a judge of the Supreme Court, and many others of less magnitude, were thus disposed of.

And what did we witness, Sir, when the administration actually commenced, in the full exercise of its authority? One universal sweep, one undistinguishing blow, levelled against all who were not of the successful party. No worth, public or private, no service, civil or military, was of power to resist the relentless greediness of proscription. Soldiers of the late war, soldiers of the Revolutionary war, the very contemporaries of the independence of the country, all lost their situations. No office was too high, and none too low; for *office* was the spoil, and "*all the spoils*," it is said, "belong to the *victors!*" If a man holding an office necessary for his daily support had presented himself covered with the scars of wounds received in every battle, from Bunker Hill to Yorktown, these would not have protected him against this reckless rapacity.[24] Nay, Sir, if [Dr. Joseph] Warren[25] himself had been among the living, and had possessed any office under government, high or low, he would not have been suffered to hold it a single hour, unless he could show that he had strictly complied with the party statutes, and had put a well-marked party collar round his own neck. Look, Sir, to the case of the late venerable Major [Thomas] Melville.[26] He was a personification of the spirit of 1776, one of the earliest to venture in the cause of liberty. He was of the Tea Party; one of the very first to expose himself to British power. And his whole life was consonant with this, its beginning. Always ardent in the cause of liberty, always a zealous friend to his country, always acting with the party which he supposed cherished the genuine republican spirit most fervently, always estimable and respectable in private life, he seemed armed against this miserable petty tyranny of party as far as man could be. But he felt its blow, and he fell. He held an office in the custom-house, and had held it for a long course of

24. *Centinel* adds "of proscription."

25. Next to the Adamses, Dr. Warren was the most influential of New England's pre-revolutionary agitators. He was killed in the battle of Bunker Hill.

26. Major Melville, in addition to the attributes Webster correctly assigns to him, was the grandfather of Herman Melville.

years; and he was deprived of it, as if unworthy to serve the country which he loved, and for whose liberties, in the vigor of his early manhood, he had thrust himself into the very jaws of its enemies. There was no mistake in the matter. His character, his standing, his Revolutionary services, were all well known; but they were known to no purpose; they weighed not one feather against party pretensions. It cost no pains to remove him; it cost no compunction to wring his aged heart with this retribution from his country for his services, his zeal, and his fidelity. Sir, you will bear witness,[27] that, when his successor was nominated to the Senate, and the Senate were informed who had been removed to make way for that nomination, its members were struck with horror. They had not conceived the administration to be capable of such a thing; and yet, they said, What can *we* do? The man is removed; *we* cannot recall him; we can only act upon the nomination before us. Sir, you and I thought otherwise; and I rejoice that we did think otherwise. We thought it our duty to resist the nomination to fill a vacancy thus created. We thought it our duty to oppose this proscription, when, and where, and as, we constitutionally could. We besought the Senate to go with us, and to take a stand before the country on this great question. We invoked them to try the deliberate sense of the people; to trust themselves before the tribunal of public opinion; to resist at first, to resist at last, to resist always, the introduction of this unsocial, this mischievous, this dangerous, this belligerent principle into the practice of the government.

Mr. President, as far as I know, there is no civilized country on earth, in which, on a change of rulers, there is such an *inquisition for spoil* as we have witnessed in this free republic. The Inaugural Address of 1829 spoke of a *searching operation* of government. The most searching operation, Sir, of the present administration, has been its search for office and place. When, Sir, did any English minister, Whig or Tory, ever make such an inquest? When did he ever go down to low-water-mark, to make an ousting of tide-waiters? When did he ever take away the daily bread of weighers, and gaugers, and measurers? When did he ever go into the villages, to disturb the little post-offices, the mail contracts, and every thing else in the remotest degree connected with government? Sir, a British minister who should do this, and should afterwards show his head in a British House of Commons, would be received by a universal hiss.

I have little to say of the selections made to fill vacancies thus created. It is true, however, and it is a natural consequence of the system which has been acted on, that, within the last three years, more nominations

27. The president of the convention was Nathaniel Silsbee, Webster's Senate colleague from Massachusetts.

have been rejected on the ground of *unfitness*, than in all the preceding forty years of the government. And these nominations, you know, Sir, could not have been rejected but by votes of the President's own friends. The cases were too strong to be resisted. Even party attachment could not stand them. In some not a third of the Senate, in others not ten votes, and in others not a single vote, could be obtained; and this for no particular reason known only to the Senate, but on general grounds of the want of character and qualifications; on grounds known to every body else, as well as to the Senate. All this, Sir, is perfectly natural and consistent. The same party selfishness which drives good men out of office will push bad men in. Political proscription leads necessarily to the filling of offices with incompetent persons, and to a consequent mal-execution of official duties. And in my opinion, Sir, this principle of claiming a monopoly of office by the right of conquest, unless the public shall effectually rebuke and restrain it, will entirely change the char-acter of our government. It elevates party above country; it forgets the common weal in the pursuit of personal emolument; it tends to form, it does form, we see that it has formed, a political combination, united by no common principles or opinions among its members, either upon the powers of the government, or the true policy of the country; but held together simply as an association, under the charm of a popular head, seeking to maintain possession of the government by a *vigorous exercise of its patronage*; and for this purpose agitating, and alarming, and dis-tressing social life by the exercise of a tyrannical party proscription. Sir, if this course of things cannot be checked, good men will grow tired of the exercise of political privileges. They will have nothing to do with popular elections. They will see that such elections are but a mere sel-fish contest for office; and they will abandon the government to the scramble of the bold, the daring, and the desperate.

It seems, Mr. President, to be a peculiar and singular characteristic of the present administration, that it came into power on a cry against abuses, *which did not exist*, and then, as soon as it was in, as if in mockery of the perception and intelligence of the people, *it created those very abuses*, and carried them to a great length. Thus the chief magis-trate himself, before he came into the chair, in a formal public paper, denounced the practice of appointing members of Congress to office.[28]

28. In a speech to the Tennessee legislature upon his resignation from the U.S. Senate, Oct. 14, 1825, Jack-son stated: "With a view to sustain, more effectually in practice, the axiom which divides the three great classes of power into independent, constitutional checks, I would im-pose a provision, rendering any member of Congress ineligible to office, under the general government, during the term for which he was elected, and for two years thereafter, except in cases of judicial office." *Niles' Register*, 29 (Nov. 5, 1825): 156–157.

He said, that, if that practice continued, *corruption would become the order of the day*; and, as if to fasten and nail down his own consistency to that point, he declared that it was *due to himself to practise what he recommended to others*. Yet, Sir, as soon as he was in power, these fastenings gave way, the nails all flew, and the promised *consistency* remains a striking proof of the manner in which political assurances are sometimes fulfilled. He has already appointed more members of Congress to office than any of his predecessors, in the longest period of administration. Before his time, there was no reason to complain of these appointments. They had not been numerous under any administration. Under this, they have been numerous, and some of them such as may well justify complaint.

Another striking instance of the exhibition of the same characteristics may be found in the sentiments of the Inaugural Address, and in the subsequent practice, on the subject of *interfering with the freedom of elections*. The Inaugural Address declares, that it is necessary to reform abuses which have *brought the patronage of the government into conflict with the freedom of elections*. And what has been the subsequent practice? Look to the newspapers; look to the published letters of officers of the government, advising, exhorting, soliciting, friends and partisans to greater exertions in the cause of the party; see all done, everywhere, which patronage and power can do, to affect, not only elections in the general government, but also in every State government, and then say, how well *this* promise of reforming abuses has been kept. At what former period, under what former administration, did public officers of the United States thus interfere in elections? Certainly, Sir, never. In this respect, then, as well as in others, that which was not true as a charge against previous administrations would have been true, if it had assumed the form of a prophecy respecting the acts of the present.

But there is another attempt to grasp and to wield a power over public opinion, of a still more daring character, and far more dangerous effects.

In all popular governments, a FREE PRESS is the most important of all agents and instruments. It not only expresses public opinion, but, to a very great degree, it contributes to form that opinion. It is an engine for good or for evil, as it may be directed; but an engine of which nothing can resist the force. The conductors of the press, in popular governments, occupy a place, in the social and political system, of the very highest consequence. They wear the character of public instructors.[29] Their daily labors bear directly on the intelligence, the morals, the taste, and the public spirit of the country. Not only are they journalists, re-

29. *Centinel* adds: "To matters of intelligence, they add matters of opinion."

cording political occurrences, but they discuss principles, they comment on measures, they canvass characters; they hold a power over the reputation, the feelings, the happiness, of individuals. The public ear is always open to their addresses, the public sympathy easily made responsive to their sentiments. It is indeed, Sir, a distinction of high honor, that theirs is the only profession expressly protected and guarded by constitutional enactments. Their employment soars so high, in its general consequences it is so intimately connected with the public happiness, that its security is provided for by the fundamental law. While it acts in a manner worthy of this distinction, the press is a fountain of light, and a source of gladdening warmth. It instructs the public mind, and animates the spirit of patriotism. Its loud voice suppresses every thing which would raise itself against the public liberty; and its blasting rebuke causes incipient despotism to perish in the bud.

But remember, Sir, that these are the attributes of a FREE press only. And is a press that is purchased or pensioned more free than a press that is fettered? Can the people look for truths to partial sources, whether rendered partial through fear or through favor? Why shall not a manacled press be trusted with the maintenance and defence of popular rights? Because it is supposed to be under the influence of a power which may prove greater than the love of truth. Such a press may screen abuses in government, or be silent. It may fear to speak. And may it not fear to speak, too, when its conductors, if they speak in any but one way, may lose their means of livelihood? Is dependence on government for bread no temptation to screen its abuses? Will the press always speak the truth, when the truth, if spoken, may be the means of silencing it for the future? Is the truth in no danger, is the watchman under no temptation, when he can neither proclaim the approach of national evils, nor seem to descry them, without the loss of his place?

Mr. President, an open attempt to secure the aid and friendship of the public press, by bestowing the emoluments of office on its active conductors, seems to me, of every thing we have witnessed, to be the most reprehensible.[30] It degrades both the government and the press. As far as its natural effect extends, it turns the palladium of liberty into an engine of party. It brings the agency, activity, energy, and patronage of government all to bear, with united force, on the means of general

30. Jackson nominated several editors for public office. Among the more prominent were Amos Kendall (1789–1869; Dartmouth, 1811) of the Frankfort, Ky. *Argus*, who served as 4th auditor of the treasury; and Isaac Hill (1789–1851) of the Concord *New Hampshire Patriot*, who served as 2nd comptroller of the treasury until he was rejected by the Senate in April, 1830. Kendall and Hill were influential members of Jackson's Kitchen Cabinet.

intelligence, and on the adoption or rejection of political opinions. It so completely perverts the true object of government, it so entirely revolutionizes our whole system, that the chief business of those in power is directed rather to the propagation of opinions favorable to themselves, than to the execution of the laws. This propagation of opinions, through the press, becomes the main administrative duty. Some fifty or sixty editors of leading journals have been appointed to office by the present executive. A stand has been made against this proceeding, in the Senate, with partial success; but, by means of appointments which do not come before the Senate, or other means, the number has been carried to the extent I have mentioned. Certainly, Sir, the editors of the public journals are not to be disfranchised. Certainly they are fair candidates either for popular elections, or a just participation in office. Certainly they reckon in their number some of the first geniuses, the best scholars, and the most honest and well-principled men in the country. But the complaint is against the *system*, against the *practice*, against the undisguised attempt to secure the favor of the press by means addressed to its pecuniary interest, and these means, too, drawn from the public treasury, being no other than the appointed compensations for the performance of official duties. Sir, the press itself should resent this. Its own character for purity and independence is at stake. It should resist a connection rendering it obnoxious to so many imputations. It should point to its honorable denomination in our constitutions of government, and it should maintain the character, there ascribed to it, of a FREE PRESS.

There can, Sir, be no objection to the appointment of an editor to office, if he is the fittest man. There can be no objection to considering the services which, in that or in any other capacity, he may have rendered his country. He may have done much to maintain her rights against foreign aggression, and her character against insult. He may have honored, as well as defended her; and may, therefore, be justly regarded and selected, in the choice of faithful public agents. But the ground of complaint is, that the aiding, by the press, of the election of an individual, is rewarded, by that same individual, with the gift of moneyed offices. Men are turned out of office, and others put in, and receive salaries from the public treasury, on the ground, either openly avowed or falsely denied, that they have rendered service in the election of the very individual who makes this removal and makes this appointment. Every man, Sir, must see that this is a vital stab at the purity of the press. It not only assails its independence, by addressing sinister motives to it, but it furnishes from the public treasury the means of exciting these motives. It extends the executive power over the press in a most daring manner. It operates to give a direction to opinion, not

favorable to the government, in the aggregate; not favorable to the Constitution and laws; not favorable to the legislature; but favorable to the executive alone. The consequence often is, just what might be looked for, that the portion of the press thus made fast to the executive interest denounces Congress, denounces the judiciary, complains of the laws, and quarrels with the Constitution. This exercise of the right of appointment to this end is an augmentation, and a vast one, of the executive power, singly and alone. It uses that power strongly against all other branches of the government, and it uses it strongly, too, for any struggle which it may be called on to make with the public opinion of the country. Mr. President, I will quit this topic. There is much in it, in my judgment, affecting, not only the purity and independence of the press, but also the character and honor, the peace and security, of the government. I leave it, in all its bearings, to the consideration of the people.

Mr. President, among the novelties introduced into the government by the present administration is the frequent use of the President's negative on acts of Congress. Under former Presidents, this power has been deemed an extraordinary one, to be exercised only in peculiar and marked cases. It was vested in the President, doubtless, as a guard against hasty or inconsiderate legislation, and against any act, inadvertently passed, which might seem to encroach on the just authority of other branches of the government. I do not recollect that, by all General Jackson's predecessors, this power was exercised more than four or five times. Not having recurred to the journals, I cannot, of course, be sure that I am numerically accurate in this particular; but such is my belief. I recollect no instance in the time of Mr. John Adams, Mr. Jefferson, or Mr. John Quincy Adams. The only cases which occur to me are two in General Washington's administration, two in Mr. Madison's, and one in Mr. Monroe's.[31] There may be some others; but we all know that it is a power which has been very sparingly and reluctantly used, from the beginning of the government. The cases, Sir, to which I have now referred, were cases in which the President returned the bill with objections. The silent veto is, I believe, the exclusive adoption of the present administration. I think, indeed, that, some years ago, a bill, by inadvertence or accident, failed to receive the President's signature, and so did not become a law. But I am not aware of any instance, before the present administration, in which the President has, by design, omitted to sign a bill, and yet has not returned it to Congress. But since that administration came into power, the veto, in both kinds, has been repeatedly applied. In the case of the Maysville Road, the Montgomery Road, and the bank, we have had the veto, *with* reasons. In an internal im-

31. *Centinel* inserts Monroe's name after Jefferson's and elimi-   nates the reference here.

provement bill of a former session, in a similar bill at the late session, and in the State interest bill, we have had the silent veto, or refusal *without* reasons.[32]

Now, Sir, it is to be considered, that the President has the power of recommending measures to Congress. Through his friends, he may and does oppose, also, any legislative movement which he does not approve. If, in addition to this, he may exercise a silent veto, at his pleasure, on all the bills presented to him during the last ten days of the session; if he may refuse assent to them all, without being called upon to assign any reasons whatever,—it will certainly be a great practical augmentation of his power. Any one, who looks at a volume of the statutes, will see that a great portion of all the laws are actually passed within the last ten days of each session. If the President is at liberty to negative any or all of these laws, at pleasure, or rather, to refuse to render the bills laws by approving them, and still may neglect to return them to Congress for renewed action, he will hold a very important control over the legislation of this country. The day of adjournment is usually fixed some weeks in advance. This being fixed, a little activity and perseverance may easily, in most cases, and perhaps in all, where no alarm has been excited, postpone important pending measures to a

32. Part of the rationale underlying Jackson's rejection of all of these bills derived from his belief that they were extravagant and unnecessary federal expenses. Jackson wanted to relieve the population of the burden of taxation, and he wanted the federal debt paid off. He justified his veto of the Maysville Road bill, May 27, 1830, by claiming that the road was of a local, not national, character. (*Messages and Papers*, 2: 483–493.) The Montgomery Road, also known as the Washington, Washington and Rockville, or Washington and Frederick Turnpike, through Montgomery County, Maryland, was rejected on similar grounds. (May 31, 1830, *Messages and Papers*, 2: 493.) For information on the Bank veto, July 10, 1832, *Messages and Papers*, 2: 576–591, see Webster's speech, pp. 501–529, above. The first internal improvement bill Webster refers to appropriated money for lighthouses, buoys, and other harbor improvements. Jackson vetoed this bill at the end of the 1st session of the 21st Congress, and in his annual message of Dec. 6, 1830, indicated that he could not approve the measure because it contained money for surveys of a purely local character. (*Messages and Papers*, 2: 508.) The bill from the late session was also a bill for the improvement of harbors and rivers. Jackson applied the pocket veto in July, and subsequently issued a veto message on Dec. 6, 1832, citing his denial of unlimited federal power over internal improvements. (*Messages and Papers*, 2: 638–639.) The veto message on the state interest bill was also issued on Dec. 6, 1832. Jackson explained that he rejected it because the principle of the bill varied for no apparent reason from the established accounting practices, and from legislation enacted by Congress previously in the case of South Carolina. (*Messages and Papers*, 2: 637–638.)

period within ten days of the close of the session; and this operation subjects all such measures to the discretion of the President, who may sign the bills or not, without being obliged to state his reasons publicly.

The bill for rechartering the bank would have been inevitably destroyed by the silent veto, if its friends had not refused to fix on any term for adjournment before the President should have had the bill in his possession so long as to be required constitutionally to sign it, or to send it back with his reasons for not signing it. The two houses did not agree, and would not agree, to fix a day for adjournment, until the bill was sent to the President; and then care was taken to fix on such a day as should allow him the whole constitutional period. This seasonable presentment rescued the bill from the power of the silent negative.

This practical innovation on the mode of administering the government, so much at variance with its general principles, and so capable of defeating the most useful acts, deserves public consideration. Its tendency is to disturb the harmony which ought always to exist between Congress and the executive, and to turn that which the Constitution intended only as an extraordinary remedy for extraordinary cases into a common means of making executive discretion paramount to the discretion of Congress, in the enactment of laws.

Mr. President, the executive has not only used these unaccustomed means to prevent the passage of laws, but it has also refused to enforce the execution of laws actually passed. An eminent instance of this is found in the course adopted relative to the Indian intercourse law of 1802. Upon being applied to, in behalf of the MISSIONARIES, to execute that law, for their relief and protection, the President replied, that, *the State of Georgia having extended her laws over the Indian territory, the laws of Congress had thereby been superseded.* This is the substance of his answer, as communicated through the Secretary of War. He holds, then, that the law of the State is paramount to the law of Congress. The Supreme Court has adjudged this act of Georgia to be void, as being repugnant to a constitutional law of the United States.[33] But the President pays no more regard to this decision than to the act of Congress itself. The missionaries remain in prison, held there by a condemnation under a law of a State which the supreme judicial tribunal has pronounced to be null and void. The Supreme Court have decided that the act of Congress is constitutional; that it is a binding statute; that it has the same force as other laws, and is as much entitled to be obeyed and executed as other laws. The President, on the contrary, declares that the law of Congress has been superseded by the law of the State, and therefore he will not carry its provisions into effect. Now we

33. *Worcester* v. *Georgia,* 6 Peters 515 (1832).

know, Sir, that the Constitution of the United States declares, that that Constitution, and all acts of Congress passed in pursuance of it, shall be the supreme law of the land, any thing in any State law to the contrary notwithstanding. This would seem to be a plain case, then, in which the law should be executed. It has been solemnly[34] decided to be in actual force, by the highest judicial authority; its execution is demanded for the relief of free citizens, now suffering the pains of unjust and unlawful imprisonment; yet the President refuses to execute it.

In the case of the Chicago Road, some sessions ago, the President approved the bill, but accompanied his approval by a message, saying how far he deemed it a proper law, and how far, therefore, it ought to be carried into execution.[35]

In the case of the harbor bill of the late session, being applied to by a member of Congress for directions for carrying parts of the law into effect, he declined giving them, and made a distinction between such parts of the law as he should cause to be executed, and such as he should not; and his right to make this distinction has been openly maintained, by those who habitually defend his measures. Indeed, Sir, these, and other instances of liberties taken with plain statute laws, flow naturally from the principles expressly avowed by the President, under his own hand. In that important document, Sir, upon which it seems to be his fate to stand or to fall before the American people, the veto message, he holds the following language:—"Each public officer who takes an oath to support the Constitution, swears that he will support it as he understands it, and not as it is understood by others." Mr. President, the general adoption of the sentiments expressed in this sentence would dissolve our government. It would raise every man's private opinions into a standard for his own conduct; and there certainly is, there can be, no government, where every man is to judge for himself of his own rights and his own obligations. Where every one is his own arbiter, force, and not law, is the governing power. He who may judge for himself, and decide for himself, must execute his own decisions; and this is the law of force. I confess, Sir, it strikes me with astonishment, that so wild, so disorganizing, a sentiment should be uttered by a President of the United States. I should think it must have escaped from its author through want of reflection, or from the habit of little reflection on such subjects, if I could suppose it possible, that, on a question exciting so

34. *Centinel* reads "recently."

35. The bill, an internal improvement act, contained money for a road from Detroit to Chicago. (May 31, 1830; 4. *U.S. Stat.* 427.) Jackson sent a message to Congress on May 30, 1830, stating that he only approved the bill on the understanding that the road would not be extended beyond the limit of the Michigan Territory. See *Messages and Papers,* 2: 483.

much public attention, and of so much national importance, any such extraordinary doctrine could find its way, through inadvertence, into a formal and solemn public act. Standing as it does, it affirms a proposition which would effectually repeal all constitutional and all legal obligations. The Constitution declares, that every public officer, in the State governments as well as in the general government, shall take an oath to support the Constitution of the United States. This is all. Would it not have cast an air of ridicule on the whole provision, if the Constitution had gone on to add the words, "as he understands it"? What could come nearer to a solemn farce, than to bind a man by oath, and still leave him to be his own interpreter of his own obligation? Sir, those who are to execute the laws have no more a license to construe them for themselves, than those whose only duty is to obey them. Public officers are bound to support the Constitution; private citizens are bound to obey it; and there is no more indulgence granted to the public officer to support the Constitution only *as he understands it*, than to a private citizen to obey it only *as he understands it*; and what is true of the Constitution, in this respect, is equally true of any law. Laws are to be executed, and to be obeyed, not as individuals may interpret them, but according to public, authoritative interpretation and adjudication. The sentiment of the message would abrogate the obligation of the whole criminal code. If every man is to judge of the Constitution and the laws for himself, if he is to obey and support them only as he may say he understands them, a revolution, I think, would take place in the administration of justice; and discussions about the law of treason, murder, and arson should be addressed, not to the judicial bench, but to those who might stand charged with such offences. The object of discussion should be, if we run out this notion to its natural extent, to enlighten[36] the culprit himself how he ought to understand the law.

Mr. President, how is it possible that a sentiment so wild, and so dangerous, so encouraging to all who feel a desire to oppose the laws, and to impair[37] the Constitution, should have been uttered by the President of the United States at this eventful and critical moment? Are we not threatened with dissolution of the Union? Are we not told that the laws of the government shall be openly and directly resisted? Is not the whole country looking, with the utmost anxiety, to what may be the result of these threatened courses? And at this very moment, so full of peril to the state, the chief magistrate puts forth opinions and sentiments as truly subversive of all government, as absolutely in conflict with the authority of the Constitution, as the wildest theories of nullification. Mr. President, I have very little regard for the law, or the logic,

36. *Centinel* reads "convince."

37. *Centinel* reads "to quarrel with."

of nullification. But there is not an individual in its ranks, capable of putting two ideas together, who, if you will grant him the principles of the veto message, cannot defend all that nullification has ever threatened.

To make this assertion good, Sir, let us see how the case stands. The Legislature of South Carolina, it is said, will nullify the late revenue or tariff law, because, *they say*, it is not warranted by the Constitution of the United States, *as they understand the Constitution*. They, as well as the President of the United States, have sworn to support the Constitution. Both he and they have taken the same oath, in the same words. Now, Sir, since he claims the right to interpret the Constitution as he pleases, how can he deny the same right to them? Is his oath less stringent than theirs? Has he a prerogative of dispensation which they do not possess? How can he answer them, when they tell him, that the revenue laws are unconstitutional, *as they understand the Constitution*, and that therefore they will nullify them? Will he reply to them, according to the doctrines of his annual message in 1830, that *precedent* has settled the question, if it was ever doubtful? They will answer him in his own words in the veto message, that, in such a case, *precedent* is not binding. Will he say to them, that the revenue law is a law of Congress, which must be executed until it shall be declared void? They will answer him, that, in other cases, he has himself refused to execute laws of Congress which had not been declared void, but which had been, on the contrary, declared valid. Will he urge the force of judicial decisions? They will answer, that he himself does not admit the binding obligation of such decisions. Sir, the President of the United States is of opinion, that an individual, called on to execute a law, may himself judge of its constitutional validity. Does nullification teach any thing more revolutionary than that? The President is of opinion, that judicial interpretations of the Constitution and the laws do not bind the consciences, and ought not to bind the conduct, of men. Is nullification at all more disorganizing than that? The President is of opinion, that every officer is bound to support the Constitution only according to what ought to be, in his private opinion, its construction. Has nullification, in its wildest flight, ever reached to an extravagance like that? No, Sir, never. The doctrine of nullification, in my judgment a most false, dangerous, and revolutionary doctrine, is this; that *the State*, or *a State*, may declare the extent of the obligations which its citizens are under to the United States; in other words, that a State, by State laws and State judicatures, may conclusively construe the Constitution for its own citizens. But that every individual may construe it for himself is a refinement on the theory of resistance to constitutional power, a sublimation of the right of being disloyal to the Union, a free charter for

the elevation of private opinion above the authority of the fundamental law of the state, such as was never presented to the public view, and the public astonishment, even by nullification itself. Its first appearance is in the veto message. Melancholy, lamentable, indeed, Sir, is our condition, when, at a moment of serious danger and wide-spread alarm, such sentiments are found to proceed from the chief magistrate of the government. Sir, I cannot feel that the Constitution is safe in such hands. I cannot feel that the present administration is its fit and proper[38] guardian.

But let me ask, Sir, what evidence there is, that the President is himself opposed to the doctrines of nullification: I do not say to the political party which now pushes these doctrines, but to the doctrines themselves. Has he anywhere rebuked them? Has he anywhere discouraged them? Has his influence been exerted to inspire respect for the Constitution, and to produce obedience to the laws? Has he followed the bright example of his predecessors? Has he held fast by the institutions of the country? Has he summoned the good and the wise around him? Has he admonished the country that the Union is in danger, and called on all the patriotic to come out in its support? Alas! Sir, we have seen nothing, nothing, of all this.

Mr. President, I shall not discuss the doctrine of nullification. I am sure it can have no friends here. Gloss it and disguise it as we may, it is a pretence incompatible with the authority of the Constitution. If direct separation be not its only mode of operation, separation is, nevertheless, its direct consequence. That a State may nullify a law of the Union, and still remain *in* the Union; that she may have Senators and Representatives in the government, and yet be at liberty to disobey and resist that government; that she may partake in the common councils, and yet not be bound by their results; that she may control a law of Congress, so that it shall be one thing with her, while it is another thing with the rest of the States;—all these propositions seem to me so absolutely at war with common sense and reason, that I do not understand how any intelligent person can yield the slightest assent to them. Nullification, it is in vain to attempt to conceal it, is dissolution; it is dismemberment; it is the breaking up of the Union. If it shall practically succeed in any one State, from that moment there are twenty-four States in the Union no longer. Now, Sir, I think it exceedingly probable that the President may come to an open rupture with that portion of his original party which now constitutes what is called the Nullification party. I think it likely he will oppose the proceedings of that party, if they shall adopt measures coming directly in conflict with the laws of the United States.

38. *Centinel* reads "safe."

But how will he oppose? What will be his course of remedy? Sir, I wish to call the attention of the Convention, and of the people, earnestly to this question,—How will the President attempt to put down nullification, if he shall attempt it at all?

Sir, for one, I protest in advance against such remedies as I have heard hinted. The administration itself keeps a profound silence, but its friends have spoken for it. We are told, Sir, that the President will immediately employ the military force, and at once blockade Charleston! A military remedy, a remedy by direct belligerent operation, has been thus suggested, and nothing else has been suggested, as the intended means of preserving the Union. Sir, there is no little reason to think, that this suggestion is true. We cannot be altogether unmindful of the past, and therefore we cannot be altogether unapprehensive for the future. For one, Sir, I raise my voice beforehand against the unauthorized employment of military power, and against superseding the authority of the laws, by an armed force, under pretence of putting down nullification. The President has no authority to blockade Charleston; the President has no authority to employ military force, till he shall be duly required so to do, by law, and by the civil authorities. His duty is to cause the laws to be executed. His duty is to support the civil authority. His duty is, if the laws be resisted, to employ the military force of the country, if necessary, for their support and execution; but to do all this in compliance only with law, and with decisions of the tribunals. If, by any ingenious devices, those who resist the laws escape from the reach of judicial authority, as it is now provided to be exercised, it is entirely competent to Congress to make such new provisions as the exigency of the case may demand. These provisions undoubtedly would[39] be made. With a constitutional and efficient head of the government, with an administration really and truly in favor of the Constitution, the country can grapple with nullification. By the force of reason, by the progress of enlightened opinion, by the natural, genuine patriotism of the country, and by the steady and well-sustained operations of law, the progress of disorganization may be successfully checked, and the Union maintained. Let it be remembered, that, where nullification is most powerful, it is not unopposed. Let it be remembered, that they who would break up the Union by force have to march toward that object through thick ranks of as brave and good men as the country can show, men strong in character, strong in intelligence, strong in the purity of their own motives, and ready, always ready, to sacrifice their fortunes and their lives to the preservation of the constitutional union of the States. If we can relieve the country from an administration which

39. *Centinel* reads "will."

denies to the Constitution those powers which are the breath of its life; if we can place the government in the hands of its friends; if we can secure it against the dangers of irregular and unlawful military force; if it can be under the lead of an administration whose moderation, firmness, and wisdom shall inspire confidence and command respect,—we may yet surmount the dangers, numerous and formidable as they are, which surround us.

Sir, I see little prospect of overcoming these dangers without a change of men. After all that has passed, the reëlection of the present executive will give the national sanction to sentiments and to measures which will effectually change the government; which, in short, must destroy the government. If the President be reëlected, with concurrent and coöperating majorities in both houses of Congress, I do not see, that, in four years more, all the power which is suffered to remain in the government will not be held by the executive hand. Nullification will proceed, or will be put down by a power as unconstitutional as itself. The revenues will be managed by a treasury bank. The use of the veto will be considered as sanctioned by the public voice. The Senate, if not "cut down," will be bound down, and, the President commanding the army and the navy, and holding all places of trust to be party property, what will then be left, Sir, for constitutional reliance?

Sir, we have been accustomed to venerate the judiciary, and to repose hopes of safety on that branch of the government. But let us not deceive ourselves. The judicial power cannot stand for a long time against the executive power. The judges, it is true, hold their places by an independent tenure; but they are mortal. That which is the common lot of humanity must make it necessary to renew the benches of justice. And how will they be filled? Doubtless, Sir, they will be filled by judges[40] agreeing with the President in his constitutional opinions. If the court is felt as an obstacle,[41] the first opportunity and every opportunity will certainly[42] be embraced to give it less and less the character of an obstacle. Sir, without pursuing these suggestions, I only say that the country must prepare itself for any change in the judicial department such as it shall deliberately sanction in other departments.

But, Sir, what is the prospect of change? Is there any hope that the national sentiment will recover its accustomed tone, and restore to the government a just and efficient administration?

Sir, if there be something of doubt on this point, there is also something, perhaps much, of hope. The popularity of the present chief magistrate, springing from causes not connected with his administration of the government, has been great. Public gratitude for military service

40. *Centinel* reads "incumbents." 42. *Centinel* omits "certainly."
41. *Centinel* adds "doubtless."

has remained fast to him, in defiance of many things in his civil administration calculated to weaken its hold. At length there are indications, not to be mistaken, of new sentiments and new impressions. At length, a conviction of danger to important interests, and to the security of the government, has made its lodgement in the public mind. At length, public sentiment begins to have its free course and to produce its just effects. I fully believe, Sir, that a great majority of the nation desire a change in the administration; and that it will be difficult for party organization or party denunciation to suppress the effective utterance of that general wish. There are unhappy differences, it is true, about the fit person to be successor to the present incumbent in the chief magistracy; and it is possible that this disunion may, in the end, defeat the will of the majority. But so far as we agree together, let us act together. Wherever our sentiments concur, let our hands coöperate. If we cannot at present agree who should be President, we are at least agreed who ought not to be. I fully believe, Sir, that gratifying intelligence is already on the wing. While we are yet deliberating in Massachusetts, Pennsylvania is voting. This week,[43] she elects her members to the next Congress. I doubt not the result of that election will show an important change in public sentiment in that State; nor can I doubt that the great States adjoining her, holding similar constitutional principles and having similar interests, will feel the impulse of the same causes which affect her. The people of the United States, by a countless majority, are attached to the Constitution. If they shall be convinced that it is in danger, they will come to its rescue, and will save it. It cannot be destroyed, even now, if THEY will undertake its guardianship and protection.

But suppose, Sir, there was less hope than there is, would that consideration weaken the force of our obligations? Are we at a post which we are at liberty to desert[44] when it becomes difficult to hold it? May we fly at the approach of danger? Does our fidelity to the Constitution require no more of us than to enjoy its blessings, to bask in the prosperity which it has shed around us and our fathers? and are we at liberty to abandon it in the hour of its peril, or to make for it but a faint and heartless struggle, for the want of encouragement and the want of hope? Sir, if no State come to our succor, if everywhere else the contest should be given up, here let it be protracted to the last moment. Here, where the first blood of the Revolution was shed, let the last effort be made for that which is the greatest blessing obtained by the Revolution, a free and united government. Sir, in our endeavors to maintain our existing forms of government, we are acting not for ourselves alone, but

43. *Centinel* reads "Today."   44. *Centinel* reads "abandon."

for the great cause of constitutional liberty all over the globe. We are trustees holding a sacred treasure, in which all the lovers of freedom have a stake. Not only in revolutionized France, where there are no longer subjects, where the monarch can no longer say, I am the state; not only in reformed England, where our principles, our institutions, our practice of free government, are now daily quoted and commended; but in the depths of Germany, also, and among the desolated fields and the still smoking ashes of Poland, prayers are uttered for the preservation of our union and happiness. We are surrounded, Sir, by a cloud of witnesses. The gaze of the sons of liberty, everywhere, is upon us, anxiously, intently, upon us. They may see us fall in the struggle for our Constitution and government, but Heaven forbid that they should see us recreant.

At least, Sir, let the star of Massachusetts be the last which shall be seen to fall from heaven, and to plunge into the utter darkness of disunion. Let her shrink back, let her hold others back if she can, at any rate, let her keep herself back, from this gulf, full at once of fire and of blackness; yes, Sir, as far as human foresight can scan, or human imagination fathom, full of the fire and the blood of civil war, and of the thick darkness of general political disgrace, ignominy, and ruin. Though the worst may happen that can happen, and though she may not be able to prevent the catastrophe, yet let her maintain her own integrity, her own high honor, her own unwavering fidelity, so that with respect and decency, though with a broken and a bleeding heart, she may pay the last tribute to a glorious, departed, free Constitution.

The Constitution Not a Compact, February 16, 1833

The dogma of nullification was derived from an interpretation of the Constitution as a compact between sovereign states. It went back to Jefferson's Kentucky Resolutions of 1798, aimed at the Alien and Sedition Acts; received a nod from the Hartford Convention; and was refined and restated in Calhoun's *South Carolina Exposition and Protest* of 1828, targeted on the tariff of that year. It was against Calhoun's doctrine that Webster argued in his second Reply to Hayne, but all of the ingredients were not there. Calhoun's elaboration in his Fort Hill Address of July 26, 1831, brought no concession in the tariff of 1832, and South Carolina prepared to fall back upon her sovereignty. Calhoun tried once more, with a letter to Governor James Hamilton, Jr., dated August 28, 1832. Calling it "far the ablest & most plausible, and therefore the most dangerous vindication of that particular *form of Revolution*, which has yet appeared," (DW to Kent, Oct. 29, 1832, *Correspondence*, 3: 195), Webster prepared to reply by way of a letter to Chancellor Kent. He had delayed too long. South Carolina had already elected a legislature dominated by nullifiers. A state convention was called for November 19, which declared the tariff acts of 1828 and 1832 to be null and void. Jackson, meanwhile, had been reelected by a large majority, and his Proclamation against the Nullifiers, issued on December 10, followed closely Webster's own arguments. In South Carolina Hayne was chosen governor, and Calhoun resigned the vice presidency to accept the Senate seat thus vacated. Webster prepared to deliver his belated answer on the Senate floor.

The sequence of events in the crucial short session of the 22nd Congress is of critical importance. Both the rebellious South and the hard-headed, nationalistic president were seeking face-saving solutions that would not leave lasting scars. On January 16, 1833 Jackson asked Congress for authority to collect the revenue by force if necessary. The appropriate measure, known thereafter as the Force Bill, was reported on January 21 from the Judiciary Committee, on which Webster was the ranking National Republican. After some discussion the following day, January 28 was fixed for debate. Calhoun then took the floor, not to argue the merits of the Force Bill but to introduce three resolutions which restated the compact theory of the Constitution. Felix Grundy

of Tennessee, an administration spokesman, proposed a substitute; then on Webster's motion both Calhoun's resolutions and Grundy's amendment were postponed. A few days later both were tabled, to make way for the opening of debate on the Force Bill.

Modification of the tariff, meanwhile, had been the subject of anxious conferences between Clay, Calhoun, and various other Senators. On February 12 Clay introduced a bill to that purport, which Calhoun promptly endorsed. Tariff revision was then referred to a select committee of Clay, Calhoun, Clayton of Delaware, Dallas of Pennsylvania, Grundy, Rives of Virginia, and Webster. Webster opposed a compromise, did not attend meetings of the committee, and gave his full attention to the Force Bill, which to him represented the crux of the problem. Administration senators were glad to yield, letting the Massachusetts senator act in effect as floor leader for the Jacksonians. It was this situation that brought on the long-heralded debate between Webster and Calhoun over the nature of the Constitution. One after another, senators spoke on either side, while the champions tried to wait each other out for the benefit of the rebuttal position. Calhoun was the one to yield, announcing his intention to speak on February 15. His argument, which Webster and others thought to be weak, carried over for two hours on the 16th, after which Webster delivered in answer the speech reproduced below. He took as his point of departure the resolutions Calhoun had introduced nearly a month earlier, but he was also answering the Fort Hill Address, the letter to Hamilton, and the whole body of nullification doctrine.

There the matter rested for another ten days, while the Senate cleared its docket. The tariff compromise from Clay's select committee was introduced on February 19, but not debated until after the Force Bill had passed on February 20. On the 25th Webster spoke against the compromise. Then, on February 26 as the session hurried to its predetermined end, Calhoun called up his resolutions. Using the same vehicle his opponent had used, he delivered a damaging reply to Webster's earlier speech. It was one of the very few times in his career that an overconfident Webster had underestimated an opponent. There was no time left to cross swords again. The compromise tariff of 1833, rerouted so as to become a House bill as the Constitution required of revenue measures, passed on March 1, and at 5 o'clock in the morning of March 3, the Senate adjourned. Jackson signed both the Force Bill and the tariff later that day, the last of his first term as president.

In retrospect, however vulnerable Webster might have appeared to a generation brought up to believe that the Constitution was indeed a compact, the argument reproduced below has proved in the long run valid. Only on such a basis could a nation endure in the nationalistic world of the nineteenth century. Whatever the Constitution may have

meant to the founding fathers, it meant after the 1830's what Daniel Webster said it meant.

The text used here from *Writings and Speeches*, 6: 181–238, is for all practical purposes the only one, handed down with no more than trifling changes from its original publication in the *National Intelligencer* of March 14, 1833. It was issued simultaneously in pamphlet form by the *Intelligencer*, which was also the source for the *Register of Debates*, 22d Cong., 2d sess., pp. 553–587. The pamphlet was presumably the text followed in the second volume of *Speeches and Forensic Arguments*, pp. 160–208, which in turn was the convenient basis for *Works*, 3: 448–505. *Writings and Speeches* reproduces the text from *Works*. Minor variations between the text here reproduced and that of the *Register of Debates*, when they appear to have any significance, are footnoted.

Calhoun's speech of February 15–16, to which Webster is replying, and the South Carolina senator's reply to Webster of February 26 are both conveniently published in volume 12 of *The Papers of John C. Calhoun*, edited by Clyde N. Wilson, Columbia, S.C., 1979.

Mr. President,—The gentleman from South Carolina has admonished us to be mindful of the opinions of those who shall come after us. We must take our chance, Sir, as to the light in which posterity will regard us. I do not decline its judgment, nor withhold myself from its scrutiny. Feeling that I am performing my public duty with singleness of heart and to the best of my ability, I fearlessly trust myself to the country, now and hereafter, and leave both my motives and my character to its decision.

The gentleman has terminated his speech in a tone of threat and defiance towards this bill, even should it become a law of the land, altogether unusual in the halls of Congress. But I shall not suffer myself to be excited into warmth by his denunciation of the measure which I support. Among the feelings which at this moment fill my breast, not the least is that of regret at the position in which the gentleman has placed himself. Sir, he does himself no justice. The cause which he has espoused finds no basis in the Constitution, no succor from public sympathy, no cheering from a patriotic community. He has no foothold on which to stand while he might display the powers of his acknowledged talents. Every thing beneath his feet is hollow and treacherous. He is like a strong man struggling in a morass: every effort to extricate himself only sinks him deeper and deeper. And I fear the resemblance may be carried still farther; I fear that no friend can safely come to his relief, that no one can approach near enough to hold out a helping hand, with-

out danger of going down himself, also, into the bottomless depths of this Serbonian bog.

The honorable gentleman has declared, that on the decision of the question now in debate may depend the cause of liberty itself. I am of the same opinion; but then, Sir, the liberty which I think is staked on the contest is not political liberty, in any general and undefined character, but our own well-understood and long-enjoyed *American* liberty.

Sir, I love Liberty no less ardently than the gentleman himself, in whatever form she may have appeared in the progress of human history. As exhibited in the master states of antiquity, as breaking out again from amidst the darkness of the Middle Ages, and beaming on the formation of new communities in modern Europe, she has, always and everywhere, charms for me. Yet, Sir, it is our own liberty, guarded by constitutions and secured by union, it is that liberty which is our paternal inheritance, it is our established, dear-bought, peculiar American liberty, to which I am chiefly devoted, and the cause of which I now mean, to the utmost of my power, to maintain and defend.

Mr. President, if I considered the constitutional question now before us as doubtful as it is important, and if I supposed that its decision, either in the Senate or by the country, was likely to be in any degree influenced by the manner in which I might now discuss it, this would be to me a moment of deep solicitude. Such a moment has once existed. There has been a time, when, rising in this place, on the same question, I felt, I must confess, that something for good or evil to the Constitution of the country might depend on an effort of mine.[1] But circumstances are changed. Since that day, Sir, the public opinion has become awakened to this great question; it has grasped it; it has reasoned upon it, as becomes an intelligent and patriotic community, and has settled it, or now seems in the progress of settling it, by an authority which none can disobey, the authority of the people themselves.

I shall not, Mr. President, follow the gentleman, step by step, through the course of his speech. Much of what he has said he has deemed necessary to the just explanation and defence of his own political character and conduct. On this I shall offer no comment. Much, too, has consisted of philosophical remark upon the general nature of political liberty, and the history of free institutions; and upon other topics, so general in their nature as to possess, in my opinion, only a remote bearing on the immediate subject of this debate.

But the gentleman's speech made some days ago, upon introducing his resolutions, those resolutions themselves, and parts of the speech now just concluded, may, I presume, be justly regarded as containing

1. The reference is to the debate with Robert Y. Hayne of January 1830. See pp. 285–348, above.

the whole South Carolina doctrine. That doctrine it is my purpose now to examine, and to compare it with the Constitution of the United States. I shall not consent, Sir, to make any new constitution, or to establish another form of government. I will not undertake to say what a constitution for these United States ought to be. That question the people have decided for themselves; and I shall take the instrument as they have established it, and shall endeavor to maintain it, in its plain sense and meaning, against opinions and notions which, in my judgment, threaten its subversion.

The resolutions introduced by the gentleman were apparently drawn up with care, and brought forward upon deliberation. I shall not be in danger, therefore, of misunderstanding him, or those who agree with him, if I proceed at once to these resolutions, and consider them as an authentic statement of those opinions upon the great constitutional question, by which the recent proceedings in South Carolina are attempted to be justified.

These resolutions are three in number.[2]

The third seems intended to enumerate, and to deny, the several opinions expressed in the President's proclamation, respecting the nature and powers of this government. Of this third resolution, I propose, at present, to take no particular notice.

The first two resolutions of the honorable member affirm these propositions, viz. : —

1. That the political system under which we live, and under which Congress is now assembled, is a *compact*, to which the people of the several States, as separate and sovereign communities, are *the parties*.

2. That these sovereign parties have a right to judge, each for itself, of any alleged violation of the Constitution by Congress; and, in case of such violation, to choose, each for itself, its own mode and measure of redress.

It is true, Sir, that the honorable member calls this a "constitutional" compact; but still he affirms it to be a compact between sovereign States. What precise meaning, then, does he attach to the term *constitutional*? When applied to compacts between sovereign States, the term *constitutional* affixes to the word *compact* no definite idea. Were we to hear of a constitutional league or treaty between England and France, or a constitutional convention between Austria and Russia, we should not understand what could be intended by such a league, such a treaty, or such a convention. In these connections, the word is void of all meaning; and yet, Sir, it is easy, quite easy, to see why the honorable gentleman has

2. Calhoun's resolutions, and his speech on the Force Bill to which Webster is replying, are reprinted in Clyde N. Wilson, ed., *The Papers of John C. Calhoun*, 12:18–26, 45–94.

used it in these resolutions. He cannot open the book, and look upon our written frame of government, without seeing that it is called a *constitution*. This may well be appalling to him. It threatens his whole doctrine of compact, and its darling derivatives, nullification and secession, with instant confutation. Because, if he admits our instrument of government to be a *constitution*, then, for that very reason, it is not a compact between sovereigns; a constitution of government and a compact between sovereign powers being things essentially unlike in their very natures, and incapable of ever being the same. Yet the word *constitution* is on the very front of the instrument. He cannot overlook it. He seeks, therefore, to compromise the matter, and to sink all the substantial sense of the word, while he retains a resemblance of its sound. He introduces a new word of his own, viz. *compact*, as importing the principal idea, and designed to play the principal part, and degrades *constitution* into an insignificant, idle epithet, attached to *compact*. The whole then stands as a *"constitutional compact"*! And in this way he hopes to pass off a plausible gloss, as satisfying the words of the instrument. But he will find himself disappointed. Sir, I must say to the honorable gentleman, that, in our American political grammar, CONSTITUTION is a noun substantive; it imports a distinct and clear idea of itself; and it is not to lose its importance and dignity, it is not to be turned into a poor, ambiguous, senseless, unmeaning adjective, for the purpose of accommodating any new set of political notions. Sir, we reject his new rules of syntax altogether. We will not give up our forms of political speech to the grammarians of the school of nullification. By the Constitution, we mean, not a "constitutional compact," but, simply and directly, the Constitution, the fundamental law; and if there be one word in the language which the people of the United States understand, this is that word. We know no more of a constitutional compact between sovereign powers, than we know of a *constitutional* indenture of copartnership, a *constitutional* deed of conveyance, or a *constitutional* bill of exchange. But we know what the *Constitution* is; we know what the plainly written, fundamental law is; we know what the bond of our Union and the security of our liberties is; and we mean to maintain and to defend it, in its plain sense and unsophisticated meaning.

The sense of the gentleman's proposition, therefore, is not at all affected, one way or the other, by the use of this word. That proposition still is, that our system of government is but a *compact* between the people of separate and sovereign States.

Was it Mirabeau, Mr. President, or some other master of the human passions, who has told us that words are things? They are indeed things, and things of mighty influence, not only in addresses to the passions and high-wrought feelings of mankind, but in the discussion of legal

and political questions also; because a just conclusion is often avoided, or a false one reached, by the adroit substitution of one phrase, or one word, for another. Of this we have, I think, another example in the resolutions before us.

The first resolution declares that the people of the several States "*acceded*" to the Constitution, or to the constitutional compact, as it is called. This word "accede," not found either in the Constitution itself, or in the ratification of it by any one of the States, has been chosen for use here, doubtless, not without a well-considered purpose.

The natural converse of *accession* is *secession*; and, therefore, when it is stated that the people of the States acceded to the Union, it may be more plausibly argued that they may secede from it. If, in adopting the Constitution, nothing was done but acceding to a compact, nothing would seem necessary, in order to break it up, but to secede from the same compact. But the term is wholly out of place. *Accession*, as a word applied to political associations, implies coming into a league, treaty, or confederacy, by one hitherto a stranger to it; and *secession* implies departing from such league or confederacy. The people of the United States have used no such form of expression in establishing the present government. They do not say that they *accede* to a league, but they declare that they *ordain* and *establish* a Constitution. Such are the very words of the instrument itself; and in all the States, without an exception, the language used by their conventions was, that they "*ratified the Constitution*"; some of them employing the additional words "assented to" and "adopted," but all of them "ratifying."

There is more importance than may, at first sight, appear, in the introduction of this new word by the honorable mover of these resolutions. Its adoption and use are indispensable to maintain those premises, from which his main conclusion is to be afterwards drawn. But before showing that, allow me to remark, that this phraseology tends to keep out of sight the just view of a previous political history, as well as to suggest wrong ideas as to what was actually done when the present Constitution was agreed to. In 1789, and before this Constitution was adopted, the United States had already been in a union, more or less close, for fifteen years. At least as far back as the meeting of the first Congress, in 1774, they had been in some measure, and for some national purposes, united together. Before the Confederation of 1781, they had declared independence jointly, and had carried on the war jointly, both by sea and land; and this not as separate States, but as one people. When, therefore, they formed that Confederation, and adopted its articles as articles of perpetual union, they did not come together for the first time; and therefore they do not speak of the States as *acceding* to the Confederation, although it was a league, and nothing but a league, and rested on nothing but

plighted faith for its performance. Yet, even then, the States were not strangers to each other; there was a bond of union already subsisting between them; they were associated, united States; and the object of the Confederation was to make a stronger and better bond of union, Their representatives deliberated together on these proposed Articles of Confederation, and, being authorized by their respective States, finally *"ratified and confirmed"* them. Inasmuch as they were already in union, they did not speak of *acceding* to the new Articles of Confederation, but of *ratifying and confirming* them; and this language was not used inadvertently, because, in the same instrument, *accession* is used in its proper sense, when applied to Canada, which was altogether a stranger to the existing union. "Canada," says the eleventh article, "*acceding* to this Confederation, and joining in the measures of the United States, shall be admitted into the Union."

Having thus used the terms *ratify* and *confirm*, even in regard to the old Constitution, it would have been strange indeed, if the people of the United States, after its formation, and when they came to establish the present Constitution, had spoken of the States, or the people of the States, as *acceding* to this Constitution. Such language would have been ill-suited to the occasion. It would have implied an existing separation or disunion among the States, such as never existed since 1774. No such language, therefore, was used. The language actually employed is, *adopt, ratify, ordain, establish.*

Therefore, Sir, since any State, before she can prove her right to dissolve the Union, must show her authority to undo what has been done, no State is at liberty to *secede,* on the ground that she and other States have done nothing but *accede.* She must show that she has a right to *reverse* what has been *ordained*, to *unsettle* and *overthrow* what has been *established*, to *reject* what the people have *adopted*, and to *break up* what they have *ratified*; because these are the terms which express the transactions which have actually taken place. In other words, she must show her right to make a revolution.

If, Mr. President, in drawing these resolutions, the honorable member had confined himself to the use of constitutional language, there would have been a wide and awful *hiatus* between his premises and his conclusion. Leaving out the two words *compact* and *accession*, which are not constitutional modes of expression, and stating the matter precisely as the truth is, his first resolution would have affirmed that *the people of the several States ratified this Constitution, or form of government.* These are the very words of South Carolina herself, in her act of ratification. Let, then, his first resolution tell the exact truth; let it state the fact precisely as it exists; let it say that the people of the several States ratified a constitution, or form of government; and then, Sir, what will become

of his inference in his second resolution, which is in these words, viz. "that, as in all other cases of compact among sovereign parties, each has an equal right to judge for itself, as well of the infraction as of the mode and measures of redress"? It is obvious, is it not, Sir? that this conclusion requires for its support quite other premises; it requires premises which speak of *accession* and of *compact* between sovereign powers; and, without such premises, it is altogether unmeaning.

Mr. President, if the honorable member will truly state what the people did in forming this Constitution, and then state what they must do if they would now undo what they then did, he will unavoidably state a case of revolution. Let us see if it be not so. He must state, in the first place, that the people of the several States adopted and ratified this Constitution, or form of government; and, in the next place, he must state that they have a right to undo this; that is to say, that they have a right to discard the form of government which they have adopted, and to break up the Constitution which they have ratified. Now, Sir, this is neither more or less than saying that they have a right to make a revolution. To reject an established government, to break up a political constitution, is revolution.

I deny that any man can state accurately what was done by the people, in establishing the present Constitution, and then state accurately what the people, or any part of them, must now do to get rid of its obligations, without stating an undeniable case of the overthrow of government. I admit, of course, that the people may, if they choose, overthrow the government. But, then, that is revolution. The doctrine now contended for is, that, by *nullification* or *secession*, the obligations and authority of the government may be set aside or rejected, without revolution. But that is what I deny; and what I say is, that no man can state the case with historical accuracy, and in constitutional language, without showing that the honorable gentleman's right, as asserted in his conclusion, is a revolutionary right merely; that it does not and cannot exist under the Constitution, or agreeably to the Constitution, but can come into existence only when the Constitution is overthrown. This is the reason, Sir, which makes it necessary to abandon the use of constitutional language for a new vocabulary, and to substitute, in the place of plain historical facts, a series of assumptions. This is the reason why it is necessary to give new names to things, to speak of the Constitution, not as a constitution, but as a compact, and of the ratifications by the people, not as ratifications, but as acts of accession.

Sir, I intend to hold the gentleman to the written record. In the discussion of a constitutional question, I intend to impose upon him the restraints of constitutional language. The people have ordained a Constitution; can they reject it without revolution? They have established a form

of government; can they overthrow it without revolution? These are the true questions.

Allow me now, Mr. President, to inquire further into the extent of the propositions contained in the resolutions, and their necessary consequences.

Where sovereign communities are parties, there is no essential difference between a compact, a confederation, and a league. They all equally rest on the plighted faith of the sovereign party. A league, or confederacy, is but a subsisting or continuing treaty.

The gentleman's resolutions, then, affirm, in effect, that these twenty-four United States are held together only by a subsisting treaty, resting for its fulfilment and continuance on no inherent power of its own, but on the plighted faith of each State; or, in other words, that our Union is but a league; and, as a consequence from this proposition, they further affirm that, as sovereigns are subject to no superior power, the States must judge, each for itself, of any alleged violation of the league; and if such violation be supposed to have occurred, each may adopt any mode or measure of redress which it shall think proper.

Other consequences naturally follow, too, from the main proposition. If a league between sovereign powers have no limitation as to the time of its duration, and contain nothing making it perpetual, it subsists only during the good pleasure of the parties, although no violation be complained of. If, in the opinion of either party, it be violated, such party may say that he will no longer fulfil its obligations on his part, but will consider the whole league or compact at an end, although it might be one of its stipulations that it should be perpetual. Upon this principle, the Congress of the United States, in 1798, declared null and void the treaty of alliance between the United States and France, though it professed to be a perpetual alliance.

If the violation of the league be accompanied with serious injuries, the suffering party, being sole judge of his own mode and measure of redress, has a right to indemnify himself by reprisals on the offending members of the league; and reprisals, if the circumstances of the case require it, may be followed by direct, avowed, and public war.

The necessary import of the resolution, therefore, is, that the United States are connected only by a league; that it is in the good pleasure of every State to decide how long she will choose to remain a member of this league; that any State may determine the extent of her own obligations under it, and accept or reject what shall be decided by the whole; that she may also determine whether her rights have been violated, what is the extent of the injury done her, and what mode and measure of redress her wrongs may make it fit and expedient for her to adopt. The result of the whole is, that any State may secede at pleasure; that any State

his opinions sweeps him along, he knows not whither. To begin with nullification, with the avowed intent, nevertheless, not to proceed to secession, dismemberment, and general revolution, is as if one were to take the plunge of Niagara, and cry out that he would stop half way down. In the one case, as in the other, the rash adventurer must go to the bottom of the dark abyss below, were it not that that abyss has no discovered bottom.

Nullification, if successful, arrests the power of the law, absolves citizens from their duty, subverts the foundation both of protection and obedience, dispenses with oaths and obligations of allegiance, and elevates another authority to supreme command. Is not this revolution? And it raises to supreme command four-and-twenty distinct powers, each professing to be under a general government, and yet each setting its laws at defiance at pleasure. Is not this anarchy, as well as revolution? Sir, the Constitution of the United States was received as a whole, and for the whole country. If it cannot stand altogether, it cannot stand in parts; and if the laws cannot be executed everywhere, they cannot long be executed anywhere. The gentleman very well knows that all duties and imposts must be uniform throughout the country. He knows that we cannot have one rule or one law for South Carolina, and another for other States. He must see, therefore, and does see, and every man sees, that the only alternative is a repeal of the laws throughout the whole Union, or their execution in Carolina as well as elsewhere. And this repeal is demanded because a single State interposes her veto, and threatens resistance! The result of the gentleman's opinion, or rather the very text of his doctrine, is, that no act of Congress can bind all the States, the constitutionality of which is not admitted by all; or, in other words, that no single State is bound, against its own dissent, by a law of imposts. This is precisely the evil experienced under the old Confederation, and for remedy of which this Constitution was adopted. The leading object in establishing this government, an object forced on the country by the condition of the times and the absolute necessity of the law, was to give to Congress power to lay and collect imposts *without the consent of particular States*. The Revolutionary debt remained unpaid; the national treasury was bankrupt; the country was destitute of credit; Congress issued its requisitions on the States, and the States neglected them; there was no power of coercion but war, Congress could not lay imposts, or other taxes, by its own authority; the whole general government, therefore, was little more than a name. The Articles of Confederation, as to purposes of revenue and finance, were nearly a dead letter. The country sought to escape from this condition, at once feeble and disgraceful, by constituting a government which should have power, of itself, to lay duties and taxes, and to pay the public debt, and provide for the general

welfare; and to lay these duties and taxes in all the States, without asking the consent of the State governments. This was the very power on which the new Constitution was to depend for all its ability to do good; and without it, it can be no government, now or at any time. Yet, Sir, it is precisely against this power, so absolutely indispensable to the very being of the government, that South Carolina directs her ordinance. She attacks the government in its authority to raise revenue, the very mainspring of the whole system; and if she succeed, every movement of that system must inevitably cease. It is of no avail that she declares that she does not resist the law as a revenue law, but as a law for protecting manufactures. It is a revenue law; it is the very law by force of which the revenue is collected; if it be arrested in any State, the revenue ceases in that State; it is, in a word, the sole reliance of the government for the means of maintaining itself and performing its duties.

Mr. President, the alleged right of a State to decide constitutional questions for herself necessarily leads to force, because other States must have the same right, and because different States will decide differently; and when these questions arise between States, if there be no superior power, they can be decided only by the law of force. On entering into the Union, the people of each State gave up a part of their own power to make laws for themselves, in consideration that, as to common objects, they should have a part in making laws for other States. In other words, the people of all the States agreed to create a common government, to be conducted by common counsels. Pennsylvania, for example, yielded the right of laying imposts in her own ports, in consideration that the new government, in which she was to have a share, should possess the power of laying imposts on all the States. If South Carolina now refuses to submit to this power, she breaks the condition on which other States entered into the Union. She partakes of the common counsels, and therein assists to bind others, while she refuses to be bound herself. It makes no difference in the case, whether she does all this without reason or pretext, or whether she sets up as a reason, that, in her judgment, the acts complained of are unconstitutional. In the judgment of other States, they are not so. It is nothing to them that she offers some reason or some apology for her conduct, if it be one which they do not admit. It is not to be expected that any State will violate her duty without some plausible pretext. That would be too rash a defiance of the opinion of mankind. But if it be a pretext which lies in her own breast; if it be no more than an opinion which she says she has formed, how can other States be satisfied with this? How can they allow her to be judge of her own obligations? Or, if she may judge of her obligations, may they not judge of their rights also? May not the twenty-three entertain an opinion as well as the twenty-fourth? And if it be their right, in their own opinion, as

expressed in the common council, to enforce the law against her, how is she to say that her right and her opinion are to be every thing, and their right and their opinion nothing?

Mr. President, if we are to receive the Constitution as the text, and then to lay down in its margin the contradictory commentaries which have been, and which may be, made by different States, the whole page would be a polyglot indeed. It would speak with as many tongues as the builders of Babel, and in dialects as much confused, and mutually as unintelligible. The very instance now before us presents a practical illustration. The law of the last session is declared unconstitutional in South Carolina, and obedience to it is refused. In other States, it is admitted to be strictly constitutional. You walk over the limit of its authority, therefore, when you pass a State line. On one side it is law, on the other side a nullity; and yet it is passed by a common government, having the same authority in all the States.

Such, Sir, are the inevitable results of this doctrine. Beginning with the original error, that the Constitution of the United States is nothing but a compact between sovereign States; asserting, in the next step, that each State has a right to be its own sole judge of the extent of its own obligations, and consequently of the constitutionality of laws of Congress; and, in the next, that it may oppose whatever it sees fit to declare unconstitutional, and that it decides for itself on the mode and measure of redress,—the argument arrives at once at the conclusion, that what a State dissents from, it may nullify; what it opposes, it may oppose by force; what it decides for itself, it may execute by its own power; and that, in short, it is itself supreme over the legislation of Congress, and supreme over the decisions of the national judicature; supreme over the constitution of the country, supreme over the supreme law of the land. However it seeks to protect itself against these plain inferences, by saying that an unconstitutional law is no law, and that it only opposes such laws as are unconstitutional, yet this does not in the slightest degree vary the result; since it insists on deciding this question for itself; and, in opposition to reason and argument, in opposition to practice and experience, in opposition to the judgment of others, having an equal right to judge, it says, only, "Such is my opinion, and my opinion shall be my law, and I will support it by my own strong hand. I denounce the law; I declare it unconstitutional; that is enough; it shall not be executed. Men in arms are ready to resist its execution. An attempt to enforce it shall cover the land with blood. Elsewhere it may be binding; but here it is trampled under foot."

This, Sir, is practical nullification.

And now, Sir, against all these theories and opinions, I maintain,—

1. That the Constitution of the United States is not a league, confed-

eracy, or compact between the people of the several States in their sovereign capacities; but a government proper, founded on the adoption of the people, and creating direct relations between itself and individuals.

2. That no State authority has power to dissolve these relations; that nothing can dissolve them but revolution; and that, consequently, there can be no such thing as secession without revolution.

3. That there is a supreme law, consisting of the Constitution of the United States, and acts of Congress passed in pursuance of it, and treaties; and that, in cases not capable of assuming the character of a suit in law or equity, Congress must judge of, and finally interpret, this supreme law so often as it has occasion to pass acts of legislation; and in cases capable of assuming, and actually assuming, the character of a suit, the Supreme Court of the United States is the final interpreter.

4. That an attempt by a State to abrogate, annul, or nullify an act of Congress, or to arrest its operation within her limits, on the ground that, in her opinion, such law is unconstitutional, is a direct usurpation on the just powers of the general government, and on the equal rights of other States; a plain violation of the Constitution, and a proceeding essentially revolutionary in its character and tendency.

Whether the Constitution be a compact between States in their sovereign capacities, is a question which must be mainly argued from what is contained in the instrument itself. We all agree that it is an instrument which has been in some way clothed with power. We all admit that it speaks with authority. The first question then is, What does it say of itself? What does it purport to be? Does it style itself a league, confederacy, or compact between sovereign States? It is to be remembered, Sir, that the Constitution began to speak only after its adoption. Until it was ratified by nine States, it was but a proposal, the mere draught of an instrument. It was like a deed drawn, but not executed. The Convention had framed it; sent it to Congress, then sitting under the Confederation; Congress had transmitted it to the State legislatures; and by these last it was laid before conventions of the people in the several States. All this while it was inoperative paper. It had received no stamp of authority, no sanction; it spoke no language. But when ratified by the people in their respective conventions, then it had a voice and spoke authentically. Every word in it had then received the sanction of the popular will, and was to be received as the expression of that will. What the Constitution says of itself, therefore, is as conclusive as what it says on any other point. Does it call itself a "compact"? Certainly not. It uses the word *compact* but once, and that is when it declares that the States shall enter into no compact. Does it call itself a "league," a "confederacy," a "subsisting treaty between the States"? Certainly not. There is not a particle of such language in all its pages. But it declares itself a CONSTITU-

TION. What is a *constitution*? Certainly not a league, compact, or confederacy, but a *fundamental law*. That fundamental regulation which determines the manner in which the public authority is to be executed, is what forms the *constitution* of a state. Those primary rules which concern the body itself, and the very being of the political society, the form of government, and the manner in which power is to be exercised,—all, in a word, which form together the *constitution of a state*,—these are the fundamental laws. This, Sir, is the language of the public writers. But do we need to be informed, in this country, what a *constitution* is? Is it not an idea perfectly familiar, definite, and well settled? We are at no loss to understand what is meant by the constitution of one of the States; and the Constitution of the United States speaks of itself as being an instrument of the same nature. It says, this *Constitution* shall be the law of the land, any thing in any State *constitution* to the contrary notwithstanding. And it speaks of itself, too, in plain contradistinction from a confederation; for it says that all debts contracted, and all engagements entered into, by the United States, shall be as valid under this *Constitution* as under the *Confederation*. It does not say, as valid under this *compact*, or this league, or this confederation, as under the former confederation, but as valid under this *Constitution*.

This, then, Sir, is declared to be a *constitution*. A constitution is the fundamental law of the state; and this is expressly declared to be the supreme law. It is as if the people had said "We prescribe this fundamental law," or "this supreme law," for they do say that they establish this Constitution, and that it shall be the supreme law. They say that they *ordain* and *establish* it. Now, Sir, what is the common application of these words? We do not speak of *ordaining* leagues and compacts. If this was intended to be a compact or league, and the States to be parties to it, why was it not so said? Why is there found no one expression in the whole instrument indicating such intent? The old Confederation was expressly called a *league*, and into this league it was declared that the States, as States, severally entered. Why was not similar language used in the Constitution, if a similar intention had existed? Why was it not said, "the States enter into this new league," "the States form this new confederation," or "the States agree to this new compact"? Or why was it not said, in the language of the gentleman's resolution, that the people of the several States acceded to this compact in their sovereign capacities? What reason is there for supposing that the framers of the Constitution rejected expressions appropriate to their own meaning, and adopted others wholly at war with that meaning?

Again, Sir, the Constitution speaks of that political system which is established as "the government of the United States." Is it not doing strange violence to language to call a league or a compact between sov-

ereign powers a *government*? The government of a state is that organization in which the political power resides. It is the political being created by the constitution or fundamental law. The broad and clear difference between a government and a league or compact is, that a government is a body politic; it has a will of its own; and it possesses powers and faculties to execute its own purposes. Every compact looks to some power to enforce its stipulations. Even in a compact between sovereign communities, there always exists this ultimate reference to a power to insure its execution; although, in such case, this power is but the force of one party against the force of another; that is to say, the power of war. But a *government* executes its decisions by its own supreme authority. Its use of force in compelling obedience to its own enactments is not war. It contemplates no opposing party having a right of resistance. It rests on its own power to enforce its own will; and when it ceases to possess this power, it is no longer a government.

Mr. President, I concur so generally in the very able speech of the gentleman from Virginia near me [William Cabell Rives], that it is not without diffidence and regret that I venture to differ with him on any point. His opinions, Sir, are redolent of the doctrines of a very distinguished school, for which I have the highest regard, of whose doctrines I can say, what I can also say of the gentleman's speech, that, while I concur in the results, I must be permitted to hesitate about some of the premises. I do not agree that the Constitution is a compact between States in their sovereign capacities. I do not agree, that, in strictness of language, it is a compact at all. But I do agree that it is founded on consent or agreement, or on compact, if the gentleman prefers that word, and means no more by it than voluntary consent or agreement. The Constitution, Sir, is not a contract, but the result of a contract; meaning by contract no more than assent. Founded on consent, it is a government proper. Adopted by the agreement of the people of the United States, when adopted, it has become a Constitution. The people have agreed to make a Constitution; but when made, that Constitution becomes what its name imports. It is no longer a mere agreement. Our laws, Sir, have their foundation in the agreement or consent of the two houses of Congress. We say, habitually, that one house proposes a bill, and the other agrees to it; but the result of this agreement is not a compact, but a law. The law, the statute, is not the agreement, but something created by the agreement; and something which, when created, has a new character, and acts by its own authority. So the Constitution of the United States, founded in or on the consent of the people, may be said to rest on compact or consent; but it is not itself the compact, but its result. When the people agree to erect a government, and actually erect it, the thing is done, and the agreement is at an end. The compact is executed, and the

end designed by it attained. Henceforth, the fruit of the agreement exists, but the agreement itself is merged in its own accomplishment; since there can be no longer a subsisting agreement or compact *to form* a constitution or government, after that constitution or government has been actually formed and established.

It appears to me, Mr. President, that the plainest account of the establishment of this government presents the most just and philosophical view of its foundation. The people of the several States had their separate State governments; and between the States there also existed a Confederation. With this condition of things the people were not satisfied, as the Confederation had been found not to fulfill its intended objects. It was *proposed*, therefore, to erect a new, common government, which should possess certain definite powers, such as regarded the prosperity of the people of all the States, and to be formed upon the general model of American constitutions. This proposal was assented to, and an instrument was presented to the people of the several States for their consideration. They approved it, and agreed to adopt it, as a Constitution. They executed that agreement; they adopted the Constitution as a Constitution, and henceforth it must stand as a Constitution until it shall be altogether destroyed. Now, Sir, is not this the truth of the whole matter? And is not all that we have heard of compact between sovereign States the mere effect of a theoretical and artificial mode of reasoning upon the subject? a mode of reasoning which disregards plain facts for the sake of hypothesis?

Mr. President, the nature of sovereignty or sovereign power has been extensively discussed by gentlemen on this occasion, as it generally is when the origin of our government is debated. But I confess myself not entirely satisfied with arguments and illustrations drawn from that topic. The sovereignty of government is an idea belonging to the other side of the Atlantic. No such thing is known in North America. Our governments are all limited. In Europe, sovereignty is of feudal origin, and imports no more than the state of the sovereign. It comprises his rights, duties, exemptions, prerogatives, and powers. But with us, all power is with the people. They alone are sovereign; and they erect what governments they please, and confer on them such powers as they please. None of these governments is sovereign, in the European sense of the word, all being restrained by written constitutions. It seems to me, therefore, that we only perplex ourselves when we attempt to explain the relations existing between the general government and the several State governments, according to those ideas of sovereignty which prevail under systems essentially different from our own.

But, Sir, to return to the Constitution itself; let me inquire what it relies upon for its own continuance and support. I hear it often sug-

gested, that the States, by refusing to appoint Senators and Electors, might bring this government to an end. Perhaps that is true; but the same may be said of the State governments themselves. Suppose the legislature of a State, having the power to appoint the governor and the judges, should omit that duty, would not the State government remain unorganized? No doubt, all elective governments may be broken up by a general abandonment, on the part of those intrusted with political powers, of their appropriate duties. But one popular government has, in this respect, as much security as another. The maintenance of this Constitution does not depend on the plighted faith of the States, as States, to support it; and this again shows that it is not a league. It relies on individual duty and obligation.

The Constitution of the United States creates direct relations between this government and individuals. This government may punish individuals for treason, and all other crimes in the code, when committed against the United States. It has power, also, to tax individuals, in any mode, and to any extent; and it possesses the further power of demanding from individuals military service. Nothing, certainly, can more clearly distinguish a government from a confederation of states than the possession of these powers. No closer relations can exist between individuals and any government.

On the other hand, the government owes high and solemn duties to every citizen of the country. It is bound to protect him in his most important rights and interests. It makes war for his protection, and no other government in the country can make war. It makes peace for his protection, and no other government can make peace. It maintains armies and navies for his defence and security, and no other government is allowed to maintain them. He goes abroad beneath its flag, and carries over all the earth a national character imparted to him by this government, and which no other government can impart. In whatever relates to war, to peace, to commerce, he knows no other government. All these, Sir, are connections as dear and as sacred as can bind individuals to any government on earth. It is not, therefore, a compact between States, but a government proper, operating directly upon individuals, yielding to them protection on the one hand, and demanding from them obedience on the other.

There is no language in the whole Constitution applicable to a confederation of States. If the States be parties, as States, what are their rights, and what their respective covenants and stipulations? And where are their rights, covenants, and stipulations expressed? The States engage for nothing, they promise nothing. In the Articles of Confederation, they did make promises, and did enter into engagements, and did plight the faith of each State for their fulfilment; but in the Constitution there

is nothing of that kind. The reason is, that, in the Constitution, it is the *people* who speak, and not the States. The people ordain the Constitution, and therein address themselves to the States, and to the legislatures of the States, in the language of injunction and prohibition. The Constitution utters its behests in the name and by authority of the people, and it does not exact from States any plighted public faith to maintain it. On the contrary, it makes its own preservation depend on individual duty and individual obligation. Sir, the States cannot omit to appoint Senators and Electors. It is not a matter resting in State discretion or State pleasure. The Constitution has taken better care of its own preservation. It lays its hand on individual conscience and individual duty. It incapacitates any man to sit in the legislature of a State, who shall not first have taken his solemn oath to support the Constitution of the United States. From the obligation of this oath, no State power can discharge him. All the members of all the State legislatures are as religiously bound to support the Constitution of the United States as they are to support their own State constitution. Nay, Sir, they are as solemnly sworn to support it as we ourselves are, who are members of Congress.

No member of a State legislature can refuse to proceed, at the proper time, to elect Senators to Congress, or to provide for the choice of Electors of President and Vice-President, any more than the members of this Senate can refuse, when the appointed day arrives, to meet the members of the other house, to count the votes for those officers, and ascertain who are chosen. In both cases, the duty binds, and with equal strength, the conscience of the individual member, and it is imposed on all by an oath in the same words. Let it then, never be said, Sir, that it is a matter of discretion with the States whether they will continue the government, or break it up by refusing to appoint Senators and to elect Electors. They have no discretion in the matter. The members of their legislatures cannot avoid doing either, so often as the time arrives, without a direct violation of their duty and their oaths; such a violation as would break up any other government.

Looking still further to the provisions of the Constitution itself, in order to learn its true character, we find its great apparent purpose to be, to unite the people of all the States under one general government, for certain definite objects, and, to the extent of this union, to restrain the separate authority of the States. Congress only can declare war; therefore, when one State is at war with a foreign nation, all must be at war. The President and the Senate only can make peace; when peace is made for one State, therefore, it must be made for all.

Can any thing be conceived more preposterous, than that any State should have power to nullify the proceedings of the general government respecting peace and war? When war is declared by a law of Congress,

can a single State nullify that law, and remain at peace? And yet she may nullify that law as well as any other. If the President and Senate make peace, may one State, nevertheless, continue the war? And yet, if she can nullify a law, she may quite as well nullify a treaty.

The truth is, Mr. President, and no ingenuity of argument, no subtilty of distinction can evade it, that, as to certain purposes, the people of the United States are one people. They are one in making war, and one in making peace; they are one in regulating commerce, and one in laying duties of imposts. The very end and purpose of the Constitution was, to make them one people in these particulars; and it has effectually accomplished its object. All this is apparent on the face of the Constitution itself. I have already said, Sir, that to obtain a power of direct legislation over the people, especially in regard to imposts, was always prominent as a reason for getting rid of the Confederation, and forming a new Constitution. Among innumerable proofs of this, before the assembling of the Convention, allow me to refer only to the report of the committee of the old Congress, July, 1785.

But, Sir, let us go to the actual formation of the Constitution; let us open the journal of the Convention itself, and we shall see that the very first resolution which the Convention adopted, was, "THAT A NATIONAL GOVERNMENT OUGHT TO BE ESTABLISHED, CONSISTING OF A SUPREME LEGISLATIVE, JUDICIARY, AND EXECUTIVE."

This itself completely negatives all idea of league, and compact, and confederation. Terms could not be chosen more fit to express an intention to establish a national government, and to banish for ever all notion of a compact between sovereign States.

This resolution was adopted on the 30th of May, 1787. Afterwards, the style was altered, and, instead of being called a national government, it was called the government of the United States; but the substance of this resolution was retained, and was at the head of that list of resolutions which was afterwards sent to the committee who were to frame the instrument.

It is true, there were gentlemen in the Convention, who were for retaining the Confederation, and amending its Articles; but the majority was against this, and was for a national government. Mr. [William] Patterson's propositions, which were for continuing the Articles of Confederation with additional powers, were submitted to the Convention on the 15th of June, and referred to the committee of the whole. The resolutions forming the basis of a national government, which had once been agreed to in the committee of the whole, and reported, were recommitted to the same committee, on the same day. The Convention, then, in committee of the whole, on the 19th of June, had both these plans before them; that is to say, the plan of a confederacy, or compact, between States, and

the plan of a national government. Both these plans were considered and debated, and the committee reported, "That they do not agree to the propositions offered by the honorable Mr. Patterson, but that they again submit the resolutions formerly reported." If, Sir, any historical fact in the world be plain and undeniable, it is that the Convention deliberated on the expediency of continuing the Confederation, with some amendments, and rejected that scheme, and adopted the plan of a national government, with a legislature, an executive, and a judiciary of its own. They were asked to preserve the league; they rejected the proposition. They were asked to continue the existing compact between States; they rejected it. They rejected compact, league, and confederation, and set themselves about framing the constitution of a national government; and they accomplished what they undertook.

If men will open their eyes fairly to the lights of history, it is impossible to be deceived on this point. The great object was to supersede the Confederation, by a regular government; because, under the Confederation, Congress had power only to make requisitions on States; and if States declined compliance, as they did, there was no remedy but war against such delinquent States. It would seem, from Mr. Jefferson's correspondence, in 1786 and 1787, that he was of opinion that even this remedy ought to be tried. "There will be no money in the treasury," said he, "till the confederacy shows its teeth"; and he suggests that a single frigate would soon levy, on the commerce of a delinquent State, the deficiency of its contribution.[3] But this would be war; and it was evident that a confederacy could not long hold together, which should be at war with its members. The Constitution was adopted to avoid this necessity. It was adopted that there might be a government which should act directly on individuals, without borrowing aid from the State governments. This is clear as light itself on the very face of the provisions of the Constitution, and its whole history tends to the same conclusion. Its framers gave this very reason for their work in the most distinct terms. Allow me to quote but one or two proofs, out of hundreds. That State, so small in territory, but so distinguished for learning and talent, Connecticut, had sent to the general Convention, among other members, [William] Samuel Johnson and Oliver Ellsworth. The Constitution having been framed, it was submitted to a convention of the people of Connecticut for ratification on the part of that State; and Mr. Johnson and Mr. Ellsworth were also members of this convention. On the first day of the debates, being called on to explain the reasons which led the Convention at Philadelphia to recommend such a Constitution, after showing the insufficiency of the

3. Jefferson to James Monroe, Aug. 11, 1786; and to Edward Carrington, Aug. 4, 1787. Julian P. Boyd, ed., *The Papers of Thomas Jefferson* (21 vols. to date, Princeton, 1950–), 10: 223–225; 11: 678–680.

existing confederacy, inasmuch as it applied to States, as States, Mr. Johnson proceeded to say,—

> The Convention saw this imperfection in attempting to legislate for States in their political capacity, that the coercion of law can be exercised by nothing but a military force. They have, therefore, gone upon entirely new ground. They have formed one new nation out of the individual States. The Constitution vests in the general legislature a power to make laws in matters of national concern; to appoint judges to decide upon these laws; and to appoint officers to carry them into execution. This excludes the idea of an armed force. The power which is to enforce these laws is to be a legal power, vested in proper magistrates. The force which is to be employed is the energy of law; and this force is to operate only upon individuals who fail in their duty to their country. This is the peculiar glory of the Constitution, that it depends upon the mild and equal energy of the magistracy for the execution of the laws.[4]

In the further course of the debate, Mr. Ellsworth said,—

> In republics, it is a fundamental principle, that the majority govern, and that the minority comply with the general voice. How contrary, then, to republican principles, how humiliating, is our present situation! A single State can rise up, and put a *veto* upon the most important public measures. We have seen this actually take place; a single State has controlled the general voice of the Union; a minority, a very small minority, has governed us. So far is this from being consistent with republican principles, that it is, in effect, the worst species of monarchy.
>
> Hence we see how necessary for the Union is a coercive principle. No man pretends the contrary. We all see and feel this necessity. The only question is, Shall it be a coercion of law, or a coercion of arms? There is no other possible alternative. Where will those who oppose a coercion of law come out? Where will they end? A necessary consequence of their principles is a war of the States one against another. I am for coercion by law; that coercion which acts only upon delinquent individuals. This Constitution does not attempt to coerce sovereign bodies, States, in their political capacity. No coercion is applicable to such bodies, but that of an armed force. If we should attempt to execute the laws of the Union by sending an armed force against a delinquent State, it would involve the good and bad, the innocent and guilty, in the same calamity. But this legal coercion singles out the guilty individual, and punishes him for breaking the laws of the Union.[5]

4. Jan. 3, 1788. See *The Public Records of the State of Connecticut* (11 vols., Hartford, 1894–1967), 6: 557–558.

5. Elliot, *Debates*, 2: 196–197.

Indeed, Sir, if we look to all contemporary history, to the numbers of the Federalist, to the debates in the conventions, to the publications of friends and foes, they all agree, that a change had been made from a confederacy of States to a different system; they all agree, that the Convention had formed a Constitution for a national government. With this result some were satisfied, and some were dissatisfied; but all admitted that the thing had been done. In none of these various productions and and publications did any one intimate that the new Constitution was but another compact between States in their sovereign capacities. I do not find such an opinion advanced in a single instance. Everywhere, the people were told that the old Confederation was to be abandoned, and a new system to be tried; that a proper government was proposed, to be founded in the name of the people, and to have a regular organization of its own. Everywhere, the people were told that it was to be a government with direct powers to make laws over individuals, and to lay taxes and imposts without the consent of the States. Everywhere, it was understood to be a popular Constitution. It came to the people for the adoption, and was to rest on the same deep foundation as the State constitutions themselves. Its most distinguished advocates, who had been themselves members of the Convention, declared that the very object of submitting the Constitution to the people was, to preclude the possibility of its being regarded as a mere compact. "However gross a heresy," say the writers of the Federalist, "it may be to maintain that a party to a *compact* has a right to revoke that *compact*, the doctrine itself has had respectable advocates. The possibility of a question of this nature proves the necessity of laying the foundations of our national government deeper than in the mere sanction of delegated authority. The fabric of American empire ought to rest on the solid basis of THE CONSENT OF THE PEOPLE."[6]

Such is the language, Sir, addressed to the people, while they yet had the Constitution under consideration. The powers conferred on the new government were perfectly well understood to be conferred, not by any State, or the people of any State, but by the people of the United States. Virginia is more explicit, perhaps, in this particular, than any other State. Her convention, assembled to ratify the Constitution, "in the name and behalf of the people of Virginia, declare and make known, that the powers granted under the Constitution, *being derived from the people of the United States*, may be resumed by them whenever the same shall be perverted to their injury or oppression."[7]

Is this language which describes the formation of a compact between States? or language describing the grant of powers to a new government, by the whole people of the United States?

6. *The Federalist*, No. 22.   7. Elliot, *Debates*, 1: 327.

Among all the other ratifications, there is not one which speaks of the Constitution as a compact between States. Those of Massachusetts and New Hampshire express the transaction, in my opinion, with sufficient accuracy. They recognize the Divine goodness "in affording THE PEOPLE OF THE UNITED STATES an opportunity of entering into an explicit and solemn compact with each other, *by assenting to and ratifying a new Constitution.*"[8] You will observe, Sir, that it is the PEOPLE, and not the States, who have entered into this compact; and it is the PEOPLE of all the United States. These conventions, by this form of expression, meant merely to say, that the people of the United States had, by the blessing of Providence, enjoyed the opportunity of establishing a new Constitution, *founded in the consent of the people.* This consent of the people has been called, by European writers, the *social compact*; and, in conformity to this common mode of expression, these conventions speak of that assent, on which the new Constitution was to rest, as an explicit and solemn compact, not which the States had entered into with each other, but which the *people* of the United States had entered into.

Finally, Sir, how can any man get over the words of the Constitution itself?—"WE, THE PEOPLE OF THE UNITED STATES, DO ORDAIN AND ESTABLISH THIS CONSTITUTION." These words must cease to be a part of the Constitution, they must be obliterated from the parchment on which they are written, before any human ingenuity or human argument can remove the popular basis on which that Constitution rests, and turn the instrument into a mere compact between sovereign States.

The second proposition, Sir, which I propose to maintain, is that no State authority can dissolve the relations subsisting between the government of the United States and individuals; that nothing can dissolve these relations but revolution; and that, therefore, there can be no such thing as *secession* without revolution. All this follows, as it seems to me, as a just consequence, if it be first proved that the Constitution of the United States is a government proper, owing protection to individuals, and entitled to their obedience.

The people, Sir, in every State, live under two governments. They owe obedience to both. These governments, though distinct, are not adverse. Each has its separate sphere, and its peculiar powers and duties. It is not a contest between two sovereigns for the same power, like the wars of the rival houses in England; nor is it a dispute between a government *de facto* and a government *de jure*. It is the case of a division of powers between two governments, made by the people, to whom both are responsible. Neither can dispense with the duty which individuals owe to the other; neither can call itself master of the other: the people are masters

8. Ibid., 1: 322, 326.

of both. This division of power, it is true, is in a great measure unknown in Europe. It is the peculiar system of America; and, though new and singular, it is not incomprehensible. The State constitutions are established by the people of the States. This Constitution is established by the people of all the States. How, then, can a State secede? How can a State undo what the whole people have done? How can she absolve her citizens from their obedience to the laws of the United States? How can she annul their obligations and oaths? How can the members of her legislature renounce their own oaths? Sir, secession, as a revolutionary right, is intelligible; as a right to be proclaimed in the midst of civil commotions, and asserted at the head of armies, I can understand it. But as a practical right, existing under the Constitution, and in conformity with its provisions, it seems to me to be nothing but a plain absurdity; for it supposes resistance to government, under the authority of government itself; it supposes dismemberment, without violating the principles of union; it supposes opposition to law, without crime; it supposes the violation of oaths, without responsibility; it supposes the total overthrow of government, without revolution.

The Constitution, Sir, regards itself as perpetual and immortal. It seeks to establish a union among the people of the States, which shall last through all time. Or, if the common fate of things human must be expected at some period to happen to it, yet that catastrophe is not anticipated.

The instrument contains ample provisions for its amendment, at all times; none for its abandonment, at any time. It declares that new States may come into the Union, but it does not declare that old States may go out. The Union is not a temporary partnership of States. It is the association of the people, under a constitution of government, uniting their power, joining together their highest interests, cementing their present enjoyments, and blending, in one indivisible mass, all their hopes for the future. Whatsoever is steadfast in just political principles; whatsoever is permanent in the structure of human society; whatsoever there is which can derive an enduring character from being founded on deep-laid principles of constitutional liberty and on the broad foundations of the public will,—all these unite to entitle this instrument to be regarded as a permanent constitution of government.

In the next place, Mr. President, I contend that there is a supreme law of the land, consisting of the Constitution, acts of Congress passed in pursuance of it, and the public treaties. This will not be denied, because such are the very words of the Constitution. But I contend, further, that it rightfully belongs to Congress, and to the courts of the United States, to settle the construction of this supreme law, in doubtful cases. This is denied; and here arises the great practical question, *Who is to construe*

finally the Constitution of the United States? We all agree that the Constitution is the supreme law; but who shall interpret that law? In our system of the division of powers between different governments, controversies will necessarily sometimes arise, respecting the extent of the powers of each. Who shall decide these controversies? Does it rest with the general government, in all or any of its departments, to exercise the office of final interpreter? Or may each of the States, as well as the general government, claim this right of ultimate decision? The practical result of this whole debate turns on this point. The gentleman contends that each State may judge for itself of any alleged violation of the Constitution, and may finally decide for itself, and may execute its own decisions by its own power. All the recent proceedings in South Carolina are founded on this claim of right. Her convention has pronounced the revenue laws of the United States unconstitutional; and this decision she does not allow any authority of the United States to overrule or reverse. Of course she rejects the authority of Congress, because the very object of the ordinance is to reverse the decision of Congress; and she rejects, too, the authority of the courts of the United States, because she expressly prohibits all appeal to those courts. It is in order to sustain this asserted right of being her own judge, that she pronounces the Constitution of the United States to be but a compact, to which she is a party, and a sovereign party. If this be established, then the inference is supposed to follow, that, being sovereign, there is no power to control her decision; and her own judgment on her own compact is, and must be, conclusive.

I have already endeavored, Sir, to point out the practical consequences of this doctrine, and to show how utterly inconsistent it is with all ideas of regular government, and how soon its adoption would involve the whole country in revolution and absolute anarchy. I hope it is easy now to show, Sir, that a doctrine bringing such consequences with it is not well founded; that it has nothing to stand on but theory and assumption; and that it is refuted by plain and express constitutional provisions. I think the government of the United States does possess, in its appropriate departments, the authority of final decision on questions of disputed power. I think it possesses this authority, both by necessary implication and by express grant.

It will not be denied, Sir, that this authority naturally belongs to all governments. They all exercise it from necessity, and as a consequence of the exercise of other powers. The State governments themselves possess it, except in that class of questions which may arise between them and the general government, and in regard to which they have surrendered it, as well by the nature of the case as by clear constitutional provisions. In other and ordinary cases, whether a particular law be in conformity to the constitution of the State is a question which the State

legislature or the State judiciary must determine. We all know that these questions arise daily in the State governments, and are decided by those governments; and I know no government which does not exercise a similar power.

Upon general principles, then, the government of the United States possesses this authority; and this would hardly be denied were it not that there are other governments. But since there are State governments, and since these, like other governments, ordinarily construe their own powers, if the government of the United States construes its own powers also, which construction is to prevail in the case of opposite constructions? And again, as in the case now actually before us, the State governments may undertake, not only to construe their own powers, but to decide directly on the extent of the powers of Congress. Congress has passed a law as being within its just powers; South Carolina denies that this law is within its just powers, and insists that she has the right so to decide this point, and that her decision is final. How are these questions to be settled?

In my opinion, Sir, even if the Constitution of the United States had made no express provision for such cases, it would yet be difficult to maintain, that, in a Constitution existing over four-and-twenty States, with equal authority over all, *one* could claim a right of construing it for the whole. This would seem a manifest impropriety; indeed, an absurdity. If the Constitution is a government existing over all the States, though with limited powers, it necessarily follows that, to the extent of those powers, it must be supreme. If it be not superior to the authority of a particular State, it is not a national government. But as it is a government, as it has a legislative power of its own, and a judicial power coextensive with the legislative, the inference is irresistible that this government, thus created *by* the whole and *for* the whole, must have an authority superior to that of the particular government of any one part. Congress is the legislature of all the people of the United States; the judiciary of the general government is the judiciary of all the people of the United States. To hold, therefore, that this legislature and this judiciary are subordinate in authority to the legislature and judiciary of a single State, is doing violence to all common sense, and overturning all established principles. Congress must judge of the extent of its own powers so often as it is called on to exercise them, or it cannot act at all; and it must also act independent of State control, or it cannot act at all.

The right of State interposition strikes at the very foundation of the legislative power of Congress. It possesses no effective legislative power, if such right of State interposition exists; because it can pass no law not subject to abrogation. It cannot make laws for the Union, if any part of the Union may pronounce its enactments void and of no effect. Its forms

of legislation would be an idle ceremony, if, after all, any one of four-and-twenty States might bid defiance to its authority. Without express provision in the Constitution, therefore, Sir, this whole question is necessarily decided by those provisions which create a legislative power and a judicial power. If these exist in a government intended for the whole, the inevitable consequence is, that the laws of this legislative power and the decisions of this judicial power must be binding on and over the whole. No man can form the conception of a government existing over four-and-twenty States, with a regular legislative and judicial power, and of the existence at the same time of an authority, residing elsewhere, to resist, at pleasure or discretion, the enactments and the decisions of such a government. I maintain, therefore, Sir, that, from the nature of the case, and as an inference wholly unavoidable, the acts of Congress and the decisions of the national courts must be of higher authority than State laws and State decisions. If this be not so, there is, there can be, no general government.

But, Mr. President, the Constitution has not left this cardinal point without full and explicit provisions. First, as to the authority of Congress. Having enumerated the specific powers conferred on Congress, the Constitution adds, as a distinct and substantive clause, the following, viz.: "To make all laws which shall be necessary and proper for carrying into execution the foregoing powers, and all other powers vested by this Constitution in the government of the United States, or in any department or officer thereof." If this means any thing, it means that Congress may judge of the true extent and just interpretation of the specific powers granted to it, and may judge also what is necessary and proper for executing those powers. If Congress is to judge of what is necessary for the execution of its powers, it must, of necessity, judge of the extent and interpretation of those powers.

And in regard, Sir, to the judiciary, the Constitution is still more express and emphatic. It declares that the judicial power shall extend to all *cases* in law or equity arising under the Constitution, laws of the United States, and treaties; that there shall be *one* Supreme Court, and that this Supreme Court shall have appellate jurisdiction of all these cases, subject to such exceptions as Congress may make. It is impossible to escape from the generality of these words. If a case arises under the Constitution, that is, if a case arises depending on the construction of the Constitution, the judicial power of the United States extends to it. It reaches *the case, the question*; it attaches the power of the national judicature to the *case* itself, in whatever court it may arise or exist; and in this *case* the Supreme Court has appellate jurisdiction over all courts whatever. No language could provide with more effect and precision than is here done, for subjecting constitutional questions to the ultimate de-

cision of the Supreme Court. And, Sir, this is exactly what the Convention found it necessary to provide for, and intended to provide for. It is, too, exactly what the people were universally told was done when they adopted the Constitution. One of the first resolutions adopted by the Convention was in these words, viz.: "That the jurisdiction of the national judiciary shall extend to cases which respect the *collection of the national revenue*, and questions which involve the national peace and harmony." Now, Sir, this either had no sensible meaning at all, or else it meant that the jurisdiction of the national judiciary should extend to these questions, *with a paramount authority*. It is not to be supposed that the Convention intended that the power of the national judiciary should extend to these questions, and that the power of the judicatures of the States should also extend to them, *with equal power of final decision*. This would be to defeat the whole object of the provision. There were thirteen judicatures already in existence. The evil complained of, or the danger to be guarded against, was contradiction and repugnance in the decisions of these judicatures. If the framers of the Constitution meant to create a fourteenth, and yet not to give it power to revise and control the decisions of the existing thirteen, then they only intended to augment the existing evil and the apprehended danger by increasing still further the chances of discordant judgments. Why, Sir, has it become a settled axiom in politics that every government must have a judicial power coextensive with its legislative power? Certainly, there is only this reason, namely, that the laws may receive a uniform interpretation and a uniform execution. This object cannot be otherwise attained. A statute is what it is judicially interpreted to be; and if it be construed one way in New Hampshire, and another way in Georgia, there is no uniform law. One supreme court, with appellate and final jurisdiction, is the natural and only adequate means, in any government, to secure this uniformity. The Convention saw all this clearly; and the resolution which I have quoted, never afterwards rescinded, passed through various modifications, till it finally received the form which the article now bears in the Constitution.

It is undeniably true, then, that the framers of the Constitution intended to create a national judicial power, which should be paramount[9] on national subjects. And after the Constitution was framed, and while the whole country was engaged in discussing its merits, one of its most distinguished advocates, Mr. [James] Madison, told the people that it *was true, that, in controversies relating to the boundary between the two jurisdictions, the tribunal which is ultimately to decide is to be established under the general government.* Mr. [Luther] Martin, who had been

9. *Register of Debates* reads "permanent."

a member of the Convention, asserted the same thing to the legislature of Maryland, and urged it as a reason for rejecting the Constitution. Mr. [Charles] Pinckney, himself also a leading member of the Convention, declared it to the people of South Carolina. Everywhere it was admitted, by friends and foes, that this power was in the Constitution. By some it was thought dangerous, by most it was thought necessary; but by all it was agreed to be a power actually contained in the instrument. The Convention saw the absolute necessity of some control in the national government over State laws. Different modes of establishing this control were suggested and considered. At one time, it was proposed that the laws of the States should, from time to time, be laid before Congress, and that Congress should possess a negative over them. But this was thought inexpedient and inadmissible; and in its place, and expressly as a substitute for it, the existing provision was introduced; that is to say, a provision by which the federal courts should have authority to overrule such State laws as might be in manifest contravention of the Constitution. The writers of the Federalist, in explaining the Constitution, while it was yet pending before the people, and still unadopted, give this account of the matter in terms, and assign this reason for the article as it now stands. By this provision Congress escaped the necessity of any revision of State laws, left the whole sphere of State legislation quite untouched, and yet obtained a security against any infringement of the constitutional power of the general government. Indeed, Sir, allow me to ask again, if the national judiciary was not to exercise a power of revision on constitutional questions over the judicatures of the States, why was any national judicature erected at all? Can any man give a sensible reason for having a judicial power in this government, unless it be for the sake of maintaining a uniformity of decision on questions arising under the Constitution and laws of Congress, and insuring its execution? And does not this very idea of uniformity necessarily imply that the construction given by the national courts is to be the prevailing construction? How else, Sir, is it possible that uniformity can be preserved?

Gentlemen appear to me, Sir, to look at but one side of the question. They regard only the supposed danger of trusting a government with the interpretation of its own powers. But will they view the question in its other aspect? Will they show us how it is possible for a government to get along with four-and-twenty interpreters of its laws and powers? Gentlemen argue, too, as if, in these cases, the State would be always right, and the general government always wrong. But suppose the reverse; suppose the State wrong (and, since they differ, some of them must be wrong); are the most important and essential operations of the government to be embarrassed and arrested, because one State holds the contrary opinion? Mr. President, every argument which refers the

constitutionality of acts of Congress to State decision appeals from the majority to the minority; it appeals from the common interest to a particular interest; from the counsels of all to the counsel of one; and endeavors to supersede the judgment of the whole by the judgment of a part.

I think it is clear, Sir, that the Constitution, by express provision, by definite and unequivocal words, as well as by necessary implication, has constituted the Supreme Court of the United States the appellate tribunal in all cases of a constitutional nature which assume the shape of a suit, in law or equity. And I think I cannot do better than to leave this part of the subject by reading the remarks made upon it in the convention of Connecticut, by Mr. [Oliver] Ellsworth; a gentleman, Sir, who has left behind him, on the records of the government of his country, proofs of the clearest intelligence and of the deepest sagacity, as well as of the utmost purity and integrity of character. "This Constitution," says he, "defines the extent of the powers of the general government. If the general legislature should, at any time, overleap their limits, the judicial department is a constitutional check. If the United States go beyond their powers, if they make a law which the Constitution does not authorize, it is void; and the judiciary power, the national judges, who, to secure their impartiality, are to be made independent, will declare it to be void. On the other hand, if the States go beyond their limits, if they make a law which is a usurpation upon the general government, the law is void; and upright, independent judges will declare it to be so."[10] Nor did this remain merely matter of private opinion.[11] In the very first session of the first Congress, with all these well-known objects, both of the Convention and the people, full and fresh in his mind, Mr. [Oliver] Ellsworth, as is generally understood, reported the bill for the organization of the judicial department, and in that bill made provision for the exercise of this appellate power of the Supreme Court, in all the proper cases, in whatsoever court arising; and this appellate power has now been exercised for more than forty years, without interruption, and without doubt.

As to the cases, Sir, which do not come before the courts, those political questions which terminate with the enactments of Congress, it is of necessity that these should be ultimately decided by Congress itself. Like other legislatures, it must be trusted with this power. The members of Congress are chosen by the people, and they are answerable to the people; like other public agents, they are bound by oath to support the Constitution. These are the securities that they will not violate their duty, nor transcend their powers. They are the same securities that prevail in other popular governments; nor is it easy to see how grants of power can

10. Elliot, *Debates*, 2: 196.
11. *Register* reads "Let me only add, sir, that, in the very first session . . ."

be more safely guarded, without rendering them nugatory. If the case cannot come before the courts, and if Congress be not trusted with its decision, who shall decide it? The gentleman says, each State is to decide it for herself. If so, then, as I have already urged, what is law in one State is not law in another. Or, if the resistance of one State compels an entire repeal of the law, then a minority, and that a small one, governs the whole country.

Sir, those who espouse the doctrines of nullification reject, as it seems to me, the first great principle of all republican liberty; that is, that the majority *must* govern. In matters of common concern, the judgment of a majority *must* stand as the judgment of the whole. This is a law imposed on us by the absolute necessity of the case; and if we do not act upon it, there is no possibility of maintaining any government but despotism. We hear loud and repeated denunciations against what is called *majority government*. It is declared, with much warmth, that a majority government cannot be maintained in the United States. What, then, do gentlemen wish? Do they wish to establish a *minority* government? Do they wish to subject the will of the many to the will of the few? The honorable gentleman from South Carolina has spoken of absolute majorities and majorities concurrent; language wholly unknown to our Constitution, and to which it is not easy to affix definite ideas. As far as I understand it, it would teach us that the absolute majority may be found in Congress, but the majority concurrent must be looked for in the States; that is to say, Sir, stripping the matter of this novelty of phrase, that the dissent of one or more States, as States, renders void the decision of a majority of Congress, so far as that State is concerned. And so this doctrine, running but a short career, like other dogmas of the day, terminates in nullification.

If this vehement invective against *majorities* meant no more than that, in the construction of government, it is wise to provide checks and balances, so that there should be various limitations on the power of the mere majority, it would only mean what the Constitution of the United States has already abundantly provided. It is full of such checks and balances. In its very organization, it adopts a broad and most effective principle in restraint of the power of mere majorities. A majority of the people elects the House of Representatives, but it does not elect the Senate. The Senate is elected by the States, each State having, in this respect, an equal power. No law, therefore, can pass, without the assent of the representatives [12] of the people, and a majority of the representatives of the States also. A majority of the representatives of the people must concur, and a majority of the States must concur, in every act of Congress;

12. *Register* reads "a majority of the representatives."

and the President is elected on a plan compounded of both these principles. But having composed one house of representatives chosen by the people in each State, according to their numbers, and the other of an equal number of members from every State, whether larger or smaller, the Constitution gives to majorities in these houses thus constituted the full and entire power of passing laws, subject always to the constitutional restrictions and to the approval of the President. To subject them to any other power is clear usurpation. The majority of one house may be controlled by the majority of the other; and both may be restrained by the President's negative. These are checks and balances provided by the Constitution, existing in the government itself, and wisely intended to secure deliberation and caution in legislative proceedings. But to resist the will of the majority in both houses, thus constitutionally exercised; to insist on the lawfulness of interposition by an extraneous power; to claim the right of defeating the will of Congress, by setting up against it the will of a single State,—is neither more nor less, as it strikes me, than a plain attempt to overthrow the government. The constituted authorities of the United States are no longer a government, if they be not masters of their own will; they are no longer a government, if an external power may arrest their proceedings; they are no longer a government, if acts passed by both houses, and approved by the President, may be nullified by State vetoes or State ordinances. Does any one suppose it could make any difference, as to the binding authority of an act of Congress, and of the duty of a State to respect it, whether it passed by a mere majority of both houses, or by three fourths of each, or the unanimous vote of each? Within the limits and restrictions of the Constitution, the government of the United States, like all other popular governments, acts by majorities. It can act no otherwise. Whoever, therefore, denounces the government of majorities, denounces the government of his own country, and denounces all free governments. And whoever would restrain these majorities, while acting within their constitutional limits, by an external power, whatever he may intend, asserts principles which, if adopted, can lead to nothing else than the destruction of the government itself.

Does not the gentleman perceive, Sir, how this argument against majorities might here be retorted upon him? Does he not see how cogently he might be asked, whether it be the character of nullification to practise what it preaches? Look to South Carolina, at the present moment. How far are the rights of minorities there respected? I confess, Sir, I have not known, in peaceable times, the power of the majority carried with a higher hand, or upheld with more relentless disregard of the rights, feelings, and principles of the minority;—a minority embracing, as the gentleman himself will admit, a large portion of the worth and respect-

ability of the State; a minority comprehending in its numbers men who have been associated with him, and with us, in these halls of legislation; men who have served their country at home and honored it abroad; men who would cheerfully lay down their lives for their native State, in any cause which they could regard as the cause of honor and duty; men above fear, and above reproach; whose deepest grief and distress spring from the conviction, that the present proceedings of the State must ultimately reflect discredit upon her. How is this minority, how are these men, regarded? They are enthralled and disfranchised by ordinances and acts of legislation; subjected to tests and oaths, incompatible, as they conscientiously think, with oaths already taken, and obligations already assumed, they are proscribed and denounced, as recreants to duty and patriotism, and slaves to a foreign power. Both the spirit which pursues them, and the positive measures which emanate from that spirit, are harsh and prospective beyond all precedent within my knowledge, except in periods of professed revolution.

It is not, Sir, one would think, for those who approve these proceedings to complain of the power of majorities.

Mr. President, all popular governments rest on two principles, or two assumptions: —

First, That there is so far a common interest among those over whom the government extends, as that it may provide for the defence, protection, and good government of the whole, without injustice or oppression to parts; and

Secondly, That the representatives of the people, and especially the people themselves, are secure against general corruption, and may be trusted, therefore, with the exercise of power.

Whoever argues against these principles argues against the practicability of all free governments. And whoever admits these, must admit, or cannot deny, that power is as safe in the hands of Congress as in those of other representative bodies. Congress is not irresponsible. Its members are agents of the people, elected by them, answerable to them, and liable to be displaced or superseded, at their pleasure; and they possess as fair a claim to the confidence of the people, while they continue to deserve it, as any other public political agents.

If, then, Sir, the manifest intention of the Convention, and the contemporary admission of both friends and foes, prove any thing; if the plain text of the instrument itself, as well as the necessary implication from other provisions, prove any thing; if the early legislation of Congress, the course of judicial decisions, acquiesced in by all the States for forty years, prove any thing,—then it is proved that there is a supreme law, and a final interpreter.

My fourth and last proposition, Mr. President, was, that any attempt

by a State to abrogate or nullify acts of Congress is a usurpation on the powers of the general government and on the equal rights of other States, a violation of the Constitution, and a proceeding essentially revolutionary. This is undoubtedly true, if the preceding propositions be regarded as proved. If the government of the United States be trusted with the duty, in any department, of declaring the extent of its own powers, then a State ordinance, or act of legislation, authorizing resistance to an act of Congress, on the alleged ground of its unconstitutionality, is manifestly a usurpation upon its powers. If the States have equal rights in matters concerning the whole, then for one State to set up her judgment against the judgment of the rest, and to insist on executing that judgment by force, is also a manifest usurpation on the rights of other States. If the Constitution of the United States be a government proper, with authority to pass laws, and to give them a uniform interpretation and execution, then the interposition of a State, to enforce her own construction, and to resist, as to herself, that law which binds the other States, is a violation of the Constitution.

If that be revolutionary which arrests the legislative, executive, and judicial power of government, dispenses with existing oaths and obligations of obedience, and elevates another power to supreme dominion, then nullification is revolutionary. Or if that be revolutionary the natural tendency and practical effect of which are to break the Union into fragments, to sever all connection among the people of the respective States, and to prostrate this general government in the dust, then nullification is revolutionary.

Nullification, Sir, is as distinctly revolutionary as secession; but I cannot say that the revolution which it seeks is one of so respectable a character. Secession would, it is true, abandon the Constitution altogether; but then it would profess to abandon it. Whatever other inconsistencies it might run into, one, at least, it would avoid. It would not belong to a government, while it rejected its authority. It would not repel the burden, and continue to enjoy the benefits. It would not aid in passing laws which others are to obey, and yet reject their authority as to itself. It would not undertake to reconcile obedience to public authority with an asserted right of command over that same authority. It would not be in the government, and above the government, at the same time. But though secession may be a more respectable mode of attaining the object of nullification, it is not more truly revolutionary.[13] Each, and both, resist the constitutional authorities; each, and both, would sever the Union, and subvert the government.

13. In the *Register of Debates* this sentence reads: "But however more respectable a mode of secession may be, it is not more truly revolutionary than the actual execution of the doctrines of nullification."

Mr. President, having detained the Senate so long already, I will not now examine at length the ordinance and laws of South Carolina. These papers are well drawn for their purpose. Their authors understand their own objects. They are called a peaceable remedy, and we have been told that South Carolina, after all, intends nothing but a lawsuit. A very few words, Sir, will show the nature of this peaceable remedy, and of the lawsuit which South Carolina contemplates.

In the first place, the ordinance declares the law of last July, and all other laws of the United States laying duties, to be absolutely null and void, and makes it unlawful for the constituted authorities of the United States to enforce the payment of such duties. It is therefore, Sir, an indictable offence, at this moment, in South Carolina, for any person to be concerned in collecting revenue under the laws of the United States. It being declared, by what is considered a fundamental law of the State, unlawful to collect these duties, an indictment lies, of course, against any one concerned in such collection; and he is, on general principles, liable to be punished by fine and imprisonment. The terms, it is true, are, that it is unlawful "to enforce the payment of duties"; but every custom-house officer enforces payment while he detains the goods in order to obtain such payment. The ordinance, therefore, reaches every body concerned in the collection of the duties.

This is the first step in the prosecution of the peaceable remedy. The second is more decisive. By the act commonly called the *replevin* law, any person, whose goods are seized or detained by the collector for the payment of duties, may sue out a writ of replevin, and, by virtue of that writ, the goods are to be restored to him. A writ of replevin is a writ which the sheriff is bound to execute, and for the execution of which he is bound to employ force, if necessary. He may call out the *posse*, and must do so, if resistance be made. This *posse* may be armed or unarmed. It may come forth with military array, and under the lead of military men. Whatever number of troops may be assembled in Charleston, they may be summoned, with the governor, or commander-in-chief, at their head, to come in aid of the sheriff. It is evident, then, Sir, that the whole military power of the State is to be employed, if[14] necessary, in dispossessing the custom-house officers, and in seizing and holding the goods, without paying the duties. This is the second step in the peaceable remedy.

Sir, whatever pretences may be set up to the contrary, this is the direct application of force, and of military force. It is unlawful, in itself, to replevy goods in the custody of the collectors. But this unlawful act is to be done, and it is to be done by power. Here is a plain interposition, by

14. Instead of "if," *Register* reads "whenever."

physical force, to resist the laws of the Union. The legal mode of collecting duties is to detain the goods till such duties are paid or secured. But force comes, and overpowers the collector and his assistants, and takes away the goods, leaving the duties unpaid. There cannot be a clearer case of forcible resistance to law. And it is provided that the goods thus seized shall be held against any attempt to retake them, by the same force which seized them.

Having thus dispossessed the officers of the government of the goods, without payment of duties, and seized and secured them by the strong arm of the State, only one thing more remains to be done, and that is, to cut off all possibility of legal redress; and that, too, is accomplished, or thought to be accomplished. The ordinance declares, *that all judicial proceedings, founded on the revenue laws* (including, of course, proceedings in the courts of the United States), *shall be null and void.* This nullifies the judicial power of the United States. Then comes the test-oath act. This requires all State judges and jurors in the State courts to swear that they will execute the ordinance, and all acts of the legislature passed in pursuance thereof. The ordinance declares, that no appeal shall be allowed from the decision of the State courts to the Supreme Court of the United States; and the replevin act makes it an indictable offence for any clerk to furnish a copy of the record, for the purpose of such appeal.

The two principal provisions on which South Carolina relies, to resist the laws of the United States, and nullify the authority of this government, are, therefore, these: —

1. A forcible seizure of goods, before duties are paid or secured, by the power of the State, civil and military.

2. The taking away, by the most effectual means in her power, of all legal redress in the courts of the United States; the confining of judicial proceedings to her own State tribunals; and the compelling of her judges and jurors of these her own courts to take an oath, beforehand, that they will decide all cases according to the ordinance, and the acts passed under it; that is, that they will decide the cause one way. They do not swear to *try* it, on its own merits; they only swear to *decide* it as nullification requires.

The character, Sir, of these provisions defies comment. Their object is as plain as their means are extraordinary. They propose direct resistance, by the whole power of the State, to laws of Congress, and cut off, by methods deemed adequate, any redress by legal and judicial authority. They arrest legislation, defy the executive, and banish the judicial power of this government. They authorize and command acts to be done, and done by force, both of numbers and of arms, which, if done, and done by force, are clearly acts of rebellion and treason.

Such, Sir, are the laws of South Carolina; such, Sir, is the peaceable

remedy of nullification. Has not nullification reached, Sir, even thus early, that point of direct and forcible resistance to law to which I intimated, three years ago, it plainly tended?[15]

And now, Mr. President, what is the reason for passing laws like these? What are the oppressions experienced under the Union, calling for measures which thus threaten to sever and destroy it? What invasions of public liberty, what ruin to private happiness, what long list of rights violated, or wrongs unredressed, is to justify to the country, to posterity, and to the world, this assault upon the free Constitution of the United States, this great and glorious work of our fathers? At this very moment, Sir, the whole land smiles in peace, and rejoices in plenty. A general and a high prosperity pervades the country; and, judging by the common standard, by increase of population and wealth, or judging by the opinions of that portion of her people not embarked in these dangerous and desperate measures, this prosperity overspreads South Carolina herself.

Thus happy at home, our country, at the same time, holds high the character of her institutions, her power, her rapid growth, and her future destiny, in the eyes of all foreign states. One danger only creates hesitation; one doubt only exists, to darken the otherwise unclouded brightness of that aspect which she exhibits to the view and to the admiration of the world. Need I say, that that doubt respects the permanency of our Union? and need I say, that that doubt is now caused, more than any thing else, by these very proceedings of South Carolina? Sir, all Europe is, at this moment, beholding us, and looking for the issue of this controversy; those who hate free institutions, with malignant hope; those who love them, with deep anxiety and shivering fear.

The cause, then, Sir, the cause! Let the world know the cause which has thus induced one State of the Union to bid defiance to the power of the whole, and openly to talk of secession. Sir, the world will scarcely believe that this whole controversy, and all the desperate measures which its support requires, have no other foundation than a difference of opinion upon a provision of the Constitution, between a majority of the people of South Carolina, on one side, and a vast majority of the whole people of the United States, on the other. It will not credit the fact, it will not admit the possibility, that, in an enlightened age, in a free, popular republic, under a constitution[16] where the people govern, as they must always govern under such systems, by majorities, at a time of unprecedented prosperity, without practical oppression, without evils such as may not only be pretended, but felt and experienced,—evils not slight or temporary, but deep, permanent, and intolerable,—a single State should rush into conflict with all the rest, attempt to put down the power of the

15. See Reply to Hayne, pp. 285–348, above.

16. *Register* reads "Government."

Union by her own laws, and to support those laws by her military power, and thus break up and destroy the world's last hope. And well the world may be incredulous. We, who see and hear it, can ourselves hardly yet believe it. Even after all that had preceded it, this ordinance struck the country with amazement. It was incredible and inconceivable that South Carolina should plunge headlong into resistance to the laws on a matter of opinion, and on a question in which the preponderance of opinion, both of the present day and of all past time, was so overwhelmingly against her. The ordinance declares that Congress has exceeded its just power by laying duties on imports, intended for the protection of manufactures. This is the opinion of South Carolina; and on the strength of that opinion she nullifies the laws. Yet has the rest of the country no right to its opinion also? Is one State to sit sole arbitress? She maintains that those laws are plain, deliberate, and palpable violations of the Constitution; that she has a sovereign right to decide this matter; and that, having so decided, she is authorized to resist their execution by her own sovereign power; and she declares that she will resist it, though such resistance should shatter the Union into atoms.

Mr. President, I do not intend to discuss the propriety of these laws at large; but I will ask, How are they shown to be thus plainly and palpably unconstitutional? Have they no countenance at all in the Constitution itself? Are they quite new in the history of the government? Are they a sudden and violent usurpation on the rights of the States? Sir, what will the civilized world say, what will posterity say, when they learn that similar laws have existed from the very foundation of the government, that for thirty years the power was never questioned, and that no State in the Union has more freely and unequivocally admitted it than South Carolina herself?

To lay and collect duties and imposts is an *express power* granted by the Constitution to Congress. It is, also, an *exclusive power*; for the Constitution as expressly prohibits all the States from exercising it themselves. This express and exclusive power is unlimited in the terms of the grant, but is attended with two specific restrictions: first, that all duties and imposts shall be equal in all the States; second, that no duties shall be laid on exports. The power, then, being granted, and being attended with these two restrictions, and no more, who is to impose a third restriction on the general words of the grant? If the power to lay duties, as known among all other nations, and as known in all our history, and as it was perfectly understood when the Constitution was adopted, includes a right of discriminating while exercising the power, and of laying some duties heavier and some lighter, for the sake of encouraging our own domestic products, what authority is there for giving to the words used in the Constitution a new, narrow, and unusual meaning? All the limita-

tions which the Constitution intended, it has expressed; and what it has left unrestricted is as much a part of its will as the restraints which it has imposed.

But these laws, it is said, are unconstitutional on account of the *motive*. How, Sir, can a law be examined on any such ground? How is the motive to be ascertained? One house, or one member, may have one motive; the other house, or another member, another. One motive may operate to-day, and another to-morrow. Upon any such mode of reasoning as this, one law might be unconstitutional now, and another law, in exactly the same words, perfectly constitutional next year. Besides, articles may not only be taxed for the purpose of protecting home products, but other articles may be left free, for the same purpose and with the same motive. A law, therefore, would become unconstitutional from what it omitted, as well as from what it contained. Mr. President, it is a settled principle, acknowledged in all legislative halls, recognized before all tribunals, sanctioned by the general sense and understanding of mankind, that there can be no inquiry into the motives of those who pass laws, for the purpose of determining on their validity. If the law be within the fair meaning of the words in the grant of the power, its authority must be admitted until it is repealed. This rule, everywhere acknowledged, everywhere admitted, is so universal and so completely without exception, that even an allegation of fraud, in the majority of a legislature, is not allowed as a ground to set aside a law.

But, Sir, is it true that the motive for these laws is such as is stated? I think not. The great object of all laws is, unquestionably, revenue. If there were no occasion for revenue, the laws would not have been passed; and it is notorious that almost the entire revenue of the country is derived from them. And as yet we have collected none too much revenue. The treasury has not been more reduced[17] for many years than it is at the present moment. All that South Carolina can say is, that, in passing the laws which she now undertakes to nullify, *particular imported articles were taxed, from a regard to the protection of certain articles of domestic manufacture, higher than they would have been had no such regard been entertained.* And she insists that, according to the Constitution, no such discrimination can be allowed; that duties should be laid for revenue, and revenue only; and that it is unlawful to have reference, in any case, to protection. In other words, she denies the power of DISCRIMINATION. She does not, and cannot, complain of excessive taxation; on the contrary, she professes to be willing to pay any amount for revenue, merely as revenue; and up to the present moment there is no surplus of revenue. Her grievance, then, that plain and palpable violation of the Constitu-

17. *Register* reads "exhausted."

tion which she insists has taken place, is simply the exercise of the power of DISCRIMINATION. Now, Sir, is the exercise of this power of discrimination plainly and palpably unconstitutional?

I have already said, the power to lay duties is given by the Constitution in broad and general terms. There is also conferred on Congress the whole power of regulating commerce, in another distinct provision. Is it clear and palpable, Sir, can any man say it is a case beyond doubt, that, under these two powers, Congress may not justly *discriminate*, in laying duties, *for the purpose of countervailing the policy of foreign nations, or of favoring our own home productions*? Sir, what ought to conclude this question for ever, as it would seem to me, is, that the regulation of commerce and the imposition of duties are, in all commercial nations, powers avowedly and constantly exercised for this very end. That undeniable truth ought to settle the question; because the Constitution ought to be considered, when it uses well-known language, as using it in its well-known sense. But it is equally undeniable, that it has been, from the very first, fully believed that this power of discrimination was conferred on Congress; and the Constitution was itself recommended, urged upon the people, and enthusiastically insisted on in some of the States, for that very reason. Not that, at that time, the country was extensively engaged in manufactures, especially of the kinds now existing. But the trades and crafts of the seaport towns, the business of the artisans and manual laborers,—those employments, the work in which supplies so great a portion of the daily wants of all classes,—all these looked to the new Constitution as a source of relief from the severe distress which followed the war. It would, Sir, be unpardonable, at so late an hour, to go into details on this point; but the truth is as I have stated. The papers of the day, the resolutions of public meetings, the debates in the conventions, all that we open our eyes upon in the history of the times, prove it.

Sir, the honorable gentleman from South Carolina has referred to two incidents connected with the proceedings of the Convention at Philadelphia, which he thinks are evidence to show that the power of protecting manufactures by laying duties, and by commercial regulations, was not intended to be given to Congress. The first is, as he says, that a power to protect manufactures was expressly proposed, but not granted. I think, Sir, the gentleman is quite mistaken in relation to this part of the proceedings of the Convention. The whole history of the occurrence to which he alludes is simply this. Towards the conclusion of the Convention, after the provisions of the Constitution had been mainly agreed upon, after the power to lay duties and the power to regulate commerce had both been granted, a long list of propositions was made and referred to the committee, containing various miscellaneous powers, some or all

of which it was thought might be properly vested in Congress. Among these was a power to establish a university; to grant charters of incorporation; to regulate stage-coaches on the post-roads; and also the power to which the gentleman refers, and which is expressed in these words: "To establish public institutions, rewards, and immunities, for the promotion of agriculture, commerce, trades, and manufactures." The committee made no report on this or various other propositions in the same list. But the only inference from this omission is, that neither the committee nor the Convention thought it proper to authorize Congress "to establish public institutions, rewards, and immunities," for the promotion of manufactures, and other interests. The Convention supposed it had done enough,—at any rate, it had done all it intended,—when it had given to Congress, in general terms, the power to lay imposts and the power to regulate trade. It is not to be argued, from its omission to give more, that it meant to take back what it had already given. It had given the impost power; it had given the regulation of trade; and it did not deem it necessary to give the further and distinct power of establishing public institutions.

The other fact, Sir, on which the gentleman relies, is the declaration of Mr. [Luther] Martin to the legislature of Maryland.[18] The gentleman supposes Mr. Martin to have urged against the Constitution, that it did not contain the power of protection. But if the gentleman will look again at what Mr. Martin said, he will find, I think, that what Mr. Martin complained of was, that the Constitution, by its prohibitions on the States, had taken away from the States themselves the power of protecting their own manufactures by duties on imports. This is undoubtedly true; but I find no expression of Mr. Martin intimating that the Constitution had not conferred on Congress the same power which it had thus taken from the States.

But, Sir, let us go to the first Congress; let us look in upon this and the other house, at the first session of their organization.

We see, in both houses, men distinguished among the framers, friends, and advocates of the Constitution. We see in both, those who had drawn, discussed, and matured the instrument in the Convention, explained and defended it before the people, and were now elected members of Congress, to put the new government into motion, and to carry the powers of the Constitution into beneficial execution. At the head of the government was WASHINGTON himself, who had been President of the Convention; and in his cabinet were others most thoroughly acquainted with the history of the Constitution, and distinguished for the part taken in its discussion. If these persons were not acquainted with the meaning of

18. Remarks of Jan. 27, 1788, Elliot, *Debates*, 1: 368–369.

the Constitution, if they did not understand the work of their own hands, who can understand it, or who shall now interpret it to us?

Sir, the volume which records the proceedings and debates of the first session of the House of Representatives lies before me. I open it, and I find that, having provided for the administration of the necessary oaths, the very first measure proposed for consideration is, the laying of imposts; and in the very first committee of the whole into which the House of Representatives ever resolved itself, on this its earliest subject, and in this its very first debate, the duty of so laying the imposts as to encourage manufactures was advanced and enlarged upon by almost every speaker, and doubted or denied by none. The first gentleman who suggests this as the clear duty of Congress, and as an object necessary to be attended to, is Mr. [Thomas] Fitzsimons, of Pennsylvania; the second, Mr. [Alexander] White, of VIRGINIA; the third, Mr. [Thomas Tudor] Tucker of SOUTH CAROLINA.

But the great leader, Sir, on this occasion, was Mr. [James] Madison. Was *he* likely to know the intentions of the Convention and the people? Was *he* likely to understand the Constitution? At the second sitting of the committee, Mr. Madison explained his own opinions of the duty of Congress, fully and explicitly. I must not detain you, Sir, with more than a few short extracts from these opinions, but they are such as are clear, intelligible, and decisive. "The States," says he, "that are most advanced in population, and ripe for manufactures, ought to have their particular interest attended to, in some degree. While these States retained the power of making regulations of trade, they had the power to cherish such institutions. By adopting the present Constitution, they have thrown the exercise of this power into other hands; they must have done this with an expectation that those interests would not be neglected here."[19] In another report of the same speech, Mr. Madison is represented as using still stronger language; as saying that, the Constitution having taken this power away from the States and conferred it on Congress, it would be a *fraud* on the States and on the people were Congress to refuse to exercise it.[20]

Mr. Madison argues, Sir, on this early and interesting occasion, very justly and liberally, in favor of the general principles of unrestricted commerce. But he argues, also, with equal force and clearness, for certain important exceptions to these general principles. The first, Sir, respects those manufactures which had been brought forward under encouragement by the State governments. "It would be cruel," says Mr. Madison, "to neglect them, and to divert their industry into other channels; for it is not possible for the hand of man to shift from one employment to

19. Apr. 9, 1789, *Annals*, 1st
Cong., 1st sess., p. 116.

20. Not found.

another without being injured by the change." Again: "There may be some manufactures which, being once formed, can advance towards perfection without any adventitious aid; while others, for want of the fostering hand of government, will be unable to go on at all. Legislative provision, therefore, will be necessary to collect the proper objects for this purpose; and this will form another exception to my general principle." And again: "The next exception that occurs is one on which great stress is laid by some well-informed men, and this with great plausibility; that each nation should have, within itself, the means of defence, independent of foreign supplies; that, in whatever relates to the operations of war, no State ought to depend upon a precarious supply from any part of the world. There may be some truth in this remark; and therefore it is proper for legislative attention."[21]

In the same debate, Sir, Mr. [Aedanus] Burk[e], from SOUTH CAROLINA, supported a duty on hemp, for the express purpose of encouraging its growth on the strong lands of South Carolina. "Cotton," he said, "was also in contemplation among them, and, if good seed could be procured, he hoped might succeed."[22] Afterwards, Sir, the cotton was obtained, its culture was protected, and it did succeed. Mr. [William L.] Smith, a very distinguished member from the SAME STATE, observed: "It has been said, and justly, that the States which adopted this Constitution expected its administration would be conducted with a favorable hand. The manufacturing States wished the encouragement of manufactures, the maritime States the encouragement of ship-building, and the agricultural States the encouragement of agriculture."[23]

Sir, I will detain the Senate by reading no more extracts from these debates. I have already shown a majority of the members of SOUTH CAROLINA, in this first session, acknowledging this power of protection, voting for its exercise, and proposing its extension to their own products. Similar propositions came from Virginia; and, indeed, Sir, in the whole debate, at whatever page you open the volume, you find the power admitted, and you find it applied to the protection of particular articles, or not applied, according to the discretion of Congress. No man denied the power, no man doubted it; the only questions were, in regard to the several articles proposed to be taxed, whether they were fit subjects for protection, and what the amount of that protection ought to be. Will gentlemen, Sir, now answer the argument drawn from these proceedings of the first Congress? Will they undertake to deny that that Congress did act on the avowed principle of protection? Or, if they admit it, will they tell us how those who framed the Constitution fell, thus early, into this great

21. *Annals*, 1st Cong., 1st sess.,
p. 118.
22. Apr. 16, 1789, *Annals*, 1st
Cong., 1st sess., p. 162.
23. May 7, 1789, *Annals*, 1st
Cong., 1st sess., p. 298.

mistake about its meaning? Will they tell us how it should happen that they had so soon forgotten their own sentiments and their own purposes? I confess I have seen no answer to this argument, nor any respectable attempt to answer it. And, Sir, how did this debate terminate? What law was passed? There it stands, Sir, among the statutes, the second law in the book. It has a *preamble*, and that preamble expressly recites, that the duties which it imposes are laid "for the support of government, for the discharge of the debts of the United States, and *the encouragement and protection of manufactures*." Until, Sir, this early legislation, thus coeval with the Constitution itself, thus full and explicit, can be explained away, no man can doubt of the meaning of that instrument, in this respect.[24]

Mr. President, this power of *discrimination*, thus admitted, avowed, and practised upon in the first revenue act, has never been denied or doubted until within a few years past. It was not at all doubted in 1816, when it became necessary to adjust the revenue to a state of peace. On the contrary, the power was then exercised, not without opposition as to its expediency, but, as far as I remember or have understood, without the slightest opposition founded on any supposed want of constitutional authority. Certainly, SOUTH CAROLINA did not doubt it. The tariff of 1816 was introduced, carried through, and established, under the lead of South Carolina. Even the minimum policy is of South Carolina origin. The honorable gentleman himself supported, and ably supported, the tariff of 1816.[25] He has informed us, Sir, that his speech on that occasion was sudden and off-hand, he being called up by the request of a friend. I am sure the gentleman so remembers it, and that it was so; but there is, nevertheless, much method, arrangement, and clear exposition in that extempore speech. It is very able, very, very much to the point, and very decisive. And in another speech, delivered two months earlier, on the proposition to repeal the internal taxes, the honorable gentleman had touched the same subject, and had declared "*that a certain encouragement ought to be extended at least to our woollen and cotton manufactures.*" I do not quote these speeches, Sir, for the purpose of showing that the honorable gentleman has changed his opinion: my object is other and higher. I do it for the sake of saying that that cannot be so plainly and palpably unconstitutional as to warrant resistance to law, nullification, and revolution, which the honorable gentleman and his friends have heretofore agreed to and acted upon without doubt and without hes-

24. *Register* omits "in this respect."

25. See Robert L. Meriwether, ed., *The Papers of John C. Calhoun* (Columbia, S.C., 1959), 1: 347–357.

Webster does not mention his own part in that debate. See *Annals*, 14th Cong., 1st sess., pp. 1257, 1270–1272.

itation. Sir, it is no answer to say that the tariff of 1816 was a revenue bill. So are they all revenue bills. The point is, and the truth is, that the tariff of 1816, like the rest, *did discriminate*; it did distinguish one article from another; it did lay duties for protection. Look to the case of coarse cottons under the minimum calculation: the duty on these was from sixty to eighty per cent. Something beside revenue, certainly, was intended in this; and, in fact, the law cut up our whole commerce with India in that article.

It is, Sir, only within a few years that Carolina has denied the constitutionality of these protective laws. The gentleman himself has narrated to us the true history of her proceedings on this point. He says, that, after the passing of the law of 1828, despairing then of being able to abolish the system of protection, political men went forth among the people, and set up the doctrine that the system was unconstitutional. *"And the people,"* says the honorable gentleman, *"received the doctrine."* This, I believe, is true, Sir. The people did then receive the doctrine; they had never entertained it before. Down to that period, the constitutionality of these laws had been no more doubted in South Carolina than elsewhere. And I suspect it is true, Sir, and I deem it a great misfortune, that, to the present moment, a great portion of the people of the State have never yet seen more than one side of the argument. I believe that thousands of honest men are involved in scenes now passing, led away by one-sided views of the question, and following their leaders by the impulses of an unlimited confidence. Depend upon it, Sir, if we can avoid the shock of arms, a day for reconsideration and reflection will come; truth and reason will act with their accustomed force, and the public opinion of South Carolina will be restored to its usual constitutional and patriotic tone.

But, Sir, I hold South Carolina to her ancient, her cool, her uninfluenced, her deliberate opinions. I hold her to her own admissions, nay, to her own claims and pretensions, in 1789, in the first Congress, and to her acknowledgments and avowed sentiments through a long series of succeeding years. I hold her to the principles on which she led Congress to act in 1816; or, if she have changed her own opinions, I claim some respect for those who still retain the same opinions. I say she is precluded from asserting that doctrines, which she has herself so long and so ably sustained, are plain, palpable, and dangerous violations of the Constitution.

Mr. President, if the friends of nullification should be able to propagate their opinions, and give them practical effect, they would, in my judgment, prove themselves the most skilful "architects of ruin," the most effectual extinguishers of high-raised expectation, the greatest blasters of human hopes, that any age has produced. They would stand up to proclaim, in tones which would pierce the ears of half the human race, that

the last great experiment of representative government had failed. They would send forth sounds, at the hearing of which the doctrine of the divine right of kings would feel, even in its grave, a returning sensation of vitality and resuscitation. Millions of eyes, of those who now feed their inherent love of liberty on the success of the American example, would turn away from beholding our dismemberment, and find no place on earth whereupon to rest their gratified sight. Amidst the incantations and orgies of nullification, secession, disunion, and revolution, would be celebrated the funeral rites of constitutional and republican liberty.

But, Sir, if the government do its duty, if it act with firmness and with moderation, these opinions cannot prevail. Be assured, Sir, be assured, that, among the political sentiments of this people, the love of union is still uppermost. They will stand fast by the Constitution, and by those who defend it. I rely on no temporary expedients, on no political combination; but I rely on the true American feeling, the genuine patriotism of the people, and the imperative decision of the public voice. Disorder and confusion, indeed, may arise; scenes of commotion and contest are threatened, and perhaps may come. With my whole heart, I pray for the continuance of the domestic peace and quiet of the country. I desire, most ardently, the restoration of affection and harmony to all its parts. I desire that every citizen of the whole country may look to this government with no other sentiments than those of grateful respect and attachment. But I cannot yield even to kind feelings the cause of the Constitution, the true glory of the country, and the great trust which we hold in our hands for succeeding ages. If the Constitution cannot be maintained without meeting these scenes of commotion and contest, however unwelcome, they must come. We cannot, we must not, we dare not, omit to do that which, in our judgment, the safety of the Union requires. Not regardless of consequences, we must yet meet consequences; seeing the hazards which surround the discharge of public duty, it must yet be discharged. For myself, Sir, I shun no responsibility justly devolving on me, here or elsewhere, in attempting to maintain the cause. I am bound to it by indissoluble ties of affection and duty, and I shall cheerfully partake in its fortunes and its fate. I am ready to perform my own appropriate part, whenever and wherever the occasion may call on me, and to take my chance among those upon whom blows may fall first and fall thickest. I shall exert every faculty I possess in aiding to prevent the Constitution from being nullified, destroyed, or impaired; and even should I see it fail, I will still, with a voice feeble, perhaps, but earnest as ever issued from human lips, and with fidelity and zeal which nothing shall extinguish, call on the PEOPLE to come to its rescue.

Calendar, 1800–1833

Formal writings may be defined as pieces written for publication. They were relatively few in number, consisting for the most part of book reviews and Congressional committee reports. Letters to various editors and other correspondents intended for newspaper publication, and drafts of editorials, have been included in the *Correspondence* series. Speeches are more difficult to identify. On the one hand are the widely advertised set speeches in and out of Congress. On the other extreme are remarks in debate, usually confined to a single aspect of the subject under discussion and generally brief. They may be easily picked up by the interested reader in the volumes of the *Annals of Congress*, the *Register of Debates*, and the *Congressional Globe*. In between these two categories is a gray area that could belong to either. Whether these are to be listed as speeches or passed over as remarks in debate is in the end a matter of editorial judgment. The editors can only hope that their classification will be acceptable to most readers.

(Items in italics are included in this volume.)

1800

July 4   An Oration pronounced at Hanover, N.H. Printed. Hanover: Moses Davis, 1800. W & S, 15: 475–484. Independence Day address.
October 6   An Oration on Ambition. Dartmouth College. ADS. NhD. mDW 18. Short address prepared "for the Fraternity."
December 15   Acquisition of the Floridas. Dartmouth College. ADS. MHi. mDW 21. Massachusetts Historical Society *Proceedings*, 1st Series 11 (1869–1870): 329–330. W & S, 15: 485–486. College exercise.

1801

August 25   Oration on Opinion. Dartmouth College. AD. NhHi. mDW 42. Copy, revised. NhD. mDW 58. W & S, 15: 494–504. "For the Anniversary of the United Fraternity."
[August 26?]   A Funeral Oration, Occasioned by the Death of Ephraim Simonds, of Templeton, Massachusetts, a Member of the Senior Class in Dartmouth College; who died at Hanover, on the 18th of June, 1801, AET. 26. AD incomplete. NhHi. mDW 78. Pamphlet, Hanover: Moses Davis, 1801. W & S, 15: 487–493

1802

July 5   An Oration delivered at Fryeburg, Maine. AD. NhHi. mDW 136.
  W & S, 15: 505–512. Same, but text widely at variance, pamphlet,
  Boston: A. Williams & Co., and Fryeburg: A.F. & C.W. Lewis,
  1882. DLC. W & S, 15: 513–524. Independence Day address.

1805

February   An Appeal to the Old Whigs of New Hampshire, by "An Old
  Whig." Essay. Copy. NhHi. Pamphlet, [n.p., 1805]. W & S, 15:
  522–531. Supports Whig John Taylor Gilman over Republican
  John Langdon in the New Hampshire gubernatorial campaign.
April   Review of the First Canto of "Terrible Tractoration." The
  Monthly Anthology, 2 (April 1805): 167–170; W & S, 15:532–536.

1806

July 4   Oration delivered at Concord, N.H. Pamphlet, Concord: George
  Hough, 1806. W & S, 15: 537–547. Contains passages identical
  with the 1882 version of the Fryeburg address, above. Indepen-
  dence Day address.
August 26   The State of Our Literature. AD. DLC. mDW 776. Misdated
  1809 in W & S, 15: 575–582. Phi Beta Kappa address.
October   Review of "A Treatise concerning Political Inquiry, and the
  Liberty of the press. By Tunis Wortman. New York: George For-
  man, 1800." The Monthly Anthology, 3(October 1806): 344–346.
  Reproduced in Legal Papers, 1: 169–171.

1807

April   Review of "Vol. I. part I. Feb. term, 1806. Reports of cases
  argued, and determined, in the Supreme Court of Judicature of
  the State of New York. By William Johnson, esquire, counsellor
  at law. New York, I. Riley & Co., 1806." The Monthly Anthology,
  4(April 1807): 206–208. W & S, 15: 552–555. Reproduced in
  Legal Papers, 1: 172–174.
December   The French Language. The Monthly Anthology, 4(December 1807): 647–649. W & S, 15: 556–558. Discusses the French
  affinity for extravagant compliment.

1808

March   Review of "An elementary Treatise on Pleading in Civil Actions. By Edward Lawes, of the Inner Temple. First American

from the First London edition. Portsmouth, (N.H.) published by
Thomas & Tappan, from the press of S. Sewall. 1808. 8 vo. pp.
246." *The Monthly Anthology*, 5(March 1808): 162–165. *W & S*,
15: 559–563. Reproduced in Legal Papers, 1: 174–178.
[October?]   Considerations on the Embargo Laws. Essay. Pamphlet,
[Walpole, N.H.?]: [n.p., October, 1808]. NhD. mDWs. *W & S*, 15:
564–574. Denounces the embargo laws.

1812

July 4   Address delivered before the Washington Benevolent Society at
Portsmouth, N.H. Pamphlet, Portsmouth: Oracle Press, 1812.
W & S, 15: 583–598. Opposes war with England; criticizes the ad-
ministration's failure to protect U.S. commerce.
August 5   The Rockingham Memorial

1813

June 10   Resolutions on the French Decrees, and supporting argument.
Boston *Messenger*, June 18, 1813. *W & S*, 14: 3–7. Summary in
Annals, 13th Cong., 1st sess., pp. 149–152. Seeks to determine
whether France did indeed repeal the Berlin and Milan Decrees
in April 1811.

1814

January 14   Encouragement of Enlistments. Speech in H.R., *Annals*,
13th Cong., 2d sess., pp. 940–951. Numerous pamphlet versions.
W & S, 14: 18–34. Opposes enlistment bill because there is no
assurance that forces raised will be used for defense.
January 22   Modification of the Embargo. Speech in H.R., *Annals*, 13th
Cong., 2d sess., p. 1121. Opposes the modification of the embargo
law, which he considers unconstitutional and thus void.
April 6   Repeal of the Embargo. Speech in H.R. *Annals*, 13th Cong., 2d
sess., pp. 1966–1973. *Lansingburgh* (N.Y.) *Gazette*, April 26,
1814. *W & S*, 14: 35–46. Denounces the embargo; welcomes
repeal.
October 24   Increase of Direct Taxes. Speech in H.R., *Annals*, 13th
Cong., 3d sess., pp. 459–465. Boston *Columbian Centinel*, November 5, 1814 (speech misdated November 24). *W & S*, 14: 47–54.
Places responsibility for tax increases with those who began the
war.
November 23, 25   Bank of the United States. Speech in H.R., *Annals*,
13th Cong., 3d sess., pp. 639, 642–646. Opposes pending bill; states
own views.
November 29   Investigation into Causes of Success of the Enemy.

Speech in H.R., *Annals*, 13th Cong., 3d sess., pp. 689–691. Criticizes a committe report.
December 9   The Conscription Bill

1815

January 2   Bill to Incorporate the Bank of the United States. Speech in H.R., *Annals*, 13th Cong., 3d sess., pp. 1014–1023. W & S, 5: 35–47. Urges amendment to avoid paper money not adequately backed by specie.

1816

February 28   National Bank Bill. Speech in H.R., *Annals*, 14th Cong., 1st sess., pp. 1091–1094. W & S, 14: 70–75. Argues that proposed bank will not solve problem of depreciated paper.
April 5   National Bank. Speech in H.R., *Annals*, 14th Cong., 1st sess., pp. 1341–1342 (summary) and subsequent debate. W & S, 14: 75–76. Argues that National Bank should be free of government influence or control.
April 26   The Legal Currency.
November   Review of "Extraordinary Red Book; a List of all places, pensions, sinecures, etc., etc., with the salaries and emoluments arising therefrom. Exhibiting also a complete view of the National Debt, etc., etc., the whole comprising the strongest body of evidence to prove the necessity of retrenchment, etc., etc. London, 1816." *North American Review* 4(November 1816): 107–112. Misdated December 1816 in W & S, 15: 3–8.

1817

April 25   Defense of the Kennistons. Legal argument before MassSJC,E. No court citation. Pamphlet, Boston: Joseph T. Buckingham, 1817. W & S, 10: 177–193.
May   Argument in *Gilman* v. *Brown*. USCC,DMass. 1 Mason 191 (1817). W & S, 15: 249–253.

1818

March 10   Argument in *Dartmouth College* v. *Woodward*. Argument for plaintiff in U.S. Supreme Court. 4 Wheaton 551. W & S, 10: 194–233. *Legal Papers*, 3.
May   Argument in *Harvey* v. *Richards*. USCC, DMass. 1 Mason 381 (1818). W & S, 15: 254–260.
July   Review of "An account of the Battle of Bunker Hill," by H.

Dearborn; and of "A letter to Major General Dearborn, repelling his unprovoked attack on the character of the late Major General Israel Putnam," by David Putnam. *North American Review* 7(July 1818): 225–258. A series of articles on the same theme appear in the Boston *Columbian Centinel* for July 4, 8, 11, 15, 22, 25, 1818, later attributed to Webster. See also *Correspondence*, 1: 226.

December   Review of "Reports of Cases argued and adjudged in the Supreme Court of the United States. February Term, 1818," by Henry Wheaton. Vol. 3. *North American Review* 8(December 1818): 63–71. Praises Wheaton's work; uses it as a vehicle for defending the common law against efforts to supercede it by statutes.

1819

February   Argument in *McCulloch* v. *Maryland*. U.S. Supreme Court, February term 1819. 4 Wheaton 322. W & S, 15: 261–267. See *Legal Papers*, 3. The Bank of the United States, as an instrumentality of the national government, may not be taxed by the states.

March   Argument in *King* v. *Dedham Bank*. MassSJC,S. 15 Tyng 451 (1819). W & S, 15: 268–270.

December 15   Memorial to Congress on Restraining the Increase of Slavery.

1820

March   Argument in *Foster* v. *Essex Bank*. MassSJC,S. 16 Tyng 266 (1821). W & S, 15: 271–274.

July   Examination of Some Remarks in the *Quarterly Review* on the Laws of Creditor and Debtor in the United States. *North American Review* 11 (July 1820): 197–208. *Legal Papers*, 2: 283–290 (extract). U.S. laws of creditor and debtor no worse than those of other countries; limitations are inherent in a difficult subject.

October 2   Speech on the Tariff. Faneuil Hall, Boston. *Boston Daily Advertiser*, October 11, 1820. W & S, 13: 5–21. Opposes any increase in tariffs; fears artificially induced industries may require permanent government support.

December 22   First Settlement of New England. Oration delivered at Plymouth, Massachusetts. Pamphlet, Boston: Wells & Lilly, 1821. W & S, 1: 181–226. Commemorative address devoted to history, character, and development of the region.

1820–1821

November 15–January 9   Massachusetts Constitutional Convention. AD. M-Ar, Constitutional Convention Papers. mDWs. *Journal of the Massachusetts Constitutional Convention*. 1821, reprint 1853. An

active delegate, Webster participated in discussion of almost every question raised. His nephew and first editor, Charles Brickett Haddock, in *Speeches and Forensic Arguments* (1830), identified three "speeches," with Webster's concurrence. We follow this classification here, as have other editors, but without in any way discounting other "remarks" or "arguments" to be found in the *Journal*.

December 4   Qualifications for Office. Remarks on the test oath question. *Journal*, pp. 160–163. *W & S*, 5: 4–7. Opposes a requirement that state officers be required to profess Christianity.

December 15   Basis of the Senate.

December 30   Independence of the Judiciary. *Journal*, pp. 481–486. *W & S*, 5: 26–32. Opposes removal of judges by the legislature without showing cause or affording opportunity of defense.

1821

April 24   Defense of Judge James Prescott. Before the Massachusetts State Senate sitting as a court of impeachment. *Independent Chronicle and Boston Patriot*, April 25, 28, 1821. Pamphlet, Boston: Pickering & Howland, *Boston Daily Advertiser*, 1821. *W & S*, 10: 234–277. Bases defense primarily on grounds that the charges do not constitute infractions of law or constitution.

1822

May   Case of La Jeune Eugénie. Argument in USCC,DMass. 2 Mason 409, (1822). *W & S*, 15: 279–280.

1823

December 30   System of Bankruptcy. Remarks in H.R., *Annals,* 18th Cong., 1st sess., pp. 895–896. *W & S*, 14: 77–78. Moves to table report of his own Judiciary Committee, which opposes a uniform system of bankruptcy.

1824

January 19   The Revolution in Greece.

January 24   Resolution regarding Greece. Discussion in H.R. of Webster's resolution of December 8, 1823, to which the speech above was addressed. *Annals*, 18th Cong., 1st sess., pp. 1190–1197. *W & S*, 14: 82–92.

February 4   Argument in *Gibbons* v. *Ogden.* U.S. Supreme Court, February term, 1824. 9 Wheaton 3. *W & S*, 11: 4–23. See *Legal Papers,* 3. Argues against New York's steamboat monopoly.

March   Argument in *Ogden* v. *Saunders*. U.S. Supreme Court, February
term, 1824. 12 Wheaton 237. *W & S*, 11 : 25–40. See *Legal Papers,*
3. Argues that the contract clause of the Constitution takes prece-
dence over state bankruptcy laws.
April 1–2   The Tariff.

1825

January 10   Penal laws of the United States. Short speech, H.R.,
Register of Debates, 18th Cong., 2d sess., pp. 166–168. Argues
for Federal jurisdiction over maritime crimes, even if committed
within state waters.
January 18   The Cumberland Road Bill.
March 3   National Bankruptcy Law. Short speech in H.R., *Register of
Debates,* 18th Cong., 2d sess., pp. 740–742. *W & S*, 14: 103–104.
Argues that the House should pass a national bankruptcy law at
a future session.
April 3   Speech at Faneuil Hall on the Election of 1825.
June 17   Dedication of the Bunker Hill Monument. Patriotic address
at Charlestown, Mass. Pamphlet, Boston: Cummings, Hilliard &
Co., 1825. *W & S*, 1 : 235–254. Celebrates those who fought at
Bunker Hill; evaluates influence of the U.S. upon representative
government.

1826

January 4   The Judiciary.
February 24   Case of the Marianna Flora. Argument before the U.S.
Supreme Court, February term, 1826. 11 Wheaton 24. *W & S*,
15: 282–285.
April 14   The Panama Mission.
August 2   Adams and Jefferson.

1827

January 12   Surviving Officers of the Revolution. Speech in H.R.,
Register of Debates, 19th Cong., 2d sess., pp. 685–690. Defends
pension claims of Revolutionary veterans.
January 19   Argument in *Ogden* v. *Saunders*. U.S. Supreme Court,
January term, 1827. 12 Wheaton 237. *W & S*, 11 : 25–40. Second
argument. Similar to 1824 argument. (The record in Wheaton is
actually a summary of both the 1824 and 1827 arguments.) See
Legal Papers, 3.
February 5, 9   The Presidential Message on the Creek Indians.
March 2   British Colonial Trade. Remarks in H.R., *Register of Debates,*
19th Cong., 2d sess., pp. 1514, 1522–1527. *W & S*, 14: 119–128.

Clarifies law; asks sanctions if British colonies are not opened to
U.S. trade by end of year.

April 20   Massachusetts Elections. Speech at Faneuil Hall. *Boston
Daily Advertiser*, April 23, 1827. W & S, 13: 24–30. Urges support for administration of J. Q. Adams regardless of party affiliation.

1828

April 15, 17   Graduation of the Price of Public Lands. Remarks in
Senate, *Register of Debates*, 20th Cong., 1st sess., pp. 660,
665–667. Availability of lands to settlers; suggests limiting terms
of bill to land on market ten years or more.

April 25   Survivors of the Revolution. Speech in Senate, *Register of
Debates*, 20th Cong., 1st sess., pp. 703–709. W & S, 5: 218–227.
Urges passage of a bill to provide pensions for Revolutionary
veterans.

May 2   Breakwater at Nantucket. Remarks in Senate, *Register of
Debates*, 20th Cong., 1st sess., p. 724. W & S, 14: 129–132. Urges
appropriation for breakwater.

May 9   Tariff. Speech and remarks in Senate, *Register of Debates*,
20th Cong., 1st sess., pp. 750–762, 765, 769. Pamphlet, Boston:
Boston Daily Advertiser press, 1828. W & S, 5: 228–247. Discusses certain provisions of tariff bill.

June 5   Testimonial dinner. Speech at Faneuil Hall. Boston *Columbian
Centinel*, June 7, 1828. W & S, 2: 13–24. Reviews past session
of Congress and appraises the political situation.

July 21   Speech at Dartmouth College. Concord *New Hampshire
Statesman*, August 2, 1828. Monograph, [Hanover, N.H.]: Dart-
mouth College Library, 1953. W & S, 13: 31–34 (misdated
July 28).

November 12   Boston Mechanics' Institution. Lecture. Published in
The American Library of Useful Knowledge (Boston, Stimpson
& Clapp, 1831), pp. 38–58. W & S, 2: 27–40. Surveys back-
ground and prospects of various types of engineering.

1829

March   Argument in *Charles River Bridge* v. *Warren Bridge*.
MassSJC,S. 7 Pickering 427 (1830). W & S, 15: 347–363. See
Legal Papers, 3.
———Remarks on Education. Speech at Amherst College, Amherst,
Mass. W & S, 13: 106–107 (abstract).

1830

January 20   First Speech on Foot's Resolution (First Reply to Hayne).
Speech in Senate, *Register of Debates*, 21st Cong., 1st sess.,

pp. 35–41. Pamphlet, Washington, D.C.: Gales & Seaton, 1830.
W & S, 5: 248–269.

*January 26–27   Second Speech on Foot's Resolution (Second Reply
to Hayne).*

February 5, 8   Argument in *Carver* v. *Jackson*. U.S. Supreme Court,
January term, 1830. 4 Peters 66. W & S, 15: 290–304.

March 5   Argument in *Wilcox et al.* v. *Exec. of Plummer*. U.S. Supreme
Court, January term, 1830. 4 Peters 176. W & S, 15: 305–309.

March 26, April 13   Office of the Attorney General. Remarks in Senate,
Register of Debates, 21st Cong., 1st sess., pp. 276–277, 324.
Opposes increasing duties of attorney general or reorganizing
the office.

August 11–12   The Salem Murder Trial.

October 30–31   The Tariff. Speech at Faneuil Hall meeting in support
of Nathan Appleton's candidacy for Congress. Notes for speech.
NhD. mDW 8975. See Boston *Columbian Centinel*, November 1,
1830.

1831

February 25   Turkish Commission. Remarks in Senate, summarized in
Register of Debates, 21st Cong., 2d sess., pp. 310–311.

March 1   Insolvent Debtors. Remarks in Senate, *Register of Debates*,
21st Cong., 2d sess., pp. 323–325. W & S, 14: 139–143. Explains
and supports provisions of a bill.

March 24   Public Dinner at New York.

October 18   Imprisonment for Debt. Paper transmitted by letter to
Alexander H. Everett, for Faneuil Hall meeting. Boston *Columbian
Centinel*, October 22, 1831. Opposes imprisonment for debt
except where debtor has means but refuses to pay.

1832

January 24, 25   The Nomination of Van Buren.

February 22   The Character of Washington. Eulogy at public dinner in
Washington, D.C. Pamphlet, Washington, D.C.: Jonathan Elliot,
1832. W & S, 2: 69–82.

March 1, 7, 12   Apportionment Bill. Remarks in Senate, *Register of
Debates*, 22d Cong., 1st sess., pp. 487–490, 513–515, 526–530.

April 5   Report on Apportionment.

May 25   Bank of the United States. Speech in Senate, *Register of
Debates*, 22d Cong., 1st sess., pp. 954–964. Pamphlet, Washington, D.C.: Gales & Seaton, 1832. W & S, 6: 124–140. Reviews
history and usefulness of the BUS.

May 28, June 5   Bank of the United States. Remarks in Senate on
aspects of the Bank recharter bill. *Register of Debates*, 22d Cong.,
1st sess., pp. 979–985, 1031–1033. Remarks of May 28 in
pamphlet, Washington, D.C.: Gales & Seaton, 1832. W & S,
6: 141–148.

July 11   Veto of the Bank Bill.
October 12   National Republican Convention at Worcester.
December 17   Nullification. Speech at Faneuil Hall. *Boston Daily Advertiser,* December 18, 1832. *W & S,* 13: 40–42. Supports Jackson's policy opposing nullification.

1833

January 14   French Spoliations. Speech in Senate, *Register of Debates,* 22d Cong., 2d sess., pp. 98–99. Explains principles of a bill; agrees to table it.
January 28   Calhoun's Resolutions. Remarks in Senate, *Register of Debates,* 22d Cong., 2d sess., pp. 237, 240–241, 243–244. Pamphlet, New York: Bergen & Tripp, 1861. *W & S,* 14: 149–151.
February 8   Revenue Collection Bill. Remarks in Senate, *Register of Debates,* 22d Cong., 2d sess., pp. 409–413. *W & S,* 14: 152–155. Reminds the Senate that the bill originated in a presidential request; attempts to deflect criticism from Judiciary Committee.
February 12, 13   Modification of the Tariff. Remarks in Senate, *Register of Debates,* 22 Cong., 2d sess., pp. 478–479, 483–484. *W & S,* 14: 156–159. Unwilling to support Clay's compromise.
February 16   The Constitution Not a Compact.
February 22, 25, March 1   The Tariff. Remarks in Senate, *Register of Debates,* 22d Cong., 2d sess., pp. 709–710, 722–724, 726, 727–729, 801–802. *W & S,* 14: 160–165. Criticizes compromise tariff.
February 26   Calhoun's Resolutions. Speech in Senate, *Register of Debates,* 22d Cong., 2d sess., pp. 774–784. *W & S,* 14: 166–171. Defends his position of February 16.
c. June 1   Reception at Buffalo, N.Y. Address at launching of steamboat "Daniel Webster." *W & S,* 2: 131–134. Extols the Union; praises the tariff.
July 8   Reception at Pittsburgh, Pa. Address. Pamphlet, Boston: Joseph T. Buckingham, 1833. *W & S,* 2: 141–156. Recalls his support of Jackson's response to Nullification. Speaks of tariff, internal improvements, public education.
December 23   Steamboat Accidents. Remarks in Senate, *Register of Debates,* 23d Cong., 1st sess., pp. 54–57. *W & S,* 14: 172–176. Proposes legislation designed to prevent steamboat accidents.

Index

Daniel Webster is abbreviated DW in the index. The entry for Webster is limited to material in the introductory sections; the speeches and topics discussed in them appear as main headings. Identification of names is indicated by page numbers set in boldface type. Individuals identified in the *Dictionary of American Biography* are denoted by an asterisk immediately following the name. Those identified in the *Biographical Dictionary of the American Congress* are denoted by a dagger.

LIBRARY OF CONGRESS CATALOGING IN PUBLICATION DATA
(REVISED FOR SER. 4, V. I)

Webster, Daniel, 1782–1852.
    The papers of Daniel Webster.
    Includes indexes.

    CONTENTS: ser. I. Correspondence: v. I, 1798–1824.
v. 2, 1825–1829—[etc.]—ser. 4, speeches and
formal writings: v. I, 1800–1833.
    I. Webster, Daniel, 1782–1852. 2. United States—
History—1801–1809—Collected works. 3. United States
—History—1809–1817—Collected works. 4. United
States—History—1815–1861—Collected works.
I. Wiltse, Charles Maurice, 1907–   . II. Moser,
Harold D. III. Dartmouth College.
E337.8.w24   1974   973.5'092'4   73–92705
ISBN 0–87451–096–I (ser. I, v. I)